Communications
in Computer and Information Science   1833

Rationale

The CCIS series is devoted to the publication of proceedings of computer science conferences. Its aim is to efficiently disseminate original research results in informatics in printed and electronic form. While the focus is on publication of peer-reviewed full papers presenting mature work, inclusion of reviewed short papers reporting on work in progress is welcome, too. Besides globally relevant meetings with internationally representative program committees guaranteeing a strict peer-reviewing and paper selection process, conferences run by societies or of high regional or national relevance are also considered for publication.

Topics

The topical scope of CCIS spans the entire spectrum of informatics ranging from foundational topics in the theory of computing to information and communications science and technology and a broad variety of interdisciplinary application fields.

Information for Volume Editors and Authors

Publication in CCIS is free of charge. No royalties are paid, however, we offer registered conference participants temporary free access to the online version of the conference proceedings on SpringerLink (http://link.springer.com) by means of an http referrer from the conference website and/or a number of complimentary printed copies, as specified in the official acceptance email of the event.

CCIS proceedings can be published in time for distribution at conferences or as post-proceedings, and delivered in the form of printed books and/or electronically as USBs and/or e-content licenses for accessing proceedings at SpringerLink. Furthermore, CCIS proceedings are included in the CCIS electronic book series hosted in the SpringerLink digital library at http://link.springer.com/bookseries/7899. Conferences publishing in CCIS are allowed to use Online Conference Service (OCS) for managing the whole proceedings lifecycle (from submission and reviewing to preparing for publication) free of charge.

Publication process

The language of publication is exclusively English. Authors publishing in CCIS have to sign the Springer CCIS copyright transfer form, however, they are free to use their material published in CCIS for substantially changed, more elaborate subsequent publications elsewhere. For the preparation of the camera-ready papers/files, authors have to strictly adhere to the Springer CCIS Authors' Instructions and are strongly encouraged to use the CCIS LaTeX style files or templates.

Abstracting/Indexing

CCIS is abstracted/indexed in DBLP, Google Scholar, EI-Compendex, Mathematical Reviews, SCImago, Scopus. CCIS volumes are also submitted for the inclusion in ISI Proceedings.

How to start

To start the evaluation of your proposal for inclusion in the CCIS series, please send an e-mail to ccis@springer.com.

Constantine Stephanidis · Margherita Antona ·
Stavroula Ntoa · Gavriel Salvendy
Editors

HCI International 2023 Posters

25th International Conference
on Human-Computer Interaction, HCII 2023
Copenhagen, Denmark, July 23–28, 2023
Proceedings, Part II

 Springer

Editors

Constantine Stephanidis
University of Crete and Foundation for
Research and Technology - Hellas (FORTH)
Heraklion, Crete, Greece

Margherita Antona
Foundation for Research and Technology -
Hellas (FORTH)
Heraklion, Crete, Greece

Stavroula Ntoa
Foundation for Research and Technology -
Hellas (FORTH)
Heraklion, Crete, Greece

Gavriel Salvendy
University of Central Florida
Orlando, FL, USA

ISSN 1865-0929   ISSN 1865-0937 (electronic)
Communications in Computer and Information Science
ISBN 978-3-031-35991-0   ISBN 978-3-031-35992-7 (eBook)
https://doi.org/10.1007/978-3-031-35992-7

This Springer imprint is published by the registered company Springer Nature Switzerland AG
The registered company address is: Gewerbestrasse 11, 6330 Cham, Switzerland

Foreword

Human-computer interaction (HCI) is acquiring an ever-increasing scientific and industrial importance, as well as having more impact on people's everyday lives, as an ever-growing number of human activities are progressively moving from the physical to the digital world. This process, which has been ongoing for some time now, was further accelerated during the acute period of the COVID-19 pandemic. The HCI International (HCII) conference series, held annually, aims to respond to the compelling need to advance the exchange of knowledge and research and development efforts on the human aspects of design and use of computing systems.

The 25th International Conference on Human-Computer Interaction, HCI International 2023 (HCII 2023), was held in the emerging post-pandemic era as a 'hybrid' event at the AC Bella Sky Hotel and Bella Center, Copenhagen, Denmark, during July 23–28, 2023. It incorporated the 21 thematic areas and affiliated conferences listed below.

A total of 7472 individuals from academia, research institutes, industry, and government agencies from 85 countries submitted contributions, and 1578 papers and 396 posters were included in the volumes of the proceedings that were published just before the start of the conference, these are listed below. The contributions thoroughly cover the entire field of human-computer interaction, addressing major advances in knowledge and effective use of computers in a variety of application areas. These papers provide academics, researchers, engineers, scientists, practitioners and students with state-of-the-art information on the most recent advances in HCI.

The HCI International (HCII) conference also offers the option of presenting 'Late Breaking Work', and this applies both for papers and posters, with corresponding volumes of proceedings that will be published after the conference. Full papers will be included in the 'HCII 2023 - Late Breaking Work - Papers' volumes of the proceedings to be published in the Springer LNCS series, while 'Poster Extended Abstracts' will be included as short research papers in the 'HCII 2023 - Late Breaking Work - Posters' volumes to be published in the Springer CCIS series.

I would like to thank the Program Board Chairs and the members of the Program Boards of all thematic areas and affiliated conferences for their contribution towards the high scientific quality and overall success of the HCI International 2023 conference. Their manifold support in terms of paper reviewing (single-blind review process, with a minimum of two reviews per submission), session organization and their willingness to act as goodwill ambassadors for the conference is most highly appreciated.

This conference would not have been possible without the continuous and unwavering support and advice of Gavriel Salvendy, founder, General Chair Emeritus, and Scientific Advisor. For his outstanding efforts, I would like to express my sincere appreciation to Abbas Moallem, Communications Chair and Editor of HCI International News.

July 2023   Constantine Stephanidis

HCI International 2023 Thematic Areas and Affiliated Conferences

Thematic Areas

- HCI: Human-Computer Interaction
- HIMI: Human Interface and the Management of Information

Affiliated Conferences

- EPCE: 20th International Conference on Engineering Psychology and Cognitive Ergonomics
- AC: 17th International Conference on Augmented Cognition
- UAHCI: 17th International Conference on Universal Access in Human-Computer Interaction
- CCD: 15th International Conference on Cross-Cultural Design
- SCSM: 15th International Conference on Social Computing and Social Media
- VAMR: 15th International Conference on Virtual, Augmented and Mixed Reality
- DHM: 14th International Conference on Digital Human Modeling and Applications in Health, Safety, Ergonomics and Risk Management
- DUXU: 12th International Conference on Design, User Experience and Usability
- C&C: 11th International Conference on Culture and Computing
- DAPI: 11th International Conference on Distributed, Ambient and Pervasive Interactions
- HCIBGO: 10th International Conference on HCI in Business, Government and Organizations
- LCT: 10th International Conference on Learning and Collaboration Technologies
- ITAP: 9th International Conference on Human Aspects of IT for the Aged Population
- AIS: 5th International Conference on Adaptive Instructional Systems
- HCI-CPT: 5th International Conference on HCI for Cybersecurity, Privacy and Trust
- HCI-Games: 5th International Conference on HCI in Games
- MobiTAS: 5th International Conference on HCI in Mobility, Transport and Automotive Systems
- AI-HCI: 4th International Conference on Artificial Intelligence in HCI
- MOBILE: 4th International Conference on Design, Operation and Evaluation of Mobile Communications

List of Conference Proceedings Volumes Appearing Before the Conference

1. LNCS 14011, Human-Computer Interaction: Part I, edited by Masaaki Kurosu and Ayako Hashizume
2. LNCS 14012, Human-Computer Interaction: Part II, edited by Masaaki Kurosu and Ayako Hashizume
3. LNCS 14013, Human-Computer Interaction: Part III, edited by Masaaki Kurosu and Ayako Hashizume
4. LNCS 14014, Human-Computer Interaction: Part IV, edited by Masaaki Kurosu and Ayako Hashizume
5. LNCS 14015, Human Interface and the Management of Information: Part I, edited by Hirohiko Mori and Yumi Asahi
6. LNCS 14016, Human Interface and the Management of Information: Part II, edited by Hirohiko Mori and Yumi Asahi
7. LNAI 14017, Engineering Psychology and Cognitive Ergonomics: Part I, edited by Don Harris and Wen-Chin Li
8. LNAI 14018, Engineering Psychology and Cognitive Ergonomics: Part II, edited by Don Harris and Wen-Chin Li
9. LNAI 14019, Augmented Cognition, edited by Dylan D. Schmorrow and Cali M. Fidopiastis
10. LNCS 14020, Universal Access in Human-Computer Interaction: Part I, edited by Margherita Antona and Constantine Stephanidis
11. LNCS 14021, Universal Access in Human-Computer Interaction: Part II, edited by Margherita Antona and Constantine Stephanidis
12. LNCS 14022, Cross-Cultural Design: Part I, edited by Pei-Luen Patrick Rau
13. LNCS 14023, Cross-Cultural Design: Part II, edited by Pei-Luen Patrick Rau
14. LNCS 14024, Cross-Cultural Design: Part III, edited by Pei-Luen Patrick Rau
15. LNCS 14025, Social Computing and Social Media: Part I, edited by Adela Coman and Simona Vasilache
16. LNCS 14026, Social Computing and Social Media: Part II, edited by Adela Coman and Simona Vasilache
17. LNCS 14027, Virtual, Augmented and Mixed Reality, edited by Jessie Y. C. Chen and Gino Fragomeni
18. LNCS 14028, Digital Human Modeling and Applications in Health, Safety, Ergonomics and Risk Management: Part I, edited by Vincent G. Duffy
19. LNCS 14029, Digital Human Modeling and Applications in Health, Safety, Ergonomics and Risk Management: Part II, edited by Vincent G. Duffy
20. LNCS 14030, Design, User Experience, and Usability: Part I, edited by Aaron Marcus, Elizabeth Rosenzweig and Marcelo Soares
21. LNCS 14031, Design, User Experience, and Usability: Part II, edited by Aaron Marcus, Elizabeth Rosenzweig and Marcelo Soares

47. CCIS 1836, HCI International 2023 Posters - Part V, edited by Constantine Stephanidis, Margherita Antona, Stavroula Ntoa and Gavriel Salvendy

https://2023.hci.international/proceedings

Preface

Preliminary scientific results, professional news, or work in progress, described in the form of short research papers (4–8 pages long), constitute a popular submission type among the International Conference on Human-Computer Interaction (HCII) participants. Extended abstracts are particularly suited for reporting ongoing work, which can benefit from a visual presentation, and are presented during the conference in the form of posters. The latter allow a focus on novel ideas and are appropriate for presenting project results in a simple, concise, and visually appealing manner. At the same time, they are also suitable for attracting feedback from an international community of HCI academics, researchers, and practitioners. Poster submissions span the wide range of topics of all HCII thematic areas and affiliated conferences.

Five volumes of the HCII 2023 proceedings are dedicated to this year's poster extended abstracts, in the form of short research papers, focusing on the following topics:

- Volume I: HCI Design - Theoretical Approaches, Methods and Case Studies; Multimodality and Novel Interaction Techniques and Devices; Perception and Cognition in Interaction; Ethics, Transparency and Trust in HCI; User Experience and Technology Acceptance Studies
- Volume II: Supporting Health, Psychological Wellbeing, and Fitness; Design for All, Accessibility and Rehabilitation Technologies; Interactive Technologies for the Aging Population
- Volume III: Interacting with Data, Information and Knowledge; Learning and Training Technologies; Interacting with Cultural Heritage and Art
- Volume IV: Social Media - Design, User Experiences and Content Analysis; Advances in eGovernment Services; eCommerce, Mobile Commerce and Digital Marketing - Design and Customer Behavior; Designing and Developing Intelligent Green Environments; (Smart) Product Design
- Volume V: Driving Support and Experiences in Automated Vehicles; eXtended Reality - Design, Interaction Techniques, User Experience and Novel Applications; Applications of AI Technologies in HCI

Poster extended abstracts are included for publication in these volumes following a minimum of two single-blind reviews from the members of the HCII 2023 international Program Boards. We would like to thank all of them for their invaluable contribution, support, and efforts.

July 2023

Constantine Stephanidis
Margherita Antona
Stavroula Ntoa
Gavriel Salvendy

25th International Conference on Human-Computer Interaction (HCII 2023)

The full list with the Program Board Chairs and the members of the Program Boards of all thematic areas and affiliated conferences of HCII2023 is available online at:

http://www.hci.international/board-members-2023.php

HCI International 2024 Conference

The 26th International Conference on Human-Computer Interaction, HCI International 2024, will be held jointly with the affiliated conferences at the Washington Hilton Hotel, Washington, DC, USA, June 29 – July 4, 2024. It will cover a broad spectrum of themes related to Human-Computer Interaction, including theoretical issues, methods, tools, processes, and case studies in HCI design, as well as novel interaction techniques, interfaces, and applications. The proceedings will be published by Springer. More information will be made available on the conference website: http://2024.hci.international/.

General Chair
Prof. Constantine Stephanidis
University of Crete and ICS-FORTH
Heraklion, Crete, Greece
Email: general_chair@hcii2024.org

https://2024.hci.international/

Contents – Part II

Design for All, Accessibility and Rehabilitation Technologies

Supporting Health, Psychological Wellbeing, and Fitness

Evaluating a Hospital Smart Notification System in a Simulated Environment: The Method

Haneen Ali[1,2]($\boxtimes$) (iD), Yasin Fatemi[1] (iD), Miranda Batchelor[2], Cordelia Capodiferro[2],
Logan Marler[2], and Sa'd Hamasha[1]

[1] Department of Industrial and Systems Engineering, Auburn University, Auburn, AL, USA
{hba0007,yzf0024,smh0083}@auburn.edu
[2] Health Services Administration Program, Auburn University, Auburn, AL, USA
{mlb0153,czc0187,lrm0047}@auburn.edu

Abstract. The call light system is a central communication technology linking care providers and patients. Call light systems in hospital settings help reduce the likelihood and severity of adverse events and ambulatory conditions by allowing nurses to quickly respond to patient needs. However, the call light system was found to be associated with major challenges and usability issues that negatively impacted patients' safety and quality of care.

This study aims at evaluating the effectiveness of a high-fidelity prototype of a previously designed smart communication system in a simulated environment. College students were invited to mimic the role of patients, and nursing students were invited to perform routine tasks using a traditional call light system and the smart system. Participants were instructed to perform routine tasks using pre-designed scenarios in a simulated environment using the traditional call light system and the smart system. Results show that the smart system reduced the overall response time by more than 50%.

Keywords: Quality of care · Patient experience · Information and communication technology · Call light technology · Patient satisfaction

1 Introduction

Notification and communication technology, such as the call light system, helps reduce the likelihood and severity of adverse events and ambulatory conditions by allowing nurses to quickly respond to patient needs (Ali and Li, 2020). The call light system is a two-way communication system that enables the patient to indicate that they have a need, or perceived need, requiring the attention of the nurses on duty (Ali, Cole, Sienkiewicz, et al., 2020). The traditional system consists of a handheld device with a singular button in the patients' room, which alerts the nursing staff to the patient's need for attention with an alarm.

Effective communication technology is essential to providing exceptional patient care. Studies find that any breakdowns in patient-provider communication can lead to poor outcomes, such as patient complications or deaths, contributing over 7,000 incidents in 2015, totaling up to $1.7 (Ali and Li, 2016) billion in malpractice and legal

C. Stephanidis et al. (Eds.): HCII 2023, CCIS 1833, pp. 3–9, 2023.
https://doi.org/10.1007/978-3-031-35992-7_1

damages (Ali and Li, 2019). The call light system is indispensable for the interaction between the nurse and the patient: an interaction that is crucial for the caring relationship (Galinato et al. 2015). The call light system has been described as a 'lifeline' for hospitalized patients (Cm et al. 2006) as it has a direct influence on patient safety, satisfaction, and quality of care outcomes (Cardoso and Martin, 2003; Cm et al. 2006; Deitrick et al., 2006). However, the traditional system was found to be associated with major challenges and usability issues that negatively impacted patients' outcomes, such as lack of prioritization and low/no discriminability (Ali et al., 2017). Despite recent advancements in healthcare technology, traditional call light systems have failed to modernize and encompass all the concerns that arise in healthcare: including determining patient care priorities, usability issues, increased mental workload, and false alarms.

1.1   The Proposed Smart System Design

The healthcare industry has an ever-growing need to adopt advanced technologies that help reduce costs, medical errors, and improve the quality of care. Advancements in patient-provider communication are needed in order to improve patient and staff experiences and keep pace with technological advancements. Improvements in patient and staff experiences via patient-provider communication are vital in the race to keep pace with the advances in communication technology (Wharton et al. 1994). Further, updating patient rooms is necessary to improve comfort levels and access to health information. The study finds that one way of addressing these concerns simultaneously is by developing a smart system consisting of a tablet, a hands-free device such as smartwatches, and a voice assistant technology such as Alexa.

Introducing information and communication technology (ICT) to the healthcare industry as a smart room layout has the capability of improving communication efficiency and nursing workflow, as such devices are compact, provide greater access to information, entertainment, and social interaction, and provide patients a diverse array of methods to engage with their providers (Ae et al. 2018; Wharton et al. 1994; Wu & Cheng, 2018). In addition to improving patient satisfaction, the proposed system allows patients to alert staff of pain or discomfort directly, which helps to improve the patient safety function of the call light system (Greysen et al. 2014).

The application of hands-free devices in the healthcare industry is in its early stages, however the literature suggests that their use is promising, especially for communication, and can improve workflow (Friend et al. 2017; Kent et al. 2015). Tablets, smartwatches, smart apps, and voice assistant devices such as Alexa, allow staff to receive alarms and updates quickly, to engage with a patient remotely, and to organize and prioritize patient alarms based on more meaningful indicators such as current vitals, reported pain levels, and patient acuity (Ali, Cole, & Panos, 2020). The smart system (Figs. 1 and 2) will incorporate smart devices in patients' rooms and hands-free communication devices for the staff to wear with multi-modal interfaces (visual, auditory/voice assistant device, and tactile.) This way they will be able to prioritize alarms by weighing the severity of patient condition and the call type.

The system will replace the traditional patient call buttons with a smart device consisting of a touchscreen display, as well as voice assistant technology to overcome accessibility and cultural challenges, such as language barriers. Three iterations were completed. Heuristic evaluation and cognitive walkthrough were used with each proto-type. Paper prototypes were created for the first design, which was tested by the research team and nursing students. Significant improvements were added to the design after the first cognitive walkthrough such as changing locations of apps, as well as adding more apps for the patient to use the smart device in patients' rooms as an entertainment device in addition to communicating patients' needs and accessing medical records.

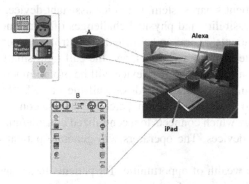

Fig. 1. In the patient room, two smart devices; Alexa, B: iPad.

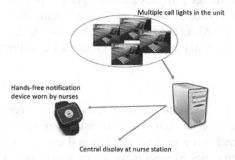

Fig. 2. In-patients' rooms devices will send notification to the unit's server and hands-free devises worn by nurses.

The study proposes a smart system utilizing three devices to improve communication with the medical staff and boost patient satisfaction. The first device in the patients' room is an iPad. It will be used by the patient to communicate their specific needs directly to hands-free devices worn by hospital staff. Further, a voice assistant device, such as Alexa, will be installed in each room to serve as a hands-free support device for patients. Patients will be able to verbally communicate their needs by asking the voice assistant to call a nurse or deliver messages. The device in the patients' rooms will also be utilized as a form of entertainment for patients.

In the past, patients have passed the time in their hospital room by watching cable TV or playing board games with guests. With the current innovations in mobile devices, patients are increasingly more familiar with a variety of streaming platforms and mobile games. As a result, patients are less likely to utilize, and therefore enjoy, the amenities currently available in hospital settings. The study, therefore, proposes a smart system whereby patients are able to not only notify hospital staff, but also watch streaming services like Netflix and Hulu, access the internet, shop, play video games, order food, and access any book at the touch of a button.

Further, such a device could be utilized to watch patient education videos and hospital introduction videos. This allows patients greater access and therefore more opportunities to retain their pertinent health information. While the tablet and smart apps provide the foundation of the patient smart system, the voice assistant device, Alexa, will be used to overcome the accessibility and physical challenges of using mobile devices. Alexa will be installed in patients' rooms and adjusted to control the amenities of that specific room: such as climate control, TV, lights, and the call light smart app. As Alexa will be assigned to each patient's room, the device will be programmed to deliver a specific message to the nursing staff such as "Alexa, call the nurse", "Alexa, I am in pain", "Alexa, I need help to go to the bathroom", etc. Upon these commands, the device will then deliver a message which connects to a centralized console/unit that serves as a hub for the unit's Alexa devices. The operators will generate patient requests and assign prioritization weight.

Alexa provides a wealth of opportunities for patients to engage directly with their healthcare by providing an interface function to receive and respond to the patient's requests and concerns. Further, Alexa now comes in a HIPAA compliant version and this study finds that the device provides adequate privacy protection safeguards for any sensitive information recorded by the device (Perez, Sarah, 2019). The study also finds that the implementation of Alexa or a similar voice assistant device is a crucial component in ensuring the widest range of physical and cognitive accessibility for patients engaging in a call light system.

Nurse Devices
The nursing staff will receive notifications via smartwatches concerning alarms and call lights in the unit. The hospital staff will have access to the most recent information thanks to the smartwatch's use as a notification and communication tool. In order to demonstrate a significant improvement in workflow, a reduction in perceived effort, and a shorter response time, a study was conducted in a mock nursing home environment to test smartwatches as notification and communication devices for the nursing staff (Ali and Li, 2020; Randazzo, Vincenzo et al. 2018).

A major function that the existing call light systems lack, according to the study, is prioritization, which features provide. Simulation modeling will be used to create an alarm prioritization system. Patients will be divided into groups according to the severity of their conditions, call lights will be prioritized according to the type of call light or alarm, and information about walking distances (such as from the patient room to the medication cart and from the patient room to the nurse station), walk rates, and the anticipated time it will take the nurse to fulfill the patient's request will also be provided. The calls will be sent to the nurse and placed in a priority queue. Setting priorities for alerts will aid nursing staff in making decisions by focusing their attention on patients who have the most urgent requirements. By keeping the nursing staff informed of any changes in the patient's health and minimizing the number of trips they must make to the patient's room, the algorithm responsible for prioritizing alerts is predicted to lessen their burden and risk of burnout. The wristwatch will show the action sequences as well as the type of alarm, room number, assigned nurse, and time since the alarm was triggered. Depending on the patient's condition, urgent alarms like discomfort and the need for restroom help will be displayed on the wristwatch display. For additional details on the system, kindly refer to (Ali and Li, 2016).

2 Methods

The study was approved by Auburn University's Institutional Review Board. Participants were notified about the aims of the experiment and the risks that might be associated with it. Additionally, participants were notified that no identifiable information will be collected, their participation is voluntary, they signed consent form before the experiment, and were compensated for their time if they choose to continue and take the survey ($95).

Ten nursing students from Auburn University were recruited to perform regular tasks, all female students were doing their clinical practice. The ten participants used iPads, smartwatches, and smartphones with multiple notifications and auditory alarms on their devices.

Two L shaped hallways with four rooms (two on each hallway) were used to simulate a hospital unit. The traditional call light system was installed in two of these rooms, while the two other rooms were equipped with a high-fidelity prototype of the smart system. This consisted of a tablet and a voice-activated system, Alexa. Undergraduate students were recruited to participate in the study and play the roles of patients (actors). Twenty actors were trained on specific medical care plans/conditions to mimic the role of patients in the unit and were instructed to perform specific tasks, such as activating the call light. Then, nursing students were instructed to perform routine tasks utilizing both the traditional call light and smart systems. The response time to the call light was recorded for both systems, as well as the communication method used by the patients (Alexa, tablet, or request help by pushing the call light button).

Six different scenarios were created to conduct the evaluation, two scenarios were used to train the participants, and four scenarios were used for the experiment. All these scenarios are equivalent and similar in terms of the number of alarms, distance nurses must move through to respond to alarms, time a nurse is expected to stay in the patient's room. Each scenario has ten alarms in six groups (pain medication and management, bathroom assistance, intravenous problems or pump alarm, personal assistance, accidental pressing of the call light, and repositioning or transfer) (Ali & Li, 2019), and Axure was used to design the smartwatch interface of alarms based on the scenarios.

3 Results

Results in Fig. 3 show a significant improvement in response times with the use of the smart system. Figure 3 shows that response to pain medication and bathroom assistance alarms were reduced by more than 50% with the smart system, and intravenous problems such as pump alarm were reduced 47%. Figure 3 also shows that no accidental alarms were recorded with the smart system. In addition, patients used the iPad and Alexa to communicate their requests with the smart system, and the voice-activated Alexa was used 47% more than the iPad with no single use of the call light button when the smart system was installed.

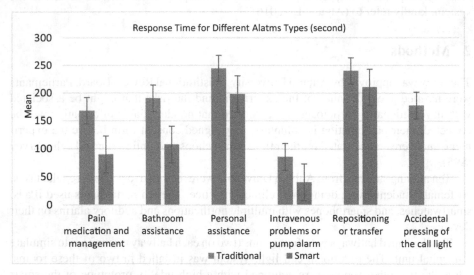

Fig. 3. Response time to alarms in the simulated environment.

4 Conclusion

In conclusion, the assessment of the high-fidelity prototype shows an improved communication between the care team and patients. The call light system reduces patient response times in multiple cases. This includes requests for pain medication, bathroom help, personal queries, and repositioning. In addition, the authors believe this improved process could facilitate the reduction of perceived mental and physical stressors of the nursing staff as the majority of the nursing students reported feelings of efficiency and easiness while using the smart system. To improve the quality of care and patient satisfaction, as well as reduce the stress the nursing staff experiences due to the traditional system, improving and testing the smart system will continue in the university nursing simulation lab. Local nurses in the field will be invited to participate and provide feedback for additional data.

References

Chung, A.E., Griffin, A.C., Selezneva, D., Gotz, D.: Health and fitness apps for hands-free voice-activated assistants: content analysis. JMIR Mhealth Uhealth **6**(9), e9705 (2018)

Ali, H., Cole, A., Panos, G.: Transforming patient hospital experience through smart technologies. In: Marcus, A., Rosenzweig, E. (eds.) HCII 2020. LNCS, vol. 12202, pp. 203–215. Springer, Cham (2020). https://doi.org/10.1007/978-3-030-49757-6_14

Ali, H., Cole, A., Sienkiewicz, A., Ho, T.: Perspectives of nursing homes staff on the nature of residents-initiated call lights. SAGE Open Nursing **6**, 2377960820903546 (2020). https://doi.org/10.1177/2377960820903546

Ali, H., Li, H.: Designing a smart watch interface for a notification and communication system for nursing homes. In: Zhou, J., Salvendy, G. (eds.) ITAP 2016. LNCS, vol. 9754, pp. 401–411. Springer, Cham (2016). https://doi.org/10.1007/978-3-319-39943-0_39

Ali, H., Li, H.: Evaluating a smartwatch notification system in a simulated nursing home. Int. J. Older People Nurs. **14**(3), e12241 (2019). https://doi.org/10.1111/opn.12241

Ali, H., Li, H.: Use of notification and communication technology (call light systems) in nursing homes: observational study. J. Med. Internet Res. **22**(3), e16252 (2020). https://doi.org/10.2196/16252

Ali, H., Li, H., Wong, J.: Evaluating a smartwatch-based notification system in a simulated nursing home: the method. In: Proceedings of the International Symposium on Human Factors and Ergonomics in Health Care, vol. 6(1), pp. 132–138 (2017). https://doi.org/10.1177/2327857917061029

Cardoso, G., Martin, N.: The patient connection: improving call bell response at cambridge memorial hospital. Healthc. Manage. Forum **16**(3), 47–50 (2003). https://doi.org/10.1016/S0840-4704(10)60235-9

Cm, M., Al, B., L, K. Effects of nursing rounds: On patients' call light use, satisfaction, and safety. Am. J. Nursing **106**(9) (2006). https://doi.org/10.1097/00000446-200609000-00029

Deitrick, L., Bokovoy, J., Stern, G., Panik, A.: Dance of the call bells: using ethnography to evaluate patient satisfaction with quality of care. J. Nurs. Care Qual. **21**(4), 316 (2006)

Friend, T.H., Jennings, S.J., Copenhaver, M.S., Levine, W.C.: Implementation of the vocera communication system in a quaternary perioperative environment. J. Med. Syst. **41**(1), 1–6 (2016). https://doi.org/10.1007/s10916-016-0652-9

Galinato, J., Montie, M., Patak, L., Titler, M.: Perspectives of nurses and patients on call light technology. Comput. Informat. Nursing : CIN **33**(8), 359–367 (2015). https://doi.org/10.1097/CIN.0000000000000177

Greysen, S.R., Khanna, R.R., Jacolbia, R., Lee, H.M., Auerbach, A.D.: Tablet computers for hospitalized patients: a pilot study to improve inpatient engagement. J. Hospital Med. An Official Publicat. Soc. Hospital Med. **9**(6), 396–399 (2014). https://doi.org/10.1002/jhm.2169

Kent, B., et al.: Exploring nurses' reactions to a novel technology to support acute health care delivery. J. Clin. Nurs. **24**(15–16), 2340–2351 (2015). https://doi.org/10.1111/jocn.12881

Perez, S.: Amazon Alexa launches its first HIPAA-compliant medical skills | TechCrunch (2019). https://techcrunch.com/2019/04/04/amazon-alexa-launches-its-first-hipaa-compliant-medical-skills/

Randazzo, V., Pasero, E., Navaretti, S.: VITAL-ECG: A portable wearable hospital (2018). https://doi.org/10.1109/SAS.2018.8336776

Wharton, C., Rieman, J., Lewis, C., Polson, P.: The cognitive walkthrough method: A practitioner's guide. In: Usability inspection methods, pp. 105–140. John Wiley & Sons, Inc. (1994)

Wu, H.-C., Cheng, C.-C.: Relationships between technology attachment, experiential relationship quality, experiential risk and experiential sharing intentions in a smart hotel. J. Hosp. Tour. Manag. **37**, 42–58 (2018). https://doi.org/10.1016/j.jhtm.2018.09.003

Interaction and Service Design of a Virtual Health Hub for Patients with Cardiovascular Disease

Kyle Boyd[1](✉), Justin Magee[1], and Aaron Peace[2]

[1] Belfast School of Art, Ulster University, 2-24 York Street, Coleraine BT15 1AP, Belfast, Ireland
ka.boyd@ulster.ac.uk

[2] MDEC Building, Altnagelvin Area Hospital, Glenshane Road, BT47 6SB Londonderry, Ireland

Abstract. Interaction and Service Design research was applied to synthesise the complex issues associated with cardiac assessment. A design demonstrator prototype was produced to rationalise how a virtual assistant might enable objective assessments clinical assessment questioning and vital signs monitoring. This led to a concept design prototype called Heart Hub, developed from a telephone triage service for patients with cardiovascular disease.

Through a co-design framework and the positive design methodology, a series of user experience techniques were used including clinician contextual laddering video interview, user personas, empathy-journey mapping, user interviews and task analysis. Secondly, we will report on the various design phases from sketching, wireframes, high resolution mock-ups to prototypes. Lastly, we report on the challenges of working on design within a healthcare setting in times of public health crisis and the effects of that). This ongoing research demonstrates the application of design c to tackle wicked problems within a healthcare context.

Keywords: Cardiology · Cardiovascular Disease · Interaction Design · Service Design · User Experience · Co-design · Digital Healthcare

1 Introduction

During the COVID-19 pandemic the delivery of healthcare in hospitals changed dramatically over a relatively short space of time. Many health resources were stretched and reorganisation of resources was necessary [1]. This has had a significant impact on cardiology care services, where risk of substantial and avoidable excess deaths occurred [2]. There is a rising epidemic of heart failure within the ageing population in the UK [3]. The elderly required shielding from normal hospital environments because of their vulnerability, especially during the pandemic.

Building upon an innovative Cardiology Triage Telephone system, which achieved over 1000 beneficial engagements [4], it was identified that a more immersive experience was desirable. This potentially could provide additional benefits in tackling the burden

© The Author(s), under exclusive license to Springer Nature Switzerland AG 2023
C. Stephanidis et al. (Eds.): HCII 2023, CCIS 1833, pp. 10–15, 2023.
https://doi.org/10.1007/978-3-031-35992-7_2

of travel, parking, and long walking distances for elderly patients leaving patients feeling breathless. Furthermore, the NHS NetZero strategy [5] identifies that carbon emissions from travel accounts for 14% overall, with 10% directly from patient travel (5%), staff (4%) and visitor travel (1%). Clinicians were further concerned about 'did not attend' rates (DNA) and the opportunity to give patients more options for personalised virtual healthcare.

To tackle this wicked problem [6] we applied design thinking with a cardiologist co-investigator and their Cardiac Assessment Unit (CAU) team, using positive design [7] and user experience techniques to synthesise the problem. The aim was to provide an effective cardiac patient monitoring service through a NetZero adaptation approach.

2   User Experience Research

Healthcare design presents unique challenges due to the complex and sensitive nature of healthcare environments. One major difficulty is balancing the needs of patients, medical professionals, and staff while effectively and safely delivering services. Healthcare spaces must be designed to meet the specific needs of each user group, while also ensuring that medical equipment is easily accessible and can be effectively operated.

Co-design is evidenced as having significant benefit as a healthcare improvement tool [8]. Here, we provide examples of the practical ways in which applied design facilitates co-design. The Design Council's Double Diamond framework (2004), was applied to discover and define problems more clearly. User experience (UX) research can visually define the needs, goals, and behaviors of healthcare users. The methods used included contextual laddering video interview, task analysis and empathy-journey mapping, providing insights into diverse user needs and pain points (patient, family, clinical professionals). This information is critical in creating digital healthcare solutions that are tailored to personalised care.

2.1   Understanding the Patients Needs

A series of user personas were created to assimilate indicative patients who would use a virtual heart hub. A range of ages, conditions, lifestyles, needs, and goals were considered, from discussion with clinical staff. These were then used to create a series of empathy maps to model patients' experiences and emotions. Within a healthcare context, these allows clinicians to gain a deeper understanding of their patients' needs and perspectives informing personalized care. This can lead to better patient outcomes and satisfaction. A hybrid empathy-journey map (Fig. 1) was created to try and visualize the process a patient goes through to get to a cardiology appointment specifying the high and low points of that experience.

2.2   Personalised Healthcare, Positive Design and Task Analysis

During the 'Discover' phase it was critical to get the insights of the healthcare professionals who deliver the primary care. We conducted a contextual laddering video interview using a Socratic approach, with a cardiologist investigating their current approaches,

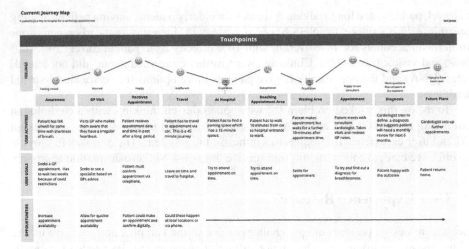

Fig. 1. An empathy-journey map documenting the current process of a patient experience for a cardiology appointment.

workflows, procedures and discourse used during patient assessment. Thereafter, a Positive Design workshop, using the happiness deck tool, helped shape our understanding of how Cardiologists envisaged values for a digital support product. Retrospective analysis of the interview informed the co-creation of design wireframes and initial prototypes of the proposed system. This was then visualised as a task analysis (Fig. 2).

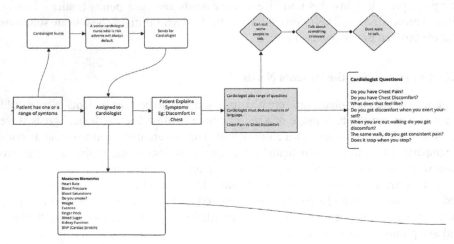

Fig. 2. A task analysis which highlights the workflow of a cardiologist when a patient is referred to them from a GP surgery.

The cardiologist interviews highlighted two main points:

1. There is significant opportunity for different clinicians to ask different questions, repeat questions or sequenced differently during health checks such as weight, lifestyles questions and kidney function, which are supported with routine vital signs monitoring. A digital tool could provide consistency and sequential flow.
2. Patients value the opportunity to talk with their cardiologist. This need not be face-to-face, it may be a phone or video call, reaffirming patient confidence. A digital tool affords multimedia interventions for simulated interpersonal communication.

3 Heart Hub

The 'Define' stage, in response to the research discovery involves conceptual design for what has been called a 'Heart Hub' providing a support tool to order clinical information and store vital signs data. Sketches were progressed to lo-fi prototypes created in the software Figma (Fig. 3). The locational context for the product would be within a public space in the heart of the community, such as a health centre, a pharmacy or public building. Following secure sign-in, patients would be guided through vital signs measurements, using existing medical IoT technology. Design fiction was used here to imagine and explore possible futures and to stimulate discussion around other ideal technologies, currently under developed. Following data collection, a clear summary would be visualized for the doctor and patient. The patient would then wait a few minutes (virtual waiting room) while the cardiologist makes a diagnosis or health status update, comparing previous serial monitored data. They then meet the patient on a video call to discuss the results. Visual brand guidelines were developed with a component library considering typography, color, and information architecture. This was then applied to an iterative design as a hi-fi prototype (Fig. 4). This simulated the real system for future usability testing.

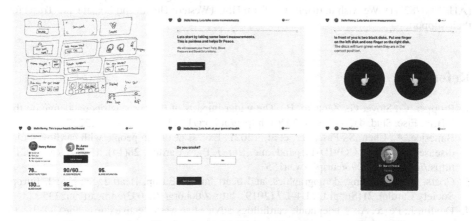

Fig. 3. A series of low and mid fidelity user interfaces for the heart hub

Fig. 4. The high-fidelity user interface that was developed for Heart Hub

4 Conclusion

This design demonstrator provokes further discussion and considerations about the potential of digital healthcare in a changing healthcare system. Research challenges within clinical settings during times of crisis were amplified between busy clinical teams and academic staff, where each operated under different delivery adaptions and human resourcing issues. This meant that timing and synchronizing meetings to discuss prototypes for feedback and testing was limited or the duration of collaboration elongated. Nevertheless, Heart Hub shows the role of design thinking, user experience design and speculative design for clinical problem solving. Its potential affords patient engagement with the consultant without the need to physically visit a hospital, and has applications beyond cardiology.

Acknowledgments. This work is part of a Design Exchange Partnership funded by AHRC (AH/W007827/1). We wish to thank staff from HSC (Western Health and Social Care Trust) for their support.

References

1. Propper, C., Stoye, G., Zaranko, B.: The wider impacts of the coronavirus pandemic on the NHS*. Fisc. Stud. **41**, 345–356 (2020). https://doi.org/10.1111/1475-5890.12227
2. Banerjee, A., Chen, S., Pasea, L., et al.: (2021) Excess deaths in people with cardiovascular diseases during the COVID-19 pandemic. Eur. J. Prev. Cardiol. **28**(14), 1599–1609 (2021). https://doi.org/10.1093/eurjpc/zwaa155
3. Coats, A.J.S.: Ageing, demographics, and heart failure. Europ. Heart J. Suppl. : J. Europ. Society Cardiol. **21**(Suppl L), L4–L7 (2019). https://doi.org/10.1093/eurheartj/suz235
4. Devlin, J., Peace, A.: A telephonic cardiology advice line was effective during the COVID-19 pandemic in both reassuring patients and in ensuring patients received optimal urgent care, ESC Congress 2021 - The Digital Experience, Session: Congress committee e-posters choice in cardiovascular nursing and allied professions: Advanced Clinical Practice, 27th August 2021 (2021)

5. NHS (2020) Delivering a NetZero National Health Service: PAR133, NHS England and NHS Improvement, October 2020
6. Buchanan, R.: Wicked Problems Thinking in Design. Des. Issues **8**, 5–21 (1992)
7. https://doi.org/10.2307/1511637
8. Desmet, P.M.A., Pohlmeyer, A.E.: Positive design: An introduction to design for subjective well-being. Int. J. Des. **7**(3), 5–19 (2013)
9. Fylan, B., Tomlinson, J., Raynor, D.K., Silcock, J.: Using experience-based co-design with patients, carers and healthcare professionals to develop theory-based interventions for safer medicines use. Res. Social Adm. Pharm. **17**(12), 2127–2135 (2021). https://doi.org/10.1016/j.sapharm.2021.06.004

Design of a Respiratory Biofeedback Serious Game for Stress Management Based on HRV Analysis

Nan Chao(✉), Wei Huang, and Xingjun Wang

Shenzhen International Graduate School, Tsinghua University,
Shenzhen 518055, China
chaon20@mails.tsinghua.edu.cn

Abstract. In today's world, individuals are encountering increasingly serious stress problems, which calls for useful self-regulation tools. Biofeedback training is a powerful technique for stress management and relaxation training. However, current biofeedback training systems still lack users' motivation as well as engagement in practicing due to abstract display and tedious tasks. Serious game is an effective tool being used in health care and medical treatment, which shows the potential to improve motivation and performance in biofeedback training while its application in this field is still in its infancy. This study intends to provide valuable strategies for biofeedback game design. And according to the design considerations, we developed a respiratory biofeedback serious game based on heart rate variability analysis. The results demonstrated that the game performed well in system usability and user experience, and it greatly improved user's motivation and engagement in biofeedback training.

Keywords: Biofeedback training · Respiratory training · Serious game · Heart rate variability analysis · Stress management

1 Introduction

Nowadays, the anxiety disorders and stress of young people have become increasingly serious, leading to severe health problems on both personal and social levels. According to the World Health Organization, since the outbreak of the COVID-19 pandemic, the global incidence of anxiety and depression increased by 25 percent. Therefore, it is of great significance to develop effective self-regulation tools for daily use.

Biofeedback plays an effective role in stress management. It assists people to learn how to regulate their physiological activities in order to restore or maintain autonomic balance and promote personal well-being [1].

Traditional applications of biofeedback training primarily involve presenting physiological information through abstract numbers or charts. Although this

C. Stephanidis et al. (Eds.): HCII 2023, CCIS 1833, pp. 16–24, 2023.
https://doi.org/10.1007/978-3-031-35992-7_3

method shows some effectiveness in relaxation therapy, these basic visual or auditory displays are often too abstract to understand. Users may find it difficult to gain effective control over them and tend not to use them in the long term. This can lead to negative user experiences and lack of motivation to continue practicing.

Therefore, how to improve the effectiveness of biofeedback training through human-computer interaction design and enhance users' motivation to practice biofeedback training are the problems that we try to address in our research.

In this paper, we designed a respiratory biofeedback serious game based on HRV analysis combining gamification and visualization to help users relax. And we utilized psychoengineering paradigm as design theory and draw specific design considerations for future research.

2 Concept and Related Work

2.1 Serious Game for Health

Serious games are defined as games that are designed for a specific purpose beyond entertainment, the use of serious games can provide an additional means to increase interest in training, education and evaluation of user performance. For instance, Serious games can be developed with the purpose of instructing and preparing healthcare practitioners on how to prevent medical mistake or to assist patients in rehabilitation by simulating the recurring activities they need to perform [2].

In the context of game design, four key components are essential to create an engaging and motivating game experience. The first component is rule, which establish a framework of patterns that connects the player to the game. The second component is challenge, which is critical for creating various difficulty levels that arouse player's motivation. The third component, interaction design, encompasses the various ways in which players communicate with and engage with the game. The last component is the goal, which represents the expected outcome of the game. Collectively, these four components form the basis for creating engaging and entertaining games, and offer satisfying experiences for players

2.2 Biofeedback Training for Self-regulation

Biofeedback is a technique used to help people monitor and gain control over physiological processes in their body. A biofeedback system measures physiological processes such as heart rate, heart rate variability, and galvanic skin response, and provides related feedback to the user about their current state. This feedback can help the user to learn how to control these physiological processes, and ultimately improve their overall health and well-being.

However, current biofeedback systems such as Polar Flow and Elite HRV, which make use of abstract graphical or numerical display to present the feedback parameters have many problems, which may hinder people from long-term use, since the parameters have complex meanings. Consequently, users might be frustrated and lack motivation to continue the training.

In this case, serious games have the potential to provide a fun and interactive way for individuals to learn to control their body's responses to anxiety and stress. However, both the theory and design of biofeedback game are still in need of research [3].

3   Methodology

3.1   Design Consideration Based on Psychoengineering Paradigm

In order to fill the research gap in game design theory of biofeedback training. This research utilized psychoengineering paradigm as the theoretical basis. Psychoengineering paradigm is a comprehensive model developed to instruct the design of biofeedback training system with five key characteristics in biofeedback learning, which are motivation, perceptibility, autonomy, mastery and learnability [4]. With consideration of the main components of serious game and biofeedback characteristics, we concluded with the following design strategies(see Fig. 1).

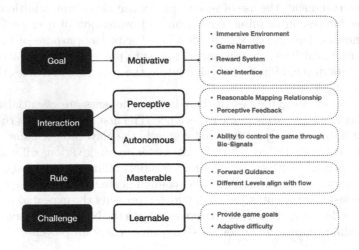

Fig. 1. Design Strategy of Biofeedback Game

The Goal of the Biofeedback Game Should Be Motivational. First, the virtual environment of the game should be immersive and relaxing which is helpful to restore the user's attention during the training. Meanwhile, it is important to provide clear and well-organized interfaces, by which the cognitive load on users could be reduced. A built-in reward systems and a game narrative and are also of necessity to make the game more motivational.

The Interaction of the Biofeedback Game Should Be Perceptive and Autonomous. The game should established a reasonable mapping between the rule of the game and physiological signals and based on the mapping relationship, a solid feedback should be provided in the game so that users can perceive their real-time states through feedback. At the same time, the interaction should be autonomous. The user need to be able to control the game by managing his or her physiological signals to acquire self-regulation methods.

The Rule of the Biofeedback Game Should Be Learnable. The mechanics of biofeedback training should be reflected in the game rules, so that users can learn how to regulate themselves through the game. Before started, appropriate materials should be provided to help users understand the meaning of physiological signals, how to control them in the game, and the meaning of feedback. In addition, personalized and adaptive guidance are also helpful to assist novice users by adaptively adjusting the difficulty of the game in response to their real-time state [6].

The Challenge of the Biofeedback Game Should Be Masterable. Since repetitive sessions are not beneficial for long-term biofeedback training, it is of necessity to set challenge in biofeedback games with consideration of flow theory [7]. In addition, applying goals into the game is also helpful. Game goals can be divided into non-compulsory and compulsory goals. Non-compulsory goals do not necessarily affect the progress of the game.While compulsory goals require the user to complete game tasks in order to keep the game going. Non-compulsory objectives are less stressful but less challenging for the user, whereas mandatory objectives are more challenging but more stressful. Depending on the goal in specific context, the game experience can vary.

It is important to note that not all of these design strategies need to be incorporated into every biofeedback game. It is of importance to take into account the specific target population and their unique needs and preferences.

3.2 HRV Analysis

Respiration Training and HRV Analysis. As previously mentioned, there are various bio-signals that can be utilized in a biofeedback system. Here we narrow down the research scope to respiration training based on HRV analysis, which is a useful technique for relaxation. Normally, a user who consciously keeps his or her breathing at around 6 breaths per minute may regulate his or her heart rate at a resonant frequency, which promotes relaxation in the responses of the autonomic nervous system. During the respiration training, the reaction of a user experiencing stress can be observed through heart rate variability [8].

As shown in Fig. 2, Heart rate variability is a method of measuring the extent of change in a continuous pulse signal, which is Inter-beat Intervals (IBI).Studies have shown that by analyzing HRV in ECG signals, it is possible to effectively identify changes in mental health. This method provides valuable insights into an individual's physiological response to stress, allowing for a more comprehensive understanding of their well-being [9].

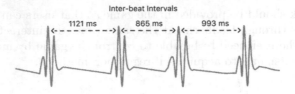

Fig. 2. Inter-beat Intervals.

Short-term HRV Analysis Algorithm. Through analysing IBI, several HRV parameters could be extracted, among which SDNN is the standard deviation of normal heartbeats. It reflects the variability between adjacent normal heartbeats, that is, the overall level of heart rate variability. The larger the SDNN value, the higher the heart rate variability, indicating that the activity of the autonomic nervous system of the heart is more flexible.

In this study, in order to provide short-term feedback to users in breath training. We used SDNN with Moving Window Analysis to indicate short-term HRV. A moving window of 15 heartbeats is applied and the HRV_{15} is calculated with the following formula, updating with each heartbeat.

$$HRV_{15} = \sqrt{\frac{1}{15} \sum_{i=n}^{n+15}(IBI_i - IBI_{avg})^2}$$
$$IBI_{avg} = \frac{\sum_{i=n}^{n+15} IBI_i}{15} \tag{1}$$

Figure 3 shows the relationship between the performance of breath training and HRV_{15}. When the user is concentrating on breath training (100s-200s), the IBI value changes from an irregular state into a sinus state, and HRV_{15} will reach a high level. And if the user did not focus on breath(0–100s and 200–300s), HRV_{15} will fall into a relatively low level. Based on the HRV_{15} algorithm we proposed, we developed a respiratory biofeedback in the following session.

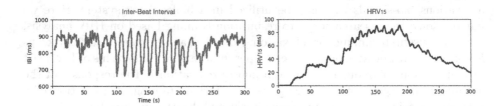

Fig. 3. HRV_{15} during breath training.

4   Serious Game Design

4.1   System Framework and Instrument

Figure 4 presents the framework of the game. The pulse signal is measured by a PPG sensor placed on the finger, which is connected to an Arduino board as a unit for data acquisition. The program on Arduino processes the raw pulse signal into IBI, and transmits the data to the PC game program developed on the Unity3D platform, transforming the IBI data and calculated HRV_{15} in real time.

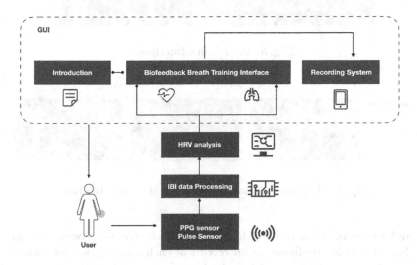

Fig. 4. Framework of HRV biofeedback game

4.2   Interaction Design

Breath Guide. Before started, the user first selects a desired breath pattern. Once started, an animated circle appears in the center of the game interface, whcih expands and shrinks in accordance with the user's chosen breath pattern, providing clear guidance for resonance breathing Fig. 5.

Biofeedback. The main objective of the game is to cultivate a tree by focusing on deep breathing. The game uses responsive biofeedback to visualize the user's breath training performance through the growth of the tree. As shown in Fig. 6, we have established a positive mapping relationship between HRV and the growth of the tree. For instance, if the user concentrates on breath training, their HRV will increase, and the tree will grow and remain in a thriving state. Conversely, if the user becomes absent-minded or anxious and doesn't focus on breath training, the leaves will fall, and the tree will become withered due to a low HRV value.

Fig. 5. Main Game Interface.

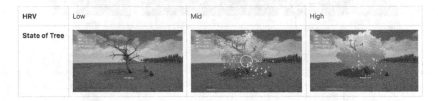

Fig. 6. Mapping Relationship between HRV and the tree.

Reward System. After the user has completed the training session, the system will plant a tree in the forest as an record of each training session, which will motivate the user to keep practicing. And key factors such as the change of HRV or heart rate during the training are also recorded and presented to the user.

5   User Experiment

5.1   Procedure

To investigate the user experience and usability of the system. We conducted a preliminary user test with 6 students from University of Geneva.GEQ questionnaire was utilized to evaluate the immersion, motivation, flow and other aspects of the game. We also used System Usability Scale(SUS) and User Experience Questionnaire (UEQ) to evaluate the system.

The participants were divided into two groups. Group 1 tried traditional biofeedback system in the first session, and then experienced the game in the second session, while Group 2 experienced both session as well but in reverse order. Each session lasted three minutes. After each session, the participants took a three-minute break and completed the questionnaires.

5.2 Results

The research results are shown in Fig. 7. In SUS test, the biofeedback game had an average score of 64 (total score=80), which is relatively higher than control group. This indicates that they considered the game to be user-friendly in terms of usability. In UEQ test, the biofeedback game significantly outperforms the control group in terms of reliability, immersion, novelty, and efficiency. This demonstrates that the system provides a better user experience. As for GEQ evaluation, the experiment group has a significant advantage over the control group in terms of flow, immersion and positive emotions. Overall, the results indicated that the game performed well in system usability and provided a more enjoyable user experience. And it has the potential to enhance user's motivation and engagement in respiratory training.

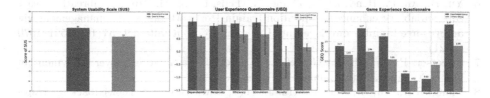

Fig. 7. Results of user experiments.

6 Conclusion

In this paper, we presented the design of a respiratory biofeedback game, which aimed to make it motivational and relaxing for user to practice self-regulation skills. To achieve this goal, we first derived specific design strategies in the context of serious game based on psychoengineering paradigm. Using these design considerations, we developed a respiratory biofeedback game based on HRV analysis and conducted a user experiment to evaluate its effectiveness. Results demonstrate that the game has the potential to enrich people's motivation in biofeedback training. We believe it is essential to arouse people's attention in mental health and provide ubiquitous and convenient tools for self-regulation, and we hope our work could attract more attention to game design in biofeedback training.

7 Future Work

Future studies need to evaluate the long-term effectiveness of the design. We would also try to utilize virtual reality to provide a more immersive and enjoyable game environment. Furthermore, we hope that our work can provide valuable insights for researchers in the field of biofeedback training.

References

1. Yu, B., Funk, M., Hu, J., Wang, Q., Feijs, L.: Biofeedback for everyday stress management: a systematic review. Frontiers in ICT **5**, 23 (2018)
2. Wattanasoontorn, V., Hernández, R.J.G., Sbert, M.: Serious games for e-health care, Simulations, Serious Games and Their Applications, pp. 127–146 (2014)
3. Lüddecke, R., Felnhofer, A.: Virtual reality biofeedback in health: a scoping review. Appl. Psychophysiol. Biofeedback **47**(1), 1–15 (2022)
4. Gaume, A., Vialatte, A., Mora-Sánchez, A., Ramdani, C., Vialatte, F.B.: A psychoengineering paradigm for the neurocognitive mechanisms of biofeedback and neurofeedback. Neurosci. Biobehav. Rev. **68**, 891–910 (2016)
5. Parnandi, A., Ahmed, B., Shipp, E., Gutierrez-Osuna, R.: Chill-Out: Relaxation Training through Respiratory Biofeedback in a Mobile Casual Game. In: Memmi, G., Blanke, U. (eds.) MobiCASE 2013. LNICST, vol. 130, pp. 252–260. Springer, Cham (2014). https://doi.org/10.1007/978-3-319-05452-0_18
6. Yu, B., An, P., Hendriks, S., Zhang, N., Feijs, L., Li, M., Hu, J.: Vibreathe: heart rate variability enhanced respiration training for workaday stress management via an eyes-free tangible interface. Int. J. Human-Comput. Interact. **37**(16), 1551–1570 (2021)
7. Sweetser, P., Wyeth, P.: Gameflow: a model for evaluating player enjoyment in games. Comput. Entertainment (CIE) **3**(3), 3 (2005)
8. Liang, R.H., Yu, B., Xue, M., Hu, J., Feijs, L.M.: Biofidget: Biofeedback for respiration training using an augmented fidget spinner. In: Proceedings of the 2018 CHI Conference On Human Factors In Computing Systems, pp. 1–12 (2018)
9. Matsumae, A., Luo, R., Wang, Y., Nishimura, E., Motomura, Y.: Emotional data visualization for well-being, based on HRV analysis. In: Ahram, T., Karwowski, W., Vergnano, A., Leali, F., Taiar, R. (eds.) IHSI 2020. AISC, vol. 1131, pp. 1270–1276. Springer, Cham (2020). https://doi.org/10.1007/978-3-030-39512-4_194

Promoting the Mediterranean Diet: A Co-design Game Approach

Aikaterina Chatziavgeri[1]([✉]) [iD], Metin Guldas[2] [iD], Noemi Boqué Terré[3] [iD],
Asmaa EL Hamdouchi[4], Lazaros Gymnopoulos[1] [iD], and Kosmas Dimitropoulos[1] [iD]

[1] Information Technologies Institute, Centre for Research and Technology Hellas,
57001 Thessaloniki, GR, Greece
{kchatz,lazg,dimitrop}@iti.gr
[2] Nutrition and Dietetics, Faculty of Health Sciences, Bursa Uludag University,
Gorukle Campus, 16059 Nilufer, Bursa, Turkey
mguldas@uludag.edu.tr
[3] Technological Unit of Nutrition and Health, Eurecat, Technology Centre of Catalonia, 43204
Reus, Spain
noemi.boque@eurecat.org
[4] National Center for Energy Sciences and Nuclear Techniques, Nutrition and Food Research
Unit, BP 1382 RP 10001, Rabat, Morocco

Abstract. In the past few years, a plethora of serious games concerning eating habits have been developed aiming to help improve people's diet and prevent chronic diseases. However, little emphasis has been placed on the Mediterranean diet and the Mediterranean way of life. In this paper we propose a novel educational game that promotes the Mediterranean diet among school students in Mediterranean countries. The work was conducted within the PRIMA SWITCH-toHEALTHY project [1], with a focus on food groups, healthy ingredients, water intake, not skipping meals, and physical activity. The game design followed a co-design approach which is based on the educational game design principles [2]. A related questionnaire regarding game factors was adopted and adjusted to the requirements of the proposed game. Each factor consists of up to three questions, certain questions were updated and a new factor that reflects "Transfer to real life" was introduced. The purpose of this process is to gather end-user feedback, with the goal of optimizing and validating the game design. To avoid bias, respondents were diverse in terms of age, nationality, and status. Children, parents, researchers, and nutritionists from Turkey, Spain, Lebanon, Morocco, and Greece participated in the survey. The higher the score, the more satisfied the user is with each question; nevertheless, low scores can occasionally be justified. The game was revised in consideration to the responses, resulting in a co-designed game.

Keywords: Game-based learning · Nutrition · Mediterranean diet · Educational game

© The Author(s), under exclusive license to Springer Nature Switzerland AG 2023
C. Stephanidis et al. (Eds.): HCII 2023, CCIS 1833, pp. 25–32, 2023.
https://doi.org/10.1007/978-3-031-35992-7_4

1 Introduction

In recent years, busy lifestyles and fast paced life have resulted in a shift away from home-cooked meals towards consumption of unhealthy, processed foods. This trend has led to an increase in malnutrition, which is characterized by inadequate, excessive, or imbalanced intake of vital nutrients. It encompasses not only being overweight or obese but also non-communicable diseases related to diet. Undernutrition is another type of malnutrition and can manifest in four forms: wasting, stunting, underweight, and micronutrient deficiencies [3]. Typically, both children and adults usually consume packed meals and fast food from their school or workplace canteens. Inadequate nutrition education, which should begin in the early childhood years, is another major factor leading to unhealthy dietary habits.

Recognizing the need for innovative approaches to address poor dietary habits, serious games have emerged as a promising educational tool designed to enhance traditional teaching methods. By combining engaging gameplay with educational content, serious games offer an opportunity to promote healthy behaviors and improve nutrition outcomes [4]. They have been successfully used in various fields, including healthcare and business, to encourage physical activity, prevent sedentary lifestyles, and promote healthy behaviors [5–7]. In the context of nutrition, serious games can teach players about food groups, balanced diets, and simulate real-world scenarios, such as meal preparation and food selection, to help players make informed decisions about their diets. "Barty" and "Space Adventures" are serious games aiming to prevent obesity in children [8, 9]. The "Robo-cook's Path" is a multiplayer board game where the players gain points when answering correctly in questions that show up depending on the tile the player is placed [10]. Research has demonstrated that educational games can improve children's eating habits in various ways. These games have been shown to enhance children's attitudes about nutrition and increase fruit and vegetable consumption. Additionally, through these game-based approaches new foods are introduced to children, leading to a more varied diet [11].

Thus far, concerning educational games, little emphasis has been placed on promoting the Mediterranean diet. The contribution of this paper lies in the design and development of a digital learning experience, the "SWITCHtoHEALTHY" "Tamagotchi"-like [12] game, a potential solution to help "revive" the Mediterranean diet and promote healthy eating habits. The game facilitates nutrition education, as it teaches players about balanced, varied diets and food groups, it focuses on reducing poor dietary intake and encourages physical activity. To engage the user in the game experience, a co-design approach was followed, allowing the incorporation of user feedback and preferences. The game also incorporates a unique "Transfer to Real Life" factor, which evaluates the player's retention and application of the knowledge gained during gameplay.

2 Methodology

The "SWITCHtoHEALTHY" game was designed following the game-based learning design model proposed by Yen-Ru Shi and Ju-Ling Shih [2]. This model comprises eleven design factors that have been verified for usability in two application examples.

Each factor has been thoroughly examined, analyzed, and verified with the help of a user questionnaire, which includes up to three questions for each factor. It is important to note that not all factors are essential for every game genre; for instance, puzzle games may not place emphasis on "Sociality". This design model offers flexibility in its application to various game genres, including our own game. It can also assist educational game developers in integrating teaching content into their game design. The authors elaborate on the significance of each factor and how they interconnect between them.

In the next two subsections we first present an overview of the design factors and then discuss how we adapted them to create a customized design model for the "SWITCHto-HEALTHY" game. Overall, we describe the process of developing an end-user question-naire aimed at evaluating our game, based on the crucial game-design factors outlined in the design model.

2.1 Game Design Factors

In the following we provide an overview of the eleven factors of the game-design model [2]. i) *"Game goals"* are the fundamental basis of game design. It is important to provide clear and achievable goals and to reward the player upon their completion. ii) The *"Game Mechanism"* plays a crucial role in achieving the game goals by providing methods for players to interact with the game world. iii) The *"Interaction"* as the name implies, refers to game and player engagement and affects player satisfaction though the progress, assistance, and feedback they get. iv) *"Freedom"* is the component of players' immersion being enhanced by providing them with the ability to act freely (e.g. Choose and design their own avatar). v) *"Game Fantasy"* is enhanced when the story, environment, and educational material are harmoniously integrated in the game. vi) *"Narrative"* differs depending on the game genre and includes the storytelling through words or media. It must align with the teaching content. vii) *"Sensation"* of serious games, including audiovisual content, icons, colors, and layout, can enhance player motivation. viii) The *"Game Value"* is increased when designers consider user preferences to help them accomplish their objectives. ix) Although *"Challenge"* is not mandatory, it can increase players' immersion and motivation in their effort to reach their goals. x) *"Sociality"* of a game can be categorized into communication, cooperation and competition between players that can influence players' motivation. xi) *"Mystery"* factor is not necessary and gives the player a sense of curiosity and the desire to explore.

2.2 Game Co-Design Using User Feedback Questionnaire

In our game, we utilized 10 of the 11 variables (*Mystery* is excluded) and added an extra feature called *"Transfer to Real Life"*. The selection of design factors and their relative importance is a result of extensive discussions and meetings with the design team. Prior to game design, the focus was on the teaching content and specific goals of the game. The game emphasizes on the importance of food groups and a balanced diet, while also insists on reducing the intake of processed food and encourages players to work out regularly. Overall, the main target of the game is to promote the Mediterranean diet, which is known for its health benefits. Our design approach emphasizes on *Game goals, Game mechanisms, Narrative* and *Interaction* to engage and motivate players while they adopt healthier eating habits. Providing positive and negative feedback through speech bubbles reinforces learning and encourages players to make healthier choices in the game. Considering the game's audience, we prioritized the graphics, audio, and overall game environment (*Sensation* and *Game fantasy*) aiming to design a visually appealing, user-friendly, and up-to-date game.

Depending on the genre of a game, certain design factors may warrant a shift in focus to better suit its specific requirements. Since "Tamagotchi"-like games usually offer less *Freedom* and *Challenge*, we tried to strike a balance between these two factors. A key element of the *Challenge* factor is the sense of capability in successfully completing game tasks [2]. In our game, achievable objectives are offered, and players are allowed to make choices without becoming overwhelmed or disheartened. The *Sociality* factor in this game is exhibited through players' responsibility to nurture their virtual friend and their desire to compete with friends and family members to achieve high scores. Although the *Mystery* factor is a prevalent feature in many games and involves surprises that stimulate player exploration, it was not our intention to incorporate this aspect.

The new introduced *Transfer to Real Life* factor, assesses whether the players can retain and apply the knowledge gained in their everyday lives. This factor measures the extent to which a game can offer a valuable and applicable experience for its players. The primary objective of this game is not only to educate children on the principles of the Mediterranean diet and healthy eating, but rather to facilitate their adoption of these dietary habits and encourage them to maintain a balanced diet throughout their lives.

The questionnaire provided in [2], comprises up to three questions for each game factor. Based on this questionnaire, several modifications were made to better align the questions with the context of the game. In consideration of the game's specific parameters, certain questions were deemed irrelevant and therefore excluded from the questionnaire. Most of the questions have been simplified to ensure comprehension and facilitate ease of response for all users. The questionnaires and videos were provided in four languages: English, Spanish, French and Arabic. All game factor related questions are 5-point Likert scale, where 5 is translated to strong agreement.

To ensure that our game effectively incorporates educational content related to the Mediterranean diet, a co-design approach was adopted leading to an end-user questionnaire, consisting of three sections: demographic data, a simulation of the game (video) to introduce the game to the users, and game design questions. Through this approach, we aim to gain insights into how effectively our game incorporates the design factors and to identify areas for improvement. Our online questionnaire was delivered to participants in five Mediterranean countries, providing a diverse range of feedback.

3   The "SWITCH to HEALTHY" Game

Our game is a "Tamagotchi"-like [12] game addressed to families, where the players are responsible for the well-being of their virtual friend. It will be developed in Unity game engine, and it will be available as a mobile app for both android and iOS.

Some of the primary teaching objectives in the game are the familiarization with food groups, the avoidance of skipping meals, the adoption of balanced dietary habits, and the promotion of physical activity. To achieve these goals, all the fundamental factors mentioned in Sect. 2 were observed. Research has shown that players' engagement is increased when they can customize their avatar [13]. This feature is incorporated in our game since the player can select a color for their avatar at the beginning of the game. To maintain the interest, after several level upgrades, the possibility to add and change avatar accessories also unlocks.

When initializing the game, some guidelines are given regarding the gameplay and the daily goals. The player should feed the avatar at least three meals per day and lead it to work out at least once. To monitor progress, the game includes three basic daily metrics displayed at the top of the User Interface (UI): daily meals, daily food groups, and daily workout (Fig. 1.). An additional metric is shown as stars in the top right corner, measuring whether a meal contains "Choose rarely" products or not. One star is given per meal when "Choose rarely" ingredients are not selected. At the end of the day, if these metrics are above predetermined values, the player gains a daily medal (displayed at the top right corner of the UI). These values are verified for nutritionists and game designers. At the end of the week, if the collected medals are more than five, the player gets a level upgrade. Using the bottom buttons, the player can navigate between the three different game locations, namely the kitchen, gym, and closet.

Fig. 1. Breakfast screen; positive feedback after completing meal; workout mini game

To ensure a balanced diet, not only it is important to consume appropriate food, but also to adhere to a consistent meal schedule. It is worth noting that the game utilizes the mobile device's time to determine which meal to display (breakfast, lunch, afternoon snack, dinner). Therefore, depending on the current time, the player can select meal ingredients from a diverse list of foods that varies daily and promotes the consumptions of olive oil. The available choices differ depending on the meal type. To discourage the consumption of processed food and sugar, some ingredients are tagged with a "Choose rarely" tag. If ingredients with the "Choose rarely" tag are selected, the player does not earn a star for that meal. When the "Meal ready" button is clicked, the UI metrics are updated and a positive or negative feedback about the dietary choices is given through speech bubbles. Workout options (such as running and jumping rope) are presented as fun mini games.

Given the importance of sleep in the Mediterranean lifestyle particularly for children the game is programmed to freeze during nighttime to discourage excessive mobile phone use. Meal preparation will be time restricted according to the current mobile time and players will be limited to a maximum of two workouts per day. These measures aim to cultivate moderation in children's lives and to avoid unnecessary phone usage.

4   Results

The questionnaire described in Sect. 2.2 was disseminated to gather user feedback about the game design. The survey included 108 participants from five Mediterranean countries, 13 from Morocco, 8 from Greece, 36 from Spain, 12 from Lebanon and 39 from Turkey. Of the participants, 75% were between 18–45 years old, 17% were older than 45 years old, and 8% were younger than 18 years old. Most of the respondents (98.14%) use a smartphone while almost one out of three participants (35%) use a tablet.

Each design factor is assessed with up to three questions and the average value of each factor is calculated as the average of its corresponding questions. The results in Fig. 2 demonstrate that all factors have average values greater than 3.5, except for the *Game Value* factor (3.44). The introduced factor named *Transfer to Real Life* exhibits notably high values that are particularly encouraging for the game effectiveness. The crucial factors that we emphasized on the game design appear to have higher values compared with *Sociality*, *Freedom*, and *Challenge*.

Figure 3 displays the factors of *Challenge* and *Game Value*, along with their respective questions and values, which are worthy of further discussion. The *Challenge* factor exhibited significant variability across individual questions. This variability is desirable in our case due to the distinct meanings of these questions. However, it is important to note that a mean score of 2.86 for this factor is reasonable in game genres where *Challenge* is not a core element. In any case, players must feel capable of completing game tasks for the game to be engaging, as reflected by the average score of 4.08 for this factor. In contrast, the individual values of the *Game Value* do not appear to differ as greatly as those of the *Challenge* factor. As mentioned in Sect. 3, our intention is to discourage excessive mobile phone use, even for educational purposes. This is reflected in the value of the respective question in the *Game Value* factor (3.30).

The overall average of all factors is 3.90 (Fig. 2), and these results have been thoroughly analyzed to identify areas of improvement in game design; we focused on questions with the lowest values that were deemed unreasonable (according to the decisions described in Sect. 2.2). Most of these questions refer to the color, layout, and appearance of the game. Although their values were above 3.7, we still aim to enhance the game design. We have considered changing the workout games and potentially transforming it to a 3D format to improve the overall gaming experience.

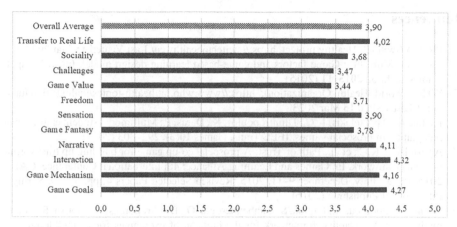

Fig. 2. Average user evaluation overall and per game factor (5-point Likert scale)

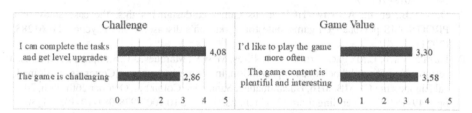

Fig. 3. User evaluation for individual questions of Challenge and Game Value factors

5 Conclusions

Game-based methods can effectively influence the behavior of children in either a positive or negative way. The "SWITCHtoHEALTHY" game is designed to encourage players to make better food choices and engage them in appropriate physical activities daily. The educational material and goals are related to the Mediterranean diet, with a focus on achieving balance in food groups and promoting the consumption of olive oil. This study utilized a questionnaire to confirm that educational games can effectively promote healthier dietary habits. The questionnaire was completed by a significant number of potential users to gather their feedback. The study also aimed to validate the incorporation of essential game factors such as *Game goals* and *Game mechanism* and to improve game design to enhance player engagement. The results of the survey were encouraging about both the design and the game efficiency.

Future work involves using the study results to redesign the game and then proceed to the development of the game. Once ready, the game will be tested to determine user satisfaction and knowledge retention and application. This will help to assess the effectiveness of the game in promoting long-term change in children's dietary behavior.

Acknowledgments. This paper is supported by the PRIMA program under grant agreement No 2133, project SWITCHTOHEALTHY. The PRIMA program is supported by the European Union.

References

1. PRIMA SwitchToHealthy project, https://switchtohealthy.eu/ Last Visited 15 Mar 2023
2. Shi, Y.R., Shih, J.L.: Game factors and game-based learning design model. Int. J. Comput. Games Technol. **2015**, 11 (2015)
3. WHO (World Health Organization), https://www.who.int/health-topics/malnutrition#tab=tab_1 Last visited 15 Mar 2023
4. Psaltis, A., Apostolakis, K.C., Dimitropoulos, K., Daras, P.: Multimodal student engagement recognition in prosocial games. IEEE Trans. Games **10**(3), 292–303 (2017)
5. Apostolakis, K.C., et al.: Path of Trust: A prosocial co-op game for building up trustworthiness and teamwork. In: Games and Learning Alliance: 4th International Conference, GALA 2015, Rome, Italy, December 9–11, 2015, Revised Selected Papers 4, pp. 80–89. Springer International Publishing (2016)
6. Grammatikopoulou, A., Laraba, S., Sahbenderoglu, O., Dimitropoulos, K., Douka, S., Grammalidis, N.: An adaptive framework for the creation of exergames for intangible cultural heritage (ICH) education. J. Comput. Educ. **6**(3), 417–450 (2018). https://doi.org/10.1007/s40692-018-0115-z
7. Dias, S.B., et al.: Assistive HCI-serious games co-design insights: the case study of i-PROGNOSIS personalized game suite for Parkinson's disease. Front. Psychol. **11**, 612835 (2021)
8. Parra Navarro, L.M., Paez Ardila, D.R., Pires, M.M.S., Marques, J.L.B.: Space adventures: a serious game for childhood obesity prevention. In: VII Latin American Congress on Biomedical Engineering CLAIB 2016, Bucaramanga, Santander, Colombia, October 26th-28th, 2016, pp. 149–152. Springer Singapore (2017) .https://doi.org/10.1007/978-981-10-4086-3_38
9. Gonçalves, F., Carvalho, V., Matos, D., Soares, F.: Development of a serious game to fight childhood obesity: "barty". In: 2020 IEEE Global Engineering Education Conference (EDUCON), pp. 1641–1646. IEEE (2020)
10. Kalvourtzis, T., Gymnopoulos, L., Milli, E., Cobello, S., Dimitropoulos, K., Daras, P.: Robocook's Path: An online multiplayer board dietary game. In: Proceedings of the 15th International Conference on PErvasive Technologies Related to Assistive Environments, pp. 330–335 (2022)
11. Chow, C.Y., Riantiningtyas, R.R., Kanstrup, M.B., Papavasileiou, M., Liem, G.D., Olsen, A.: Can games change children's eating behaviour? a review of gamification and serious games. Food Qual. Prefer. **80**, 103823 (2020)
12. Wikipedia (search: Tamagotchi), https://en.wikipedia.org/wiki/Tamagotchi, Accessed 14 Mar 2023
13. Ng, R., Lindgren, R.: Examining the effects of avatar customization and narrative on engagement and learning in video games. In: Proceedings of CGAMES'2013 USA, pp. 87–90. IEEE (2013)

Developing an Emotional Interaction Design for Social Anxiety Disorders (SAD)

HsiangTing Chien[1]([✉]), Hsin-Yi Huang[1], Teng-Wen Chang[1], Chi-Chi Shih[1], Jia-Rong Li[1], Zih-Syuan Wang[2], and Ching-Chih Chang[1]

[1] Department of Digital Media Design, National Yunlin University of Science and Technology Yunlin, Douliu, Taiwan
zoranachienht@gmail.com, tengwen@softlab.tw,
d11030001@yuntech.edu.tw
[2] Department of Computer Science and Information Engineering, National Yunlin University of Science and Technology Yunlin, Douliu, Taiwan

Abstract. This study focuses on using books in libraries as an interactive medium, aiming to help individuals with social anxiety disorder alleviate their anxiety and establish positive social experiences. The research background and literature review explore the relationship between social anxiety disorder and books, utilizing narrative frameworks and mirroring psychotherapy techniques to design an experience related to books, book reviews, and social experiences. Through case studies, needs exploration, scenario mapping systems, and interactive process design, we provide an innovative approach for individuals with social anxiety disorder who desire socialization, allowing them to find like-minded partners and engage in social interactions with reduced anxiety interference. Finally, this study summarizes system design, interface design, and user testing and evaluation.

Keywords: User experience · Social Anxiety Disorder · Information Visualization · Interactive Design · Experience Design

1 Research Issues and Literature

1.1 Users Group: Social Anxiety Disorder and Reading

Patients with Social Anxiety Disorder (SAD) have a lower willingness to seek medical treatment, but our investigation reveals that the involvement of digital media can increase patients' willingness to seek help. Social Anxiety Disorder presents common physiological and psychological characteristics. Physiological characteristics include dry mouth, sweating, rapid heartbeat, palpitations (irregular heartbeat), frequent or infrequent urination, gastrointestinal discomfort, facial and ear flushing, stuttering, and elevated blood pressure. Psychological characteristics involve excessive worry about social situations, excessive concern about others' evaluations, avoidance of social settings, worry about poor performance, cognitive bias, heightened self-consciousness, and fear of rejection.

C. Stephanidis et al. (Eds.): HCII 2023, CCIS 1833, pp. 33–40, 2023.
https://doi.org/10.1007/978-3-031-35992-7_5

These symptoms are defined according to the fifth edition of the Diagnostic and Statistical Manual of Mental Disorders (DSM-5) [1], The diagnostic criteria for Social Anxiety Disorder can be summarized into the following seven points:

1. Persistent fear of single or multiple social or performance situations, stemming from concerns about being scrutinized or humiliated by others.
2. Exhibiting discomfort when exposed to social situations.
3. Awareness that the fear is unreasonable or excessive.
4. Intolerable intense anxiety and distress.
5. Avoidance of social situations or exhibiting withdrawal, severely impacting daily life, work, or interpersonal relationships.
6. Persistent fear lasting six months or longer.
7. The fear is not attributable to the effects of medication or better explained by another mental disorder.

There are two main approaches to treating social anxiety disorder: cognitive-behavioral therapy and medication. Cognitive-behavioral therapy aims to help patients adjust their perceptions of their physical and mental states to face social situations with a healthier mindset. Medication therapy, on the other hand, uses anti-anxiety medications to regulate physiological conditions, reduce sympathetic nervous system activity, and alleviate anxiety and fear. Both approaches emphasize the importance of anxiety relief and stress reduction in improving symptoms. Many studies suggest that reading can alleviate anxiety and promote mental and physical well-being. [2, 3]. Thus, this study chose books as a medium to explore a healthy social approach. The research setting is a library, providing an ideal environment for patients to find partners with common interests in a safe atmosphere and engage in social interactions with other readers.

The aim of this study is to use reading and books as a medium to help patients divert their attention and find partners with common interests through book reviews. Engaging in alternative social interactions in the tranquil library environment can help inspire individuals with social anxiety disorder to increase their willingness to socialize.

1.2 Experience Design

Experience Design (XD) encompasses various fields such as physical, online, virtual reality, and augmented reality. This study focuses on the design related to social experiences. By adopting the five major aspects of User Experience (UX) design methodology, we find that individuals with social anxiety disorder have unmet social needs due to anxiety and automatic thinking. They avoid social interactions, but what they fear is not socializing itself but rather negative social experiences. Therefore, we draw upon cognitive behavioral therapy techniques and combine them with narrative frameworks to design a blended virtual and real-world interactive experience that can reduce anxiety and cater to the habits of patients. The cognitive-behavioral therapy and narrative framework will be discussed in detail in subsequent chapters.

1.3 Experience Design Cases

According to the research cases conducted by Bian, Chang, Lu, Yu, and Chang et al. [4–6], the relationship between reading, interactive spaces, the Internet of Things, and experience design is demonstrated. In [4], an interactive reading space is created, utilizing collective drawing to provide a diverse form of reading output. [5] employs horticultural therapy as a medium to facilitate emotional interaction experiences between elderly caregivers in skipped-generation families and their grandchildren who are away from their hometown. [6] develops an experience design that provides a warm embrace to alleviate the loneliness of young Chinese people who have left their hometowns. These cases illustrate that numerous fields have already begun to comprehensively develop towards experience design and will further develop more innovative interactive design solutions.

1.4 Comprehensive Induction of Cases

In addition to the experience design in Sect. 1.2, this section incorporates a comprehensive summary of existing social anxiety-related app cases. The Challenger app [7] encourages users to write notes after completing challenges, which are called "messages in a bottle." Miloff emphasizes that these notes are not meant to become chat rooms, but rather to encourage users to re-engage with challenging tasks. This concept is also borrowed in our study. Furthermore, research by Eysenbach et al. [8] shows that patients with social anxiety disorder who spend more time online perceive stronger online social support and encouragement. These cases demonstrate the application of experience design across multiple fields, highlighting the relationship between reading, interactive spaces, the Internet of Things, and experience design. It is evident that experience design has begun to provide more innovative solutions and can be applied across various fields, such as education, health, gaming, etc., to enhance user experience and satisfaction.

2 Research Design

2.1 Cognitive Behavioral Therapy (CBT)

Cognitive Behavioral Therapy (CBT) is a psychological treatment approach aimed at resolving problems by changing an individual's maladaptive cognitive and behavioral patterns. The therapy focuses on two core elements: cognition and behavior. During the treatment process, therapists collaborate with clients to explore the mutual influence between negative thoughts, emotions, and behaviors, and provide corresponding strategies to facilitate change. Through this method, clients can learn self-regulation, achieving psychological well-being and functional improvement. Cognitive Behavioral Therapy has been widely applied in treating various psychological disorders (such as anxiety, depression, obsessive-compulsive disorder, etc.) and has achieved significant therapeutic effects.

2.2 Narrative Framework

Joseph Campbell's "Hero's Journey" (Monomyth) is a universal narrative framework that describes the heroic adventures in myths and legends. This framework consists of three stages: initiation, trials, and return. The hero departs from the familiar world, explores unknown territories, faces challenges, and eventually brings back valuable achievements. In the initiation stage, the hero receives a call to adventure, initially refuses the call, and finally accepts the call to enter a new world. The trials stage includes facing challenges on the path, confronting the ultimate crisis, and obtaining the final reward. In the return stage, the hero experiences a rebirth, brings wisdom and treasures back to the original world, and becomes a paradigm or savior.

2.3 Social Interaction Methods

Effective social methods can help improve the quality of interpersonal interactions. These include good listening skills, appropriate self-disclosure, friendly body language, respecting others, timely greetings and expressions of gratitude, communication skills, emotional intelligence, empathy, sense of humor, and teamwork. These skills involve effective communication, empathic ability, adaptability, and situational awareness. By understanding and respecting the needs of others, as well as adapting to different social situations, individuals can make appropriate behavioral choices. Integrating these methods can help alleviate social anxiety and improve an individual's adaptability and success rate in social situations. For most people, it's not difficult to flexibly apply these skills, but for individuals with social anxiety disorder, these skills need to be learned. Therefore, this study aims to test whether experiential interaction design can effectively achieve such outcomes.

3 Research Results

3.1 Demand Exploration

In this study, the interview method and AEIOU observation method [9] were used to gather information from library staff about how patrons use related equipment and the process of borrowing and returning books in the library. Based on these interviews, three personas were created: the Book Seeker, the Book Collector, and the Other Type. These three personas were then organized into a Table 1 [10] using the AEIOU observation method framework [9].

Through Table 1, we can clarify the representative tasks, task contents, tools used, and areas passed through for each of the three persona types. It can also be seen that before the Fate system intervention, these three types of readers were exploring the field at different times and spaces, using different strategies. This is quite inconvenient for the book-seeking and book-collecting readers. Therefore, this study draws on one of the treatment methods for social anxiety disorder cases in the field of psychology: Cognitive Behavioral Therapy (CBT), and a treatment technique under this method: Introduction to Imagery Rescripting (ImRs). This technique has three stages: revisiting, mastering, and empathizing. By using the alternative experiences generated through these three stages, this study combines them with Joseph Campbell's Monomyth[11]framework to design the Scenario Map System. The content of the Scenario Map System will be explained in the next section.

Table 1. AEIOU comparison table for the three personas.

Activities 活動	找書	藏書	協助找書
Environments 環境	宿舍、圖書館、圖書館5樓	圖書館、圖書館7樓	圖書館座位區
Interactions 互動	在宿舍用筆電查詢館藏、較速圖書館能走到對應樓層、發現找不到書，下樓詢問工作人員。	在圖書館用電腦查詢館藏、走到對應樓層、拿起書本走到其他樓層藏這。	原本在看書、發現王伯書在藏書、從旁觀察幫書舉動、協助就熏要找書
Objects 物件	筆電、手機、書架	手機、書架、書	書本、書架
Users 使用者	尋書型	藏書型	其他型

3.2 Scenario Map System

This system refers to Imagery Rescripting and Joseph Campbell's Monomyth [11] to assist the narrative turning points of the Scenario Map System. The system starts with creating a virtual avatar, and then, through the three stages of Imagery Rescripting, it allows the socially eager individual to immerse themselves in the virtual avatar and generate self-empathy (Aymerich-Franch et al., 2014). During the book-collecting and book-seeking process, participants take clue photos, create clues, and return book photos after finding the book. By writing messages to their partner, they provide an imaginative space for the waiting socially eager individual. After completing the book-seeking task, the other socially eager individual writes a reply to the book-collecting participant, initiating a continued social connection.

3.3 Interaction Process

From the previous section, we can understand that the Scenario Map System is formed by constructing a virtual avatar, Monomyth, and the framework of Imagery Rescripting. In this section, we will focus on describing the interactive processes under these frameworks and how they meet the needs of socially eager individuals, as shown in Fig. 1.

The biggest difference between the book hiding and book searching processes lies in the second stage of challenges and temptations. When hiding a book and creating clues, the person also needs to write a message to their future partner. Since the corresponding book searching behavior does not happen immediately, writing a message to the partner allows the person hiding the book to imagine their future partner while waiting. At the same time, the message provides immediate feedback for the person who eventually finds the book, as well as serving as a basis for both parties to decide whether they want to continue this connection.

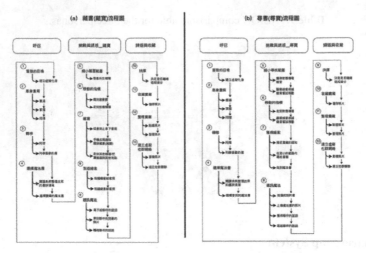

Fig. 1. (a) Book hiding process diagram, (b) Book searching process diagram

4 Conclusion and Analysis

4.1 System Design

The Fate system structure (Fig. 2) centers around the library, with book searchers and book hiders on the left and right sides, respectively. Both parties establish a connection through the Scenario Map System and carry out interactive behaviors at different stages, such as creating virtual avatars, making book recommendations, taking photos for hiding and searching for books, leaving messages for each other, and finally opening a chat room. The entire process revolves around books as the core element.

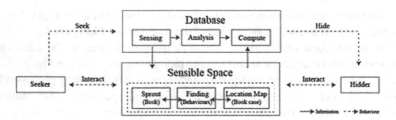

Fig. 2. Fate System Structure

4.2 Interface Design

In this study, based on the theory of Aymerich-Franch and others, an interactive process is designed for individuals with social anxiety to create virtual avatars, which helps to alleviate anxiety and generate resonance. Using the three steps of imagery rescripting, the socially anxious individuals are assisted in narrating their past experiences, thereby building self-compassion. Then, six dimensions are created, and books are recommended to those who desire social interaction. These dimensions were derived through repeated testing by the researchers and participants using the KJ method. Additionally, the interaction of hiding and searching for books is designed, requiring the input of hiding and finding locations, as well as providing clues and evidence. Finally, with both parties' consent, a chat room is opened for subsequent communication and social interaction.

4.3   User Testing and Evaluation

In this user test, two female digital media graduate students were invited to participate, using both the LINE mobile app and the computer version of Meet. The aim was to explore the differences in user experience on different devices. Test participants pointed out that button and link operations were difficult, causing confusion. Another participant was curious about the upper limit for the number of recommended books, as well as the number of books for hiding and searching. Currently, the limit is set to three or five books, as odd numbers help users make decisions. The number of books depends on the countdown time for hiding and searching for books.

References

1. Shapse, S.N.: The diagnostic and statistical manual of mental disorders. Last modified, 2008
2. Lewis, D.: How Reading Can Reduce Stress. Mindlab International, Sussex University, UK, Galaxy Stress Research (2009)
3. Adler, K.A.: Reading: the key to addressing students' social emotional needs in the time of COVID-19. New Jersey English J. **2021**(10), 2 (2021)
4. Yu, T.-T., Chang, T.W.: A Designer Embedded Book Space Experiment', in Editor (Ed.)^(Eds.): 'Book A Designer Embedded Book Space Experiment' (Springer, 2021, edn.), pp. 661–670 (2021)
5. Bian, Y., Chang, T.-W.: AMISA: A Pilot Study of an Emotional Supporting Device Between Friends Over Long-Distance', in Editor (Ed.)^(Eds.): 'Book AMISA: A Pilot Study of an Emotional Supporting Device Between Friends Over Long-Distance' (Springer, 2020, edn.), pp. 471–482 (2020)
6. Lu, J.-R.R., Chang, T.-W., Wu, Y.-S., and Chen, C.-Y.: 'Multimodal coexistence environment design to assist user testing and iterative design of higame emotional interaction design for elderly', in Editor (Ed.)^(Eds.): 'Book Multimodal coexistence environment design to assist user testing and iterative design of higame emotional interaction design for elderly' (Springer, 2020, edn.), pp. 197–209
7. Miloff, A., Marklund, A., Carlbring, P.: The challenger app for social anxiety disorder: New advances in mobile psychological treatment. Internet Interv. **2**(4), 382–391 (2015)
8. Eysenbach, G., Powell, J., Englesakis, M., Rizo, C., Stern, A.: Health related virtual communities and electronic support groups: systematic review of the effects of online peer to peer interactions', Bmj, 2004, 328, (7449), p. 1166
9. Martin, B., Hanington, B., Hanington, B.M.: 'Universal methods of design: 100 ways to research complex problems, develop innovative ideas, and design effective solutions' (Rockport Pub, 2012. 2012)

10. Hsiang-Ting Chien, H.-Y.H., Teng-Wen Chang, Ching-Chih Chang: 'Fate - Assist emotional interaction of social disorders through library behavior design', in Editor (Ed.)^(Eds.): 'Book Fate - Assist emotional interaction of social disorders through library behavior design' (ICTIK & DMD, 2022, edn.), pp. pp.810–819
11. Bär, E., Boshouwers, S.: 'Worlds of Wonder–Experience Design for Curious People', in Editor (Ed.)^(Eds.): 'Book Worlds of Wonder–Experience Design for Curious People' (Amsterdam: BIS Publishers, 2019, edn.)

Gamification of Self-care by Type 2 Diabetic Patients

Y. M. Choi[1] and W. Wilson[2]([✉])

[1] School of Design, Royal College of Art, Princeton 08544, NJ, UK
`christina.choi@rca.ac.uk`
[2] School of Industrial Design, Georgia Institute of Technology, Atlanta, GA 30332, USA
`ww25@gatech.edu`

Abstract. The project addressed by this paper was undertaken by graduate students in a healthcare-related design studio course within the MID program in the School of Industrial Design at the Georgia Institute of Technology.

After being briefed on the problem, students began with background research intended to help identify and understand the needs of various users, existing solutions, the use environment, as well as specific developmental requirements. In researching this problem further, the team that is the focus of this paper narrowed their attention from general medication adherence to the specific issue of medication adherence in Type 2 Diabetic patients. The team wished to address this population segment after discovering that the required adjustments to lifestyle & medication adherence are particularly problematic and challenging to the newly diagnosed.

This paper details the process of how this team leveraged "gamification" of the self-care process to ease the process of updating diet, medication and lifestyle habits. The design encouraged the patient to care for a virtual pet which moved the focus away from oneself and towards the virtual companion. By caring for this virtual pet, the patient could improve his/her self-care, presumably resulting in improved exercise, diet & medication adherence.

This "gamification" contrasted with more traditional conceptual solutions proposed by other teams that included improved medication organizers, medication dispensers, and reminder Apps. The lifestyle adjustments required by a Type 2 Diabetes diagnosis are largely a psychological and emotional challenge; addressing these problems through providing care for a virtual companion was a novel approach.

Keywords: Gamification · Virtual Pet · Industrial Design · Type 2 Diabetes

1 Introduction and Background

More than 37 million people in the United States have diabetes, with 90–95% of them having type 2. With Type 2 diabetes, the body does not respond to insulin normally, resulting in abnormally high levels of blood sugar. Type 2 diabetes often develops in people over 45, but it is increasingly prevalent in children and teens (CDC 2022). Successfully managing Type 2 diabetes requires a number of significant lifestyle changes.

© The Author(s), under exclusive license to Springer Nature Switzerland AG 2023
C. Stephanidis et al. (Eds.): HCII 2023, CCIS 1833, pp. 41–44, 2023.
https://doi.org/10.1007/978-3-031-35992-7_6

These changes can be difficult and lead to social or psychological problems that get in the way of a person's ability to self-manage their diabetes (Garrett and Doherty 2014). The need to perform glucose monitoring for example, has been described by adolescents as the least favorite task, leading some to avoid testing in social environments due the associated stigma (McCarthy et al. 2017).

Behavioral factors are an important component of successful diabetes self-management. There is a high prevalence of depression with diabetes and an opportunity to integrate mental health treatment with diabetes care in order to improve patient and public health outcomes (Ducat et al. 2014). Generalized anxiety disorder and eating disorders have been found to be more prevalent in people with diabetes (Robinson et al. 2013).

Gamification is an approach that has been successful for behavioral and educational intervention in a number of contexts. In children for example it has been shown to have significant impacts on nutritional knowledge and promoting good nutritional habits (Suleiman-Martos et al. 2021). It has shown highly satisfactory results in helping to develop healthy eating habits (González et al. 2016). With relation to diabetes, gamification and virtual environments have shown positive results in promoting behavior changes to reduce diabetes related risk, increased extrinsic motivation and provided positive reinforcement (Theng et al. 2015). This paper outlines how "gamification" was used in the design of an App to facilitate changes in diet, medication and lifestyle habits by newly diagnosed Type 2 Diabetic patients.

2   Method

The problem addressed by students was identified and presented to the class by Cognizant, which supported the student's efforts throughout the semester.

In one of several project prompts distributed to the students, Cognizant outlined the general problem of assuring medication adherence in individuals suffering from chronic diseases. Students formed teams of three to address specific prompts of their choosing. A virtual panel discussion was conducted in which experts from Cognizant provided additional detail and fielded questions related to the various prompts to help students identify specific problem areas to undertake and to define the scope for the resulting projects.

After being briefed on the problem, the team that is the focus of this paper narrowed their attention from general medication adherence to medication adherence in Type 2 Diabetic patients since this diagnosis typically occurs later in life after habits and lifestyle preferences are already established. In conducting background research, the team discovered that the most common causes for treatment non-adherence can be attributed to 1) Financial; 2) Mental; 3) Emotional; 4) Knowledge; and 5) Social factors. Based on their preliminary research, students developed specific design goals & design criteria to guide subsequent design development.

Students generated a wide range of ideas and used morphological matrices for concept mapping, resulting in three solution concepts that were presented to Cognizant and the class. Based largely on feedback received during this presentation, the team decided to move forward with the design of an App featuring a virtual pet to encourage the newly diagnosed to follow medication routines and make lifestyle adjustments such as diet & exercise. The journey that newly diagnosed patients typically undergo was examined in order to identify pain points to be addressed by the App (Fig. 1).

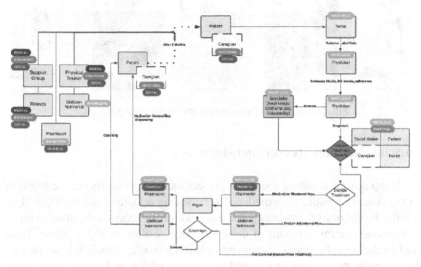

Fig. 1. Patient Journey from Diagnosis.

This App was developed and underwent preliminary usability testing with HCI students who evaluated the usability of the app (vs. the efficacy of the app in actually improving the habits of diabetic patients). Recommended adjustments were made to the App design and a final version was presented to Cognizant and the class at semester's end.

3   Results and Discussion

In theory an App based on interaction with a virtual companion could ease the transition to a healthier lifestyle for patients by shifting the focus from making required changes in one's own diet, medication and exercise to caring for another entity (in the form of the digital pet).

The team's design was an innovative approach to easing the difficult lifestyle transition faced by newly diagnosed Type 2 Diabetic patients and represented a more complete solution than most developed by other teams in the class – in that it addressed all the adjustments that must be made to one's lifestyle after a Type 2 Diabetes diagnosis, diet, medication adherence and exercise (Fig. 2).

Fig. 2. Selected Screenshots from the final App design.

4   Conclusions and Recommendations

The final App design resulting from this project focused primarily on the needs of the patient vs. those of healthcare providers. To be widely adopted (and as originally envisioned), the design must provide targeted users with easy access to healthcare providers by incentivizing the involvement of those providers. Solutions to this issue should be explored further in subsequent refinement of this approach. Clearly it is recommended that the design be prototyped further and that testing with actual users, Type 2 Diabetic patients, be conducted in order to provide a more objective measure of the potential usefulness of the App proposed by students.

References

CDC 2022. https://www.cdc.gov/diabetes/basics/type2.html. Accessed 1 Jul 2022

Ducat, L., Philipson, L.H., Anderson, B.J.: The mental health comorbidities of diabetes. JAMA **312**(7), 691–692 (2014)

Garrett, C., Doherty, A.: Diabetes and mental health. Clin. Med. **14**(6), 669 (2014)

González, C.S., et al.: Learning healthy lifestyles through active videogames, motor games and the gamification of educational activities. Comput. Hum. Behav. **55**, 529–551 (2016)

McCarthy, G.M., Rodriguez Ramírez, E.R., Robinson, B.J.: Participatory design to address stigma with adolescents with type 1 diabetes. In: Proceedings of the 2017 Conference on Designing Interactive Systems, pp. 83–94 (June 2017)

Robinson, D.J., Luthra, M., Vallis, M.: Diabetes and mental health. Can. J. Diab. **37**, S87–S92 (2013)

Suleiman-Martos, N., et al.: Gamification for the Improvement of diet, nutritional habits, and body composition in children and adolescents: a systematic review and meta-analysis. Nutrients **13**(7), 2478 (2021)

Theng, Y.L., Lee, J.W., Patinadan, P.V., Foo, S.S.: The use of videogames, gamification, and virtual environments in the self-management of diabetes: a systematic review of evidence. Games Health J. **4**(5), 352–361 (2015)

Artificial Intelligence Enhancement for Remote Virtual Consultations in Healthcare Provision for Patients with Chronic Conditions

Pranavsingh Dhunnoo[1](✉) (iD), Karen McGuigan[2] (iD), Vicky O'Rourke[3] (iD), and Michael McCann[1] (iD)

[1] Faculty of Engineering & Technology, Department of Computing, Atlantic Technological University, Donegal Campus, County Donegal, Letterkenny, Republic of Ireland
`pranavsingh.dhunnoo@research.atu.ie, michael.mccann@lyit.ie`
[2] School of Nursing and Midwifery, Queen's University Belfast, Belfast, UK
`k.mcguigan@qub.ac.uk`
[3] Faculty of Business, Atlantic Technological University, Donegal Campus, County Donegal, Letterkenny, Republic of Ireland
`vicky.orourke@lyit.ie`

Keywords: artificial intelligence · healthcare · remote consultation · chronic conditions · cyberpsychology · digital health

1 Introduction

The need for healthcare provision while being constrained by physical restrictions during the COVID-19 pandemic encouraged a rise in the adoption of virtual consultations [1, 2]. For instance, in the United Kingdom alone, remote care modalities ranging from audio to video calls made up around 90% of primary care provision amidst the public health crisis [3].

In particular, virtual consultations proved essential to provide continuity of care for patients with chronic conditions [4, 5]. For the latter demographic, such modes of care delivery can help alleviate the pain associated with travelling to receive healthcare while facilitating their disease management and treatment [6, 7]. Physicians treating such patients also favour the technology-mediated consultation for its ability to increase productivity and improve patients' health and management [7]. The convenience offered and the support provided by virtual consultations indicate that they will persist as viable options in the post-pandemic paradigm [8].

However, this increase in adoption of remote care models also highlighted pertinent challenges that need to be addressed as they become more routine [3, 9]. Issues around privacy, reliability, safety and accessibility have been raised [10–13], as have difficulties in identifying non-verbal cues and emotional distress [14]. Moreover, the associated perceptions, experiences and outcomes with virtual consultations remains unclear [9, 15].

Such inherent challenges require a better understanding of the technical and psychological factors at play during virtual consultations, and the extent to which they can be addressed through new technological approaches [7]. These can be investigated through a cyberpsychology approach, which can inform the development of digital, evidence-based solutions to address those relevant needs and challenges with the aim of improving interactions during those modalities as well as outcomes [16].

The relevant challenges and potential approaches are explored in this PhD study being conducted at the Atlantic Technological University (ATU) which aims to: 1) identify relevant psychological factors and technological challenges presented by virtual consultations; 2) assess the impact of emerging technologies in enhancing virtual healthcare provision for patients with chronic conditions; and 3) discover if the design and implementation of an artificial intelligence (AI) toolkit can provide valuable insight to address these challenges, enhance the patient experience, and improve outcomes.

2 Methods

In order to achieve its research aims, this PhD project adopts a mixed-method study design including qualitative and quantitative techniques at various stages. The development of the study is guided by the Integrate Design Assess and Share (IDEAS) framework in order to ensure that the prototype considers the human-technology interaction aspects and delivers an effective implementation [17]. The IDEAS framework integrates steps that require in-depth understanding of the end-users; an iterative development cycle of the proposed intervention through end-user input and feedback; evaluates and refines the developed prototype; whilst adopting principles of behaviour change theory [18–20]. Thus, appropriate methodologies have been proposed to achieve those aims during the course of the study.

The initial step of the PhD project involves conducting a scoping review that explores the associated behaviours of patients and healthcare professionals (HCPs) during synchronous virtual consultations and how supplemental technology can provide assistance. At the time of writing, this PhD study is at the scoping review stage which is being conducted according to the Preferred Reporting Items for Systematic reviews and Meta-Analyses extension for Scoping Reviews (PRISMA-ScR) guidelines [21]. From the selected databases and repositories, namely PubMed, MEDLINE, CINAHL, APA PsycNet, Web of Science, IEEE and ACM Digital, relevant literature have been identified based on a pre-defined search string. The search results are being screened independently by two researchers based on the inclusion criteria summarized in Table 1.

In the next step, the perspectives of HCPs and patients will be sought further through surveys and interviews to review existing remote provision modalities. Participants will be sought from healthcare organisations within ATU's network and will likely include patients with chronic conditions such as cardiovascular diseases, respiratory illnesses and diabetes, and the corresponding HCPs. Participants will be invited to initially complete a survey that explores their experiences of remote care provision.

Based on the latter findings and insights from the scoping review, semi-structured interviews will be conducted with a subset of the participants [22]. An interview guide will assist in the appropriate discussions [23]. Through these interviews, the study aims to

Table 1. Inclusion and exclusion criteria based on PCC framework for study selection

PCC Element	Include	Exclude
Population	Adults with non-malignant, non-communicable chronic conditions	Patients with no/any other condition Below 18 years of age Malignant and/or communicable conditions
Concept	Attitude towards synchronous virtual consultations between patient and healthcare professional Aspects around experiences, engagement, behaviours, intentions and barriers during such interactions	Traditional/face-to-face/non-virtual means of consultations Interactions with non-healthcare professionals
Context	Clinical settings and beyond Research centres	

identify the key psychological behaviours and engagement measures for successful virtual healthcare provision and management of patients with chronic conditions. Insights will be sought around experiences and perceptions when employing remote consultations to provide an overview of the current state of the technology by adopters. The interview results will also help highlight the relevant needs and challenges around aspects of privacy, reliability, safety, and accessibility when it comes to remote consultation modalities in practice.

To generate insights from the perspective of HCPs, focus groups will be designed with a snowball sampling approach to include HCPs employing remote care provision for those living with chronic illness [22]. Discussions in the focus groups will revolve around topics such as the benefits and challenges of current remote care provision, patient diagnosis, treatment and management, and opportunities for supplemental technologies to improve virtual consultations.

Based on the findings from the steps above, an appropriate AI toolkit will be designed and implemented in the study's third step to provide real-time assistance and post-consultation insights for virtual consultations. The specific AI model under-pinning the toolkit will be based on the insights from the earlier steps and the resources available. Thus, the model to be adopted can range from machine vision with deep learning interface to generative language models.

Once functional, feasibility testing of the prototype will commence. The toolkit will be implemented into the current system adopted by consenting participants who took part in the earlier qualitative phase of the study. Similar to the type of AI model developed, the type of assistance and post-consultation insights provided will focus on the needs identified in the earlier steps of this PhD project.

Subsequently, the effectiveness of the toolkit will be assessed through a further phase of qualitative research. Semi-structured interviews will be carried out with participants in order to gain feedback to refine the prototype and obtain a continuity of their assessment of the technology in the remote consultation process pre- and post-implementation of the AI toolkit. Whether the supplement of the toolkit enhanced the patient experience and improved outcomes will also be investigated. The follow-up investigation will also aid in assessing the success factors of the AI solution developed in order to gauge its effectiveness as well as inform future improvements that could potentially lead to wider adoption.

3 Discussion

This PhD project has as its objectives to investigate the challenges and factors involved in delivering the most effective patient experience and clinical confidence in remote consultations through a mixed methods study to identify these nuanced factors. Based on the primary research findings, the study will develop a novel AI toolkit to provide insight and direction to guide HCPs in order to ensure the maximum effectiveness to enable positive clinical outcomes from their online virtual patient interactions. The project involves a strong interdisciplinary research ethos bringing together the fields of data science, psychology, and innovation development to solve the complex challenges presented by this accelerated mode of healthcare delivery.

The aims and subsequent findings of this study are in line with recommended investigations in the field highlighted by researchers. The qualitative steps will shed light on relevant needs regarding current remote consultation offerings ranging from associated psychological behaviours to accessibility and privacy [10–13] and whether – and to what extent - the proposed AI toolkit will address those needs.

Embedding such a toolkit is relevant in the current healthcare provision paradigm. A 2021 analysis by McKinsey & Company identified that only around 40% of consumers surveyed wish to employ telehealth post-pandemic [24]. However, around 40%-60% consumers showed interest in virtual healthcare solutions with broader offerings such as a "digital front door" or lower-cost virtual-first health plan. This indicates the potential to deliver a more compelling remote care experience through supplemental technologies that could address telemedicine adoption barriers.

The assistance of supplemental technologies represents an opportunity for change with current modalities, including online and telephone options. For instance, Yuan *et al.*'s investigation on the remote care outcomes of heart failure patients during the pandemic identified increased mortality associated with telephone consultations, which is one of the current modalities of virtual consultations [25]. Supplementing this modality with other technologies, such as an assistive AI, could potentially contribute to better outcomes.

However, there are limitations to the project that need to be highlighted. Firstly, the PhD study is in its early stages, currently in the scoping review process. Thus, the planned methodological approaches detailed in this extended abstract may evolve as the project progresses.

Furthermore, the qualitative phases of this study rely on the recurring engagement of consenting participants. While this approach facilitates the assessment of the success factors of the AI solution provision, the possibility of attrition remains.

In addition, based on the scope and resources of the study, the bespoke AI toolkit developed will be more akin to a prototype than a ready-to-market tool; and may only be able to address a fraction of the spectrum of challenges inherent to virtual consultations [10–13]. Nevertheless, the investigation and application of emerging AI and data analytics from this study has the potential to inform the direction of development for future commercialised digital transformation strategies in healthcare provision.

However, the potential of virtual consultations to enhance the healthcare experience [26, 27], coupled with the need to improve the modality further with supplemental technology [24] and understand the relevant nuanced factors [9, 15] posit this PhD project as a timely and highly relevant study. It provides an avenue for applying and adopting novel technologies in the paradigm shift in healthcare provision practices that the field has experienced in recent years.

References

1. Grata-Borkowska, U., Sobieski, M., Drobnik, J., Fabich, E., Bujnowska-Fedak, M.M.: Perception and attitude toward teleconsultations among different healthcare professionals in the era of the covid-19 pandemic. Int. J. Environ. Res. Pub. Health 19(18), 11532 (2022)
2. Jiménez-Rodríguez, D., Santillán García, A., Montoro Robles, J., Rodríguez Salvador, M.D., Muñoz Ronda, F.J., Arrogante, O.: Increase in video consultations during the COVID-19 pandemic: healthcare professionals' perceptions about their implementation and adequate management. Int. J. Environ. Res. Pub. Health 17(14), 5112 (2020)
3. Murphy, M., et al.: Implementation of remote consulting in UK primary care following the COVID-19 pandemic: a mixed-methods longitudinal study. Br. J. Gen. Pract. 71(704), e166–e177 (2021)
4. Omboni, S., et al.: The worldwide impact of telemedicine during COVID-19: current evidence and recommendations for the future. Connected health. 1(1), 7 (2022)
5. Wang, H., Yuan, X., Wang, J., Sun, C., Wang, G.: Telemedicine maybe an effective solution for management of chronic disease during the COVID-19 epidemic. Primary Health Care Res. Dev. 22, e48 (2021)
6. Li, J., Chen, G., De Ridder, H., Cesar, P.: Designing a social VR clinic for medical consultations. In: Extended Abstracts of the 2020 CHI Conference on Human Factors in Computing Systems, 2020 April 25, pp. 1–9 (2020)
7. Rego, N., Pereira, H.S., Crispim, J.: Perceptions of patients and physicians on teleconsultation at home for Diabetes Mellitus: survey study. JMIR Hum. Factors 8(4), e27873 (2021)
8. Shaver, J.: The state of telehealth before and after the COVID-19 pandemic. Prim. Care Clin. Off. Pract. 49(4), 517–530 (2022)
9. Mann, C., Turner, A., Salisbury, C.: The impact of remote consultations on personalised care. Personalised Care Institute (May 2021)
10. Baker, D.C., Bufka, L.F.: Preparing for the telehealth world: navigating legal, regulatory, reimbursement, and ethical issues in an electronic age. Prof. Psychol. Res. Pract. 42(6), 405 (2011)
11. Caffery, L.J., Smith, A.C.: Investigating the quality of video consultations performed using fourth generation (4G) mobile telecommunications. J. Telemed. Telecare 21(6), 348–354 (2015)
12. van Eck, C.F.: Web-based follow-up after total joint arthroplasty proves to be cost-effective, but is it safe?: commentary on an article by Jacquelyn Marsh, PhD, et al. "Economic evaluation of web-based compared with in-person follow-up after total joint arthroplasty". JBJS 96(22), e192 (2014)
13. Litchfield, I., Shukla, D., Greenfield, S.: Impact of COVID-19 on the digital divide: a rapid review. BMJ Open 11(10), e053440 (2021)

14. Kilvert, A., Wilmot, E.G., Davies, M., Fox, C.: Virtual consultations: are we missing anything? Pract. Diab. **37**(4), 143–146 (2020)
15. Rodgers, M., Raine, G.A., Thomas, S., Harden, M., Eastwood, A.J.: Informing NHS policy in 'digital-first primary care': a rapid evidence synthesis. Health Serv. Deliv. Res. **7**, 1–54 (2019)
16. Dunn, R.S.: The Fourth Industrial Revolution: Cyberpsychology & Well-being (2021)
17. Mummah, S.A., Robinson, T.N., King, A.C., Gardner, C.D., Sutton, S.: IDEAS (Integrate, Design, Assess, and Share): a framework and toolkit of strategies for the development of more effective digital interventions to change health behavior. J. Med. Internet Res. **18**(12), e317 (2016)
18. Kumar, S., et al.: Mobile health technology evaluation: the mHealth evidence workshop. Am. J. Prev. Med. **45**(2), 228–236 (2013)
19. Pagoto, S., Schneider, K., Jojic, M., DeBiasse, M., Mann, D.: Evidence-based strategies in weight-loss mobile apps. Am. J. Prev. Med. **45**(5), 576–582 (2013)
20. Tate, E.B., et al.: mHealth approaches to child obesity prevention: successes, unique challenges, and next directions. Transl. Behav. Med. **3**(4), 406–415 (2013). https://doi.org/10.1007/s13142-013-0222-3
21. Tricco, A.C., et al.: PRISMA extension for scoping reviews (PRISMA-ScR): checklist and explanation. Ann. Intern. Med. **169**(7), 467–473 (2018)
22. Bryman, A.: Social Research Methods. Oxford University Press (2016)
23. Kvale, S., Brinkmann, S.: Interviews: Learning the Craft of Qualitative Research Interviewing. Sage (2009)
24. Bestsennyy, O., Gilbert, G., Harris, A., Rost, J.: Telehealth: a quarter-trillion-dollar post-COVID-19 reality. McKinsey & Company (9 July 2021)
25. Yuan, N., et al.: Practice patterns and patient outcomes after widespread adoption of remote heart failure care. Circ. Heart Fail. **14**(10), e008573 (2021)
26. Alsaif, S.S., et al.: Virtual consultations for patients with obstructive sleep apnoea: a systematic review and meta-analysis. Eur. Respir. Rev. **31**(166), 220180 (2022)
27. Richardson, E., Aissat, D., Williams, G.A., Fahy, N.: Keeping what works: remote consultations during the Covid-19 pandemic. Eurohealth **26**(2), 73–76 (2020)

Facilitating Student Counseling Through the Chatbot

Chia Min Ho[✉]

National Taipei University of Education, Jinan Rd., Zhongzheng, Taipei 100025, Taiwan
(R.O.C.)
shiloh10146@gmail.com

Abstract. Adolescents' psychological problems have become a global public health problem, and the age of teenage suicides in schools is gradually decreasing. However, many teens on campus are afraid to disclose their status to counselors and advisor. In the study, we interviewed Six university advisor and five students. Their thoughts and suggestions on functions such as "conversation response", "menu guidance", "push broadcast function", "improved student usage rate", "providing chatbot data to tutors as evidence for tutoring" of chatbots supporting tutoring. The study pointed out that the introduction of chatbots can help students express their emotions, and adding the option of chatting with teachers can increase students' ability to explain their own situation to teachers through chatbots, and help teachers manage class management while providing more accurate counseling resources. Based on the research results, we also discuss the functions that help to provide counseling effectiveness, such as introducing chatbots, counseling and counseling chatbot response methods, personalized broadcasting, increasing student usage, precise counseling, and counseling warnings. propose.

Keywords: Chatbot · Counseling · User Experience

1 Introduction

In recent years, adolescents in various countries have exhibited non-suicidal self-injury (NSSI) or suicidal behavior due to excessive stress. Many news reports have highlighted the serious public health issue of adolescent suicide that many countries are facing [1]. Related studies have pointed out that adolescence is a transitional period of physical and psychological growth, during which teenagers begin to develop self-awareness. However, literature also suggests that many adolescents experience negative emotional stress due to external factors during this stage of development, leading to adolescent suicide problems [2]. According to Duffy et al.'s [3] research, from 2007 to 2019, more and more adolescents worldwide have been suffering from different emotional disorders such as stress, depression, and suicide. Despite global efforts to address this public health crisis, the reality is that very few people are willing to seek professional help, with only about one-third of young people seeking assistance from professional medical resources [4]. In response to this situation, Olivari et al.'s [5] study suggests that the

C. Stephanidis et al. (Eds.): HCII 2023, CCIS 1833, pp. 51–59, 2023.
https://doi.org/10.1007/978-3-031-35992-7_8

reason why most young people are unwilling to seek professional medical resources is due to external social attitudes and social stigma-related issues. Similarly, Mojtabai's [6] research has also indicated that the majority of patients refuse medical treatment due to economic conditions, transportation, and other related high medical costs.

According to reports and data related to Taiwan's six major cities, about 13.3% of junior high and high school students show signs of significant depression, but less than 20% actively seek help, and 60.5% of those surveyed were unaware that their school has dedicated on-site psychologists. According to regulations under the Student Counseling Act for colleges and universities, the ratio of psychologists to students should be 1:1200, but due to the increasing demand for counseling in recent years, the ratio of psychologists to students in universities is significantly unequal. As a result, students often have to wait for months for counseling appointments, which further discourages them from seeking help and worsens their mental health conditions.

Furthermore, many teachers, who are often the ones closest to the students, are not aware of their students' mental and emotional conditions. Interviews with university teachers found that most of them rely on grades and attendance records to confirm students' conditions. However, potential issues such as bullying, relationships, family, academics, college admissions, and finances can only be addressed if the students disclose them. Therefore, teachers are often in a passive position when it comes to obtaining relevant information.

Given these circumstances, students are often deterred from seeking professional help due to the lack of timely counseling and concerns about social stigmas and negative perceptions. Clark et al. [8] pointed out that many people are afraid of face-to-face conversations in real life, which can lead to social anxiety because they fear that they will not be able to establish normal social relationships. However, through text-based communication, individuals can fully express their thoughts and emotions, and online chat can reduce their emotional anxiety. Dysthe et al. [9] found that many depressed adolescents are unwilling to share their mental health conditions with family, friends, or professionals, and often prefer to search for relevant information online or disclose their condition to strangers on the internet. Birnbaum's [10] research also found that about 30% of adolescents with emotional disorders have discussed their conditions on social media. Approximately 74.3% of these adolescents prefer to receive help or advice from professionals through social media or online software rather than face-to-face consultations.

Given that the internet and social media can increase teenagers' willingness to seek counseling, many companies have developed chatbots with counseling services [11]. Alm & Nkomo's [12] study found that young people today tend to prefer using chatbots for counseling over face-to-face counseling. Research found that most people choose online communication because they believe that strangers can provide objective advice without knowing them, and they do not have to worry about being recognized in real life. Sharing secrets and feelings with strangers online will not be leaked. Lee et al.'s [13] study found that social media technology can help people release their stress, depression, and anxiety. As chatbot technology becomes more sophisticated, natural conversation can enhance users' self-disclosure.

In the past, there have been many applications of chatbots in counseling to enhance users' level of self-disclosure. Through the technology of instant feedback from chatbots, students can have a stress-relieving space when facing emotional pressures, and the conversation also maintains confidentiality, allowing for the immediate release of negative emotions. Subsequently, the data from the conversations between students and chatbots are organized and classified and provided to class teachers who have more frequent contact with the students. Students with mild symptoms can receive immediate counseling intervention from the class teacher, while those with severe symptoms can be referred to a psychologist for counseling. This enables teachers to effectively manage the classroom and monitor students' physical and mental conditions, detect potential problems, and intervene and provide counseling in a timely manner, while also reducing the burden on psychologists. For students, the instant response of chatbots can effectively reduce their negative emotions, and counseling can be accessed anytime and anywhere.

2 Related Work

The Age of Teenage Suicide is Gradually Getting Younger. From 2007 to 2019, more and more young people worldwide have experienced different emotional disorders, such as anxiety, depression, suicide, and mood disorders due to various emotional stressors [3]. De la Serna et al. [14] have mentioned in their related studies on the age of onset of psychiatric illnesses among children (≤ 18 years old), adolescents (19–24 years old), and adults (≥ 25 years old) that most psychiatric illnesses occur before the age of 25 and are prevalent during childhood and adolescence. Long-term exposure to these negative emotions may cause mental health problems. According to the World Health Organization (WHO) report in 2021, there are more than 700,000 suicides annually, with the majority occurring among 15–29-year-olds [15]. The data from the Ministry of Health and Welfare in Taiwan also indicated that youth suicide has become a global public health issue and even a crisis. In recent years, the reported suicide cases among 15–24-year-old students in Taiwan have been decreasing year by year [16]. Previous studies have also revealed that in 2005, a study conducted on fourth-grade students in a primary school in northern Taiwan found that about 19.77% of children around the age of 10 had clear and obvious suicidal ideation. However, influenced by traditional Oriental culture, parents would not talk about related issues with their children. Even when children exhibited deviant behavior, parents would only think that the child was seeking attention from adults and would not give more attention to meet the child's emotional needs, leading to the aggravation of the child's psychological symptoms and more severe deviant behavior. Related studies have shown that the main causes of youth suicide are setbacks in school performance, campus bullying, peer pressure, social anxiety, and family relationships [17].

Chatbots used for Counseling and Guidance. From the above literature, it can be seen that adolescent psychological counseling has become a global public health issue. Birnbaum et al. [10] also found that about 74.3% of people prefer to receive online help or advice from professionals through social media rather than face-to-face consultations. Alm & Nkomo [12] also mentioned that young people nowadays prefer counseling through chatbots rather than FTF counseling. Previous studies have shown that the current social media technology and information dissemination help people release their stress, and the natural interactive dialogue experience of chatbots greatly enhances users' willingness to use them [13].We can see that most people prefer to transmit their information through the Internet mainly because the people in the online world are strangers to them, and they don't have to worry about their secrets being revealed. The biggest reason why most people like to talk to chatbots is their confidentiality. They can tell their troubles to the chatbot, and the chatbot will not tell others. In addition, some people prefer to talk to chatbots because they are better at communicating their thoughts through text than speaking. Therefore, many people who are not good at expressing themselves verbally like to talk to others through online chat. In recent years, countries have realized the importance of online counseling and remote treatment, and have developed chatbots with counseling services, such as Woebot and Wysa [11].

3   Method

User Needs Interview. According to previous studies, teenagers prefer to talk to chatbots rather than adults, and many studies have focused on improving teenagers' self-disclosure to chatbots. However, if the content of the conversation with the chatbot cannot be provided to counselors or homeroom teachers, there will be a gap between reality and ideal in the implementation of counseling.

For this reason, to design a chatbot that can support student counseling, we conducted interviews with 6 professors and 5 students who agreed to participate in the interviews in the researcher's workplace. The 6 professors served as homeroom teachers for different age groups of students, and the 5 students were between 16 and 20 years old. The interview process was recorded with the consent of the interviewees, and the interview could be terminated at any time if the interviewee felt uncomfortable.

We obtained the actual situation, difficulties, and system development needs of the students that the 6 teachers usually counsel, and also asked the 5 students about their reasons for not seeking help from teachers when they encounter stress or difficulties, as well as their needs for system development (Table 1).

Design Concept. The proposed design of this study is to provide emotional expression guidance to students who need to express their emotions. Through a guided menu, students can input and organize their emotions and clarify the source and situation of their stress. Additionally, the push notification function enhances the intimacy and stickiness between the students and the chatbot. Finally, the teacher can understand the student's situation by reviewing the content of the selected menu and the inputted text and intervene in counseling in a timely manner.

System Design. After confirming user requirements, the Evolutionary Prototyping or Evolutionary Development Strategy will be used to discuss and determine user requirements and create a prototype interface. The system prototype will be provided to users for use and modifications and expansions to user requirements. The developed chatbot prototype will be provided to students, and semi-structured interviews will be conducted with teachers and students to gather feedback and suggestions on the acceptability,

Table 1. Teachers' and Students' Perspectives and Needs for Tutoring

	Professor	Student
Reality	Teachers can only observe students' grades, classroom performance and status. There is no other way to understand a student's sources of stress and abnormal states	Students like to share their secrets with their friends, but they choose to process their negative emotions on their own rather than ask others for help
Predicament	1. The student is too young can not initiative the teacher for help 2. In the past, no relevant tutoring records were left, and the relationship with students needs to be re-cultivated during the handover 3. Not knowing exactly what the student is currently experiencing under stress	1. The student does not get along well with the advisor, and is unwilling to trust the advisor or ask for help 2. There is no contact information for the advisor and no channel for help 3. Fear of bringing negative emotions to others
User Needs	Understand the source of students' current troubles and provide the counseling information students need	There is a window to resolve emotions and respond to yourself immediately, and others cannot peek at what you express

usage status, and functional aspects of the counseling support chatbot. At the same time, teachers will be consulted on adjusting the backend data presentation and improving the requirements (Fig. 1).

Student Responses and Suggestions. After using the chatbot prototype interface, five students showed a high level of interest and willingness to use the chatbot as a means of expressing their emotions. They appreciated the fact that there were no time or space limitations to using the chatbot and that it was a machine, meaning they did not have to worry about negative emotions having any impact on the chatbot's impression of them. Regarding the chatbot's response, most students felt that the chatbot should use more kind, friendly, and caring language in its responses. Currently, the chatbot mainly asks about their situation, but the students hoped that the chatbot's responses would make them feel like they were talking to a friend. The students highly appreciated the option-based response feature, as it helped them avoid inputting incorrect information when they were emotionally overwhelmed, and they could check for any necessary supplement later. In terms of the chatbot pushing articles, the students hoped that a recommendation system could be integrated to push only articles that they were interested in and that the frequency of article pushing should not be too high, as it would make them refuse to use the chatbot. The students believed that if the chatbot could be integrated with school affairs to have personal assistant-like features, it would increase its usage frequency. Finally, regarding providing input data to teachers as a counseling basis, half of the students expressed support because they were afraid to talk to teachers and seek help due to fear of social judgment. The other half hoped that not all conversation content would be visible to teachers, but they would be willing to communicate with teachers if

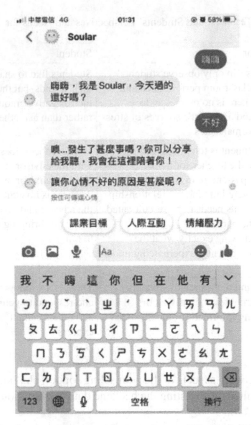

Fig. 1. Teachers' and Students' Perspectives and Needs for Tutoring [7]

there were additional options to talk with them or if the teacher saw the menu options they had chosen and was willing to initiate a conversation. The students said that they often just needed someone to talk to and did not want all their trivial matters to be known to teachers, but they would be more willing to seek help from teachers if there were more options available to talk with them.

Teacher's Responses and Suggestions. Six teachers believe that the introduction of a counseling chatbot can help both students and teachers, but they suggest integrating it with other school affairs to reduce the threshold for student use and increase the usage rate. Regarding the chatbot's responses, teachers believe that the current response method is too rational, and the chatbot should respond to students' input and improve the accuracy of its responses. At the same time, the needs of students with disabilities should be considered, and a voice conversation section should be provided. As for the chatbot's guided menu, all teachers believe that introducing a menu can help students provide a more organized explanation of their situation and current reactions. However, teachers suggest that the chatbot should provide some feedback based on students' input to help them relieve their emotions in real-time.

Regarding article push notifications, teachers also believe that personalized push notifications can improve student click rates. Regarding the integration of the chatbot with school affairs, most teachers believe that it can indeed increase students' usage rate, but the chatbot's purpose must be defined to avoid students using it for non-emotional relief purposes. All teachers hope that they can access the conversation data between students and the chatbot, which can help them manage their classes and provide more precise counseling assistance to students. Some teachers mentioned that in the past, they spent a lot of time building a relationship with students because they were not familiar with the students and did not dare to reveal their situation to the teacher. With this system, teachers can better understand their students and provide timely help. However, teachers also mentioned that for students in emergency situations, if the chatbot detects keywords from the conversation, it must immediately notify the teacher. In terms of data presentation, teachers also indicated that they do not want to see all conversation records, only the content of the menu, which can help them better understand the direction of the student's current difficulties, and they will pay more attention to observation.

Discussion. Regarding the overall design of the chatbot, most teachers and students express anticipation for further development, and many students feel troubled by the lack of channels to contact their teachers. Teachers also believe that through the chatbot, they can not only comfort students and provide them with an outlet to express their emotions but also the recorded data can help them quickly understand the students' situation, reduce the difficulties encountered by teachers in counseling students in the past, and provide a more accurate channel to understand the students' situation.

In terms of feedback mechanisms, according to the interview content, artificial intelligence still needs to be introduced in subsequent development. The current chatbot does not have enough intelligence to provide students with professional counseling and guidance. The interaction in the dialogue is also inadequate. In addition to adjusting and improving the content of questioning and response, professional counselors or medical professionals need to be consulted to help with the chatbot's conversation training when judging the student's urgent situation. In addition to the above, the responses also need to be adjusted to be more empathetic or caring in order to reduce the user's current anxious emotions, and to provide relevant advice or solutions based on the user's input.

Regarding the push function, artificial intelligence needs to be introduced to create personalized recommendation articles and push them based on the user's usual chat content, which can increase the user's click-through rate and create a direction for users to talk to the chatbot after reading the full article.

In addition to increasing the user's usage rate through the push function, it is also possible to plan to combine the chatbot that supports counseling guidance with school coursework or student interests to improve the student's usage rate. By constantly searching for information on the chatbot, students can be timely asked about their current situation and whether they have any worries to talk about, which can support the function of counseling guidance for students.

Finally, although most students are afraid that their teachers will see their conversation records with the chatbot, if there is a menu that allows students to choose whether these conversations should be shared with their teachers, it will not affect their willingness to continue using the chatbot for stress relief. It may even increase their willingness to use it. This can help them provide information they want to convey to their teachers, avoiding problems such as not being able to find their teachers or not having their teachers' contact information. Both students and teachers also mentioned that if the chatbot only records the content on the current menu, it can also help students release distress messages, and teachers can pay attention to what counseling resources the students may need at the moment.

4   Conclusion

In this study, we used an Evolutionary Prototyping or Evolutionary Development Strategy to continuously discuss, test, and improve the prototype system with users. We needed to adjust the chatbot's response style to make it more personable. Additionally, recommending relevant articles based on individual needs and integrating the chatbot with school-related affairs can increase its usage. Finally, students were willing to provide data on their menu selections to teachers or add an option to chat with them. They were also willing to view the chatbot as a communication channel between teachers and students. From the teacher's perspective, they could better understand student situations to facilitate classroom management and provide counseling resources more accurately.

References

1. Chen, X.Y., et al.: Influential factors of non-suicidal self-injury in an eastern cultural context: a qualitative study from the perspective of school mental health professionals. Front. Psychiatry 12, 681985 (2021). https://doi.org/10.3389/fpsyt.2021.681985
2. Ross, S.G., Dehay, T., Deiling, M.: The suicide prevention for college student gatekeepers program - a pilot study. Crisis J. Crisis Interv. Suicide Prev. 42, 48–55 (2021). https://doi.org/10.1027/0227-5910/a000686
3. Duffy, M.E., Twenge, J.M., Joiner, T.E.: Trends in mood and anxiety symptoms and suicide-related outcomes among US undergraduates, 2007–2018: evidence from two national surveys. J. Adolesc. Health 65(5), 590–598 (2019). https://doi.org/10.1016/j.jadohealth.2019.04.033
4. Radez, J., Reardon, T., Creswell, C., Lawrence, P.J., Evdoka-Burton, G., Waite, P.: Why do children and adolescents (not) seek and access professional help for their mental health problems? A systematic review of quantitative and qualitative studies. Eur. Child Adolesc. Psychiatry 30(2), 183–211 (2020). https://doi.org/10.1007/s00787-019-01469-4
5. Olivari, C., Mendez-Bustos, P., Nunez, R.: Confidentiality and help-seeking behavior for adolescent mental health problem. Acta Bioethica 28(1), 59–66 (2022)
6. Mojtabai, R.: Unmet need for treatment of major depression in the United States. Psychiatr. Serv. 60(3), 297–305 (2009). https://doi.org/10.1176/ps.2009.60.3.297
7. Ho, C.M.: Facilitating Student Counseling through the Chatbot: Perceptions of Teachers and Students (2022)
8. Beaudry, J., Consigli, A., Clark, C., Robinson, K.J.: Getting ready for adult healthcare: designing a Chatbot to coach adolescents with special health needs through the transitions of care. J. Pediatr. Nurs. Nurs. Care Child. Families 49, 85–91 (2019). https://doi.org/10.1016/j.pedn.2019.09.004
9. Dysthe, K.K., Haavet, O.R., Rossberg, J.I., Brandtzaeg, P.B., Folstad, A., Klovning, A.: Finding relevant psychoeducation content for adolescents experiencing symptoms of depression: content analysis of user-generated online texts. J. Med. Internet Res. 23(9), e28765 (2021). https://doi.org/10.2196/28765

10. Birnbaum, M.L., Rizvi, A.F., Correll, C.U., Kane, J.M., Confino, J.: Role of social media and the Internet in pathways to care for adolescents and young adults with psychotic disorders and non-psychotic mood disorders. Early Interv. Psychiatr. **11**(4), 290–295 (2017). https://doi.org/10.1111/eip.12237

11. Meadows, R., Hine, C., Suddaby, E.: Conversational agents and the making of mental health recovery. Digit. Health 6 (2020). https://doi.org/10.1177/2055207620966170

12. Alm, A., Nkomo, L.M.: Chatbot experiences of informal language learners: a sentiment analysis. In: Research Anthology on Implementing Sentiment Analysis Across Multiple Disciplines, pp. , 933–948. IGI Global (2022)

13. Lee, Y.C., Yamashita, N., Huang, Y., Fu, W.: "I Hear You, I Feel You": encouraging Deep self-disclosure through a chatbot. In: CHI Conference on Human Factors in Computing Systems (CHI). ACM (2020). https://doi.org/10.1145/3313831.3376175

14. Camprodon-Boadas, P., et al.: Cognitive reserve and its correlates in child and adolescent off-spring of patients diagnosed with schizophrenia or bipolar disorder. Eur. Neuropsychopharmacol. **53**, S552–S552 (2021). https://doi.org/10.1016/j.euroneuro.2021.10.822

15. World Health Organization. Suicide (17 June 2021). https://www.who.int/news-room/fact-sheets/detail/suicide

16. Ministry of Health and Welfare. Suicide Report (26 August 2021). https://www.cy.gov.tw/CyBsBoxContent.aspx?n=133&s=17592

17. Cuesta, I., et al.: Risk factors for teen suicide and bullying: an international integrative review. Int. J. Nurs. Pract. **27**(3), e12930 (2021). https://doi.org/10.1111/ijn.12930

18. John Tung Foundation. Young people become more emotional and less resilient due to COVID-19 (07 December 2022). https://www.etmh.org/News/news_more?id=800e133a51c744f1aa1201b925d941a9

On Developing an Intelligent AIoT Urine Bag by Integrating AHP and QFD

Jing-Jie Huang[1(✉)] and Chia-Hui Feng[2,3]

[1] Hillsborough High School, 466 Raider Boulevard, Hillsborough Township, Somerset County, NJ 08844, USA
`ashleyhuang093@gmail.com`
[2] Department of Creative Product Design, Southern Taiwan University of Science and Technology, No. 1, Nan-Tai Street, Yongkang District, Tainan, Taiwan R.O.C.
[3] Department of Information and Learning Technology, National University of Tainan, 3, Sec. 2, Shu-Lin St., Tainan 700, Taiwan

Abstract. In 2022, the World Health Organization reported that 1 in 6 people worldwide will be aged 60 years or older by 2030. By 2050, the global population of people aged 60 years or older will double. The demand for long-term health care for older adults is increasing. In particular, the rate of urinary tract infection in older adults in long-term health care institutions is increasing. In this study, a smart health care strategy was proposed for preventing sepsis caused by urinary tract infections. A smart AIoT urine bag was designed to monitor the urine bacterial levels of older patients who are confined to bed for an extended time. To design the bag, a questionnaire was first administered to 19 medical professionals. Semistructured interviews with three health-care professionals were then conducted for further analysis, and the analytic hierarchy process (AHP) was used to perform a quantitative calculation of functional weights and to extract key product criteria. Quality functional deployment evaluation was used to define the design in terms of the house of quality and to verify the AHP results by quantifying the AHP-identified criteria for the design of the AIoT smart urine bag. Posture sensing, one-way valve, out-of-bed displacement warning, and emptying equipment were the four most important criteria for consideration during product development.

Keywords: AIoT · QFD · AHP · CAUTI

1 Introduction

Population aging has been accelerating, which poses challenges for the care of older adults. According to statistics from the United States Census Bureau, 16.8% of the United States population were 65 years old or older in 2022 [1]. This population is expected to outnumber younger adults by 2034 and reach 23.4% of the population by 2060 [2]. This increase will burden long-term care services due to both the increasing demand for medical personnel and the high cost of medical care for older adults. The phenomenon will affect both national medical care systems and individual families.

C. Stephanidis et al. (Eds.): HCII 2023, CCIS 1833, pp. 60–67, 2023.
https://doi.org/10.1007/978-3-031-35992-7_9

Indwelling urethral catheters are the most commonly used catheters for treating older patients with disease. However, long-term use of these catheters often results in bacteria entering the bladder through the urinary tract, resulting in catheter-associated urinary tract infection (CAUTI) [3]. CAUTI comprises approximately 1 in 10 of all hospital infections [4]. In severe cases, patients may also experience septicemia; this is known as urosepsis. Moreover, antibiotics are usually prescribed by doctors to treat urinary infections; these treatments risk increases in antibiotic resistance. If CAUTI could be prevented, the associated risks, costs, and patient discomfort could be avoided.

The integration of artificial intelligence with the Internet of Things (AIoT) has been widely used in the medical industry for disease diagnosis, patient monitoring, or expanding access to health services in distant regions. Applications of AIoT for measuring blood coagulation, providing asthma-related alerts, and determining blood sugar levels have already been introduced and are widely accepted. For example, one smart medical device was created to detect substances in blood using an electrode implant, reducing the time physicians spend performing blood laboratory work [5]. AIoT has excellent potential for alleviating hospital burden by preventing CAUTI.

Motivated by both the need to decrease the number of medical staff required for elderly care and to prevent urosepsis and antibiotic resistance resulting from CAUTI, this study investigated the development of an AIoT urine bag that can determine whether a patient has CAUTI on the basis of white blood cell levels. Engineering verifications and validations were performed to ensure that the design of the innovative AIoT urine bag meets the needs of both patients and doctors.

2 Literature Review

2.1 Analytic Hierarchy Process and Quality Functional Deployment

The analytic hierarchy process (AHP) was first proposed by Saaty [7] in 1990 as a method of decision-making for problem-solving. Decision makers use literal judgment and numerical values for different criteria to evaluate which factors to prioritize while solving a problem. AHP has been expanded to product development in business as a method of assessing various product components and increasing product quality to improve market competitiveness. Applications of AHP for product development include the sustainable technology product proposed by Vinodh [8].

Quality functional deployment (QFD) is a quality system proposed by Yoji Akao that attempts to identify customer needs in the product design stage to enable the designer to focus on those features and reduce or eliminate unnecessary spending. QFD can be applied to direct discussions, written reflections from customers or professionals, or other data after these data have been quantized [9].

2.2 AIoT and Super-Resolution Generative Adversarial Networks (SRGAN) in Health Care

AIoT has been applied in the medical field to monitor and track patient progress both at home and in hospital settings. For example, remote patient monitoring is an AIoT application that has enabled monitoring of the health of patients with COVID-19 at home to ease the burden on understaffed hospitals during the COVID-19 pandemic. Gopinath [10] proposed an AIoT-based biosensing monitor that used dual probes to detect blood clotting factor IX to prevent hemophilia.

Super-resolution generative adversarial networks (SRGAN) can be used to recover details in images by upscaling the image to almost four times its original size [11]. This technique has been applied to the medical field to increase the accuracy of disease diagnosis. In 2021, several researchers proposed using SRGAN in dentistry to obtain higher quality and resolution for radiographic images to better identify com-mon oral diseases, such as caries and periapical disease [12]. The SRGAN method was also being used to improve cardiac magnetic resonance (CMR) imaging by producing a clearer and more precise heart structure for assessing heart disease [13]. The method can reduce misdiagnosis by avoiding false images caused by factors such as arrhythmia or breath-holding while an CMR image is being taken.

Zhang used SRGAN to increase the resolution of low-resolution images acquired from lens-free imaging modalities that use magnification, which may cause pixelation [14]. SRGAN is both more cost-effective and efficient than the pixel super-resolution technique often used by scientists, which requires special hardware and has a slower image processing speed. Zhang successfully used a CMOS chip to extract cell images, placed them under regular LED illumination, and input them into an SRGAN algorithm to acquire a higher-resolution image. The SRGAN method has been demonstrated to be effective for obtaining high-resolution images. In this study, this algorithm was proposed for improving the quality of images of white blood cells extracted from urine samples. Machine learning was then used to identify the level of infection.

3 Research Methodology

To develop the product for preventing urinary tract infections and urosepsis, a question-naire was designed and sent to medical professionals to determine the critical functions of the product. Moreover, semistructured interviews with three medical professionals were conducted to better understand the relevant medical procedures and requirements. The AHP pairwise comparison matrix was then applied for weight function quantization. Project managers, engineers, and product designers have used QFD to define function quality, verify features, and ultimately achieve quality accession in the design process; hence, this method was used to quantify the design of the AIoT urine bag [15, 16]. The research procedure is presented in Fig. 1.

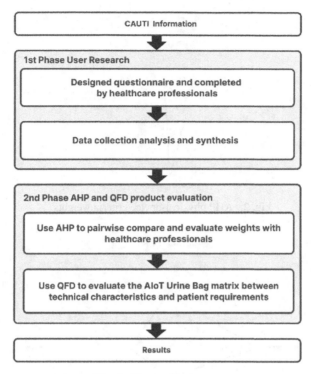

Fig. 1. Research process.

4   Results

Questionnaires were collected from 19 health care professionals to determine the criteria that should be included. The questionnaires comprised multiple-choice questions, and responders could choose one or more product features for each question. The top eight most-desired features (criteria) were chosen from the survey as follows: SRGAN/AI white blood cell count monitor (79.1%), notification to change the urine bag (79%), antibacterial urine bag (78.9%), alerting a nurse (68.4%), backflow prevention (63.2%), reporting of infection level in an application (63.2%), an emptying valve for the urine bag (57.9%), and nursing staff placement training (52.6%).

The AHP pairwise comparison process requires 5 ± 2 criteria in total [7]; hence, the eight criteria were distributed into two groups: technology criteria and physical-device criteria, and the AHP method was applied. In the technology group, backflow prevention was the top feature (67.9%), followed by placement training (18%), anti-bacterial urine bag (10.3%), and an emptying valve (3.8%). In the physical device group, notification to change the urine bag was the top feature (42.0%) followed by SRGAN/AI white blood cell count (25.5%), reporting infection levels (18.4%), and alerting a nurse (14.1%), as show in Fig. 2 and 3.

In the semistructured interviews, three medical professionals shared their opinions. They all had a positive attitude toward smart medical care regarding its convenience and ability to reduce demand for staff. They agreed that such devices can reduce the need

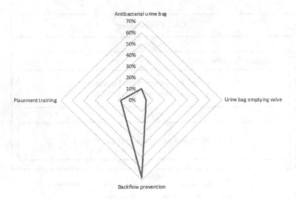

Fig. 2. AHP physical-device criteria weights

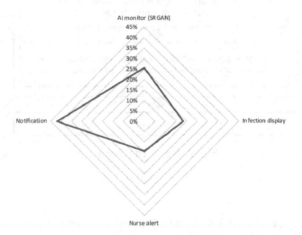

Fig. 3. AHP technique criteria weights

to perform routine tasks, which is particularly beneficial if a hospital has many patients. Smart medical care can identify meaningful data for analysis, such as the proposed urine measurement in this research. The device can also increase data accuracy; for example, patients are less precise than the device when recording urine output, and they may lose samples. They also stated that sensitivity and specificity are key metrics for a successful smart medical device. Moreover, they provided their opinions regarding conventional urine bags. Conventional urine bags must be changed regularly to avoid the accumulation of bacteria; this requires work from staff. Hence, they agreed that an application notification to change the urine bag would lower infection rates. If the AIoT urine bag could help monitor infection levels, the likelihood of serious disease could be reduced.

Finally, six product development experts collaborated to produce the QFD house of quality relationship matrix for 13 criteria: antibacterial material, emptying equipment, urine bag volume, urine bag fixed position, out-of-bed displacement warning, posture sensing, one-way urine valve, hygiene procedures and wear protection, indwelling tube replacement notification, SRGAN medical images, white blood cell range analysis, upper and lower urinary tract infection (UTI) infection level, and notification to change the urine bag. According to the weight and relative weight, these rank from high to low (weight importance/relative weight) as follows: posture sensing (671.6/10), one-way valve (655.3/9.7), out-of-bed displacement warning (617.6/9.2), emptying equipment (600.1/8.9), changing urine bag notification (600.0/8.9), upper and lower UTI infection level (544.9/8.1), hygiene procedure and wear protection (511.9/7.6), urine bag fixed position (502.6/7.5), indwelling tube replacement notification (492.8/7.3), urine bag volume (459.7/6.8), SRGAN (390.8/5.8), white blood cell range analysis (388.5/5.8), and antibacterial material (298.2/4.4), as show in Table 1. Hence, the critical product features are posture sensing, one-way valve, and out-of-bed displacement warning; these are all key for preventing backflow. The weight for SRGAN AI technology may be lower because the product development staff were unfamiliar with this technology for improving image quality. Providing a more detailed and thorough explanation of the technology might improve the expert ratings.

Table 1. QFD house of quality relationship matrix

Relative Weight	Weight / Importance	Demanded Quality	Antibacterial material	Emptying equipment	Urine bag volume	Urine bag fixed position	Out-of-bed displacement warning	Posture sensing	One-way valve	Hygiene procedure and wear protection	Indwelling tube replacement notification	SRGAN	White blood cell range analysis	Upper and lower UTI infection level	Changing urine bag notification
5.1	10.3	Antibacterial urine bag	Θ	Θ	O	Θ	▲	▲	Θ	▲	O	Θ	Θ	Θ	▲
1.9	3.9	Urine bag emptying valve	Θ	Θ	O	O	O	O	O	O	▲	▲	O	O	Θ
33.9	67.9	Backflow prevention	O	Θ	Θ	Θ	Θ	Θ	Θ	O	O	▲	O	▲	O
9.0	18.0	Placement training	▲	▲	O	Θ	O	Θ	Θ	Θ	Θ	O	▲	▲	Θ
12.7	25.5	AI monitor	▲	▲	▲	▲	▲	▲	O	O	▲	Θ	Θ	Θ	Θ
9.2	18.4	Infection display	Θ	Θ	▲	▲	▲	▲	Θ	O	O	Θ	Θ	Θ	O
7.0	14.1	Nurse alert	▲	Θ	O	O	Θ	Θ	O	Θ	Θ	O	▲	Θ	Θ
21.0	42.0	Notification	▲	O	O	▲	Θ	Θ	O	Θ	Θ	O	▲	Θ	Θ
		Weight / Importance	298.2	600.1	459.7	502.6	617.6	671.6	655.3	511.9	492.8	390.8	388.5	544.9	600.0
		Relative Weight	4.4	8.9	6.8	7.5	9.2	10.0	9.7	7.6	7.3	5.8	5.8	8.1	8.9

5 Discussion and Conclusion

In this preliminary study, AHP was used to determine the priority hierarchy matrix of medical requirements to evaluate the weight function for various factors; QFD was used to convert these requirements into technical specifications. The AHP and QFD methods were critical in the AIoT urine bag development and research processes because they ensure that the product will be medically sound and meet patient needs. Desirable product features were identified, and their functional importance was validated by health care professionals. The proposed AIoT urine bag monitors and records patient urine volume, color, and temperature. The medical professionals suggested that the AI technology should determine infection on the basis of increased white blood cell count range instead of the number of white blood cells. The product could then alert medical professionals and provide valuable information for their initial decision-making. The product's technical features can improve medical management quality, reduce the workload of medical staff, and prevent bacterial infection for older adults who are confined to bed or in long-term care. In the interviews, the medical professionals mentioned that antibacterial urine bags can be costly; whether this method would be cost-effective for AIoT products should be considered in a future study. Furthermore, SRGAN could be included in the product to improve the quality of white blood cell images extracted from urine samples, increasing the precision and accuracy of diagnosis. The generalizability of the results is limited by the small sample size of medical professionals involved. In the future, AIoT urine bag product prototypes could be produced to verify their effectiveness and reliability.

References

1. U.S. Census Bureau: United States Quick Facts (2022). https://www.census.gov/quickfacts/fact/table/US/AGE775221. Accessed 16 Jan 2023
2. U.S. Census Bureau: An Aging Nation: Projected Number of Children and Older Adults. https://www.census.gov/library/visualizations/2018/comm/historic-first.html. Accessed 16 Jan 2023
3. Nicolle, L.E.: Catheter associated urinary tract infections. Antimicrob. Resist. Infect. Control **3**, 23. (2014)
4. Van Decker, S.G., Bosch, N., Murphy, J.: Catheter-associated urinary tract infection reduction in critical care units: a bundled care model. BMJ Open Qual. **10**(4), e001534 (2021)
5. Pise, A., Yoon, B., Singh, S.: Enabling Ambient Intelligence of Things (AIoT) healthcare system architectures. Comput. Commun. **198**, 186–194 (2023)
6. Karasan, A., Ilbahar, E., Cebi, S., Kahraman, C.: Customer-oriented product design using an integrated neutrosophic AHP & DEMATEL & QFD methodology. Appl. Soft Comput. **118**, 108445 (2022)
7. Saaty, T.L.: How to make a decision: The analytic hierarchy process. Eur. J. Oper. Res. **48**(1), 9–26 (1990)
8. Vinodh, S., Kamala, V., Jayakrishna, K.: Integration of ECQFD, TRIZ, and AHP for innovative and sustainable product development. Appl. Math. Model. **38**(11), 2758–2770 (2014)
9. Kiran, D.R.: Quality function deployment, Chap. 30. In: Kiran, D.R. (ed.) Total Quality Management, pp. 425–437. Butterworth-Heinemann (2017)
10. Gopinath, S.C., Ismail, Z.H., Shapiai, M.I., Sobran, N.M.M.: Biosensing human blood clotting factor by dual probes: evaluation by deep long short-term memory networks in time series forecasting. Biotechnol. Appl. Biochem. **69**(3), 930–938 (2022)
11. Ledig, C., et al.: Photo-realistic single image super-resolution using a generative adversarial network. In: Proceedings of the IEEE Conference on Computer Vision and Pattern Recognition (2017)
12. Moran, M.B., Faria, M.D., Giraldi, G.A., Bastos, L.F., Conci, A.: Using super-resolution generative adversarial network models and transfer learning to obtain high resolution digital periapical radiographs. Comput. Biol. Med. **129**, 104139 (2021)
13. Zhao, M., Wei, Y., Wong, K.K.L.: A Generative Adversarial Network technique for high-quality super-resolution reconstruction of cardiac magnetic resonance images. Magn. Reson. Imaging **85**, 153–160 (2022)

14. Zhang, H., Zhu, T., Chen, X., Zhu, L., Jin, D., Fei, P.: Super-resolution generative adversarial network (SRGAN) enabled on-chip contact microscopy. J. Phys. D Appl. Phys. **54**(39), 394005 (2021)
15. Altuntas, S., Kansu, S.: An innovative and integrated approach based on SERVQUAL, QFD and FMEA for service quality improvement: a case study. Kybernetes **49**(10), 2419–2453 (2020)
16. Frizziero, L., Francia, D., Donnici, G., Liverani, A., Caligiana, G.: Sustainable design of open molds with QFD and TRIZ combination. J. Ind. Prod. Eng. **35**(1), 21–31 (2018)

Gamification App Design Based on Augmented Reality Technique for Depression Rehabilitation

Yukun Xia, Zijie Ding, and Yan Gan(⊠)

Huazhong University of Science and Technology, Wuhan 430074, Hubei, China
ganyan@hust.edu.cn

Abstract. Depression is one of the most common psychological disorders nowadays, and its causes are influenced by many factors such as family, personality, emotions, upbringing, and learning process. Usually, depressed patients are sensitive and pessimistic about all kinds of things, and they will show extreme emotions such as pain and misanthropy, and finally they may even have suicidal tendencies and behaviors. Gamification, on the other hand, is considered a reliable way to regulate depression and enhance the sense of experience and accomplishment; meanwhile, in the medical field, gamification has been used as a method to improve treatment compliance and participation. Therefore, in order to address the emotional regulation and self-management of depressed patients in the recovery pathway, augmented reality technology will be combined with the recovery process to design a gamified recovery aid. The design will use audience population interview method, follow-up interview method, questionnaire method, and literature search method for research verification, in-depth analysis of the psychological and realistic needs of depressed patients, formulation of software framework, rehabilitation model and game mechanics through their mapped design points, and enhancement of the visibility and participation of the rehabilitation game through emerging augmented reality means. The software consists of five main modules: game, daily plan, achievement, communication, and record, which regulates patients' depression through gamification and adjusts the game process based on daily records to reduce their depression and increase their motivation for recovery, thus assisting their self-management and recovery.

Keywords: Gamification Design · Depression Treatment · Augmented Reality · Application Design

1 Introduction

1.1 Depression Overview

Depression is a mental condition that impacts human emotions, cognition, orientation, and behavior. Depression is characterized by a sense of abandonment, isolation, and loss of self-worth, a heart that is battling and complex internal sentiments, and profound sadness lasting days to weeks, which can lead to suicidal ideation [1]. The difficulty in diagnosis or therapy stems from the patient's illness's cause, which is frequently a lengthy,

© The Author(s), under exclusive license to Springer Nature Switzerland AG 2023
C. Stephanidis et al. (Eds.): HCII 2023, CCIS 1833, pp. 68–76, 2023.
https://doi.org/10.1007/978-3-031-35992-7_10

complex, and highly individual matter. There may be psychological, depressed, social disengagement, and emotional imbalance effects. This ultimately impairs the effective coordination of a person's psychological state, resulting in a persistently negative disposition [2].

And when industrialization progresses and the degree of social production rises, people prefer to raise their stress and strain in order to obtain more value, which contributes to a rise in the pathogenicity of mental disorders such as depression. Depression is now the fourth most prevalent disease in the world [3]. Moreover, the frequency of depression is especially high among college students and those young adults who have recently begun working [4, 5]. When these groups have depressed symptoms, it is frequently difficult for them to recognize the need to see a professional psychologist in order to resolve their issues. Currently, the number of science-based software or gaming applications for assisting in the treatment of depression is limited, and their use is plagued by numerous issues, such as the absence of visual features, the inability to pinpoint the exact causative variables, and their ineffectiveness. Moreover, gamification and augmented reality (AR) are the fundamental design tenets of this program for addressing the aforementioned issues. The application of augmented reality technology and gamification design can boost patients' visual experience and sense of accomplishment, hence reducing depressive patients' bad emotions and allowing them to enjoy their life. It also allows individuals to improve their capacity for self-adjustment in order to lessen their reliance on external treatment.

2 Literature Review

2.1 Depression Overview

Gamification can be defined as a game application represented in other non-game domains or the use of game elements in a non-game environment [6]. Education, self-management, fitness, health, and early intervention for autism spectrum disorders are examples of field applications where gamification has been proved to be advantageous and an effective technique to encourage the user experience and foster a sense of accomplishment. Consequently, the frequency of gamification usage has surged in recent years and shows no signs of slowing [7].

Respecting the private psychological needs of depressed patients, gamification was used as the primary design objective in this study, combining the scientific approach of psychological guidance with the fun and entertainment of games, and integrating positive thinking habits and emotional control techniques into interactive games from which it is easy to derive a sense of accomplishment, in order to improve patients' self-esteem and emotional stability. This study employs a gamified and unique guidance paradigm, as well as augmented reality as a tool for information display. It is a crucial application tool that allows patients to meet their supplementary communication demands, obtain emotional value, and alleviate their emotions.

2.2 Pathological Features of Depression and Treatment Strategies

Depression is caused by dysfunctional families, unforeseen circumstances, developmental stress, previous injuries, and genetic factors. Depression is characterized by weight loss, apathy, irritability, bodily pain, anxiety, and suicidal ideation [8]. People with depression have difficulties thinking broadly and are unable to derive enjoyment from everyday activities in order to alter their mental state. People with depression typically experience a cycle of depression that reaches intense levels of sadness at various times and causes others to experience emotions of discomfort, dullness, and unhappiness. Depression causes numerous mental alterations. People with depression no longer think optimistically and will overthink self-created scenarios and logic, making it difficult for them to break out of their melancholy cycle and way of thinking, thereby increasing their aggravation. People with depression may feel helpless, useless, hopeless, and worthless; they lack friendship and communication; they have difficulties finding daily joy; and in extreme circumstances, they may want to end their life [9].

Cognitive behavioral therapy (CBT) is a psychotherapy method that teaches patients how to recognize and alter unhelpful or stressful thought patterns that negatively affect their behavior and emotions. Four of the most prominent cognitive-behavioral therapies include cognitive therapy, dialectical behavior therapy, multimodal therapy, and rational emotive behavior therapy. This style of therapy focuses largely on the patient's dysfunctional thoughts and leads to healthy thinking; it is the most well-researched form of psychotherapy accessible [10] and has a high rate of success.

2.3 Current Research on Gamification + Augmented Reality in the Field of Depression Treatment

The majority of research have demonstrated that gamification is an effective technique to increase user achievement and access, and it has proven successful in fields such as education and healthcare. Werbach and Hunter define gamification in game systems as a method that uses game features to enhance user experience and user engagement in For the Win [11]. In the treatment of depression, there is a significant demand for self-awareness and recognition, and the gamification approach is intended to fill this void.

Syed Ali Hussain et al. utilized an interactive virtual reality video as a visual environment for depressed patients, guiding them to name their life trauma and depressive experiences in order to access their key emotional points and use them for long-term treatment of depression, a move that aids depressed patients in enhancing their future communication intentions [12].

Oluwasefunmi Arogundade et al. addressed the psychotherapy of depression in adolescents using video games, and a questionnaire evaluation of the study revealed an 80% approval rating [1]. In the field of mood and depression detection, researchers led by Gali Amoolya developed an EEG recognition-based mood detection system that links the processed data of EEG signals to a virtual world for the basic diagnosis of depressed patients' mood states and provides calming feedback [13]. As a result of the general environment and technology advancements, people are beginning to adopt AR/VR techniques to treat psychological issues. A team of researchers at the University of Oxford created virtual reality therapies targeting psychological characteristics for the diagnosis and treatment of agoraphobia, which successfully reduced patients' concerns by 70 percent [14]. AR/VR technologies were utilized by scholars such as S. B. Goyal to reduce stress in depressed individuals during the COVID-19 era in order to improve their mental and emotional wellbeing. AR/VR games are utilized as an efficient means of alleviating stress, despair, and anxiety. Using deep learning, their team was able to diagnose early depressive disorders in patients and predict the level of treatment necessary to provide early alleviation and cure [15]. Using neurolinguistic programming, scholars such as antidepressant and antisuicide programs replace the previous professional therapies for depression. Using Microsoft Cognitive Services, experts such as Syed M. Nabeel Mustafa built antidepressant and antisuicide programs with powerful features for mood recognition, with the goal of providing users with individualized treatment services to help patients fight depression [9]. Additionally, the aforementioned findings imply that gamification and AR/VR have enormous promise in the field of psychotherapy, particularly the treatment of depression.

3 Emotion-Based Design Strategies for Intelligent Medical Systems

3.1 User Needs Research

Since the needs of depression groups are more individualized and each patient has different reasons for the formation of the disease, the author's team conducted group needs research through the interview method + questionnaire method. We screened out the typical common needs and made a targeted design for individual needs. The author's team interviewed 10 depressed patients of different ages in China and recorded and labeled the interviews, and the results are now divided into the following categories.

Visual Needs. The game's graphic design encompasses color, shape, and elemental patterns. The interviewed depressed people's demand for color is more inclined to low saturation of various colors with a soft feeling. In terms of shape, it is not advisable to use too sharp borders, which tend to cause stiffness and bring discomfort to the user group. In the selection of element patterns, try to choose illustrations or icons in a cute and fresh style. The above choices can give positive thinking guidance in the visual effect.

Auditory Needs. The majority of responders fear low or sharp sounds, which will cause them to feel insecure. More piano music or natural sounds should be included to the design of the gamified application to provide a sense of calm and safety.

Emotional Needs. People with depression are typically unable to effectively regulate their emotions, and emotional instability can easily lead to extreme sadness and other illnesses. In order to regulate their emotions, greater attention must be directed to their emotional needs; this is the foundation of depression treatment. It is proposed to include more sophisticated question-and-answer and voice functions to the design of the gamification program to assist the user group. Due to the fact that each user's growth experience and causes are unique, the application will listen to the user's conversation, develop more positive components of the user's memories, and borrow these elements to complete the learning process in order to connect with and motivate the user. To help the user through the learning process, the application must also present a hierarchy of rewards.

Interaction Requirements. Interaction is essential to the design of gamification. Before designing interaction flow and functions, design psychology, ergonomics, and user behavior should be investigated. Depressed individuals are prone to impatience and anxiety when operating; hence, it is preferable to eliminate intricate operation flows and difficult-to-understand interaction effects in gamification applications, and good instruction will put them at ease. Therefore, during the design phase of the gamified application, the interaction buttons must be intuitive and visually appealing, and the operation method must be straightforward and engaging. Additionally, engaging interactions contribute to the improvement of the user's thinking.

3.2 User Group Characteristics Analysis

Depression is characterized by fast and cyclical mood swings and frequently negative thought patterns. At the same time, the manner of thinking influences a variety of daily actions. Patients' psychological and behavioral features are distinguished by their sensitivity to external stimuli and low adaptability. Additionally, patients frequently experience self-doubt and anxiety, which can readily show as exhaustion and insomnia.

In order to verify the need classification and common behavioral characteristics in the interview results, and at the same time to understand more diverse individualized needs. The author's team conducted further research using a questionnaire method, designing question and answer options based on the interview results and expanding the research to the world. 512 questionnaires were distributed and 498 questionnaires were returned, of which 490 were valid. From the questionnaire results, it is concluded that the above visual, auditory, emotional and interactive needs are basically met, and most depressed people want a gentler interface style, more make natural and pleasant auditory effect, more personalized emotional function and more rich and interesting interactive effect.

Also among the responses, many more interesting personalized needs were received: adding more white noise to the audio for soothing mood or solving insomnia problems. In the social mode, activities with fewer people were preferred. In emotional expression, abstract expressions were preferred.

Based on the above research, a user portrait map was created using crowd clustering analysis (see Fig. 1). This can better help designers focus on problems and needs for the purpose of targeted design.

3.3 User Group Characteristics Analysis

Through the above research, we identified the target audience as youth and children, who are in a period of difficult self-judgment, and wanted to guide them as positively as possible to help heal from depression when it does not have a profound impact. We named the app "Love and Emotions".

The purpose of the design is as follows. Guide the user to think in a positive way; Use augmented reality to educate users about proper healing; To help users recognize themselves in different emotions through learning tasks; Reduce users' resistance to therapy and social interaction.

Process and Information Architecture Design. The application has four main functional sections: emotional, communication, science, and personal.

After identity login, the application will conduct some simple voice quiz or let the user create a picture, listen to the personal experience and sad things that the user tells,

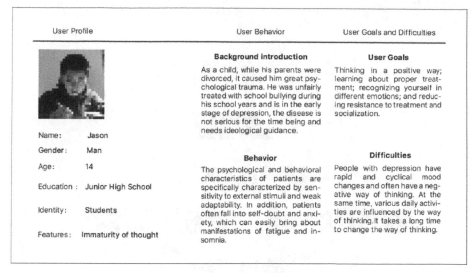

User Profile	User Behavior	User Goals and Difficulties

Background introduction

As a child, while his parents were divorced, it caused him great psychological trauma. He was unfairly treated with school bullying during his school years and is in the early stage of depression, the disease is not serious for the time being and needs ideological guidance.

User Goals

Thinking in a positive way; learning about proper treatment; recognizing yourself in different emotions; and reducing resistance to treatment and socialization.

Name: Jason

Gender: Man

Age: 14

Education : Junior High School

Identity: Students

Features: Immaturity of thought

Behavior

The psychological and behavioral characteristics of patients are specifically characterized by sensitivity to external stimuli and weak adaptability. In addition, patients often fall into self-doubt and anxiety, which can easily bring about manifestations of fatigue and insomnia.

Difficulties

People with depression have rapid and cyclical mood changes and often have a negative way of thinking. At the same time, various daily activities are influenced by the way of thinking. It takes a long time to change the way of thinking.

Fig. 1. A user profile analyzed from four aspects

the application will give answers and will record emotional data, and will improve the data in multiple game tasks and communication (see Fig. 2).

Communication Section. The application contains many types of games. The application represents different emotions through visual and auditory levels according to the user's cognitive level and personal experience, in order to improve the user's understanding of different emotions and reduce the level of resistance to others. In the mood section, users can first record their daily mood, and if the app picks up depression or other unusual moods, the app will generate a corresponding mood theme based on the analysis. The app will generate pictures, colors or sounds that feel similar to the emotions, and slowly change from the initial recorded negative mood expressions to positive ones, guiding users to recognize and change their emotions through visual and auditory shifts. At the end of each game, the app rewards the user with a badge, and at the end of the game, the user receives an email report of the mood change.

Communication Section. The application will generate a low-saturation, soft environment and play soothing piano music or white noise such as rain in the environment to help users relax their thinking and reduce defensiveness. In order to feel safe and private, users will use virtual images to confide in a psychiatrist or a friend to communicate in a way that guides them out of mental internal conflict and reduces resistance to treatment.

Science Section. The application will show the science content in the form of augmented reality, and will assign gamification tasks at the end of the science, the user needs to complete the game level by swiping and other gestures to increase the user's patience

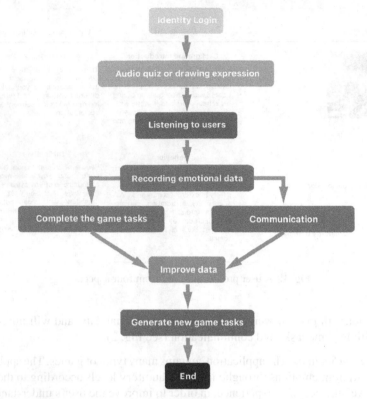

Fig. 2. Functional flow chart

and sense of achievement in the game. At the same time, the augmented reality function can be used to scan medicines or objects to obtain more information.

Personal Section. There are functions such as personal information, settings, my achievements, my mood report, and feedback.

3.4 Design Development

The interface of "love and emotions" application is shown (Fig. 3)

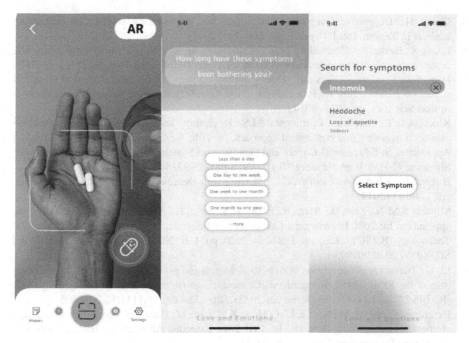

Fig. 3. Interface effect display

4 Conclusion

The "Love and Emotions" app combines gamification design and augmented reality technologies to deliver depression therapy ideas through literature study, interviews, questionnaires, and user group profiling. It can assist people in comprehending and realizing the correct style of thinking.

Due to the short development period, there are still some flaws in the design, resulting in a slightly different effect than anticipated. The design of the application must be continuously updated and iterated, and additional sample testing must be undertaken to confirm practicality. Through this work, the author hopes to provide light on depression treatment and improve the illness through gamification.

References

1. Arogundade, O., et al.: Psychotherapeutic tool for addressing depression in teenagers through video games. In: Abraham, A., et al. (eds.) HIS 2021. LNNS, vol. 420, pp. 483–492. Springer, Cham (2022). https://doi.org/10.1007/978-3-030-96305-7_45
2. Sarokhani, D., Delpisheh, A., Veisani, Y., Sarokhani, M.T., Manesh, R.E., Sayehmiri, K.: Prevalence of depression among university students: a systematic review and meta-analysis study. Depression Res. Treat. **2013**, 1–7 (2013)
3. Hassan, A.U., Hussain, J., Hussain, M., Sadiq, M., Lee, S.: Sentiment analysis of social networking sites (SNS) data using machine learning approach for the measurement of depression. In: 2017 International Conference on Information and Communication Technology Convergence (ICTC), pp. 138–140 (October 2017)

4. Chang, H.: Depressive symptom manifestation and help-seeking among Chinese college students in Taiwan. Int. J. Psychol. **42**, 200–206 (2007)
5. Lucas, S., Berke, A.: Counseling needs of students who seek help at a university counseling center: a closer look at gender and multicultural issues. J. Coll. Stud. Dev. **46**, 251–266 (2005)
6. Hamari, J., Koivisto, J., Sarsa, H.: Does gamification work?-A literature review of empirical studies on gamification. In: Proceedings of the Annual Hawaii International Conference on System Sciences, pp. 3025–3034 (2014)
7. Klock, A.C.T., Gasparini, I., Pimenta, M.S.: Designing, developing and evaluating gamification: an overview and conceptual approach. In: Tlili, A., Chang, M. (eds.) Data Analytics Approaches in Educational Games and Gamification Systems. SCI, pp. 227–246. Springer, Singapore (2019). https://doi.org/10.1007/978-981-32-9335-9_12
8. Hughes, R., Kinder, A., Cooper, C.L.: "Living with Depression", The Wellbeing Workout, pp. 139–143 (2019)
9. Mustafa, S.M.N., Zaki, H., Alam, S., Khan, M.S., Zafar, H.: Anti depression and anti suicidal application. In: 2020 International Conference on Information Science and Communication Technology (ICISCT), Karachi, Pakistan, 2020, pp. 1–6 (2020). https://doi.org/10.1109/ICISCT49550.2020.9079936
10. Li, D.: Treatment of depression from both biological and psychological aspects. In: Proceedings of the SPIE 12458, International Conference on Biomedical and Intelligent Systems (IC-BIS 2022), 124581G (6 December 2022). https://doi.org/10.1117/12.2660405
11. Deterding, S., Sicart, M., Nacke, L., O'Hara, K., Dixon, D.: Gamification: using game-design elements in non-gaming contexts. In: CHI 2011 Extended Abstracts on Human Factors in Computing Systems, pp. 2425–2428 (2011)
12. Hussain, S.A., Park, T., Yildirim, I., Xiang, Z., Abbasi, F.: Virtual-reality videos to relieve depression. In: Chen, J.Y.C., Fragomeni, G. (eds.) VAMR 2018. LNCS, vol. 10910, pp. 77–85. Springer, Cham (2018). https://doi.org/10.1007/978-3-319-91584-5_6
13. Amoolya, G., KK, A., Sai Venkata Swetha, G., Das, G., Geeta, J., George, S.N.: EEG-based emotion recognition and its interface with augmented reality. In: Thampi, S.M., Lloret Mauri, J., Fernando, X., Boppana, R., Geetha, S., Sikora, A. (eds.) Applied Soft Computing and Communication Networks. LNNS, vol. 187, pp. 41–56. Springer, Singapore (2021). https://doi.org/10.1007/978-981-33-6173-7_4
14. https://www.med-technews.com/news/five-ways-virtual-reality-is-transforming-mental-health/#:~:text=VR%2Denabled%20therapy%20is%20the,to%20treat%20a%20specific%20ailment.&text=VR%2Denabled%20therapy%20is%20a,lasting%20improvements%20in%20mental%20health
15. Goyal, S.B., Bedi, P., Garg, N.: AR and VR and AI Allied technologies and depression detection and control mechanism. In: Kautish, S., Peng, S.-L., Obaid, A.J. (eds.) Computational Intelligence Techniques for Combating COVID-19. EICC, pp. 203–229. Springer, Cham (2021). https://doi.org/10.1007/978-3-030-68936-0_11

Augmented Mirror Hand (MIRANDA): Advanced Training System for New Generation Prosthesis

Alexander Kovalev[1](✉) ⓘD, Anna Makarova[1] ⓘD, Matvey Antonov[1] ⓘD,
Petr Chizhov[3] ⓘD, Vladislav Aksiotis[1], Andrey Tsurkan[1] ⓘD, Alexey Timchenko[1,2],
Viacheslav Gostevskii[3], Vladislav Lomtev[4], Gleb Duplin[1] ⓘD, and Alex Ossadtchi[1] ⓘD

[1] National Research University Higher School of Economics, 101000 Moscow, Russia
koval.alvi@gmail.com
[2] Eberhard Karls University of Tübingen, 72074 Tübingen, Germany
[3] Lomonosov Moscow State University, 119991 Moscow, Russia
[4] Bauman Moscow State Technical University, 105005 Moscow, Russia

Abstract. This paper presents a novel training system called the Augmented Mirror Hand (MIRANDA) for advanced prosthetic devices. MIRANDA utilizes virtual reality technology and electromyographic data to train the control system of the prosthesis. The system includes an experimental environment, a hand reflection module, and an aggregation module to collect and store synchronized data. A machine learning algorithm is then trained on the collected data to predict the expected movements of the arm. The experiment was conducted with 10 healthy volunteers, and the results showed a prediction error of around 7 degrees accuracy with a CNN-based decoder. MIRANDA has the potential to be used in combination with other paradigms to record muscle electrical activity data in amputees and support the learning of controlling advanced bionic prosthetic devices, which can lead to more intuitive prosthetic control. The proposed system can also contribute to improving the economic and social outcomes for amputees by better preparing them for the use of advanced prosthetic devices.

Keywords: Artificial Intelligence · Healthcare · Human-Robot Interaction · Machine Learning · Tracking Technologies

1 Introduction

People who have undergone an upper limb amputation face significant difficulties in everyday life while performing routine daily activities. Amputation also results in a substantial load on the economy as only a small fraction of amputees keep their occupations. The use of standard prosthetics only partly alleviates the problem as only 27–56% of amputees keep using them within the year time [1]. Most robotic prostheses have a limited set of gestures and a primitive control system. Even the most modern robotic prosthesis results in low agency experience due to a lack of feedback and a limited range of gestures with an unnatural switching strategy [2]. More natural control is possible

C. Stephanidis et al. (Eds.): HCII 2023, CCIS 1833, pp. 77–83, 2023.
https://doi.org/10.1007/978-3-031-35992-7_11

when the signals from the remaining muscles are utilized. However, in order to train the control system, one needs the ground truth trajectories that are obviously unavailable when dealing with amputees. This creates a considerable gap between the reported EMG-based hand movements recognition accuracy obtained in healthy subjects and what can be achieved with amputees. Moreover, most of the modern approaches decode discrete intentions and gestures. For example, authors in [3] reported a model for decoding finger movements in real-time from surface electromyography (sEMG) with the median error of 6.24 degrees in healthy people. Here we propose a novel experimental virtual reality (VR) environment and a pipeline of methods for collecting data and control system training. The VR environment contributes to the involvement in the training process and gives visual feedback to the user while collecting the data required to train the decoder.

2   Methods

2.1   Experimental Environment

To facilitate the performance of the movements, we provide subjects with real-time visual feedback. The feedback is provided in two ways: first, the subject sees the model of their virtual hands performing the movement on the screen in front of them, and secondly, the augmented mirror hand system reflects the position of their healthy hand to the absent hand location, creating the projection of the amputated wrist.

The VR environment consists of the screen where the guiding movements and instructions are shown, the control button which allows starting each trial, and the progress bar. The experimental environment was developed in the cross-platform game development environment Unity3D using open-source assets by Meta the for hand-tracking part. 3D objects for the environment were created in 3DsMax using Substance 3D Painter for the texture development and embedded into the scene.

In order to ensure the accuracy of the collected data, we take measures to minimize the noise that may interfere with the EMG signal. Each movement's hand coordinates are recorded with high temporal resolution of 40 Hz, and the corresponding EMG signals are collected simultaneously.

Overall, our experimental environment provides a comprehensive and immersive training experience for the subjects, allowing them to practice a wide range of movements in a controlled environment while providing real-time visual feedback. The collected data serves as a crucial resource for training machine learning algorithms to predict the expected movements of the amputated arm and control advanced bionic prosthetic devices (Fig. 1).

2.2   Hand Reflection Module

In our study, we developed a hand reflection module to obtain the target finger position of the absent hand accurately. This module utilizes an augmented mirror hand system that symmetrically reflects the position of the healthy hand. By doing so, we were able to create an accurate representation of the target finger movements for the patient to emulate. The system operates by recording the healthy hand finger coordinates in real-time using an Oculus Quest 2 hand-tracking system. These coordinates are then mirrored

Fig. 1. Experimental VR environment.

to the absent hand location, which is obtained from the standard elbow position of the avatar. The use of the avatar allows for a virtual environment where both hands are rendered, creating the illusion of the amputated wrist being present.

The hand reflection module is a crucial component of our experimental setting, as it allows for the precise tracking and replication of finger movements.

2.3 Aggregation Module

The aggregation module in our system plays a main role in facilitating the synchronization of target hand positions with EMG recordings obtained from the stump via the EMG armband with the sampling frequency of 200 Hz. Through its functionality, the system is able to collect and store data in a specialized format, which enables us to flexibly tune our EMG decoder offline, based on the dataset of each movement task. The module uses open-source networked middleware ecosystem Lab Streaming Layer (LSL) [4] that allows on-the-fly streaming of the EMG and coordinates data. The collected synchronized data is stored in the module and can be used for further analysis and processing. The module also facilitates the creation of separate datasets for each movement task, enabling us to evaluate and tune our decoder's performance for each movement (Fig. 2).

2.4 Experiment

The movements range from simple movements of separate fingers to more complex gestures often encountered in real-life settings. The experiment lasts for 1–1.5 h, and each movement is repeated several times over one minute. Subjects were also provided with an opportunity to become familiar with the movement and practice its implementation. The subjects were instructed to avoid unnecessary movements and distractions during the experiment. The experimental setting also includes combinations of simple and complex gestures to ensure smooth transitions between different movements. This is necessary to ensure the collection of the most informative dataset (Figs. 3 and 4).

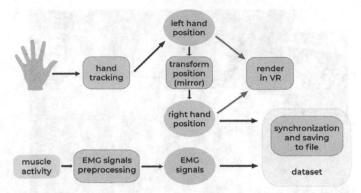

Fig. 2. Scheme for recording and aggregating EMG data from the armband and fingers position data. Synchronization of recorded signals.

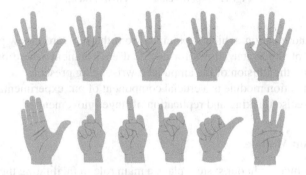

Fig. 3. Examples of gestures performed by subjects during the experiment.

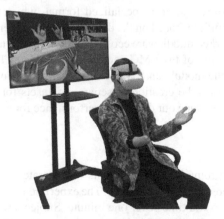

Fig. 4. Experiment setting applied to the study on amputee.

2.5 EMG-Decoding Model

In the article [3], the authors set the task of converting the EMG sensor signals into 3D finger coordinates. They use different machine learning architectures such as: recurrent neural networks (RNN), encoder-decoder networks, and residual neural networks (ResNet). The authors distinguish the encoder-decoder architecture as the best approach.

One of the closest problems to our task of signal-to-signal transformation is text-to-speech synthesis (TTS) [5, 6]. Speech synthesis aims to generate natural speech according to a given context. In the article [7], the authors use the architecture encoder-attention-decoder based on Transformer by [8] for generating mel-spectrograms from phonemes. They argue that RNN-based models also suffer from several problems that are relevant to our problem.

Based on the above, we settled on the architectural approaches of convolutions and attention [8]. The best results were demonstrated by convolutional neural network (CNN) based on the architecture introduced in FastSpeech2 [9].

As input, the model takes a time window of EMG activity of arbitrary length and returns the corresponding window of predicted movements; however, in the learning process, the length of such a window is fixed and equal to 256 time points (1.2 s). The average deviation between the prediction and the actual position of the fingers was calculated for each bone in degrees and then averaged over all bones and over the entire duration of the experiment.

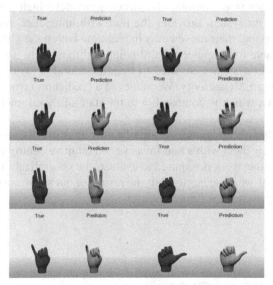

Fig. 5. Illustration decoding model inference performance in a healthy subject. The actual position of the fingers is shown on the left. The model prediction is shown on the right.

3 Results

This study was conducted with a cohort of 10 healthy volunteers to evaluate the performance of our CNN-based decoder in predicting finger movements using EMG signals. Our best result shows a prediction error of 7 degrees, which is comparable to the results reported by [3].

We also collected data from 3 amputees in the presented virtual environment for future implementation of our finger movements decoding model. To evaluate the usability of our solution, we collected subjective feedback from our participants through questionnaires. The questionnaires were designed to assess the ergonomics of our solution and the level of user satisfaction. The data collected from the questionnaires will be analyzed to provide insights into the usability and effectiveness of our system.

Our study contributes to the development of a reliable and accurate method for predicting finger movements using EMG signals, which could be applied to modern intuitive prosthetic devices to improve the quality of life for individuals with limb amputation. Future work will focus on improving the accuracy and speed of our decoder and expanding the range of finger movements that can be predicted (Fig. 5).

4 Conclusion

We have developed a virtual reality-based system that provides a real-time intuitive interface to collect data from amputees for decoding model which could be applied to control prostheses. Our system provides the user with immediate visual feedback on their actions by reflecting their movements in real-time within the virtual environment. This system is suitable for amputee rehabilitation and training to use their prosthesis. Data collected via our system were used to train the neural network model to predict finger positions using EMG activity. We achieved a prediction error of 7 degrees in a health subjects study, which is comparable to the state-of-the-art methods reported in the literature.

Our approach has the potential to significantly improve the quality of life for amputees by providing them with a non-invasive and intuitive control interface for their prosthetic limbs. Further work is required to evaluate the generalizability and feasibility of our solution in real-world scenarios, but the results of our study are encouraging and provide a promising avenue for future research.

References

1. Raichle, K.A., et al.: Prosthesis use in persons with lower- and upper-limb amputation. J. Rehabil. Res. Dev. **45**(7), 961–972 (2008)
2. Parr, J., Wright, D.W., Uiga, L., Marshall, B.R., Mohamed, M.A., Wood, G.: A scoping review of the application of motor learning principles to optimize myoelectric prosthetic hand control. Prosthet. Orthot. Int. **46**(3), 274–281 (2022)
3. Liu, Y., Zhang, S., Gowda, M.: NeuroPose: 3D hand pose tracking using EMG wearables. In: Proceedings of the Web Conference 2021, Ljubljana, Slovenia, pp. 1471–1482. ACM, New York (2021)

4. LSL. https://labstreaminglayer.org/. Accessed 17 Mar 2023
5. Taylor, P.D.: Text-to-Speech Synthesis. Cambridge University Press (2009)
6. Tan, X., Qin, T., Soong, F., Liu, T.-Y.: A survey on neural speech synthesis. arXiv preprint arXiv:2106.15561 (2021)
7. Li, N., Liu, S., Liu, Y., Zhao, S., Li, M.: Neural speech synthesis with transformer network. Proc. AAAI Conf. Artif. Intell. **33**(01), 6706–6713 (2019)
8. Vaswani, A., et al.: Attention is all you need. Neural Inf. Process. Syst. **30**, 5998–6008 (2017)
9. Ren, Y., et al.: FastSpeech 2: Fast and High-Quality End-to-End Text to Speech. ArXiv (Cornell University) (2021)

Psychosocial Risk and Work Stress in Logistics and Distribution

Andrés Lara-Calle(✉) ⓘ and Danny Prado

SISAu Research Group, Facultad de Ingeniería, Industria y Producción,
Universidad Indoamérica, Ambato 180103, Ecuador
andreslara@uti.edu.ec

Abstract. The research is focused on studying the psychosocial risk factors and work stress in the logistics and distribution personnel of a company in the city of Latacunga, Ecuador. It contributes to the thematic area of the Psychology of Engineering, and the methodology follows a quantitative approach with a cross-sectional design and correlational scope. For data collection, the evaluation method of psychosocial factors designed by the National Institute of Safety and Health at Work of Spain through the FPSICO 4.0 software and the Work Stress Questionnaire developed by the World Health Organization are used. The study is conducted on 25 workers. The results show a 70% presence of psychosocial risk with a moderate to a high level, and there is low work stress of 68%. To identify if there is a possible relationship between psychosocial risk and work stress, the variables are analyzed. Initially, the Shapiro-Wilk normality test is performed, obtaining values less than 0.05, and there is no homogeneity between variables. Therefore, the non-parametric statistical test of Spearman's correlation is established, in which a value of 0.38 is obtained, accepting the alternative hypothesis with a low correlation between the variables. In this sense, this demonstrates the importance of evaluating the work environment to identify the existence of risks that may be affecting the performance of workers and the fulfillment of business objectives. Finally, these results allow for creating awareness in the country to reduce or mitigate the existing risks and prioritize the health of workers.

Keywords: Environment · Performance · Prevention · Psychosocial risk · stress work

1 Introduction

The study of human factors has been developed for a long time, such as in the case of Texas Tech University, where professionals are trained to focus on human factors both from a research and application perspective. They are oriented toward human factors in Industrial Engineering and ergonomics, consequently generating postgraduate courses in Stress and Fatigue in Human Performance [1].

One branch of industrial engineering is industrial safety and hygiene, which generates studies on human factors and the changes they undergo due to risks present in job positions. These risks can affect workers' health. Moreno (2022) states that, from

© The Author(s), under exclusive license to Springer Nature Switzerland AG 2023
C. Stephanidis et al. (Eds.): HCII 2023, CCIS 1833, pp. 84–89, 2023.
https://doi.org/10.1007/978-3-031-35992-7_12

a sample of 55 teachers, the prevalence of overweight is 42%, and the prevalence of obesity is 18.0%, being more critical for men, caused by virtual work generated during the pandemic [2]. In turn, the development of a low-cost WBGT index meter to measure thermal comfort variables allows determining temperature values to control work environments that can be graphically visualized from a web browser and from anywhere in the world, observable on an IoT platform of ThingSpeak through the internet access [3].

An important human factor is a stress, which could be produced by the psychological risks generated by job positions. Therefore, research is important to determine the effect of risk presence on the stress generated by Logistics and Distribution area workers of a company that sells household products. In addition, a survey of work content from the Copenhagen Psychosocial Questionnaire and the Medical Outcomes Study Short Form-36 health survey, conducted with a total of 647 doctors, showed that a quarter of the surveyed doctors were classified as having low discretion and authority to make decisions, and supervisor support was weak [4], On the other hand, the Danish Psychosocial Work Environment Questionnaire, compared to two criterion variables - the occurrence of depressive disorders and long-term sickness absence - was applied to 4,340 workers, and the results were able to identify that high work demands, poorly organized work conditions, poor relationships with colleagues and superiors, and negative reactions to the work situation predicted the occurrence of depressive disorders in the follow-up and the occurrence of long-term illnesses [5].

Stress is present in every activity that human beings carry out. Thus, in medicine, for example, the work of nurses can be mentioned, who carry out their daily and nocturnal activities with high levels of distress, anxiety, and gastrointestinal disorders caused by the level of stress generated by the lack of nocturnal rest and low support from supervisors during the day [6], similarly, in educational centers both students and teachers experience stress, where stress factors such as challenges and obstacles were significant negative predictors of teacher job satisfaction [7], likewise, the mechanism of the effect of academic stress on the sleep quality of adolescents is revealed, and a chain mediation model of anxiety and school burnout is developed [8], on the other hand, stress is also present in activities that take place at home, as happened during the pandemic where leaders had to have a broad vision of work design, taking into account the physical and psychosocial aspects of work, to effectively support employees working from home [9]. From what has been said so far, it is assumed that in the industry, workers are also exposed to risks that cause them work-related stress due to the work environment, which in turn leads to alcohol consumption in the working population [10].

The purpose of this study was to identify whether the presence of psychosocial risks is related to the stress presented by workers in the logistics and distribution area.

2 Materials and Methods

This section will present the materials and methodology developed in the present research study, first with a detailed description of the materials and tools used, and then the methodology used to attain the data of the study variables.

2.1 Materials and Tools

The data will be obtained using FPSICO 4.0, a tool for evaluating psychosocial factors developed by the National Institute of Safety and Health at Work in Spain. Its first version was created in 1998 and has been updated since then. We will be using version 4.0, and this software handles technical and functional criteria outlined in NTP 926: Psychosocial factors - Assessment methodology. The reliability and validity requirements of the instrument can be consulted in the document "Psychometric properties of the psychosocial risk assessment instrument" [11].

To determine data on the variable of job stress, the Occupational Stress Indicator (OSI) questionnaire developed by the International Labor Organization (ILO) and the World Health Organization (WHO) was used.

2.2 Methods

The FPSICO 4.0 tool is an evaluation method that addresses 9 components and consists of 44 questions that allow obtaining quantitative values based on measuring psychosocial risk, in addition to guiding and structuring preventive measures. The questionnaire allows identifying Time of work (TT), Autonomy of work (AU), Workload (CT), Psychological demands (DP), Variety/content (VC), Participation/supervision (PS), Worker interest compensation (ITC), Role performance (DR) and Social support relationships (RAS), according to the structuring and distribution of work activities in a given time. Once the questionnaire is executed with the FPSICO 4.0 tool, numerical values are obtained, which allow contrasting the results according to the identified level of psychosocial risk.

The Instrument for Occupational Stress of the ILO-WHO consists of 25 items related to the work context, intrinsic factors of the job, temporary factors, leadership and management styles, human resource management, new technologies, organizational structure, and even aspects related to the organizational climate. The stress results allow identifying the level at which workers are based on the sum of each item of the questionnaire according to the weights assigned by the ILO-WHO.

3 Results

After having completed the questionnaire, the working time was recorded in the FPSICO 4.0 software, obtaining the following results in relation to the 9 components related to psychosocial risk (see Fig. 1).

The data is presented as a percentage of psychosocial risk and occupational stress for each of the twenty-five workers (see Fig. 2).

The studied variables are independent, quantitative interval, or ratio samples. The data on psychosocial risk and work stress do not follow a normal distribution, as indicated by the Shapiro-Wilk test, which resulted in 0.026 for psychosocial risk and 0 for work stress, with values less than 0.05. Additionally, there is no homogeneity of variances between the variables, with a value of 0.765. Therefore, to determine the correlation, the non-parametric Spearman test was applied. A weak correlation was found between the studied variables, with a p-value ≤ 0.05 and a Spearman correlation coefficient of 0.388, indicating a low relationship between psychosocial risk and work stress.

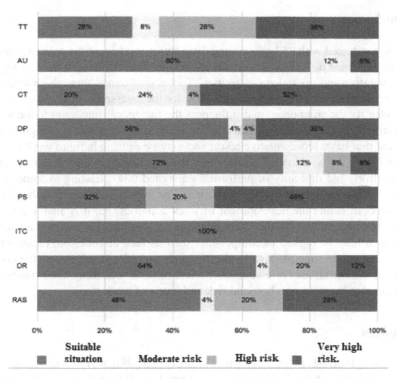

Fig. 1. The figure shows the assessment of exposure, with the distribution of the 4 levels of risk for each of the 9 factors measured by the method. The result is expressed as a percentage of exposed people.

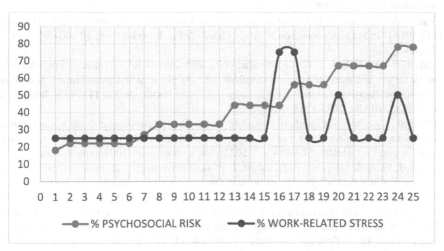

Fig. 2. After applying the psychosocial risk and occupational stress assessment instruments, the individually identified results have been obtained, as detailed below.

4 Conclusion

The study conducted with 25 logistics and distribution workers in the company demonstrates the existence of 70% psychosocial risk and 68% work stress in the development of administrative and operational activities. This was obtained through an evaluation using questionnaire-type instruments that allow for the assessment of the work environment to identify the component that influences the factors causing harm to the worker. The identified psychosocial risk index in the workers is moderate and high, and the component that has a representative result and may be causing harm to work activities was found to be the workload. This indicates that workers have high demand, causing pressure, effort, and difficulty in performing assigned tasks, leading to some type of harm. Regarding the level of work stress, it is low, which indicates that there are no direct factors affecting the development of work activities, but it is also necessary to consider that the results show that there are workers who have an intermediate level of stress, which may be related to components such as lack of cohesion, organizational structure, and group support. Finally, the research variables in relation to the contrast obtained by the Spearman correlation coefficient of 0.388 determine the existence of a low relationship between psychosocial risk and levels of work stress.

References

1. Klein, M.I., Halcomb, C., DeLucia, P.R., Liddell, G., Chaparro, B., Endsley, M.: 50 Years of human factors psychology at Texas Tech University. Proc. Human Factor. Ergon. Soc. Annu. Meet. **61**, 430–434 (2017). https://doi.org/10.1177/1541931213601589
2. Moreno Medina, V., Bermudez, L., Lara-Calle, A.: Presented at the Effects of Teleworking on the Body Mass Index of the Teachers of an Educational Institution (2022). https://doi.org/10.1007/978-3-031-19682-9_41
3. Varela-Aldás, J., Buele, J., Mosquera, H., Palacios-Navarro, G.: Presented at the Development of a WBGT Index Meter Based on M5Stack Core2 (2022). https://doi.org/10.1007/978-3-031-21704-3_23
4. Zutautiene, R., Kaliniene, G., Ustinaviciene, R., Radisauskas, R.: Prevalence of psychosocial work factors and stress and their associations with the physical and mental health of hospital physicians: A cross-sectional study in Lithuania. Front Public Health. **11** (2023). https://doi.org/10.3389/fpubh.2023.1123736
5. Clausen, T., et al.: The predictive validity of the Danish psychosocial work environment questionnaire with regard to onset of depressive disorders and long-term sickness absence. Ann. Work. Exp. Health. **67**, 195–207 (2023). https://doi.org/10.1093/annweh/wxac069
6. Amiard, V., Telliez, F., Pamart, F., Libert, J.-P.: Health, occupational stress, and psychosocial risk factors in night shift psychiatric nurses: The influence of an unscheduled night-time nap. Int. J. Environ. Res. Publ. Health. **20**, 158 (2022). https://doi.org/10.3390/ijerph20010158
7. Xu, L., Guo, J., Zheng, L., Zhang, Q.: Teacher well-being in Chinese Universities: Examining the relationship between challenge—hindrance stressors, job satisfaction, and teaching engagement. Int. J. Environ. Res. Publ. Health. **20**, 1523 (2023). https://doi.org/10.3390/ijerph20021523
8. Wang, H., Fan, X.: Academic stress and sleep quality among Chinese adolescents: Chain mediating effects of anxiety and school burnout. Int. J. Environ. Res. Publ. Health. **20**, 2219 (2023). https://doi.org/10.3390/ijerph20032219

9. Oakman, J., Lambert, K.A., Weale, V.P., Stuckey, R., Graham, M.: Employees working from home: Do leadership factors influence work-related stress and musculoskeletal pain? Int. J. Environ. Res. Publ. Health. **20**, 3046 (2023). https://doi.org/10.3390/ijerph20043046
10. Cruz-Zuñiga, N., Alonso Castillo, M.M., Armendáriz-García, N.A., Lima Rodríguez, J.S.: Clima laboral, estrés laboral y consumo de alcohol en trabajadores de la industria. Una revisión sistemática. Rev Esp Salud Publica. **95** (2021)
11. Lara, A.A.: Prediction of psychosocial occupational risk in urban transport applying machine learning techniques. RISTI – Rev. Iber. Sist. Tecnol. Inf. **2020**, 153–165 (2020)

Research on the Design of Children's Infusion Medical Auxiliary Products Based on Emotional Design

Ningning Le[(✉)]

School of Design, South China University of Technology, No. 382, Guangzhou, People's Republic of China
120812439@qq.com

Abstract. In order to effectively improve the pain and fear of children's intravenous infusion process, and effectively maintain a good relationship between children, parents, medical staff and medical products, this study will design and research on children's intravenous infusion medical auxiliary products based on Professor Norman's three-level theory of emotional design, combined with the Children's Medical Fear Scale (CMFS) and the Facial Pain Scale (Wong-baker). The study will visualize the fear of infusion in children, find the root causes and peak stages of children's fear of intravenous infusion, and finally do a preliminary design of infusion medical auxiliary products in the form of pain transfer to guide intravenous infusion to a more relaxed and pleasant direction, and provide methodological guidance and data support for future related medical design research.

Keywords: Emotional design · Intravenous infusion · Fear factor · Medical auxiliary products

1 Introduction

With the advancement of science and technology and the improvement of living standards, new generations of parents are paying special attention to the health of their children. In recent years, the safety problems caused by improperly designed children's medical products have led to a higher demand and concern for the design of children's medical field.

And as the modern medical model gradually moves toward a comprehensive medical model, paying attention to human emotional needs has become a popular theme in medical product design. Children's infusion as an important part of children's medical care, has received strong attention from major hospitals. Currently, improper medical operations, depressing medical environment, cold appearances of medical devices and other factors greatly affect the emotions of children, making them have an extremely bad experience during infusion. Therefore, research and design of medical auxiliary products for children's infusion is crucial.

C. Stephanidis et al. (Eds.): HCII 2023, CCIS 1833, pp. 90–98, 2023.
https://doi.org/10.1007/978-3-031-35992-7_13

2 Research Objective and Significance

Applying the three-level theory of emotional design to design of children's infusion medical auxiliary products, centering on the needs of children, the final products implemented are hoped to effectively alleviate children's fear of infusion, reduce the psychological pressure of parents, improve the efficiency of hospitals, and it is important to further improve the current state of healthcare for children in China.

3 Current Research on Emotional Design

3.1 Market Background of Emotional Design

With the upgrading of consumption and experience, today's market has become a "consumer-oriented" buyer's market [1]. In front of the same price, similar appearance, and similar functions, consumers tend to choose products that can touch their emotions [2].

3.2 Theoretical Background of Emotional Design

In 2004, Donald Norman proposed a specific "emotional design" model in his book "Emotional Design", arguing that design should be focused on three levels: instinctive, behavioral and reflective [3].

In this study, the three levels are interpreted as the following three kinds of experiences: intuitive experience - the sensory feelings generated by the appearance of the product; process experience - the experience feelings triggered by using products; emotional experience - involves deep feelings such as emotion, awareness, memory, understanding, self-image, personal satisfaction, etc. The three levels progress in layers, and eventually, users will have deep emotional reactions such as recognition, empathy and dependence obtained at the reflective level.

4 Current Status of Children's Medical Field

4.1 Analysis of Current Situation of the Application of Emotional Design in the Domestic CHIldren's Medical Field

The 2010 China Medical Services Industry Investment Research Report, published by the Research Center of Tsinghua University, shows that outpatient visits are expected to exceed 40 million in 2015 [4]. The national investment in outpatient clinics is increasing, but there are few infusion spaces specifically created for children.

4.2 Focus and Trends in CHIldren's Medical Field

The focus of design in the field of children's medical care has gradually shifted from satisfying the physiological level of children to satisfying the psychological level. The ultimate development trend of medical products will also realize the integration of aesthetic value, use value and cultural value of products.

5 Design Research

5.1 Research Subjects

The study population was selected from children requiring intravenous infusions from July 24 to July 31, 2022, in the Third Hospital of Ningbo, Zhejiang Province. The age group of children was controlled between 3 to 10, and in order to increase the subjectivity and credibility of the study, children in this age group were divided into two study groups: preschool children aged 3 to 6, school-aged children aged 7 to 10. Let them score the fear factor subjectively and objectively.

5.2 User Research (1)

Research Purpose. To understand the fear factors during intravenous infusion in children.

Research Methodology. The scale used in this study was modified from the "Children's Medical Fear Scale" developed by Broom ME (1995) (scale provided by Broom ME himself) [5]. The scale consists of four subscales: fear of medical procedures, fear of the medical environment, fear of interpersonal relationships, and fear of self. Each item is scored on a 3-point scale, with "no fear" scoring 1, "some fear" scoring 2, and "very fearful" scoring 3. The internal consistency reliability coefficient of the scale was 0.93 and the expert validity was 85%. The scoring points were based on the behavioral journey of children's intravenous infusion, and 12 scoring points were finalized, as shown in Fig. 1.

1. What is your age			
2. What is your gender	Male	Female	
3. Where you live	Cities & Towns	Rural	
4. Please rate the **medical environment** for intravenous infusion (1-3 points)	Not scared-1	A little scared-2	Very scared-3
When you are waiting for an infusion in the infusion waiting area, you feel			
When you sit at the infusion table, you feel			
When you return to the rest area after the infusion, you feel			
5. Please rate your interpersonal **relationship** with intravenous infusion (1-3 points)	Not scared-1	A little scared-2	Very scared-3
When you see other children who are strangers and need infusions, you feel			
How do you feel about the infusion nurse's expression and tone of voice			
6. Please rate the content of your **self-fear** in intravenous infusion (1-3 points)	Not scared 1	A little scared 2	Very scared 3
When you hear your doctor say you need an infusion, you feel			
When you feel the pain of a skin puncture, you feel			
When you see blood flowing out of your veins, you feel			
7. Please rate your **medical practice** in intravenous infusion (1-3 points)	Not scared-1	A little scared-2	Very scared-3
When the nurse ties the band fixation rubber strip, you feel			
When the nurse swabs your skin with an alcohol swab, you feel			
When the nurse taps the back of your hand to find the infusion vessel, you feel			
When the nurse takes the infusion needle and punctures the skin and samples the blood, you feel			

Fig. 1. Children's intravenous infusion medical fear content scoring table

The total number of questionnaires: 47 offline questionnaires, 63 online questionnaires. One hundred valid questionnaires were retained. Statistical analysis of the data was done with the help of SPSS 26.0 software package.

5.3 Results

In this study, there were 60 children aged 3 to 6 years old and 40 children aged 7 to 10 years old among 100 subjects, with a male to female ratio of 51 to 49 and an urban to rural population ratio of 72 to 28. The scores of the four components of children's fear of intravenous infusion were statistically analyzed, as shown Table 1. The correlation between children's fear of intravenous infusion and age, gender, and place of residence was statistically analyzed, as shown in Table 2.

Table 1. Children's intravenous infusion fear score.

Medical fear content	Score ($\bar{x} \pm s$)
Fear of medical environment	1.51 ± 0.46
Enter the infusion waiting area	1.40 ± 0.55
Enter the infusion area	2.00 ± 0.75
Back to the rest area	1.14 ± 0.38
Fear of relationships	1.48 ± 0.53
Meet strangers	1.43 ± 0.62
Nurse's attitude and expression	1.52 ± 0.64
Self-fear	2.20 ± 0.65
Learn of the need for infusion	1.94 ± 0.66
Painful piercing of skin	2.36 ± 0.75
Bleeding	2.29 ± 0.80
Fear of medical operations	2.02 ± 0.70
Tie rubber strips	1.76 ± 0.79
Slap the back of hand	1.99 ± 0.81
Alcohol pads for skin wiping	1.93 ± 0.78
Needle and blood collection	2.39 ± 0.75

The SPSS multivariate test showed that intravenous infusion fear had a significant effect on children of different ages ($P < 0.01$) and no significant effect on children of different genders and residence ($P > 0.05$).

The Pearson correlation coefficient showed that age was significantly correlated with four infusion fear factors, with an overall negative trend, in descending order: fear of medical operations, fear of self, fear of medical environment, and fear of interpersonal relationships (from Table 3).

5.4 User Research (2)

Research Purpose. To further understand children's fear of various aspects of intravenous infusion.

Table 2. Correlation of intravenous infusion fear in children with age, gender, and residence

	Age		Gender		Residence	
	(3–6)	(7–10)	Male	Female	Cities/towns	Rural
Total score	24.03 ± 2.42	18.90 ± 1.32	21.20 ± 5.29	23.14 ± 7.11	21.89 ± 6.32	22.82 ± 6.29
Medical environment	4.88 ± 0.46	4.05 ± 0.25	4.33 ± 1.07	4.76 ± 1.63	4.57 ± 1.43	4.46 ± 1.26
Relationships	3.15 ± 0.42	2.68 ± 0.34	2.69 ± 0.93	3.22 ± 1.41	2.96 ± 1.11	2.93 ± 0.98
Self-fear	7.15 ± 0.54	5.55 ± 0.70	6.49 ± 1.86	6.69 ± 2.05	6.47 ± 1.94	6.89 ± 1.97
Medical operations	8.85 ± 1.08	6.63 ± 0.53	7.69 ± 2.40	8.47 ± 3.11	7.89 ± 2.73	8.54 ± 2.92
P	<0.01		>0.05		>0.05	

Table 3. Correlation between children's age and various fear factors of intravenous infusion.

Medical fear content	Pearson Correlation Analysis (−1,1)	P
Fear of medical environment	−0.376	<0.01
Fear of relationships	−0.364	<0.01
Self-fear	−0.471	<0.01
Fear of medical operations	−0.493	<0.01

Research Methodology. The Wong-Baker Facial Pain Scale was chosen to assess the changes in children's fear level during each infusion session (from Fig. 2). This scale is suitable for young children with low cognitive abilities [6]. A 6-point scale was used to score from no pain to severe pain [7]. The color of each pain expression was differentiated with reference to child color psychology.

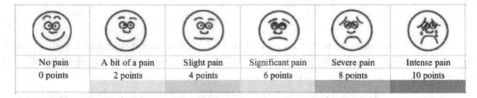

No pain	A bit of a pain	Slight pain	Significant pain	Severe pain	Intense pain
0 points	2 points	4 points	6 points	8 points	10 points

Fig. 2. Wong-Baker Facial Pain Scale (assigned colors based on child color psychology)

In this study, the researchers objectively recorded and analyzed children's expressions at various points of infusion through an observational method. For the observation of children's intravenous infusion expressions, consent was sought from parents and children to record videos and collect relevant materials. Sixty videos were recorded and 54 videos were selected and retained.

5.5 Results

Based on the behavioral journey of children's intravenous infusions, the scores of facial-pain for children aged 3 to 10 corresponded to specific infusion sessions, as shown in Fig. 3.

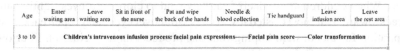

Age	Enter waiting area	Leave waiting area	Sit in front of the nurse	Pat and wipe the back of the hands	Needle & blood collection	Tie handguard	Leave infusion area	Leave the rest area
3 to 10	Children's intravenous infusion process: facial pain expressions——Facial pain score——Color transformation							

Fig. 3. Facial pain scores for each segment of children's intravenous infusion process

Age	Enter waiting area	Leave waiting area	Sit in front of the nurse	Pat and wipe the back of the hands	Needle & blood collection	Tie handguard	Leave infusion area	Leave the rest area
3								
4								
5								
6								
7								
8								
9								
10								

Fig. 4. Intravenous infusion facial pain color stacking chart in children aged 3–10

Comparing the fear level of preschoolers aged 3 to 6 and school-age children aged 7 to 10 for the infusion session (shown in Fig. 4), it was concluded from the color stacking chart:

(1) the preschoolers aged 3 to 6 had much higher severe fear values than the school-age children aged 7 to 10. (Large percentage of color saturation)
(2) Children aged 3 to 6 had an earlier initial point of fear and a later point of fear reduction compared to children aged 7 to 10; the duration of fear (range of fluctuation) lasted longer.
(3) Fear peaks in preschoolers were concentrated at the venipuncture node, and fear increased significantly from the time they left the waiting area; fear peaks in school-age children were concentrated from sitting in front of the nurse to the preparation of the infusion, while they were less fearful during the infusion.

5.6 Design Position

The key problem to be solved by this design is how to help children alleviate the fear of intravenous infusion, reduce resistance and behavior of sudden jerking and struggling during infusion by means of visual masking, auditory transfer and tactile soothing. The specific product to be implemented is the children's intravenous infusion head-mounted musical eye mask.

6 Product Design

6.1 Design Concept

It has been observed that parents often cover their children's eyes with their hands and offer them warm words of encouragement in order to help ease their fear of intravenous infusions. When children are in deep fear, they tend to close their eyes tightly and turn their heads toward their most trusted loved ones. So "cover eyes" and "open ears" become the inspiration for this design, hoping that this product can help children filter out the fearful images in the infusion and listen to more warm voices.

6.2 Sketch

See Figs. 5 and 6.

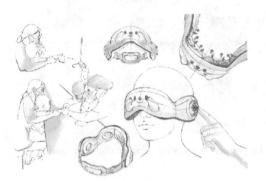   

Fig. 5. Sketch 1.0   Fig. 6. Sketch 2.0

6.3 Product Emotional Design Innovation Point

Emotionalization of instinctive level: n appearance, the rounded cloud shape of the eye mask contrasts with the sharp shape of the infusion products; in material, the shell environmentally friendly ABS resin material, the internal massage pad and head guard pad mesh breathable fabric, with easy to clean, fit the skin, high safety; in color, choose to meet the hospital tone of baby blue, both lively and not irritating (Fig. 7).

Emotionalization of behavior level: The product fits the face line of children aged 3–10 years old, with 5 micro airbags built in around the eye points to cover and massage at the same time; the music can output a variety of modes, up and down, left and right, in the order of forest, water, sleep, vitality, parents can choose the child's favorite music to help them transfer their fear. The head protector pad is easy to wear while enhancing safety.

Emotionalization of reflective level: firstly, the round and lovely cartoon image of the product makes children not reject wearing the product during infusion; secondly, through the action of "covering eyes", children have a sense of being protected by "someone will cover my eyes", thus building up a certain confidence in infusion; thirdly,

Fig. 7. Product modeling diagram (1. Massage micro-airbag 2. "Cover the eyes" action 3. Head protection pad 4. Elastic band 5. Eye-mask lining 6. Music modes)

the comprehensive intervention of visual, tactile and auditory senses, while soothing the fear of infusion, also makes them have a certain psychological comfort and emotional dependence.

6.4 Product Renderings

See Fig. 8.

Fig. 8. Renderings

7 Children's Intravenous Infusion Medical Auxiliary Product Design Inspiration

In the study of the design of medical auxiliary products for children's infusion, the emotional design theory was used as a basis to focus on the child's position, narrowing down the specific design aspects to the preparation before the infusion to the completion of blood collection, relieving stress and diverting fear, allowing the child to transform his or her fear of infusion into an optimistic experience through the positive guidance of emotional products.

References

1. Qi, G.N., Gu, X.J., Tan, J.R.: Principles and Key Technologies of Mass Customization. Mechanical Industry Press, Beijing (2003)
2. Ding, J.W., Yang, D.T., Cao, Y.D., Wang, L.: The main theories, methods and research trends of emotional design. Journal 17(01), 12–18 (2010)
3. Norman, D.A.: Emotional Design. Electronic Industry Press, Beijing (2016)
4. Chen, Y.B., Zhang, L.H.: Research on the service design based on HCD of waiting facilities in children's hospital. Design J. (2014)
5. Hamed, A.: Nurses' Knowledge and Practices toward Caring for Children undergoing Blood Transfusion (2019)
6. Liu, J., Liu, H.: Exploring the effect of psychological care in pediatric intravenous infusion. Shanxi Med. J. 49(07), 914–915 (2020)
7. Li, G.M.: Effect of comprehensive nursing intervention on pediatric intravenous infusion compliance and successful puncture rate. J. Pract. Med. Techniq. 25(06), 683–684 (2018)

Research on Immersive Virtual Reality Healing Design Based on the Five Senses Theory

Haoyu Li and Hong Chen(✉)

School of Art Design and Media, East China University of Science and Technology, Shanghai, China

y81210107@mail.ecust.edu.cn, engoy2008@163.com

Abstract. In the context of increasing social competition, life pressure, and COVID-19 epidemic, the psychological subhealth issues of young and middle-aged individuals are becoming more prevalent. In light of this, the study of psychological relaxation has become crucial. The rapid development of virtual reality technology in recent years has enabled visiting virtual environments to be a convenient means of achieving physical and mental healing. Nevertheless, the combination of healing environments and virtual reality is currently limited to virtual scenes shaped by sound and light, and the use of tactile, olfactory, and gustatory simulation technologies is minimal. Therefore, innovative research is required. In this paper, theories and technologies related to five-sense healing around the world are analyzed, and the psychological healing needs of young and middle-aged groups are investigated. On this basis, immersive virtual re-ality healing designs based on the five senses are proposed. This enlightens immersive virtual reality healing design and provides a more immersive healing experience for young and middle-aged people with mental sub-health.

Keywords: Virtual Reality · Five Senses · Psychological Healing · Immersive Experience

1 Introduction

Since the outbreak of COVID-19, there has been a sharp increase in the prevalence of depression and anxiety disorders, and the psychological burden on individuals has been boosted. It is urgent to provide people with relaxation in daily life. In recent years, the development of virtual reality technology has provided a convenient way of relaxation and stress reduction. VR utilizes computers to generate simulated three-dimensional environments, establishing an immersive experience for users. Virtual reality healing systems primarily simulate natural environments, accompanied by natural sounds and soothing music, so as to cultivate a peaceful atmosphere and promote relaxation. Additionally, VR relaxation healing can effectively reduce stress and regulate emotional states within a short time [1].

The human body possesses five senses: vision, hearing, smell, taste, and touch, which collectively allow individuals to form a comprehensive representation of the objective

C. Stephanidis et al. (Eds.): HCII 2023, CCIS 1833, pp. 99–106, 2023.
https://doi.org/10.1007/978-3-031-35992-7_14

environment and emotional experiences. Multisensory experiences can effectively stimulate relaxation and weaken anxiety and depression. Nonetheless, current VR healing
creates virtual environments majorly through audiovisual simulation, with limited use
of touch, smell, and taste simulation techniques. This is a field to be widely explored.

This study involves psychological healing, VR, and multisensory experience to
explore the new possibilities of immersive VR healing from the perspective of the five
senses. In this work, the application of the five senses in psychological healing is investigated, followed by the VR five-sense simulation technology and user needs. On this
basis, the future development directions of VR psychological healing are discussed, and
immersive virtual reality healing design solutions are proposed, contributing to a more
immersive relaxation experience for young and middle-aged groups.

2 Psychotherapy Theories Based on the Five Senses

In this section, theories related to psychological healing are analyzed from the perspective
of the five senses by conducting a literature search on the five senses and psychological
healing. According to the collected literature, the classification of the five senses healing
elements is summarized in Fig. 1.

Fig. 1. Elements of psychological healing based on the five senses theory

2.1 Analysis of Visual-Based Healing Theory

Vision is the main sensory organ of human beings. Currently, VR relaxation healing scenes are mostly natural scenes such as forests and lakes. Studies have suggested that the vitality of plants is beneficial for people to relieve stress. In addition to natural landscapes, urban environments such as cafes, monasteries, and museums have been revealed to have healing effects. The differences in color, texture, lighting, and shape in the scene can bring different emotional experiences. For example, green and white plants allow people to feel relaxed, while green and yellow plants provide people with a cheerful feeling. Rough-textured plants make the space appear stable, while fine-textured plants leave a tranquil impression on people. Bright natural light can help increase vitality and lessen depression [2]. Curves bring a sense of pleasure, while sharp shapes create threatened and unpleasant feelings. Understanding the physiological characteristics of various visual elements and using them appropriately contribute to alleviating users' stress and regulating their emotions.

2.2 Analysis of Auditory-Based Healing Theory

Healing sounds can be classified into natural sounds, music, and human voice. Studies have unveiled that natural sounds such as birdsong can alleviate people's stress. Compared to subjects in virtual environments without natural sounds, those in natural sound environments recovered from stress more quickly [3]. Gaston, one of the earliest researchers to discover the influence of music on emotions, identified that calm music is characterized by continuous melody, non-percussive instruments, and a uniform and simple rhythm [4]. Additionally, the listener's preference can also impact the relaxation effects of music [5]. Cerwén discovered that non-interactive human voices, such as the calm and slow voice of a therapist, can help individuals relax [6]. These three types of sounds can be employed in virtual reality therapy systems to enhance auditory enjoyment for users.

2.3 Analysis of Tactile-Based Healing Theory

Positive olfactory experiences can soothe emotions and accelerate functional recovery. Aromatherapy utilizes extracts from aromatic plants, such as lavender and rose, to relieve anxiety and depression while improving physical and mental health. Smelling nostalgic scents, which can trigger pleasant recollections, can also increase happiness and reduce anxiety [7]. Experiments by Hedblom demonstrated that olfactory stimuli may be more effective in lessening stress than visual stimuli [1]. Installing olfactory sensors in VR devices that release soothing scents during film playback can further enhance sensory experiences and deepen relaxation effects.

2.4 Analysis of Olfactory-Based Healing Theory

Tactile sensation is a direct perceptual experience of human contact with the external world. Through touch, people can perceive the shape, material, hardness, temperature, and humidity of objects. Touch is discovered to be highly correlated with emotions.

Positive touch allows people to feel relaxed and comfortable, helping to release positive hormones such as dopamine and oxytocin. Human-nature touches, such as touching wood with a hand, can also assist people in calming and relaxing [8]. By adding tactile-enhanced reality devices to virtual reality healing systems to simulate the tactile sensations of plants and gentle breezes, users can feel the refinements of VR scenes, generating a complete relaxation experience.

2.5 Analysis of Gustatory-Based Healing Theory

Compared with olfactory sensation, gustatory experience is more stimulating and intuitive and has a significant guiding effect on emotions. Taste elements comprise type, temperature, and concentration of food. It has been unveiled that sweetness can promote positive emotions. Temperature also affects the emotions of consumers. For example, 65 °C coffee and green tea are more likely to evoke positive emotions such as happiness and warmth compared to similar drinks at 25 °C or 5 °C [9]. In real life, taste healing is frequently applied in healing gardens and ecological wellness centers, where people eat ecological food to nourish body and minds. With the introduction of a gustatory experience in a suitable VR scene, users can better immerse themselves in the relaxing atmosphere of virtual reality.

3 Analysis of VR Five Senses Simulation Technology

Virtual reality technology has achieved significant progress in simulating visual and auditory experiences. In this section, the development of simulation techniques for olfactory, tactile, and gustatory senses is primarily discussed. Currently, olfactory simulation typically uses an odor generator that stores multiple scents and spreads them through a ventilation system. In 2015, FeelReal launched a multisensory VR device composed of scent capsules, an ultrasonic ionizing system for generating mist, a micro-heater for producing warmth, a miniature cooler for producing wind, and a tactile motor for generating vibration, providing users with an immersive multisensory experience.

Common VR haptic simulation devices also consist of gloves and vests such as Cybertouch and adopt actuators to generate vibrations of different frequencies and intensities to simulate various tactile sensations such as wind and rain. Additionally, some researchers have used muscle electrical stimulation technology to more realistically simulate force feedback effects.

The simulation of taste sensation can be achieved through both chemical and physical methods. Chemical methods involve the spraying of liquid chemicals that mimic food flavors into the mouth, while physical methods involve the use of electrodes to stimulate taste receptors on the tongue. However, careful consideration is required when incorporating taste into virtual reality healing design, due to the invasiveness and lack of user-friendliness of taste simulation.

Currently, many technical challenges should be overcome in multimodal simulation. With the development and improvement of technology, more new interactive experiences will emerge to provide the public with a more complete immersive healing experience.

4 Healing Needs of Young and Middle-Aged Groups

4.1 Psychological Healing Needs of Young and Middle-Aged Groups

With the increasingly improved quality of life, people's demand for health is no longer limited to treating diseases, whereas more attention is paid to the healing of the mind. The young and middle-aged group is in the rising and confused period of career and education, faces challenges such as low happiness, exhaustion, lack of confidence, and anxiety, and has a higher demand for psychological healing. Through user research, the psychological healing needs of this group are summarized as follows.

Relax and Decompress. The young and middle-aged group is confronted with multi-faceted pressures from work, education, family, and society, which can result in sustained high-stress levels that inflict irreversible harm on their physical and mental well-being. Therefore, stress relief measures are urgent in this group.

Emotional Expression. When young and middle-aged people face pressure and challenges in work and study, they may experience negative emotions such as unease and tension. If it is not vented in time, it may result in emotional loss, anxiety, and depression. Thus, this group necessitates a safe space for emotional expression.

Self-Mindfulness. Young and middle-aged people are usually busy with work and study and lack the capability of reflection and deep thinking, leading to self-disgust and confusion. Meditation can help this group better understand themselves, uncover inner potential, and improve self-awareness and psychological resilience.

Enhancing Self-Confidence. Attributed to the high intensity of work and study pressure, young and middle-aged groups sometimes feel a decrease in self-worth and require appropriate encouragement to strengthen their self-confidence.

4.2 Sensory Needs of Young and Middle-Aged Groups

Young and middle-aged people tend to satisfy their sensory needs through various means, promote physical and mental relaxation, and enhance their quality of life and work efficiency. According to user research, the sensory needs are summarized as follows.

Visual Needs. This group pursues aesthetic pleasure and visual enjoyment to relieve stress and increase mood by appreciating beautiful scenery and visiting art exhibitions.

Auditory Needs. This group is eager to use music to regulate emotions in different situations, such as listening to lively pop music during leisure time to release emotions and boost spirits; listening to white noise or light music to relax and reduce stress when feeling exhausted or needing concentration.

Olfactory Needs. Seeking pleasurable olfactory experiences is an emerging way for this group to soothe emotions. Using perfume, scented candles, or essential oils to relieve stress and enhance pleasure has become a potential need for them.

Tactile Needs. This group seeks various activities such as massage, hot springs, and yoga to alleviate the tension and fatigue of both the body and mind. Additionally, they desire to evoke a relaxing tactile experience, such as stroking soft pet fur.

Taste Needs. This group has higher dietary requirements, emphasizing the intake of nutritionally, healthy, and delicious food. They would also adjust their mood by desserts to bring positive emotions through pleasant taste experiences.

By developing a thorough understanding of the needs of the target audience, the design goals of immersive virtual reality healing systems were further clarified to better satisfy the expectations and requirements of the target users.

5   Design of VR Psychological Healing Based on Five Senses

The design ideas of virtual reality healing were broadened through literature analysis from the perspective of the five senses. It has been revealed that future virtual immersive healing systems can not only be limited to pure relaxation and stress relief but also provide various healing experiences, such as converging thoughts and uplifting moods, which are suitable for users with different psychological needs. Thus, the following three immersive virtual reality healing design schemes were proposed based on the five senses.

5.1   Soothing and Stress-Relieving, Immersive Natural Experience

Beautiful natural landscapes are conducive to relieving stress, eliminating fatigue, and restoring attention. This proposal adopts the five-sense enhanced reality technology to simulate natural scenery, sounds, smells, and tactile sensations, allowing users to immerse themselves in nature and deeply relax and relieve stress. With the purpose of providing users with more relaxation options, this proposal covers a range of natural beauty experiences from different regions, consisting of themes such as "Summer Rainforest", "Peach Blossom Sea", and "Sunlight Coast", to meet the preferences of different users. With "Summer Rainforest" as an example, a brief description of the user experience scene is provided.

Upon wearing the VR device, the user is immersed in a lush forest. Tall and verdant trees tower overhead, with sunlight filtering through the leaves and casting speckled patterns on the ground, creating a tranquil and leisurely atmosphere. The grass beneath the trees is luxuriant and has a velvety texture that users can feel when they reach out to touch it. A winding stream meanders through the forest, accompanied by the sound of gurgling water and shimmering under the sun's rays. In this forest, users can feel the full vitality of nature, hear the rustling of leaves in the breeze and the cheerful birdsong, and smell the fresh air and fragrance of the grass and trees. Occasionally, a few squirrels play in the forest. Users can interact with them using the hand-held controller and experience the pleasure of interacting with wildlife. Walking along the stream, the user will see a magnificent waterfall, with water pouring down from a height, and the haptic simulation equipment provides a refreshing feeling of water mist for the user. In the distance, mist rises and lingers like a landscape painting. Users stop here for a moment to completely relax their minds.

In this natural environment, users can immerse themselves in the beauty and vitality of nature, escape from the busy city life, fully relax, and enjoy a delightful time through a comprehensive sensory experience of sight, sound, smell, and touch.

5.2 Spiritual Sublimation, Immersive Meditation Experience

Meditation is a spiritual practice involving discarding chaotic thoughts and seeking self-awareness, assisting individuals in returning to the present moment and confronting the self. This design plan creates a pure meditation space through clean colors, calming music, and elegant fragrances, providing a resting environment for young and middle-aged people to purify tired bodies and calm their minds. In our study, multiple meditation scenes are provided for users to deepen their meditation, such as "Quiet Lakeside", "Breath of the Wilderness", and "Church of Light", so as to keep users engaged and explore different meditation experiences in different settings. With "Quiet Lakeside" as an example, a brief description of the user experience scene is provided as follows.

Upon wearing the VR device, the user is immersed in a serene lakeside surrounded by lush mountains, creating a peaceful and tranquil atmosphere. Facing the lake, the user sits on the ground with only a clear blue in view. At the meeting point of water and sky, distant mountains appear faintly reflected as if seen through a veil. Accompanied by the rippling waves, the user gradually releases their anxiety and worries, with increasingly deep and calming breathing, as if the whole person merges with the lake water. The lakeside becomes more silent as the meditation progresses, blocking out external noise through the VR device while leaving only the faint sound of water and meditation guidance. The air is filled with a hint of minty aroma, which makes people calm down. The tactile simulation device guides the user to the correct breathing rhythm through gentle vibration, enabling them to maintain concentration during meditation and relax from daily stress.

In this pure lake, users can get rid of the distractions and fully immerse themselves in meditation. Through various sensory experiences such as visual, auditory, olfactory, and tactile, users can develop a deeper understanding of themselves, achieve a state of physical and mental balance, and attain spiritual tranquility.

5.3 Artistic Healing, Immersive Interactive Experience

Art healing is a psychological treatment method encompassing various forms of art such as painting, dancing, gaming, and drama. It provides individuals with a safe emotional expression channel. This proposal combines multisensory design with various art forms, such as painting, dancing, and gaming, to create a diversified VR art healing program. Specifically, it consists of various interactive themes such as "Painting Magic", "Dance

Power", and "Journey of the Wind". It aims to provide users with a more personalized and comprehensive art healing experience based on their preferences and needs for releasing pressure and eliminating emotional distress.

In the "Painting Magic" theme, users are immersed in a colorful and imaginative art space where they can freely engage in artistic creation. Through painting, users can express their emotions and the inner world while releasing stress. In the "Dance Power" theme, users dance to their heart's content following the movements of the virtual characters with cheerful dance music, releasing the pressure and tension and experiencing relaxation and joy. In the "Journey of the Wind" theme, users explore the magical Wind Canyon, collect treasures such as crystals and flowers, complete game tasks, and unlock new storylines, contributing to a sense of achievement and satisfaction in exploration and collection. Each interactive theme provides music and scents matching the environment to evoke positive emotions. The tactile simulation device will give vibration feedback to enhance immersion when users interact with items such as paintbrushes and props, or complete dance movements.

Through these creative and engaging artistic interactions, users can fully express their emotions, release psychological pressure, and reach a sense of accomplishment and increased confidence through wholehearted immersion.

6 Conclusion

Amidst the fierce competition in today's society, multisensory healing experiences can assist young and middle-aged people in better relaxing and releasing pressure. This paper proposes design schemes for immersive virtual healing through the integration of multisensory elements to introduce olfactory, tactile, and gustatory senses into virtual reality healing research beyond audio and visual senses. This work guides VR developers in creating more immersive virtual reality healing experiences for users.

References

1. Hedblom, M., et al.: Reduction of physiological stress by urban green space in a multisensory virtual experiment. Sci. Rep. 9(1), 10113 (2019)
2. Partonen, T., Lönnqvist, J.J.J.o.A.d.: Bright light improves vitality and alleviates distress in healthy people. J. Affect. Disord. 57(1–3), 55–61 (2000)
3. Annerstedt, M., et al.: Inducing physiological stress recovery with sounds of nature in a virtual reality forest—Results from a pilot study. Physiol. Behav. 118, 240–250 (2013)
4. Gaston, E.T.J.M.E.J.: Dynamic music factors in mood change. Music Educat. J. 37(4), 42–44 (1951)
5. Stratton, V.N., Zalanowski, A.H.J.J.o.M.T.: The relationship between music, degree of liking, and self-reported relaxation. J. Music Therapy 21(4), 184–192 (1984)
6. Cerwén, G., Pedersen, E., Pálsdóttir, A.M.J.I.j.o.e.r..: The role of soundscape in nature-based rehabilitation: A patient perspective. Int. J. Environ. Res. Publ. Health 13(12), 1229 (2016)
7. Matsunaga, M., et al.: Psychological and physiological responses to odor-evoked autobio-graphic memory. Neuro Endocrinol. Lett. 32(6), 774–780 (2011)
8. Ikei, H., Song, C., Miyazaki, Y.J.I.j.o.e.r..: Physiological effects of touching wood. Int. J. Environ. Res. Publ. Health 14(7), 801 (2017)
9. Pramudya, R.C., Seo, H.-S.J.F.i.P.: Influences of product temperature on emotional responses to, and sensory attributes of, coffee and green tea beverages. Front. Psychol. 8, 2264 (2018)

The Use of Telehealth for Clinical and Laboratory Teaching in Healthcare Professional Education During Covid-19: Findings of a Scoping Review

Radia Mardiatan, Puteri Dianti, and Erna Rochmawati(✉)

Master of Nursing, Universitas Muhammadiyah Yogyakarta, Kasihan, Indonesia
`erna.rochmawati@umy.ac.id`

Abstract. This research aims to map the available evidence on teaching strategies for clinical and laboratory in healthcare professional education during the COVID-19 pandemic and their impacts on students. PubMed, Science Direct, JSTOR, ProQuest, and Springer Nature were searched for relevant articles with queries that combine keywords related to healthcare professional students, clinical learning, laboratory learning and Covid-19. Included studies focused on clinical and laboratory education during the Covid-19 pandemic and their impacts. We excluded reviews or study protocols. The retrieved articles were screened at the title, abstract, and full-text stages. Studies were selected based on relevancy with the inclusion criteria. Findings then were extracted, and the reported based on the PRISMA guidelines. A total of 3237 studies were identified following a comprehensive search, and eight studies were included after removing duplicates and screening. We found several teaching methods utilized during Covid-19 pandemic including blended learning, virtual and online learning, online simulated learning, and the use of telehealth. The learning methods received a mixed response from students, some rated positive responses, and some assumed that this online approach was not enough to support clinical and laboratory learning for health students. The scoping review maps out that majority of used methods are online and virtual clinical and laboratory learning. There is a need for further research designing more quasi-experimental studies to assess the effectiveness of standalone digital education interventions for the remote training of nursing or medical interns to be fully prepared for emergencies.

Keywords: Covid-19 · Healthcare Students · Clinical Teaching · Telehealth · Virtual Learning

1 Introduction

The coronavirus outbreak has rapidly expanded to nearly all regions of the globe, and confirmed cases of COVID-19 continue to rise each week. Globally, until March 2021, there will be 122,536,880 covid-19 cases, with 2,703,780 deaths [1]. The Covid-19 pandemic has affected in all aspects of human life and activities and caused behavioural, social and lifestyle changes [2].

C. Stephanidis et al. (Eds.): HCII 2023, CCIS 1833, pp. 107–112, 2023.
https://doi.org/10.1007/978-3-031-35992-7_15

This rapid educational transition encourages health care professional educators to strive, adopt and adapt to new technologies [3]. The pandemic situation has initiated digital developments and distance learning through online resources in higher health-care profession education [4, 5]. The new technologies provided in the education include online media and platforms such as websites, online forums, communication applications, videos, podcasts, discussion boards and considering the use of Augmented Reality (AR) and Virtual Reality (VR). Changing face-to-face learning methods to online methods has resulted in the loss of collaborative learning experiences, clinical rotations, medical conferences, and opportunities to upgrade skills, which will have an impact on the education and careers of health care professional students [3]. Although this online learning approach is fairly success, this approach has limitations in developing laboratory skills and clinical abilities of students. These skills can be obtained from direct activities and practice on health instruments as well as to patients and the clinical environment directly, but with distance learning laboratory skills practice and clinical learning cannot be done properly [6, 7].

Since the COVID-19 pandemic is recent, literature is limited regarding the methods on clinical education and laboratory learning on higher education for healthcare profession. Existing literature identifies type of teaching methods in clinical education, but none has mapped the available methods. Therefore, the purpose of this paper is to map what methods are used during the pandemic to facilitate clinical and laboratory learning of healthcare professional students and how the outcomes of these learning methods are.

2   Methods

This scoping review adopted the methodological framework proposed by Arskey and O'Malley [8]. The Preferred Reporting Items for Systematic Reviews and Meta-Analyses extension for Scoping Reviews (PRISMA-ScR) checklist was used as a guideline in reporting the results of the study. Identifying relevant studies, To accomplish the aims of the study, the following research questions were identified:What teaching methods were used in clinical education during Covid-19 pandemic?. What are the impacts on the methods used in clinical education and laboratory learning?

Identifying relevant studies using predetermined criteria. The databases used in the literature search were Science Direct, PubMed, ProQuest, and JStor. The search was carried out using the keywords "health professional student", "clinical learning", "laboratory", and "covid-19" were all utilized together in a MeSH search. The terms were individually searched before being joined using the Boolean term AND. The inclusion criteria were: papers with all study designs; published between 2020 to present; using English language; and articles discussing clinical and laboratory education during the Covid-19 pandemic. Reviews or study protocols were excluded for the scoping review.

All records found in the initial search were transferred to Endnote X9 Software (Clarivate Analytics, PA, USA), where duplicates were deleted automatically. Two reviewers independently examined the publications based on titles and abstracts for relevance. Following this, all reviewers met to discuss the review considering the inclusion criteria. We then independently assessed the retrieved full texts to confirm they met the inclusion criteria.

Charting and extracting data. We charted the data at the fourth stage of the review using a table that was developed based on the Joanna Briggs model to extract details, attributes, and results from investigations [9]. Each of the eight full-text papers was meticulously read several times by the two authors to capture all important information was included. The following categories were included in the data extraction tool and spreadsheet: authors and year; participants; type of study; teaching methods and results. The data were extracted to a table. A summary of review findings is presented in Table 1 (supplement).

3 Result

Characteristics of the included studies. A total of 4442 papers were identified. After removing duplicates, screening title and abstract and full texts to examine with the eligibility criteria, a total of eight studies were reviewed. Methods to facilitate clinical and laboratory learning. There were several methods to facilitate healthcare profession students in their clinical and laboratory education including virtual simulation [10-13]; tele-rotation [14]; zoom teleconferencing [15] and e-learning [16]. The virtual simulations were conducted using online meeting platform to manage patient-based cases. The medical students were provided simulated e-health record and opportunity to conduct online virtual medical interviews [13]. The virtual simulation was facilitated by physicians. The virtual simulation was adopted in nursing education to manage psychiatric patients [12]. Of the eight articles, there is one article that has a slightly different approach, apart from utilizing online and virtual learning, some virtual experiences are replaced with clinical hours, but the substitution does not exceed 50%, so the method used is to combine virtual and online learning with clinical teaching directly [17].

Outcomes of the clinical teaching methods Of the eight included studies, three studies developed, implemented and measured the effects of virtual simulations. After the virtual simulations program, students' knowledge, comprehension, and skills improved [11, 13, 14]. There are two articles that look at how the results of student evaluations of the clinical abilities they acquire during the pandemic with the learning methods used [13, 14]. In addition, there was also improvement on students' openness and confidence in managing patients using telemedicine [12], and increased teamwork [11]. Other studies were cross-sectional studies to measure student's perception and satisfaction on e-learning method. Most of the outcomes from these articles were to see how students' perceptions, satisfaction, and responses to the learning methods used during the article pandemic [10, 15, 17]. In addition to satisfaction, some students face difficulties for online learning due to technical issues [10].

4 Discussion

The impact of the pandemic is causing changes to clinical and laboratory learning systems and methods, many educational institutions and clinic practice lands respond to this condition by changing face-to-face classes and moving to a virtual learning environment [18]. The change of clinical learning to online learning is not easy, but several ways can be considered to ensure students are exposed to as much clinical environment as possible [19]. Studies on learning methods during this pandemic have not been done too much. Most of the articles in this review discuss virtual and online distance learning methods for clinical and laboratory learning in health students. Distance learning is considered suitable to be applied given development of technology that supports the implementation of online and virtual learning, and the availability of various learning platforms [2]. The current scoping review confirms previous studies that digital education is the most common method implemented in health care education and is considered as being effective for learning knowledge and practice [20].

The use of telemedicine services and virtual treatments was applied in two studies [12, 14]. During the shift, the students review the patient's electronic medical records using a checklist developed by the university. Students provide interventions as per patient needs through Tele-ICU such as education, patient safety, drug regulation, ventilator settings, lab results re-examination, by using checklists as guidelines in implementing protocols and practices.

Another alternative to clinical placement is the use of teleteaching and telemedicine. For example, universities in London provide access to a library that provides recordings of online interviews with patients, cases, and online lectures from doctors via computers on the hospital's website. The use of telemedicine can minimize the risk of exposure to covid-19. Students can interact with patients in isolation rooms through tablets that have been provided [21]. Virtual simulations improved students' knowledge, skills, comprehension, and confidence. The improvement could be due to exposure to cases and facilitated and supervised by the faculty as stated in Ho et.al's study [14]. In fact, not all institutions are currently ready to anticipate this, but adaptation must still be implemented [22, 23]. Virtual learning in system learning management during pandemics makes the learning experience more flexible despite some shortcomings, so it is expected that improvements and developments are expected to overcome some of the problems and shortcomings of the system [24].

Although the scoping review has mapped available teaching methods for clinical and laboratory in health profession education, there were limitations present. First, there is limited quantity of peer-reviewed research within this area that cause a limited strength in providing a more thorough finding. Due to the sudden pandemic situation, high standard of published was scarce and therefore limited relevant and rigorous insight on the topic.

5   Conclusion

The Covid-19 pandemic caused a change in approaches and methods in learning in nursing education. The scoping review maps out that majority of used methods are most of online and virtual clinical and laboratory learning. This learning method received a mixed response from students, some rated positively, and some assumed that this online approach was not enough to support clinical and laboratory learning for health students, so it requires other approaches and methods in facilitating clinical and laboratory learning in health profession students. The implementation of virtual simulation should be facilitated and supervised by the faculty and followed with student's reflections.

References

1. World Health Organization. "COVID-19 Weekly Epidemiological Update. https://www.who.int/publications/m/item/weekly-epidemiological-update-on-covid-19. Accessed 21 Mar 2021
2. Romli, M.H., Cheema, M.S., Mehat, M.Z., Hashim, N.F.M., Hamid, H.A.: Exploring the effectiveness of technology-based learning on the educational outcomes of undergraduate healthcare students: an overview of systematic reviews protocol. BMJ Open **10**(11), e041153 (2020). https://doi.org/10.1136/bmjopen-2020-041153
3. Haslam, B.M.: What might COVID-19 have taught us about the delivery of Nurse Education, in a post-COVID-19 world?. Nurse Educ. Today **97**, 104707 (2021). (in eng). https://doi.org/10.1016/j.nedt.2020.104707
4. Di Gennaro, F., et al.: Coronavirus diseases (COVID-19) current status and future perspectives: a narrative review. Int. J. Environ. Res. Public Health **17**(8) (2020). (in eng). https://doi.org/10.3390/ijerph17082690
5. Khodaei, S., Hasanvand, S., Gholami, M., Mokhayeri, Y., Amini, M.: The effect of the online flipped classroom on self-directed learning readiness and metacognitive awareness in nursing students during the COVID-19 pandemic. BMC Nurs. **21**(1), 22 (2022). https://doi.org/10.1186/s12912-022-00804-6
6. Gamage, K.A.A., Wijesuriya, D.I., Ekanayake, S.Y., Rennie, A.E.W., Lambert, C.G., Gunawardhana, N.: Online delivery of teaching and laboratory practices: continuity of university programmes during COVID-19 pandemic. Educ. Sci. **10**(10), 291 (2020). https://doi.org/10.3390/educsci10100291
7. Nourkami-Tutdibi, N., Hofer, M., Zemlin, M., Abdul-Khaliq, H., Tutdibi, E.: TEACHING MUST GO ON: flexibility and advantages of peer assisted learning during the COVID-19 pandemic for undergraduate medical ultrasound education - perspective from the "sonoBY students" ultrasound group. GMS J. Med. Educ. 38(1), Doc5 (2021). (in eng). https://doi.org/10.3205/zma001401
8. Arskey, H., O'Malley, L.: Scoping studies: towards a methodological framework. Int. J. Soc. Res. Methodol. **8**(1), 19–32 (2005). https://doi.org/10.1080/1364557032000119616
9. Peters, M.D.J., Godfrey, C., McInerney, P., Munn, Z., Tricco, A.C., Khalil, H.: Chapter 11: scoping reviews. In: Aromataris, E., Munn, Z. (eds.) JBI Manual for Evidence Synthesis. The Joanna Briggs Institute (2020)
10. De Ponti, R., Marazzato, J., Maresca, A.M., Rovera, F., Carcano, G., Ferrario, M.M.: Pre-graduation medical training including virtual reality during COVID-19 pandemic: a report on students' perception. BMC Med. Educ. **20**(1), 332 (2020). https://doi.org/10.1186/s12909-020-02245-8
11. Esposito, C.P., Sullivan, K.: Maintaining clinical continuity through virtual simulation during the COVID-19 pandemic. J. Nurs. Educ. **59**(9), 522–525 (2020). https://doi.org/10.3928/01484834-20200817-09
12. Abram, M.D., Guilamo-Ramos, V., Lobelo, A., Forbes, M.O., Caliendo, G.: Telehealth simulation of psychiatric and chronic disease comorbidity: response to the COVID-19 national epidemic. Clin. Simul. Nurs. **54**, 86–96 (2021). https://doi.org/10.1016/j.ecns.2021.02.001
13. Kasai, H., et al.: Alternative approaches for clinical clerkship during the COVID-19 pandemic: online simulated clinical practice for inpatients and outpatients—a mixed method. BMC Med. Educ. **21**(1), 149 (2021). https://doi.org/10.1186/s12909-021-02586-y
14. Ho, J., et al.: Developing the eMedical Student (eMS)-a pilot project integrating medical students into the tele-ICU during the COVID-19 pandemic and beyond. Healthcare (Basel) **9**(1), 73 (2021). (in eng). https://doi.org/10.3390/healthcare9010073

15. Lieberman, J.A., Nester, T., Emrich, B., Staley, E.M., Bourassa, L.A., Tsang, H.C.: Coping with COVID-19: emerging medical student clinical pathology education in the pacific northwest in the face of a global pandemic. Am. J. Clin. Pathol. **155**(1), 79–86 (2021). https://doi.org/10.1093/ajcp/aqaa152

16. Al-Balas, M., et al.: Distance learning in clinical medical education amid COVID-19 pandemic in Jordan: current situation, challenges, and perspectives. BMC Med. Educ. **20**(1), 341 (2020). https://doi.org/10.1186/s12909-020-02257-4

17. Zerwic, J.J., Montgomery, L.A., Dawson, C., Dolter, K.J., Stineman, A.: Planning and implementing a practice/academic partnership during COVID-19. J. Prof. Nurs. **37**(1), 24–28 (2021). https://doi.org/10.1016/j.profnurs.2020.11.007

18. Owolabi, J.O.: Virtualising the school during COVID-19 and beyond in Africa: infrastructure, pedagogy, resources, assessment, quality assurance, student support system, technology, culture and best practices. Adv. Med. Educ. Pract. **11**, 755–759 (2020)

19. Dedeilia, A., Sotiropoulos, M.G., Hanrahan, J.G., Janga, D., Dedeilias, P., Sideris, M.: Medical and surgical education challenges and innovations in the COVID-19 era: a systematic review. In Vivo **34**(3 Suppl), 1603–1611 (2020). (in eng). https://doi.org/10.21873/invivo.11950

20. Hao, X., et al.: Application of digital education in undergraduate nursing and medical interns during the COVID-19 pandemic: a systematic review. Nurse Educ. Today **108**, 105183 (2022). https://doi.org/10.1016/j.nedt.2021.105183

21. Mian, A., Khan, S.: Medical education during pandemics: a UK perspective. BMC Med. **18**(1), 100 (2020). https://doi.org/10.1186/s12916-020-01577-y

22. Henry, J.A., Black, S., Gowell, M., Morris, E.: Covid-19: how to use your time when clinical placements are postponed. BMJ **369**, m1489 (2020). https://doi.org/10.1136/bmj.m1489

23. O'Byrne, P., Holmes, D.: Researching marginalized populations: ethical concerns about ethnography. Can. J. Nurs. Res. **40**(3), 144–159 (2008). http://proxy.library.adelaide.edu.au/login?url=http://search.ebscohost.com/login.aspx?direct=true&db=c8h&AN=2010059249&site=ehost-live&scope=site

24. Uchejeso, O., Chinaza, I., Ejinaka, O.: COVID-19: the stimulus for virtual learning in medical laboratory science. J. Bio Innov. **9**, 812–820 (2020). https://doi.org/10.46344/JBINO.2020.v09i05.17

A Contextual Design Approach for Creating a Holistic Fitness Application

Chandni Murmu$^{(\boxtimes)}$ [iD]

Clemson University, Clemson, NSC 29634, USA
chandni2104@gmail.com

Abstract. With the rising popularity of fitness and the growing need to record workouts for analytical or social purposes, there is an increasing demand for fitness application(s) that would cater to the requirements of the emerging lifestyle. Looking at the available applications, there are only a few of them, namely, Garmin Connect, Strava, RunKeeper, Map My Ride, Zombie Run and Zwift. From the reviews received on their websites or applications, multiple issues were identified. A few of them are syncing issues, notification issues, GPS issues, fitness goal update issues, and many more. Motivated by these shortcomings in a market of high demand, a contextual design approach was used to design a new fitness application that would benefit the fitness enthusiast without these issues. Intermediary steps in achieving this goal were - experience model construction, grand vision development, identification of persons, product concepts and their cool drilldowns, storyboarding, Generalized Transition Network (GTN), wireframing, prototyping, creating Usability Aspect Report (UAR) based on persona, and improvements made according to the UARs. Along with these, a few suggestions for further improvement have been made.

Keywords: Human Computer Interaction · HCI · Contextual Design · Application · User Centered Design

1 Introduction and Related Work

Revolutionary advancements in technology have empowered individuals to monitor and gather copious amounts of data pertaining to their personal fitness endeavors, providing unprecedented opportunities for self-improvement and optimization [8,12,14,15,21–24]. Several websites and mobile applications have utilized this method to establish a platform for social interaction, whereby users can upload, exchange, and observe personal fitness-related activities (examples: [1,3,10,13]). However, there exists a diverse range of individuals who seek to enhance the dissemination of their physical exercise routines through means that cater to their specific requirements [2]. This necessitates conventional fitness-sharing platforms to develop functionalities that can cater to the needs of a heterogeneous user population.

C. Stephanidis et al. (Eds.): HCII 2023, CCIS 1833, pp. 113–120, 2023.
https://doi.org/10.1007/978-3-031-35992-7_16

To address the aforementioned challenge, a contextual inquiry was conducted to investigate the underlying reasons and patterns behind how users of STRAVA, a popular fitness-sharing platform, choose to share certain physical activities and with whom. The contextual design method specifically centered on the sharing aspects (like [16,20]) that users customize when creating or reviewing their accounts on the platform. STRAVA was selected as the focus of our investigation, owing to its widespread popularity and the absence of any necessity for proprietary fitness-tracking equipment. Users can conveniently record their activities solely through GPS-enabled devices, including their smartphones.

Contextual Design was chosen as the guiding process because it has been built upon in-depth field research. Its emphasis on user-centeredness fosters innovative design solutions. First developed in 1988, Contextual Design has been widely applied across various industries and has become a staple in university curricula worldwide [9]. Designing applications that meet users' needs and expectations requires a deep understanding of the context in which they will be used [9]. This includes understanding users' goals, tasks, and activities, as well as the environmental and technological constraints that may affect their interactions with the application. The Contextual Design process provides a framework for gathering this information and using it to create a user-centered design. Following this process ensures that the designed application is tailored to the specific needs of its users, making it more intuitive, efficient, and effective [6,7,17]. Additionally, applications are often used in a variety of contexts, such as: while commuting or multitasking [11,19]. Contextual Design process can help anticipate and address these different usage scenarios [5,9]. It provides a comprehensive approach for designing applications that are both user-centered and contextually appropriate, making it a valuable tool to follow [4].

2   Design Process and Outcome

Contextual Inquiry: The master and apprentice model of inquiry was employed to understand the context of STRAVA usage, with users acting as the masters and researchers as the apprentices. Initial semi-structured interviews were conducted to gather demographic information and insight into app usage. Users were then asked to perform tasks on the app, explaining each step as needed, in 1.5–2 hour Zoom meetings. Screen sharing allowed for observation, and Zoom transcripts were used for subsequent stages of the contextual design process.

Interpretation: After the contextual inquiry, the design team had immersive interpretation sessions lasting 1.5 to 2 h each, where they discussed each inquiry and gained multiple perspectives. These sessions were held a week after the inquiry, and recordings and transcripts were revisited to document user preferences, pain points, and design ideas on yellow sticky notes. Each interpretation generated 50 to 100 notes and 3 to 8 insights.

Affinity Diagram: The affinity diagram was constructed by shuffling and distributing the yellow affinity notes amongst the design team. A random note was chosen and placed on a wall, which served as the starting point. The other team members sorted through their notes and added related ones to the initial note, based on underlying implications. This grouping process was repeated for each unique note until all the affinity notes were displayed on the wall. The affinity groups were assessed and labeled using blue sticky notes, with short, user-friendly labels containing a key point. Associated issues were then identified and noted on pink sticky notes. Similar pink notes were grouped together to form themes, which were represented by green sticky notes. These themes provided insight into the users' perspective of fitness-sharing tasks and conveyed a core story. The left section of Fig. 1 shows the process and outcome for this step.

Fig. 1. (Left section) Affinity Diagram Obtained: (Top Left) Step 1 with Yellow notes, (Bottom Left) Step 2 and 3 with Blue and Pink notes and (Right Large image) Step 4 with Green notes. (Right section) Experience Model Obtained: (A) Identity Model, (B) Day-in-the-life Model, (C) Decision Point Model, (D) Relationship Model and (E) Sensation Board. (Color figure online)

Building Experience Models: Contextual design has 8 models, namely, Day-in-the-life model (how things get done throughout the day), Identity model (what matters to the user), Relationship model (how closeness to others is affected through the activity), Collaboration model (how collaboration gets things done and improves relationships), Sensation board (aesthetic and emotional experiences), Sequence model (the order of work tasks over time), Decision Point model (what influences the user's decisions), and Physical model (the constraints of the physical environment). The right section of the Fig. 1 shows the outcome for each of the chosen models and the following subsections describes how they were obtained.

Identity: Sources of pride, self-esteem, value, anything that indicated user's identity relating to the task or characterized the users were considered as identity elements. Unique identity elements were given descriptive name ("I am", "I do", etc.) and related elements were grouped and placed under these names. **Day-in-the-life:** Around 2 to 4, for each inquiry, organizing contexts were selected which constituted the main locations or phases of the activity. Common things,

things that are important, items associated with the location or activity phase were grouped by time and location. These were put in such a way that the overall collection told an insightful story that fit the fitness-sharing activity. **Decision Point:** The moment in task or activity where the users had to make decisions where considered as the decision points. Either side of these points positive and negative columns were placed which were filled with their respective decisions. **Relationship:** To captures closeness, three levels of relationship: intimates, friends, acquaintances; were focused. People who interacted with the users for the activity were placed in either of these levels along with short explanation on why they were placed in that level. **Sensation Board:** The affinity diagram was revisited to identify emotional themes. 4 to 8 groups of similar emotions were created. The groups were given emotional themes of the feeling that were evoked when looking at these groups and would carried forward for designing the application. Relevant, free stock, images were found that expressed these groups.

Personas: Using the affinity diagram and experience model, specifically, the identity model, unique groups of users who use the product the same way were identified. These unique groups became the personas for the new fitness sharing app. The uniqueness of the groups was decided by the users' goals, which were experience goals, end goals, or life goals. Figure 2 shows the five unique personas and their respective scenarios which were the results of this step.

Lee Hao is a 32-year-old attorney who lives in Philadelphia, Pennsylvania. He is an avid runner who uses a variety of fitness devices to track his runs, including a Garmin watch and heart rate monitor. Lee's work schedule keeps him very busy, so he is trying to make junior partner this year, and for this reason he likes to get his morning run in first thing in the morning. He is currently training for the Philadelphia marathon in November, along with a few of his colleagues at his firm.

Scenario: Lee's alarm goes off promptly at 5am on Monday morning and alerts him to the morning workout on his training schedule, which this morning is a 6-mile tempo run. He gets into his running clothes, drinks his electrolytes drink, and heads out the door for his run. Before he starts, he navigates on his Garmin watch to his run workout and hits "start." It is important that he be able to monitor and review his workout later to ensure he is hitting the right paces for his marathon training. When the run is complete he saves the workout and it automatically uploads to a fitness app. After showering and changing into his work clothes, he takes the bus to the firm and takes his morning meetings. Over his lunch break he logs onto the fitness app on his phone and reviews the statistics from his run, specifically his paces and heart rate. He also reads the

Susan Brook is a 22-year-old, female, university student who lives in New Hampton, New Hampshire. As she is a student, she depends on free stuff and try to save as much as possible. She likes to run and walk to decompress from the school and relax and refresh herself. She lives in a dormitory and she is friends with most of her roommates. She often go for walks, like, everyday after dinner, with friends and sometimes alone. She is a member of a running club in the university and goes for running with the club members on Mondays, Wednesdays and Fridays, at a time convenient for most of the club members. She is an Android phone user and she needs an application that would provide facilities to record her group walking and running activities and share them with friends and group members, respectively. Through these, she wants to encourage competitive spirit among her friends and club members. She does want to record her solo walks and runs, if any, but prefers not to share them with others. She does not like notifications flooding her inbox or making her phone beep all the time, hates ambiguous content or features that makes no sense, and tries to maintain a boundary between her personal and social life. The only content she shares on public platforms are those activities that she do with friends or other groups. However, if she has achieved something that she would want to show off, she would share them over public platforms.

Scenario: Susan's running club decided that the club members will go for running at 7 pm on Wednesday, 4 pm on Friday. She gets this notification on Sunday and set schedules her week accordingly. On Monday, when she gets some free time, she logs into the fitness application and sets up a challenge where she defines a route on a map and gives caption: 'Let's see who can complete this route first were we start today evening!'. She shares this challenge with her club-mates with an option to 'Accept Challenge'. In the evening, when all the club members meet, Susan logs into the application again to see who all have accepted the challenge. She reminds her club-mates to start tracking activity in their respective devices from which the route completion information will be drawn into the challenge. Susan starts GPS tracking in her mobile application and starts running. At the end of the route, when all of the participating club members have completed the route, the fitness application shows the leaderboard with the top three performers highlighted, which they could share with their friends and followers in the same fitness-app or any other sharing app.

Minerva McGonagall is a 63 years old woman who recently retired from a lifelong career as an educator. Minerva puts great value on her health and fitness and makes an effort to stay active. She likes to start her days with a morning walk with her walking group and, on her daughter's suggestion, now uses a fitness app to record her activities. She is not a premium user, and thinks Premium features are a bit much and not worth the money. She likes to look at her performance, but perceives these stats as a way to evaluate herself. She loves to encourage her friends and likes all their posts on the fitness app. She also likes to look at her health stats to check on her physical health, but finds it hard to navigate through all the options. On weekends, she likes to go hiking or biking with her partner and would be thrilled if she could see the hike routes her friends may have been to, for some inspiration.

Scenario: It is the early hours of Friday morning. Minerva heads out for her morning walk, and drives to the neighborhood park where she meets up with her walking group. Before they set off, she opens her fitness app on her Android phone and starts recording her activity. Her friends and she finish off their walk with their daily ritual of a morning cup of coffee at their favorite local roasters. Minerva's friend Dumbledore shows the group pictures from his last hike. She is impressed with the fall colors in the photo and asks him what Park it was. Later at home, she tells her partner that they could go on the same trail for their weekend hike, and shows him the photos Dumbledore uploaded on the fitness app. She wishes the app would let them navigate Dumbledore's route so they could be sure to see the same colors. She spends some time looking at posts from her friends, and liking comments on her own post from that morning before retiring to bed.

Heather Jones is a 27 years old Executive Assistant. She finds a lot of joy in staying active. She specifically enjoys going on runs and hiking as she strives to improve her health. She often frequents the town park to run some laps after she gets off from work, and she walks the nearby trails during the weekends, sometimes even travels for variety. She keeps track of all her activities through her fitness tracker which is paired up to a fitness app and her mobile phone. She is very protective of her data that is collected, so she does not share her activities with anyone as she just wants to use the data to analyze her progress on her weight-loss journey.

Scenario: The clock strikes 5 on a Friday and Heather's work day at the office ends, so she drives to her house that is located near her favorite park. She gets changed out of her work attire into some more appropriate athletic attire and sets out on a run with her fitness tracker. She sets the settings to her liking and selects the route she created that she normally uses, and starts the run to the nearby park. Her route consists of the directions to her favorite park as she has to navigate through multiple winding roads; this route also depicts the path that surrounds the entire 400 acre park, which she runs twice before heading back home. Once she arrives back home, she stops her activity on her fitness app and double checks all of the sharing options to make sure it is set to private, as she is tracking her activities for her personal gain, not for sharing. After that, she then analyzes her run to see how long it took and other various health statistics her fitness tracker compiled. She also compares the run to her past runs to see if there was any improvement to her previous runs.

Jake Strong is a 24 year old man who is a recent college graduate and has recently started his career in accounting. Jake played sports throughout high school and into college, and is looking to maintain his high level of fitness. He goes for a 30-minute run at least four times a week during the morning, before he goes into work. Jake has recently started using a fitness app to record his runs. He believes that it is worth it to pay for a premium membership, as he enjoys to challenge himself and compete with others. Jake is currently training to compete in a triathlon in the near future.

Scenario: Jake's alarm awakes him at 6:00 A.M. sharp. He gets out of bed, puts on his running clothes, and eats his breakfast. By 6:30, he is set to go on a 5 mile run. He unlocks his iPhone, opens the fitness app, and tracks the statistics of his run. He then showers and heads to work after his run, and posts his results on the app. By the time Jake gets off of work, he notices that he has a notification from the fitness app. His friend liked his post, and left a comment stating that he wants to try to beat the amount of time Jake took on his 5 mile run. Jake is motivated by his friend's comment, and goes to bed soon after he goes home to eat dinner, looking to improve his run time for tomorrow morning.

Fig. 2. Personas and their respective Scenarios.

Product Concepts: The green notes in the affinity diagram served as the foundation for ideating product concepts. The design team revisited the diagram and experience model during brainstorming sessions to refine initial ideas into more satisfying concepts using the cool-drill-down process described in the "Contextual Design" book by Holtzblatt and Bayer (1998). Among the refined and processed product concepts were Anonymous Profile (share and compete anonymously), Visibility Meter (adjust public settings easily), Social Circle (control followers' access), Customizable Feeds (control feed content), and Trophy Case (motivate users to achieve fitness goals). Left 2 columns in the Fig. 3 shows one of the product concepts that was the outcome of this step.

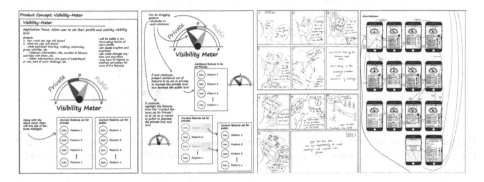

Fig. 3. (From left: 2 columns) Visibility Meter; one of the product concepts, (3rd column) Storyboard for Visibility Meter and (4th column) a section of the GTN corresponding to this product concept.

Storyboard and Generalized Transition Network (GTN): The new application's product concepts and interaction components were developed based on the diverse goals of users who use fitness tracking and sharing applications. The app catered to users who wanted to store data, compete, or socialize with others interested in fitness. Storyboards were created for each persona with their specific goals in mind, and GTN was constructed to provide all possible options for users to achieve their goals while allowing them to ignore irrelevant features. The rightmost column in the Fig. 3 shows the storyboard for one of the product concepts, i.e. Visibility Meter, and its corresponding GTN.

Wireframing and Prototyping: Adobe Illustrator was used for wireframing the states/nodes of the above GTN and Adobe XD was used to prototype the navigation and interaction flow of the new app where all the elements of the GTN and wireframe were connected to form a holistic app. Figure 4 shows a few of the wireframes pertaining to Anonymous Profile product concept and Creating New Challenge with anonymous profile feature.

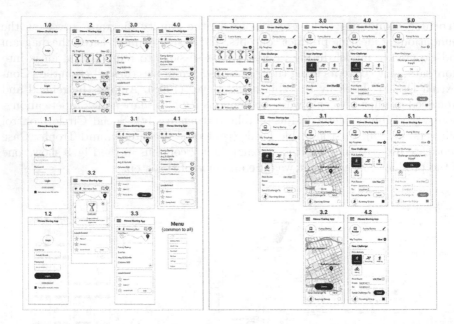

Fig. 4. Few wireframes: Left block corresponds to Anonymous Profile after Login and the right block corresponds to Creating New Challenge feature with anonymous profile.

Usability Aspect Report (UAR): Nielsen's usability heuristics [18] were used to test the usability of the prototype and generate a UAR for each problem or good aspect. Each UAR comprised of Number, Problem/Good Aspect, Name, Evidence (heuristic name), Description of the interface where the heuristic was violated/adhered, Explanation (argument on why the particular heuristic was violated/adhered in this interface), Severity/Benefit (NA: good aspect, 1: cosmetic problem, does not matter too much, 2: minor problem, would be nice to solve, but not a high priority, 3: major problem, a problem that should definitely be solved with high priority, 4: usability catastrophe, a problem that renders the website/app useless), Motivation for severity rating (a justification for that rating in terms of frequency: does it occur for everyone or just in some specific cases?, impact: is it a minor inconvenience or a huge hurdle?, and persistence: is it easily fixed/avoided or does it keep happening?, each rated low, medium, or high), and Possible solution and/or trade-offs (How would you solve the problem? What are potential downsides of your solution? For good aspects, list potential downsides of the current solution), Relationships (How is this aspect related to other usability aspects found?). 6 problematic aspects were found and reported. They were: (1) "Where am I?" or "What am I suppose to do next?" feeling, (2) Does not prevent clicking "ADD" button, (3) Visibility of the conversation or chat status missing, (4) Course related action needs clicking the course name, (5) Have to recall the course number, and (6) No "Forgot Password" option. A separate UAR was provided for each of the problems.

3 Discussions and Conclusion

In this study, contextual techniques were employed to gain an understanding of the target market's needs, which enabled the development of innovative product concepts and brought them to life through storyboarding and prototyping. However, in order to transform the prototype into a marketable product, it is suggested to validate the design with the user base through inclusive design iteration, scoping, prioritization, planning, and staffing [9].

Despite the user-centered focus of contextual design, the design process only involved direct communication with users during the contextual inquiry stage. Therefore, it is essential to return to the field with the prototype in hand, allowing the designers to test the design in the rich environment of their users and gain valuable insights for further improvement. Moreover, the significance of expanding the user base by interviewing new users with the prototype to ensure that the product addresses the market's broader needs, rather than catering solely to a select few, has been acknowledged.

Acknowledgement. I would like to thank the users, colleagues, and mentors who contributed to this study. The institution's resources and facilities allowed us to conduct the design process efficiently. The larger HCI research community's work inspired this study, and I hope it will contribute to the growing knowledge in this field and inspire future innovation.

References

1. Anderson, I., et al.: Shakra: tracking and sharing daily activity levels with unaugmented mobile phones. Mobile Netw. Appl. **12**, 185–199 (2007)
2. Attig, C., Franke, T.: Why do people abandon activity trackers? the role of user diversity in discontinued use. Int. J. Human-Comput. Interact. **39**(8) 1–13 (2022)
3. Feldvari, K., Dremel, A., Stanarević Katavić, S.: Virtual fitness community: Online behavior on a croatian fitness forum. In: Social Computing and Social Media. Design, Ethics, User Behavior, and Social Network Analysis: 12th International Conference, SCSM 2020, Held as Part of the 22nd HCI International Conference, HCII 2020, Copenhagen, Denmark, July 19–24, 2020, Proceedings, Part I 22, pp. 459–474. Springer (2020)
4. Hainess, E.R., et al.: Harmonizing evidence-based practice, implementation context, and implementation strategies with user-centered design: a case example in young adult cancer care. Implement. Sci. Commun. **2**(1), 45 (2021)
5. Haines, E.R.,et al.: Ethnography and user-centered design to inform context-driven implementation. Trans. Behav. Med. **12**(1), ibab077 (2022)
6. Hartson, H.R.: Human-computer interaction: Interdisciplinary roots and trends. J. Syst. Softw. **43**(2), 103–118 (1998)
7. Hartson, R., Pyla, P.S.: The UX Book: Process and guidelines for ensuring a quality user experience. Elsevier (2012)
8. He, Z., et al.: Effects of smartphone-based interventions on physical activity in children and adolescents: systematic review and meta-analysis. JMIR Mhealth Uhealth **9**(2), e22601 (2021)

9. Holtzblatt, K., Beyer, H.: Contextual design: defining customer-centered systems. Elsevier (1997)
10. Izadi, S., Brignull, H., Rodden, T., Rogers, Y., Underwood, M.: Dynamo: a public interactive surface supporting the cooperative sharing and exchange of media. In: Proceedings of the 16th annual ACM symposium on User interface software and technology, pp. 159–168 (2003)
11. Judd, T.: Making sense of multitasking: key behaviours. Comput. Educ. **63**, 358–367 (2013)
12. Kim, H.N., Seo, K.: Smartphone-based health program for improving physical activity and tackling obesity for young adults: a systematic review and meta-analysis. Int. J. Environ. Res. Public Health **17**(1), 15 (2020)
13. Liu, S., Perdew, M., Lithopoulos, A., Rhodes, R.E.: The feasibility of using instagram data to predict exercise identity and physical activity levels: Cross-sectional observational study. J. Med. Internet Res. **23**(4), e20954 (2021)
14. Liu, Y., Kashian, N.: Sharing workout experiences on social networking sites: its moderating factors and well-being outcomes. Health Commun. **36**(11), 1309–1319 (2021)
15. Mishra, A., Baker-Eveleth, L., Gala, P., Stachofsky, J.: Factors influencing actual usage of fitness tracking devices: Empirical evidence from the utaut model. Health Marketing Quarterly, pp. 1–20 (2022)
16. Nakhasi, A., Shen, A.X., Passarella, R.J., Appel, L.J., Anderson, C.A.: Online social networks that connect users to physical activity partners: a review and descriptive analysis. J. Med. Internet Res. **16**(6), e153 (2014)
17. Nesset, V., Large, A.: Children in the information technology design process: a review of theories and their applications. Lib. Inform. Sci. Res. **26**(2), 140–161 (2004)
18. Nielsen, J.: Ten usability heuristics (2005)
19. Sohn, T., Li, K.A., Griswold, W.G., Hollan, J.D.: A diary study of mobile information needs. In: Proceedings of the Sigchi Conference on Human Factors in Computing Systems, pp. 433–442 (2008)
20. Stragier, J., Mechant, P.: Mobile fitness apps for promoting physical activity on twitter: the# runkeeper case. In: Etmaal van de Communicatiewetenschap (2013)
21. Teixeira, E., et al.: Wearable devices for physical activity and healthcare monitoring in elderly people: a critical review. Geriatrics **6**(2), 38 (2021)
22. Wang, J.B., et al.: Mobile and wearable device features that matter in promoting physical activity. J. Mobile Technol. Med. **5**(2), 2 (2016)
23. Wayment, H.A., McDonald, R.L.: Sharing a personal trainer: personal and social benefits of individualized, small-group training. J. Strength Condition. Res. **31**(11), 3137–3145 (2017)
24. Xie, J., Wen, D., Liang, L., Jia, Y., Gao, L., Lei, J., et al.: Evaluating the validity of current mainstream wearable devices in fitness tracking under various physical activities: comparative study. JMIR Mhealth Uhealth **6**(4), e9754 (2018)

Proposal for a Food Selection App at a Convenience Store for CKD Patients

Tetsuya Nakatoh[✉] [iD], Haruka Abe, Nagisa Ogawa, and Erina Sakata

Faculty of Nutritional Sciences, Nakamura Gakuen University, 5-7-1 Befu, Jounan-ku, 814-0198 Fukuoka, Japan
nakatoh@nakamura-u.ac.jp

Abstract. Convenience stores (hereafter referred to as "C-stores") are popular due to their convenient locations and the ability to easily purchase a variety of goods. However, the food available for takeout at these stores tends to be high in energy, fat, and salt. This makes it difficult for chronic kidney disease (CKD) patients who have dietary restrictions to maintain a balanced diet while utilizing C-stores. In this study, we propose a nutrition balance confirmation application to be used at C-stores for CKD patients. By inputting age, gender, height, and physical activity level beforehand, the application calculates the user's appropriate nutritional balance. Based on the nutrition information stored in the database, the application can immediately display and confirm the nutritional balance of the food selected at C-stores, making it easy for the user to select appropriate food items. We present the results of a simulated experiment using this application and discuss future challenges.

1 Introduction

Chronic Kidney Disease (CKD) is a general term for various kidney diseases in which kidney function gradually decreases. The name was proposed to actively prevent. If CKD progresses, end-stage renal failure occurs and artificial dialysis or kidney transplantation becomes necessary. Currently, there are approximately 320,000 artificial dialysis patients in Japan, and the medical expenses per patient are enormous, at about 5 million yen per year. Under Japan's national health insurance system, 95% to 97.5% of these treatment costs are covered by medical insurance. Additionally, the burden on patients, such as the long confinement time, is not insignificant. Therefore, it is important to halt the progression of the disease at an early stage, and nutrition education is implemented for this purpose.

C-stores are abundant in urban areas and are widely used for purchasing meals due to their high convenience. However, food sold in C-stores (C-store food) tends to be high in energy, fat, and salt, and it is not easy for CKD patients who have strict dietary restrictions to maintain a balanced diet while using C-stores. This may require patients to cook for themselves at every meal, or they may give up a balanced diet altogether. Our goal is to provide a tool that allows users to select appropriate food combinations without specialized knowledge when choosing meals at C-stores. This study targets the early stage (stages 1–2) of CKD, where patients have insufficient knowledge of dietary management. The system calculates the recommended nutrients by inputting age, gender, height, and physical activity level in advance. In addition, the database of individual nutrient components of C-store food is maintained. When selecting food at the C-store, the system calculates the nutritional content from this data, presents the user with the current nutritional balance, and allows the user to select food while checking the nutritional balance, thereby attempting to build a system that can easily select meals tailored to each individual user.

2 Methods

2.1 Data Collection

C-stores in Japan are dominated by three major companies, namely Seven-Eleven, FamilyMart, and Lawson, which account for 90% of all C-stores. However, FamilyMart did not display nutrition information about their food products on their website. Therefore, this study collected nutrient data for foods sold by Seven-Eleven and Lawson in the target cities. As indicators of nutrition, energy and the three major nutrients (carbohydrates, protein, and fat) are generally emphasized, but due to the importance of salt restriction in CKD, salt content was also collected.

2.2 Design of Nutrient Intake Allowance

The recommended energy intake for each user was set based on the lower limit of age-specific basal metabolic rate [1], which is calculated by multiplying the standard weight of the user (BMI 22) by an individual activity level (low, moderate, or high). The upper limits were set as follows: protein should be no more than 1.3 g per standard weight, and salt should be less than 6 g [2]. The ratios of carbohydrates (50–65% of total energy) and lipids (20–30% of total energy) were determined based on energy intake. As these nutrient intake values were per day, one-third of these values were used during the operation of the system.

2.3 Prototype System

At the initial screen of the application, users input their age, height, gender, restrictions, and physical activity level to register. Using this information and the basal metabolic rate standards based on age and individual activity levels for a standard weight (BMI 22), the recommended intake of nutrients and salt is calculated. Next, when users choose a C-store at the C-store selection screen, the categories of products are displayed. Tapping on a category displays a list of product names in that category from the database. This two-stage product selection method allows for efficient selection of products on a narrow screen of a smartphone or other device.

When a product is selected, its nutritional content is displayed, with individual nutrient amounts displayed in red if excessive and in green if within the appropriate range. To simplify the screen display, the chosen products are displayed only by their category name in the list, and their actual product name can be confirmed by tapping the category name to bring up a pop-up. To delete a product, users tap on the leftmost " × ". To add more products, users tap on the category name at the top and the list is displayed again. The selected products are added to the list display, and the total amounts of nutrients are shown at the bottom. The upper limits of some nutrients are displayed at the very bottom as a guideline for food selection. The total amounts of each nutrient are displayed in green if within the appropriate range and in red if exceeding the limits. Figure 1 shows an example of the actual screen when four foods are selected.

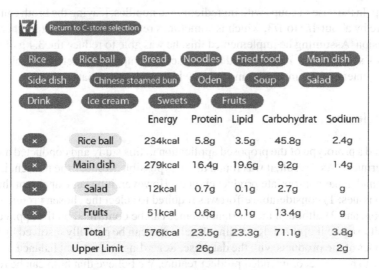

Fig. 1. Screenshot of the application

3 Results of the Simulation Experiment

A simulation experiment was conducted using this system. Four students assumed the role of CKD patients and selected and purchased lunch items at a convenience store. Two examples out of these are presented here.

First example: A 55-year-old male CKD patient with a height of 168 cm, working as an office worker with low physical activity due to commuting by car. This male selected food for lunch at Seven Eleven. Initially, he selected shrimp tempura rice ball, grilled salmon belly in soy sauce, mixed salad, and pineapple. However, the system indicated that the fat and salt content was excessive (Table 1-A). Therefore, when he changed the rice ball to packed rice, he was able to select a well-balanced meal without exceeding the standard values (Table 1-B).

Second example: A male CKD patient, 56 years old, 176 cm tall, and with normal physical activity, was assumed to have gone to Seven-Eleven to select lunch items. He chose retort pouch rice, Japanese pork soup, octopus and broccoli basil salad, packaged sliced pineapple, and peeled apples. However, the system displayed that the sodium content was excessive. Therefore, he decided to leave some of the soup portion of the

Table 1. Results of choosing onigiri (A) and choosing cooked rice (B)

	Energy(kcal)	Protein(g)	Lipid(g)	carbohydrat(g)	Sodium(g)
A	576	23.5	23.3*	71.1	3.8*
B	622	22.3	19.8	90.3	1.4

Note: * is over the limit

pork soup. In the case of soups with ingredients and noodles, leaving the broth can reduce salt intake by about 1/2 to 1/3, which is sometimes recommended in dietary therapy for hypertension. Assuming he implemented this, he was able to reduce the 3.4 g of sodium in the pork soup by 2/3. This resulted in a reduction of approximately 2. of salt, and the total salt content of the meal became 2.0 g, which was appropriate.

4 Conclusion

We created a prototype of the proposed application in this study and conducted a simulation experiment. As a result, it was found that it is possible to check the nutrient intake in the store and make appropriate product choices. However, it became apparent that there were two issues: 1) considerable effort was required to select the chosen products on the application, and 2) although the nutrient balance can be confirmed on the application, it is difficult to make it optimal. Regarding the effort, it can be partially resolved by linking the barcodes of the products with the database. Regarding the nutrient balance, it may be necessary to have a recommended product feature. We believe that both can be resolved with existing technology. Another challenge is that the application does not set an upper limit on energy intake, so it cannot consider the possibility of obesity or other diseases caused by energy excess. Providing support for patients with other diseases, enhancing data collection, and improving usability of the application are future tasks.

References

1. Ministry of Health, Labor and Welfare: Dietary Reference Intakes for Japanese (2020 Edition) Review Committee Report, https://www.mhlw.go.jp/stf/newpage_08517.html, (Japanese)
2. Japanese Society of Nephrology: Dietary Reference Intakes for Chronic Kidney Disease 2014 Edition, Japanese Journal of Nephrology, **56**(5), 553–599, ISSN:0385–2385, Tokyo Igakusha Co., Ltd. (2014). (Japanese)

Immersive Virtual Reality Simulation of the Nine-Hole Peg Test for Post-Stroke Patients

Wanjoo Park[1], Muhammad Hassan Jamil[1], Sabahat Wasti[2], and Mohamad Eid[1(✉)]

[1] Engineering Division, New York University Abu Dhabi, Saadiyat Island, Abu Dhabi, United Arab Emirates
{wanjoo,hassan.jamil,mohamad.eid}@nyu.edu
[2] Neurological Institute, Cleveland Clinic Abu Dhabi, Al Maryah Island, Abu Dhabi, United Arab Emirates
WastiS@clevelandclinicabudhabi.ae

Abstract. The Nine-Hole Peg Test (NHPT) is a standard clinical tool to assess the hand dexterity of a subject with impaired mobility. Virtual reality (VR) offers several advantages in evaluating the user's performance (such as upper limb mobility, movement coordination, precision, and stability) and customizing the rehabilitation task. However, the VR-based NHPT may require more time to complete due to the unfamiliarity of the VR environment and the lack of haptic feedback. In the study, 40 participants were recruited to compare the execution time between conventional NHPT and VR NHPT. The results revealed that participants spend significantly more time in VR than in the physical test (Wilcoxon Rank Sum test, $p < 0.0001$). This study demonstrates the need for new norms for the virtualized NHPT in order to evaluate hand dexterity.

Keywords: Nine-Hole Peg Test · Virtual reality · Rehabilitation

1 Introduction

The Nine Hole Peg Test (NHPT) is a quantitative physiotherapy tool for rehabilitating and evaluating hand motor functions and is considered a gold standard measure of manual dexterity [1]. The NHPT is made of a rectangular board composed of a shallow round dish on one side and nine deep holes on the other side, and nine pegs (7 mm diameter, 32 mm length) stored in the shallow round dish. The NHPT is administered by asking the patient to pick up the pegs from the container and place them into the holes, one by one as quickly as possible. They shall then remove the pegs from the holes and put them back in the container, one by one. A physician records the time taken to complete the test using a stopwatch. It takes 26–30 seconds to complete the test for an individual with normal finger dexterity [2].

W. Par and M. H. Jamil—These authors contributed equally to this work.

C. Stephanidis et al. (Eds.): HCII 2023, CCIS 1833, pp. 125–129, 2023.
https://doi.org/10.1007/978-3-031-35992-7_18

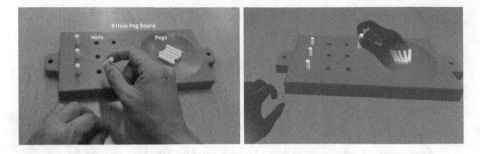

Fig. 1. The conventional NHPT (left) and the VR-based NHPT (right).

However, the NHPT does not provide any information on other parameters such as the reaction time, stability or speed of hand movement that could help the physicist assess the rehabilitation process [3]. It also requires the presence of a physician for every patient performing the test in order to manually measure the execution time using a stopwatch. A good alternative is to simulate the test in virtual reality (VR). Virtualizing the NHPT significantly reduces the costs of the assessment/treatment, allows for customizing the task to meet the specific patient's needs, and evaluate finger dexterity in a comprehensive way, at any time, in any location. For instance, the VR-based NHPT, as opposed to the physical test, can automatically record, analyze, and send feedback to the physician electronically while patients perform the test at home.

Nonetheless, the VR-based NHPT certainly does not take the same amount of time to be completed as the conventional test, due to a variety of factors such as an unfamiliar environment and a lack of haptic feedback. In this paper, we study the feasibility of the VR-based NHPT by comparing the execution time for the VR simulation to that of the physical test. The results of this study motivate the need for developing norms for the VR-based NHPT.

2   Methods

2.1   Experimental Setup and Protocol

To simulate the virtual representation of the NHPT, a VR application was developed using Unity 3D engine (Unity Technologies, USA). All virtual 3D models (for both pegs and the peg board with nine holes) were rendered to match the same scale and colors as in physical instrument. The application was deployed onto the Meta Quest 2 headset and the hand-tracking feature was used to enable realistic hand interactions within the VR environment. The participants could pick up and place the pegs using grasping gestures similar to the physical NHPT. The data collection process was automated inside the VR application. The execution time was recorded for each task and was stored in a data file inside the headset. Figure 1 highlights the conventional NHPT setup (left) and the virtual NHPT application (right).

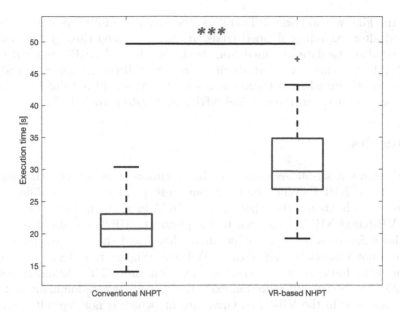

Fig. 2. Comparison between the execution time in physical NHPT test and VR-based NHPT. Wilcoxon Rank Sum test,***$p < 0.0001$. (Color figure online)

A total of 40 subjects participated in the experiment: 20 participants evaluated the conventional NHPT and 20 participants evaluated the VR-based NHPT. Participants had no history of hand motion-related illnesses and ranged in age from 18 to 30 years old. The study was conducted after obtaining approval on the experimental protocol from New York University Abu Dhabi Institutional Review Board (IRB: #HRPP-2022-93).

For the conventional NHPT, participants were asked to perform the NHPT with the dominant and the non-dominant hands, and the experimenter recorded their execution times with the help of a stopwatch. For the VR-based NHPT, a training session was performed to get familiarity with the VR setup followed by the main experiment. The VR-based NHPT was completed for four trials each for the dominant and non-dominant hands per participant in a counterbalanced order. The total execution time was recorded automatically inside the data file for every trial.

We also got a focus group evaluation at the Cleveland Clinic Abu Dhabi. Doctors and therapists in the department of rehabilitation evaluated the feasibility of the VR-based NHPT.

2.2 Data Analysis

The data of 20 participants from the physical NHPT were used as a benchmark to compare the results of the VR-based NHPT. Unlike the physical NHPT, the VR-based NHPT had a skip button that allowed users to skip a trial if they felt that something was abnormal. Therefore, the average of four repeated trials was obtained after excluding skipped trials. It was confirmed through the Jarque-Bera test that the data obtained from both the physical NHPT and VR-based NHPT did not follow a normal distribution. The Wilcoxon Rank Sum test was used to investigate whether there was a statistically significant difference in the execution time between the physical NHPT and VR-based NHPT.

3   Results

Figure 2 shows a significant difference in execution time between the physical and VR-based NHPT (Wilcoxon Rank Sum test, $p < 0.0001$). The difference in median values is about 10 s. That means a 50 % increase in the execution time in the VR-based NHPT compared to the physical NHPT. We also investigated potential differences between the dominant hand and the non-dominant hand. Although not statistically significant (Wilcoxon Signed rank test, $p = 0.057$), the dominant hand showed a shorter execution time. This demonstrates the possibility to observe differences in execution time between dominant and non-dominant hands in the VR-based environment, which is not typically observed in the physical NHPT.

From the focus group evaluation, we confirmed that the VR-based NHPT is suitable to be completed by post-stroke patients. We confirmed a need to build new norms for the VR-based NHPT. Interviews with therapists revealed that patients tend to drop pegs very often, and therapists spend a lot of time picking them up. VR-based NHPT eliminated this issue since whenever a peg is accidentally dropped, it is automatically returned to its initial position.

4   Discussion

Through this study, we found that VR-based NHPT took significantly more time to execute the NHPT as compared to the conventional NHPT. In addition, the VR-based NHPT showed a difference in execution time between dominant and non-dominant hands (although not statistically significant). This is not seen with conventional physical NHPT [1], therefore potential differences between dominant and non-dominant hand performance should be further examined.

There is considerable potential to improve the VR-based NHPT. First, adding haptic feedback to simulate contact with the peg would improve the performance and/or the quality of user experience. Furthermore, by utilizing the data collected through the VR headset about hand movement, a quantitative and automatic evaluation of the hand dexterity can be developed (perhaps using machine learning). Finally, the VR-based NHPT simulation can be used to develop rehabilitation exercises where the properties of the task can be customized for the specific needs of the patient (such as the number and size of the pegs/holes).

Acknowledgements. This work is supported in part by the NYUAD Center for Artificial Intelligence and Robotics, funded by Tamkeen under the NYUAD Research Institute Award CG010.

References

1. Mathiowetz, V., Weber, K., Kashman, N., Volland, G.: Adult norms for the nine hole peg test of finger dexterity. Occup. Ther. J. Res. **5**(1), 24–38 (1985)
2. Feys, P., et al.: Multiple Sclerosis Outcome Assessments Consortium: The nine-hole peg test as a manual dexterity performance measure for multiple sclerosis. Mult. Scler. J. **23**(5), 711–720 (2017)
3. Emery, C., Samur, E., Lambercy, O., Bleuler, H., Gassert, R.: Haptic/VR assessment tool for fine motor control. In: Kappers, A.M.L., van Erp, J.B.F., Bergmann Tiest, W.M., van der Helm, F.C.T. (eds.) EuroHaptics 2010. LNCS, vol. 6192, pp. 186–193. Springer, Heidelberg (2010). https://doi.org/10.1007/978-3-642-14075-4_27

Design of a Medical Accompanying Bed Based on the FBS Model

Yadie Rao and RongRong Fu$^{(\boxtimes)}$

College of Art Design and Media, East China University of Science and Technology, Shanghai, China
1109226815@qq.com

Abstract. Caeregivers undertake the important work of taking care of patients'daily life in hospital. But the hospital accompanying bed has the problems of unreasonable size setting and too hard bed surface, which makes the accompanying person unable to get a good rest after a large amount of physical consumption, thus affecting the treatment of patients. In view of this situation, this study firstly investigated the internal space of the ward and the demand points of the accompanying bed. Secondly, the Kano model is constructed through user interviews and questionnaires, and the key user needs are obtained. At the same time, based on the framework of situational FBS model, the structural framework and related technical principles of the accompanying bed are constructed, and the design principles of the accompanying bed are derived. Then the Jack simulation system was used to carry out the experiment, and the size of the accompanying bed was determined, and the design scheme was produced. Finally, evaluate the design scheme through user interviews. According to the results, a multi-functional medical accompanying bed which can meet the needs of caregivers for all-day rest is obtained.

Keywords: Accompanying bed · Situational FBS model · Jack · Kano model

1 Introduction

China has a large rigid demand for medical services and relatively tight medical resources. But the hospital management system in China is still imperfect compared with the developed countries, with unreasonable ward space and poor accompanying facilities [1]. Accompanying family members are important participants in the treatment process of patients, but their needs are generally neglected. Although the ward accompanying bed is a public facility provided by the hospital for the accompanying person to rest, its size is too small and the bed surface is too hard, which will increase the fatigue of the accompanying person's lumbar spine. Ergonomic intervention can effectively alleviate the fatigue of lumbar spine of caregivers. Therefore, Jack simulation, Carnot model, and FBS model are used to improve the design of ward accompanying beds in this paper.

C. Stephanidis et al. (Eds.): HCII 2023, CCIS 1833, pp. 130–137, 2023.
https://doi.org/10.1007/978-3-031-35992-7_19

2 Desktop Research

2.1 Analysis of Available Space in Ward

The wards in China are divided into single ward, double ward, triple ward and multi-ward. This paper focuses on solving the rest problem of caregivers in three-person and multi-person wards. The rest area of the caregiver in the ward is usually the bed nursing area and the aisle area. The state stipulates that the usable area of each bed in the ward shall not be less than 6 square meters. The width of the nursing area around the bed is generally 1200 mm, the width of the corridor area is generally more than 1400 mm, and the overall length of the ward is 3200–3900 mm [2].

2.2 Analysis of the Characteristics and Needs of Caregivers

Because of the large age span of caregivers, this paper divides caregivers into three groups according to the WHO international age classification standard: the youth group aged 18–44, the middle-aged group aged 45–59, and the elderly group aged over 60 [3]. Under the same work intensity, the needs of each group of caregivers are different. Young people's caregivers can recover quickly after fatigue, but they will have the need to deal with work and study affairs. Middle-aged caregivers have low physical fitness and slow energy recovery. They generally have joint problems such as lumbar and cervical vertebrae, and need a good rest environment. The caregivers of the elderly group generally suffer from basic diseases, poor physical condition, unable to bear heavy nursing work, and difficult to recover their energy. This type of caregiver has high requirements for the comfort and safety of the rest environment [4].

According to the literature analysis of the above two parts, it is preliminarily determined that the demand points of the ward accompanying bed are strong stability, easy storage, small size and light weight. At the same time, it is set that the escort can be used as a seat when it is folded.

3 Determination of the Size of the Accompanying Bed

3.1 Establishment of Digital Person and Accompanying Bed Model

Jack is recognized as a successful human body virtual simulation model and ergonomic evaluation software [5]. According to the body data of Chinese adult males built in Jack 8.0, three mannequins (P5, P50 and P95) conforming to the body size of the caregiver are established. Referring to the size of the mainstream accompanying bed in the current market, the size of the model bed is set as 2000 mm * 1000 mm * 500 mm, and the thickness of the mattress is 100 mm Fig. 1.

3.2 Experimental Process and Conclusion

Firstly, the bed model and three mannequins P5, P50, P95 are imported into the Jack system. Then adjust the three models according to the lying posture, and check whether the size of the bed model is suitable for the three types of caregivers.

Secondly, the height of the chair back, the length of the chair surface and the height of the chair when the accompanying bed is folded into a chair form are respectively determined by measuring the sitting shoulder height, the sitting hip knee distance and the sitting leg bending part height of a human body model. Adjust the three mannequins P5, P50 and P95 to the correct sitting posture and place them on the seat model. The size of the seat surface is set as 400 mm * 600 mm * 100 mm, and the size of the seat back is 600mm * 600 mm * 100 mm, and the height of the chair is 400 mm. The sitting shoulder height of the human body model is L1, the sitting hip knee distance is W, and the sitting leg bending height is L2 Table 1.

Thirdly, determine the size of the armrest of the bed. Adjust the three mannequins to lie flat and place them right above the bed model. The range of motion of the palm was simulated by Jack simulation system, and the distance from the intersection point of the range of motion and the edge of the bed to the head of the bed was L3. At the same time, the distance from the top of the head to the head of the bed is L4 when the mannequin is lying flat. And the height H of the armrest is obtained by measuring the chest thickness of the human body model when lying flat (as shown in Table 2).

Fig. 1. Measurement process of L3 and L4

Table 1. Final Values of Chair Back Height, Chair Surface Length and Chair Height (Unit: cm)

Human body size model	P5	P50	P95	Final value
L1	59.7	64.2	67.6	70
L2	32.8	35.7	37.2	37
W	42.3	46.9	51.1	40–50

Table 2. Final Values of Handrail Height and Length (Unit: cm)

Human body size model	P5	P50	P95	Final value
L3	98.6	102.4	107.0	50
L4	42.5	46.1	40.2	
H	24.8	26.3	28.7	25–30

4   Determination of the Function of the Accompanying Bed

4.1   Establishment of the Kano Model

In this section, semi-structured interviews were conducted among three groups of caregivers. The summarized interview results were used to design the questionnaire, and the contents of the questionnaire are shown in Table 3.

Table 3. Question Number and Content

Issue number	Content of the question
Q1	Accompanying bed size can meet the vast majority of caregivers, not too narrow and too short
Q2	Protect the shoulder and neck of the caregiver to ensure comfortable sleep
Q3	Make it easy for the caregiver to eat or work
Q4	It can store articles
Q5	Flexible unfolding and folding (if there is a pulley at the bottom, it is easy to move)
Q6	Good safety (if there is a guardrail and the corners are rounded)
Q7	High degree of cleanliness and hygiene (such as the use of disposable bed surface or bed surface is easy to clean material)
Q8	Small space, convenient storage and stacking
Q9	Metal or mattress and other accessories can be replaced separately, with strong durability
Q10	Can be converted into a chair for up
Q11	It can assist patients to get out of bed or change wards

Questionnaires were distributed online and offline, and 200 valid questionnaires were collected. Based on the better worse coefficient diagram (Fig. 2), mandatory requirements Q1 and Q6 should be firstly implemented. Secondly, expectant requirements Q2 and Q7 should be implemented. Finally, charismatic needs Q3, Q4, and Q11 should be implemented. Q5, Q6, Q9 and Q10 belong to undifferentiated requirements, which should be realized on the premise of meeting other functions.

4.2   Situational FBS Model Mapping Analysis

The contextual FBS model, first proposed by Professor Gero, is an innovative methodology used to describe the product conceptual design process [6]. This article will use the situational FBS model to map "function behavior structure" and construct the structural framework and related technical principles of the accompanying bed.

1. Determine the product function

According to the results of the questionnaire survey, three types of requirements that should be implemented first are obtained. ①Necessary requirements: Q1 - the size of

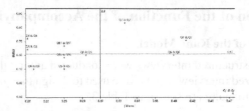

Fig. 2. Better-Worse Coefficient Plot

the accompanying bed can meet the needs of the vast majority of caregivers, and it will not be too narrow or too short; Q6 - Good security. ②Expectation demand: Q2 - protect the shoulder and neck of the caregiver to ensure comfortable sleep; Q7 - high degree of cleanliness and hygiene. ③Charismatic needs: Q3 - convenient for caregivers to eat or work; Q4 - able to store articles; Q11 - able to assist patients to get out of bed or change wards. Preset the functions according to the requirements, and determine that the accompanying bed has six functions of safety, comfort, hygiene, folding, storage and assistance.

2. Function mapping behavior

In the process of functional behavior transformation, the preset function corresponds to the demand. Among other things, safety features include appropriately sized handrails, bed fixation, and edge rounding. Comfortable functions include air mattress and head bed adjustment. Sanitary features include an easy to clean surface. The folding function is divided into two States: folding into a seat and completely folding. Stowage features include side hooks and bottom storage. Auxiliary functions include pulley control and support for standing up and sitting down.

3. Behavior Mapping Structure

There is a one-to-many relationship between behavior and structure mapping, for example, different behaviors may be implemented with the same structure. Therefore, in the design practice, the man-machine size should be fully considered, and the functional modules should be reasonably arranged to prevent the disorder of the relationship between behavior and structure (Fig. 3).

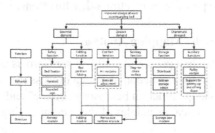

Fig. 3. Hierarchical mapping of function-behavior-structure

5 Design Practice

5.1 Design Principles

1. Safety: According to the user survey results, safety is the most important point, such as edge fillet treatment, installation of handrails, etc.
2. Convenience: Reduce the difficulty of using the accompanying bed and increase its flexibility and the number of functions.
3. Humanization: fully consider the living needs of the caregivers in the ward to meet their basic living needs.

5.2 Design Scheme

The design scheme is mainly divided into the following four parts.

A. Folding module: The head of the accompanying bed adopts a separate adjustable structure, which is convenient for the accompanying person to adjust to the angle suitable for the cervical vertebra. The whole bed body has four adjustable modules, which can adjust the angle and fold all of them.
B. Detachable mattress module: In order to ensure the hygiene of the accompanying bed, each mattress can be disassembled for cleaning and disinfection. The surface of the mattress is PU artificial leather.
C. Storage box module: The storage box at the bottom of the accompanying bed not only supports the bed body, but also can be opened to store sundries. It also has a folding table inside, which can be used as a temporary table on the armrest. Pulleys at the bottom of the storage box allow the bed to move easily.
D. Armrest module: Handrails on both sides shall be 300 mm high and 500 mm long. The armrest not only can be used as a supporting structure of the folding table board, but also can provide an additional supporting point when a patient is transferred.

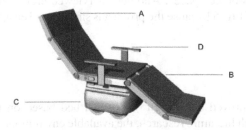

Fig. 4. Hierarchical mapping of function-behavior-structure

6 Design Evaluation

In order to evaluate the effectiveness of the design scheme, user interviews are conducted in the evaluation section. The interview first introduced the design scheme and the functions of the two main accompanying beds on the market to the interviewees in detail, and then asked the interviewees about their views and reasons for the three-hour accompanying bed Figs. 4 and 5.

Fig. 5. Two accompanying beds for comparison

There were 6 participants in this interview, including 2 young people, 2 young and middle-aged people and 2 elderly people. The main contents of the interviews are shown in Table 4 below.

Table 4. Interview Content

Number	Content of the interview
1	Show the three images shown in Fig. 666
2	Respondents were briefed on each type of bed
3	"Which bed do you prefer?"
4	"What is your reason for choosing/not choosing this bed?"

In the interview, five interviewees chose the design scheme of this paper. Their reasons are "more comfortable to look at", "more functional, easy to move in the ward", "more labor-saving to move the accompanying bed", "to meet the needs of rest during the day" and "more storage space". Another interviewee preferred the accompanying bed on the left side of Fig. 5 because the product is simpler and easy to manage centrally in the hospital.

7   Conclusion

In this paper, we improved the design of hospital bed based on the situational FBS model. Firstly, through literature research, the available environment in the ward and the characteristics of caregivers were analyzed. Secondly, Jack simulation system is used to determine the size of the accompanying bed. At the same time, the Kano model is established by using user interviews and questionnaire survey to determine the priority of demand. Then the function and structure of the accompanying bed are determined by mapping the situational FBS model. Finally, the output design scheme is evaluated. In this paper, we propose a design framework for hospital bed, hoping to improve the rest conditions of caregivers, improve the efficiency of rest, and promote the rational use of internal space in the ward.

References

1. Shi, J., et al.: Connotation of modern hospital management system and implementation path of hospital. China Hospital Manage. **40**(01), 1–4 (2020)
2. Zhang, M.: Design and research of ward accompanying bed. Hebei University of Science and Technology (2018).
3. Zhang, C., Liang, H.: Age stage, physical and mental health and subjective well-being -- analysis of mediating effect based on CGSS2017. Theor. Observ. **194**(10), 86-91 (2022).
4. Zhao, C., Zhang, M., Bai, Y.: Research on the design of ward accompanying bed. Western Leather **42**(08), 19 (2020)
5. Li, X., Tang, F., Xie, Y.: Ergonomic design of surgical transfer bed based on Jack simulation. Machine Design, 2020, **37**(05), 130–133. https://doi.org/10.13841/j.cnki.jxsj.2020.05.022
6. Su, C., Tang, P., Song, R., Luo, G.: Intelligent bed design based on requirement analysis and situational FBS model. Mech. Des. Res. **37**(06), 7–12 + 17 (2021) https://doi.org/10.13952/j.cnki.jofmdr.2021.0227

Interactions Afforded by Mobile Telepresence Robots in Health Care Settings

Alejandra Rojas(✉) and Sladjana Nørskov

Department of Business Development and Technology, Aarhus University, Herning, Denmark
rojas@btech.au.dk

Abstract. Mobile telepresence robots (MTRs) allow communication and mobility to interact from a distant location. In health care settings, these robots are used to enhance interactions between physicians, patients, and family members. MTRs can thus be effective in improving quality and efficiency in health care; however, the interactions that MTRs afford need to be studied to address issues related to their design, development, and implementation in line with the physical affordance space by looking not only at the features but also at the relationships they create. Therefore, this study aims to identify the types of interactions offered by two different types of MTRs in health care settings, the relevance of each interaction depending on the type of health care setting, and the perceived differences between the two MTRs. Empirical data were collected in Spain, in two hospitals, a nursing home and with professionals from private clinics. With a qualitative approach, the main data source were 25 semi-structured interviews with informants that used CLARC and GoBe tests in situ and video recorded as stimulus. Additionally, observations, two focus groups and archival data were collected. Findings show two types of interactions: displacement and simultaneity. Furthermore, perceived differences related to the appearance of the two MTRs result in different evoked feelings that are either appropriate or inappropriate depending on the type of patient. This study improves the understanding of how to design, develop, and implement MTRs in health care settings by expanding knowledge on the proper fit between type of interaction and setting.

Keywords: Mobile Telepresence Robots · Human-Robot Interaction · Health Care

1 Introduction

As a result of their use in health care settings, robots may impact patients' health positively by facilitating access and speed of caregiving tasks [1]. Mobile telepresence robots (MTRs) are a type of robot that can be controlled remotely by users to interact with local informants [2]. Therefore, MTRs that are implemented and used in health

---

The original version of this chapter was previously published non-open access. The correction to this chapter is available at
https://doi.org/10.1007/978-3-031-35992-7_74

C. Stephanidis et al. (Eds.): HCII 2023, CCIS 1833, pp. 138–145, 2023.
https://doi.org/10.1007/978-3-031-35992-7_20

care settings may enable remote interactions between health care workers, patients, and family members while supporting physical presence [3]. MTRs may thus provide emotional and physical support [4] in health care settings by allowing social interaction and by enabling in situ mobility for remote users. For example, telepresence can promote well-being, increase self-esteem and reduce loneliness in the elderly [5]. In situations such as infectious disease outbreaks, telepresence can help alleviate the negative effects of social distancing on the elderly and patients [6]. Furthermore, healthcare processes can be improved in terms of efficiency because robots can facilitate access and speed of care tasks, for example, with telemedicine practices. Even when the health sector measures performance mainly with the well-being of patients and not with the maximization of profits [7], the use of robots such as MTRs is relevant due to the benefits for effective performance.

1.1 Relational Approach for the Study of Interactions

MTRs can be effective in improving quality and efficiency in health care [1]; however, the interactions that emerge when health care staff, patients, and family members communicate through such robots need to be studied to address issues related to the design, development, and implementation of MTRs. The study of interactions provides an opportunity to address issues related to the design and development of robots in line with the physical affordance space by looking not only at the features but also at the relationships they create [8, 9]. Focusing on interactions will allow a relational approach to MTRs' design and development, which considers aspects of the social environment, context characteristics, users, stakeholders and robot features [10]. Therefore, this study aims to identify: (i) the types of interactions offered by two different types of MTRs in healthcare settings, (ii) the relevance of each interaction depending on the type of setting, and (iii) the perceived differences between the two MTRs. In doing so, the study contributes both theoretically and practically by providing insights to inform discussions among interdisciplinary teams and stakeholders who are researching, designing, developing, implementing, and using MTRs in health care settings.

2 Methodology

Data was collected from different sources of information and analyzed with the help of qualitative case study methodology, which is particularly appropriate for fields that are not mature [11, 12]. As part of a larger exploratory research that investigated the safety and effectiveness of MTRs in health care settings, test environments were created in which one or two different MTRs, CLARC and GoBe were tested. CLARC (see Fig. 1) has a humanoid form that includes a touch screen at the torso, a shotgun microphone, speakers, and a webcam developed by the University of Malaga and was, at the time, being tested in a nursing home located in Malaga, Spain. GoBe (see Fig. 2) is an MTR with a touch display, multiple cameras, speakers, and microphone developed by the Danish company Blue Ocean Robotics and was being tested in the nursing home and in two hospitals located in Seville, Spain. Moreover, the study included independent professionals working in private clinics in the south of Spain that were selected using snowball sampling.

Fig. 1. CLARC at the nursing home.   **Fig. 2.** GoBe at the nursing home.

2.1 Data Collection and Analysis

The first author visited the health care settings three to four times per week between April and May 2022 to collect primary and secondary data. While onsite, the researcher (i) observed daily health care practices, (ii) participated in the MTR tests, and (iii) conducted the interviews with staff. The main primary data source were 25 semi-structured interviews with health care staff working in the selected health care settings. Only interviews with private clinic informants were conducted via Zoom, where MTRs were presented via a video recording. The informants had various occupations, e.g., nurses, physiotherapists, psychologists, social workers, and psychiatrists. Each interview lasted between 20 to 30 min. The first part of the interview was related to the MTR being tested at the time to elucidate the health care staff's perspectives and then about the second MTR, which created the basis for comparison. Reflective notes were taken based on the onsite observations and the informal conversations.

The secondary data included two 40-min focus groups, one with four staff members and one with four residents, that were conducted in the nursing home as part of the larger assessment to evaluate the strengths and weaknesses of GoBe and CLARC. Other sources of secondary data were three media articles related to the MTR project at the nursing home and five emails exchanged between CLARC developers and the nursing home director. These sources provided insights about the perspectives of the nursing home residents and top management.

As we transcribed the interviews and collected the reflective field notes and secondary data transcripts, we followed a coding process that involved first-order concepts, second-order themes leading to aggregated dimensions. This process was done in NVivo to identify patterns, determine categories, analyze them, and interpret them in-depth [13]. Several strategies were employed in interpreting the data including constant comparison and replication logic to find common topics between the cases and facilitate abstraction [11].

3 Findings and Discussion

3.1 The Types of Interactions

Displacement Interaction. This interaction type occurs when video calls between patients or nursing home residents and family members are handled by MTRs instead of health care staff. With CLARC, a family member can log into the system and choose a time slot for the call. With GoBe, they can connect immediately to start the video call. Hospital patients and nursing home residents may require communicating remotely with family members and thus health care workers must organize video calls, i.e., find a convenient time, hold the mobile device throughout the call and support in case of technical issues. This task became a challenge in the nursing home during the COVID-19 lockdown due to the larger number of residents compared to the number of employees. This resulted in health care staff abandoning their core caretaking tasks, which created a feeling of dissatisfaction. In a displacement interaction, health care staff are no longer organizing the patient-family member video call and may focus on job-related tasks. As illustrated by an informant "having that ability to make more video calls without taking time away from professionals [...] this way they are not limiting the work of the physiotherapist, the psychologist" (P17). Furthermore, the analysis showed that patients benefit from the privacy during the video calls with their families in the displacement interaction, given that there is no health care worker standing next to them to hold the device or assist.

Simultaneity Interaction. This interaction type takes place when health care staff connects to the MTR to communicate with patients or nursing home residents, e.g., a psychiatrist located in a capital city can connect remotely to an MTR situated in a rural area hospital to give consultation. Some informants mentioned that using MTRs for a first diagnosis could be very effective in emergency cases, and later they can proceed with the treatment in-person. MTRs add value in the emergency room (ER) because there are cases that need the assistance of different medical specialties that might not be physically present. There are some medical specialties such as physiotherapists that need to manipulate patients physically, however, the interviewees from this field of medicine mentioned that there is an opportunity for educating patients through a simultaneity interaction by showing them how to perform exercises and monitoring remotely. Additionally, using MTRs instead of other mobile devices may improve the diagnosis. As put by an informant, "it will give the health professionals behind it a vision they do not normally have during an emergency call, many factors could be seen (P11)". Hospital nurses mentioned that using MTRs for communicating with patients that are in different rooms could help them avoid unnecessary movements and optimize work time given that they usually walk back and forth from the nursing station to the patient's room to exchange a few words, which is sometimes perceived as unnecessary. MTRs can thus help healthcare staff add more value within their core tasks.

3.2 The Relevance of Each Interaction Depends on the Type of Health Care Setting

The identified types of interactions afforded by MTRs in health care settings are (i) displacement and (ii) simultaneity. Each interaction will bring different benefits to the quality and efficiency of healthcare depending on the context characteristics and stakeholders involved. Therefore, increasing the quality and effectiveness of health practices with MTRs may be easier if healthcare providers have a clear understanding of which types of interactions most appropriately fit the type of setting, whether it be a nursing home, hospital, or private clinic.

The Displacement Interaction is More Relevant in the Nursing Home. Informants from the nursing home appeared to be more disrupted by the burden of organizing video calls compared to hospital and private clinic interviewees. As some informants explained, elderly people are usually dependent on health care staff to communicate with their family members because they might not be familiar with technology or might be physically impaired. Therefore, the displacement interaction that emerges when MTRs can manage video calls independently appears to be highly relevant in nursing homes. On the other hand, this type of interaction is relevant in hospitals when patients who are isolated or physically disabled need to make video calls with family members. Some informants' opinion was that video calls to family members through an MTR may evoke a feeling of closeness that may contribute to the patient's wellbeing, which is perceived as highly relevant when they have been isolated. Finally, the informants from the private clinics mentioned that MTRs for displacement interactions add no value in outpatient clinics because patients receive treatment without staying there overnight.

The Simultaneity Interaction is More Helpful in Hospitals. Informants working in private clinics and nursing homes mentioned that this type of interaction is more useful in hospitals given that in private clinics and nursing homes the attention is usually face-to-face, characterized by being more personalized and well-planned than in hospitals, and thus in-person interactions are considered more appropriate for these health care settings. However, some informants mentioned that medical attention via MTRs could be done sporadically in private clinics and nursing homes only if the patient agrees in advance. On the other hand, informants working in hospitals argued that MTRs may be more useful in such settings than in nursing homes or private clinics because hospitals usually have a large number of patients, who are not always expected to come for consultation, and only a few health workers to assist them. Therefore, the use of MTR could help alleviate the workload of local doctors by facilitating mobile telepresence to other health professionals who are not present in hospitals but have time to see patients, resulting in a more effective health care service. Table 1 summarizes the reasons for the relevance of each interaction in nursing homes, hospitals, and private clinics.

3.3 Perceived Differences Between the MTRs

The main perceived difference between GoBe and CLARC is related to their appearance, which in turn created a difference in the evoked feelings. To illustrate, while CLARC is perceived as "informal" and "toy-like", GoBe is perceived as "sophisticated", and "more

Table 1. Relevance of each interaction in each case.

Case	Displacement Interaction	Simultaneity Interaction
Nursing Home	**High Relevance** Elderly people are dependent on health care staff to use mobile devices for video calls	**Low Relevance** Medical attention is well-planned and personalized, and thus considered more appropriate in-person
Hospital #1 and #2	**Medium Relevance** Physically impaired or isolated patients depend on health care staff to use mobile devices for video calls	**High Relevance** Reaching remote patients who need urgent medical attention improves health care effectiveness
Private Clinics	**Low Relevance** Patients usually receive treatment without staying there overnight	**Low Relevance** Medical attention is well-planned and personalized, and thus considered more appropriate in-person

functional". The appearance of each MTR makes it more appropriate for some patients and less appropriate for others. As put by an informant, "For mental health patients, CLARC can trigger fear or hallucinations, that is why I think the other [GoBe] is more neutral" (P12). Observations revealed that the nursing home residents called CLARC by the name "Felipe" and had conversations with the MTR when turned off, while no conversations were observed with GoBe. Thus, CLARC may evoke a feeling of presence of an ascribed identity, while GoBe may be better at evoking a feeling of closeness, as if the person operating the MTR is present in the room, "It gives the feeling of company, being tall, because it is the height of a person, it seems to me that it can be of great help for some people, especially in isolation" (P22). "It seems that it is the family member who approaches [the resident], then I think it is easier for them to recognize them" (P5). In the nursing home, GoBe's screen size resulted an advantage compared to CLARC's, given that elderly people might be visually impaired. However, some informants believed that CLARC may be more beneficial for elderly people because it has a familiar form, "For older patients perhaps a robot in human form would be more friendly […], for young patients who are more used to technology, I think the screen would be good" (P13).

3.4 Considerations for the Design, Development, and Implementation of MTRs in Health Care Settings

Design and Development Implications. Some participants proposed new features or ways in which both MTRs could be improved to contribute more effectively to the quality and effectiveness of health care. The proposals did not distinguish between the MTRs but, rather, addressed them in general. Related to the hardware, some participants mentioned the relevance of having a button to call staff when assistance is needed, as well as an emergency button to turn off the MTR immediately. Also, hospital nurses preferred the MTRs to have a space to carry objects that patients may need, e.g., tissues. As for the software, input from interviewees and observations revealed that MTRs should be able to detect objects while navigating to avoid accidents or an autonomous navigation mode, mainly in the nursing home, because residents are usually walking around with no supervision. Also, some clinicians would like to share relevant information through the screen with the patients during remote consultations, similar to sharing their screens with other tools such as Zoom.

Effective Implementation of MTRs in Health Care Settings. For an effective implementation of MTRs in health care settings, the fit between type of interaction and setting should be considered. This requires taking into account the relevance of each interaction depending on the type of health care setting, which implies analyzing what a certain group of users and stakeholders may require. For instance, a nursing home may highly benefit from a displacement interaction because patients are dependent on health care workers to communicate, while hospitals may benefit more from a simultaneity interaction because health care staff's workload may be decreased if remote clinicians join with the MTRs to assist onsite patients. Private clinics might not be the most appropriate setting for MTRs interactions, as can be seen in Table 1. Moreover, choosing GoBe or CLARC for a given health care setting may depend on whether patients should be attached to the MTR or not. Findings showed that patients may build an affective relationship with CLARC due to the humanoid form, whereas GoBe has a neutral form that is less likely to trigger such social reactions.

4 Conclusion

This study covers implications for the design, development, and implementation of MTRs in health care settings by looking not only at the features but also at the relationships created with patients, nursing home residents, health workers and family members. It also highlights the relevance of identifying a suitable fit between the type of interaction and the type of health care setting to increase the benefits of implementing MTRs in such settings. Future research may examine the effects of using MTRs in health care settings with particular medical specialties and types of patients to understand differences and best practices.

Acknowledgements. This project has received funding from the European Union's Horizon 2020 research and innovation programme under the Marie Skłodowska-Curie grant agreement No 956745. The content of this publication does not reflect the official opinion of the European Union. Responsibility for the information and views expressed in the publication lies entirely with the author(s).

References

1. Sætra, H.S.: The foundations of a policy for the use of social robots in care. Technol. Soc. **63**, 101383 (2020). https://doi.org/10.1016/j.techsoc.2020.101383

2. Lee, M.K., Takayama, L.: "Now, i have a body": uses and social norms for mobile remote presence in the workplace. In: Proceedings of the SIGCHI Conference on Human Factors in Computing Systems, pp. 33–42. ACM, Vancouver BC Canada (2011). https://doi.org/10.1145/1978942.1978950

3. Koceski, S., Koceska, N.: Evaluation of an assistive telepresence robot for elderly healthcare. J. Med. Syst. **40**(5), 1–7 (2016). https://doi.org/10.1007/s10916-016-0481-x

4. Sparrow, R., Sparrow, L.: In the hands of machines? the future of aged care. Mind. Mach. **16**, 141–161 (2006). https://doi.org/10.1007/s11023-006-9030-6

5. Cesta, A., Cortellessa, G., Orlandini, A., Tiberio, L.: Long-term evaluation of a telepresence robot for the elderly: methodology and ecological case study. Int. J. Soc. Robot. **8**(3), 421–441 (2016). https://doi.org/10.1007/s12369-016-0337-z

6. Scassellati, B., Vázquez, M.: The potential of socially assistive robots during infectious disease outbreaks. Sci. Robot. **5**, eabc9014 (2020). https://doi.org/10.1126/scirobotics.abc9014

7. Kim, R.H., Gaukler, G.M., Lee, C.W.: Improving healthcare quality: a technological and managerial innovation perspective. Technol. Forecast. Soc. Chang. **113**, 373–378 (2016). https://doi.org/10.1016/j.techfore.2016.09.012

8. Fischer, K., et al.: Integrative Social Robotics Hands-on. IS. **21**, 145–185 (2020). https://doi.org/10.1075/is.18058.fis

9. Seibt, J., Flensborg Damholdt, M., Vestergaard, C.: Integrative social robotics, value-driven design, and transdisciplinarity. IS. **21**, 111–144 (2020). https://doi.org/10.1075/is.18061.sei

10. Prescott, T.J., Robillard, J.M.: Designing Socially-Assistive Robots. ICCHP-AAATE 2022 Open Access Compendium "Assistive Technology. Accessibility, 8 pages (2022). https://doi.org/10.35011/ICCHP-AAATE22-P2-36

11. Eisenhardt, K.M.: Building theories from case study research. Acad. Manag. Rev. **14**, 532 (1989). https://doi.org/10.2307/258557

12. Yin, R.K.: Case study research: design and methods. Sage Publications, Los Angeles, Calif (2009)

13. Gioia, D.A., Corley, K.G., Hamilton, A.L.: Seeking qualitative rigor in inductive research: notes on the gioia methodology. Organ. Res. Methods **16**, 15–31 (2013). https://doi.org/10.1177/1094428112452151

Visualising Health: A Survey Exploring the Attitudes, Behaviours and Problems Faced Towards Personal Health Data Visualisations of Patients Living with Chronic Conditions in the UK

Zhonghan Sheng$^{(\boxtimes)}$ ⓘ, Gyuchan Thomas Jun ⓘ, and Panagiotis Balatsoukas ⓘ

Loughborough University, Loughborough LE11 3TU, UK
z.sheng@lboro.ac.uk

Abstract. While existing wearable technologies and mobile health apps make easy the collection of personal health data, they do not provide the means necessary for patients to visualise, better understand and make use of this data. Our research examined the following question: What are the behaviours and attitudes of patients living with chronic conditions when viewing personal health data (PHD) visualisations? A cross-sectional online questionnaire survey was conducted in the UK in the spring of 2022. A total of 152 patients with chronic conditions participated. Data was analysed descriptively and using Chi-square tests. The results showed that patients with diabetes viewed PHD more frequently compared to other conditions ($p = .011$). Patients with musculoskeletal diseases were more likely to have problems understanding PHD visualisations ($p = .056$). The most frequently viewed types of self-generated data were physical activity ($p < .001$), mental well-being ($p < .001$), sleep ($p < .001$), BMI or weight ($p < .001$) and healthy lifestyle data ($p = .031$), such as diet/nutrition plans, alcohol and smoking habits. The most common problems patients faced when viewing their PHD were: "Presence of too much or too little data" (40.7%), "Lack of customisation of the data visualisation" (40%), and "Lack of personalised information" (38%).

Keywords: Personal health data visualisation · Chronic conditions · Human–computer interaction · Experience design · Online survey

1 Introduction

Chronic conditions, such as cardiovascular diseases, diabetes or depression put heavy burdens on societies, national health services, carers and patients themselves. The patients living with chronic conditions were about 15 million in England [1]. Health information technologies (HIT) have been proven to play an important role in involving patients in the self-management and monitoring of their conditions [2, 3]. For example, currently, patients in the UK and abroad can access personal health information, like laboratory test results and medication, via patient portals and electronic health records

(EHRs) [4, 5]. Also, the wide availability of smartphone applications and wearable technologies has made it possible for patients suffering from different chronic conditions to collect, store and retrieve their health data [6, 7]. This type of patient-generated health data (PGHD) is defined as health data collected by patients themselves, which can be either self-reported, like electronic patient report outcomes (e-PROs), or objectively measured, like blood pressure, blood glucose or heart rate. In the context of the present article. In the context of this study, PGHD, together with data stored in EHRs or patient portals, is defined as Personal Health Data (PHD).

While existing technologies make it easy for the collection and integration of PHD, they do not provide the means necessary for patients to visualise this in a way that can facilitate understanding, and this is the case, especially for people with low literacy and numeracy skills [8–10]. For example, modern EHR systems and patient portals present test results to patients in tables, which is a format that is difficult for many of them to interpret [11]. Also, most of the visualisations tend to be health provider-oriented rather than patient-friendly [12] and there are few widely accepted guidelines or standards about how to visualise information for different patient-facing situations and needs [13].

1.1 Research Aim

The aim of this study was to explore the behaviours and attitudes towards personal health data visualisations of patients with chronic conditions and with varying levels of health literacy, graph literacy, and numeracy.

2 Method

An online, UK-wide, questionnaire survey was conducted in the spring of 2022 and administered through the Prolific [14].

Survey Design. The main body of the questionnaire included a total of 33 questions. These questions were divided into 3 sections. Section 1 contained 7 questions about respondents' background characteristics including demographic information (age, gender, ethnicity) and information about their conditions e.g., types of chronic health conditions and years since diagnosis. Section 2 contained 15 questions about respondents' behaviours and attitudes towards personal health data visualisations. Section 3 contained 9 questions about respondents' level of graph literacy (7 questions), health literacy (1 question), and numeracy (1 question). The graph literacy questions were adopted from Zikmund-Fisher [10]'s adaption of Galesic and Garcia-Retamero [15]'s graph literacy scale. The health literacy questions were adapted from Chew [16] and the numeracy questions were adapted from Fagerlin [17]. There were 2 attention-check questions. The purpose of which was to remove from the sample participants who responded to the items of the questionnaire randomly.

Sampling Strategy and Participant Recruitment. Non-probability strategic sampling was conducted because there was little information about the demographic information of patients living with different types of chronic conditions in the UK.

The target population was 15 million [1]. We calculated the sample size based on Charan [18]. A total of 151 participants were needed for a 95% confidence interval because it is widely accepted and practised in academic research in the PHD visualisation domain [10, 11, 19, 20]. In addition, an 8% margin of error was selected.

The inclusion criteria for participants were: 1. They should be above 18 years old and have the capacity to provide their consent to participate; 2. They should have been diagnosed with at least one chronic condition in their life, including both current and recovered patients; 3. They should have viewed their personal health data at least once in the past 30 days; 4. They should be, by the time of the survey, living in the UK.

Data Analysis. A descriptive analysis was performed. Because participants in the survey were asked to self-report the type of chronic conditions they had been diagnosed with, during the processing of these responses we used the classification used by the NHS website and the International Classification of Diseases (ICD-11) for Mortality and Morbidity Statistics [21, 22]. The self-reported diseases/conditions that were too few to be classified into a broader group were classified as "others".

Also, Chi-square tests (with 95% confidence intervals) were conducted to identify differences in attitudes and behaviours towards personal health data visualisations across different types of individual characteristics, such as age, gender, type of chronic condition, and level of health and graph literacy or numeracy skills.

Answers from open-ended questions were analysed thematically and were categorised into broader themes.

The survey was piloted before launching, to test potential problems, and to calculate the completion time.

Ethical Approval. Ethics were approved by the Ethics Review Sub-Committee in the School of Design & Creative Arts at Loughborough University.

3   Summary of Findings

A total of 152 people responded to the survey, and none of the participants failed the attention questions, however, 2 participants reported that they did not use or view their personal health data last month, and their responses were excluded from the analysis. Therefore, a final set of 150 responses were included in the final dataset.

The results showed that the patients with diabetes viewed PHD more frequently compared to other conditions ($p = .011$). Patients with musculoskeletal diseases were more likely to have problems understanding PHD visualisations ($p = .056$). Patients with integumentary system disease were more likely to have problems with too many or too few tables ($p = 0.058$). Whether patients had comorbidity or not did not relate to the frequency of viewing, or the problems they faced when viewing, PHD visualisations.

The most frequently viewed types of self-generated data were physical activity ($p < .001$), mental well-being ($p < .001$), sleep ($p < .001$), BMI or weight ($p < .001$) and healthy lifestyle data, such as diet/nutrition plans, and alcohol and smoking habits ($p = .031$).

The most common problems patients faced when viewing their PHD were the "Presence of too much or too little data" (40.7%), "Lack of customisation of the data visualisation" (40%), and "Lack of personalised information" (38%). Lack of customisation was more likely to be reported by patients who viewed their PHD visualisations more frequently ($p = .011$), had a higher level of graph literacy ($p = .031$) and higher technological literacy ($p < .001$). Also, the lack of customisation was reported more frequently by patients who viewed physical activity data ($p < .001$), and weight-related data ($p = .015$) at a higher frequency. The lack of personalised information was reported more frequently among patients who viewed PHD visualisations at a higher frequency ($p = .013$), and especially among those who viewed sleep ($p = .032$) and healthy lifestyle data ($p = .023$).

4 Conclusions

The findings of this survey showed that patients with different types of chronic conditions may have different needs and may face different problems when viewing their PHD. Therefore, it is important for designers of consumer-facing health information technology (HIT) systems to rely not only on generic usability principles and guidelines when designing PHD visualisations and dashboards. Instead, they should involve patients themselves in the design of such visualisations to make sure that their needs and requirements are taken into account and not hindered by the lack of existing disease-specific design principles. Thus, attention should be paid to the specific patient needs and requirements of specific conditions when designing PHD visualisations.

From the findings of this survey, it also became clear that patients perceived existing data visualisation interfaces to be poor in terms of customisation and personalisation. Lack of customisation and personalisation were the two most frequently reported problems faced by patients when viewing their personal health data. Personalisation is key to helping participants understand their PHD, while customisation is critical to help them interrogate and explore this data.

Finally, the findings of the survey showed that patients were interested in understanding their PHD in context. This means that they were interested in understanding how contextual information collected about themselves, such as physical activity, weight, diet plans and smoking or drinking habits influenced their vital signs and other physiological data that were critical to the self-management of their conditions. This suggests that allowing patients the option to view their various types of health data individually and not in combination hinders their ability to understand this data. Of course in this case a critical question that needs to be addressed in future research is how much information/data should be presented to the patients.

References

1. Long Term Conditions Compendium of Information: Third Edition. https://www.gov.uk/government/publications/long-term-conditions-compendium-of-information-third-edition
2. Farinango, C.D., Benavides, J.S., Cerón, J.D., López, D.M., Álvarez, R.E.: Human-centered design of a personal health record system for metabolic syndrome management based on the ISO 9241–210:2010 standard. J. Multidisc. Healthc. **11**, 21–37 (2018). https://doi.org/10.2147/JMDH.S150976
3. Shneiderman, B.: Improving health and healthcare with interactive visualization methods. J. Chem. Inf. Model. **53**, 1689–1699 (2013)

4. NHS website. https://www.england.nhs.uk/2019/08/nhs-launches-accredited-suppliers-for-electronic-patient-records/
5. Fraccaro, P., Vigo, M., Balatsoukas, P., Buchan, I.E., Peek, N., Van Der Veer, S.N.: Patient portal adoption rates: a systematic literature review and meta-analysis. Stud. Health Technol. Inform. **245**, 79–83 (2017). https://doi.org/10.3233/978-1-61499-830-3-79
6. Onyeaka, H., Firth, J., Kessler, R.C., Lovell, K., Torous, J.: Use of smartphones, mobile apps and wearables for health promotion by people with anxiety or depression: an analysis of a nationally representative survey data. Psychiat. Res. **304**, 114120 (2021). https://doi.org/10.1016/j.psychres.2021.114120
7. Balatsoukas, P., et al.: In the wild pilot usability assessment of a connected health system for stroke self management. 2020 IEEE International Conference on Healthcare Informatics, ICHI 2020, pp. 2–4 (2020). https://doi.org/10.1109/ICHI48887.2020.9374338
8. Arcia, A., et al.: Method for the development of data visualizations for community members with varying levels of health literacy. AMIA Annu. Symp. Proc. **2013**, 51–60 (2013)
9. Fraccaro, P., et al.: Presentation of laboratory test results in patient portals: influence of interface design on risk interpretation and visual search behaviour. BMC Med. Inf. Decis. Mak. **18**, 11 (2018). https://doi.org/10.1186/s12911-018-0589-7
10. Zikmund-Fisher, B.J., et al.: Graphics help patients distinguish between urgent and non-urgent deviations in laboratory test results. J. Am. Med. Inform. Assoc. **24**, 520–528 (2017). https://doi.org/10.1093/jamia/ocw169
11. Zikmund-Fisher, B.J., Scherer, A.M., Witteman, H.O., Solomon, J.B., Exe, N.L., Fagerlin, A.: Effect of harm anchors in visual displays of test results on patient perceptions of urgency about near-normal values: experimental study. J. Med. Internet Res. **20** (2018). https://doi.org/10.2196/jmir.8889
12. Wood, E., et al.: Diabetes mobile care: aggregating and visualizing data from multiple mobile health technologies. AMIA Jt. Summits Transl. Sci. **2019**, 202–211 (2019)
13. Ola, O., Sedig, K.: Beyond simple charts: design of visualizations for big health data. Online J. Public Health Inf. **8** (2016). https://doi.org/10.5210/ojphi.v8i3.7100
14. Home page of Prolific. https://www.prolific.co/
15. Galesic, M., Garcia-Retamero, R.: Graph literacy: a cross-cultural comparison. Med. Decis. Mak. **31**, 444–457 (2011). https://doi.org/10.1177/0272989X10373805
16. Chew, L.D., et al.: Validation of screening questions for limited health literacy in a large VA outpatient population. J. Gen. Intern. Med. **23**(5), 561–566 (2008). https://www.ncbi.nlm.nih.gov/pmc/articles/PMC2324160/
17. Fagerlin, A., et al.: Measuring numeracy without a math test: development of the subjective numeracy scale. Med. Decis. Mak. **27**, 672–680 (2007). https://doi.org/10.1177/0272989X07304449
18. Charan, J., Biswas, T.: How to calculate sample size for different study designs in medical research? Indian J. Psychol. Med. **35**, 121–126 (2013). https://doi.org/10.4103/0253-7176.116232
19. Morrow, D., et al.: Contextualizing numeric clinical test results for gist comprehension: implications for EHR patient portals. J. Exp. Psychol. Appl. **25**, 41–61 (2019). https://doi.org/10.1037/xap0000203
20. Tao, D., Yuan, J., Qu, X.: Effects of presentation formats on consumers' performance and perceptions in the use of personal health records among older and young adults. Patient Educ. Couns. **102**, 578–585 (2019). https://doi.org/10.1016/j.pec.2018.10.007
21. NHS website. https://www.datadictionary.nhs.uk/nhs_business_definitions/long_term_physical_health_condition.html
22. World Health Organisation. ICD-11. https://icd.who.int/en

Development of a Home-Visit Nursing Practice Information Sharing System that Transitions from Text to Images and Video

Sachiko Somaki[1,2]($\boxtimes$), Yukie Majima[3], Seiko Masuda[3], and Yumiko Nakamura[4]

[1] Faculty of Nursing, Osaka Medical and Pharmaceutical University, Osaka, Japan
sachiko.somaki@ompu.ac.jp
[2] Graduate School of Humanities and Sustainable System Sciences,
Osaka Prefecture University, Osaka, Japan
[3] Graduate School of Informatics, Osaka Metropolitan University, Osaka, Japan
[4] Research Institute for Advanced Nursing Technology,
Osaka Metropolitan University, Osaka, Japan

Abstract. Japan's aging population is among the largest in the world. The increase in the number of people requiring medical and nursing care has resulted in a shortage of home care nurses. Despite an increasing number of home-visit nursing stations and the introduction of electronic medical records, information is still text-input, making it difficult to visualize nursing practice for each patient. Insufficient information sharing increases the risk of medical accidents. Therefore, we developed an information sharing system that uses images and videos on a tablet (iPad). This system consists of an administration screen and a user screen: (1) The administration screen allows "Patient Registration," "User Registration," and "Category Registration." In the "Patient Registration" section, users register by entering the name and date of birth of the patient with whom they wish to share information. "Nurse Registration" registers visiting nurses who will use the system and assigns them an ID and password. "Category Registration" allows users to set categories according to the nature of the nursing practice they wish to share information about. (2) The user screen is used by visiting nurses to log in and use the system. They upload images and videos of nursing practice taken at home and view these images and videos on a tablet. This system is expected to teach nursing practice prior to the visit. In addition, the accumulation of images and videos can be arranged according to the category of nursing practice and used as a continuous learning tool for home-visiting nurses.

Keywords: Prior Learning · Learning Content · Continued Education

1 Research Background and Purpose

Currently, the Japanese population has one of the highest average ages in the world. The aging rate in Japan is estimated to be 28.8% in 2020 and 38.4% in 2065. Meanwhile, the population peaked in 2010, has been declining since, and is expected to continue declining every year [4].

C. Stephanidis et al. (Eds.): HCII 2023, CCIS 1833, pp. 151–156, 2023.
https://doi.org/10.1007/978-3-031-35992-7_22

The Japanese government has been promoting a comprehensive community care system that provides home care to people receiving medical and nursing care. Consequently, the demand for home care nurses has increased dramatically, and the shortage of human resources has become more serious.

In recent years, home medical care has provided advanced medical care such as ventilator and dialysis management. In addition, the number of cases in which end-of-life care is provided at home has increased.

Therefore, home care nurses require advanced skills to accurately assess patients' situations, provide appropriate care, and collaborate with other professionals.

However, home care nurses are busy, making it difficult for them to find time for education. In addition, home-visit nursing stations have a large amount of clerical work and an increasing number of facilities have introduced electronic medical records. However, even with electronic medical records, it is difficult to visualize each patient's nursing practice because the input is text-based. These situations require home care nurses to check patients' situation during their visits. Furthermore, the quality of nursing care may deteriorate because it is difficult to grasp patients' situation in advance and make the necessary preparations for nursing practice.

2 Definition of Terms

1) **Home-Visit Nursing Station**: A station is a facility from which nurses visit homes to provide medical and nursing care for patients receiving home healthcare under the direction of their family physician. The service is available through medical and long-term care insurance. The stations should have an average of at least 2.5 full-time nurses. Thus, there are numerous micro-enterprises.
2) **Patient**: A patient who uses a nursing station.
3) **User**: A nurse who uses a tablet (iPad).
4) **Category**: Classification of nursing practices.

3 Specifications of the Home-Visit Nursing Practice Information Sharing System

3.1 Screen Type

There are two types of screens: administration and user (Table 1).

The administration screen allows for "Patient Registration," "User Registration," and "Category Registration." The administration screen is logged into using a predefined administrator-specific ID and password. Patients can be registered by clicking "Create New" and entering their names and dates of birth. Nurses can be registered as a user by entering the name, an ID, and a password of up to eight alphanumeric characters. Category registration is divided into "Large Category," "Medium Category," and "Small Category." For example, "Nursing Practice for Daily Living" is set in the large category; <dietary assistance>, <oral care>, <cleanliness care>, and <elimination care> in the medium category; and the contents in the small category are set according to the medium category. Furthermore, these categories can be edited or deleted (Fig. 1).

Table 1. Screen type

	Screen Type	Function
1	Administration Screen	This screen allows "Patient Registration," "User Registration," and "Category Registration."
2	User Screen	This screen is used by home care nurses to log in and use the system. They upload images and videos of nursing practice taken at home, and view these images and videos on a tablet

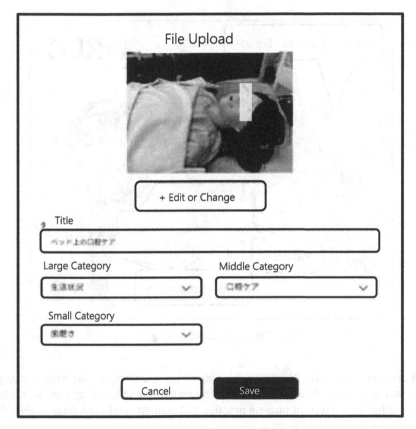

Fig. 1. Uploading images and videos

The user screen allows log-in using the ID and password registered on the administration screen. When logged in, the user will see a list of names, dates of birth, and last updated dates of the patients registered on the administration screen. Users can search for patients via their names or date of birth. Once they click on a patient, the registered image or video and the category name (large, medium, or small), registrant name, and date of registration are displayed. Users can click on the image to enlarge the screen.

To add an image or video, the user can click "New" and then "Create Image or Video. Images and videos are added via "Photo Library" or "Take Photo or Video" or "Select File."

3.2 Filming and System Utilization

Figure 2 shows the method of capturing a picture or video. The user can take pictures of the patient using a wearable camera while performing their usual nursing practice. Pictures can also be taken directly with a tablet device (iPad) with a camera function.

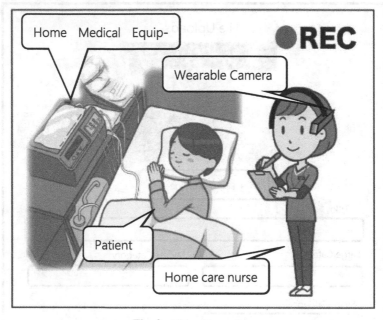

Fig. 2. Video Recording

In addition, the ability to search the patient list according to the title or category (large, medium, or small) allows users to view various patient nursing practices side by side according to the type of nursing practice and compare and view images (Fig. 3).

4   Expected Effects of Using the Information Sharing System

4.1   Pre-learning for Nursing Practice

Home care nurses must enter the patient's medical records after visiting a patient's home. However, they are often too busy with their nursing practice and have no time to enter medical records while at the patients' homes. This causes the home care nurse to fill out the records upon returning to the station. This results in multiple patients' medical records being filled out at once, which sometimes simplifies or obscures the details.

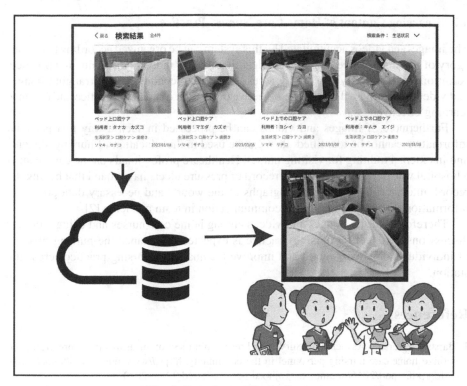

Fig. 3. Learning to Use the System

In addition, home care nurses are required to prepare patient reports at the end of each month for other agencies related to home care, which involves considerable paperwork. Therefore, to make time for visiting nurses' education, it is necessary to simplify their work.

In recent years, as more stations have transitioned from paper-based to electronic medical records, the efficiency of reporting and reimbursement statements has improved. However, patient information is still input by text, and a shift to voice input and recording of images and videos will lead to a reduced workload by shortening the time required for input and accurately conveying information.

In addition, although the education of home care nurses is primarily through on-the-job training, there is a tendency toward immediate employment as there is not enough time to adequately educate them [1]. However, new hires have been reported to be highly anxious about visiting alone [3]. Therefore, using this system to view nursing practices prior to a visit would reduce visiting nurses' anxiety and help them learn in advance. This will also provide an opportunity to check the nursing practices of home care nurses who are anxious and obtain advice from other home care nurses.

4.2   Learning Content of Home Care Nurses' Practice

The images and videos accumulated by this system can be organized according to the category of nursing practice and used as a learning tool for individualized nursing practice. Additionally, the ability to visually assess changes in conditions by arranging images and videos over time will lead to an objective evaluation of nursing practice and enhance learning effectiveness.

Furthermore, if images and videos can be processed in such a way that personal information cannot be identified, they can be used in the education of nursing students and in external training for visiting nurses. Healthcare professionals on the care team at a hospital who developed their own record of pressure ulcers have stated that having the record automatically include photographs of the wound and necessary data promoted information sharing and facilitated communication in team medicine [2].

Therefore, sharing images and videos among home care nurses and using them for discussions to reflect on nursing practice is expected to enhance the nursing practice of individual home care nurses and improve the quality of nursing practice across the station.

References

1. Japanese Nursing Association, Survey and research project on measures to secure, train, and utilize home care nursing personnel in the community. https://www.nurse.or.jp/home/public ation/pdf/report/2016/houmonkangojinzai.pdf. Accessed 9 Mar 2023
2. Kazuhiro, A., Masako, A., Noboru, M., Miyuki, T., Keiko, T., Akiko, N.: Pressure ulcer care chart by information technology. Jpn. Soc. Pressure Ulcers 6(4), 652–655 (2004)
3. Miyuki, M., Naoko, M.: Competencies required by new visiting nurses to make a visit without assistance -a comparison of attitudes among new home care nurses and nurse managers- Japan Red Cross Hiroshima Coll. Nurse 17, 43–52 (2017)
4. White Paper on Aging Society, Cabinet Office Homepage. https://www8.cao.go.jp/kourei/whi tepaper/w-2021/gaiyou/03pdf_indexg.html. Accessed 1 Mar 2023

Investigating User Requirements: A Participant Observation Study to Define the Information Needs at a Hospital Reception

Domenic Sommer(✉)[iD], Tobias Greiler[iD], Stefan Fischer[iD],
Sebastian Wilhelm[iD], Lisa-Marie Hanninger[iD], and Florian Wahl[iD]

Deggendorf Institute of Technology, Dieter-Görlitz-Platz 1, 94469 Deggendorf,
Germany
{Domenic.Sommer,Tobias.Greiler,Stefan.Fischer2,Sebastian.Wilhelm,
Lisa-Marie.Hanninger,Florian.Wahl}@th-deg.de

Abstract. The hospital reception (HR) is one of the first contact points for information about treatment stays, visits, or administrative matters, and thus has influence on the perceived hospital quality. In Dec. 2022, we investigated the information needs during a one week participant observation of the entrance hall at a rural Bavarian hospital. We aim to understand the HRs information needs and how these requests are answered. Previous studies show that the information needs can vary significantly among patients, visitors and employees, impacting the overall hospital experience. There is a lack of research on the information requirements at hospital receptions, with most studies focusing on emergency admissions. In our literature search, we couldn't locate studies that addressed information needs at a hospital reception. We conducted a participant observation using a standardized form. Over the seven day observation period, N = 1,499 requests were made at HR. The requests were examined by summarizing qualitative content analysis in different categories about locations or concerns. *Visitors* account for 51.3% (n = 769) of all requests, followed by *patients* at 38.5% (n = 577), *employees* at 5.3% (n = 79), and other stakeholder at 1.6% (n = 24). The highest utilization of the reception is due to *visitors* showing a COVID-19 test certificate (n = 289) and asking the reception staff for a patient room number (n = 204). *Patients* most frequently asked about their appointment registration (n = 148), the procedure in case of an emergency (n = 98), and orientation (n = 79). The minor requests came from *employees* in the form of administrative requests like borrowing keys (n = 39). On average, the staff needs 65 s to attend to one person. New technologies, like service robots in the entrance hall, can reduce the number of requests in the future. Our study helps to meet user needs through designing service robots. Follow-up studies are planned to validate our findings.

Keywords: User Requirement Analysis · Information Needs · User Requests · Empirical Study · Hospital Reception

This research was supported by the *German Federal Ministry for Digital and Transport* under grant number 45FGU120.

C. Stephanidis et al. (Eds.): HCII 2023, CCIS 1833, pp. 157–166, 2023.
https://doi.org/10.1007/978-3-031-35992-7_23

1 Introduction

Hospital receptions (HRs) and emergency rooms (ERs) are crucial contact points for patients, visitors, and external groups (e.g., suppliers). The HR with the reception staff serves as a generalized information provider about hospital operations, including directions in and around the hospital, available departments, contact details of doctors and nurses, additional services and forwarding to ER or outpatient medical services. For many people, the HR is the first vital impression, which influences the overall hospital experience and perceived quality [16]. Moreover, some experts stating that patient-outcomes improve due to the contribution by HRs to the field of patient-centeredness [1].

Little has been published assessing HR, leading to a research gap that makes it hard to improve the service and enhance patient-experience about HRs. Technical solutions become increasingly important and show the potential to relief and support HRs, due to clarify frequently asked questions, provide route guidance, and direct patients to affiliated practices. Despite economic benefits, technical solutions are not commonly used at HRs. Understanding the information needs and interaction patterns at HRs is crucial for user-centered deployment of humanoid robots [13]. By identifying the specific questions and concerns that patients, visitors, and employees have at the HRs, developers can create tech solutions that effectively address these needs. This, in turn, can improve the overall hospital experience, increase staff efficiency, and reduce the workload on reception staff.

In particular this paper provides the following contributions: We examine the information needs at HRs of different stakeholder, and how these needs are met. Therefore, we conducted an observational study between December 5th and 11th, 2022 in a HR, answering the question: What information do patients, visitors, and employees need from the hospital reception (HR), and how these requests are answered? This includes the following sub-questions:

1. Which questions are asked how often from whom in which language or dialect at which time at the HR staff?
2. How (in terms of content, language, gestures) are the individual questions answered by the HR?
3. Does the information needs variate between certain stakeholder types (e.g., patients, employees, visitors, or suppliers)?
4. How often do people with handicaps ask questions at the HR and what are their handicaps?

Our paper is structured as follows: In Sect. 2, we outline the HRs relevant literature, esp. the information needs. Section 3 presents the methodology of our observation study, and the main findings are shown in Sect. 4. In Sect. 5, we discuss our findings and highlight some major limitations before concluding and providing some outlook for future work in Sect. 6.

2 Related Work

The HR is an essential contact point for patients, their families, and other stakeholder. Previous research by Dominik et al. [5], Carpman et al. [2] and Garg et al. [6] focuses on the architecture of ERs, but there is a research gap regarding HRs, which are crucial for hospital's stakeholder.

Hospital Reception: Karakut [8] and Wong et al. [16] found that HR is the first impression and information platform that can impact hospital quality. HRs comprise usually shops, kiosks, pharmacies, post offices, ATM's, and reception desk services (including help or inquiry desks). Staff at HRs also registers patients or visitors, provides information, provide support to anxious patients, and offers orientation to e.g., treatments as stated by Grag et al. [6]. Face-to-face interaction is, according to Veimeir et al. [15], essential in the information process. Philipp et al. [11] and Prochnow et al. [12] describe the HR as vital for wayfinding and health assistance because reception clerks interact with patients and guide them e.g., to therapies. Usually, building illustrations are placed in the HR area to facilitate finding the floors [2]. Focus of designing HRs is on guiding patients and providing a welcoming atmosphere, such as choosing a color concept and avoiding noise [3]. Noise is the main difficulty to consider in the HR area and is actively avoided in such places. Although technology, such as humanoid robots with the ability for face-to-face interaction, touch-terminals or smart light guiding systems, is seen as potentially useful for extended services and relieving HR staff, it is not yet commonly used at the HR in line with Prochnow et al. [12] and Radic et al. [13].

Information Needs: Information needs in hospital processes are as reported by Philipp et al. [11] particularly high, esp. in diagnosis and treatment, but little is known about medical supporting areas such as the HR. However, Szpiro et al. [14] reports, that providing information may have positive impacts on patients due to health education that HRs can promote. In consonance with Miele [10] the Health advice can be given, and the HRs also act as a kind of gatekeeper, guiding stakeholder to the proper place. Nonetheless, empirical studies have yet to examine the particular information requirements in the setting of HRs. The needs and satisfaction vary among hospital stakeholder, with visitors being the most unsatisfied with the information policies and feeling neglected [11]. Hospital information needs are diverse due to social, cultural, and educational backgrounds of inquirers. According to Dominik et al. an user-centered approach must be employed to address these requirements [5]. In summary, conducting research on information needs in HRs is crucial for designing hospitals and deploying new technologies in accordance with Mathiasen et al. [9] and Gawlak et al. [7].

3 Methodology

To address the gap in empirical research on investigating the HR information needs as described in Sect. 2, we performed a *participatory observation*.

Table 1. Overview of recorded interaction data.

Data	Description
Timestamp	Timestamp at the beginning and end of an interaction
Question	Note on the main topic of an interaction
Language & Dialect	Language and dialect of the inquirer
Answer	Notes on the kind of response
Answer style	Contextual information about the response type
Stakeholder type	Assignment of the inquirer to a group (patient, employee, visitor)
Handicap	Identification of obvious handicaps
Interaction Duration	Calculated duration, from question to complete answer
Waiting Que	Number of people waiting with a request to HR

Study Design: We utilized a *participatory observation* with low complexity level to study information needs at a HR for seven consecutive days. Trough HR opening hours, we documented all interactions using a predefined observation sheet quantitatively evaluate on-site events directly [4]. Items recorded on observation sheet are listed in Table 1. To organize collected data, we used a spreadsheet program. For evaluation we then classified all requests into 17 categories based on the primary question content listed in Table 2.

Study Execution: The participatory observation was conducted from December 5th to 11th, 2022 at the HR of *Kliniken Am Goldenen Steig*, a hospital in Freyung, Bavaria, Germany. This hospital is a typical rural Bavarian hospital, with more than 1,000 employees, 365 planned beds, and multiple treatment sites. The hospital provides care to approximately 40,000 patients annually. The observation was conducted during an average week, avoiding public holidays or other disruptive factors such as construction work. However, during the observation period, wearing masks and showing a valid COVID-19 test certificate for visitors was mandatory by law. The HR was open from Monday to Friday between *06:45* and *20:00* and on Saturday/Sunday between *08:00* and *18:00* during the observation period. Six observers recorded all interactions and rotated in a shift system. For comprehensive data collection the standardized protocol was used, including a pre-test training for all observers.

4   Results

In this Section the insights into the types of requests made to HR by different stakeholder types and the answer by HR are presented. All numbers are rounded to one decimal place. During the seven day study period, 1,170 people-interactions were observed and a total of 1,499 requests were registered at the HR. It is important to note that individuals could make multiple requests within one interaction.

Table 2. Requests to HR per category by stakeholder type.

Category	All		Patients		Visitors		Employees	
	n	%	n	%	n	%	n	%
Show COVID-19 test certificate	313	20.9	23	4.0	289	37.6	0	0.0
Information about patient	218	14.5	9	1.6	204	26.5	2	2.5
Appointment registration	162	10.8	148	25.7	7	0.9	3	3.8
General staff administration	126	8.4	27	4.7	48	6.2	29	36.7
Arriving person with pain	104	6.9	89	15.4	10	1.3	1	1.3
Orientation question	101	6.7	79	13.7	17	2.2	2	2.5
Patients registration	97	6.5	72	12.5	19	2.5	0	0.0
Information on visitation rules	71	4.7	6	1.0	65	8.5	0	0.0
Information about doctors	49	3.3	39	6.8	5	0.7	3	3.8
Payment / Billing	39	2.6	26	4.5	11	1.4	1	1.3
Deposit personal items	38	2.5	4	0.7	23	3.0	9	11.4
Deposit documents	35	2.3	10	1.7	9	1.2	6	7.6
Pick up patient	29	1.9	2	0.4	24	3.1	0	0.0
Patients deregistration	26	1.7	21	3.6	4	0.5	0	0.0
Lending keys	25	1.7	4	0.7	3	0.4	10	12.7
Receive hygiene materials	24	1.6	11	1.9	10	1.3	2	2.5
Other (e.g., Small Talk)	42	2.8	7	1.2	21	2.7	11	13.9
Sum	**1,499**		**577**		**769**		**79**	

4.1   Characterization of the Information Needs and Questioners

Varying Information Needs: In our study terminology, *interactions* refer to any communication between HR staff and hospital stakeholder, while *requests* pertain to specific inquiries or demands made by stakeholder, such as questions about directions, appointments or general information. During a single interaction, multiple requests on different topics can be made by the same person.

Table 2 presents all HR requests categorized by stakeholder type. *Visitors* account for 51.3% (n = 769) of all requests, followed by *Patients* at 38.5% (n = 577), employees at 5.3% (n = 79), and other stakeholder at 1.6% (n = 24). Across all stakeholder types, presenting a COVID-19 test certificate (20.2%, n = 318) was the most common request, followed by inquiries about patients (14.5%, n = 218) and appointment registration (10.8%, n = 162). Other notable categories included requests for assistance with pain management (6.9%, n = 104), orientation and navigation (6.7%, n = 101), and general patient registration (6.5%, n = 97).

Patients primarily require assistance with appointment registration (25.7%, n = 148). Moreover, patients arrive with pain at the HR and need to be forwarded to the ER (15.4%, n = 89). Wayfinding, meaning inquiring guide or orientation to an treatment section, is also a common HR request (13.7%, n = 79).

For *Visitors*, submitting a COVID-19 test certificate is the most common request (37.6%, n = 289), followed by inquiries about a specific patient (26.5%, n = 204), such as their location or health status. Visitors also frequently ask about visitation rules (8.5%, n = 65) and request assistance with depositing personal items, picking up patients, and receiving hygiene materials.

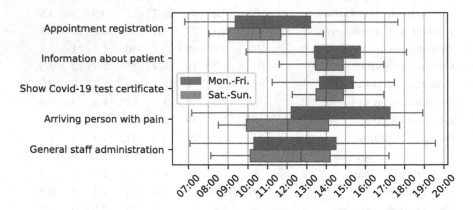

Fig. 1. Temporal distribution of most frequent request types.

Employees or staff members have the fewest inquiries, primarily requesting general staff administration (36.7%, n = 29), small talk (13.9%, n = 11), and depositing or lending keys (12.7%, n = 10).

Frequency and Timing of Information Needs at the HR: Figure 1 shows that HR information needs depend on stakeholder type and time of day. The majority of requests occur between 10:30 and 15:30, with appointment registrations being the most common in the morning and typically completed by lunchtime. Requests in the afternoon, particularly those related to COVID-19 test certificates and patient information, are more frequent, with a higher number of visitors making these requests. General staff administration requests e.g., mailing and handling orders are typically made between 10:00 and 14:00. Weekdays and weekends do not significantly differ in terms of the majority of requests. However, there is a noticeable difference in requests related to patients arriving with pain, with more patients coming in later on weekdays, possibly due to work schedules.

Information Needed by Language and Accessibility: Out of the 1,170 interactions recorded, 98.8% (n = 1,156) were conducted in German, while 0.2% (n = 2) were conducted in English, and 1.0% (n = 12) were conducted in other languages. Regarding the language variations within the interactions, 79.4% (n = 929) were conducted in Bavarian dialect, 13.4% (n = 157) were conducted in standard German, 6.1% (n = 71) were conducted with a foreign accent, and 1.1% (n = 13) were conducted in other dialects. A small percentage of interactions involved individuals with disabilities, including those in wheelchairs (0.7%, n = 8), using crutches (0.6%, n = 7), or walking aids (0.1%, n = 1), emphasising the importance of accessibility of information for individuals with disabilities.

4.2   Characterization of the Answers

Content and Style of HR Answers: In total, 393 concrete answers were recorded, as trivial answers to short questions were not listed. Among them, all requests could be solved by route descriptions (53.9%, n = 212), data exchange (16.8%, n = 66), item exchange (8.9%, n = 35), phone calls (8.1%, n = 32), visiting rules (5.1%, n = 20), in-person guidance (4.6%, n = 18) and other (2.5%, n = 10). HR staff additionally used gestures, cell phones and slips of paper for assistance.

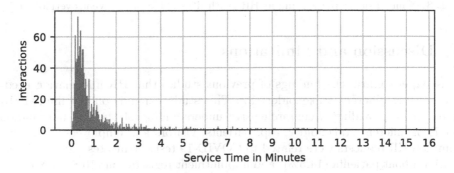

Fig. 2. Number of HR-interactions with use of HR-service time.

Duration of HR Interactions: On average, one HR interaction needs 65 s and a median of 33 s 90.0% of the interactions (n = 1,053) were made within 147 s, according Fig. 2. The majority of requests can be solved without a long answer or high complexity. The shortest interaction took 2 s and the longest took 928 s (14.5 min) of HR service time (Fig. 2).

Temporal Distribution Queue Length: The queue length at the HR was short during the observation period. Out of 1,170 interactions, 898 cases (76.8%) where first in the waiting queue. 206 interactions (17.6%) were second in line, 51 interactions (4.4%) were third in line, and only 15 (1.3%) third or more in line (Fig. 3).

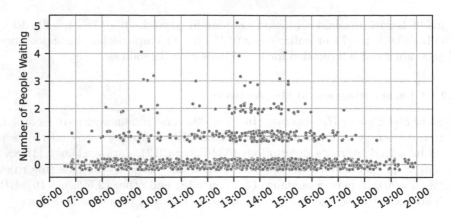

Fig. 3. Number of people waiting at HR (with jitter added to prevent overplotting).

5   Discussion and Limitations

This paper confirm the findings of previous studies that HR information needs vary among different stakeholder [13]. This study expands on the limited HR research by providing a comprehensive understanding of the HR information needs of different stakeholder, esp. patients, visitors and employees. The most common HR requests were related to COVID-19 test certificates (20.9%), information about patients (14.5%), and appointment registration (10.8%). Notably, most requests were resolved with short answers within a minute.

Our study provides valuable insights into the development of technical user-centered solutions for the understudied field of HR. However, our study has several limitations. First, we used an ad-hoc sample, which may not accurately represent the entire population due to unknown and uncontrolled selection probabilities [4]. Second, potential bias from multiple observers and our cross-sectional view of a rural Bavarian hospital may limit the generalizability of our findings. Finally, regional factors and the obligations related to COVID-19 during the observation period may have influenced our results, highlighting the need for further studies in this area. Despite limitations, our study contributes to the understanding of HR information needs and suggests potential for future research.

6   Conclusion and Future Work

We indicate that there is a range of different information needs, as seen in Table 2 which need to be addressed by the HR. Visitors (46.1%) made the most requests, followed by patients (42.6%), employees (6.0%) and others (5.4%). The most common request was for a COVID-19 test certificate (20.9%), followed by information about patients (14.5%) and appointment registration (10.8%). Requests were concentrated between 10:30 and 15:30, with most being resolved within

147 s. The waiting queue was short, with only 1.3% of interactions having three or more people waiting in line.

This article extends the limited research on HR by revealing the information needs of patients, visitors, and employees, as well as how they were addressed. Our findings suggest that user-centered technologies, such as touch terminals for frequently asked questions and service robots, could help support many of the tasks observed, including queries about visitation rules, payment, and way-finding, as well as patient registration and appointment scheduling. Implementing such technologies could alleviate the workload of HR staff, reduce waiting times, and improve communication.

Further studies in other hospitals and regions could investigate the effectiveness of such solutions and explore the potential of technology at the HR to improve communication and relieve staff.

References

1. Bromley, E.: Building patient-centeredness: hospital design as an interpretive act. Social Sci. Med. **75**(6), 1057–1066 (2012)
2. Carpman, J.R., Grant, M.A.: Design that Cares: Planning Health Facilities for Patients and Visitors. John Wiley & Sons, Hoboken (2016)
3. Dalke, H., et al.: Colour and lighting in hospital design. Opt. Laser Technol. **38**(4–6), 343–365 (2006)
4. Doering, N.: Forschungsmethoden und Evaluation in den Sozial- und Humanwissenschaften. Springer, Heidelberg (2023). https://doi.org/10.1007/978-3-642-41089-5
5. Dominik, P., et al.: Emergency room as primary point of access in the German healthcare system. Eur. J. Trauma Emerg. Surg. **47**(2), 453–460 (2021)
6. Garg, A., Dewan, A.: Manual of Hospital Planning and Designing: For Medical Administrators, Architects and Planners. Springer, Heidelberg (2022). https://doi.org/10.1007/978-981-16-8456-2
7. Gawlak, A., Stankiewicz, M.: Specific needs of patients and staff reflected in the design of an orthopaedic and rehabilitation hospital-design recommendations based on a case study (poland). In. J. Environ. Res. Public Health **19**(22), 15388 (2022)
8. Karakurt, A.S.: Critical analysis and evaluation of hospital main entrances according to design and performance criteria in the case of Turkey. Master's thesis, Middle East Technical University (2003)
9. Mathiasen, N., Frandsen, A. (eds.): ARCH17: 3rd International Conference on Architecture, Research, Care and Health. Conference Proceedings. Polyteknisk Boghandel og Forlag, 1 edn (2017)
10. Miele, R.: Tales from a hospital entrance screener: an autoethnography and exploration of covid-19, risk, and responsibility. J. Contemp. Ethnography (2022)
11. Philipp, R., Hughes, A., Wood, N., Burns-Cox, C., Cook, N., Fletcher, G.: Information needs of patients and visitors in a district general hospital. J. Royal Soc. Health **110**(1), 10–12 (1990)
12. Prochnow, A.G., dos Santos, J., Pradebon, V.M., Schimith, M.D.: Reception in the hospital environment: perspectives of companions of hospitalized patients. Revista Gaucha de Enfermagem **30**(1), 11–18 (2009)

13. Radic, M., Vosen, A., Graf, B.: Use of robotics in the German healthcare sector. In: Salichs, M.A., et al. (eds.) ICSR 2019. LNCS (LNAI), vol. 11876, pp. 434–442. Springer, Cham (2019). https://doi.org/10.1007/978-3-030-35888-4_40
14. Szpiro, K.A., Harrison, M.B., Van Den Kerkhof, E.G., Lougheed, M.D.: Patient education in the emergency department: a systematic review of interventions and outcomes. Adv. Emerg. Nurs. J. **30**(1), 34–49 (2008)
15. Vermeir, P., et al.: Communication in healthcare: a narrative review of the literature and practical recommendations. Int. J. Clin. Pract. **69**(11), 1257–1267 (2015)
16. Wong, E.L.Y., Poon, C.M., Cheung, A.W.L., Chen, F.Y., Yeoh, E.K.: Relationship between patient experience and hospital readmission: system-level survey with deterministic data linkage method. BMC Med. Res. Methodol. **22**(1), 1–10 (2022)

Understanding User Preferences for Gaining Trust, When Utilising Conversational Agents for Mental Health Data Disclosures

Deborah Taylor[✉][iD], Oliver Buckley[iD], and Hane Aung[iD]

School of Computing Sciences, University of East Anglia, Norwich NR4 7TJ, UK
{debbie.taylor,o.buckley,min.aung}@uea.ac.uk
https://www.uea.ac.uk/

Abstract. Encouraging humans to disclose personal information is a complex process that is built upon trust, and this is especially true when related to sensitive topics such as mental health. Currently, this data is collected through trained professionals but COVID-19 has seen an increasing demand for support. This paper looks at maximising trust in mental health conversational agents. The study collected data from 177 participants, using survey questionnaires, to examine what human-like features help cultivate and encourage trust. Analysis suggests respondents prefer something that reflects themselves. For example, 78% stated a conversational agent should display a static avatar they can shape to their own preferences. Other factors found to have an impact were friendly greetings (preferred by 76%) and patience (99%). This initial study establishes that humans believe mental health conversational agents can, and should, exhibit a range of human-like features. Some preferences are largely universal across all demographics, whereas others are more specific. This study then delivers a framework of desirable attributes, traits and characteristics, which will be used to test if these features are more successful at establishing trust than standard online forms.

Keywords: Personal disclosure · Conversational agents · Trust

1 Introduction

Utilising conversational agents for data collection is becoming increasingly prevalent across all sectors of industry, but less so for mental health, despite technological innovations increasing usability and functionality [1,2].

Gaggioli et al. [13] established there was a lack of generic processes for eliciting a patient's sensitive mental health personal data and, since the COVID-19 pandemic started, this has become a greater concern for healthcare providers, government and industry, across the globe. In 2021, Cardno et.al. [17] identified a reduced capacity for mental health support and this was verified when

C. Stephanidis et al. (Eds.): HCII 2023, CCIS 1833, pp. 167–174, 2023.
https://doi.org/10.1007/978-3-031-35992-7_24

shadowing trained professionals at a UK mental health charity, in November 2021. They confirmed initial disclosures are extracted via human conversations and this impacts their ability to complete the required number of counselling sessions [3,16,17].

In order to release trained professionals to focus on counselling, it is essential to consider utilising conversational agents when completing initial data disclosures. This initial study aimed to understand what human-like attributes, characteristics, and traits people believe cultivate and encourage trust, when utilising conversational agents for mental health. A software engineering MoSCoW framework was then designed to test these features in a second study.

2   Related Work

COVID-19 has increased the need for trained counsellors to support mental health conditions with extra counselling. With over 3 billion smartphone, and 4.66 billion web-based internet users, worldwide it is logical to consider utilising conversational agents to complete initial sensitive data disclosures. This would enable patients to log their information at any time and free up counsellors to complete the growing number of counselling sessions [4,12,15–17].

Currently the top 3 mental health conversational agents are Wysa, Youper and Woebot. Each one utilises a different level of data disclosure and human-like features.

Wysa was created in 2015 by Jo Aggarwal and Ramakant Vempati, for use on both Android and iOS mobile phones. It integrates artificial intelligence (AI) with human interaction and was designed to collect basic demographic and daily routine data, such as date of birth, age, contact information, addresses, financial identifiers and medical information. Users decide how much, or little, they wish to share and the data is automatically analysed to help its users combat stress, support sleep management and mindfulness, via motivational interviews, positive reinforcement and mindfulness suggestions. In 2022 Malik et.al. [22] completed a study to review Wysa. It identified the low level data disclosures enabled some users to feel more secure, while others found it caused misunderstanding, but using friendly human-like interactions improved the system and helped with user engagement [5,6].

Youper was founded in 2016 by psychiatrist Dr. Jose Hamilton as a free and payable conversational agent with a 'mission to cure the world of anxiety and depression' [7]. It is available in over 150 countries with the free version tracking moods, promoting journal writing to identify triggers, offering personality tests, recommending goals and a providing a one-off emotional health check. The paid version includes advanced AI conversations, upgraded journal writing and support for mindfulness, relaxation, breathing and improved sleep. It also tracks and diagnoses social phobias, anxiety, panic and depression. The data collected involves email addresses, names, passwords, features used within Youper and some health information. In 2021 Mehta et.al [23] designed a study to analyse how effective Youper was at supporting anxiety and depression, based on age and gender demographics. The results established that Youper's utilisation of real-time interventions, using some human-like emotional features and disclosures, supported both engagement and a reduction in user symptoms [8, 9].

Woebot is a free iOS and Android application, created in 2017, by a team of AI specialists and psychologists at Stanford University. It incorporates talk-therapy to help patients analyse, monitor and learn about their emotions. Woebot utilises ten-minute conversations to support patients via the use of age specific contractions, Natural Language Processing, a sense of humour and low level human-like questioning. The data collected includes email addresses, personal identifiers such as name, age and date of birth, passwords, data already authorised with partner companies, operating systems, access codes and time zones. In 2017 Fitzpatrick et.al [24] conducted a study to review the effectiveness of Woebot and the results established that Woebot, versus a standard control group, reduced symptoms to a greater degree. This was believed to be a result of utilising empathetic techniques, but this human-like approach should be explored in more depth, to fully understand how it helped users [10, 11].

The Above Conversational Agents emphasise the requirement to utilise some human-like characteristics, attributes and traits, but require further exploration to establish exactly which features cultivate and encourage trust. This paper presents a preliminary understanding of which human-like features people believe are essential for improving trust, when designing mental health conversational agents. It then provides a simple MoSCoW software engineering framework for designing these systems.

3   Methodology

This study utilised Leo Goodman's [19] statistical snowball data sampling and Braun, V et.al.'s [20] thematic data analysis. Thematic analysis was chosen as this was utilised, to some extent, when each of the above systems were reviewed. Snowball enabled the study to reach a wide ranging demographic, which would be difficult to do with standard in-person data sampling.

This study commenced with in-person and online discussions, with 20 industry and health contacts, then expanded to shadow trained professionals at a UK-based mental health charity. Ethical considerations were undertaken and non-disclosure agreements were signed when visiting the mental health charity. These discussions were designed to better understand what people believed human-like features mean and identify exactly how current initial data disclosures are processed.

This resulted in a set of 25 questions, for data collection via a Microsoft 365 survey questionnaire, across multiple demographics around the globe. We recruited 177 participants by advertising the survey across social media platforms on LinkedIn, Facebook and Twitter (chosen to reach the widest possible demographics [14]), along with the University of East Anglia's (UEA) School of Computing Sciences.

As mental health requirements can differ across ages, genders and nationalities these 3 themes were chosen for the thematic data analysis [21]. Participant ages ranged from 18 to over 80, gender identification was female, male, other and prefer not to say and continental nationality included UK, Europe, North America, South America, Asia and Africa.

A MoSCoW software engineering prioritisation technique was then chosen for the features framework, as this is an essential design tool for development projects and enabled the features to be prioritised into Must have, Should have, Could have and Won't have requirements [18].

4   Results and Framework

The analysis established that some human-like feature preferences are largely universal across all demographics, but others were more specific. See Table 1 for universal human-like feature requirements and Table 2 for divergences across demographics.

Table 1. Universal human-like features across demographics

Feature	Percentage	Universal Data
Patience	99%	Required partially or fully patient conversation
Decisiveness	98%	Required a high level of decisiveness
Focus and Consistency	98%	Required partial or fully focused and consistent questions and answers
Sentence length	95%	Required either medium or full sentences
Empathy and Compassion	95%	Required some empathy and compassion. Could encompass some language shortcuts, such as emoji's
Humour	90%	Required some humour throughout, as this would improve engagement with the system
Text or Voice or	86%	Required text rather than voice-based conversation. Evidenced by UK charity - text only preferred
Formal or informal language	80%	Required a mix of formal and informal language, as this would make the system feel more human
Small talk	76%	Required some small talk, especially at start as this is standard for human conversations
Greeting	76%	Required a friendly greeting. Further 10% dependent on what the agent relating to, e.g. mental health = friendly, but financial = formal
Biography	71%	Stated a biography not required, as most organisations don't offer this feature
End conversation	60%	Required a friendly end to a conversation

Table 2. Diverging human-like features across demographics

Feature	Percentage	Diverging Data
Language Shortcuts:Phrases	75%	Required phrases such as 'I believe'. Divergences for South American and Asian participants. These required zero phrases
Optimism or Pessimism	63%	Required a mix. Divergences for 80+, African and Prefer not to say. These required zero use of either
Language Shortcuts: Colloquialisms	51%	Required some colloquialisms. Divergences for 60–69 and African participants. These required zero colloquialisms
Language Shortcuts: Emojis	49%	Required some emojis. Divergences for 70+ and African participants. These required zero emoji use
Spelling and grammar	43%	Required zero errors. Divergences for African, Other and Prefer not to say. These required some errors
Language Shortcuts: Pop Culture	43%	Required some pop culture references. Divergences for 60–64 and African participants. These required zero pop culture references
Language Shortcuts: Abbreviations	37%	Required some abbreviations. Divergences for 70+, South American and African participants. These required zero abbreviations

The feature with the **greatest divergence across demographics** was a **static avatar**. See Fig. 1 for the divisions across the themes of age ranges, nationalities and gender identification.

4.1   MoSCoW Features Framework

A software engineering MoSCoW framework, see Fig. 2, was then designed for UK utilisation. This prioritised all the human-like features, based on their percentage scores, across Must have, Should have, Could have and Won't have design requirements.

If future development requires a non-UK, or demographic specific, conversational agent to be designed the MoSCoW feature framework would need altering, based on the information provided in Table 1 and 2. For example, African only systems would need to move multiple features to Won't have, but South American and over 70's would only need to move abbreviations.

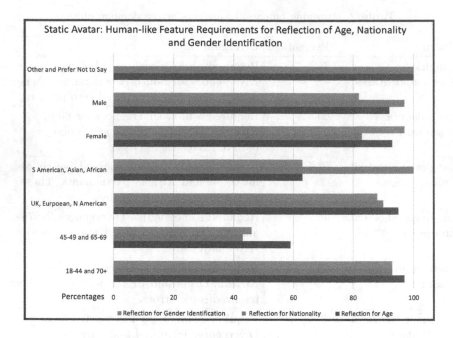

Fig. 1. Static avatar demographic divergence

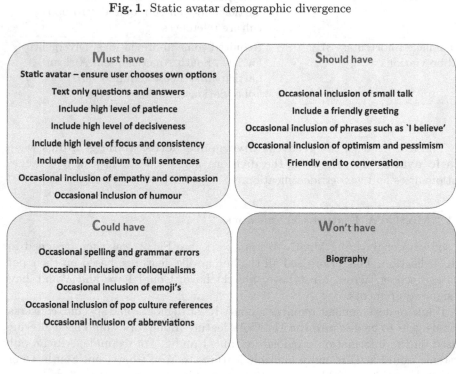

Fig. 2. MoSCoW framework for human-like features in conversational agents

5   Conclusion

The results from this study established that respondents believe conversational agents can, and should, exhibit a range of human-like features, when designed for mental health purposes. Several features are required across all demographics, but some need to be considered based on age, gender identification or nationality.

Collating the data enabled a simple UK human-like MoSCoW feature framework, Fig. 2, to be designed. This will be used in a second study to test if a conversational agent displaying these features, is more successful at encouraging and cultivating trust than a standard online form.

References

1. Sharma, V., Goyal, M., Malik, D.: An intelligent behaviour shown by chatbot system. Int. J. New Technol. Res. **3**(4), 263312 (2017)
2. Shawar, B.A. Atwell, E.: Chatbots: are they really useful? In: Ldv Forum, vol. 22, pp. 137–140. IEEE (2020)
3. Molodynski, A., McLellan, A., Craig, T., Bhugra, D.: What does COVID mean for UK mental health care? Int. J. Soc. Psychiat. **67**, 823–1825 (2021)
4. Global digital population as of January 2021. https://ico.org.uk/for-organisations/guide-to-data-protection/guide-to-the-general-data-protection-regulation-gdpr/key-definitions/what-is-personal-data/. Accessed 14 Apr 2021
5. The wisdom of Wysa-Mental health apps, the (AI) friend who is always there. https://blogs.wysa.io/blog/most-read/best-mental-health-apps-for-employees. Accessed 28 Feb 2023
6. How Indian Startup Wysa Built an Empathetic AI Bot to Offer Mental Support to Millions. https://www.news18.com/news/tech/how-indian-startup-wysa-built-an-empathetic-ai-bot-to-offer-mental-support-to-millions-2681669.html. Accessed 27 Feb 2023
7. The Startup That Wants to Cure Social Anxiety. https://www.theatlantic.com/health/archive/2015/05/the-startup-that-wants-to-end-social-anxiety/392900/. Accessed 10 Mar 2023
8. Youper. https://www.crunchbase.com/organization/youper. Accessed 3 Mar 2023
9. Youper App Review: What's Offered, Cost, and Who It's Right For. https://www.choosingtherapy.com/youper-app-review/. Accessed 3 Mar 2023
10. Chew, A.M.K., et al.: Digital health solutions for mental health disorders during covid-19. Front. Psychiat. **11**, 898 (2020)
11. Welch, C., et al.: Digital Health Solutions for Mental Health Disorders During COVID-19. arXiv preprint arXiv:2007:0381 (2020)
12. Inkster, B.: Digital mental health data insights group (DMHDIG): early warning signs of a mental health tsunami: a coordinated response to gather initial data insights from multiple digital services providers. Front. Dig. Health **2**, 64 (2021)
13. Gaggioli, A., et al.: A mobile data collection platform for mental health research. Pers. Ubiq. Comput. **17**, 241–251 (2013)
14. Mazur, E.: Collecting data from social networking Web sites and blogs. American Psychological Association (2010)
15. Molodynski, A., McLellan, A., Craig, T., Bhugra, D.: What does COVID mean for UK mental health care. Int. J. Soc. Psychiat. **67**(7), 823–825 (2021)

16. Yarrington, J.S., et al.: Impact of the COVID-19 pandemic on mental health among 157,213 Americans. J. Affect. Disord. **286**, 64–70 (2021)
17. Cardno, S., Sahraie, A.: The expanding backlog of mental health patients: time for a major rethink in COVID-19 policy. PsyArXiv (2021)
18. Moran, A.: Managing Agile: Strategy, Implementation, Organisation and People. Springer, Heidelberg (2015). https://doi.org/10.1007/978-3-319-16262-1
19. Goodman, L.A.: Snowball sampling. In: The Annals of Mathematical Statistics, pp. 148–170. JSTOR (1961)
20. Braun, V., Clarke, V.: Thematic Analysis. American Psychological Association (2012)
21. Baker, C.: Mental health statistics for England: prevalence, services and funding. UK Parliament (2020)
22. Malik, T., Ambrose, A.J., Sinha, C.: Evaluating user feedback for an artificial intelligence-enabled, cognitive behavioral therapy-based mental health app (Wysa): qualitative thematic analysis. JMIR Hum. Fact. **9**(2), e35668 (2022)
23. Mehta, A., Niles, A.N., Vargas, J.H., Marafon, T., Couto, D.D., Gross, J.J.: Acceptability and effectiveness of artificial intelligence therapy for anxiety and depression (Youper): Longitudinal observational study. J. Med. Internet Res. **23**(6), e26771 (2021)
24. Fitzpatrick, K.K., Darcy, A., Darcy, A.: Delivering cognitive behavior therapy to young adults with symptoms of depression and anxiety using a fully automated conversational agent (Woebot): a randomized controlled trial. JMIR Mental Health **4**(2), e7785 (2017)

Guidance Method of Arm Movement for Care Prevention on Game Based Shoulder Joint ROM Measurement

Tomoji Toriyama[1]([✉]), Yoshinobu Ichihashi[1], Naoya Matsusaka[1], Tasuku Hanato[1],
Yuto Minagawa[1], Shin Morishima[1], Akira Urashima[1], and Kotoku Mizukami[2]

[1] Toyama Prefectural University, Toyama, Japan
{toriyama,morisima,a-urasim}@pu-toyama.ac.jp
[2] Toyama Prefecture International Health Complex, Toyama, Japan
mizukami@toyama-pref-ihc.or.jp

Abstract. We are developing a game-based nursing-care prevention system, which promotes physical exercise among the elderly by requiring them to wipe or clean a virtual window displayed on a screen. This game can accurately measure the range of motion(ROM) of the shoulder joint, which is one of the main measurement items for activity of daily life (ADL) evaluation. However, this game has its limitations in that there are rare occurrences of side elevation and forward elevation movements. Therefore, this time, we devised the three following methods for obtaining suitable movements for measuring the shoulder joint ROM without impairing players' enjoyment of the game with more than 100 elderly people. We implemented, 1. A method with voice or video guidance, 2. a method of varying the unclean part of the window, 3. a method of presenting parallel projection images transformed from camera images so that players have an advantage in the game when they extend their hands broadly. As a result, the necessary movements for measuring the typical shoulder joint ROM were induced.

Keywords: Preventive Care System · Game Based Design · ROM Measurement

1 Background

The growing number of elderly people is resulting in an increased number of care-receivers, which in turn is increasing the cost of nursing care and intensifying the shortage of caregivers. In order to tackle this issue, the Japanese government is actively implementing preventative measures to maintain the health condition of the elderly so that they do not become care-receivers. It is important to understand the ADL for the elderly population and to support them in maintaining ADL so that they may be socially active [1]. Recently, some local communities have approached this issue through "Kayoi-no-ba" or community of connection, social gatherings that practiced physical exercises [2]. ROM of the shoulders is one of the major standards for assessing ADL. However, this assessment requires specialist knowledge and implementation, meaning that regular assessments would be difficult without the constant availability of professional assessors.

© The Author(s), under exclusive license to Springer Nature Switzerland AG 2023
C. Stephanidis et al. (Eds.): HCII 2023, CCIS 1833, pp. 175–183, 2023.
https://doi.org/10.1007/978-3-031-35992-7_25

To overcome this problem, several preventative care support methods that automatically measure ROM without specialist interventions are proposed [6, 7]. These studies raise several prerequisites including the inducement and guidance of player actions suitable for assessment, and the ability to measure with accuracy. We devise several more effective guidance methods, describe the results of evaluation and discuss these multiple inducement methods.

2   Related Works

2.1   Measurement of Shoulder ROM

Figure 1 shows the method of measuring shoulder ROM (abduction, forward flexion). As shown in Fig. 1, shoulder abduction is the angle between arm and vertical line drawn through shoulder joint. Flexion is the angle captured between the arm raised forward and vertical line through the shoulder. These angles are measured in this study [3].

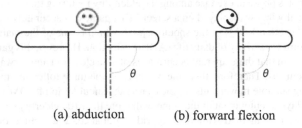

(a) abduction   (b) forward flexion

Fig. 1. Method of measuring abduction and forward flexion on shoulder joint

2.2   ROM Measurement Using Sensors

Several measurement methods using sensors are proposed, mainly with the methods of applying wearable contact sensors and non-contact depth sensors [4, 5]. When comparing these methods, contact sensors are highly accurate, as Qi et al. achieved its accuracy within ±5% to the results of measurement on shoulder and elbow ROM for 80% of subjects [4]. On the other hand, non-contact depth sensors have the benefit of relieving its subjects from unnecessary physical burden. Nan et al. achieved its accuracy within ±13.5% to the test result of measuring shoulder joint ROM with Microsoft's Kinect angle gauge as one of the depth sensors [5]. Nan et al. gamified some parts of their measuring process and at the time of measurement, provided players with precise direction according to each measurement item, which is unlike our study that attempts to measure players' unconscious actions through game contents.

2.3   ROM Measuring System with Game

ROM measurement system emulating a window cleaning game, called "window wiping game" is proposed [6]. This system consists of a screen to show the game, depth sensors

Kinect, and a computer. Player sit in front of Kinect and play the game in their seats. Figure 2 shows this screen shows the player own image overlaid with yellow paint as an imitation of a grimy window. The overlaid yellow paint becomes clear when players move their arms to "clean" the window. Once the first window becomes clean, the next one appears, and this process continues until the time limit. This game seeks to measure shoulder ROM by capturing cleaning movements as well as learning how many windows a player can clean in a given amount of time. This game has a function to adjust the window frame size to fit the limit of the player's arm before the main part of game begins. As players try to clear the windows to their edges, they are forced to stretch their arms outwards, which induces movements at the maximum ROM. In this game, the player's joint angles are measured, therefore the elevation angle of their arms can be calculated based on its joint angles. Figure 3 is a picture of joint positions Kinect v2 captured. As thick lines indicate, the elevation angle of arms is calculated by setting up the vector that goes through the shoulder and spine center, and one that goes through the right or left shoulder and the elbow. This system succeeded in measurement with average 21.6 degrees error compared to the measurement conducted by professionals on shoulder abduction and forward flexion.

Fig. 2. Screen of "window wiping game"

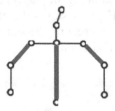

Fig. 3. Joint positions Kinect v2 captures

2.4 ROM Measurement Conducted as E-sports for the Elderly

It is common to compete and gain points or beat other teams, or watch someone play and defeat others as part of regular E-sports. However, it is difficult to simply apply the common E-sports principles to elderly players for reasons such as varied cognitive capacity. Therefore, one study loosened the competitive elements of E-sports, and measured ROM as a means of facilitating social interaction and communications among the elderly through E-sports.

Interaction through E-sports includes conversations as follows; advice given when playing games, cheering and exchanging comments after games. In our study, we boosted these conversations and signs of communications by assigning groups, requiring each member of the group to take turns to play a game, and also by encouraging others to participate through viewing or watching another group play. Participants could see the score counted by the number of windows they cleaned at the end of the game. The elderly who gathered could exchange ideas and communicate as a community through E-sports and developed a competitive spirit. That led them to generate abduction/forward flexion movement, or even more accurate measurements.

3   Methodology

This study aims to obtain accurate ROM of abduction and forward flexion of shoulders based on the previous studies [6, 7]. The following discusses how we induce movements and measure ROM.

3.1   Movement Inducing Method

Method of Using Multiple Media Display.   Previous studies have confirmed that elevation movements can be induced with videos guidance [7]. However, in our subsequent research, we found that video guidance, which means the viewing of videos prior to the start of the game, would become necessary each time. Also, it has been confirmed that the induction effect decreased with each repetition. Therefore, a motion guidance method using a robot or voice was chosen as a method to guide players' movements during the game. In addition, we introduced two more methods, 1) a model example motion of 'cleaning' movements, and 2) an interactive presentation of information on how to wipe the window in various ways.

Method of Leaving Grimy Parts.   By placing some grimy parts on the window, as indicated in Fig. 4, players can be motivated to stretch out their arms to reach specific areas. Figure 4 shows the effects of two patterns; (a) rectangular pattern to induce up and down linear movement for leading forward flexion, and (b) dome-shaped pattern to induce abduction.

(a) Rectangle shape   (b) Dome shape

Fig. 4. Grime on window

Method of Presenting the Converted Player Image.   This aims to induce abduction. The regular screen shows what is captured on a camera as seen in Fig. 2. In contrast, when the player image is generated by parallel projection of the player 3D model created from the camera and the depth image, the motion of spreading player's hands without bringing them forward will allow the hands to spread more on the screen.

3.2   ROM Measuring Method

Methods of obtaining shoulder ROM using Kinect depth sensor, have already been proposed as mentioned in Sect. 2.3. The depth sensor measures ROM by calculating the variation range of angles that occur with elevated arms. In the study, the elevation movements are defined as movements that are kept over 0.5 s. From the arm movement during the game, we extracted all angles of the arms and spine when deemed as elevation movements. The shoulder ROM is the maximum value of those angles. As explained in Fig. 1, an angle of abduction is generally the angle when the arm is raised laterally. Also, angle of flexion is the angle when the arm is raised from the front. However, actual automatic ROM measurement is slightly deviated from the forefront or lateral as shown in Fig. 5. In this study, as Fig. 5 shows, these angles are defined respectively as "forward deviating angle" and "lateral deviating angle."

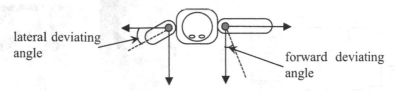

Fig. 5. Angle of spreading arms

4 Experiment and Results

As shown in Table 1, An experimental "E-sports gaming event" involving elderly people aged 65 years old and above was conducted at several municipalities or local health care centers with the intended purpose of premature nursing care prevention. The experiment conducted in each venue used one of those methods of three inductive motions described in 3.2. These experiments have been approved by the ethics board composed of on and off-campus members in Prefectural University of Toyama, to consider privacy protection.

Table 1. Experiment Specifications

Experiment	1–1	1–2	1–3	2–1	2–2	3–1
Inductive method	Video guidance	Robot's motion	Robot's motion + voice	Dome shape grime	Rect. Shape grime	Image conversion
Inductive timing	All time	All time	Interactive	All time	All time	All time
Number of participants	56	67	13	19	24	8
Kinds of induction	Flexion / Abduction	Flexion / Abduction	Abduction	Abduction	Flexion	Abduction

4.1 Experiment

Figure 6 shows an overview layout of the actual gaming event. The game was operated and data collection was also conducted using Kinect v2. A screen large enough for not only the players but also those waiting could watch the game was chosen. As shown in Fig. 6, players sat in front of the screen and played the game while the groups who were waiting for their turn sat in the seats behind the players. In addition, the humanoid robot "Sota" manufactured by Vstone Co., Ltd. Shown in Fig. 7 was used for robot motion guidance in the experiments 1–2 and 1–3.

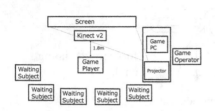

Fig. 6. Overview layout of the gaming event   **Fig. 7.** Humanoid robot "Sota"

4.2 Results and Discussion

Table 2 shows the result of experiment 1–1. It indicates that abduction and flexion motions were induced by showing guidance video. With analyzing the video of experiment, elderly subjects who underwent multiple experiments on the same day watched the guidance video with less frequency as experiments continued over time. Also, it is confirmed that fewer elderly subjects were induced on the second game of abduction guidance, when the experiments were conducted repeatedly on the same subjects after some days later. This suggests that subjects master how to play the game after several trials, which faded the inductive effects on a gaming style with guidance videos.

Table 2. Results of inductive motion with video

	Exp. 1–1(induce flexion)		Exp. 1–1(induce abduction)	
Exp. Date	21.07.20	21.11.15	21.07.08	21.10.14
Flexion	15/15(100%)	10/10 (100%)	3/15 (20%)	8/16 (50%)
Abduction	0/15(0%)	0/10 (0%)	12/15 (80%)	8/16 (50%)

Table 3 is the result of experiment 1–2. Inducing flexion motion was successful although inducing for abduction was not sufficient. The following results of the experiment explains subjective evaluation and maximum elevation angle within 0–45 degrees of forward and side deviation angle. On the result, the elevation motion angle is large when inducing flexion motion, while it is small when inducing abduction motion. Video analysis shows entire screens were wiped in most of the cases, therefore it is assumed that five consecutive frames of elevation motion were seldom conducted on elevation motion when inducing abduction.

Table 3. Inducing motion by robot motion

| | Exp. 1–2(induce flexion) | | Exp. 1–2(induce abduction) | |
	Subjective Eval.	Ave. of Elevation Angle (deg)	Subjective Eval.	Ave. of Elevation Angle (deg)
Flexion	45/57 (80%)	162	4/10 (40%)	87
Abduction	12/57 (20%)	148	6/10 (60%)	85

Table 4 shows the result of experiment 1–3, which uses an interactive method of robot's motion and voice to induce abduction motion when the unwiped area is large. It is difficult to say that induction effects for abduction are clearly confirmed since the number of subjects induced were less than that of experiment 1–2. As a result of video analysis, it is assumed that elevation motions were conducted with left and right movements and were not always lifted consecutively, therefore the elevation angle became smaller. Those reasons above could suggest motion induction with a robot did not work on elderly subjects as possibly the robot itself or its motions were not similar enough. With these reasons and with the limitations of the actual size of the robot lead us to believe that the induction for abduction motion with actual robot is difficult.

Table 4. Inducing motion by robot motion and voice

| | experiment 1–3(induce abduction) | |
	Subjective Eval	Ave. of Elev. Angle (deg)
Flexion	7/13 (54%)	104
Abduction	6/13 (46%)	108

Table 5 shows the result of experiment 2–1 and 2–2. Subjects were surely inducing forward flexion when rectangle grimy windows were shown on the screen, which was our intended purpose. However, forward flexion was induced when subjects were induced for abduction with dome shaped windows. In the video analysis of experiment 2–2, we found that subjects wiped the windows completely when their arms were at the top position of forward flexion and lowered them from that point, and not in elevation motions. This indicates that inducing the angles of arm motion is difficult, even if it is possible to induce arm positions with window grimes.

Table 6 shows the result of experiment 3–1. This method induced forward flexion more sharply than expected. It became clear that subjects wiped the windows when their arms lowered after they reached the top with forward flexion as in the experiment 2–2. Moreover, it indicated to us that some motions were not large enough to be categorized as elevation.

Table 5. Results of inductive motion by window grime

	experiment 2–1 (Rectangle Shape)		experiment 2–2 (Dome Shape)	
	Subjective Eval.	Ave. of Elev. Angle (deg)	Subjective Eval.	Ave. of Elev. Angle (deg)
Flexion	24/24 (100%)	142	19/20 (95%)	140
Abduction	0/24 (0%)	52	1/20 (5%)	41

Table 6. Inducing motion by arm image conversion

	Experiment 3–1	
	Subjective Eval.	Ave. of Elev. Angle (deg)
Flexion	6/8 (75%)	116
Abduction	2/8 (25%)	88

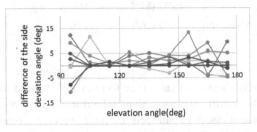

Fig. 8. Transition of subjects' spread arms

The results examined above indicate that inducing the motion of abduction with window grimes and image conversion has difficulty since it cannot indicate the angle of arm motion clearly. Figure 8 showed the difference of the side deviation angle between normal image and converted image used in experiment 3–1 on the same elderly subjects. On these two values, T-test was conducted and significant difference was found on side deviation angle, which suggests that the windows are wiped with slightly "lateral deviating angle". In other words, the elderly subjects' arms are passing near the lateral area when lowered. This movement is apparently not abduction from subjective evaluation's point of view. However, it is possible to measure abduction angle more precisely as arms are passing close to lateral position when lowered. Currently, abduction angles are measured in the abduction process. It is thought that there is a possibility that the abduction angle can be measured from the descent movement by clarifying the relationship between the elevation angle measured during elevation and the angle measured during descent on further experiments.

5   Conclusion and Future Work

We have investigated the movement guidance method for acquiring the abduction/flexion angles of the shoulder ROM with high accuracy in a window cleaning game that aims to prevent premature nursing care. As a result, we have found that the method with guidance video has a clear effect, although the effect fades as the number of iterations increases. Another method with grime windows can induce forward flexion. The method with image conversion could hardly induce abduction, though it was effective to reduce "lateral deviating angle". The possibility of measuring abduction angle on lowering process is considered our future work.

References

1. Ministry of Health, Labour and Welfare. Care Prevention. https://www.mhlw.go.jp/stf/seisak unitsuite/bunya/hukushi_kaigo/kaigo_koureisha/yobou/index.html/. Accessed 28 Feb 2023
2. Ministry of Health, Labour and Welfare. Long-term care preventive activity dissemination and development project. https://www.mhlw.go.jp/file/06-Seisakujouhou-12300000-Rouken kyoku/hukyuutenkai.pdf. Accessed 28 Feb 2023
3. Fukuda, O.: ROM Measurement, 2 edn., Miwa Shoten Ltd. (2010)
4. Bozhao, Q., Suman, B.: GonioSense: a wearable-based range of motion sensing and measurement system for body joints: poster. In: Proceedings of the 22nd Annual International Conference on Mobile Computing and Networking, pp. 441–442 (2016)
5. Peng, N., Amnad, T., Theeraphong, W.: Evaluation of upper limb joint's range of motion data by kinect sensor for rehabilitation exercise game. In: Proceedings of the Third International Conf. on Medical and Health Informatics 2019, pp. 92–98 (2019)
6. Li, M., Tsuchiya, T., Urashima, A., Morishima, S., Toriyama, T.: A game-based upper limb AROM measurement system for older adults. J. Inf. Commun. Eng. (JICE) 5(1), 294–300 (2019)
7. Morishima, S., Souna, K., Ofusa, R., Toriyama, T.: Automatic measurement of shoulder joint ROM conducted on elderly eSports. IEICE Tech. Rep. 121(203), 12–17 (2021)

Design Considerations for a Robotic Hand Sanitizer Encouragement Platform

Evgenios Vlachos[1,2(✉)] [iD] and Iraklis Amoiridis[3]

[1] University Library of Southern Denmark, University of Southern Denmark, Campusvej 55, 5230 Odense, Denmark
evl@bib.sdu.dk
[2] The Mærsk Mc-Kinney Møller Institute, University of Southern Denmark, Campusvej 55, 5230 Odense, Denmark
[3] Offshore, Operations, Technology and Standards, Blades, Casting, Siemens Gamesa Renewable Energy, Assensvej 11, 9220 Aalborg, Denmark

Abstract. We present the initial design, and development of a wheeled mobile robot that encourages people to sanitize their hands. The aim is to help people make hand hygiene part of their daily routine, as hand hygiene is perhaps the most important measure to prevent healthcare related infections. The laws that regulate machinery, and robots deployed in public spaces affected the design, and determined the equipment mounted on the robot. Safety, and accessibility where the main drivers behind all design considerations in order to allow for side, and forward secure approaches. For a wheeled mobile robot to be able to navigate in complex, and populated indoor environments, and assist humans in sanitizing their hands, a combination of multiple sensors, equipment, and accessories is needed. We tried to keep the budget of the robot to a minimum by equipping it with low-cost equipment whenever possible, and by allowing those who helped us build the robot to be advertised on the robot. We have decided to use hard materials for three reasons: to have a more stable design; to indicate that this is not a robot for communication purposes; and to be able to clean/disinfect it easier. The first iteration of our robotic platform is 1415 mm tall, has max speed 0,7 m/s, is mostly build of stainless-steel material, and involves a contactless hand sanitizer dispenser built on top of a Slamtec platform. Our proposed robotic solution can be deployed in private spaces also, and can be further upgraded with more and better quality equipment to serve in different needs/contexts.

Keywords: Assistive robotics · Wellness · Hand hygiene · Public space · Interface design prototyping

1 Introduction

Robots can be spotted in all sorts of populated private and public spaces, from airports, museums, and shopping malls, to schools, libraries, and hospitals, working together with humans, or independently, or even collaborating with other robots [1–5]. How robots shape our experience of these spaces, how human-robot interaction (HRI) can

C. Stephanidis et al. (Eds.): HCII 2023, CCIS 1833, pp. 184–189, 2023.
https://doi.org/10.1007/978-3-031-35992-7_26

affect our place attachment (even leading to place aversion) [20], and how public policy approaches are trying to regulate such disruptive technology [6] are three topics that are under-researched.

Among the plethora of robots developed over the last years, a large portion of them was devoted to assist in the fight against the COVID-19 pandemic. Notable application areas include promoting hand hygiene in hospital settings [7, 8], hand sanitation [9], carrying out throat swabs so that healthcare professionals are not exposed to the risk of infection[1], assisting nurses as their workload has significantly increased [10], non-contact disinfection of open spaces with ultraviolet light [11], accelerating the acceptance of service robots [12], supplementing distance learning and supporting in-home tutoring [13], and mitigating loneliness with companion robots [14]. Most of the hand hygiene/sanitation robots are either products of a start-up company and overpriced, or are experimental prototypes not for sale. Therefore, we decided to build our own robotic hand sanitizer encouragement platform using as many off-the-self equipment as possible, and custom-made components based on accessible manufacturing processes (laser cut), and effortless assembling. Our aim is to deploy the robot in a public space, and specifically in a university library. This is a preliminary study, and all design consideration presented could serve as inspiration for similar robotic platforms.

In the following sections we present various safety concerns for deploying a robot in a public space, describe the appearance and functionalities of our robot, discuss various design considerations, materials used, and its mechanical design.

2   Safety

Tan et al. [15] showed that participants felt safer observing the HRI rather than actively interacting with the robot even though they were all in the same room, and in close proximity to the robot. It seems that in HRI perceived safety, and actual safety matters equally. In the real world, however, only the latter matters as potential psychological hazard is not taken yet into account. Almost any robot equipped with wheels-in the eyes of the European law at least-is considered similar in terms of safety regulations with the heavy industrial machineries when deployed in a public space. Even the smallest social wheeled mobile robots.

To deploy our robot into a public library in Denmark, we had to consider collision, and other hazards deriving from intentional, or unintentional physical contact between the robot, and a human. To minimize, and if possible eliminate, these hazards we had to comply with the following:

- Mount audiovisual signals indicating that the robot is moving. Red, or orange flashing lights and preferably beeping sounds must be used.
- There must be signs placed across the operating space of the robot warning of a running robot.
- The floor where the robot is moving must be marked with tracks.
- There needs to be a red emergency stop button on top of a yellow base (Machinery Directive 2006/42/CE).

---

[1] Lifeline Robotics, https://www.lifelinerobotics.com, last accessed 2023/03/17.

- The robots' charging station must be located in a sheltered place where there is no public access, and where one cannot accidentally get an electric shock.
- All loads, and movable/floating items must be secured firmly.
- A fire procedure must be prepared.
- There must be an accessible folder containing the robots' manual and a safety data sheet.

3   The Robotic Hand Sanitizer Encouragement Platform

For a wheeled mobile robot to be able to navigate in complex, and populated indoor environments, and assist humans in sanitizing their hands, a combination of multiple sensors, equipment, and accessories is needed. We tried to keep the budget of the robot to a minimum by equipping it with low-cost equipment whenever possible, and by allowing those who helped us build the robot to be advertised on the robot. Accessibility, and safety are the cornerstones to any considerations made for the robots' physical appearance and capabilities, and this section is dealing with it.

3.1   Design and Components

The design of the robot can be seen in Fig. 1, including the distribution of sensors, equipment, and size specifications. The height of the robot is 1415 mm to make HRI comfortable with both seated, and standing users. A demonstration video of the robot can be seen at this link[2].

To accommodate users with limited reach range, we mounted a commercial non-contact hand sanitizer dispenser at a height where the dispensing mechanism is at 1035 mm with less than 250 mm reach depth. We followed the 2010 ADA (American Disabilities Act) Standards and 2009 ICC/ANSI Standards that state any operable parts should be maximum at 1120–1220 mm above the finish floor and less than 250–280 mm reach depth for both forward and side reach (obstructed and unobstructed) [16, 17]. The location of the dispenser allows for both side, and forward approaches with the use of one hand without requiring any force.

To comply with the safety regulations, we installed an emergency stop mechanism that completely shuts down the robot, as the original stop button of the robot only immobilized the robot without switching it off. We also installed a commercial orange flashing light, and created robotic sounds inspired by R2D2 for use as audio signals.

The movement base of the robot is the APOLLO 2.0 A3M21 General Robot Platform by Slamtec[3]. It is equipped with a laser range scanner, a depth camera, a set of ultrasonic sensors and a cliff sensor. This multi-sensor fusion allows for autonomous navigation in various scenarios reliably as it has a detection range of more than 15 m. It scans the environment in real time and creates a high precision map where virtual walls and virtual tracks can be planned (see Fig. 2). The virtual track technology can make the robot move on a fixed track intelligently and smoothly, avoiding obstacles until it gets to its target,

---

[2] Demonstration video of the envisioned usage of the robot, https://youtu.be/Q9mAA2A5qCY, last accessed 2023/03/17.

[3] Slamtec, https://www.slamtec.com/en, last accessed 2023/03/17.

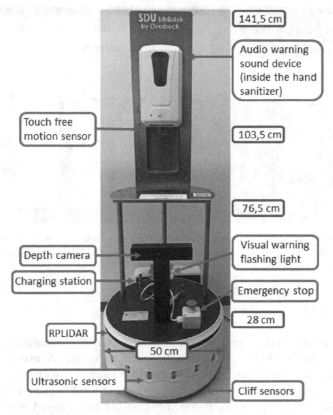

Fig. 1. Robot sensors, equipment, and size specifications.

or move on a specified loop. It is autonomously recharged finding its way to the docking station by itself when the battery runs low. The maximum speed reached is 0.7 m/s that is considered a slow, and safe walking speed.

3.2 Materials

We have decided to use hard materials for three reasons: to have a more stable design; to indicate that this is not a robot for communication purposes; and to be able to clean/disinfect it easier. The payload capacity of the base (35 kg) of the robot allowed us to have all the custom-made materials from stainless steel (AISI 304-1.4301)[4]. Stainless steel has been used extensively in hospitals as it can be thoroughly cleaned, and disinfected with minimum degradation, or corrosion [18]. In [19], it was reported that after 7 days no infectious virus could be detected on stainless steel platforms, on the contrary the virus could still be present on the outer layer of a surgical mask.

---

[4] Stainless steel sheet, design, and cutting by Overbeck Staal Aps, https://overbeckstaal.dk, last accessed 2023/03/17.

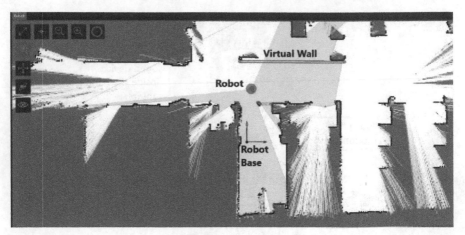

Fig. 2. Screenshot of the floormap as perceived by the robot sensors showing the position of the robot, its base, the range of its sensors (pink shade), and virtual walls that the interface allowed to be added. (Color figure Online)

4 Conclusion

This paper presents work in progress on the design, and implementation of a robotic hand sanitizer platform to be used in a public space. Pandemics do eventually end, but hand sanitizers are here to stay. Despite the lessons learned from the recent COVID-19 pandemic, there is always room for improvement in hand hygiene encouragement, and/or compliance. Our proposed robotic solution can be deployed in private spaces also, and can be further upgraded with more and better quality equipment to serve in different needs/contexts. With a more playful design, it could -for example- be deployed in a school, or a kindergarten. Future improvements will focus on making the robot "smarter", and more "attentive" via sound/speech localization, and orientation.

References

1. Tonkin, M., Vitale, J., Herse, S., Williams, M.A., Judge, W., Wang, X.: Design methodology for the UX of HRI: a field study of a commercial social robot at an airport. In: Proceedings of the 2018 ACM/IEEE International Conference on Human-Robot Interaction, pp. 407–415 (2018)
2. Herath, D.C., et al.: An experimental study of embodied interaction and human perception of social presence for interactive robots in public settings. IEEE Trans. Cogn. Dev. Syst. **10**(4), 1096–1105 (2017)
3. Karunarathne, D., Morales, Y., Kanda, T., Ishiguro, H.: Understanding a public environment via continuous robot observations. Robot. Auton. Syst. **126**, 103443 (2020). https://doi.org/10.1016/j.robot.2020.103443
4. Meghdari, A., Shariati, A., Alemi, M., et al.: Arash: a social robot buddy to support children with cancer in a hospital environment. Proc. Inst. Mech. Eng. Part H J. Eng. Med. **232**(6), 605–618 (2018)

5. Vlachos, E., Hansen, A.F., Holck, J.P.: A robot in the library. In: Rauterberg, M. (ed.) HCII 2020. LNCS, vol. 12215, pp. 312–322. Springer, Cham (2020). https://doi.org/10.1007/978-3-030-50267-6_24
6. Mintrom, M., Sumartojo, S., Kulić, D., Tian, L., Carreno-Medrano, P., Allen, A.: Robots in public spaces: implications for policy design. Policy Des. Pract. 5(2), 123–139 (2022)
7. Worlikar, H., et al.: Is it feasible to use a humanoid robot to promote hand hygiene adherence in a hospital setting? Infect. Prev. Pract. 4(1), 100188 (2022). https://doi.org/10.1016/j.infpip.2021.100188
8. Couto, B.R.G.M., et al.: Using Ozires, a humanoid robot, to continuing education of healthcare workers: a pilot study. CSEDU (2), 293–299 (2017)
9. Beck, S.K., Gade, S.K., Høj, H., Thielsen, M.G., Fischer, K., Palinko, O.: Speed and speech impact on the usage of a hand sanitizer robot. In: Companion of the 2021 ACM/IEEE International Conference on Human-Robot Interaction, pp. 382–386 (2021)
10. Nambiappan, H.R., Kodur, K.C., Kyrarini, M., Makedon, F., Gans, N.: MINA: a multitasking intelligent nurse aid robot. In: The 14th PErvasive Technologies Related to Assistive Environments Conference, pp. 266–267 (2021)
11. Sanchez, A.G., Smart, W.D.: Towards verifiable COVID-19 aerosol disinfection using ultraviolet light with a mobile robot. In: The 14th PErvasive Technologies Related to Assistive Environments Conference, pp. 300–305 (2021)
12. Kim, S.S., Kim, J., Badu-Baiden, F., Giroux, M., Choi, Y.: Preference for robot service or human service in hotels? Impacts of the COVID-19 pandemic. Int. J. Hospitality Manag. 93, 102795 (2021). https://doi.org/10.1016/j.ijhm.2020.102795
13. Scassellati, B., Vázquez, M.: The potential of socially assistive robots during infectious disease outbreaks. Sci. Rob. 5, eabc9014 (2020)
14. Odekerken-Schröder, G., Mele, C., Russo-Spena, T., Mahr, D., Ruggiero, A.: Mitigating loneliness with companion robots in the COVID-19 pandemic and beyond: an integrative framework and research agenda. J. Serv. Manag. 31(6), 1149–1162 (2020). https://doi.org/10.1108/JOSM-05-2020-0148
15. Tan, Z.-H., et al.: iSocioBot: a multimodal interactive social robot. Int. J. Soc. Robot. 10(1), 5–19 (2017). https://doi.org/10.1007/s12369-017-0426-7
16. Department of Justice (United States): 2010 ADA standards for accessible design (2010). https://www.ada.gov/regs2010/2010ADAStandards/2010ADAstandards.htm#General. Accessed 17 Mar 2023
17. 2009 ICC/ANSI Standards. https://codes.iccsafe.org/content/icca117-12009/chapter-3-building-blocks. Accessed 17 Mar 2023
18. Bonin, L., Vitry, V., Olivier, M.G., Bertolucci-Coelho, L.: Covid-19: effect of disinfection on corrosion of surfaces. Corros. Eng. Sci. Technol. 55(8), 693–695 (2020). https://doi.org/10.1080/1478422X.2020.1777022
19. Chin, A.W., et al.: Stability of SARS-CoV-2 in different environmental conditions. Lancet Microbe 1(1), e10 (2020). https://doi.org/10.1016/S2666-5247(20)30003-3
20. Vlachos, E., Schärfe, H.: Social robots as persuasive agents. In: Meiselwitz, G. (ed.) Social Computing and Social Media, pp. 277–284. Springer, Cham (2014). https://doi.org/10.1007/978-3-319-07632-4_26

Methodology and Design for Assessing the Normative Exercise Posture of Young Females in Media-Home Fitness with Motion Capture Technology

Jing Wang(✉) iD

East China University of Science and Technology, Shanghai, China
1030987304@qq.com

Abstract. The pandemic has altered some females' perspectives on fitness, home settings have become a more popular exercise venue than gyms, particularly among young females. In this study, through a survey of 160 young females, it was found that most prefer to engage in low to moderate intensity exercises during home fitness. It is noteworthy that 86% of young females expressed that playing media content during exercise would distract their attention, leading to difficulty in maintaining proper form throughout the workout. This study aims to optimize the home exercise experience for young females and reduce the risk of physical injury caused by improper exercise posture resulting from excessive immersion in media playback content. During testing, six young female participants were recorded using the AI motion capture tool "Plask" while performing an experimental task (rotating hula hoops) with and without media playback, measuring their conscious state and body posture. The experimental results demonstrate that the use of the AI motion capture tool can effectively obtain the movement parameters and limb data of participants from different perspectives. This helps health experts better analyze participants' exercise perception behavior and identify issues in young females' home exercise routines. Based on the evaluation results, a set of exercise reminder programs has been designed in this study to assist young females in maintaining exercise regularity through periodic reminders. Through usability testing, it has been demonstrated that this design can effectively enhance the positive effects of home fitness for young females.

Keywords: home fitness · media · motion capture technology · hula hoop

1 Introduction

1.1 Home Fitness is Gaining Importance

The pandemic has led people to prefer exercising at home, which has facilitated the development of home-based fitness. In 2020, the General Administration of Sport of China issued the notice "On Promoting Scientific Home-based Fitness Methods [1]",

C. Stephanidis et al. (Eds.): HCII 2023, CCIS 1833, pp. 190–198, 2023.
https://doi.org/10.1007/978-3-031-35992-7_27

to meet the fitness needs of the public during the pandemic, and advocate for a positive and healthy lifestyle. Majid et al. [2] have demonstrated the effectiveness of home exercise, which is feasible, safe, and beneficial for individuals with high rehabilitation requirements and low exercise capacity. Chen Dexu et al. [3] pointed out that the higher quality of home fitness, the more benefits one can experience in physical fitness, and the greater the number of people who can achieve health benefits. Furthermore, among the younger population, they tend to favor home-based fitness over traditional gym workouts, due to its advantages of not being limited by space or equipment, allowing for flexible scheduling, and having a low threshold for exercise skills and physical fitness.

Due to the lack of professional knowledge and experience in daily exercise for most people, and the absence of professional guidance from coaches in the home environment, individuals may experience injuries such as irregular breathing, blind exertion, joint compensation, muscle soreness, and other issues during home fitness, which not only fail to achieve the goal of enhancing physical fitness but also pose a risk to their basic health. Therefore, it is necessary to investigate and focus on the behavior standardization of the home fitness population during the exercise process, and reasonable measures need to be proposed to protect the home fitness population.

1.2 Young Females Are the Main Population of Home Fitness

To investigate the exercise preferences of home fitness enthusiasts, this study first conducted a questionnaire of 230 individuals who habitually exercise in their home environment using a questionnaire. The results showed that females constituted 81% of the sample, and young females were the main group engaging in home fitness, accounting for 70% of the total sample across all age groups, with an age range of 20–29 years. This is due to various factors such as personal daily work, time constraints, lack of exercise facilities, and economic conditions, which limit their options and lead to home fitness being their primary choice for fitness. Due to the monotonous nature of training, they often choose music and videos with upbeat rhythms and engaging content for playback. The survey respondents are consistent with the user profile identified in the "The 2021 General Fitness Behavior and Consumption Research Report [4]", and the study conducted by Schneider Verena et al. [5]. Therefore, this study focuses on the methodology and design of a normative assessment of exercise posture in young females who prefer to play media while exercising at home.

1.3 Media (Music and Movies) Broadcasting Harms the Exercise of Postural Standardization

For many young female sports enthusiasts, playing music and videos during exercise is essential. The melody rhythm and interactive content can help them ignore the boredom and soreness caused by exercise. Regarding music and video interaction with sports, D. Tanaka, et al. [6] investigated the impact of music on the improvement of post-exercise IC following moderate-intensity exercise and suggested that listening to music may be a beneficial strategy to alleviate the perceived exertion during aerobic exercise. M. Marques et al. [7] studied the effect of self-selected music (SSM) versus no music on the mood and performance of athletes and found that SSM can enhance explosive performance and emotional state. In summary, many scholars have affirmed the efficacy of music and video in the context of sports and fitness.

However, most of the existing research focuses on professional sports with scientific interactive settings, which may not be suitable for home fitness scenarios. According to research, females mainly believe that the interaction between music and video diverts their attention and weakens their perception of time and exercise intensity at home. However, it is important to note that this habit can also pose safety risks [8]. Jacquet Thomas, et al. [9] have indicated in their study that media playback can induce dissociative thinking during physical activity. P. Franco-Alvarenga, et al. [10] considered that increased attentional distraction exacerbates dissociation during SIT and weakens feedback to afferent nerves.

Prolonged exercise with increased volume, wearing headphones, or staring at screens can reduce athletes' perception of the external environment, resulting in increased fatigue, disrupted respiratory rhythms, dizziness, hypoxia, and exercise-induced injuries (see Fig. 1). Cai et al. [11] explored the influence of motion state, spatial perception, visual fatigue, and interface color schemes on visual search performance. Regarding the negative effects of prolonged headphone use and screen staring closely, Rravis M. Moore et al. [12] summarized the problem of mental fatigue caused by continued auditory processing and pointed out that prolonged exposure to stimulating sounds can cause hearing damage. Therefore, this study attempts to provide an interactive design that better satisfies the needs of home fitness, including reminders to correct posture and reduce the risk of injury.

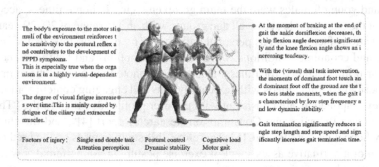

Fig. 1. For home fitness may produce negative injuries (author's drawing).

2   Experimental Design

The hula hoop, owing to its aesthetic appeal, lightweight construction, small footprint, and a high degree of amusement, is frequently employed as a preferred exercise apparatus for young females practicing home fitness routines. Its employment during physical activity can effectively enhance flexibility and suppleness of the waist and knee joints. In 2011, American Councilon Exercise published a report [13] with ample scientific data demonstrating that hula hooping is among the best fitness exercises.

This study aims to use motion capture technology based on hula hooping exercises to evaluate the standardized movement posture of young females who engage in media-home fitness, and design a methodology to remind and reduce negative injuries during home exercise for young females.

2.1 Participants

The test invited 6 female participants (mean age 21 years, range 5 years) with a BMI between 20–25, no medical history (no gastrointestinal diseases, not in the menstrual period), without significant postural symptoms, and rich experience in home fitness, including proficient hula hooping skills. Before the investigation, participants were informed of the experimental procedures and potential risks and discomfort associated with the research protocol. Subsequently, they completed a test informed consent document.

2.2 Experimental Procedure

The experimental procedure follows:

1. Participants need to undergo coordination and control ability and normal posture observation in advance, and use Magic Poser to provide standards reference (see Fig. 2) to ensure that there are no obvious problems;
2. Education on the participants' safety and hula hoop motion to standardize their initial movements;
3. A simplified warm-up before exercise to awaken muscle energy to thereby avoid injury. And The Hula hoop used in the experiment was also practiced to better simulate daily conditions and reduce the rate of hoop dropping during the experiment;
4. The experiment was divided into three groups, and participants were required to rest between each group of exercises. The group is shown in Table 1.

Fig. 2. Physical observation of subjects (standing, walking, running, squatting).

The experimentally selected a piece of video editing from the Internet media and played by APPLE IPAD AIR3, the height of the position is 60 cm, simulating the common home fitness status of young females. The content settings (see Table 2) were designed to better help observe the effects of self-selected music media on exercisers in the practice situation.

The site was set up within an area of 2.5×2.5 m^2, based on the simulation of a home environment and the size of the commonly used hula hoop (90 cm in diameter and 1.75 kg in weight). No other factors were present to interfere with the experiment.

The observation of the process was recorded with a 64M 16:9 camera set at a sideways angle to mark all conditions triggered by the music video during the exercise tests. And with the AI motion capture tool Plask to generate motion capture images (see Fig. 3), which has the advantage of detecting variation in body reactions clearly and recording the expression.

Table 1. Research Group Setting.

Group	Exercise duration	media playback	Reminder to maintain standards
Control group A	10 min	——	——
Experimental group B	10 min	play	——
Experimental group C	10 min	play	One at three-minute intervals

Table 2. Media content for the experiment.

Minutes	0	1			2		3			4	5		6	
Media schedule	12'18"	13'00"	13'13"	13'51"	14'00"	14'25"	15'00"	15'30"	15'44"	16'00"	17'30"	17'45"	18'40"	18'45"
Media content	N	N	H	N	M	N	H	N	N	N	M	H	N	M

Minutes	7	8	9				10	11	12		13	14		15
Media schedule	19'00"	20'00"	21'00"	21'14"	21'45"	21'53"	22'00"	23'45"	24'15"	24'27"	25'2"	26'19"	26'46"	27'00"
Media content	N	N	N	M	M	N	N	M	H	N	M	N	M	N

N: Mild emotion, M: Basic emotion, H: Intense emotion [14]

At the end of the test, participants were asked to take a subjective assessment (the assessment framework was created by the Borg scale and the RPE scale based on the realities of this experiment modification).

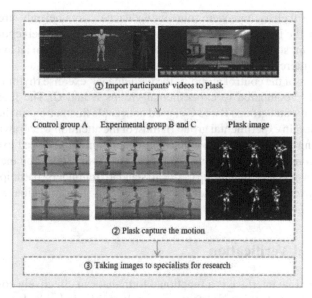

Fig. 3. Plask generates images for motion capture experiments.

3   Experimental Results and Analysis

3.1   The Participants' Motion Capture Objective Findings

The experimental procedure and results were collated, and the motion capture images and prominent experimental segments were submitted to experts for diagnosis (a bone specialist from a certain tertiary hospital and a fitness coach with 6 years of experience). The conclusions are as follows:

For control group A, self-selected music videos in self-training exercises can effectively motivate exercisers, thereby achieving better fitness purposes.

For experimental group B, self-selected music videos revealed many problems. Although they have many advantages in shifting attention, reducing fatigue, and prolonging exercise duration. However, long-term head-down screen viewing can have negative effects on exercisers' visual acuity and spinal curvature. Moreover, Intense rhythm can affect force production, especially in unconscious, habitual force production causes damage to the surrounding muscles and joints.

For experimental group C, the establishment of a reminder mechanism has greatly solved the problems mentioned by experimental group B. The intermittent reminders do not affect the experience of music videos during exercise, but also provide timely reminders when the body exhibits irregularities, helping exercisers to make adjustments and obtain positive fitness effects.

3.2   The Subjective Findings of the Participants' Exercise Scale

The participants thought that, compared to the control group A, both experimental groups B and C felt that time passed faster. The main areas of fatigue and exertion were the waist and legs, as well as there were some individual cases of unevenly stressed soreness and dizziness in the left and right legs. Additionally, the negative perception of exercise (fatigue, boredom, soreness, etc.) on a 5-point scale decreased from an average score of 4.5 to 2, while interest in exercise remained active.

In the process of the control group A, the participants' exercise rhythm and breathing were more stable compared to experimental groups B and C. The music and video played in experimental groups B and C caused noticeable fluctuations in the participants' exercise behavior. In experimental group B, most of the attention was drawn to the played content, resulting in an inability to consistently maintain the required exercise posture and the most pronounced fluctuations. At times, participants relied on inertia instead of sending force. In experimental group C, due to standard reminders, participants promptly adjusted their exercise posture after the reminder, but their attention was still easily diverted to the played content.

4 Design and Verification

The floating window interface is a functional form that can effectively convey information to users without blocking interface content. It enables individuals to use electronic devices to watch online videos without interference while exercising, and receive health prompts from the floating window simultaneously. This is a low-cost specialized operation suitable for home fitness environments, which assists users to maintain exercise standardization.

Based on users' habits, this study designed a set of floating windows composed of icons and text prompts combined with exercise feedback. The two prompts consist of "maintaining steady breathing" and "maintaining standard posture" (see Fig. 4).

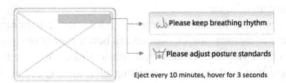

Fig. 4. The pop-up displayed briefly above the media, to maintain standards

The SD method was used to invite young females with home fitness habits to evaluate the floating window based on their real exercise experience. Results from 60 users showed that compared to a traditional media interface, the floating window prompt achieved more effective constraints on exercise posture standardization, and reminded users of exercise time. In addition, the appearance of the floating window during use did not cause a negative impact on the media entertainment experience during exercise. The improvement in user experience values demonstrates the reliability of this study's reliability of young females' home fitness behavior through motion capture. Furthermore, it confirms the effectiveness of the proposed floating window prompt method in providing health assistance for the home fitness population.

5 Summary

This study introduces that home fitness has become a popular exercise choice among young people, particularly among young females, and highlights its advantages, also acknowledges the lack of professionalism and the possibility of injury. The study identifies the negative impact of media on an exercise posture. Based on hula hoop exercise and motion capture technology, this study discusses the normative performance of young females' home fitness postures and evaluates their performance based on expert assessments and self-evaluations. The study proposes a design improvement method using an interface floating window prompter based on posture and breathing issues, which has been proven effective through user evaluations.

In the future, this study's experimental results can be used to develop more effective design solutions to enhance the positive exercise experience of young females and other home fitness enthusiasts. Moreover, the application of motion capture technology can be extended to obtain more standardized human data, which can be used for research and practice in fields such as exercise correction, rehabilitation training, and art design.

References

1. General Administration of Sport of China: The Notice from the General Office of the General Administration of Sport of China on Vigorously Promoting Scientific Home Fitness Methods (in Chinese). http://www.gov.cn/zhengce/zhengceku/2020-02/03/content_5474274.htm/,2020-01-30
2. Mardaniyan, G.M., Ebrahim, B., Raoof, N., Motl Robert, W.: Home-based exercise training in multiple sclerosis: a systematic review with implications for future research. Multiple Sclerosis Related Disord. **55** (2021)
3. Dexu, C., Bin, Z.: A home fitness satisfaction model for Chinese residents during the COVID-19 pandemic based on SEM analysis. Frontiers Public Health **10** (2022)
4. General Administration of Sport of China: The 2021 General Fitness Behavior and Consumption Research Report (in Chinese). https://www.sport.gov.cn/n20001280/n20067608/n20067635/c21043791/content.html/,2021-05-19
5. Verena, S., Dimitra, K., Aleksandra, H., Emma, B., Abigail, F., Lion, S.: UK adults' exercise locations, use of digital programs and associations with physical activity during the COVID-19 pandemic: longitudinal analysis of data from the health behaviours during the COVID-19 pandemic study. JMIR Formative Res. **6** (2022)
6. Tanaka, D., et al.: Self-selected music-induced reduction of perceived exertion during moderate-intensity exercise does not interfere with post-exercise improvements in inhibitory control. Physiol. Behav. **194** (2018)
7. Thomas, J., Bénédicte, P., Patrick, B., Joris, P., Romuald, L.: Physical activity and music to counteract mental fatigue. Neuroscience **478** (2021)
8. Liu, X.: Home fitness is actually very simple (in Chinese). China Sports News **06** (2022)
9. Marques, M., Staibano, V., Franchini, E.: Effects of self-selected or randomly selected music on performance and psychological responses during a sprint interval training session. Sci. Sports **37** (2021)
10. Franco-Alvarenga, P.E., Brietzke, C., Canestri, R., Pires, F.O., Asano, R.Y.: Psychophysiological responses of music on physical performance: a critical review. Revista Brasileira de Ciência e Movimento **27** (2019)

11. Cai, J.: Research on the influence mechanism of vibration, visual fatigue and color scheme on visual search performance. Shenzhen University (2021). (in Chinese)
12. Moore, T.M., Key, A.P., Thelen, A., Hornsby, B.W.Y.: Neural mechanisms of mental fatigue elicited by sustained auditory processing. Neuropsychologia **106** (2017)
13. American Councilon Exercise: ACE-sponsored Research: Hooping—Effective Workout or Child's Play? https://www.acefitness.org/certifiednewsarticle/1094/ace-sponsored-research-hooping-effective-workout-or-child-s-play/
14. Griffiths, P.E.: Current emotion research in philosophy. Emotion Rev. **5** (2013)

Combining Game User Types and Health Beliefs to Explore the Persuasiveness of Gamification Strategies for Fitness Systems

Tingting Wen and Yongyan Guo[✉]

East China University of Science and Technology, No. 130 Meilong Road, Xuhui District,
Shanghai, China
g_gale@163.com

Abstract. Using gamification techniques to intervene in health behaviors is a promising study. The effect of gamification varies considerably between different users. Therefore, our purpose is to understand the effect of user type and health beliefs on the effect of gamification systems. Physical activity applications are studied as an example in this paper. Firstly, we designed storyboards to explain six gamification elements commonly used in the area of encouraging physical activity. Secondly, we conducted an online study (N = 133). We counted subjects' user type and health belief by using the modified Hexad User Type Scale and HBM scale. Then we measured the perceived persuasiveness of the six gamification elements using the Perceived Persuasiveness Scale. Finally, the results of the correlation test showed a potential influence of health beliefs on the perception of gamification strategies by different users. The novelty of this study is the combination of the health beliefs with the hexad user type model which developed for gamification systems. This complements the existing correlation between Hexad user types and gamification strategies. Our findings may help system developers to select appropriate gamification strategies for different types of users to achieve better health behavior interventions.

Keywords: Gamification · Health Behavior · Hexad User Type · M-health · Personalization

1 Introduction

Sedentary behaviour has become the number one trigger for reduced functional capacity in all age groups [1]. There is growing evidence that physical inactivity is an important contributor to a wide range of diseases, including diabetes, cardiovascular disease, physical obesity and skeletal muscle dysfunction [2, 3]. Adequate Physical activity helps people to improve their health [4]. Therefore, motivating physical activity has become an important target for many studies [5].

With the increasing popularity of digital technology, digital applications are able to reach a large number of users over a long period of time. This makes them a convenient, efficient and cost-effective way to intervene in behaviour. One of the most common

C. Stephanidis et al. (Eds.): HCII 2023, CCIS 1833, pp. 199–209, 2023.
https://doi.org/10.1007/978-3-031-35992-7_28

digital interventions is gamification techniques. Gamification is a method of using game elements in a non-game environment [6]. By increasing user engagement, motivation and social interaction in digital behavioural Interventions, gamification has been successfully applied in many areas, including health [7, 8].

The positive effects of gamification in health behaviour change are highly dependent on the context in which it is applied and the users who use it [8]. The Hexad user type model, developed specifically for gamification interventions [9], has proven to be a useful tool for customising gamification persuasion systems [10]. In addition, it is necessary to consider the user's motivation for behavioural change [11]. The health belief model (HBM) is an ideal framework for explaining and predicting health behaviours [12]. However, few relevant studies promoting the gamification of physical activity have combined user types with health beliefs.

This study selected six common gamification elements based on past literature [13]. We analysed the correlation between gamification elements and user type [9]. Our findings suggest that users' perceptions of gamification elements are influenced by individual health beliefs and that health beliefs influence the attitudes of all types of users towards the relevant gamification elements. This means that the susceptibility of each user type to relevant gamification elements when using health apps is influenced by the user's personal health beliefs. This finding suggests that it is worth considering user type and health beliefs when selecting gamification elements that promote physical activity.

2   Related Work

2.1   The Hexad User Type Model

The Hexad user type model (HUM) proposed by Marczewski et al. is able to explain and understand user preferences in game systems [14]. Based on the type of motivation, HUM classifies users into the following six categories: philanthropists who are willing to share and take responsibility. Socializers who love interaction and seek a sense of belonging; Free spirits who focus on autonomy. Achievers who want to overcome challenges and seek competence. Disruptors who like to push the boundaries of the system and players who seek external rewards for personal interest [14]. The HUM has been used in several studies [15, 16] and is considered to be the most appropriate method of classifying users for personalised gaming systems [17].

2.2   The Health Belief Model

Health behaviour change in individuals is a complex process. The Health Belief Model (HBM), one of the oldest and most practical models for explaining and predicting health behaviour based on health beliefs [18], is suitable for research related to interventions in physical activity.

The HBM can explain why health behaviours vary from person to person [19]. According to the HBM, the four main factors that influence health behaviours are: perceived threat, behavioural assessment, action cues (CUA) and self-efficacy (EFF) [20]. Perceived threat can be divided into perceived susceptibility (SUS) and severity

(SEV). SUS refers to the individual's perceived vulnerability to a health problem. SEV refers to the individual's assessment of the severity of the health problem. Behavioural assessment refers to the individual's perception of the benefits (BEN) and barriers (BAR) that a healthy behaviour may bring. CUA include a variety of triggers, such as safety education and advice from others. EFF is seen as an individual's confidence and belief in the ability to take a particular action. It has been tested in a number of studies that HBM has a positive effect on promoting health behaviour change [21, 22].

2.3 Personalised Gamification Strategies

Gamification strategies have been widely used in health and fitness applications [23]. Haque et al. [24] used an mHealth app based on game elements to motivate employees to physical activity in the workplace. They concluded that gamification strategies helped to support the need for autonomy and competence. In a similar vein, Mustafa et al. [25] noted that mHealth app developers need to consider using gamification strategies to maintain psychological variables such as intrinsic motivation of users.

Although the effectiveness of gamification strategies has been widely validated, some gamification designs that use a "one-size-fits-all" strategy do not increase user satisfaction [25]. Zuckerman et al. [26] pointed out that users' preferences for game elements vary from person to person. Aldenaini et al. [27] found that close to half of the papers noted the existence of gamification strategies that had limited effect or showed counterproductive effects after reviewed 170 papers. It is therefore important to understand what factors influence the effectiveness of gamification strategies to encourage physical activity.

The demographic information of users is often cited as influencing the perception and effectiveness of gamification strategies [28]. However, these factors lack relevance to gamification applications. Gamers differ in the style of gameplay they favour. It is inappropriate to consider gamers as a whole [29]. With this in mind, we introduced the Hexad user type model. It was developed specifically for gaming systems and has great potential for tailoring personalised gaming systems [30]. According to Santos et al. [10], the preference for gamification elements differs significantly between different types of players. Further, Altmeyer et al. [31] combined Hexad user types with the dynamic process of behavioural change. In their study, they found that users' susceptibility to gamification elements changed with the stage of behavioural change. The test results showed that the approach was able to have a long-term positive impact on users' health behaviours [15].

HBM has been used to examine factors that influence intention to use mhealth apps [32]. Darville et al. [33] designed a health word game based on HBM theory to promote HPV vaccination in young men. While they considered users' health beliefs, they did not consider the impact of user types on the acceptance of gamification systems. Relevant studies combining user type with HBM are even more limited. Therefore, the research in this paper focuses on (1) the relationship between the determinants of HBM and the six player types. (2) How health beliefs and user types affect individuals' perceptions of gamification elements in the context of physical activity.

3 Methods

3.1 Story Board

The gamification strategies we chose were the six core components of healthy gamification mentioned by Lister et al. [13], which include leaderboards, achievements or levels, digital rewards, real rewards, competitions or challenges, and social or peer pressure. Storyboards were designed for each strategy to facilitate respondents' understanding of how these gamification strategies are used in the system. Each set of storyboards consisted the name of the gamification strategy, an application that used the particular gamification strategy, the character's mental activity and physical activity and the character's interaction with the application. As storyboards can recruit a large number of participants from a diverse population and provide a common visual language that is easy to understand [30]. The feasibility of this approach has been validated in past research [34].

To ensure that the storyboards accurately portrayed the intended gamification strategy and were easily understood by participants, six sets of storyboards were first reviewed by three experts in the field. Then a small-scale test (N = 6) was conducted to confirm feasibility. During the test, the researchers presented the storyboards to the participants and asked questions such as, "What is the character's goal?" and "What means does the character use to achieve his or her goal?" After ascertaining that the participants' responses matched the content of the storyboard, the storyboard was used. An example of a storyboard is shown in Fig. 1.

Fig. 1. Gamification strategy storyboard (taking leaderboard as an example).

3.2 Measurement Tools

We developed a web-based platform questionnaire study and recruited subjects. First, the researchers collected demographic information containing the subjects' gender, age, occupation and frequency of physical activity. Secondly, the study used the Hexad User Type Scale proposed by Tondello et al. [9], with 24 questions presented in random order on a 5-point Likert scale to assess the user type of the participants. And their health beliefs were counted using the HBM scale. HBM was measured with reference to the study by Ren et al. [35]. The HBM measures dimensions of SUS, SEV, BEN, BAR, EFF and CUA. Each dimension contained three question items. A Liker 5-point scale was used to assign scores to each option by degree (ranging from 1 strongly disagree to 5 strongly agree). The scores for each dimension were calculated by adding up the scores for all the items under the same dimension. The scores for all dimensions are added together to give a total health belief score. (Where perceived barriers entries are reverse scored). We used the percentage of the total score out of the full score to measure health beliefs [36]. Finally, the persuasiveness of each gamification strategies described in the storyboards was measured using the perceived persuasiveness scale proposed by Drozd et al. [37].

3.3 Participants

The online data collection was conducted over a seven-day period. After screening out incomplete responses, a total of 133 responses were accepted. Participants were at least 18 years old at the time of data collection to ensure they were able to make decisions independently. The demographic information of the subjects is shown in Table 1.

The game types of participants were: philanthropists (25%), socializers (24%), free spirits (21%), achievers (12%), disruptors (1%), and players (17%). This distribution is similar to the study by Tondello et al. [9].

Table 1. The demographic description of the subjects.

Category	Content
Total	133
Gender	Female (61%), Male (39%)
Age	Age 18–25 (22%), 26–35 (36%), 36–45 (33%), 45–55 (5%), > 56 (4%)
Occupation	Student (11%), Career (5%), Civil servant (10%), State-owned enterprise (17%), Private enterprise (57%)
Frequency of exercise	Frequency of exercise Daily (39%), Weekly (50%), Monthly (11%)

4 Results

To investigate the relationship between the six determinants of HBM and player type, we used the Kaiser-Meyer-Olkin (KMO) test of sampling adequacy and the Bartlett's sphericity test to determine the reliability and validity of our data analysis.

To determine the suitability of our data for further analysis, we measured the reliability of HBM using the Kaiser Meyer-Olkin (KMO) test of sampling adequacy and the Bartlett's sphericity test (KMO > 0.70, Bartlett's test was statistically significant p < 0.001). Cronbach alpha values for all latent variables were greater than 0.7. These results suggest that our data are suitable for further analysis.

4.1 Health Beliefs and Persuasion of Gamification Strategies

To measure the effect of health beliefs on perceived gamification measure persuasiveness, we divided participants into a low health belief group (<0.75, N = 61) and a high health belief group (>0.75, N = 72) based on their health belief scores. The Shapiro-Wilk test revealed that the gamification strategy persuasiveness items were not normally distributed, so we used non-parametric tests. Table 2 shows the perceived persuasiveness and median of the six gamification strategies in the two groups. We used Fisher-z changes to measure whether there were significant differences between the two groups. We found that the perceived persuasiveness of the gamification elements was slightly higher overall in the high health belief group than in the low health belief group. Among these, competition and challenge and social or peer pressure scored lower in the low belief group. There were also significant differences between the two groups for leaderboard, rank and achievement, competition and challenge and social or peer pressure.

Table 2. Perceived persuasiveness of gamification strategies in the high and low health belief groups (elements with significant changes in the means of the two groups are bolded.)

	Low Health Belief			High Health Belief		
	M	SD	MDN	M	SD	MDN
Leaderboard	**4.31**	**0.59**	**4.00**	**4.22**	**0.64**	**4.33**
Rank and Achievement	**4.25**	**0.69**	**4.00**	**4.03**	**0.68**	**4.00**
Digital Rewards	4.02	0.92	4.00	4.13	0.88	4.17
Real Rewards	4.36	0.70	4.33	4.39	0.77	4.66
Competition and Challenge	**3.84**	**1.01**	**4.00**	3.99	0.67	4.00
Social or Peer Pressure	**3.85**	**0.95**	**4.00**	**4.02**	**0.78**	**4.00**

We used Kendall's τ to analyse the significant correlations between health beliefs and gamification strategies. As shown in Table 3, there was a negative correlation between perceived susceptibility and rank and achievement strategies. Perceived benefits were correlated with leaderboard strategies. Self-efficacy was correlated with leaderboard, competition and challenge. The correlations between all other items were weak (τ < 0.2) [38]. In summary, health beliefs moderate the perceived persuasiveness of game design elements in physical activity environments.

4.2 Hexad User Types and Gamification Strategy Persuasion

To investigate the potential impact of HB on the perceived persuasiveness of gamification elements for each user type, we compared the correlations between gamification elements

Table 3. Kendall's τ and its significance between health beliefs and gamification strategies.

	SUS	SEV	BEN	BAR	EFF	CUA
Leaderboard	-	-	0.219**	-	0.297**	0.159*
Rank and Achievement	−0.204**	-	0.194**	-	-	-
Digital Rewards	-	-	0.172*	-	-	-
Real Rewards	-	-	-	-	-	-
Competition and Challenge	−0.152*	0.157*	-	-	0.366**	-
Social or Peer Pressure	-	0.175*	-	-	0.159*	-

* $p < 0.05$, ** $p < 0.01$

and user types for the low and high health belief groups. As shown in Table 4, the correlation between leaderboard and social or peer pressure was significantly stronger in the high health belief group than in the low group for the 'Philanthropists'. Similarly, the effect of gamification strategies on the "Socializers" and "Achievers" user types was more significant in the High Health Beliefs group. In contrast, leaderboard and social or peer pressure only had an effect on "Free spirits" in the low health belief group. The correlation between "Disruptor" and all gamification strategies was not significant. Therefore, user type should be considered when deciding which gamification elements should be included in the system.

Table 4. Kendall's τ between Hexad user type and gamification strategy and its significance.

	Low Health Belief						High Health Belief					
	PHI	SOC	FRS	ACH	DIS	PLA	PHI	SOC	FRS	ACH	DIS	PLA
Leaderboard	0.256**	-	0.248**	-	-	-	0.327**	0.230*	-	0.349**	-	-
Rank and Achievement	0.211*	-	-	-	-	0.247**	-	-	-	0.294**	-	-
Digital Rewards	-	-	-	-	-	0.264**	-	-	-	-	-	0.207*
Real Rewards	-	-	-	-	-	0.291**	-	-	-	-	-	0.336**
Competition and Challenge	-	-	-	-	-	-	-	0.343**	-	-	-	-
Social or Peer Pressure	-	-	0.215**	-	-	-	0.245*	0.359**	-	-	-	-

* $p < 0.05$, ** $p < 0.01$

5 Discussion

The results of the study revealed significant differences in the attitudes of users with low and high health beliefs towards some of the gamification elements. Competition and challenge were significantly associated with self-efficacy (($\tau = 0.366$, p < 0.01). As social competition is built on relevant motivations [14], the high health belief group had stronger health motivations and were therefore vulnerable to social competition. The low health group had slightly higher perceived persuasiveness for leaderboard versus rank and achievement than the other group. Leaderboard strategies were significantly associated with perceived benefits ($\tau = 0.219$, p < 0.01) and self-efficacy ($\tau = 0.297$, p < 0.01). This may be due to the greater influence of leaderboards on motivation compared to other game mechanics [39] and the ability of ranks and achievements to encourage user engagement [40]. In summary, health beliefs need to be taken into account when selecting gamification strategies.

There is a potential impact of health beliefs on the perception of gamification elements for each user type. As shown in Table 4, the correlation between rank and achievement and social or peer pressure was significantly stronger in the high health beliefs group than another for the philanthropists. Socializers were correlated with socially competitive strategies, which is similar to the findings of Tondello et al. [9] Due to higher health beliefs, attitudes and willingness to use gamification elements that promote healthy behaviour were also more positive [41]. Free spirits were only influenced by leaderboards and social or peer pressure in the low health belief group. This may because free spirits are reluctant to be influenced externally [42]. This characteristic may lead to a decrease in their perceived susceptibility to gamification strategies. The effect of the achievers was more pronounced in the high health belief group. Gamers were significantly associated with digital or realistic rewards. They are more susceptible to external motivation. Appropriate rewards can motivate them to change their behaviour. No correlations were reported between disruptor type and either gamification strategy.

6 Limitations and Conclusion

We investigated the impact of health beliefs on the perception of gamification elements in the physical activity field, both on their own and on each Hexad user type. We designed storyboards to explain six gamification design elements commonly used in the field of encouraging physical activity. We then conducted an online study (N = 133) which showed that subjects' health beliefs and Hexad user types influenced their perceived persuasiveness of the gamification elements. Gamification studies based on Hexad user types have suggested static or dynamic gamification elements for each user type. Our findings complement this research. The impact of health beliefs on different user types in mobile applications that promote physical activity is worth considering.

There are certain limitations to this study. Firstly, the presentation of gamification elements in this study was based on a storyboard rather than a real system, which may differ from the real user experience. Secondly, no significant correlation was found for the type of 'disruptors', possibly due to the small sample size. Therefore, more participants need to be recruited in future studies in order to be able to find more accurate results. In addition, the effect of changes in health beliefs on perceptions of gamification strategies over a longer time span could be considered. Users' willingness to use the gamification system could also provide additional insights into the potential impact of strategy choice and behaviour change. Further, it would be useful to investigate whether our findings can be replicated in other health-related contexts. To better understand the impact of personalisation on user experience, additional objective variables, such as psychophysiological measures, could be considered to better understand the findings of various user experience-related studies.

References

1. Booth, F.W., Roberts, C.K., Laye, M.J.: Lack of exercise is a major cause of chronic diseases. Compr. Physiol. **2**(2), 1143–1211 (2012)
2. de Melo, E.A.S., et al.: Nuances between sedentary behavior and physical inactivity: cardiometabolic effects and cardiovascular risk. Rev. Assoc. Med. Bras. **67**(2), 335–343 (2021)
3. Pan, X.F., Wang, L.M., Pan, A.: Epidemiology and determinants of obesity in China. Lancet Diabetes Endocrinol. **9**(6), 373–392 (2021)
4. Amagasa, S., et al.: Is objectively measured light-intensity physical activity associated with health outcomes after adjustment for moderate-to-vigorous physical activity in adults? A systematic review. Int. J. Behav. Nutr. Phys. Act. **15**(1), 65 (2018)
5. Mclaughlin, M., et al.: Associations between digital health intervention engagement, physical activity, and sedentary behavior: systematic review and meta-analysis. J. Med. Internet Res. **23**(2), e23180 (2021)
6. Deterding, S., et al.: From game design elements to gamefulness: defining gamification. MindTrek **11**, 9–15 (2011)
7. Gentry, S.V., et al.: Serious gaming and gamification education in health professions: systematic review. J. Med. Internet Res. **21**(3), e12994 (2019)
8. Hamari, J., Koivisto, J., Pakkanen, T.: Do persuasive technologies persuade? - A review of empirical studies. In: Spagnolli, A., Chittaro, L., Gamberini, L. (eds.) PERSUASIVE 2014. LNCS, vol. 8462, pp. 118–136. Springer, Cham (2014). https://doi.org/10.1007/978-3-319-07127-5_11
9. Tondello, G., Wehbe, R., Diamond, L., et al.: The Gamification User Types Hexad Scale (2016)
10. Santos, A.C.G., et al.: The relationship between user types and gamification designs. User Model. User-Adap. Inter. **31**(5), 907–940 (2021). https://doi.org/10.1007/s11257-021-09300-z
11. Wang, T., Wang, H., Zeng, Y., et al.: Health beliefs associated with preventive behaviors against noncommunicable diseases. Patient Educ. Couns. **105**(1), 173–181 (2022)
12. Saei Ghare Naz, M., et al.: Effects of model-based interventions on breast cancer screening behavior of women: a systematic review. Asian Pac. J. Cancer Prev. **19**(8), 2031–2041 (2018)
13. Lister, C., West, J.H., Cannon, B., et al.: Just a fad? gamification in health and fitness apps. JMIR Serious Games **2**(2), e9 (2014)
14. Marczewski, A.: User types. In: Even Ninja Monkeys Like to Play: Gamification, Game Thinking and Motivational Design, CreateSpace Independent Publishing Platform, North Charleston, NC (2015)
15. Altmeyer, M., Lessel, P., Jantwal, S., Muller, L., Daiber, F., Krüger, A.: Potential and effects of personalizing gameful fitness applications using behavior change intentions and Hexad user types. User Model. User-Adap. Inter. **31**(4), 675–712 (2021). https://doi.org/10.1007/s11257-021-09288-6

16. Hallifax, S., Lavoué, E., Serna, A.: To tailor or not to tailor gamification? An analysis of the impact of tailored game elements on learners' behaviours and motivation. In: Bittencourt, I.I., Cukurova, M., Muldner, K., Luckin, R., Millán, E. (eds.) AIED 2020. LNCS (LNAI), vol. 12163, pp. 216–227. Springer, Cham (2020). https://doi.org/10.1007/978-3-030-52237-7_18
17. Hallifax, S., Serna, A., Marty J.C.: Factors to Consider for Tailored Gamification, pp. 559–572 (2019)
18. Khodaveisi, M., Azizpour, B., Jadidi, A., et al.: Education based on the health belief model to improve the level of physical activity. Phys. Act. Nutr. **25**(4), 17–23 (2021)
19. Hosseini, H., Moradi, R., Kazemi, A., et al.: Determinants of physical activity in middle-aged woman in Isfahan using the health belief model. J. Educ. Health Promot. **6**, 26 (2017)
20. Becker, M.H.: The health belief model and sick role behavior. Health Educ. Monogr. **2**(4), 409–419 (1974)
21. Kim, H.Y., Shin, S.H., Lee, E.H.: Effects of health belief, knowledge, and attitude toward COVID-19 on prevention behavior in health college students. Int. J. Environ. Res. Public Health **19**(3), 1898 (2022)
22. Azadi, N.A., Ziapour, A., Lebni, J.Y., et al.: The effect of education based on health belief model on promoting preventive behaviors of hypertensive disease in staff of the Iran University of Medical Sciences. Arch. Public Health **79**(1) (2021)
23. Payne, H.E., Moxley, V.B., MacDonald, E.: Health behavior theory in physical activity game apps: a content analysis. JMIR Serious Games **3**(2), e4 (2015)
24. Haque, M.S., Kangas, M., Jamsa, T.: A persuasive mHealth behavioral change intervention for promoting physical activity in the workplace: feasibility randomized controlled trial. JMIR Formative Res. **4**(5), e15083 (2020)
25. Mustafa, A.S., Ali, Na., Dhillon, J.S., et al.: User engagement and abandonment of mHealth: a cross-sectional survey. Healthcare **10**(2), 221 (2022)
26. Zuckerman, O., Gal-Oz, A.: Deconstructing gamification: evaluating the effectiveness of continuous measurement, virtual rewards, and social comparison for promoting physical activity. Pers. Ubiquit. Comput. **18**(7), 1705–1719 (2014). https://doi.org/10.1007/s00779-014-0783-2
27. Aldenaini, N., Alslaity, A., Sampalli, S., et al.: Persuasive strategies and their implementations in mobile interventions for physical activity: a systematic review. Int. J. Hum. Comput. Interact. (2022)
28. Polo-Pena, A.I., Frias-Jamilena, D.M., Fernandez-Ruano, M.L.: Influence of gamification on perceived self-efficacy: gender and age moderator effect. Int. J. Sports Mark. Spons. **22**(3), 453–476 (2021)
29. Birk, M., Mandryk, R.L.: Control your game-self: effects of controller type on enjoyment, motivation, and personality in game. In: Proceedings of the SIGCHI Conference on Human Factors in Computing Systems, pp. 685–694. Association for Computing Machinery, Paris (2013)
30. Orji, R., Tondello, G., Nacke, L.: Personalizing Persuasive Strategies in Gameful Systems to Gamification User Types (2018)
31. Altmeyer, M., Lessel, P., Muller, L., Krüger, A.: Combining behavior change intentions and user types to select suitable gamification elements for persuasive fitness systems. In: Oinas-Kukkonen, H., Win, K.T., Karapanos, E., Karppinen, P., Kyza, E. (eds.) PERSUASIVE 2019. LNCS, vol. 11433, pp. 337–349. Springer, Cham (2019). https://doi.org/10.1007/978-3-030-17287-9_27
32. Alharbi, N.S., AlGhanmi, A.S., Fahlevi, M.: Adoption of health mobile apps during the COVID-19 lockdown: a health belief model approach. Int. J. Environ. Res. Public Health **19**(7), 4179 (2022)
33. Darville, G., Burns, J., Chavanduka, T., et al.: Utilizing theories and evaluation in digital gaming interventions to increase human papillomavirus vaccination among young males: qualitative study. JMIR Serious Games **9**(1), e21303 (2021)

34. Oyibo, K., Vassileva, J.: Investigation of the moderating effect of culture on users' susceptibility to persuasive features in fitness applications. Information **10**(11), 344 (2019)

35. Ren, C., Deng, C.: Mobile health service user acceptance model and its empirical study. Chin. J. Health Stat. **31**(6), 1015–1018, 1022 (2014)

36. Yu, B., Han, J., Yang, S., et al.: Influence of different types of AIDS knowledge on AIDS-related health beliefs of junior college students. Chin. J. Health Educ. **36**(8), 733–737 (2020)

37. Drozd, F., Lehto, T., Oinas-Kukkonen, H.: Exploring perceived persuasiveness of a behavior change support system: a structural model. In: Bang, M., Ragnemalm, E.L. (eds.) PERSUASIVE 2012. LNCS, vol. 7284, pp. 157–168. Springer, Heidelberg (2012). https://doi.org/10.1007/978-3-642-31037-9_14

38. Walker, D.A.: JMASM9: converting Kendall's tau for correlational or meta-analytic analyses. J. Mod. Appl. Stat. Methods JMASM **2**(2), 525–530 (2003)

39. Park, S., Kim, S.: Leaderboard design principles to enhance learning and motivation in a gamified educational environment: development study. JMIR Serious Games **9**(2), e14746 (2021)

40. Höllig, C.E., Tumasjan, A., Welpe, I.M.: Individualizing gamified systems: the role of trait competitiveness and leaderboard design. J. Bus. Res. **106**, 288–303 (2020)

41. Hamari, J., Koivisto, J.: "Working out for likes": an empirical study on social influence in exercise gamification. Comput. Hum. Behav. **50**, 333–347 (2015)

42. Ryan, R., Deci, E.: Self-determination theory and the facilitation of intrinsic motivation, social Schwartz, S. H. 1977. Adv. Exp. Soc. Psychol. **10**, 221–279 (2000)

Smart Mental Chatbot Platform in the Media and Cognition Course

Yi Yang[✉] and Xinyi Zhao

Tsinghua University, Beijing, China
yangyy@tsinghua.edu.cn

Abstract. The media and cognition course has evolved over ten years and is still keeping pace with the latest developments in artificial intelligence and machine learning. In order to promote this course, the teaching group specially launched one python programming course in the first year of college to help freshmen use python as a tool more proficiently, and combine their interests in the subsequent media and cognition course to propose their more attractive and innovative ideas. This process is also known as the interest-based teaching method. With the development of interest-based teaching method, more students can find interesting problems or difficulties in their study and life, and try to solve them with various intelligent means taught in the course of media and cognition. In the latest course, students independently propose a diagnostic technique for teenagers' psychological anxiety based on image cognition. In the class, the students developed one anxiety diagnosis chatbot system for teenagers to self-test their anxious level. Based on the user's description and cognition of the image, the user's language and text analysis and entity extraction are used to determine the severity of their psychological problems and analyze the causes of their anxiety and stress. The topics proposed in this paper reflect the recent development of artificial intelligence and psychology shown in this course. This kind of interest-based application project proposed by the students fully implies that as a teaching platform, this course effectively helps students to conduct independent research based on interest, and further stimulates students' innovative ability.

Keywords: Media and Cognition Course · Artificial Intelligence · Teenagers' Psychological Anxiety · Innovative Ability

1 Introduction

The media and cognition course has evolved over the years and is still keeping pace with the latest developments in artificial intelligence and machine learning. It has been developed for several years, and are still closely following the development of the state-of-the-art technologies of artificial intelligence and machine learning. By referring to the relevant knowledge of famous universities such as MIT and famous companies such as Google, this course proposes and continuously updates its respective application projects based on artificial intelligence and machine learning year by year. These projects are all developed around how to apply human cognitive methods to the existing and future media carriers [1, 2].

© The Author(s), under exclusive license to Springer Nature Switzerland AG 2023
C. Stephanidis et al. (Eds.): HCII 2023, CCIS 1833, pp. 210–217, 2023.
https://doi.org/10.1007/978-3-031-35992-7_29

In order to serve this course, we even specially launched a python programming course in the first year of college to help freshmen use python more proficiently, and combine their interests in the subsequent media and cognition courses to propose more attractive and innovative ideas. This process is also known as the interest teaching method. With the development of interest teaching method, more students can find interesting problems or difficulties in their study and life, and try to solve them with various intelligent means taught in the course of media and cognition [3].

On the other side, with the increasing pressure on the students' study and life, the psychological anxiety problem has become more and more serious. Traditional psychological research methods are more inclined to use scales to diagnose people and analyze their anxiety levels with psychological problems. However, this approach has several drawbacks: first, it is that teenagers may have a rebellious psychological resistance test, or congenitally conceal their true situation during the test, with will lead to inaccurate test results; second, this method is inconvenient to operate, and is not conducive to finding psychological problems as soon as possible; The third question is, the scale test can only judge the anxiety level from the perspective of psychological knowledge, and it is not closely related to the daily life of teenagers. It requires professional psychotherapist to analyze it.

In the latest course, students independently propose a diagnostic technique for teenagers' psychological anxiety based on image cognition. In the class, the students developed one anxiety chatbot system for teenagers to self-test their anxious level. Based on the user's description and cognition of the image, the user's language and text analysis and entity extraction are used to determine the severity of their psychological problems and analyze the causes of their anxiety and stress. This chatbot system could continuously guide users to give pictures more description information and obtain more user language description information through intelligent dialogue with users. These language information features could enrich the language features for training and analysis. Its main contents included:

Language description information feature extraction: Use natural language processing technology to extract the key information in the user's picture description; Use entity recognition and other technologies to extract keywords and key points in the user's language, and extract emotions through a large number of training samples. Analyzing information is conducive to help follow-up training.

Image information extraction: Use computer vision technology to automatically extract the main objects and features in the image; Extract the weight ratio of each object in each picture; Judge the importance of each item in image perception automatically.

Psychological anxiety prediction and diagnosis suggestion: Through the neural network training of the user's language features and image information, the gap between the user's cognitive judgments on the picture is judged. Picture information mainly comes from manual annotation, supplemented by computer vision image information extraction technology, to help people mark more accurately and quickly. According to the annotation data corresponding to the user's language description, determine the user's psychological anxiety and the cause of its anxiety.

2   The Chatbot System Architecture

The chatbot technique mainly includes three models: Text-based Information Extraction Model, Image-based Information Extraction Model and Psychological Anxiety Prediction Model. From two models, it achieved the sentimental analysis information from the texts and images. Specially, from the text-based model, it automatically extracted how people understand the picture. And from the image-based model, the third model predicts the anxiety level of adolescents by comparing the difference between the text-based analysis results and image-based analysis results. The overall process of the proposed method is illustrated in Fig. 1.

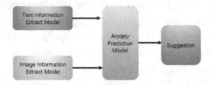

Fig. 1. The basic structure of chatbot system.

2.1   Text-Based Information Extraction Model

In this section, the Sentimental Analysis Model was adopted to analyze and extract sentimental information from the depiction that the users give for the picture. To get VAD (valence-arousal-dimension) scores of sentences, Students use the existing sentiment datasets for our training. Specially, students used BERT-Large for training for pretrained model and EmoBank [4] and SemEval for fine-tuning. EmoBank and SemEval are both classical sentimental analysis database. In order to get the valence and arousal value raning from 0 to 100, students map the value 1–9 in EmoBank equally distributed to 0 to 100 and map the 11 emotions in SemEval to the value according to the past experiment in the paper [5]. Students use transformer model [6, 7], which is the state-of-the-art sentiment analysis model. The transformer model contains positional encoding process, one encoder and one decoder. And students use hidden layer embeddings for later prediction. The Fig. 2 can show the main network architecture.

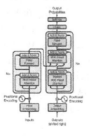

Fig. 2. The basic structure of transformer in paper [9].

The encoder consists of 6 layers, each including one multi-head self-attention mechanism and connected feed-forward network. And it could be described as Eq. 1:

$$Sub\_layer\_output = LayerNorm\ (x + (\ SubLayer\ (x))) \quad (1)$$

And Multi-head self-attention mechanism connects multi attention results, as shown in Eq. 2:

$$MultiHead(Q, K, V) = Concat\ (\ head_1, \ldots, \ head_h)W^O$$
$$head_i = Attention\ \left(QW_i^Q, KW_i^K, VW_i^V\right) \quad (2)$$

The position-wise feed-forward networks gives the non-linear transformation for the output of multi-attention networks. The decoder's input is the output of the encoder and the output of the first $i - 1$ positions. The K, V from the encoder and Q from the decoder is to form attention sublayers. And through linear layers, it will give the probability of each word in each position. Finally, the system ne-tune the model trained on Bert-large on EmoBank and SemEval to predict the valence and arousal of the picture.

2.2 Image-Based Information Extraction Model

Dimensional Emotion Space is the common sentimental model which depicts the valence, arousal and dominance information for the picture. It reflects how people react when seeing the picture. The labels for the picture are often obtained by averaging the scores provided by many experiment testers. There exist some datasets like IASP and GAPED and we can use these datasets and machine learning method to train the model and predict the V(valence), A(arousal) and D(dominance) of the picture. In this way, it can increase the number of pictures and use for the system by including more pictures that are not included in the datasets. The method mainly follows the model in the paper [4] to predict the valence and arousal of the picture. Specially, valence represents the pleasure through the scale from 0(negative) to 100(positive). And arousal is the level of excitement, which ranges from 1 (calm) to 100 (excited). The overall process is shown in Fig. 3. For one picture, it first gets a 150-dimension vector from semantic segmentation and a 1000-dimension vector from object classification and a 1938-dimension vector for low-level features. And then uses four layers of neural networks to train the overall 3088 features and predict the valence and arousal of the picture.

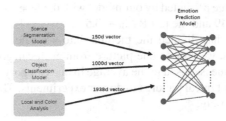

Fig. 3. The basic structure of image sentimental analysis.

The semantic segmentation model [8] mainly classifies each pixel of an image into one of 150 semantic categories. It mainly extracts the information in the background of the picture and gives the ratio of some scenes like sky, sea and buildings. The Object classification model mainly extracts the objects in the picture and these objects can help decide the emotion of the pictures. The CNN models of various structures using ImageNet dataset is designed for the image classification. The probabilities of 1000 object categories is to form a 1000-dimension vector, which can be used for later classification.

For the low-level features, it includes color features and local features. For color features, the system extracts the mean values of RGB and HSV color space as the basic color characteristics. And we exploit two kinds of local features used in the [9]. We use a 512-dimensional GIST descriptor and a 59-dimensional local binary pattern (LBP) descriptor to depict the local features. And all the color features and local features are all the low-level features. And combing all the features above, the three layers and one output layers with rectified linear unit (ReLU) [10] is to form emotion prediction model. The function can be written as Eq. 3:

$$F(X, \theta) = f^4 g^3 f^3 g^2 f^2 g^1 f^1(X) \tag{3}$$

where X is input vector which unions the features from the models before and θ. is the train parameters.

2.3 Anxiety Prediction Model

Text-based model and image-based model will provide the valence and arousal value from both the text and picture. One classification model with input above and other information like users' basic information and its own quantitative judgement are built for the picture. And the probability that the people have anxiety problems is defined and predicted the intensity of the anxiety.

3 The Experimental Results

3.1 Picture Selection and Analysis

The first step of experiments is to select the pictures. The Geneva affective picture database (GAPED) [11] provides a set of pictures with sentimental reaction value labeled by people. First, it proves that the effects of our image-based model by comparing the valence and arousal value predicted by our model with the labels given by GAPED itself. The test MSE is 1006.49 and the test R2 is -0.5.

Notice that GAPE has divided the pictures into six categories. To minimize the workload of the testers, we choose one picture from each category in the way that the arousal and valence value is closed to the average in one category. And then from the six pictures, we select four typical pictures to do our experiments. The basic information of the pictures is shown in Fig. 4.

3.2 Data Collection

We gave the questionnaires to the adolescents aged from 18 to 24 in the universities in China. The universities include Tsinghua University, Chinese Academy of Sciences University and Beijing Foreign Studies University. And we asked students to answer the question: Please use the sentences to describe the feeling and thoughts after seeing the picture. And gave the valence and arousal scores for the picture. After answering the questions for four pictures, we then asked students to do The General Anxiety Disorder 7-item scale [12], which gives the anxiety level for the people. And finally, we collect 230 effective questionnaires.

Fig. 4. The pictures for test and its valence and arousal results.

Table 1. The valence and arousal from the text sentimental analysis. Valence-1 means the valence score for the first picture while arousal-1 means the variance score for the second picture.

	valence-1	arousal-1	valence-2	arousal-2	valence-3	arousal-3	valence-4	arousal-4
average	47.164502	46.705628	71.870130	63.930736	35.432900	45	35.489177	41.735931
variance	25.950769	26.052287	23.714617	25.029278	26.265758	28.009315	24.822126	25.198938

3.3 Results and Analysis

We calculate the arousal and valence of the sentences provided by the students and the overall statistic information is shown in Table 1. We use the anxiety classification from 1–5 based on the sum of the scores that the students answer after the questionnaire. It simply checks whether the anxiety score is correlated with the text-based valence and arousal with linear regression analysis. The standardized residual histogram is shown in Fig. 5 and the deviation analysis is in Table 2. It could be seen that the correlation between the scores and features extracted.

And if the database increases, it could improve the training model and thus improve the results.

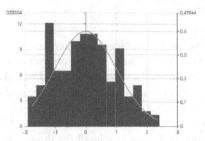

Fig. 5. The standardized residual histogram of the linear regression.

Table 2. The deviation analysis.

Deviation Sources	df	SS	MS	F-value	p-value	F crit
Regression	303.888711	16	18.993044	1.306947	0.617792	1.690958
Residual	3109.929471	214	14.532381			

4 Conclusion

Because the actual problems faced by young people are simpler than adults, the pressure is more concentrated on problems such as learning, emotions, and family. Students in the media and cognition course put forward a chatbot system that can make suggestions to users by guiding users to analyze anxiety and other psychological problems to help users understand psychological probability correctly and reduce their pressure in time. Through machine learning and artificial intelligence methods, through data training, provide more accurate, faster and more effective preliminary analysis and suggestions of psychological problems to help users find problems earlier, recognize and solve problems faster, and help young people decompress, which is more conducive to their physical and mental development. By analyzing the performance characteristics of teenagers' language cognition under different anxiety problems, which could find out more valuable psychological information. It can find that there is correlation between people's reaction to the picture and its own anxiety level. This system includes many machine learning architectures and uses these models to solve real world problems. In the future, the increase of the database could help the prediction. And we can add more models and extract more features to increase the training effect.

The media and cognition course itself involves multiple directions of artificial intelligence, such as computer vision, image content understanding, natural language processing, etc. The topics proposed in this paper reflect the recent advantages of this course and psychology. This kind of interest-based application project proposed by the students fully implies that as a teaching platform, this course effectively helps students to conduct independent research based on interest, and further stimulates students' innovative ability.

References

1. MIT OpenCourseWare Homepage. https://ocw.mit.edu/courses/6-034-artificial-intelligence-fall-2010/. Accessed 1 Mar 2023
2. Jordan, M.I., Mitchell, T.M.: Machine learning: trends, perspectives, and prospects. Science **349**(6245), 255–260 (2015)
3. Yi, Y., Shengjin, W., Jiasong, S., et al.: Interest-based learning for teaching a human-computer interaction course: media and cognition course. In: Proceedings of the International Conference on Frontiers in Education: Computer Science and Computer Engineering (FECS), pp. 62–67 (2017)
4. Buechel, S., Hahn, U.: EmoBank: studying the impact of annotation perspective and representation format on dimensional emotion analysis. In: Proceedings of the 15th Conference of the European Chapter of the Association for Computational Linguistics: Volume 2, Short Papers, pp. 578–585 (2017)
5. Park, S., Kim, J., Jeon, J., Park, H., Oh, A.: Toward dimensional emotion detection from categorical emotion annotations. arXiv preprint arXiv:1911.02499 11 (2019)
6. Liu, S., Shuai, P., Zhang, X., Chen, S., Li, L., Liu, M.: Fine-tuned transformer model for sentiment analysis. In: Li, G., Shen, H.T., Yuan, Y., Wang, X., Liu, H., Zhao, X. (eds.) Knowledge Science, Engineering and Management, pp. 336–343. Springer International Publishing, Cham (2020)
7. Vaswani, A., et al.: Attention is all you need. In: Advances in Neural Information Processing Systems, vol. 30 (2017)
8. Wu, Z., Shen, C., van den Hengel, A.: Wider or deeper: revisiting the resnet model for visual recognition. Pattern Recogn. **90**, 119–133 (2019)
9. Borth, D., Ji, R., Chen, T., Breuel, T., Chang, S.F.: Large-scale visual sentiment ontology and detectors using adjective noun pairs. In: Proceedings of the 21st ACM International Conference on Multimedia, pp. 223–232 (2013)
10. Krizhevsky, A., Sutskever, I., Hinton, G.E.: Imagenet classification with deep convolutional neural networks. Commun. ACM **60**(6), 84–90 (2017)
11. Dan-Glauser, E.S., Scherer, K.R.: The Geneva affective picture database (gaped): a new 730-picture database focusing on valence and normative significance. Behav. Res. Methods **43**(2), 468–477 (2011)
12. Spitzer, R.L., Kroenke, K., Williams, J.B.W., Löwe, B.: A brief measure for assessing generalized anxiety disorder. Arch. Internal Med. **166**(10), 1092 (2006)

Research on Gamified Design of Introductory Core Muscle Training

Dongxu Yang, Jiayuan Lu, Xiangyu Liu$^{(\boxtimes)}$, and Hao Tang$^{(\boxtimes)}$

College of Communication and Art Design, University of Shanghai for Science and Technology,
Shanghai 200093, China
{Liuxiangyu,th}@usst.edu.cn

Abstract. This study sought to evaluate the effectiveness of gamified design as a means of introductory core muscle training. A gamified design session incorporated surface electromyogram (sEMG) technology and game-like elements to facilitate core muscle training to achieve this objective. The study examined participants' core muscle surface electromyography, endurance, and engagement levels before and after the training. The findings indicated that individuals who underwent gamified design training demonstrated significantly enhanced core muscle strength and endurance compared to those who received formal training.

Furthermore, the participants reported higher levels of engagement and motivation during the training sessions. In conclusion, this study suggests that gamified design can effectively enhance introductory core muscle training. Incorporating game-like elements and sEMG technology may increase participant engagement and motivation, improving training outcomes.

Keywords: Core Muscle Training · Human-Computer Interaction · Motion Recognition · Gamified Design

1 Introduction

1.1 The Importance of Core Muscle

Core muscle training is crucial in maintaining overall physical health and preventing injuries by stabilizing and supporting the body during movement [1]. Strengthening the core muscles in the abdomen, pelvis, and lower back can improve posture, balance, and coordination while reducing the likelihood of back pain and injuries [2]. Additionally, incorporating core muscle training into a workout regimen can enhance sports performance and serve as an effective preventive measure against injuries [3].

Despite the benefits of traditional core muscle training, maintaining a consistent training routine can be challenging due to low engagement and motivation levels [4]. To overcome this issue, gamification, which involves integrating game-like features into non-game situations, has increased engagement and motivation in various domains. Although limited research has explored the efficacy of gamification in core muscle training programs, it can enhance engagement and motivation, resulting in improved adherence and better health outcomes [5].

C. Stephanidis et al. (Eds.): HCII 2023, CCIS 1833, pp. 218–223, 2023.
https://doi.org/10.1007/978-3-031-35992-7_30

As individuals age, their core muscle strength naturally diminishes, resulting in poor posture, balance, and mobility [6]. To combat this, integrating minimum-intensity core muscle training into the workout routine of older adults can effectively maintain core strength and improve overall physical function [7].

In conclusion, gamification can increase engagement and motivation in core muscle training programs, leading to better health outcomes. Core muscle training is crucial for maintaining physical health, preventing injuries, enhancing sports performance, and improving overall function, particularly among older adults.

1.2 Surface Electromyography (sEMG) Application in Core Muscle Training

Surface electromyography (sEMG) is a valuable tool for evaluating and enhancing core muscle function, which is crucial for stabilizing the spine and pelvis during movement [8]. By assessing the activation levels of the core muscles during different exercises and activities, sEMG can identify weak or underactive muscles that require attention in a training program [9]. Furthermore, sEMG biofeedback can provide real-time feedback during core muscle training, enabling athletes and trainers to ensure that the correct muscles are engaged and exercises are executed accurately. Research has indicated that incorporating sEMG biofeedback into core muscle training can lead to better outcomes, such as increased muscle activation and improved performance [10, 11].

However, it is essential to note that sEMG should be combined with other techniques as part of a comprehensive training program and under the supervision of a qualified professional. Moreover, integrating sEMG into core muscle game training can further enhance performance and reduce the risk of injury. During core muscle game training, sEMG can assess muscle activation levels and provide feedback on the effectiveness of movements. It can also ensure that athletes use the correct muscles and maintain proper form, thereby reducing the likelihood of injury and improving performance.

Furthermore, sEMG can add a competitive element to core muscle game training by measuring muscle activation levels and generating a leaderboard or competition. This can motivate athletes to challenge themselves and achieve superior results. Overall, sEMG is a valuable tool for enhancing performance and reducing the risk of injury during core muscle training and core muscle game training [12]. It provides real-time feedback on muscle activation levels, allowing athletes and trainers to identify weaknesses and optimize their training programs.

1.3 The Benefits of Gamified Muscle Training

Gamification is a powerful tool to enhance muscle training programs' engagement, motivation, and adherence [13]. By incorporating game-like elements such as points, badges, leaderboards, and challenges into exercise programs, participants can experience instant feedback and encouragement, making the program more enjoyable and rewarding [14].

Muscle training programs can incorporate gamification elements, including point systems, leaderboards, challenges, and progress tracking. This approach can increase engagement, motivation, and adherence, ultimately improving health outcomes [15]. Moreover, by designing games tailored to their interests and skills, gamification can be customized to meet specific populations' unique needs and abilities, such as children or older adults.

The benefits of gamified muscle training programs include increased adherence, motivation, performance, personalization, and better outcomes [16]. Gamification makes muscle training more fun and rewarding, which can lead to better compliance and reduced dropout rates. Additionally, by providing instant feedback and rewards, gamification can increase motivation and encourage participants to push themselves harder. By incorporating game-like elements into muscle training programs, gamification can make muscle training more enjoyable and effective, leading to better overall health and fitness.

2   Method

This study invited 12 healthy participants (Table 1) to investigate the effectiveness of gamified design in core muscle training. The participants were recruited from the University of Shanghai for Science and Technology. The sessions used OT Sessantaquattro (Italy) to record the sEMG incorporating game-like elements to deliver core muscle training.

Table 1. Personal information of participants in the experiment six

Subject	Gender	Age	Height (CM)	Weight (kg)	BMI
1	Male	22	175	85	27.7
2	Male	22	177	88	25.5
3	Male	22	175	67.5	22
4	Male	22	175	47.5	15.5
5	Male	33	175	70	22.9
6	Male	22	190	100	26.8
7	Male	22	177	69	22
8	Male	21	178	80	25.2
9	Male	21	178	63	19.9
10	Male	22	168	57.4	20.3
11	Male	22	175	47.5	15.5
12	Male	21	177	63	20.1

* For privacy concerns, we used numbers as the index of the participants.

The training program consisted of two exercises targeting the core muscles, including half-crunches and leg raises. The participants completed five-game trials in a session (Fig. 1). The study measured the participants' core muscle surface EMG, endurance, and engagement level before and after the training.

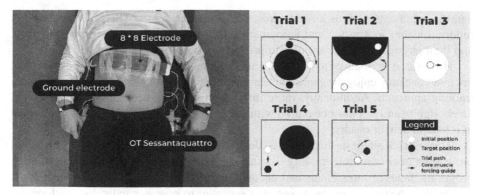

Fig. 1. Experimental setup and game guide session

3 Results

Based on our analysis of the collected data, incorporating gamified core muscle training impacted the participants' muscle strength and endurance. Compared to their prior training experience, the gamified approach led to notable improvements in both areas. These results suggest that integrating gamification into core muscle training programs could be a highly effective strategy for improving program outcomes.

In addition, the participants reported feeling more engaged and motivated throughout the training. The Game Engagement Questionnaire results indicated that the participants had a higher average score, which suggests they felt more inspired, immersed, and enjoyed the training program. These findings suggest that gamification enhances the physical outcomes of training and improves the overall training experience for participants.

4 Discussion

Firstly, it is essential to note that gamification has emerged as a popular trend in fitness training. Gamification involves incorporating game elements into non-game contexts to motivate and engage users. In the case of core muscle training, gamification can be used to make the exercise more enjoyable, interactive, and rewarding, which may encourage people to adhere to their fitness regimen over the long term.

Several studies have explored the effectiveness of gamified design in core muscle training. For instance, a study by researchers at the University of Helsinki investigated the impact of a gamified mobile application on core muscle strength and balance in older adults. The app included games focused on core muscle training, such as planking and balancing exercises. The participants in the study reported enjoying the app and found it motivating, and their core muscle strength and balance improved significantly throughout the study.

Another study, published in the Journal of Sports Science and Medicine, examined the impact of a gamified core muscle training program on physical fitness and motivation in college students. The program consisted of a 10-week training course incorporating gamified elements such as leaderboards, badges, and rewards. The study participants reported higher motivation and enjoyment levels than a traditional training program, and their physical fitness levels also improved significantly.

However, it is essential to note that gamification has some limitations. For instance, not everyone may enjoy the game-like elements, and some may prefer a more traditional training approach. Additionally, more than gamification is needed to improve fitness levels significantly; it must be paired with effective training techniques and progressive overload to deliver results.

The research suggests that gamified design can effectively promote engagement and motivation in core muscle training. By incorporating game-like elements into training programs, fitness professionals can encourage people to adhere to their fitness goals and achieve better results. However, it is essential to consider individual preferences and needs while designing gamified fitness programs and to pair gamification with effective training techniques. The research suggests that gamified design can effectively promote engagement and motivation in core muscle training. By incorporating game-like elements into training programs, fitness professionals can encourage people to stick with their fitness goals and achieve better results.

5   Conclusion

The results of our study suggest that gamified design can effectively increase engagement and motivation in introductory core muscle training. Specifically, participants demonstrated significantly improved core muscle strength and endurance compared to their prior training experience. Additionally, participants reported feeling more engaged and motivated throughout the training. Our findings are essential for designing effective and engaging core muscle training programs to help people maintain a healthy and active lifestyle. However, further research is needed to investigate the long-term effects of gamified design in core muscle training and its potential for reducing the risk of injury and enhancing sports performance.

Acknowledgment. This work is sponsored by the Shanghai Rising-Star Program (Sailing Program) (22YF1430800).

References

1. Hibbs, A.E., Thompson, K.G., French, D., Wrigley, A., Spears, I.: Optimizing performance by improving core stability and core strength. Sports Med. **38**, 995–1008 (2008). https://doi.org/10.2165/00007256-200838120-00004
2. Martuscello, J.M., Nuzzo, J.L., Ashley, C.D., Campbell, B.I., Orriola, J.J., Mayer, J.M.: Systematic review of core muscle activity during physical fitness exercises. J. Strength Cond. Res. **27**, 1684–1698 (2013). https://doi.org/10.1519/JSC.0b013e318291b8da
3. Akuthota, V., Nadler, S.F.: Core strengthening11No commercial party having a direct financial interest in the results of the research supporting this article has or will confer a benefit upon the author(s) or upon any organization with which the authors is/are associated. Arch. Phys. Med. Rehabil. **85**, 86–92 (2004). https://doi.org/10.1053/j.apmr.2003.12.005

4. Kraemer, W.J., Ratamess, N.A.: Fundamentals of resistance training: progression and exercise prescription. Med. Sci. Sports Exerc. **36**, 674–688 (2004). https://doi.org/10.1249/01.MSS. 0000121945.36635.61
5. Bitrián, P., Buil, I., Catalán, S.: Gamification in sport apps: the determinants of users' motivation. EJMBE **29**, 365–381 (2020). https://doi.org/10.1108/EJMBE-09-2019-0163
6. Boccia, G., Dardanello, D., Rosso, V., Pizzigalli, L., Rainoldi, A.: The application of sEMG in aging: a mini review. Gerontology **61**, 477–484 (2015). https://doi.org/10.1159/000368655
7. CDC TUFTS: Growing Stronger - Strength Training for Older Adults (2002)
8. Reiman, M.P., Bolgla, L.A., Loudon, J.K.: A literature review of studies evaluating gluteus maximus and gluteus medius activation during rehabilitation exercises. Physiother. Theory Pract. **28**, 257–268 (2012). https://doi.org/10.3109/09593985.2011.604981
9. Gong, Q., Jiang, X., Liu, Y., Yu, M., Hu, Y.: A flexible wireless sEMG system for wearable muscle strength and fatigue monitoring in real time. Adv. Elect. Mater., 2200916 (2023). https://doi.org/10.1002/aelm.202200916
10. Chmielewska, D., et al.: Electromyographic characteristics of pelvic floor muscles in women with stress urinary incontinence following sEMG-assisted biofeedback training and Pilates exercises. PLoS ONE **14**, e0225647 (2019). https://doi.org/10.1371/journal.pone.0225647
11. Drysdale, C.L., Earl, J.E., Hertel, J.: Surface electromyographic activity of the abdominal muscles during pelvic-tilt and abdominal-hollowing exercises (2004)
12. Liu, X., et al.: Changes in synchronization of the motor unit in muscle fatigue condition during the dynamic and isometric contraction in the Biceps Brachii muscle. Neurosci. Lett. **761**, 136101 (2021). https://doi.org/10.1016/j.neulet.2021.136101
13. González-González, C., Río, N.G., Navarro-Adelantado, V.: Exploring the benefits of using gamification and videogames for physical exercise: a review of state of art. IJIMAI **5**, 46 (2018). https://doi.org/10.9781/ijimai.2018.03.005
14. Mazeas, A., Duclos, M., Pereira, B., Chalabaev, A.: Evaluating the effectiveness of gamification on physical activity: systematic review and meta-analysis of randomized controlled trials. J. Med. Internet Res. **24**, e26779 (2022). https://doi.org/10.2196/26779
15. Toth, A., Logo, E.: The effect of gamification in sport applications. In: 2018 9th IEEE International Conference on Cognitive Infocommunications (CogInfoCom), pp. 000069–000074. IEEE, Budapest (2018). https://doi.org/10.1109/CogInfoCom.2018.8639934
16. Johnson, D., Deterding, S., Kuhn, K.-A., Staneva, A., Stoyanov, S., Hides, L.: Gamification for health and wellbeing: a systematic review of the literature. Internet Interv. **6**, 89–106 (2016). https://doi.org/10.1016/j.invent.2016.10.002

Designing At-Home Workout Products to Improve Sub-health of Young People

Sunxiya Zhang[1], Emiran Kaisar[1], Ting Han[1], Ruoyu Liang[2], and Shi Qiu[1(✉)]

[1] Department of Design, Shanghai Jiao Tong University, Shanghai, China
{zhangsunxiya,imarsemiran,hanting,qiushi11}@sjtu.edu.cn
[2] Department of Design, Jiangnan University, Wuxi, China
8201801018@jiangnan.edu.cn

Abstract. This paper describes an at-home workout product, aiming at improving the sub-health situation of young people and decreasing their low back pain (LBP), and guiding them to actively complete the training in the correct posture in the interaction with music game to achieve continuous improvement of their physical condition. In consideration of young people's physical condition, the crawling exercises were added to the overall training program which contains upper limb exercises, lower limb exercises, and core exercises. In addition, music games with a strong sense of rhythm are applied to stimulate young people's interest in daily training and core muscle rehabilitation training of a certain intensity. The movements of young people are captured with a range of sensors and they can control the movements of game characters by their movement in real-time. The design process, the rehabilitation program, and the implementation of the game mechanics are presented in this paper.

Keywords: Low back pain · At-home workouts · Social interaction · Young adults

1 Introduction

Due to the increase in at-home working time, the sedentary screen-time activities of young people have greatly increased. The phenomenon of sub-health and LBP of young people caused by sedentary behavior is also more popular and getting more attention [1]. Researchers argued that crawl training therapy has an effective influence on the treatment of patients with LBP [2]. The combination of crawling exercise and upper body exercise can help relieve the symptoms of LBP and increase young people's body flexibility and enhances organism resistance [3].

Interactive exergame can not only help young people improve their physical fitness, increase motivation and participation in sports, but also improve the mental health of young people by increasing interaction between people [4].

In previous studies, we conducted reviews to summarize research findings of using exercise therapy to solve LBP and of using social exergame to improve young people's mental sub-health. Next, we designed a set of home fitness products to solve a series of physical health problems of young people, including LBP, and improve their mental health by increasing interpersonal communication. In the following study, we presented an evaluation plan to evaluate the improvement data of the workout products on the health level of young people.

2   Related Work

2.1   Crawling Exercise Therapy

Numerous studies support the role of core training in the prevention and rehabilitation of LBP. It is found that taking specific exercises designed to strengthen the muscles that support the back and improve back flexibility can reduce the chances of acute attack of LBP [5]. Crawling is an effective exercise for pain reduction and functional restoration as a core and stabilization exercise (SE), which is aimed at improving neuromuscular control to maintain spinal stability [6]. Crawling exercises are as effective as manual therapy in terms of decreasing LBP and improving spinal sub-health and highlighted that crawling should be a part of musculoskeletal rehabilitation for LBP, based on clinical control experiments on patients [2].

In the market, there are also several crawling training devices based on this theory such as crawling exercise devices (FITCRAWL®FC-518) from FITOW CROWE (SHANGHAI) INDUSTRIAL Co Ltd. Patients can alternatively crawl on the devices in a kneeling position [7].

2.2   Application of Gamification

Many studies presented the value of exergame in motivating their initiative in training resulting in the creation of a sound psychological state in them. Skjæret et al. found exergame may have fundamental advantages compared to traditional exercise, as they easily allow for task-specific exercises to be delivered across a range of difficulty levels [8]. Exergame makes sports more interactive and enjoyable by adding game elements, increasing the attractiveness of sports. This helps to enhance the motivation of patients to participate in sports and reduces the symptoms of depression [9].

Numerous authors have advocated including social play in exergames to foster interaction and increase motivation. It is proved that social exergame can help sustain physical activity (PA) [10]. Researchers have also suggested that social play in exergames can transfer the quality of the game from 'hard fun' to 'social fun' [11]. When players are involved in a common social activity, the social interaction between them increases, which contributes to their sense of belonging and positive emotions [12].

In prior work, we investigated socially assistive systems from system design and evaluation to find HCI technologies that supported social interactions [13]. A review of data gathering methods for evaluating socially assistive systems is also summarized for people with special needs [14]. Aside from systematic reviews, we also conducted empirical studies. For example, the Social Balance Ball was designed to enhance intergenerational interaction and at-home balance training [15]. Qiu et al. [16] also performed a user experiment with 18 unfamiliar young-old pairs to evaluate this social exergame. Results demonstrated that older participants perceived significantly higher social interaction than younger participants.

In this study, we focus on the design and implementation of the exergame to improve physical sub-health and LBP of young people. In the further study, we intend to apply social interaction into the exergame and focus on the effects of the exergame on the mental health of young people.

3 Concept Design

Based on the existing physical and mental health status of young people, the design goals include the following two aspects.

- Allocate different exercise plans to young adults according to their sub-health condition.
- Find an effective game mechanism that can guide young people to complete the exercise plan and supports different interactions between players and the game.

The design contains two parts of hardware as shown in Fig. 1. The intelligent dumbbell can be held by the player to control the game characters with different movements according to the music direction. Players can do crawling exercises on the crawling devices to control the crawling speed to make the game character forward. They can change the tilt direction and angle of the acrylic board to connect with the game characters. The pattern links daily workouts to rehabilitation training which may relieve symptoms of LBP [17].The daily workouts include upper limb exercises and lower limb exercises. The rehabilitation training contains crawling movements. Players can choose a suitable workout mode according to their health condition.

Fig. 1. The design involves two parts: the crawling devices and the intelligent dumbbell.

4 Music Game System Implementation

4.1 Hardware and Software

Figure 2 presents the workflow of the music game system. In this process, players' motion will be captured by different arduino sensors of and then the signal from will be input into Unity as keyboard signal to control the movement of the game character.

Figure 3 presents the hardware such as acceleration sensors, pull switches and pressure sensors is used to monitor players' movement to control game characters' movement. Upper limb movement game, crawling exercise game and stretch guidance page are all embedded in the APP. Acceleration sensors can monitor players' right and left hand movement to control characters turning right or left in upper limb movement game. Pull switches can monitor players' crawling movement to control planes up and down to avoid barriers in crawling exercise game. Pressure sensors can monitor players' stretching movement to feed back to the stretching guidance system.

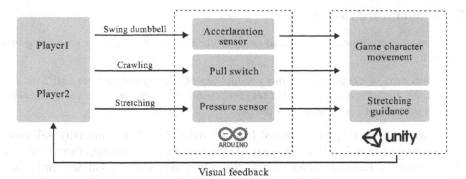

Fig. 2. The system overview

Fig. 3. Users can follow do stretching exercises, crawling exercises, and upper limb exercises.

4.2 Social Play

Players can either complete the exercise on their own or with other players with the LBP. Players can work in pairs to control game characters' movement as shown in Fig. 4. Sensors will capture the pairs' movement and feedback the effect superimposed on the game characters' movement.

Fig. 4. The pair can work together to control the character movement.

5 Evaluation Scheme

We propose a preliminary scheme to analyze the system. We focus on answering two research questions:

- Whether the workout mode of this product can efficiently help relieve LBP?
- Whether the intervention of this exergame could efficiently increase social connectedness between young and older people?

Young adult participants recruited from Shanghai Jiao Tong University will complete a questionnaire in advance to evaluate whether they are suffering form LBP. The questionnaire includes questions such as "I can lift heavy weights without extra pain", "Pain does not prevent me walking any distance", "I can sit in any chair as long as I like" [18]. Finally, twenty participants born after 1995 who are suffering from the LBP will be recruited to complete the exergame and fill in Post-Game questionnaires.

Both quantitative and qualitative data will be collected through the user experiment. Before the test, we will collect the participants' demographic information as well as their sedentary screen-time activities in daily routines through the subjective questionnaires. After that, the first 10 participants are invited to complete exergame on their own for 8 min and complete Post-Game questionnaire 1 before and after the experiment. And the other 10 participants will be invited to work alone and in pairs respectively to complete exergame and fill in Post-Game questionnaire 2 after experiments.

Visual Analogue Scale (VAS) is adopted in questionnaire 1 to evaluate whether the LBP is relieved [19]. Intrinsic Motion Inventory would be adopted in questionnaire 2 to evaluate the social engagement of young adult participants in the exergame. It contains a total of six subscales including Interest/Enjoyment, Perceived Competence, Effort/Importance, Pressure/Tension, Value/Usefulness, Relatedness [15].

6 Conclusion

Our work was inspired by the increased focus on LBP in young people. Our previous study also includes the application of the social play between players in the exergame to foster interaction and increase motivation. In response, we introduced an at-home exergame that can help improve LBP and mental health of young people. We added crawling exercises and upper limb exercises into exergame system and intend to add social play in it in the further study.

We are intrigued by the possibility that focusing on interaction between young players can lead to new experiences and believe that this can be a useful design approach to motivate their initiative in training and create a sound psychological state in them. With this in mind, we proposed an evaluation scheme to improve the usability of the system, observing whether the implementation of the social exergame could efficiently help relieve LBP and bring positive feelings between young players.

References

1. ul-Haq, F., et al.: Characteristics of back pain in young adults and their relationship with dehydration: a cross sectional study. F1000Res **9**, 159 (2020). https://doi.org/10.12688/f1000research.22298.1

2. Li, M., Wang, K., Niu, W., Zhang, S.: A musculoskeletal modeling of hand-foot crawling with different heights. J. Bionic Eng. **17**(3), 591–599 (2020). https://doi.org/10.1007/s42235-020-0047-y
3. Cheung, C.Y.W., Ng, G.Y.F.: An eight-week exercise programme improves physical fitness of sedentary female adolescents. Physiotherapy **89**(4), 249–255 (2003). https://doi.org/10.1016/S0031-9406(05)60156-3
4. Wan Yunus, F., Tan, X.Z., Romli, M.H.: Investigating the feasibility of exergame on sleep and emotion among university students. Games Health J. **9**(6), 415–424 (2020). https://doi.org/10.1089/g4h.2019.0077
5. Paolucci, T., Attanasi, C., Cecchini, W., Marazzi, A., Capobianco, S.V., Santilli, V.: Chronic low back pain and postural rehabilitation exercise: a literature review. J. Pain Res. **12**, 95–107 (2019). https://doi.org/10.2147/JPR.S171729
6. Demirel, A., Oz, M., Ozel, Y.A., Cetin, H., Ulger, O.: Stabilization exercise versus yoga exercise in non-specific low back pain: pain, disability, quality of life, performance: a randomized controlled trial. Complement Ther. Clin. Pract. **35**, 102–108 (2019). https://doi.org/10.1016/j.ctcp.2019.02.004
7. FC518 Fitness Equipment (id: 5502682) Product details - View FC518 Fitness Equipment from Fitcrawl (Shanghai) Industry Co., Ltd - EC21. https://fitcrawl.en.ec21.com/FC518_Fitness_Equipment--5502571_5502682.html
8. Skjæret, N., Nawaz, A., Morat, T., Schoene, D., Helbostad, J.L., Vereijken, B.: Exercise and rehabilitation delivered through exergames in older adults: An integrative review of technologies, safety and efficacy. Int. J. Med. Inform. **85**(1), 1–16 (2016). Elsevier Ireland Ltd., https://doi.org/10.1016/j.ijmedinf.2015.10.008
9. Rosenberg, D., et al.: Exergames for subsyndromal depression in older adults: a pilot study of a novel intervention. Am. J. Geriatr. Psychiatry **18**(3), 221–226 (2010). https://doi.org/10.1097/JGP.0B013E3181C534B5
10. Caro, K., Freed, E., Fox, B., Day, T.: Understanding the Effect of Existing Positive Relationships on a Social Motion-based Game for Health
11. Mueller, F.F.: Designing for bodily interplay in social exertion games. ACM Trans. Comput.-Hum. Interact. **24**(3), 1–41 (2017). https://doi.org/10.1145/3064938
12. Kaos, M.D., Rhodes, R.E.: Social Play in an Exergame : How the Need to Belong Predicts Adherence, pp. 1–13 (2019)
13. Qiu, S., An, P., Kang, K., Hu, J., Han, T., Rauterberg, M.: Investigating socially assistive systems from system design and evaluation : a systematic review. Univ. Access Inf. Soc. 0123456789 (2021). https://doi.org/10.1007/s10209-021-00852-w
14. Qiu, S., An, P., Kang, K., Hu, J., Han, T., Rauterberg, M.: A review of data gathering methods for evaluating socially assistive systems, pp. 1–31 (2022)
15. Kaisar, E., Qiu, S., Yuan, R., Han, T.: Designing social exergame to enhance intergenerational interaction and exercise. In: Fang, X. (eds.) HCI in Games. HCII 2022. LNCS, vol. 13334. Springer, Cham (2022). https://doi.org/10.1007/978-3-031-05637-6_34
16. Qiu, S., Kaisar, E., Ding, R.B., Han, T., Hu, J., Rauterberg, M.: Social balance ball: designing and evaluating an exergame that promotes social interaction between older and younger players. Int. J. Human-Comput. Interact. 1–58 (2022). (In print)
17. Ribas, J., Gomes, M.A., Montes, A.M., Ribas, C., Duarte, J.A.: Resolution of chronic lower back pain symptoms through high-intensity therapeutic exercise and motor imagery program: a case-report. Physiother. Theory Pract. **38**(10), 1545–1552 (2020). https://doi.org/10.1080/09593985.2020.1839985
18. Roland, M., Fairbank, J.: The Roland – Morris Disability Questionnaire and the Oswestry Disability Questionnaire, vol. 25, no. 24, pp. 3115–3124 (2000)
19. Katz, J., Melzack, R.: Measurement of pain. Surg. Clin. North Am. **79**(2), 231–252 (1999). https://doi.org/10.1016/S0039-6109(05)70381-9

Design for All, Accessibility
and Rehabilitation Technologies

Accessibility – An Incremental Part of Holistic User Experience Design Process for Mobility Solutions

Huseyin Avsar[✉] and Marc Burkhardt

Siemens Mobility GmbH, Ackerstraße 22, 38126 Braunschweig, Germany
{hueseyin.avsar,marc.burkhardt}@siemens.com

Abstract. Siemens Mobility is a leading provider of sustainable and efficient transport solutions. Siemens Mobility integrates cutting-edge technologies that drive the development of accessible products and services for all potential users. There is a common misunderstanding that accessibility is relevant for only disabled people. Situational conditions may affect the accessibility of a product or a service, even if the user has no disability. The user acceptance can be affected since there is a correlation between accessibility and user experience. The visual, audible, physical, and cognitive abilities of the end user and the context of use in which the product or service is used must be considered. This paper presents how accessibility has been implemented into Siemens Mobility's holistic user experience process. The design process is described from the perspective of an accessibility specialist who reviews and supports the design team based on best practices and lessons learned from past projects.

Keywords: Accessibility · User Experience · User Acceptance · Human Centered Design Process

1 Introduction

The Siemens Mobility inclusion agreement requires compliance with the international Web Content Accessibility Guidelines (WCAG) at level AA for all IT services that are newly introduced for internal use. Siemens Mobility's goal is to make the entire product range as accessible as possible, because the portfolio consists not only of IT services for office environments, rather than hardware and software solutions for entire rail systems [1].

Lack of awareness and knowledge among user experience professionals [2] about accessibility can lead to several misconceptions [3]. The most prominent misconception might be that accessibility only affects a small group of users and they would not use the product. Accessibility definitions by the World Wide Web Consortium (W3C) [4], Microsoft [5], the International Standardization Organization (ISO) [6] and the World Health Organization (WHO) [7] show that the entire user population, whether disabled or not, can benefit from accessible products and services. The reason for this is that there are situational limitations resulting from circumstances, environments, and conditions

© The Author(s), under exclusive license to Springer Nature Switzerland AG 2023
C. Stephanidis et al. (Eds.): HCII 2023, CCIS 1833, pp. 233–239, 2023.
https://doi.org/10.1007/978-3-031-35992-7_32

that can affect all users regardless of disability [8]. For example, a noisy environment can affect hearing, being sleepy can affect cognitive capacity [9], being in a situation where both hands are needed [10] or being in a vibrating environment [11] can affect physical performance and using a device in bright sunlight can affect a person's vision.

Most hardware and software solutions from Siemens Mobility are installed, operated, and maintained under such challenging conditions. Experience has shown that working in an uncomfortable working posture and/or extreme light and temperature conditions impairs the user experience.

2   Impact of Accessibility on User Acceptance

There is a relationship between accessibility and user experience [12], which is defined as the perceptions and responses of a user resulting from the actual and/or expected use of a product or service [13]. Usability is a feature that user experience while using a product. It defines the extent to which the product or service can be used by specific users in a specific context of use to achieve defined goals effectively, efficiently, and satisfactorily [14]. Accessibility is a prerequisite of usability [15], especially for users experiencing permanent or situational disability [16]. Technology Acceptance Model (TAM) [17] and the Unified Theory of Acceptance and Use of Technology (UTAUT) [18] are models that aim to better understand why users accept or reject a particular technology and how user acceptance can be improved. Both models include the constructs perceived usability and usefulness, which determine the user's behavioral intention to use a product or service. Therefore, it is fair to say that accessibility may have a significant impact on user acceptance.

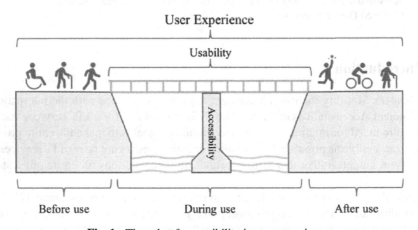

Fig. 1. The role of accessibility in user experience.

Figure 1 illustrates how Siemens Mobility perceives the importance of accessibility. An unstable bridge leaves a negative impression on people, and they will never use it again. Accessibility is the pillar that gives the bridge (usability) the necessary stability. People entering the bridge can cross it efficiently and effectively. A quick and safe crossing will leave a positive impression on people, and they are likely to use the bridge again.

This pillar should not convey the feeling that designing accessible products is costly and time-consuming, or that accessibility is something that can be added before release. Our experience is consistent with the literature, which has found that when accessibility is implemented from the beginning of the design process, there is no significant additional cost. However, if accessibility is considered late in the development process, it is almost impossible to retrofit a solution [19].

3   Accessibility at Siemens Mobility's UX Process

Accessibility related tasks must be applied as early as possible to identify and avoid potential accessibility issues. This requires constant communication with other roles in the design team and stakeholders throughout the design process. Accessibility is an incremental part of Siemens Mobility's holistic user experience process for software development, which can be divided into two phases: discovery and execution. The accessibility specialist applies best practices in each phase to ensure that the individual needs of all users are considered during the design process.

3.1   Discovery Phase

In the discovery phase (Fig. 2), the goal is to understand the user, their context of use, their workflows, and their goals to the defined focus and the corresponding overarching UX goal described by the ISO standard 9241-210 [13].

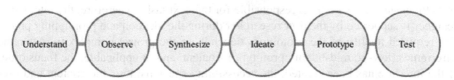

Fig. 2. Discovery phase of the holistic user experience design process

Typically, a stakeholder (project manager, product owner, motivator, client, or architect) approaches the design team with a specific project idea. At the first stakeholder meeting the accessibility specialist is interested in identifying potential user groups, the context of use, and the level of requested accessibility. Information about user groups, their specific needs and a detailed description of use context is collected during the observation phase (e.g., through interviews with potential users). If possible, it is recommended to identify and include disabled persons into the iterative design process to understand specific needs and identify creative and inclusive solutions [20]. Otherwise, experience has shown that stakeholders and users assume the highest degree of disability (e.g., blind, deaf, non-verbal or wheelchair users) and tend to say that there is no potential user group that has a disability. It is recommended to go the opposite way and ask if the user needs to have the full capacity in each category (visual, audible, physical, and cognitive) to use the product or service. This can be combined with the question exploring situational conditions that can affect the accessibility of the product. With this information and the features of the envisioned product or service the accessibility specialist can create the accessibility plan.

First, the accessibility specialist identifies the applicable WCAG requirements. Applicable requirements can be categorized into content, user experience, visual design, and integration. User researcher is responsible for the content, the interaction designer for the user experience, the user interface designer for the visual design and the developer for the integration. Since the accessibility specialist evaluates the work results of all team members, it is recommended that the person holding the role of accessibility specialist does not have any of the mentioned roles as a second role.

It is difficult to apply guidelines without having practical expertise in accessibility [21]. User experience professionals may have a knowledge gap about disabled bodies, a limited understanding of the needs of disabled people [22] and do not understand situational conditions that may affect the accessibility of a product or a service. The task of the accessibility specialist is to identify knowledge gaps related to accessibility and sensitize team members to design principles (e.g. inclusive design and universal design principles) and best practices with focus on accessibility. The awareness trainings allow the team to create inclusive and sustainable products and services [23] and should be carried out before each team member's task begins.

Based on the methods conducted during the observation phase, the user researcher creates the personas and user journeys by including the specific needs and pain points of users experiencing a permanent or situational limitation. The accessibility specialist checks whether all accessibility related information is included in the persona and user journeys and provides feedback.

It is recommended that the team member who completed the upstream tasks supports the team member who is responsible for the next tasks. Therefore, the interaction designer is supported by the user researcher during the ideation and prototyping phase. The required fidelity of the prototypes depends on the project complexity. After the wireframes (low- to mid-fidelity prototype), content, and, if applicable, the focus order of the interface has been created, the accessibility specialist tests the content and user experience for conformity with WCAG. The content includes topics such as the correct implementation of headings, instructions, captions and text equivalents for images or videos. The user experience focuses on easy-to-use navigation, ability for keyboard only usage, and whether users can notice and respond to error messages and other feedback from the system. This activity can be seen as an expert review to identify and fix accessibility related issues before the design is validated through user tests.

3.2 Execution Phase

The execution phase (Fig. 3) is about implementing the knowledge gained in the discovery phase with a good UX experience with the corresponding UI concepts and design.

The visual designer creates (high-fidelity prototypes) mockups based on the design language and guidelines agreed upon at the initial meeting with stakeholders. If the customer does not have a design language, the design language of Siemens is applied.

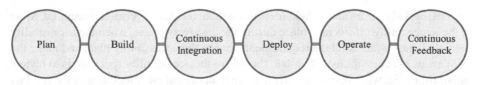

Fig. 3. Execution phase of the holistic user experience design process.

It is recommended to use established guidelines and apply the design principles as they evolve from time to time and are optimized based on the insights gained from the projects. This also includes optimizations related to accessibility. Experience has shown that the construct of user interface design must comply with the design guidelines, but there are always project-specific situations in which the visual designer must find a creative and, above all, usable solution. The visual designer is not alone in these phases and is accompanied by the interaction designer.

After mockups are created, the accessibility specialist can test the visual aspects of the user interface. The visual requirements verify the correct implementation for color and contrast of text, components, and graphics, and ensure that nobody is affected by the visual design decisions. It is beneficial for the visual designer to point out the cases where a deviation from the design guidelines is present so that the accessibility specialist can focus on these instances and see if there is a potential accessibility issue. There are various tools that identify accessibility issues related to visibility, contrast, focus, and alt text annotations, but it is recommended to manually check each case for conformance.

For projects that contain a significant amount of continuous text, a user experience writer is responsible for creating text that is clear, easy to read, and purposeful for users. Based on the information collected during the observation phase (e.g. educational background), a target readability score can be set for continuous text content. A readability score is the level of education someone needs to be able to read a text easily [24]. The accessibility specialist uses a tool to rate the text and suggests a different wording for the content to get a better score.

The European Accessibility Act [25] requires companies to ensure that newly introduced products and services covered by the law are accessible and usable with assistive technologies. Assistive technologies are essential to acquire and maintain skills for people with disabilities. It has been observed that assistive technologies lead to better accuracy and task completion [26]. Assistive technologies only work if the code meets certain requirements. Before integration, automatic tools, web extensions, and apps can be used. However, these tools do not yet replace manual compliance checking.

4 Conclusion

This paper described how accessibility is managed and implemented at Siemens Mobility. Misconceptions such as that accessibility only affects a small group of users, people with limited ability would not use the product, designing accessible products is costly and time-consuming, or that accessibility is something that can be added before release have been addressed. Accessibility related tasks are performed as early as possible to identify and avoid potential accessibility issues. A constant communication with other roles in the design team and stakeholders throughout the design process is required. Most of the accessibility efforts take place during the discovery phase, when the accessibility specialist must understand the requirements, create the accessibility plan, and make the team aware of accessibility. After that, the role of the accessibility specialist is to review and optimize the work output of other team members until the integration of the product or service begins.

References

1. Siemens Mobility GmbH. Our Siemens Mobility Portfolio. https://www.mobility.siemens.com/global/en/portfolio.html. Accessed 31 Jan 2023
2. Inal, Y., Rizvanoglu, K., Yesilada, Y.: Web accessibility in Turkey: awareness, understanding and practices of user experience professionals. In: Universal Access in the Information Society, vol. 18 (2019)
3. Krieger, S.: Accessibility Myths (2022). https://a11ymyths.com/. Accessed 27 Feb 2023
4. (WAI), W3C Web Accessibility Initiative, Introduction to Web Accessibility, 31 March 2022. https://www.w3.org/WAI/fundamentals/accessibility-intro/. Accessed 27 Feb 2023
5. Micosoft. Inclusive Design. 31 Jan 2023. https://www.microsoft.com/design/inclusive/
6. International Organization for Standardization. Ergonomics of human-system interaction – Part 171: Guidance on software accessibility (ISO 9241-171:2008) (2008)
7. Word Health Organization, Disability. https://www.who.int/health-topics/disability. Accessed 31 Jan 2023
8. Henry, S.L.: Just Ask: Integrating Accessibility Throughout Design (2007). lulu.com
9. Sethfors, H.: Statistics on disabilities – the one stat you need to know, Axesslab, 19 September 2017. https://axesslab.com/statistics-on-disabilities/. Accessed 16 Feb 2023
10. Burgstahler, S.: Distance Learning: Universal Design, Universal Access. AACE Rev. **10**(1) (2002)
11. Avsar, H., Fischer, J., Rodden, T.: Target size guidelines for interactive displays on the flight deck. In: IEEE/AIAA 34th Digital Avionics Systems Conference (DASC), Prague (2015)
12. Aizpura, A., Harper, S., Vigo, M.: Exploring the relationship between web accessibility and user experience. Int. J. Hum Comput Stud. **91**, 13–23 (2016)
13. International Organization for Standardization, Ergonomics of human system interaction – Part 210: Humancentred design for interactive systems (2020)
14. International Organization for Standardization, Ergonomics of human system interaction – Part 11: Usability: Definitions and concepts (ISO 924111:2018) (2018)
15. Pühretmair, F., Miesenberger, K.: Making sense of accessibility in IT design - usable accessibility vs. accessible. In: Proceedings of the 16th International Workshop on Database and Expert Systems Applications (DEXA 2005) (2005)
16. Wegge, K.P., Zimmermann, D.: Accessibility, usability, safety, ergonomics: concepts, models, and differences. In: International Conference on Universal Access in Human-Computer Interaction UAHCI 2007: Universal Access in Human Computer Interaction. Coping with Diversity (2007)
17. Davis, F.D.: Perceived usefulness, perceived ease of use, and user acceptance of information technology. MIS Q. **9**(1), 319–340 (1989)
18. Venkatesh, V., Morris, M.G., Davis, G.B., Davis, F.D.: User acceptance of information technology: toward a unified view. MIS Q. 425–478 (2003)
19. Petrie, H., Bevan, N.: The Universal Access Handbook. In: Stepanidis, C. (ed.) The Evaluation of Accessibility, Usability and User Experience. CRC Press (2009)

20. Narenthiran, O.P., Torero, J., Woodrow, M.: Inclusive design of workspaces: mixed methods approach to understanding users. Sustainability **14**(6) (2022)
21. Petrie, H., Hamilton, F., King, N., Pavan, P.: Remote usability evaluations with disabled people. In: CHI 2006: Proceedings of the SIGCHI Conference on Human Factors in Computing Systems (2006)
22. Oswal, S.K.: Breaking the exclusionary boundary between user experience and access: steps toward making UX inclusive of users with disabilities. In: SIGDOC 2019: Proceedings of the 37th ACM International Conference on the Design of Communication (2019)
23. Greco, A.: Social sustainability: from accessibility to inclusive design. EGE Revista de Expresión Gráfica en la Edificación (12), 18–27 (2020)
24. Kincald, P.J., Chissom, B.S., Rogers, R.L., Chissom, B.S.: Derivation of new readability formulas (automated readability index, fog count and Flesch reading ease formula) for navy enlisted personnel. Naval Technical Training Command Millington TN Research Branch (1975)
25. European Commission. European Accessibility Act: Q&A. https://ec.europa.eu/social/main.jsp?catId=1202. Accessed 5 Mar 2023
26. Sauer, A.L., Parks, A., Heyn, P.C.: Assistive technology effects on the employment outcomes for people with cognitive disabilities: a systematic review. Disabil. Rehabil. Assist. Technol. **5**(6), 377–391 (2010)

What You Need is What You Get: Adapting Word Prediction of Augmentative and Alternative Communication Aids to Youth Language

Cherifa Ben Khelil[1]([✉]), Frédéric Rayar[1], Jean-Yves Antoine[1], Lisa Hoiry[2], Mathieu Raynal[2], and Anaïs Halftermeyer[3]

[1] LIFAT, University of Tours, Tours, France
cherifa.bk@gmail.com
[2] IRIT, University of Toulouse, Toulouse, France
[3] LIFO, University of Orleans, Orleans, France

Abstract. This paper focuses on the development of prediction models for Augmentative and Alternative Communication (AAC) that are tailored specifically to child and young users. A new native-speaking corpus for child and adolescent languages is introduced, which allows the training of models that better fit the needs of this user category. The experiments conducted on real texts show that adapting the prediction models for children and young users leads to an improvement in keystroke savings, which in turn reduces the number of predicted words to be displayed. This opens up new possibilities for rethinking the virtual keyboard organization and interaction styles, with the aim of reducing cognitive load during text entry.

Keywords: Augmentative and Alternative Communication · word prediction · corpus building · user adaptation · Keystroke Saving Rate

1 Introduction

Augmentative and Alternative Communication (AAC) aims at supplementing or replacing speech and/or writing for people suffering from serious speech and motion impairments. It concerns a large diversity of physical and/or cognitive disabilities among which locked-in syndrome, cerebral palsy, amyotrophic lateral sclerosis and other neurodegenerative diseases. These disabilities are frequently accompanied by associated language disorders. Whatever the impairment, oral communication is impossible for these persons who also have serious difficulties in physically controlling their environment. In particular, most of them are not able to use the standard input devices of a computer or with strong difficulties. To answer such special needs, a typical AAC system consists of a virtual keyboard from which text is entered using a dedicated control device, and a speech synthesis. Although AAC systems restore or facilitate the communication abilities of their users, text entry remains slow and tiring. Two complementary approaches can be considered to speed up typing: fast key selection through optimized keyboards design, and keystroke saving through word prediction. Predicted words are usually displayed in a dedicated prediction list, allowing word completion and hence faster text entry. Additionally, word prediction can help in writing correct messages for people with additional language disabilities or without sufficient language competences (children, for instance). Prediction models rely on automatic machine learning techniques. They are trained on large corpora that are extracted from web or newspapers resources and are supposed to be representative of the communication language. Word prediction has proven to provide a sensible assistance during communication, even if its benefits in terms of input speed will depend strongly on the disability and the context of use [4]. The issue of the adaptation of word prediction to any kind of user remains however, largely open. Some AAC systems incorporate a user language model which is combined with a general one and allows the system's behaviour to adapt progressively to the user's input. It is important to note that if the user's language skills differ greatly from the general language model used for prediction, a considerable amount of text may be necessary for the adaptation to take effect.

In particular, standard AAC word predictions fail to adapt to child and adolescent language, mainly due to the lack of a large child corpus on which a prediction model can be trained. An effective adaptation of prediction has a double beneficial impact for the user:

1. Words that belong to the user's lexicon will be predicted more frequently.
2. Words that the user does not know will be removed from the prediction list, avoiding confusing predictions and limiting his cognitive load.

In this paper, we investigate the benefits of developing prediction models that are adapted to child and young users. At first, we introduce in Sect. 2 a new French-speaking corpus that is dedicated to child and adolescent languages which allows the training of specific prediction models that fit better the needs of child or young users. In Sect. 3, we outline the evaluation process used to assess the performance of our adapted models, while in Sect. 4 we discuss experimental results obtained from analyzing real-world texts. These results highlight the benefits of our models in terms of keystroke savings and how they can improve virtual keyboard organization and interaction styles.

2   Adaptation for Children and Adolescents Needs

The user adaptation of word prediction meets two complementary challenges:

1. *Age adaptation* - Prediction should adapt to the overall language fluency of the user. From a language learning perspective with young users, this adaptation may be achieved by creating general prediction models adapted to several language age groups.
2. *Personalization* - The prediction should also be adapted to the language preferences of each individual. For example, an adolescent who is interested in Formula 1 will appreciate a prediction promoting Formula 1 related words and

phrases such as "red flag" and "formation lap". This individual adaptation will be achieved through a dynamic user prediction model combined with the general one as well as better consideration of the current communication context by the prediction [6].

The adaptation can be limited to the system lexicon or to its whole language model. Lexicon adaptation can be manually handled by the user or speech therapists. However, the practical application of manual adaptation is progressively becoming more limiting. The automatic adaptation of the lexicon can be envisaged by considering the average frequency of occurrence of words in the general language. In a language learning perspective, this solution is not optimal, as the list of most frequent words changes with the age of the user. Additionally, lexicon adaptation can not allow a fine-tuning concerning styles and/or language registers. For these reasons, this paper focuses on adapting the language model of the prediction, and not just lexicon customization.

The development of age-based language models requires the use of adapted training corpora. Large child corpora that meet the needs of machine learning techniques are lacking for the French language. Taking these constraints into consideration, we decided to collect a corpus of texts specifically for children and adolescents to train the language model on language patterns and vocabulary that are most relevant to them. This can result in a more accurate and effective word prediction system for children and adolescents who use AAC.

2.1   Corpus and Language Model Building Process

1. **Text collection:** We begin by collecting a large number of relevant texts for children (6–11 years) and adolescents (12–17 years) using our scraping module. This includes news websites, Vikidia[1], books, and other copyright-free stories that are available online. The texts are varied in terms of content, style, and genre, to ensure that the corpus is representative of the language patterns and vocabulary used by children and adolescents. As can be seen in Table 1, there were a total of 58 237 files extracted (18 601 471 words).
2. **Text preprocessing** - Once the texts were collected, we pre-processed them, using natural language processing (NLP) techniques, to remove unwanted characters and words.

Table 1. Distribution of the collected texts according to source type.

Text source	Number of files	Number of words
Books and stories for Children	2 249	2 987 285
Children news sites	16 077	5 125 990
Adolescents news sites	20 422	976 777
Vikidia	17 240	7 403 234
Total	58 237	18 601 471

---

[1] Vikidia is a online encyclopedia adapted for children and adolescents.

3. **Text tokenization** - The next step was to split the text content into smaller units, namely words or multiword units, which are referred to as tokens. These latter are used to build our language models.

4. **Language model training** - The final step was to train age-based language models on the preprocessed and tokenized corpora. Our experiment was conducted on a stochastic N-gram prediction model, *Predict4all* (Subsect. 3.1). The fundamental premise of this approach is to use probabilistic analysis to determine the co-occurrence of words in a sequence of n tokens. This acquired knowledge is then applied to generate a ranking of likely following words for any sequence of n-1 tokens. This procedure can be followed to any machine learning techniques. We produced one model for adolescents *Adolescents_all* and three models for children *Children_stories*, *Children_info* and *Children_all*. *Adolescents_all* was trained with texts extracted from news sites for adolescents and Vikidia, resulting in a 4-gram model based on a vocabulary of 67 190 unique words. As for the models for children, they were trained as follows: *Children_stories* with texts collected from books and stories for children, *Children_info* with texts collected from news sites for children and *Children_all* with with all the texts collected for Children. These models' vocabulary sizes are 45 249, 42 982 and 67 075 distinct words.

3   Experimental Evaluation

3.1   PREDICT4ALL

The experiments reported in this paper were conducted on the *Predict4All* prediction module. *Predict4All* is an open-source library[2] that can be integrated into any AAC system (and actually any other application). In particular, the *LifeCompanion*[3] AAC system developped in the *AAC4All*[4] project of the French ANR research agency integrates the *Predict4All* prediction. As explained before, *Predict4All* is based on a standard 4-gram prediction model. It incorporates a general prediction language model combined with a dynamic user model trained on-the-fly on the messages entered by the user[5]. The general prediction model has been trained on more than 20 millions words from Wikipedia and subtitles (of films and series) corpus. It has a vocabulary of 111 880 unique words. *Predict4All* offers also the possibility of a semantic adaptation of the prediction [7] according to the current of communication. It was co-designed with speech therapists and occupational therapists and proposes an on-the-fly correction module that is fully integrated with the prediction. This correction module is particularly dedicated to young users and/or users with language disorders.

As our experiments focused specifically on the benefits of age-based prediction models, they were conducted with a minimal setting of *Predict4All*, e.g. with no user dynamic model, nor semantic adaptation and nor correction.

---

[2] https://github.com/mthebaud/predict4all.
[3] https://lifecompanionaac.org/.
[4] https://www.aac4all.org/en/home/.
[5] This dynamic adaptation must be explicitly authorized by the user.

3.2   Evaluation Metric

The Keystroke Saving Rate (KSR) is a performance indicator used to assess the effectiveness of different text input methods, including those that use word prediction and/or auto-completion. It is usually measured by comparing the amount of keystrokes needed to accomplish a given task with and without the use of an assistive tool. The higher the keystroke saving rate, the more effective the method is considered. KSR is especially useful when it comes to evaluating text input tools for people who have trouble using a standard keyboard, but it is important to note that this metric does not take into account other factors such as typing speed, accuracy, user satisfaction, etc. To compute the KSR score, we calculate the ratio of keystrokes that were accurately predicted to those that were not predicted, based on the length of the list of suggested words. This formula is typically represented as follows:

$$\text{KSR} = (1 - \frac{\text{keystrokes with prediction}}{\text{keystrokes without prediction}}) \times 100 \tag{1}$$

When using the KSR metric to evaluate the effectiveness of word prediction in AAC software for people with disabilities, it is important to distinguish between theoretical KSR and real KSR. Theoretical KSR represents the highest achievable score if users were to consistently choose words from the predicted list whenever a correct prediction is made. In contrast, real KSR reflects the actual performance, which includes any inaccuracies or errors that may be caused by the user while entering text. In this paper, we calculated the theoretical KSR as a way of assessing the performance potential in using our models.

3.3   Evaluation Procedure

We carried out an evaluation of our child- and adolescent-dedicated models for word prediction with the goal of assessing their performance and comparing them to the general prediction language model. To achieve this, we used a diverse range of test corpora that are catered to different age groups. Specifically, the test corpora included nine sets of texts, with the first three intended for adults (texts from online journal articles, lifestyle blog posts, and website threads), one for adolescents (texts from online newspaper articles specifically intended for adolescents), and the last five for children (a collection of children's stories and fables, as well as essays written by children). We recorded KSR scores for these nine test corpora, with predicted word list lengths (N) ranging from 1 to 5. By analyzing the KSR scores at different predicted word list lengths, we can evaluate the impact of the prediction strategy on performance and determine the most effective approach for different age groups and types of text. This information can guide decisions about the design of virtual keyboards and improve the user experience for young users.

4 Results and Discussion

4.1 Results

Table 2 summarizes the recorded KSR scores for the nine test corpora. The scores are organized according to the length of the predicted word list (N). The results indicate that the general model offers the highest KSR scores for the first four

Table 2. Performance evaluation of our child- and teenager-friendly models and the general one on various test corpora: KSR analysis with varying prediction list lengths.

Test Corpus	Models	Word prediction list length				
		N = 1	N = 2	N = 3	N = 4	N = 5
1- Newswire from the site "Le monde"	Children_stories	29.128%	37.265%	41.235%	44.009%	45.763%
	Children_info	33.658%	42.05%	46.116%	48.84%	50.42%
	Children_all	34.945%	43.241%	47.331%	49.913%	51.717%
	Adolescents_all	35.031%	43.533%	47.675%	50.334%	51.955%
	General model	**38.329%**	**46.846%**	**51.015%**	**53.524%**	**54.968%**
2- Text from a lifestyle blog post	Children_stories	35.338%	43.686%	48.154%	51.059%	52.692%
	Children_info	37.973%	45.713%	50.288%	52.877%	54.345%
	Children_all	39.301%	47.240%	51.601%	54.496%	56.120%
	Adolescents_all	39.782%	47.919%	51.991%	54.447%	56.074%
	General model	**40.870%**	**49.308%**	**53.411%**	**56.036%**	**57.483%**
3- Excerpt from thread on reddit	Children_stories	31.307%	38.872%	42.909%	45.741%	47.350%
	Children_info	34.932%	43.325%	47.608%	49.926%	51.732%
	Children_all	36.293%	44.849%	48.983%	51.418%	52.853%
	Adolescents_all	36.068%	44.982%	49.206%	51.726%	53.249%
	General model	**39.482%**	**47.659%**	**51.864%**	**54.195%**	**55.926%**
4- Excerpt from teenager's news sites	Children_stories	33.046%	41.269%	45.261%	47.955%	49.725%
	Children_info	35.544%	43.553%	47.721%	50.219%	51.788%
	Children_all	37.477%	45.700%	49.610%	52.132%	53.757%
	Adolescents_all	37.507%	45.586%	49.669%	52.081%	53.669%
	General model	**38.922%**	**47.210%**	**51.285%**	**53.697%**	**55.253%**
5- Excerpt from the children's story: "Sophie's Misfortunes"	Children_stories	38.301%	46.791%	**51.029%**	**53.662%**	**55.546%**
	Children_info	34.288%	42.442%	46.591%	49.211%	51.099%
	Children_all	**38.577%**	**46.893%**	50.985%	53.601%	55.426%
	Adolescents_all	34.764%	43.008%	47.296%	50.022%	51.881%
	General model	36.827%	45.175%	49.483%	52.069%	53.974%
6- Excerpt from The Fables of La Fontaine	Children_stories	33.097%	41.021%	45.36%	48.262%	50.134%
	Children_info	28.651%	37.001%	41.554%	44.575%	46.509%
	Children_all	**34.925%**	**43.128%**	**47.128%**	**49.797%**	**51.567%**
	Adolescents_all	29.745%	38.087%	42.646%	45.613%	47.532%
	General model	31.781%	40.305%	44.814%	47.800%	49.563%
7- Excerpt from children's books and stories	Children_stories	37.770%	46.018%	50.210%	52.762%	54.402%
	Children_info	32.49%	40.904%	45.056%	47.577%	49.215%
	Children_all	**38.311%**	**46.630%**	**50.746%**	**53.182%**	**54.851%**
	Adolescents_all	33.931%	42.199%	46.523%	48.954%	50.661%
	General model	36.161%	44.624%	49.062%	51.491%	53.249%
8- Collection of essays written by children (6–10 years)	Children_stories	40.859%	50,00 %	54.365%	57.167%	58.885%
	Children_info	37.535%	46.65%	51.054%	53.692%	55.382%
	Children_all	**41.235%**	49.895%	54.285%	56.735%	58.687%
	Adolescents_all	38.031%	46.186%	50.192%	52.205%	55.095%
	General model	40.409%	48.595%	53.365%	55.359%	57.285%
9- A story written by a 11 year old child	Children_stories	35.885%	44.598%	48.693%	**51.436%**	**53.227%**
	Children_info	31.965%	39.917%	43.928%	46.927%	48.607%
	Children_all	**36.159%**	**44.807%**	**48.75%**	51.393%	53.129%
	Adolescents_all	33.25%	41.254%	45.678%	48.244%	50.239%
	General model	35.086%	43.799%	47.957%	50.621%	52.33%

corpora, which are intended for adults and adolescents. These scores, obtained from the general model and the adolescent model, differ by approximately 3%, while the difference between the scores obtained from the general model and the children's models can be as high as 8%. On the other hand, when it comes to the test corpora intended for children, the general model typically yields slightly lower scores than the dedicated children's models. Specifically, the results show that the *Children_stories* and *Children_all* models offer the best scores for the last five test corpora. The difference between these models and the general model ranges from 1% to 3%.

4.2 Discussion

The experiments conducted on real texts show the potential of prediction models adapted for young users and that a general model trained on more than 20 millions words from a variety of texts may not be the best fit for specific audience groups. These findings offer a promising approach to facilitate the adaptation of AAC systems for young users. Instead of relying on a general model with a large vocabulary and combining it with a dynamic user model, it is now possible to start with a more specific general model that takes into account the user's age, and then merge it with the user's dynamic model. This approach may offer greater flexibility as it enables the AAC system to adapt more quickly and accurately to the user's unique vocabulary and language usage patterns. As the specific general model has a more constrained vocabulary, the combination with the dynamic user model is expected to yield better results, allowing for a more rapid and effective adaptation to the user's language use patterns. Additionally, the reduction in vocabulary size can have a positive impact on the memory requirements of prediction models, making them more practical to deploy on low-resource devices, such as mobile phones or tablets.

Another important finding from this study is that the adaptation of these models improves keystroke saving rates, which can reduce the number of predicted words displayed on the virtual keyboard. This finding opens up new possibilities for the organization of virtual keyboards. Traditionally, recommendations for the number of words in the prediction list are between 5 and 7 words [1–3]. However, recent research [5] has shown that users of pointing keyboards, a type of virtual keyboard that relies on eye gaze or other pointing methods for text entry, only look at the top of the prediction list and tend to choose the predicted word when it appears in the first or second position. Based on the observed improvements, we can consider reducing the size of this list to 3 words. This would make the interface lighter and thus reduce the cognitive load during the text input. There is also another type of virtual keyboard, scanning keyboards. It uses a scanning method to cycle through the keyboard keys, allowing users to select letters or other input options at the desired row and/or column. It is reasonable to expect that reducing the number of predicted words displayed would also improve the efficiency and speed of this navigation method. Limiting the number of displayed options can lead to an increase in words per minute (WPM) for users, as it reduces the scanning step.

5   Conclusion

In this paper, we investigated the effectiveness of customizing word prediction models for youth. Four models were trained on different types of text intended for children and adolescents. Our results suggest that the accuracy of these models can vary significantly depending on the intended audience and the specific text they are trained on. Especially, for texts intended for children or written by children, the specialized children's models produced better results. These findings highlight the importance of developing specialized models for specific audience groups, as this can improve the accuracy of word prediction systems. Our first experiment primarily focused on written texts and it remains to be seen whether the findings can be extended to spoken communication scenarios. To address this, other ongoing work is in progress to test the models on transcripts of discussions. Furthermore, a clinical study will be planned to further investigate the potential of these models to improve communication with an AAC system for the young users in real-life situations.

Acknowledgments. This research was funded by the French National Research Agency as part of the AAC4ALL project (ANR-21-CE19-0051).

References

1. Heinisch, B., Hecht, J.: Predictive word processors: a comparison of six programs. Tam News **8**, 4–9 (1993)
2. Norman, D.A., Fisher, D.: Why alphabetic keyboards are not easy to use: keyboard layout doesn't much matter. Human Factor **24**, 509–519 (1982)
3. Swiffin, A., Arnott, J., Pickering, J., Newell, A.: Adaptive and predictive techniques in communication prosthesis. Augmentative Alt. Commun. **3**, 181–191 (1987)
4. Pouplin, S., et al.: The effect of word prediction settings on text input speed in persons with cervical spinal cord injury: a prospective study. Disabil. Rehabil. **39**(12), 1215–1220 (2017)
5. Raynal, M., Badr, G.: Study of user behavior when using a list of predicted words. In: Computers Helping People with Special Needs: 18th International Conference, ICCHP-AAATE 2022, Lecco, Italy, 11–15 July 2022, pp. 331–337 (2022)
6. Wandmacher, T., Antoine, J.-Y., Poirier, F.: SIBYLLE: a system for alternative communication adapting to the context and its user. In: Actes ACM Conference on Assistive Technologies, ASSETS 2007, Phoenix, Arizona, pp. 203–210 (2007)
7. Wandmacher, T., Ovchinnikova, E., Alexandrov, F.: Does latent semantic analysis reflect human associations? In: 20th European Summer School in Logic, Language and Information, 4–15 August 2008, Hamburg, Germany, pp. 63–70 (2008)

Training Interface for Multimodal Data Analysis: A First Approach to Measuring Perception

Natasha Maria Monserrat Bertaina Lucero[1,2] , Johanna Casado[1,2](✉) ,
and Beatriz García[1,3]

[1] Instituto en Tecnologías de Detección y Astropartículas (CNEA, CONICET,
UNSAM), Mendoza, Argentina
`johi.ceh@gmail.com`
[2] Instituto de Bioingeniería, Facultad de Ingeniería, Universidad de Mendoza,
Mendoza, Argentina
[3] Universidad Tecnológica Nacional, Mendoza, Argentina

Abstract. During the last years different tools devoted to the sonification of astronomical data were proposed. With the aim to enhance accessibility and remove systematic barriers faced by people with disabilities, sonoUno was developed as a user centred sonification software (UCD) for its desktop and web versions [1]. After different user tests the need to understand more about sound perception came out, at hand of the need of training [2]. Perception is a process that requires a great deal of mental processing that provides the means by which one's concept of the environment is created and helps people to learn and interact with it. The compilation of previous studies throughout history has led to the conclusion that auditory performance improves when it is combined with visual stimuli and vice-versa. Taking into account the above considerations, the development of a training platform that allows to run perception tests begins. The requirements for this platform were: (1) accessibility via web; (2) co-creation with collaborators in different parts of the world; and (3) simple and effective storage of results. In this contribution, the first approach, a graphic user interface that allows users to read information about it and access to the training from the web browser, will be presented. Beyond the USD principles, the proposed framework is being tested with screen readers during each step of its development.

Keywords: Sonification training · Multimodal display · User centred design

1 Introduction

The definition of perception varies according to the branch of psychology that is studied. Despite this, all of them share a general idea where perception is

Consejo Nacional de Investigaciones Científicas y Técnicas (CONICET), Buenos Aires, AR, for the grants to the two students authors of this contribution.

considered as a process that is built with all the external stimuli captured by our senses, carrying behind a complex mental processing in order to create a concept of our environment, in order to allow the human being to function in it.

Since perception depends on our senses, over the years it has been studied how our brain processes the stimuli that reach it from the different sensory pathways. Being the most studied, the visual pathway, in combination with some of the remaining senses, corroborating that the bulk of research focuses on how vision works better when it is stimulated in conjunction with hearing. Despite this, a small percentage of articles can be found where the order is reversed, studying how auditory performance improves when accompanied by a visual stimulus [3]. Furthermore, within this small group, a few studies can be found in which the improvement in frequency discrimination is exposed when a person undergoes training from 4 to 8 h, achieving an ability similar to a professional musician [4].

From what has been observed to date, the topic of auditory training has not been studied in depth, and even less in training about the detection of astrophysical signals. That's, in addition to the detected need of training during the user exchanges in the sonoUno project (Casado et al., 2021), mark the starting point of this contribution. SonoUno starts as a user centred sonification software devoted to translate astrophysical data sets into sound. During the years and following the user recommendations, sonoUno grows. At the date, the sonoUno project count with a desktop version, a web version with almost the same functionalities (web deployment present limitations with mathematical operations and size of files to process) and an ongoing programming of a server deployment under the label 'Sonification as a service' (Chanial, P. et al. [5]).

About training in sonification, during 2022 some activities was carried out to test some of the training sessions generated with astrophysical data. In [6], authors describe a training test done with the sonification of simple mathematical functions and a galaxy spectrum downloaded from SLOAN database. During the training test, the participants could recognize easily the simple mathematical function. About the galaxy spectrum, some absorption and emission lines were presented: first only the sonification and then in multimodal display (visual and sound). From the data collected, arise that multimodal display enhance patter recognition, in comparison with only sonification.

In July 2022, a training course was carried out in Greece [7], during two days, two sessions was carried out were different data sonification was presented to the participants in multimodal display. The data in this case were Glitches [8] detected by the Virgo facility, particles from the LHC [9] at CERN and Muongraphy [10] from the IP2I. The participants remarked the benefits of training and the data collected highlight that the second session was better that the first, even when the data displayed present more difficulty.

People involved in the training activities and some difficulties found in the installation process of the training software, points out the need of a better tool to carry out the task. Taking into account the experience of the sonoUno development team and the user recommendations the requirements for the starting point of the training platform were: (1) accessibility via web; (2) co-creation with collaborators in different parts of the world; and (3) simple and effective storage of results. In this contribution the first approach for a sonification training platform was presented, with a graphic user interface centred on the user.

2   Methodology

PsychoPy [11] is a software designed for the creation of experiments in behavioral sciences (such as psychology, neuroscience, linguistics, among others) that allows precise and synchronized spatial control of different stimuli. This program provides two types of interface with different functionality, allowing the user to choose between designing their experiments graphically or programming them in Python language. PsychoPy is available for any operating system, this is not a limitation as many other software have. Finally, it has a community, which shares its experiments online, with the possibility of downloading the code in order to modify it, being able to adapt the experiment to new needs.

Recently, the software has been used to generate stimuli that are used as support in the neurorehabilitation of patients in rural areas [12]. It should be noted that there is no evidence that the software has been used for the design of training in the detection of signals through more than one sense, in the same way it is considered to be an adequate tool.

Particularly, throughout the execution of the training sessions, the difficulty of installing this software on some computers was encountered. One of the alternatives was to use the web service created by Psychopy (Pavlovia) to run the training curse online. Given the early need to be able to carry out the training within the framework of an international project (REINFORCE project, GA 872859, with the support of EC Research Innovation Action under the H2020 SwafS-2019-1 program, [13]), is that, despite being a paid resource, it was decided to use it.

However, for a project (like sonoUno) that seeks to develop long-term training, this solution is not recommended, mainly due to the cost and the dependence to an external platform. That's why the development of a web page devoted to the training materials began, to overcome the difficulties generated by resources not open to public use. This development was also part of a Final Degree Project to obtain the Bioengineering degree, at the University of Mendoza, Argentina [14].

3   Results

REACT library was used for the web design, which allows to integrate all the necessary languages for the front-end. Three different pages were programmed, which differ in content but maintain the general design of the website. The first one, called 'Home' (see Fig. 1), serves as an introduction to the project, welcoming and briefly explaining the origin of it. This display also offers a brief explanation on multimodal training. The second page, called 'Manual', is intended to show users how to perform the online workouts, to do so, a small instruction

Fig. 1. Homepage of the training web site, named 'HOME'. The image language is Spanish, but English will be available for release.

manual will be displayed, with descriptions and images. Finally, the third page lists all the training sessions available to be done on the web.

The training course were initially going to be done with the Psychopy tool, which allows to convert code written in python to javascript. The Psychojs documentation itself stated that in order to execute them in a web service the next files should be stored on the server: the psychojs library, the training code, and an index.html file (which one is created at the time of making the aforementioned language conversion). The mentioned action was programmed to be done when programming the back-end.

Once the front-end layout was finished, following the recommendations in the official documentation of the Psychojs library, the cited files started to be included on the server. Both the training file and index.html could be added, however the required library (psychojs) could not be found. In a subsequent search, the same PsychoPy developers expressed in a forum that after the availability of their online service Pavlovia, said 'psychojs' library is no longer available. For this reason, the training sessions prepared with the Psychopy tool could not be uploaded to the website designed in the way initially proposed.

Despite this, the production of a functional website makes it possible to develop and integrate own trainings, programmed from the beginning in javascript or Python. The described website is hosted on Heroku, it is not yet available to the public because the training sessions are under development. Their implementation on the website is programmed once a stable version is achieved.

4   Conclusions

Based on the results, it is highlighted that most of the development of the website has been achieved. In addition, from previous works described earlier the team acquire experience in the development of training sessions [6,7]. The complication found is not unexpected in the development of a research work on topics with little background and where, what is proposed is obviously new. It should be seen as an opportunity for future work that can be addressed in a longer period of time.

As for the training sessions developed with Psychopy described at the beginning [6,7], it was possible to understand how this tool works and get the most out of its resources, designing training sessions that meet the stated objectives. It should be noted that limitations were also found in said software, such as the impossibility of adding an auditory response in the feedback to the participant. For this reason, it is proposed to become independent of this resource in future updates of this research and proposal, developing an alternative that meets everything requested by users.

Despite the limitations found, it can be concluded that the training and the development of the web served as a precedent for already planned projects, opening a new line of development and research, being able to focus more on the investigation of how perception could be affected by the use of certain tones or melodies in the sonification of astronomical data. This investigation is proposed in the framework of the doctoral thesis, that will be carried out by the first author.

Finally, it is important to highlight that users with functional diversity have been taken into account since the beginning of this development. Following the guidelines of the sonoUno work team, the different developments obtained have taken into account the multimodal deployment of information. Achieving equity related to tools and information access should always be a priority, each person should find an equitable environment, in terms of work, education and recreation.

References

1. De La Vega, G., Dominguez, L.-M.-E., Casado, J., García, B.: SonoUno web: an innovative user centred web interface. In: Stephanidis, C., Antona, M., Ntoa, S., Salvendy, G. (eds.) HCI International 2022 – Late Breaking Posters - 24th International Conference on Human-Computer Interaction, HCII 2022, Proceedings, Part I. CCIS, vol. 1654, pp. 628–633. Springer, Cham (2022). https://doi.org/10.1007/978-3-031-19679-9_79

2. Casado, J., García, B., Gandhi, P., Díaz Merced, W.: A new approach to sonification of astrophysical data: the user centred design of SonoUno. Am. J. Astron. Astrophys. **9**(4), 1–10 (2021). Science Pub. Co
3. Opoku-Baah, C., Schoenhaut, A.M., Vassall, S.G., Tovar, D.A., Ramachandran, R., Wallace, M.T.: Visual influences on auditory behavioral, neural, and perceptual processes: a Review. J. Assoc. Res. Otolaryngol. **22**(4), 365–386 (2021). https://doi.org/10.1007/s10162-021-00789-0
4. Oxenham, A.J.: How we hear: the perception and neural coding of sound. Annu. Rev. Psychol. **69**(1), 27–50 (2018). https://doi.org/10.1146/annurev-psych-122216-011635
5. Zenodo Repository: sonoUnoTeam/sonoUno-server: v0.4.2. https://zenodo.org/record/7717567#.ZBHl6NLMJkg. Accessed 15 Mar 2023
6. Bertaina Lucero, N., Casado, J., García, B., Jaren, G.: The use of sonification in data analysis: a Psychopy training test. In: XXIII Congreso Argentino de Bioingeniería - XII Jornadas de Ingeniería Clínica, Proceedings Series de IFBME, Ed Springer, Universidad Nacional de San Juan, Argentina (2022). (in press)
7. Zenodo Repository: sonoUno Training Course, July 2022. https://zenodo.org/record/7717030#.ZBCN3tLMJkg. Accessed 14 Mar 2023
8. Zooniverse: GWitchHunters Project. https://www.zooniverse.org/projects/reinforce/gwitchhunters. Accessed 15 Mar 2023
9. Zooniverse: New Particle Search at CERN Project. https://www.zooniverse.org/projects/reinforce/new-particle-search-at-cern. Accessed 15 Mar 2023
10. Zooniverse: Cosmic Muon Images Project. https://www.zooniverse.org/projects/reinforce/cosmic-muon-images. Accessed 15 Mar 2023
11. Peirce, J., et al.: PsychoPy2: experiments in behavior made easy. Behav. Res. Methods **51**(1), 195–203 (2019). https://doi.org/10.3758/s13428-018-01193-y
12. del Angel Arrieta, F., et al.: Characterization of a Raspberry Pi as the core for a low-cost multimodal EEG-fNIRS platform. In: 43rd Annual International Conference of the IEEE Engineering in Medicine and Biology Society (EMBC), pp. 1288–1291. IEEE (2021)
13. REINFORCE Homepage. https://www.reinforceeu.eu. Accessed 15 Mar 2023
14. Bertaina Lucero, N.: Desarrollo de entrenamientos para el análisis multisensorial de datos. Degree thesis. University of Mendoza, Engineering Faculty, Mendoza, Argentina (2023)

HCI in Healthcare: Computer-Based Cognitive Rehabilitation for Individuals with Mild Traumatic Brain Injury

Liliana Oliveira da Silva[1,2]([⊠]) and Sergio Cleger-Tamayo[1,2]

[1] Escola Superior de Tecnologia – Universidade do Estado do Amazonas, Av. Darcy Vargas 1200, Manaus, Amazonas, Brazil
lods.eng@uea.edu.br
[2] Sidia Instituto de Ciência e Tecnologia, Av. Darcy Vargas 654, Manaus, Amazonas, Brazil
{liliana.silva,sergio.tamayo}@sidia.com

Abstract. This research aims to provide a tool to support an individual in the early days following a traumatic brain injury (TBI). The end user is the collective diagnosed with mild TBI. The application has two main purposes. The first is to provide useful information to the patient, who probably does not know the severity of this type of injury, generally assessed taking into account the Glasgow Coma Scale (GCS). The second main purpose is to give the patient the first step with some cognitive rehabilitation, providing a virtual space where they can put into practice their relearning process by themselves or supervised by a specialist. The research explores how the human-computer interaction principles can lead to the design and development of an effective user-flow, that can be applied to a number of virtual environments in order to bring a good place for a patient going through a rehabilitation process.

Keywords: Human computer interaction · Healthcare application · Cognitive rehabilitation

1 Introduction

Traumatic brain injuries (TBIs) can affect anyone, regardless of age, gender, or background. However, among the population that may be at a higher risk of sustaining a TBI or experiencing more severe effects are the young adults, due to their participation in sports and other physical activities. One of the most frequent sequeleas following a TBI are cognitive impairments. The goal of this research is provide a tool to support an individual in the early days following a traumatic brain injury. Within the application, the individual will have access to useful information, that is no widely know to everyone, and alongside that it will also give the patient the first step with some cognitive rehabilitation. A virtual space where they can put into practice their relearning process by themselves or supervised by a specialist will be provided. The human-computer interaction (HCI) principles will be used here to guide the application design and

C. Stephanidis et al. (Eds.): HCII 2023, CCIS 1833, pp. 254–261, 2023.
https://doi.org/10.1007/978-3-031-35992-7_35

development, as key points like design, usability, accessibility and user experience determine the potential effectiveness of the cognitive training method. A user flow, prototyped for rehabilitation purpose and that can be used in other types of virtual environment, will be described. The rest of the paper is organized as follows: Related work on computer based cognitive rehabilitation is reviewed in Sect. 2. Section 3 introduces the HCI principles and how this precepts are applicable in the design and development of an application in the healthcare field. Section 4 brings some light about computer based cognitive rehabilitation and the techniques that can be addressed to handle cognitive impairments and finally on Sect. 5 the design methodology and development stages of the software are described. The conclusions and directions for future work are outlined in Sect. 6.

2   Motivation and Related Work

Traumatic brain injury is considered the major cause of death and disability worldwide, especially among young adults. In Brazil, it is estimated that more than one million people live with neurological sequelae resulting from TBI [13]. Disabilities resulting from TBI can be divided into three categories: physical, cognitive and emotional/behavioral. Physical impairments are the most apparent, but in the longer term, problems with cognition, personality, and behavior are more important for the quality of life of the affected person [2,12].

After a head injury, most individuals either do not recognize their cognitive problems or have no understanding of what they might be [14]. In general, alterations in attention, memory and executive function are the most commonly found after TBI, with memory alteration being the most common complaint [9]. Such cognitive impairments can be addressed with cognitive rehabilitation.

Computer-based cognitive rehabilitation for people with cognitive impairment has been the focus of various studies on various fields, as the subject can be seen from various perspectives. Early studies already were concerned with the effectiveness of this technique in the medical field [3]. [15] lists various studies regarding the use of cognitive rehabilitation for the specific population targeted in this research. All studies used computer-based cognitive rehabilitation software programs. This was also the study focus of [8,11].

Looking from the computational side, [6] gave a substancial landscape of the scenario, looking for design methodologies used during the development of the computer-based training programs. From the results we can see most researches did take an UCD approach for development.

We must bring COGWEB®, as this is the closest we've seen from what we're trying to achieve within this study, looking from the computational side. In these we have intensive cognitive training, carried out in a controlled group, with exercises already tested in a real context, a clinic, although some patients were not familiar with a virtual environment [5].

Regarding the HCI principles use we can cite [1] and [10]. The first one with focus on mapping the HCI principles in order to bring a quality-in-use model to minimize human error and user frustation, as well as make healthcare professionals tasks more pleasant and effective. The second dealing with Alzheimer's patients and taking the HCI approach during design and development.

The research reported in this paper differs from the related work, as the objective is to build the cognitive training system from the user's, who may still be living with hidden disabilities, perspective. The user will acknowledge the reason why he is performing such cognitive training, with useful information about the rehabilitation process. A generic user flow for the cognitive rehabiliation task, to be used in other virtual environments will also be described. A healthcare professional assistance and watch will be recommended, but it will not be a requirement.

3   Computer Based Cognitive Rehabilitation

Computer-based cognitive rehabilitation is a type of cognitive training that uses computer programs to improve cognitive abilities in individuals with cognitive impairments [4]. It typically involves exercises and activities that target specific cognitive functions, such as attention, memory, and problem-solving.

Research has shown that computer-based cognitive rehabilitation can be effective in improving cognitive function in individuals with cognitive impairments. It is efficient for mild-to-severe injuries and beneficial at any time post-injury [16]. However, it is important to note that cognitive rehabilitation is just one aspect of a comprehensive treatment plan for individuals with cognitive impairments, and should be used in conjunction with other therapies and interventions.

In the next section we present how the HCI principles can help to overcome the challenge in designing a space for cognitive rehabilitation. Construct a space, where the patient can perform those cognitive functions, on a conscious and intentional basis, something that once occurred without the need for conscious intent. This is the most fundamental, underlying principal underlying the effects of traumatic brain injury [14].

4   HCI Principles

Human-computer interaction principles refer to a set of guidelines and best practices that help designers create interfaces and interactions that are easy to use, efficient, and enjoyable for users. The user, who in this context is not common, has to complete a set of tasks, following a cognitive training method, using technology. The healthcare technology has the potential to improve the patient outcome, reduce errors, and enhance the efficiency of the healthcare delivery. The way HCI principles are taken during a healthcare application design and development step will be decisive for its potential and effectiveness. [7] classifies these rules into three different types: principles, standards and guidelines. Here we establish a proper link between the HCI principles, precepts by [7], and wellbeing.

Visibility: the application should provide clear and concise information to the patients and healthcare providers.

Feedback: clear and useful feedback to the patient or healthcare provider must be provided when actions are taken.

Consistency: the application should be consistent in its design and functionality. This can help healthcare providers learn how to use the technology more quickly and reduce the risk of errors.

Learnability: it should be easy to learn and use. This is particularly important for patients who may be using the technology without prior training.

Efficiency: healthcare technology should be designed to save time and increase efficiency.

Error Prevention and Recovery: healthcare technology should be designed to prevent errors and provide ways to recover from mistakes.

Accessibility: healthcare technology should be accessible to all patients, including those with disabilities. This may involve designing interfaces that are compatible with screen readers or other assistive technology.

Aesthetics: healthcare technology should be designed to be visually appealing and engaging. This can help patients feel more comfortable and engaged in their healthcare.

These human-computer interaction principles can guide the build application process, regardless of the technology used. This last one ranging from the general desktop computer to a large-scale computer system, a process control system or an embedded system [7].

5 Design and Development

Once the theoretical and practical foundation were established by the HCI principals, we could lie on the on User-Centered Design (UCD) design philosophy as this one applies this understanding to the design process, ensuring that patient needs and preferences were taken into account throughout the design cycle.

To accomplish the design life cycle design thinking was chosen. A problem-solving approach, iterative and based on a user-centered design. Counting on the five stages of design thinking: empathize, define, ideate, prototype and test, here we describe the first four and its iterations needed to accomplish the computer-based cognitive training model proposed.

5.1 Empathize, Define and Ideate

The first step into this, once the patient and his needs were know, was establish a visual representation of the steps a patient takes to complete a specific exercise on the application, a user-flow. The following can help designers understand the user's journey through the product and identify areas where the user experience can be improved. This is presented in Fig. 1.

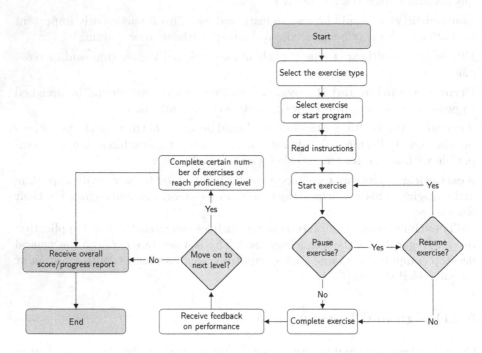

Fig. 1. User-flow for the cognitive exercise task

The user-flow provided takes into account some of the mentioned HCI principles, including:

- **User control and freedom** The pause/break option in the user flow provides users with control and freedom over their exercise routine, allowing them to take a break whenever they need to without losing progress.
- **Feedback** The feedback on performance provides users with clear information about how they are doing in the exercises and what they can do to improve.
- **Consistency** The standardized interface (e.g., instructions, start, feedback, progress report, etc.) helps users navigate the exercise program more easily and efficiently.
- **Error prevention and recovery** The pause/break option also helps prevent errors and provides users with a way to recover from mistakes or interruptions.

And then, the next task was gather which exercises would be initially available in the application. As the cognitive impairments comprehends a vary large field of possibilities, a cognitive domain was chosen for the exercise filtering task. That was the memory, as this is the most common complaint alteration after a brain injury [9]. There are plenty of cognitive exercises available at magazines, papers and books. But not all of them are targeted and could be performed by the special mild TBI patients, early after the injury. With this, the research was narrowed to exercises aimed to this group. Although its availability, these exercises are gathered by copyright, in general. So initially, for this research, five known exercises, that could be performed for this group were taken. They were generic enough, so could be adapted to a virtual space and explored in different levels, without losing its initial purpose. These are: Remember a picture, Kims's game, Word list, Remembering a number and Memorize tables.

Following the user flow, two major spaces were needed in order to provide a virtual space for the cognite training: a landing page, where the user could learn about the exercise and a exercise room, where the exercise could be performed. In the last a progress report should also be presented.

With the exercises defined, wireframes were created in order to explore the potential solutions and visualize the content and functionality of the application. Two iterations were needed to achieve a solution that met the needs of the patient. The wireframe, that represents the exercise room, for the Remember a picture exercise, can be seen in Fig. 2.

For the Remember a picture exercise, an image is presented for 30 s and after this time, the image is blurred and the patient must answer a number of questions. As the questions are answered the number of hits and errors is updated, providing a interactive feedback. The patient will also have the option to pause and resume the exercise assessment. If the patient chooses to leave the exercise room he will be warned on the exercise completion.

5.2   Prototype

With the wireframes and user-flow established the prototype phase could be started. The application prototype was constructed based on the Angular framework and TypeScript, a subset of the JavaScript programming language. With a component based approach, using the objected oriented programming paradigm, a tangible and interactive model was provided.

5.3   Evaluation of Prototype

With the prototype ready, an initial evaluation step could be taken. For this, the 10 Nielsen heuristics were considered. Some of them are listed below, following its applicability on the screen seen in Fig. 2.

1. Visibility of system status: there is an indication of the user's progress or status within the exercise overall.

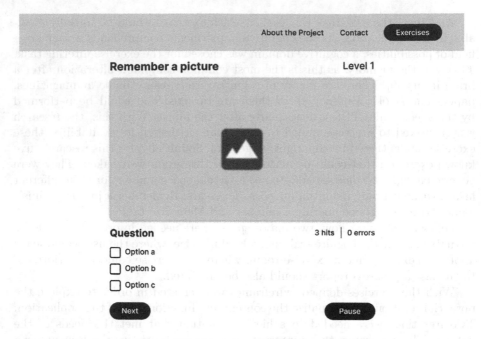

Fig. 2. Wireframe for the exercise room

2. Match between system and the real world: it does simulates a real-world memory exercise, with a picture to study and details to recall.
3. User control and freedom: there is a navigation menu that allows the user to move within the application and a pause/resume button.
4. Consistency and standards: the wireframe does use standard UI elements such as checkboxes, and navigation menu.
5. Flexibility and efficiency of use: it is fairly efficient in its use of screen real estate and presents the key elements of the exercise in a clear and organized way. A pause/resume button provides users with more control and flexibility.
6. Aesthetic and minimalist design: it is minimalist in its design, with a focus on the key elements of the exercise.

6   Conclusion and Future Work

The main goal of the application briefly described here is to support a patient regarding cognitive rehabilitation, early after a mild traumatic brain injury. Further evaluation is needed to determine the utility and acceptability of the tool. Additionally, it is important to tailor the application use to the individual needs and abilities for each patient, to ensure the best possible outcomes. A way to healthcare professionals to tailor and watch the cognite training process can also be provided.

References

1. Alnanih, R., Ormandjieva, O.: Mapping HCI principles to design quality of mobile user interfaces in healthcare applications. Procedia Comput. Sci. **94**, 75–82 (2016)
2. Burleigh, S.A., Farber, R.S., Gillard, M.: Community integration and life satisfaction after traumatic brain injury: long-term findings. Am. J. Occup. Ther. **52**(1), 45–52 (1998)
3. Chen, S., Thomas, J., Glueckauf, R., Bracy, O.: The effectiveness of computer-assisted cognitive rehabilitation for persons with traumatic brain injury. Brain Inj. **11**(3), 197–210 (1997)
4. Cicerone, K.D., et al.: Evidence-based cognitive rehabilitation: recommendations for clinical practice. Arch. Phys. Med. Rehabil. **81**(12), 1596–1615 (2000)
5. Cruz, V.T., et al.: A rehabilitation tool designed for intensive web-based cognitive training: description and usability study. JMIR Res. Protocols **2**(2), e2899 (2013)
6. Diaz Baquero, A.A., et al.: Methodological designs applied in the development of computer-based training programs for the cognitive rehabilitation in people with mild cognitive impairment (MCI) and mild dementia. systematic review. J. Clin. Med. **10**(6), 1222 (2021)
7. Dix, A., Finlay, J., Abowd, G.D., Beale, R.: Human-Computer Interaction. Pearson Education, New York (2003)
8. Fetta, J., Starkweather, A., Gill, J.M.: Computer-based cognitive rehabilitation interventions for traumatic brain injury: a critical review of the literature. J. Neurosci. Nurs. J. Am. Assoc. Neurosci. Nurses **49**(4), 235 (2017)
9. Flynn, F.G.: Memory impairment after mild traumatic brain injury. CONTINUUM: Lifelong Learn. Neurol. **16**(6), 79–109 (2010)
10. Gao, Y.: Cognitive guidance and improvement of Alzheimer's disease patients based on human-computer interaction design. Cogn. Syst. Res. **56**, 192–202 (2019)
11. Jung, H., et al.: The effectiveness of computer-assisted cognitive rehabilitation and the degree of recovery in patients with traumatic brain injury and stroke. J. Clin. Med. **10**(24), 5728 (2021)
12. Koskinen, S.: Quality of life 10 years after a very severe traumatic brain injury (TBI): the perspective of the injured and the closest relative. Brain Inj. **12**(8), 631–648 (1998)
13. Magalhães, A.L.G., Souza, L.C.D., Faleiro, R.M., Teixeira, A.L., Miranda, A.S.D.: Epidemiologia do traumatismo cranioencefálico no brasil. Rev. Bras. Neurol. **53**(2), 15–22 (2017)
14. Morris, J.: Cognitive rehabilitation: where we are and what is on the horizon. Phys. Med. Rehabil. Clin. N. Am. **18**(1), 27–42 (2007)
15. Politis, A.M., Norman, R.S.: Computer-based cognitive rehabilitation for individuals with traumatic brain injury: a systematic review. Perspect. ASHA Spec. Interest Groups **1**(2), 18–46 (2016)
16. Tsaousides, T., Gordon, W.A.: Cognitive rehabilitation following traumatic brain injury: assessment to treatment. Mount Sinai J. Med. J. Transl. Personalized Med. **76**(2), 173–181 (2009)

An Evaluation of a Hybrid STEM-Robotics Programme for Students with Special Needs in Guyana

Penelope DeFreitas[1]([✉]), Farnaz Baksh[2], Matevž Zorec[2], Joyann Todd[2],
and Obena Vanlewin[2]

[1] University of Guyana, Georgetown, Guyana
penelope.defreitas@uog.edu.gy
[2] University of Guyana Robotics Club, Georgetown, Guyana
ugrc.csi@uog.edu.gy

Abstract. Students with disabilities stand a higher chance of dropping out of school before completing their primary or secondary education. As a result, their full integration into society may be hindered. Globally, there is a movement towards addressing this issue through targeted interventions. For example, the Guyana Council of Organisations for Persons with Disabilities (GCOPD), has been operating at a national level to develop educational programmes (e.g., STEM-Robotics), which expose youngsters with disabilities to skills that are needed for the twenty-first-century. During the 2020/2021 iteration of the STEM-Robotics programme, the GCOPD leveraged the support of 7 mentors from the University of Guyana's Robotics Club and Department of Computer Science to design, develop, adapt, and execute the curriculum for 48 special needs students within the age range of 11 to 27 years old. The curriculum was delivered using a hybrid approach for approximately 12 weekly sessions. Feedback in the form of observations and experiences was collected from the mentors. Overall, the mentors observed positive improvements in the students' critical thinking, problem-solving, environmental awareness and presentation skills. Notably, the majority of the participants managed to complete class activities and graduated from the programme. The lessons learned from our study may prove useful for future related programmes.

Keywords: STEM · Robotics · Twenty-first-century skills · Special Education Needs · Hybrid training

1 Introduction

One (1) in every 10 children worldwide lives with some form of disability [1]. Alarmingly, students with disabilities are likely to drop out of school before completing their primary or secondary education [2]. As a consequence, their full integration into society may be hindered.

To address this problem, there is a global movement toward improving the lives of persons with disabilities. For instance, the UN has taken a rights-based approach toward developing and implementing inclusive policies, programmes, and practices to ensure equal educational opportunities for persons with disabilities [3]. Similarly, the Guyana Council of Organisations for Persons with Disabilities (GCOPD), has been operating at a national level to develop programmes that expose youngsters with disabilities to twenty-first-century skills (e.g., problem-solving, critical thinking) and soft skills (e.g., communicating ideas, teamwork). During COVID-19, GCOPD's inaugural 2020/2021 STEM-Robotics programme was implemented using a hybrid model to promote the safety of its participants, teachers and mentors. This presented an opportunity to adapt the curriculum for hybrid operations, and to evaluate the strengths and weaknesses of the training programme.

In this study, we provide a background to the SEN (Special Education Needs) STEM-Robotics training programme's implementation. The overall aim of this paper is to evaluate mentors' observations and experiences delivering the hybrid STEM-Robotics curriculum to students with disabilities.

2 The SEN STEM-Robotics Programme

Preliminary investigations by the researchers revealed insights into the 2020/2021 SEN STEM-Robotics programme's delivery. These are detailed in the following subsections:

2.1 Students and Mentors

Forty-eight (48) students with disabilities (i.e., physical, intellectual, visual, hearing and multiple impairments), between the ages of 11 and 27 years old, were shortlisted for the training programme. The students were attached to 5 SEN schools (Groups A, B, C, D, E) in Region 4 of Guyana (Fig. 1). Groups C, D and E joined the training sessions from their homes (i.e. virtually), whereas Groups A and B participated virtually from school (i.e. hybrid). The majority of the students were digitally literate and utilised devices such as tablets, mobile phones and laptops for participating in the sessions.

About 2 to 4 mentors were assigned to work with each student group virtually. The mentors collaboratively designed and developed lesson plans, activities and teaching materials for the programme. They were also responsible for adapting and executing the curriculum, demonstrating practical examples, and offering guidance to the students. In addition, the mentors met on a weekly basis to discuss positive outcomes, issues that arose, brainstormed ways for overcoming issues and planned for subsequent sessions.

2.2 Implementation and Curriculum

The training programme was delivered using either a fully online mode for some groups (Groups C, D, E) or a hybrid approach for others (Groups A and B). The programme was run for approximately 12 weekly sessions (September to December of 2020), with each session lasting for 2 h. Core concepts of the curriculum focused on areas such as recycling; repurposing and reusing; measurements; design thinking; algorithms and coding. In addition, the fostering of twenty-first-century skills such as critical thinking, problem-solving, and creativity were embedded into the lesson plans.

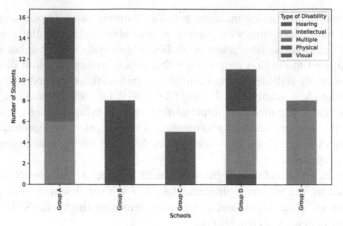

Fig. 1. Number of students per group (school), showcasing their compositions in terms of 5 simplified categories: Visual, Physical, Intellectual, Hearing or Multiple disabilities.

Credit was assigned to the students for completing homework activities (i.e., recycling and repurposing assignment, SI units, measurement and tools), presentations (i.e., recycling and repurposing assignment, Capstone project), robot assemblies (i.e., Tin-can and Solar Rover kits), Capstone project and an oral examination which tested the students' knowledge of topics covered in the curriculum. For the Capstone project, the students were required to apply their knowledge and skills acquired across the curriculum. They worked alongside their mentors to derive and shape their project ideas.

The criteria for students to graduate included: at least 50% attendance of all sessions, completion of at least 2 out of 3 hands-on activities (i.e., recycling and repurposing assignment, robot build, measurement), and delivery of at least 1 presentation.

2.3 Communication Tools

The training programme was supported by the following communication tools: Zoom, Google Classroom, email and WhatsApp. These tools were used because a significant number of the mentors, students, teachers and parents had experience interacting with them.

2.4 Academic, Management and Financial Support

The STEM-Robotics curriculum was collaboratively designed by mentors of the UG Robotics Club and an academic of the UG's Computer Science Department. In addition, teachers of the SEN schools offered weekly guidance to the mentors by reviewing lesson plans and instructional materials, and offering advice for tailoring content for specific groups.

Management support took the form of coordinating the student recruitment process, ensuring the smooth running of the programme and organising special events. To further support the training programme, financial assistance was provided by donors (i.e., Exxon

Mobil and the former Ministry of Public Telecommunications) in the form of robotic kits, tablets, stipends for mentors and rewards (i.e., medals and certificates) to the students.

3 Methodology

In this study, we determined mentors' observations and experiences implementing a STEM-Robotics curriculum for students with disabilities in the hybrid mode. Our investigation focused primarily on mentors' feedback regarding student engagement, attendance and performance, challenges encountered and support from parents and teachers.

3.1 Participants and Procedure

We collected quantitative and qualitative data from 7 mentors (M1, M2, M3,…. M7) to answer our primary research question: What were the observations and experiences of mentors hybridly delivering the STEM-Robotics curriculum to students with disabilities? Data collection was accomplished by using surveys along with collaborative tools (e.g., Google Forms and Sheets or Docs) for certain activities. During every session, the surveys were shared with mentors to improve accessibility. Using these tools, mentors tracked student progress as well as their own observations and experiences from each session. This data was analyzed and used to investigate mentors' observations and experiences while delivering the curriculum to students with disabilities.

3.2 Data Management and Analysis

The quantitative data was compiled into a spreadsheet, exported to csv format and uploaded to Google Colaboratory. This made it convenient for researchers to study the data and view results. We used Python pandas[1] to perform exploratory analysis, which included filtering and cleaning the data. The results were then visualised using seaborn[2]. By utilising these tools and techniques, we were able to gain valuable insights into our research question and draw meaningful conclusions from our data.

The qualitative dataset related to mentor observations and experiences was assessed using the Rosette Text Analysis tool[3] to determine the sentiments (i.e., negative, neutral, or positive) of each session. This process allowed the researchers to easily pinpoint particular sessions that were more successful versus challenging for the mentors. This dataset was also reviewed inductively, resulting in the following interesting themes being identified: 'Virtual Environment Constraints', 'Parental and Teacher Support', 'Learning Engagement and Altering the Teaching Strategy', 'Student Performance'. These themes were used as a basis for discussing interesting findings which stood out in the study.

---

[1] https://pandas.pydata.org/.

[2] https://seaborn.pydata.org/.

[3] https://www.rosette.com/.

4   Results and Discussion

4.1   Virtual Environment Constraints

Operating in the hybrid mode presented a number of constraints for the mentors and students. For the first few training sessions, most groups who worked from school were not fully prepared, which resulted in a significant amount of time being spent on troubleshooting issues (i.e., camera, audio, microphone, internet, interacting with the video conferencing tool) to ensure that the mentor and students could effectively communicate with each other.

> *"We encountered some initial problems with microphones, but everything was resolved. The students turned out to be very interactive". (Mentor 4)*

Another notable issue was the unsteady availability of power and internet for some students and mentors. This posed a serious threat to the training programme, but fortunately, multiple mentors were assigned to work with each group. As such, if one mentor lost access to power or the internet, another mentor was always available to guide the students. Some students who joined from home were either absent or late to sessions mainly due to internet or power failure. This disrupted the normal flow of the subsequent sessions since the mentors had to spend a significant portion of the class time recapping content that was missed. The students who worked from school experienced the most unreliable internet connectivity. As a workaround, their teachers were forced to use data plans on their mobile phones to afford the running of some sessions.

> *"The teacher was basically hosting the whole session using her mobile data plan".*
> *(Mentor 1)*

The abovementioned issues are common threats to training programmes, which involve a virtual learning component. According to [4], four core requirements that are needed to facilitate robust virtual learning include high-speed internet service, internet-enabled devices, instructional content, and support such as digital literacy, teacher readiness and technical assistance.

4.2   Parental and Teacher Support

It was observed that parents and teachers played a major supporting role in the training programme. For instance, the students who participated in the training from home were supported by their parents who ensured that they joined the sessions on time and had the required materials to complete activities.

> *"Assistance from parents was vital in the session as some students had trouble vocalising their answers and using the device [computer-related]". (Mentor 4)*

In addition, parents served as a source of encouragement and even assisted with the completion of activities (e.g., computer-related tasks, assembling the robots, using tools such as the screwdriver, and preparing for presentations). Interestingly, it was also observed that some parents passively participated in the training to learn more about STEM and Robotics. This behaviour was interpreted positively since parents' participation during sessions is a sign that they are interested in becoming involved in their children's education [5], which in turn can impact educational success [6].

Similarly, the students who participated in the training from school also benefited from their teachers' support. For example, the teachers took on the responsibility of ensuring that their students were able to access the training online, had the necessary materials, and remained focused during the sessions. Some teachers also eagerly provided assistance during activities. According to [7], teachers who are enthusiastic and engage their students in STEM development activities tend to pass on their excitement to the students.

Moreover, the teachers rendered vital assistance to the mentors by helping them to better understand the student groups and served as a main source of communication regarding potential challenges. The teachers assisted by reviewing the learning materials to ensure that they were pitched at a level for the students to understand and offered advice for improving the content and activities. The teachers who worked with Group B (i.e., hearing impaired) students also served in the capacity of a translator, since some of the learning content was not provided in a sign language format.

4.3 Learning Engagement and Altering the Teaching Strategy

Groups C (i.e., visually impaired) and D (i.e., hearing, intellectually and physically impaired) were the most engaging out of all the groups. In particular, the majority of the students participated in every session without being prompted by their mentors. Their interactions at the class level were also relatively consistent across the sessions.

"The students were very engaging and seem[ed] to have an understanding of the concepts .... Overall, the session [reuse, reduce, recycle] was [a] good one". (Mentor 3)

"The session [measurement and tools] was very interactive and students loved the activities". (Mentor 4)

For group C (i.e., visually impaired), the mentors were more conscious about making their explanations descriptive in order to improve the quality of learning and understandability of instructions, especially for the robot assembly activities. Moreover, the students were engaged in smaller breakout rooms and were encouraged to turn on their cameras to ensure that the robot assembly was done correctly. Furthermore, the learning materials were converted to an accessible format (e.g., MS PowerPoint slides by embedding alt text for images) to increase ease of understandability and readability by the students' screen readers.

Initially, the mentors found Group B (i.e., hearing impaired) to be challenging to work with because they had no prior knowledge of sign language and heavily relied on the teachers for translating the materials to the students. This issue was further compounded by the poor internet access at the school. However, by the second and third sessions, the teachers received the learning materials ahead of time for the purpose of reviewing and sharing recommendations for improvement. The mentors also used more simplistic words and embedded ASL (American Sign Language) into some of the learning content.

"We had many connection and communication issues... for the session [introduction to STEM and Robotics]....The students were not very interactive due to the time taken for translation relay and the language barrier. Likewise, question and answer pathways were limited". (Mentor 4)

"A successful session [run subsequently with the Solar Rover] ... Students were able to complete the task in less than 2 hours". (Mentor 5)

The most challenging schools to engage and sustain interest were Groups A (i.e., intellectually, physically impaired and multiple impairments) and E (i.e. multiple and intellectually impaired); however, as the mentors got to know the students and adjusted their teaching strategy, they were better able to fuel engagement among the groups. For instance, the sessions were run at a slower pace with more simplistic words, visual materials, and hands-on activities.

The modifications that were done during the SEN STEM-Robotics programme appeared to be a major contributor to improving student engagement. Similarly, [8] posited that the presence or implementation of curriculum enhancements for improving engagement was a strong predictor of positive student responses.

4.4   Student Performance

Overall, the mentors observed positive improvements in the students' critical thinking, problem-solving, environmental awareness, and presentation skills. Interestingly, the majority of the students graduated (i.e., 87.5%) from the SEN STEM-Robotics training programme. However, the remaining 12.5% of the students did not complete the programme due to schedule conflicts with competing activities, employment, or waning interest (e.g., passive participation in sessions, incomplete homework activities, and low attendance).

For those students who stayed the course of the programme, it was observed that performance did not differ based on their type of disability. Most of the students managed to complete the activities; however, the mentors revealed that a significant number of students were absent during the last few weeks of the programme due to a high volume of internet connectivity issues and conflicting activities (e.g., school examinations, Christmas holiday preparations). Nonetheless, the absentees were contacted and encouraged to make their outstanding submissions.

"The [final] session was completed on a good note. Evaluations could not be completed for more than half the students due to connectivity issues. A majority of the students[who were present] finished their final project and presented them". (Mentor 4)

Impressively, a majority of students completed their Capstone projects - many reusing components of their previous robot builds; however, they initially struggled to derive project ideas. As a result, the mentors worked closely (i.e. in-class and out-of-class) with the students to formulate and shape their individual project ideas into tangible outputs. This was heartening to note, but for future iterations of the programme, it is recommended that ideas and accompanying guidelines be provided to help students to more confidently and easily complete their projects.

All in all, the mentors enjoyed working with the students, were extremely proud of their efforts, and found the programme to be a success.

"Today in our last session … the students presented their amazing final projects. I was impressed by their effort and the attention paid to detail. I enjoyed working with these amazing students!" (Mentor 5)

5   Conclusion

This study presents key findings and lessons learned from the inaugural STEM-Robotics programme that was offered in hybrid mode to students with special needs in Guyana during 2020/2021. We observed promising development in students with different types of disabilities. In addition, guidance and support received from special needs experts, parents and mentors were key factors for delivering the programme successfully. Lessons learned from our analysis may prove crucial for future related programmes.

References

1. UNICEF: Seen, Counted, Included (2021). https://data.unicef.org/resources/children-with-dis abilities-report-2021/
2. UNESCO Institute of Statistics: Education And Disability (2017). http://unesdoc.unesco.org/images/0024/002475/247516e.pdf
3. UNESCO: What you need to know about inclusion in education (2022). https://www.unesco.org/en/education/inclusion/need-know
4. Chandra, S., et al.: Closing the K–12 digital divide in the age of distance learning. Common Sense and Boston Consulting Group (2020). https://www.bbcmag.com/broadband-applicati ons/closing-the-k-ndash-12-digital-divide-in-the-age-of-distance-learning
5. Bers, M.U.: Project InterActions: A multigenerational robotic learning environment. J. Sci. Educ. Technol. **16**, 537–552 (2007)
6. Wilder, S.: Effects of parental involvement on academic achievement: a meta-synthesis. Educ. Rev. **66**(3), 377–397 (2014)
7. McClure, E.R., et al.: STEM Starts Early: Grounding Science, Technology, Engineering, and Math Education in Early Childhood. In Joan Ganz Cooney center at sesame workshop. Joan Ganz Cooney Center at Sesame Workshop. 1900 Broadway, New York, NY 10023 (2017)
8. Lee, S.H., Wehmeyer, M.L., Soukup, J.H., Palmer, S.B.: Impact of curriculum modifications on access to the general education curriculum for students with disabilities. Except. Child. **76**(2), 213–233 (2010)

Automatic Assistance to Help Disabled Students Feel Welcomed in Their Early Days at the University

Paula Escudeiro$^{(\boxtimes)}$ (iD), Márcia Campos Gouveia(iD), and Nuno Escudeiro(iD)

Porto School of Engineering, Rua Dr. António Bernardino de Almeida, 431, 4249-015 Porto, Portugal
pmo@isep.ipp.pt

Abstract. In recent times, disabled, incoming, and Erasmus students have encountered challenges in their initial days at the University. These challenges often stem from communication or assistance difficulties, necessitating new solutions to aid them. InDoor Mapping is one such solution; it is an assistive technology that serves as a guide and navigation system for students to navigate through the ISEP school premises. The app is powered by beacons, and it displays different routes and accessible points, carefully customized to the users' requirements. The application provides vital information such as wheelchair access ramps or elevators to the users. Ultimately, this is a fresh inclusion and accessibility solution that assists in welcoming and aiding all students.

Keywords: Automatic assistance · assistive technology · indoor navigation

1 Introduction

Incoming students, Erasmus students, and disabled students often struggle to find assistance and feel welcomed in their early days at the University. Communication and assistance challenges demand for new technologies – assistive technologies – that can help welcoming all students. InDoor Mapping, an indoor navigation application, is such a technology.

The application is intended for students as a guide and navigation system within the school grounds of *Instituto Superior de Engenharia do Porto* (ISEP). When arriving at an institution such as the ISEP campus, which includes a considerable number of different buildings, an assistive technology, that serves both as a guide and indoor GPS, may allow the user to easily navigate through the facilities and quickly become familiar with them.

Furthermore, another advantage of this application is the inclusion and assistance of disabled people, as mentioned, since this indoor mapping application also provides information about easy access points, carefully adapted to their needs. Easy access points, such as an elevator or wheelchair access ramps, are highlighted on the map in order to introduce the most adequate route for each person.

C. Stephanidis et al. (Eds.): HCII 2023, CCIS 1833, pp. 270–276, 2023.
https://doi.org/10.1007/978-3-031-35992-7_37

This application falls within the prevalence of navigation systems that have nowadays become an integral part of modern life. Still, the well-known exterior GPS signal does not have the capacity to cover all areas as there is no contact with the satellite, making indoor positioning impossible.

Indoor mapping is the means of using various technologies to determine the location of a device indoors. While indoor mapping shares similarities with GPS tracking, it does not rely on satellite tracking technology as satellite waves are not strong enough to penetrate roofs and walls. Instead, indoor mapping technology and indoor mapping software offer accurate information within buildings. Indoor mapping can be achieved with the use of various location-based technologies. Together they work to help identify the position of users.

Because traditional navigation systems do not guarantee the best results in terms of indoor navigation, the technology of Beacons was used. A Bluetooth beacon is a small wireless device that works based on Bluetooth Low Energy, that repeatedly broadcasts a radio signal that other devices can find. These Beacons are used to improve orientation inside a building with turn-by-turn navigation and show the user the interior mapping of the building they are in.

The aim of this project was the creation of an indoor mapping functional project, to be available on both web and mobile devices, with the purpose to acquire data from beacons and show the user multiple paths to move inside ISEP, according to the user needs. To use the application, it is only required that location services are activated on the user's device as well as a stable Wi-Fi connection, that the institution can offer.

The application aims to provide an easy and accessible virtual "space" for students, workers, members of the institution, and visitors, to navigate through the facilities of ISEP. The core of this project is its map, which defines a specific set of directions and information to guide the user within a certain location or set of locations. In this case, a series of information regarding the campus and individual buildings is provided. Each building has a designation, geo-location, and internal data – classrooms, bathrooms, elevator locations, and all else. Combining all the data of each building, the user can experience accurate guidance between buildings, with specified alternatives for disabled students/users.

Showing concerns for inclusion, the ISEP campus is the starting point of this new assistive technology, that can be implemented in all other indoor environments, from schools to companies or public services, to ensure assistance for everyone.

2   Theoretical Framework

Indoor navigation has gained increasing importance in recent times. User-friendly indoor navigation systems have been found to be critical in this context [1]. Such systems are based on pedestrian pathfinding, which involves orientation towards a specific destination, considering both the unfamiliarity with certain environments and the location of the user, path planning, and guidance [2].

Indoor positioning systems are an extension of outdoor navigation systems, which aim to complement them in the face of greater mobility [3]. Examples of large infrastructures where indoor mapping is beneficial to include hospitals, airports, malls, and universities [4]. Indoor navigation systems can provide directions to visitors, improve their experience, and offer useful information. However, indoor spaces pose different challenges and restrictions, which necessitate the use of different technologies compared to GPS-based outdoor navigation systems [1].

2.1 Indoor Positioning and Assisted Navigation

Indoor positioning and navigation systems are technologies designed to provide location information and directions to users within indoor spaces where GPS signals are often weak or unavailable. These systems use a variety of technologies, including Wi-Fi, Bluetooth, RFID, and sensors, to determine a user's location and guide them to their destination. There are several types of indoor positioning and navigation systems, including Bluetooth-based systems, like InDoor Mapping. These systems use Bluetooth beacons to provide location information and can be used in a variety of applications, including:

1. Wayfinding: These systems can be used to provide directions to users within complex indoor spaces, such as airports, hospitals, and shopping malls.
2. Asset tracking: These systems can be used to track the location of valuable assets, such as equipment or inventory, within a building.
3. Safety and security: These systems can be used to monitor the movement of people within a building and provide alerts in the event of an emergency.
4. Marketing and advertising: These systems can be used to send targeted promotions and advertisements to users based on their location within a building.

Overall, indoor positioning and navigation systems are becoming increasingly important as more people spend time in indoor spaces and rely on technology to navigate their surroundings. Plus, they can provide several benefits for businesses and organizations that operate in indoor spaces. Some of these benefits include:

1. Improved experience: By providing accurate and reliable location information and directions, indoor positioning and navigation systems can help people navigate complex indoor spaces more easily and reduce the time and frustration associated with getting lost.
2. Increased efficiency: By tracking the movement of people and assets within a building, indoor positioning and navigation systems can help businesses optimize their operations and improve efficiency.
3. Enhanced safety and security: Indoor positioning and navigation systems can be used to monitor the movement of people within a building and provide alerts in the event of an emergency, helping to enhance safety and security.
4. Better data collection: Indoor positioning and navigation systems can collect valuable data about the movement of people and assets within a building, which can be used to optimize operations and improve customer experiences.

2.2 Bluetooth Low Energy Beacons for Indoor Positioning

Satellite technologies are not a viable option for indoor positioning as they are unable to detect the floor of a building and their position resolution is highly inaccurate due to shadowing. Instead, Bluetooth Low Energy (BLE) beacons are the most commonly used indoor positioning technology.

BLE beacons are small wireless devices that use Bluetooth technology to transmit signals to other devices, such as smartphones or tablets. These signals contain information about the beacon's location, which can be used to provide location-based services and other types of information to users.

BLE beacons work by constantly broadcasting a signal that contains a unique identifier code. When a nearby device (such as a smartphone) detects the signal, it can use the identifier code to determine the beacon's location and trigger a specific action, such as displaying a message or providing directions.

One of the key advantages of BLE beacons is their low power consumption. BLE beacons are designed to operate for months or even years on a single battery, making them a cost-effective and low-maintenance solution for providing location-based services.

To use BLE beacons, a user's device must have Bluetooth enabled and be running a compatible app or software that can detect the beacon's signal. The app or software can then use the information provided by the beacon to provide location-based services, such as indoor navigation or targeted marketing messages.

Thus, BLE beacons are a powerful tool for providing location-based services in a variety of contexts, including retail, hospitality, and healthcare. As the technology continues to evolve, we will likely see even more innovative uses for BLE beacons in the future.

2.3 Wayfinding: Access to Information in the Case of Disabled Students

The issue of promoting equal opportunities and social inclusion for people with disabilities is a complex and multifaceted challenge, and one of the main objectives of this project. While advancements in technology have facilitated the development of various tools to improve communication and accessibility for the hearing, visual, and mobility impaired, there is still a long way to go to ensure that they have equal access to information [5].

Blind individuals face numerous obstacles when it comes to independent travel, particularly when navigating unfamiliar environments. The inability to see street signs and landmarks can make it difficult for blind individuals to determine the direction they need to travel and efficiently move from place to place. Without this important information, they may become disoriented or lost [6, 7].

In the case of deaf students, communication barriers pose another challenge in educational settings. Also, in their case, information is not easily accessed, when relying on text, for instance, since not all deaf individuals can read the written language (they often depend on sign language, which is not commonly known by the non-deaf community).

As a result, wayfinding challenges for blind and visually impaired individuals can be thought of as problems of information access. Providing access to relevant information in a way that is accessible to them is critical for enabling these individuals to navigate their environments safely and independently [7].

Accessible indoor and outdoor GPS technology has the potential to eliminate a significant travel barrier experienced by individuals who are blind and visually impaired: the lack of location information [4, 7]. With an accessible indoor navigation system, blind and visually impaired individuals can obtain real-time information about their surroundings [7] – in the case of the InDoor Mapping application, audio and soon-to-be-implemented sign language are available.

3 Methodology

3.1 Concept

The activity of wayfinding, which involves navigating through indoor environments, is a common occurrence in daily life. However, students on university campuses often face challenges in navigating unfamiliar environments. To address this issue and provide access to information, the ISEP Indoor Mapping application was created. The app aims to offer an indoor positioning tool that allows users to navigate the facilities easily.

The project aimed to create a navigation tool for web and mobile devices that utilizes beacons to provide users with multiple paths for navigating through ISEP facilities, customized to their specific needs such as wheelchair accessibility and elevators. By utilizing beacons, the application displays the interior mapping of ISEP buildings and offers guidance and orientation to users based on their needs. The development of this assistive technology enables all students, including incoming, Erasmus, and disabled students, to independently navigate through the school grounds.

Like outdoor tracking systems, indoor navigation systems aim to provide users with an autonomous way to navigate through unfamiliar environments. The ISEP Indoor Mapping app is an excellent example of how technology can be used to provide accessibility and support for students with different needs. By providing customized navigation options and features, the app helps to ensure that all students can move around the campus easily and independently.

3.2 Objectives

The InDoor Mapping application aims to provide an indoor positioning tool that enables users to navigate ISEP facilities easily. To achieve this goal, the project will pursue the following specific objectives:

1. Develop an application that can be used on both web and mobile devices.
2. Utilize beacons to acquire data and create an indoor mapping of ISEP buildings.
3. Customize the navigation paths according to the user's specific needs, such as wheelchair accessibility and elevators.
4. Provide guidance and orientation to users based on their needs.
5. Ensure that the application is inclusive and accessible to all students, including incoming, Erasmus, and disabled students.
6. Enhance the autonomy and independence of all students, regardless of their abilities, to navigate ISEP facilities.
7. Promote awareness of the importance of indoor navigation tools in enhancing the student experience on campus.
8. Increase the efficiency and accuracy of navigation through ISEP facilities, resulting in better use of time and resources for students and staff.

9. Offer an accessible and user-friendly indoor navigation system that requires only location services and a stable Wi-Fi connection.
10. Improve the overall safety and security of the ISEP facilities by providing an easy and reliable navigation tool.

By creating and implementing the InDoor Mapping application, the project aims to develop a better sense of social responsibility toward welcoming and assisting all students. The project's ultimate goal is to contribute to a more equitable, inclusive, and accessible education.

4 Conclusion

The InDoor Mapping indoor navigation application appears to be a useful assistive technology for helping new students, Erasmus students, and disabled students navigate the ISEP campus. By providing accurate and reliable location information and directions, the application can help users quickly become familiar with the campus and locate important facilities and resources.

The application's ability to highlight easy access points for disabled people is particularly noteworthy, as this can help to ensure that these individuals feel welcomed and supported at the university. By providing information about wheelchair access ramps and other accommodations, the application can help to remove barriers and make it easier for disabled students to navigate the campus.

Overall, the InDoor Mapping indoor navigation application appears to be a promising tool for improving the student experience and promoting inclusivity at the ISEP campus. This assistive tool can have a significant impact on the lives of individuals with disabilities, as well as other groups who may face barriers to accessing information and resources in indoor spaces. In addition to providing navigation assistance, assistive technologies can also help to promote social inclusion and reduce stigma by creating more accessible and welcoming environments.

Also, with continued research and development, it is possible to create practical solutions that can significantly improve the quality of life for people with disabilities and enable them to navigate indoor environments more independently.

Acknowledgments. This work is being developed at the research group GILT – Games, Interaction and Learning Technologies from the Polytechnic Institute of Porto, with the support of FCT/MCTES Financiamento Plurianual Base da Unidade (UIDB/05627/2020).

References

1. Hirtle, S.C., Bahm, C.R.: Cognition for the navigation of complex indoor environments. In: Indoor Wayfinding and Navigation. CRC Press, Boca Raton, pp. 1–12 (2015)
2. Yan, J., Zlatanova, S.: Seamless 3D Navigation in Indoor and Outdoor Spaces. CRC Press, Boca Raton (2023)
3. Samama, N.: Indoor Positioning: Technologies and Performance. John Wiley & Sons Inc, New Jersey (2019)

4. Kunhoth, J., Karkar, A., Al-Maadeed, S., Al-Ali, A.: Indoor positioning and wayfinding systems: a survey. Hum.-Cent. Comput. Inf. Sci. **10**(18) (2020)
5. Escudeiro, P., Escudeiro, N., Norberto, M., Lopes, J., Soares, F.: Digital assisted communication. In: 13th International Conference on Web Information Systems and Technologies, Porto (2017)
6. Dias, M.B., Teves, E.A., Zimmerman, G.J., Gedawy, H.K., Belousov, S.M., Dias, M.B.: Indoor navigation challenges for visually impaired people. In: Indoor Wayfinding and Navigation. CRC Press, Boca Raton, pp. 141–164 (2015)
7. May, M., Casey, K.: Accessible global positioning systems. In: Assistive Technology for Blindness and Low Vision. CRC Press, Boca Raton, pp. 81–104 (2013)

Awareness, Understanding, and Attitudes of Digital Accessibility in Technology Professionals

Carie Fisher[(⊠)] [iD], Sunghyun R. Kang [iD], and Cyndi Wiley

Iowa State University, Ames, IA 50014, USA
cefisher@iastate.edu

Abstract. Digital accessibility is about designing and building digital products so that regardless of a person's mental or physical abilities, they still interact with them meaningfully and equitably. This study explores the digital accessibility awareness, understanding, and attitudes of technology professionals. As a research method, an online survey was sent to technology professionals currently working in the field to gain a clearer picture of what digital accessibility resources are being used, what limitations might exist, and attitudes and perceptions surrounding digital accessibility in the workforce.

Keywords: Digital Accessibility · Technology Professionals · Accessibility Awareness

1 Introduction

Digital accessibility is about designing and building digital products so that regardless of a person's mental or physical abilities, they can still interact with that product in a meaningful and equivalent way. The World Health Organization estimates that over 15% of the world's population self-identify as having a disability [1]. While large on its own, that number increases dramatically if you consider the variety of people who do not self-identify as having a disability but could benefit from accessible products.

The price of creating accessible digital products is high. Building digital products with inclusivity in mind requires expert knowledge of the various accessibility rules, an understanding of specialized coding/design techniques, and a deep comprehension of usability testing with both assistive technology (AT) devices and people with disabilities – not to mention the actual time and money required to implement these steps in a typical product life cycle [2, 3]. Even with the high cost, the need for technical professionals to understand digital accessibility is greater than ever [4].

Unfortunately, research has shown that many students entering the workforce do not possess even the most basic understanding of this field [5]. While many factors are at play, part of the long-standing issue is that there are no agreed-upon curriculum standards for digital accessibility instruction [5], and the existence of quality tools and resources to support instructors in higher education is not universal [6].

C. Stephanidis et al. (Eds.): HCII 2023, CCIS 1833, pp. 277–283, 2023.
https://doi.org/10.1007/978-3-031-35992-7_38

This paper explores the digital accessibility awareness, understanding, and attitudes of technology professionals through an online survey to answer the following questions: how are people with disabilities (PwD) represented in the technology industry?; what are the perceived prioritization levels and attitudes surrounding digital accessibility work in the technology industry?; which resources, tools, and assistive technology (ATs) are often used to solve digital accessibility issues today?; and how likely would a technology professional be to seek out an online resource, company, or a person with a disability to help them achieve their digital accessibility goals?

2 Methodology

Research has shown a gap in the knowledge and awareness of technical professionals regarding digital accessibility, but billions of people worldwide could benefit from more accessible designs and code. Previous surveys of technology professionals on the topic of accessibility have been conducted [7–9], but the participant numbers were small [9], or the questions were limited [8] to typical demographic questions.

By surveying a larger group of technology professionals and asking additional questions about digital accessibility in the workplace, this paper is focused on understanding why some people focus on digital accessibility even though it is costly in terms of effort and time. Conversely, we are interested in data that shows why a technical professional would not pursue digital accessibility in their products. This section outlines the methodology behind creating the online survey.

2.1 Participants

The survey participants include designers, UX/UI researchers, developers, project/program managers, consultants, and trainers. This group represents the people who have the most impact on the accessibility of current digital products. Since the focus is on current working professionals, full-time students, adults who choose to be unemployed, and retirees are excluded from the survey.

2.2 Measurements and Procedure

The online survey was built using the survey tool Qualtrics and consisted of 43 questions that took roughly 10–15 min to complete. The survey was broken into five main sections: Introduction, Employment, Demographics, Digital Accessibility, and Closing. The survey was posted publicly and open to any technology professional for over two weeks, from December 1–15, 2021. If individuals did not consent or were under 18 years old, they were directed to the end of the survey.

2.3 Data Analysis

Qualtrics data was exported in CSV format to Microsoft Excel. In Microsoft Excel, the data was cleaned-up and filtered to get numerical data for comparison and t-test purposes that were analyzed using the open-source statistics program JASP. Some Likert scale survey responses were quantified in separate columns in the CSV file. The survey received 716 submissions, and the viable survey count was 626.

3 Survey Results

This part of the paper summarizes the demographic information surrounding people in the technology industry.

3.1 General Demographics of the Technology Industry

Age, Gender, and Race/Ethnicity. Among 625 responses in total, a large number of the survey participants were in the range of 25–34 (42%, n = 262) and 35–44 (31%, n = 195), followed in sequential order by people aged 45–54 (16%, n = 100), 18–24 (5%, n = 31), 55–64 (5%, n = 31), and 65 or older (1%, n = 6).

We had 623 survey participants answer the question about gender identity. The participants were allowed to choose more than one gender identity, so the total number of valid responses for this question equaled 732. The majority of the survey participants self-identified as male (47%, n = 341), female (36%, n = 263), or non-binary/agender/transgender (15%, n = 111). Seventeen people said their gender identity was not listed or preferred not to answer the question.

A total of 622 participants answer the race/ethnicity question. The participants were allowed to choose more than one race or ethnicity, so the total number of valid responses to this question was 655. Most of the survey participants self-identified as Caucasian/White (69%, n = 450), followed by Black/African American (12%, n = 76), Hispanic/Latino (6%, n = 42), Asian (6%, n = 41), and small numbers in American Indian and Middle Eastern. Some people preferred not to answer the question.

Titles/Positions and Years of Industry Experience. We received 625 responses to the question about the primary role/position at the survey participants' current company, organization, or institution. The data showed that survey participants were primarily Front-end Engineers (33%, n = 211), Digital Accessibility Professionals (18%, n = 111), and Back-end Engineers (17%, n = 109). The rest of the survey participants were a mix of Content creators/strategists (7%, n = 46), Program/project managers (5%, n = 34), UX/UI designers (5%, n = 33), Educators/trainers (4%, n = 22), and small numbers are from UI/UX researchers/data scientists, Information architects and An additional group (5%, n = 32) identified as "Other" fields centered around support and leadership roles.

Among 626 responses to the question related to the number of years the survey participants held their current role/position was varied from 0–2 years (24%, n = 149), 3–5 years (29%, n = 180), 6–10 years (21%, n = 130), 11–15 years (12%, n = 80), 16–20 years (8%, n = 49), to 21 or more years (6%, n = 36). Two participants said they were unsure or preferred not to answer this question. This data shows that most people have worked in their current position for more than ten years.

Industry Sectors and Company Sizes. We received 625 valid responses to the question about industry sectors. The majority of the survey participants came from general Software (23%, n = 143), Information/Media (20%, n = 122), and Education (16%, n = 100) spaces. The remainder of the responses were a mix of Professional Services (6%, n = 39), Financial (6%, n = 36), and small numbers in Creative, Healthcare, Entertainment,

Agriculture, Cultural Hospitality/Leisure, Manufacturing, Real estate, Transportation, and Sports. Twenty-three (4%) people chose the "Unsure/Prefer not to answer" option. An additional group (10%, n = 63) chose the "Other" option, which included write-in responses such as Retail, Non-profit, and Government sectors.

When it comes to size (n = 625), most of the survey participants worked at companies, organizations, or institutions with more than 1000 employees (25%, n = 159), followed by 11–50 employees (16%, n = 120), 6–10 employees (12%, n = 73), 101–250 employees (10%, n = 60), 51–100 employees (8%, n = 52), less than five employees (8%, n = 50), 501–1000 employees (8%, n = 47), and 251–500 employees (7%, n = 42). Twenty-two people chose the "Unsure/Prefer not to answer" option.

3.2 Disability Representation and Digital Accessibility Prioritization/Attitudes

After establishing a baseline of demographic information for the individual and the company they work for, we asked questions about disability representation, prioritization, and attitudes in the technology industry.

Disability Representation. When we asked about disability representation in the technology industry, specifically self-identification, we had 620 valid responses where 26% (n = 161) reported "Yes," they had a disability, 64% (n = 395) responded "No," and 10% (n = 64) were "Unsure/Preferred not to answer" the question.

The disability representation numbers were higher when we asked participants about other people. Out of 619 valid responses, 73% (n = 450) reported "Yes," they knew someone with a disability, 19% (n = 120) responded "No," and 8% (n = 49) were "Unsure/Preferred not to answer."

When asked if they worked with someone with a disability, 43% (n = 269) reported "Yes," they knew someone with a disability, 38% (n = 238) responded "No," and 18% (n = 112) were "Unsure or preferred not to answer." Note: participants were never forced to self-disclose their disability status or those they knew or worked with.

Digital Accessibility Prioritization and Attitudes. We received 595 responses when we asked the survey question related to priority levels of digital accessibility work. Of those who responded, 63% (n = 372) said "Yes," 23% (n = 137) responded "No," while 12% (n = 86) were "Unsure/Preferred not to answer" if the priority level had changed over the last year.

When we focused our questioning on the attitudes surrounding digital accessibility, we received 594 responses and saw almost identical percentages to the previous question, with 62% (n = 366) said "Yes," 25% (n = 146) responded "No," while 14% (n = 82) were "Unsure/Preferred not to answer," if the attitudes had changed over the last year.

3.3 Resources, Tools, and Assistive Technology Preference and Utilization

Next, we focused on the most often used resources, tools, and assistive technology that professionals in the technology industry use today to help solve their digital accessibility issues. We also looked at how likely it would be that these professionals would use these online resources, companies, and individuals.

Most Often Used Resources, Tools, and Assistive Technology. For this topic, we asked three multiple-choice questions and one write-in question to better understand the resources, tools, and assistive technology currently used by technology industry professionals.

We asked the survey participants which resources, tools, and assistive technology they used to help solve their digital accessibility goals and received 590, 589, and 581 individual responses, respectively. The total number of valid responses is 3388, 2541, and 1906, respectively, due to the participants being allowed to choose multiple options per response.

The list of resources, tools, and assistive technology used is lengthy, so this overview will report on the top five items in each category. For resources used, the data showed 12% (n = 388) used online searches, 11% (n = 375) used WCAG specifications, 9% (n = 267) used academic articles/studies, 7% (n = 244) used non-academic articles from companies/organizations, and 7% (n = 235) used video tutorials/talks to help them resolve digital accessibility issues.

For tools used, the data showed 15% (n = 381) used automated browser extensions, 14% (n = 366) used browser inspector/tools, 13% (n = 330) used color contrast checkers/palette generators, 8% (n = 208) used code linters/checkers, and 7% (n = 166) used color contrast simulators/filters to help them resolve digital accessibility issues.

For assistive technology used, the data showed 19% (n = 360) used a keyboard, 13% (n = 238) used VoiceOver (VO) screen reader (macOS), 10% (n = 188) used magnification programs/tools, 10% (n = 182) used Non-Visual Desktop Access (NVDA) screen reader (Windows), and 8% (n = 160) used VoiceOver (VO) screen reader (iOS mobile) to help them resolve digital accessibility issues.

Likelihood of Utilizing an Online Resource, Company, or Individual for. Digital Accessibility Assistance. For this topic, we asked three multiple-choice questions and one write-in question to better understand the resources, tools, and assistive technology currently used by technology industry professionals.

First, we asked how likely it would be for a technology professional to seek out an online resource to help them achieve their digital accessibility goals, and we received 595 responses. The data showed that 65% (n = 385) were extremely likely to use them, 18% (n = 104) were neither likely nor unlikely to use them, 16% (n = 97) were somewhat likely to use them, 1% (n = 8) were somewhat unlikely to use them, and 0.17% (n = 1) were extremely unlikely to use these resources.

Next, we asked how likely it would be for a technology professional to seek out an individual or company to help them achieve their digital accessibility goals, and we received 593 responses. The data showed that 33% (n = 197) were somewhat likely to use them, 27% (n = 162) were extremely likely to use them, 27% (n = 162) were neither likely nor unlikely to use them, 11% (n = 63) were somewhat unlikely to use them, and 2% (n = 9) were extremely unlikely to use these resources.

Lastly, we asked how likely it would be for a technology professional to seek out a person with a disability to help them achieve their digital accessibility goals and received

591 responses. The data showed that 38% (n = 226) were extremely likely to use them, 31% (n = 183) were somewhat likely to use them, 25% (n = 147) were neither likely nor unlikely to use them, 5% (n = 31) were somewhat unlikely to use them, and 0.68% (n = 4) were extremely unlikely to use these resources.

The t-test data shows a technology professional's likelihood of using an online resource, company, or individual with a disability to help achieve their digital accessibility goals against their title/position. Also, the t-tests show one statistically significant result related to the developer/engineer (front-end) title/position and looking to people with disabilities to help solve their digital accessibility issues (p = 0.012). Additional tests we ran against this data included: gender identity, disability representation, and priorities/attitudes, but none of the t-tests were statistically significant.

4   Conclusion

This paper presents high-level data from our survey focused on understanding technology professionals' backgrounds, observations and attitudes about digital accessibility, as well as the overall disability representation in the current industry.

Regarding age, gender, and race, most of our survey participants (73%) were between the ages of 25–34 and 45–44. The top two gender identities were male at 47% and female at 36%. The top three races/ethnicities represented in the survey were Caucasian/White at 69%, Black/African American at 12%, and Hispanic/Latino/Spanish at 6%.

For titles/positions and years of industry experience, the data showed that survey participants were primarily Front-end Engineers at 34%, Digital Accessibility Professionals at 18%, and Back-end Engineers at 17%. Most (53%) of our survey participants had less than five years of experience. No correlation was found between a technology professional's title/position, the number of years in the industry, or gender identity.

Regarding disability representation and digital accessibility prioritization and attitudes, most survey participants (64%) indicated that they did not have a disability but did know someone with a disability (73%). However, less than half of the respondents (43%) indicated that they worked with a person with a disability. When asked about the priority level of digital accessibility work at their company, 63% said it improved over the last year, and 62% said that the attitudes surrounding such work have also increased over the last year.

When it came to resources, almost half of our survey respondents used the following types of resources to help them resolve digital accessibility issues: online searches (12%), WCAG specifications (11%), academic articles/studies (9%), non-academic articles from companies/organizations (7%), and video tutorials/talks (7%). When it came to accessibility tools, the data showed that technical professionals used automated browser extensions (15%), browser inspector/tools (14%), color contrast checkers/palette generators (13%), code linters/checkers (8%), and color contrast simulators/filters (7%) the most.

For assistive technology tools used, the majority of respondents used a keyboard (19%), VoiceOver (VO) screen reader on macOS (13%), magnification programs/tools (10%), 10% used Non-Visual Desktop Access (NVDA) screen reader for Windows OS (10%), and 8% used VoiceOver (VO) screen reader on iOS mobile (8%) to help them resolve digital accessibility issues. When asked about using such resources, tools, and assistive technology, most survey participants (65%) said they were extremely likely to use them. However, when asked about hiring a company or individual, most respondents said they were only somewhat likely to use them (33%). When asked about hiring people with disabilities specifically, 38% said they were extremely likely to use them to help resolve their digital accessibility needs.

We ran various t-tests against different independent variables/factors such as gender identity, disability representation, and priorities/attitudes but did not find anything of statistical significance. However, we did see some significant results related to a survey participant's title/position and their likelihood to use any resources, tool, or assistive technology to resolve digital accessibility issues. If a participant was a front-end developer, they were statistically more likely to seek a person with a disability to help them than in a different role/position.

Future studies will explore questions surrounding general digital accessibility knowledge, the educational backgrounds of technical professionals, and which educational resources and tools might help train the next generation of technology industry professionals.

References

1. WHO. Disability. https://www.who.int/news-room/fact-sheets/detail/disability-and-health, (Accessed 24 Feb 2023)
2. Putnam, C., Dahman, M., Rose, E., Cheng, J., Bradford, G.: Best practices for teaching accessibility in university classrooms: cultivating awareness, understanding, and appreciation for diverse users. ACM Trans. Accessible Comput. 8(4), 1–16 (2016). https://doi.org/10.1145/2831424
3. Bi, T., Xia, X., Lo, D., Grundy, J., Zimmermann, T., Ford, D.: Accessibility in Software Practice: A Practitioner's Perspective. arXiv:2103.08778 [csSE] (Mar 2021). http://arxiv.org/abs/2103.08778
4. Snider, S., Scott II, W.L., Trewin, S.: Accessibility information needs in the enterprise. ACM Trans. Accessible Comput. 12(4), 1–23 (2020). Pp. https://doi.org/10.1145/3368620
5. Conn, p., et al.: Understanding the motivations of final-year computing undergraduates for considering accessibility. ACM Trans. Comput. Educ. 20(2), 1–22 (2020). https://doi.org/10.1145/3381911
6. Baker, C.M., El-Glaly, Y.N., Shinohara, K.: A systematic analysis of accessibility in computing education research. In: Proceedings of the 51st ACM Technical Symposium on Computer Science Education, pp. pp.107–113 (2020). https://doi.org/10.1145/3328778.3366843
7. Shinohara, K., Bennett, C.L., Pratt, W., Wobbrock, J.O.: Tenets for social accessibility: towards humanizing disabled people in design. ACM Trans. Accessible Comput. 11(1), 1–31 (2018). https://doi.org/10.1145/3178855
8. WebAIM. 2021. Survey of web accessibility practitioners #3 results https://webaim.org/projects/practitionersurvey3, (Accessed 24 Feb 2023)
9. Patel, R., Breton, p., Baker, C.M., El-Glaly, Y.N., Shinohara, K.: Why software is not accessible: technology professionals' perspectives and challenges. In: Extended Abstracts of the 2020 CHI Conference on Human Factors in Computing Systems. ACM, pp. 1–9. https://doi.org/10.1145/3334480.3383103

Vibrotactile Human Machine Interface for Electric Wheelchairs to Intuitively Present the Movement Direction of Nearby Objects

Tomokazu Furuya[✉] and Mutsuki Kobayashi

Tokyo Metropolitan College of Industrial Technology, 8-17-1 Minami-Senju, Arakawa-Ku, Tokyo 116-8523, Japan

t-furuya@g.metro-cit.ac.jp

Abstract. We attempted to transmit the movement direction of nearby vehicles using "vibrotactile apparent motion," perceived as moving a vibration by two vibrations with a time difference. First, we prototyped a device in which eight linear vibration motors (four on each side) were attached to a handle grip equivalent to that on an electric wheelchair. Using the device, we performed evaluation experiments to determine vibration stimuli that could show five directions (left and right, diagonally backward left and right, and backward) and confirmed whether the directions were understood by subjects. As a result, the vibration stimuli achieved a high accuracy rate for understanding the presented directions. In the future, if we can confirm the effect of vibrotactile apparent motion on accident prevention in real-world settings, it could be applied to various mobility devices as a universal design interface for older adults.

Keywords: Electric Wheelchairs · Human Machine Interface · Tactile Apparent Motion · Vibrotactile Simulation

1 Introduction

Japan has the world's highest rate of aging, with around 30% of the population aged 65 years and over. This proportion is expected to increase further in the future. In this context, electric wheelchairs are essential assistive devices for maintaining and improving the quality of life of disabled, older adults. However, in Japan, there are many accidents involving older adults using electric wheelchairs, mostly involving automobiles while crossing a road [1]. If electric wheelchair users can become more aware of approaching cars, they should be able to avoid accidents. However, it is difficult for elderly people to hear warning sounds outside, and there is little space on a wheelchair for a warning display near the handle. We, therefore, focused on the tactile sensation between the hands, and the steering wheel, which is gripped while driving an electric wheelchair, and researched the transmission of peripheral conditions by vibrotactile stimulation from the handle.Studies on the presenting and alerting using vibrotactile stimuli have been conducted in automobile driving. Vibrotactile stimuli have been used to warn the abdomen

C. Stephanidis et al. (Eds.): HCII 2023, CCIS 1833, pp. 284–291, 2023.
https://doi.org/10.1007/978-3-031-35992-7_39

and back [2], to alert the arms, legs and back/abdomen [3], to provide directions to the thighs [4], and to transmit warnings and navigation information from the steering wheel to the palms [5, 6]. In addition, our laboratory has already attempted to transmit the direction of surrounding objects using the vibrotactile apparent motion by assembling a vibration device on the steering wheel of a car [7]. However, because this research was focused on cars, it only transmitted information about vehicles passing in lanes either side of the car and vehicles in front and behind. In Japan, electric wheelchairs are treated as pedestrians [8], and it is assumed that surrounding objects approach from various directions. Furthermore, the shape of the steering wheel of a car is different from that of the handle of an electric wheelchair. Therefore, in this study, the presentation of directions from the left and right, from the left and diagonally right backward, and from behind, coming from areas outside the wheelchair user's field of vision, was studied using tactile apparent motion.

2 Basic Concept and Methodology

2.1 Basic Concept and Use Cases

There are two main types of electric wheelchairs: handle-type and joystick-type, but because handle-type wheelchairs account for approximately 77.9% of all shipments in Japan (in 2021) [9], they were the target of this study. The peripheral state is transmitted by providing a vibration stimulus that moves in the same direction as that of a vehicle in the blind spot behind or to the side of the electric wheelchair user.

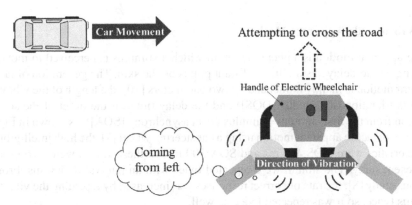

Fig. 1. Use case 1: Examples of vibrotactile stimuli to present when attempting to cross the road.

A use case is shown in Fig. 1 and 2. Given that electric wheelchairs are often involved in accidents while crossing the road, the system presents vibrotactile stimuli to warn users that a vehicle is coming when the wheelchair is about to cross, as shown in Fig. 1. Also, when a vehicle is approaching diagonally from behind, the system presents a stimulus representing diagonally behind, as shown in Fig. 2(a). When a vehicle is approaching from directly behind, the system presents a stimulus representing the front from the rear of something as shown in Fig. 2(b). Communication technologies between vehicles and between vehicles and pedestrians, such as V2X, are evolving. However, the key is the way that information is presented, and this research contributes to vehicle to electric wheelchair communication. In addition, because the direction can be transmitted by vibration, the system could be used for root navigation.

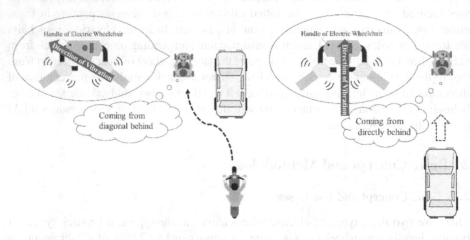

(a) Use case 2: Diagonal direction   (b) Use case 3: Rear to front

Fig. 2. Use cases of a vibrotactile human machine interface for electric wheelchairs.

2.2 Vibrotactile Apparent Motion

Tactile apparent motion is a phenomenon in which a stimulus is perceived to move by applying a time-delayed stimulus to distant points on the skin. The generation of tactile apparent motion is mainly influenced by two parameters [10]: the length of the vibration stimulus (duration of stimulus [DOS]) and the delay time for the onset of the second vibration from the first stimulus (stimulus onset asynchrony [SOA]), as shown in Fig. 3. In a study of tactile apparent motion using a car steering wheel [7], the high intelligibility characteristics were DOS 400 ms and SOA 300 ms, so these values were also used in the present study. The stimuli were repeated twice with an interval of 500 ms. From a previous study [8], the rate of correct responses was increased by repeating the vibration stimulus twice, so it was repeated twice as well.

2.3 Apparatus

Figure 4 shows the experimental apparatus, which consisted of a handle (PVC pipe) with eight linear vibration motors (LD14–002, resonance frequency: approx.150 Hz, Nidec Copal Electronics Corporation), four on each side, controlled by a motor driver (DRV2605, Adafruit Corporation) and a microcomputer (Arduino MEGA 2560). The overall width of the steering wheel was 370 mm, and the left - right distance between the two hands was 200 mm. Two prototypes were made: the minimum overall width

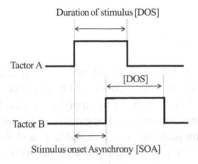

Fig. 3. Tactile apparent motion.

(370 mm), which can be reproduced with reference to an actual electric wheelchair, and a maximum overall width of 680 mm with reference to the maximum width of 700 mm specified in the JIS standard [11]. As a result of testing the prototypes, the minimum value was used, because there was no effect due to the feeling of the distance between the two hands. The position of the vibration device was set at a distance of 50 mm so that the entire vibration device would strike the palm, as the average hand width of adult men and women is 80.4 mm [12] and the width of the vibration device is 14 mm. To prevent the perception of vibrations on the palm from an unexpected location by the handle from receiving vibrations from the vibration device, urethane foam was placed between the handle and the vibration device to prevent the transmission of vibrations to the handle.

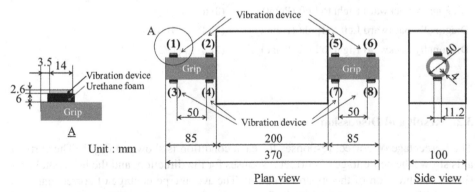

Fig. 4. Apparatus of vibrotactile human machine interface for electric wheelchairs.

The following experiments were reviewed and approved by the Research Ethics Committee of the Arakawa Campus of the Tokyo Metropolitan College of Industrial Technology, and were conducted after obtaining the informed consent of the participants.

3 Experiment 1

3.1 Design and Procedure

The vibration device applies vibration impulses to the left and right palms as a tactile apparent motion. The experiment was conducted to evaluate whether the direction of the apparent motion could be perceived by applying a vibration stimulus to the left and right palms from a vibration device. The experiment consisted of four randomized trials of the seven vibration patterns shown in Table 1, and the subjects were asked to respond with the direction they perceived. All patterns were presented to and learned by participants before the experiment. White noise was provided through headphones so as not to influence the vibration sound. For the diagonal direction, two conditions were compared: a "point" condition with one vibration device and a "plane" condition with two vibration devices. The subjects were a total of 11 males and females aged 19 - 20 years.

Table 1. Types of vibrotactile stimuli used in Experiment 1.

Direction of Apparent Motion	Vibration Device Number (See Fig. 4)
Rear to Front	(4)(7) to (2)(5)
Left to Right	(2)(4) to (5)(7)
Right to Left	(5)(7) to (2)(4)
Diagonally Backward Left to Right (Point)	(3) to (6)
Diagonally Backward Right to Left (Point)	(8) to (1)
Diagonally Backward Left to Right (Plane)	(3)(4) to (5)(6)
Diagonally Backward Right to Left (Plane)	(7)(8) to (1)(2)

3.2 Result and Discussion

The percentage of correct responses for each condition is shown in Fig. 5. The vertical axis shows the percentage of correct responses for the direction, and the horizontal axis shows the direction of the apparent motion. The average percentage of correct answers was 82.8%, which is a high result. For the diagonal direction, diagonally backward (plane) was 2.2–4.5 points higher than diagonally backward (point).

The subjects were confused because both diagonal and left-right directions vibrated both hands, and some commented that they could not make instantaneous judgments. Therefore, we considered that the left-right direction could be differentiated from the diagonal direction and misrecognition could be reduced by making the left hand only (1)(3) to (2)(4) instead of the left hand to the right hand (2)(4) to (5)(7). This condition will be confirmed in Experiment 2. The correct response rate was relatively low for the rear-to-front pattern. If even one of the vibration patterns from (4)(7) to (2)(5), which is the rear to front vibration pattern, was not perceived, it was considered to be mis-recognized as

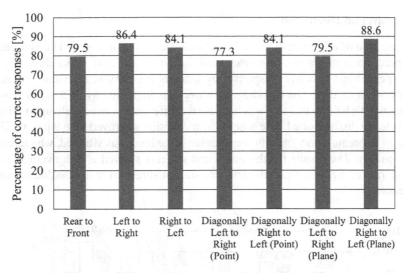

Fig. 5. Percentage of correct responses in Experiment 1 (n = 11)

diagonal or left-right. Therefore, the rear to front direction was transmitted by vibrating (3)(4)(7) and (8), which were located behind the handle, at regular intervals(500ms), without using the apparent motion. This will also be confirmed in Experiment 2.

4 Experiment 2

4.1 Design and Procedure

The same experiments in Sect 3.1 were conducted for the same 11 subjects with the five vibration patterns listed in Table 2. Alerts and warnings require an understanding of the direction of the dangerous object on the spur of the moment. Therefore, the unlearned condition was also evaluated. The subjects in the unlearned condition were five 20-year-old males, different from the previous experiments.

Table 2. Types of vibrotactile stimuli used in Experiment 2.

Direction of Apparent Motion	Vibration Device Number (See Fig. 4)
Rear to Front (Not apparent motion)	(3)(4)(7)(8)
Left to Right	(1)(3) to (2)(4)
Right to Left	(6)(8) to (5)(7)
Diagonally Backward Left to Right (Plane)	(3)(4) to (5)(6)
Diagonally Backward Right to Left (Plane)	(7)(8) to (1)(2)

4.2 Results and Discussion

The percentage of correct responses for each item is shown in Fig. 6. The vertical axis is the percentage of correct responses, and the horizontal axis is the direction. The average percentage of correct responses by learners was 90.9%, exceeding the results of the previous section. The two diagonal directions improved by 20.5 and 9.1 points, respectively. We believe that this was because the difference between left and right could now be clearly distinguished. The rear to front direction improved by 6.9 points. This is thought to be because only the vibrating device in the back was vibrated, which reduced misrecognition. The results for the unlearned subjects showed a high average correct response rate of 87.0%. Thus, the transmission of direction was possible regardless experience.

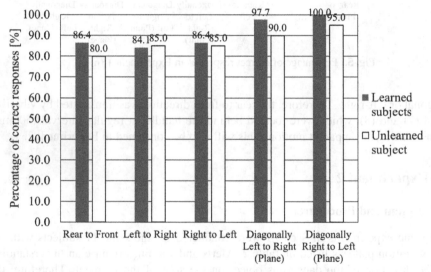

Fig. 6. Percentage of correct responses in Experiment 2 (Learned subjects: n = 11, Unlearned subjects: n = 5)

5 Conclusions

We studied the intuitive presentation of vibrotactile stimulation representing the movements of objects surrounding an electric wheelchair. As a result, the correct response rate was more than 90% in the diagonal direction for both learned and unlearned subjects, and more than 80% in the rear-front and left-right directions, indicating the possibility of transmitting information about the surroundings. In the future, a driving simulator will be used to verify whether the system can be applied as an alert or warning.

References

1. National Police Agency: The accident of electric wheelchairs - The reality of recent road accidents, https://www.npa.go.jp/koutsuu/kikaku12/shi_04jikojittai.pdf, (Accessed 25 2 2023) (in Japanese)
2. Ho, C., Tan, H.Z., Spence, C.: Using spatial vibrotactile cues to direct visual attention in driving scenes. Transp. Res. Part F **8**, 397–412 (2005)
3. Murata, A., Kemori, S., Morikawa, M.: Basic study on automotive warning presentation to front/rear danger by vibrotactile stimulation. Japanese J. Ergonom. **47**(50), 198–208. (2011) (in Japanese)
4. Okuwa, M., Nakashima, A., Fujieda, N.: Development of a tactile driver interface using seat vibrations. Trans. Hum. Interf. Soc. **10**(3), 363–371 (2008) (in Japanese)
5. Murata, A., Tanaka, K., Morikawa, M.: Basic study on effectiveness of tactile interface for warning presentation in driving environment. In: Fifth International Workshop on Computational Intelligence & Applications IEEE SMC Hiroshima Chapter, pp. 242–247 (2009)
6. Hwang, S., Ryu, J.: The haptic steering wheel: vibro-tactile based navigation for the driving environment. In: 2010 8th IEEE International Conference on Pervasive Computing and Communications Workshops (PERCOM Workshops), pp. 660–665 (2010)
7. Furuya, T., Kawashima, T.: Presenting direction of surrounding objects by steering wheel with vibrotactile apparent motion. Trans. Soc. Automot. Eng. Japan **53**(3), 567–572 (2022) (in Japanese)
8. National Police Agency: Manual on the safe use of electric wheelchairs - Legal position and methods of passage. https://www.npa.go.jp/koutsuu/kikaku12/shi_03mokuji-itiduke.pdf, (Accessed 6 March 2023) (in Japanese)
9. Dendo-kurumaisu Anzen Fukyu Kyokai (Association for the Promotion of Electric Wheelchair Safety): Number of shipments, https://www.den-ankyo.org/society/transition.html, (Accessed 6 March 2023) (in Japanese)
10. Kirman, J.B.: Tactile apparent movement: The effects of interstimulus onset interval and stimulus duration. Percept. Psychophys. **15**(1), 1–6 (1974)
11. Japanese Standard Association: JIS Handbook, vol. 38, pp.1056–1109. (2012) (in Japanese)
12. Kouchi,M.,: AIST Japanese hand dimension data (2012).https://www.airc.aist.go.jp/dhrt/hand/index.html, (Accessed 25 Feb 2023) (in Japanese)

Therapy Oriented Garden Monitoring System Gardening for Autistic Children

Rubén Galicia Mejía$^{(\boxtimes)}$, Erika Hernández Rubio, and Jorge A. Ruiz Escareño

Instituto Politécnico Nacional México, Escuela Superior de Cómputo, Av Othon de Mendizabal S/N, Ciudad de México, México
Rgaliciam@ipn.mx

Abstract. An increasing number of children with autism spectrum disorder (ASD) is linked to blend in problems like anxiety and depression, is known that visual aids make it immediately clear that electronic media can and are there to help the autistic child. This work proposes a system that helps to reduce the levels of anxiety in children with autism, since it is difficult for children to understand an instruction given by an adult and by nature such children have a better visual understanding; Due to this, their cognitive process is stimulated by colors and images, responding to the what, how, when and how long of the instruction, this system aims to help autistic children by making use of these elements, since assigning them the task of caring an orchard considerably lowers their anxiety levels, because it is a task that can be structured, thus helping children attend scheduled activities and thus reduce their anxiety, the system receives information on humidity, temperature and sunlight from different digital electronic sensors placed in the orchard, this information is constantly acquired and is obtained from the orchard, it is sent by an electronic system to the internet cloud, to later notify the child through an software on a computer or a tablet if the garden needs to be cared for by the autistic child, the data coming from the garden is to show them in a friendly and striking way, in this way the child's attention is captured, either to be irrigated by water, or to have excess of it, with these actions, the child autistic develops an understanding regarding a given instruction. Tests were carried out with the system in a period of time in a child with (ASD), in this way it was verified that this helps significantly to reduce the levels of anxiety and depression of the autistic child.

Keywords: Therapy · Garden · Autism · Tablet

1 Introduction

Autism Spectrum Disorder (ASD) is a neurobiological disorder of the development of communication and social interaction, which manifests itself during the first three years of life and will last throughout the entire life cycle of the person who suffers from it. The fundamental symptoms of autism are two: 1) Persistent deficits in communication and social interaction. 2). Restrictive and repetitive patterns of behavior, interests, or activities [1]. The Monitoring system garnering was developed focused on children with ASD, specifically with autism and Rett syndrome, autism usually occurs in the first 3 years, it can present various symptoms such as: no or very little verbal communication, the child is not very sociable and solitary or showing no interest in identifying objects or attracting the attention of the parents, just like Rett syndrome, except that it occurs almost exclusively in girls and is regressive in nature [2], the different traits that can cause this syndrome are loss of speech, balance problems, breathing problems, behavior problems, learning problems, and decreased or loss of movement in the hands [3, 4]. To contribute to better health for children with these disorders, one can use to psychosocial interventions such as: behavioral therapy, social behavior, understanding the environment, as well as therapies that stimulate motor skills and training programs. Education and learning programs, both for the individual and for family members. Among the occupational therapies that an individual with ASD and in general anyone with some type of human behavior disorder, can practice therapeutic horticulture, which has proven to have positive effects for those who carry it out [5, 6]. Despite these practices, the trend today is for children to spend less time outdoors, which sharpens the practice of horticulture as occupational therapy, demonstrating that contact with nature helps to reduce various energy deficit disorders. Attention [7, 8]. For this reason, it seeks to provide a tool that is at the hand of any person and that can assist therapy based on horticulture as a means that can be used to promote the development and/or recovery of personal autonomy, both physically and mentally integrating the development of basic and social skills [9], etc.

2 Methods

2.1 Procedure and Design

Garden monitoring system oriented to horticultural therapy for autistic children is made up of 2 main modules; hardware and software, which are made up of sub modules, hardware consists of 3 processes through which the analog variables pass; by acquisition, conversion and treatment and sending of data to the database in the cloud, while software is composed of 2 processes; acquisition of data from the database and display of data in a user-friendly way. The system works according to the diagram in Fig. 1.

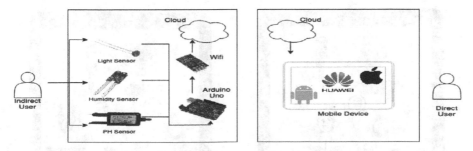

Fig. 1. System Diagram

2.2 Hardware

In this module the following 3 processes are carried out: 1) Acquisition of the variables [10, 11]: The system was subjected to variable climatic conditions to obtain the correct behavior of the sensors [12, 13]. 2) Conversion [14, 15] and treatment of the values: 3) Sending of values: The values are sent through a WIFI module using a POST request to send them quickly and safely.

2.3 Software

In this module the following 2 processes are carried out: 1) Acquisition of the values [16–18]: The values are obtained from a SQL-type database using a GET-type request [20], which returns the information in a JSON format. 2) Data sample: the data obtained from the database is used as a reference to know which image to display depending on the range in which they are found. Once the system was developed, tests were carried out to verify the different states that can be obtained through the sensors, which are documented below: State of lack of water: in this state the sensors detect low or no humidity in the soil, which shows the need to water the plant as seen in Figs. (2, 3, 4,

Fig. 2. Overexposure to the sun

Fig. 3. Lack of water

Fig. 4. High acid

Fig. 5. Alert values

5). Interfaces were developed taking into account the data bank Aragonese Center of Augmentative and Alternative Communication [21].

3 Results and Discution

Tests were carried out with a child diagnosed with ASD (Matthew), with the help of the child's family we managed to have a better idea of the improvement in the child's mood and behavior. The system being designed following data banks with images that are friendly to children, was noticed from the first approach to the system that it was of interest to the `child` as expected, when the garden lacks water, the child indicates that it has to be watered, if it is sunny and the soil in the garden is dry, it indicates that it must be watered Fig. 6. The system is configured to connect directly to the network of the house where it is being tested and is designed so that it can only be connected to a power source, either the previously mentioned battery or a direct source using an power supply to feed the prototype with 5V, depending on the type of power it has is the autonomy that the device presents Fig. 7. It should be noted that all these tests were carried out under the supervision of Matthew's parents, Tests were carried out for more than six months, which the child became interested in caring for his orchard and in this way his therapy to reduce stress and anxiety was carried out, a considerable decrease in his anxiety level was noted. The garden therapy system will be applied in the Mexican Association of Horticulture and Therapeutic Gardening [22] and the ATZAN Psychopedagogical and Psychotherapeutic Center to help more children with autism syndrome and reduce their anxiety.

Fig. 6. Matthew's interaction, with the system orchard status on the screen

Fig. 7. System working in the orchard

4 Conclusions

The work presented managed to obtain the expected results throughout its development, even at the cost of the pandemic situation and health issues. The sensors were calibrated to obtain the `most` accurate values possible and thus have greater precision when reporting the state of the orchard to the child. The interfaces were developed taking into account the database "Aragonese Center of Augmentative and Alternative Communication" which is the largest collection of visual material for children with this disorder. Taking into account the above, tests were carried out to find out if the child seemed interested in the interfaces made, which was a success, since he does seem interested and also quickly began to associate what he saw on the screen with his garden. In general, it is expected that this final work can be replicated in different associations such as the Mexican Association of Horticulture and Therapeutic Gardening¨and the ATZAN Psychopedagogical and Psychotherapeutic Center, where horticultural therapy is already used satisfactorily and it is hoped that it will be able to help as many children as possible .

Acknowledgments. Thanks to PhD. Berenice Galicia for contributing ideas to the system and testing it. This work was supported by IPN México.

References

1. World Health Organization, "Autism spectrum disorders". https://www.who.int/es/news-room/fact-sheets/detail/autism-spectrum-disorders (Accessed October 2020)
2. Project Autism la Garriga, "Autism: Definition, Symptoms and Indications (2016). Available in. https://www.autismo.com.es/autismo/que-es-el-autismo.html. (Accessed February-March 2020)
3. International University of Valencia, The different types of the autism spectrum (ASD): characteristics and forms of intervention in the classroom (2018). https://www.universid adviu.com/los-distintos-tipos-de-trastorno-del-espectro-autista-tea-caracteristicas-y-formas-de-intervencion-en-el-aula/. (Accessed August-September 2020)
4. National Institute of Neurological Disorders and Stroke, Rett Syndrome (2010). https://esp anol.ninds.nih.gov/trastornos/el_sindrome_de_rett.htm. (Accessed August-September 2020)
5. Schneider, J.: Learning Styles and Autism (2017). https://revista.redipe.org/index.php/1/art icle/download/400/397. (Accessed October 2020)
6. Rezayi, S., Tehrani-Doost, M., Shahmoradi.: Features and effects of computer-based games on cognitive impairments in children with autism spectrum disorder: an evidence-based systematic literature review https://www.scopus.com/record/ (Accessed December 2022)
7. Garrido, L.: Robot Nao: a therapy for children with neurodevelopmental disorders - Tec Transference, Tec Transfer (2020). https://transferencia.tec.mx/2018/04/08/robot-nao-una-terapia-para-ninos-con-trastornos-de-neurodesarrollo/ (Accessed October 2020)
8. Navarra Autism Association, TEACCH Learning Methodology (2016). http://www.autism onavarra.com/2016/08/metodologia-de-aprendizaje-teacch/. (Accessed October 2020.)
9. Infosalus, What is the Origin of Autism?/ https://m.infosalus.com/salud-investigacion/not icia-cual-origen-autismo-20190101075934.html. (Accessed November 2020)
10. Latam Mechatronics, Sensor What is it and types of sensors?. https://www.mecatronicalatam. com/tutorial/es/sensores (Accessed November 2020)
11. LDR, Mechatronics LATAM (2020). https://www.mecatronicalatam.com/es/tutoriales/sen sores/sensor-de-luz/ldr/. *(Accessed November 2020)
12. Relative Humidity Sensor (RHS), Cab.inta-csic.es (2020). https://cab.inta-csic.es/rems/es/ descripcion-del-instrumento/sensor-de-humedad-relativa-rhs/. (Accessed November 2020)
13. pH meters, what are they and how do they work?, Es.omega.com (2020). https://es.omega. com/prodinfo/medidor-ph.html. (Accessed November 2020)
14. PH sensor, Jenck.com (2020). https://www.jenck.com/productos/producto/dpd1p1/specific aciones. (Accessed November 2020)

15. Gironés, J.T.: Chapter 1 Overview and Development Environment, The Big Android Book. 2nd ed. Ed. Marcombo (2011)
16. Mendez, R.: Javascript. https://www.um.es/docencia/barzana/DAWEB/Lenguaje-de-progra macion-JavaScript-1.pdf. (Accessed November 2020)
17. MDN Web Docs, "HTML". https://developer.mozilla.org/es/docs/HTML/HTML5. (Accessed November 2020)
18. Web Development, "CSS". (Accessed November 2020). https://desarrolloweb.com/home/css
19. Ionic Framework, "What is Ionic Framework?". https://ionicframework.com/docs/intro. (Accessed November 2020)
20. Amazon, "What is NoSQL?". https://aws.amazon.com/es/nosql/. (Accessed November 2020)
21. Aragonese Center of Augmentative and Alternative Communication. https://arasaac.org (Accessed Octuber 2020)
22. Psychopedagogical and Psychotherapeutic Center, "ATZAN Psychopedagogical and Psychotherapeutic Center,". https://www.atzan.com.mx/ (Accessed January 2021)

PipeBlind: A Game Adaptation for Blind

Anabela Gomes[1,2(✉)], Nelson Simão[1], and Ana Rita Teixeira[3,4]

[1] Polytechnic Institute of Coimbra - ISEC, Coimbra, Portugal
anabela@isec.pt
[2] CISUC—Department of Informatics Engineering, University of Coimbra, Coimbra, Portugal
[3] Polytechnic Institute of Coimbra - ESEC, Coimbra, Portugal
ateixeira@ua.pt
[4] Institute of Electronics and Informatics Engineering of Aveiro, University of Aveiro, Aveiro, Portugal

Abstract. Video games adapted for people with any type of disability should be a growing concern for the video game production companies, programmers and researchers. Literature research reveals that there is still no systematic and structured set of guidelines being followed in order to achieve a truly accessible game. Some researchers and programmers simply follow some recommendations and not always. In this sense, we tried to follow well-known and established heuristics about usability with their mapping for accessibility to be applied in a well-known game, Pipe Mania. Although the game is not yet completely ready to be played by a blind person, it already has the basic mechanisms implemented and others defined. In addition to the recommendations found in the literature, in gathering expert opinion, in applying heuristics and guidelines, it will also be necessary to interview individuals representing potential players. Finally, the game should be tested by users including the disabled ones in order to evaluate the Player eXperience.

Keywords: Games · Accessibility · Blind · Auditory icons · Sound

1 Introduction

Nowadays, games play an important role in our society and have gained ground in recent years in all age groups and with different user profiles for very different purposes than just entertainment. However, only a few programmers and companies seem to be concerned with users with special needs or disabilities such as the blind. They do not promote equal opportunities with regard to people with disabilities and few games are adapted or designed for them [1, 2]. Nevertheless, these concerns are increasing in importance and can be seen in some of the more recent works [3].

With this concern in mind, the authors of this paper searched the literature in order to find answers or suggestions to follow in order to make a game adaptable and playable by the blind. Before starting the adaptation work itself, but already having the type of game in mind, an attempt was made to have an up-to-date situation on this topic. Thus, we searched the literature and found a systematic review on video game accessibility. This review analyzed different types of video games and interaction models [4].

In that particular systematic literature review, in the studies investigated, the authors concluded that video games are currently not developed in a fully accessible way, although these concerns and some adaptations are starting to become evident, especially with some interested researchers. They also concluded that the adaptations do not establish a generic methodology to be followed and the developers themselves do not appreciate the existing ones or do not follow them. Furthermore, the pursuit of fully accessible implementations is an arduous and unrealistic task. They also conclude that its implementation would bring benefits to people with disabilities, which are usually excluded from its use.

As there are different types and classifications of games, we decided to focus on a specific game and try to collect and follow the recommendations in [5] that suggest a set of usability, accessibility and gameplay heuristics for audio games, keeping blind people in mind. Other considerations that resulted from the investigation on auditory information were also followed in the implementation [6].

2   Game Adaptation

The game developed and presented in this article is based on the famous well-known 2D pipeline puzzle game Pipe Mania or Pipe Dream [7], which consists of placing pipes on a map in order to lead water from an origin to a destination.

The developed game has several additional aspects compared to the original game, for example, the player can stop the water for a certain period of time, there are impassable walls on the map, the algorithm for generating pieces can be changed, the game can be played on two remote machines, among others. However, the great benefit of this work resides in the efforts made in its adaptation to enable gameplay with easy interaction with a visually impaired user, taking into account accessibility aspects for blind players. Next, a more detailed description of each of the game's features and options in terms of accessibility is given, considering gameplay by blind players.

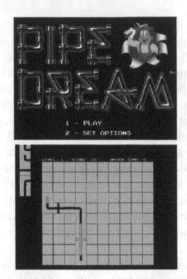

2.1 Inputs

Even though there are several considerations for handicapped people for controlling computers designing software with different input devices and equipment we considered the control of the game, mainly, by keyboard. Basically, we reflected on the recommendation for "Adjustable sensitivity/error tolerance" and "Adjustable speed and size of pointers and markers". With concerns to these recommendations it should be possible to adjust the properties for the keyboard such as, the repetition delay, repetition speed, marker blinking, slow keys, filter keys, switch keys and other keyboard configuration aspects and button configuration (left/right handed), speed of double clicking, speed of mouse pointer movement, acceleration, use of mouse keys, and other mouse configurations. It should also be possible to adjust the size and speed of the pointers and markers.

In the specific case of this game, in addition to the configuration options mentioned above, special attention was given to the first aspect considered in the developed game, text insertion. Thus, the first screen presented to the user is a screen that asks for the name. Naturally, the name is an important aspect for the online version of the network game. It is also important for the individual and offline version enabling the existence of personalized feedback.

A very important factor in the design of an application that will be used by the blind or people with visual impairments is that it is necessary to keep the user informed of where he/she is and what is happening. Thus, Heuristic 1: "Visibility of system status" will be the main one followed, with the visual part replaced by audio. Thus, the audio will be responsible for transmitting the actions that are relevant to the game. As the user cannot use his/her eyes to know which stage of the game he/she is in, the user will have to use his other senses to be able to locate himself/herself. Regarding these aspects, it was considered that when the user enters the application, the system would use text-to-speech to talk to the user and say the phrase "Type your name limited to 20 characters". For every 10 s of inactivity the system would repeat the same phrase. Related to this aspect, another important factor is to inform the user of how many characters he/she can still type as well as those he/she has already typed.

Thus, in addition to the game pronouncing the characters already typed, it also uses beeps with increasing frequency to warn the user that he/she is reaching the limit of possible characters. Naturally, when the user deletes a character, a sound representing that action will be emitted and the frequency of the beeps will decrease to tell the user that one more character can be typed. When the user reaches the maximum number of characters, a different and loud finish sound will be emitted to represent that the user has reached the maximum number of characters hc/she can type.

Informal tests carried out with these aspects reveal that the frequencies of the sounds used turned out to be very high, making it somewhat uncomfortable to hear such frequencies for a long period of time.

2.2 Menus

Essentially the same principles that were applied to entering text, presented in the previous section, also apply to the design and implementation of menus. What is important in a menu made for visually impaired users is to inform the user of what is happening and where he/she is. Thus, when the user "enters" a screen that presents him with a menu, the program should start by emitting a sentence that represents the first option and from x in x time, it should proceed to the next option and also emit the sentence that represents that option. The menu must respond to pressing the arrow keys on the keyboard and must advance through the options, emitting sounds that represent such action. An interesting addition, not yet implemented, would be pressing the specific key over an option to enable text-to-speech and inform the user of more details about the option. It was contemplated that the menu would respond to pressing all the arrows on the keyboard, with the top and left arrows having exactly the same functionality and the bottom and right arrows also having the same functionality. The reason for such logic is due to the fact that for a blind user the layout of the menu does not make sense and, therefore, the menu may have vertical and/or horizontal options that the user will not be aware of and therefore the menu should respond to all keyboard arrows. Naturally, a sound is emitted when this is done.

Another consideration concerns popup menus. During the execution of the application, there are several popups that can be shown to the user to inform him/her of any errors or other aspects considered of interest in the game. In the precise case of the implemented game, the only action that the popup would take was to use text-to-speech to indicate to the user what happened and that he/she must press any key to proceed.

2.3 Playability

Without a doubt, the gameplay issue is the most challenging part of supporting the blind and raises interesting questions from an accessibility point of view. As previously mentioned, the objective of the game is to take the water from a point of origin to a destination point, with aspects of some complexity, so we will start with the most obvious problems.

An important aspect of the gameplay is to provide information regarding the user's location, letting him/her know the cell he/she is in. A trick often used in games of this type for the user to move around on a two-dimensional map is the emission of sounds that represent the player's position. The player can use the arrow keys to move around the map and for each cell a different sound is emitted based on the player's position. Thus, each elevation (from cell 0 to n) has a different sound frequency associated with each height (y coordinate) and, each time the player moves horizontally (x coordinate), a sound is emitted by the computer on the user's side, for example the upper right corner, can produce a sound with a higher frequency on the right side of the computer. Another option also used is that the displacement to a new cell is indicated verbally by the real coordinates corresponding to the cell where the user is.

Also considered relevant is the user knowing the location of the different components on the map, as well as how to position the pieces on the map. The user obviously has to know where the source and destination of the water is. There are several possibilities, one of which is to provide shortcuts to the user to be able to move to the source and destination cell of the water. When this shortcut is activated, the cursor is positioned in that cell and emits a sound that represents the cell, as described above. The user will place pieces on the map by pressing the enter key. The recognition of the piece to be placed is identified by a unique characteristic sound and through the verbalization of its name. Recognition of pieces placed in a certain position can be performed by sounds, be they text-to-speech or beeps. Thus, when the user moves around on the map, each cell he/she passes emits the sound of the cell and the sound of the piece that is there. There are also shortcuts for the user to move to certain special positions on the map, for example, to the coordinates of the last piece he/she inserted.

In this game, it is also important that the user knows how much time is left for the water to start flowing. Thus, with each passing second, the time until the water starts flowing decreases and to indicate this effect to the user, a technique similar to the one presented for inserting characters is used. Thus, as the time approaches 0, the frequency of the beeps that are emitted increases from second to second, making a different sound when the time runs out and being additionally warned that the water is starting to flow. Each time the water advances, a specific and characteristic sound of running water will be emitted. When the user moves towards a piece containing water, he/she hears the sounds of the cell, the water and the piece. When the game ends (for various reasons) the user is notified via text-to-speech of such event.

An important aspect is that the game includes several levels so that the player can progress in the game. It is important that the game offers different difficulty levels to challenge, stimulate, and enjoy giving motivation to continue. In this case, it was considered that the game would be structured so as to progress naturally from easy (beginner) to more complex (advanced) levels.

2.4 General Considerations

Undoubtedly, the adaptation of a game for the blind should fundamentally be based on sound. Nevertheless, the user should be the one who dictates the best option for the game (text-to-speech, specific and appropriate sounds for each element and situation of the game, shortcuts, among others). Thus, some considerations about auditory information are made. Some other important aspects such as the speed at which sound/speech is played as well as the choice between a male or female voice should also be considered. Also to be noted is the possibility of switching off/on different sounds, especially if the sounds are not essential for advancing in the game. Sound can motivate, but may also be very distracting, so a distinction must be made between essential sounds and optional sounds.

In situations where there is text, it may be an advantage to use synthetic speech. In this specific game, the textual description of the symbols used may be simpler than their association with specific sounds, but it is an aspect that will be tested.

We tried to follow the 10 heuristics of Jacob Nielsen [8] for interaction design, having in consideration its adaptability for the blind. Regarding the Heuristic1: "Visibility of system status" was the most important consideration and therefore was the one given special attention. The issue of feedback was also an important aspect to consider. Thus, not only should messages be audible, but they should also be able to be repeated, either automatically when there is no response from the user after some time, or at the user's request. Also the possibility to start/stop/pause the reproduction of a message must be foreseen. The existence of other elements such as rewards and associated auditory feedback should be expected. Important aspects to keep the player challenged like checking their scores and level are important aspects. For now, this verification is done through keyboard shortcuts, giving priority to essential gameplay aspects such as identifying the location and typology of objects through 3D audio. Of course, special care must be taken to ensure that each key only performs a single function.

Heuristic 2: "Similarity between system and real world" was also followed as much as possible, trying to use language and sounds as naturally and similar to reality. The game always uses the same sounds to signal errors, to symbolize counters and the like. Similar to what happens in the Windows operating system, which always uses the same sound when the user makes a mistake, without the need for any dialog box. The study of what kind of sounds would work better to help users recall the last sequence is another aspect to test. In designing auditory cues in a user interface a distinction is made between auditory icons, earcons and speech [9]. Therefore we sought to find a compromise between the realism and the abstraction of the designed sounds, in order to provide further meaning to the user, exploring different levels of meaning either in the relationship between the sounds, or in the semantic and naturalistic relation that the sounds have in the learning process of the users.

Heuristic 3: "User control and freedom" was also followed giving the user the feeling that he/she controls the game as much as possible, for example, being able to cancel actions, stop or leave the game at any time, which is essentially done using Keyboard shortcuts.

Heuristic 4: "Consistency and standardization" was followed as much as possible essentially in the interaction elements, keeping the same for equal actions. The layout remained consistent so that there would still be a visual interface enabling people without visual problems to play.

Heuristic 5: "Error prevention" was also used as much as possible to prevent, especially blind users, from making mistakes. The essentially followed rule was to disable keys and menu options that did not make sense at a given moment. In the inactive/disabled menu options, a different tone of voice was used for visually impaired users.

In Heuristic 6: "Recognition rather than recall", there was a concern to use the same sounds for similar actions and for the same typology of objects and their location, in addition to 3D sounds whose audio translation is already known to the user.

Heuristic 7: "Flexibility and efficiency of use" was also followed as much as possible, essentially with the concern of maximizing the user's productivity, for example, not having to wait to listen to the entirety of an audio when the user already understood the input for progressing in the game.

In line with Heuristic 8: "Aesthetic and minimalistic design", we essentially tried to avoid many different types of sounds so as not to cognitively overload the user, by using distinct sounds as much as possible for the various actions and making messages shorter.

Heuristic 9: "Help users recognize, diagnose, and recover from errors" is the one that needs to be worked on the most, after evaluation with users. Therefore, checking situations such as whether the messages are clear, if there is not too much interference from sounds or messages during gameplay and if when the user does something that is not intended or makes a mistake if it is easy to get out of these situations.

Heuristic 10: "Help and documentation", despite the attempt to make the explanations succinct and clear, as already mentioned, there is the possibility of having an explanation at the beginning of the game, which the player can choose to skip. There is also always contextual information, during the game, especially about the type and location of pieces.

3   Conclusions

As researchers and citizens concerned with the production of accessible and inclusive technological solutions, in this work we proposed the adaptation of a game so that it could be completely played by the blind. The adaptation task fell on several studies, from consulting experts to researching the literature on guidelines, techniques and accessibility strategies applicable to all phases of a video game, with challenging characteristics.

Although the basic features of the game are fully implemented, after research, consultation with experts and having been tested individually, formal tests have not yet been carried out. However, tests are expected to be carried out with blind users in order to evaluate the true Player eXperience.

The fact that we thought about the possibility that the game could also be played by people without any visual impairment and have a visual interface brought another type of challenge to the compatibility of both solutions. In the near future, there is the possibility that the game could also be played by people with other types of disabilities, such as motor disabilities.

References

1. Barlet, M.C., Spohn, S.D.: A practical guide to game accessibility. The Ablegamers Foundation, Charles Town (2012)
2. Porter, J.R., Kientz, J.A.: An empirical study of issues and barriers to mainstream video game accessibility. In: Proceedings of the 15th International ACM SIGACCESS Conference on Computers and Accessibility, pp. 3:1–3:8. ACM, Bellevue (2013)
3. Khaliq, I., Torre, I.D.: A study on accessibility in games for the visually impaired. In: Proceedings of the 5th EAI International Conference on Smart Objects and Technologies for Social Good (GoodTechs 2019), pp. 142–148. Association for Computing Machinery, New York (2019). https://doi.org/10.1145/3342428.3342682
4. Aguado-Delgado, J., Gutiérrez-Martínez, J.-M., Hilera, J.R., de-Marcos, L., Otón, S.: Accessibility in video games: a systematic review. Univ. Access Inf. Soc. **19**(1), 169–193 (2018). https://doi.org/10.1007/s10209-018-0628-2
5. de Borba Campos, M., Damasio Oliveira, J.: Usability, accessibility and gameplay heuristics to evaluate audiogames for users who are blind. In: Antona, M., Stephanidis, C. (eds.) UAHCI 2016. LNCS, vol. 9737, pp. 38–48. Springer, Cham (2016). https://doi.org/10.1007/978-3-319-40250-5_4
6. Guidelines for the development of entertaining software for people with multiple learning disabilities. http://www.medialt.no/rapport/entertainment_guidelines/index.htm
7. Poitras, J.: Pipe Dreams: The Fight for Canada's Energy Future. Penguin (2018)
8. Nielsen, J.: 10 Usability Heuristics for User Interface Design Retirado de (1995). http://www.nngroup.com/articles/ten-usability-heuristics/
9. Torres, M.J.R., Barwaldt, R., Pinho, P.C.R., de Topin, L.O.H., Otero, T.F.: An auditory interface to workspace awareness elements accessible for the blind in diagrams' collaborative modeling. In: 2020 IEEE Frontiers in Education Conference (FIE), pp. 1–7. IEEE (2020)

Co-designing Virtual Environments
for People with Intellectual Disabilities
to Assess Cognitive Decline: Methodology

Matthew Harris[1]([✉]) [ID], David J. Brown[1] [ID], Pratik Vyas[1] [ID], James Lewis[1] [ID],
and Bonnie Connor[2] [ID]

[1] Department of Computer Science, Nottingham Trent University, Clifton Campus,
Clifton Lane, Nottingham NG11 8NS, UK
matthew.harris@ntu.ac.uk
[2] 1736 Picasso Avenue Suite A, 95618 Davis, CA, USA
https://isrg.org.uk/

Abstract. There is a lack of unified, standardised measures for cognitive decline in individuals with intellectual disabilities (ID), despite the fact that they can experience cognitive decline earlier and are a population in which mild neurocognitive disorder and dementia are likely under-diagnosed. Spatial navigation has been identified as a key indicator of mild cognitive decline, and Virtual Reality (VR) has been proposed as a potential tool to address this issue. However, there are a lack of VR tools aimed specifically at individuals with ID. To address this, a co-design methodology will be used to develop a VR platform to assess spatial navigational skills in individuals with ID. Additionally, EEG data will be used to validate the platform's effectiveness. A within-subjects design will be used to evaluate the system's effectiveness, and it is expected that this approach will lead to a system that can predict the onset of cognitive decline within this population.

Keywords: Virtual Reality · Cognitive decline · Co-design · Methodology · Intellectual Disabilities · Mild Neurocognitive Disorder · EEG data

1 Introduction

ICD11 specifies mild neurocognitive disorder (MND) as a mild impairment of one or more cognitive domains relative to what's expected for an individual's age. MND often progresses to dementia (major neurocognitive decline), however research indicates that lifestyle changes might slow the decline (Serrano-Pozo and Growdon 2019).

Those with Intellectual Disabilities (ID) are especially vulnerable to MND for a number of reasons. Firstly, those with Down syndrome have been shown to be genetically predisposed to experience Alzheimer's, the most common form of dementia, due to the presence of an extra copy of a chromasome which carries a

C. Stephanidis et al. (Eds.): HCII 2023, CCIS 1833, pp. 306–313, 2023.
https://doi.org/10.1007/978-3-031-35992-7_42

gene responsible for a buildup of beta-amyloid plaques involved in Alzheimer's (Fortea et al. 2021). Secondly, given a lack of knowledge in how dementia will manifest in those with ID, there can be a delay in diagnosis (Wilkinson and Janicki 2002). Under-diagnosis has been highlighted as an issue in this population (Heller et al. 2018). Additionally, decline in daily living skills has been identified as a common early symptom missed by caregivers and clinicians in this group (Livingston et al. 2007). As those with ID can now expect to live longer due to advances in medical care, they are more likely now than ever to live into older age. For these reasons, and given that (as already discussed) research indicates that lifestyle changes can slow this decline, there is a need to ensure that assessment measures for cognitive decline are sensitive with this group.

There are currently some difficulties in using screening tools for cognitive changes in those with ID. Due to floor effects, screening tools targeting the neurotypical population are often not suitable for those with ID given their pre-existing cognitive impairments (Zeilinger et al. 2020), (Krinsky-McHale and Silverman 2013). Additionally, a recent review highlights variation between measures used to screen for cognitive changes in those with ID and the need for unified, standardised measures for this group. (Paiva et al. 2020).

Current assessment measures for MND and dementia are largely questionnaire and paper based. 2009 point out that table-top tests for navigational skills may have limited generalisability to real-world tasks. More ecologically valid assessment measures might better predict performance in the cognitive domains used for MND diagnosis.

Various neuroimaging measures can be used to screen for dementia and cognitive decline in the neurotypical population. However, it has been identified that these techniques may not currently be suitable for use with those with ID due to the difficulty in interpreting the scans in this group as the brain can appear differently to the general population (Strydom et al. 2002). Alpha frequencies (as measured by EEG) have also been shown to decline in the early stages of dementia in both the neurotypical population (Neto et al. 2015) and those with Down syndrome (Musaeus et al. 2021). This highlights the potential role EEG and neuroimaging measures could play in assessing cognitive decline.

This paper will discuss a methodology that will be used to co-design and develop a virtual environment to assess spatial navigation for use with those with intellectual disabilities, and how EEG data will be used to validate the sensitivity of the measure.

2   Spatial Navigational Skill to Indicate MND

MND (and normally physiological ageing) are associated with structural changes in the brain. Areas affected include the retrosplenal cortex (Tan et al. 2013) which has been implicated in spatial navigation (Lin et al. 2015). Many studies have explored spatial navigational skills in older adults and found they have more difficulties in learning routes compared to younger adults (Barrash 1994,

Hilton et al. 2020). Gazova et al. suggest that computer based tests could be used as part of an early diagnosis tool for Alheimer's disease, the most common form of dementia (Gazova et al. 2012).

Zakzanis et al. (2009) suggest that Virtual Reality (VR) could provide a more ecologically valid environment in which to assess spatial navigation, and by extension cognitive decline. Those with Alzheimer's made more mistakes on a recognition task. This study used seated immersive VR in which the participants navigated using a joystick. This paper shows that VR can be used to assess differences in spatial navigation. A virtual environment in which the participant can walk naturally may introduce more vestibular cues and even more closely resemble a real world task.

Current generation immersive VR not only provides a more convincing Virtual environment for the user, but can also be used in conjunction with data collection methods such as head tracking, eye gaze data and EEG. "Untethered" VR devices make setup of these devices much simpler than previous devices. Previous studies have highlighted the potential for using VR with this group (Lewis et al. 2020, Brown et al. 2022).

2.1   Co-design and Co-development

'NICER', a local research governance group consisting of those with intellectual disabilities, have been aiding in the co-design and development of a VR based spatial navigation platform. The NICER group consists of adults with varying intellectual disabilities (including William's syndrome, Down syndrome and moderate to severe intellectual disabilities) who have prior experience in participating in academic research. These adults all have some experience in using VR before in a previous study (Lewis et al. 2020). Additionally, this group also consists of teachers and researchers experienced in using interactive technologies with those with ID. Previous fieldwork and preparation work has identified guidelines in co-designing Virtual Environments for this group. It also highlighted that due to the heterogeneity of this population, a VR application for this group should be accessible to those with a range of coordination and physical disabilities. This methodology will form the ideation and validation phases of the co-design process. As with these previous studies, these participants will in actuality be treated as co-researchers. Their voices will be treated as equally important, with the aim to design and develop the platform'with' rather than'for' them as much as possible.

Co-design sessions last year focused on preparing the user group for the co-design sessions, and getting their ideas on what use cases they envisioned for VR. Two co-design sessions have been held so far this year iterating on two early versions of the spatial navigation task.

The triangle completion task has been chosen as the spatial navigation task to implement in Virtual Reality. This is a commonly used task for assessing spatial navigation involving path integration without visual cues. Participants are guided through two sides of a triangle, and are then asked to navigate back to where they started from (completing the final side of the triangle). The distance of the participant from the starting point and the angle between the user's trajectory and the correct trajectory is recorded. The trajectory and position data is recorded using the VR headset's 6DoF (6 degrees of freedom) tracking functionality which is how the device knows where it is in 3D space. This information is recorded automatically when the user indicates they have finished the task.

The VR headset being used for this is the PICO Neo3, which is a standalone immersive VR capable of running VR applications without the need for any external hardware. Previous work with the NICER group has used the Oculus Quest 2 which is similar in this regard. The PICO Neo3 was chosen due to having a slightly more ergonomic strap.

The NICER group are being consulted at their monthly meeting to gain valuable feedback on the controls, the presentation of the task, the wording used in the instructions, and any other issues. They will be given the opportunity to try the environment at various stages in its development, and their ideas will be directly incorporated into the next stage. A summary of the feedback will be presented to the group along with how this feedback was implemented to promote transparency. The language used in this feedback will be reviewed by the experienced teachers and researchers skilled in facilitating co-design sessions with this group to ensure they are easily understood by all co-researchers (Fig. 1).

Fig. 1. Members of the NICER group trying an early version of the spatial navigation task during the second co-design session

It was fed back by the co-researchers at the first co-design session that the task was initially presented in too much of an abstract manner. The environment initially used glowing circles to guide the user to the first two points on the triangle. It was also suggested that its difficult to explain what these are and their relevance to the task, and that a practice mode involving a more grounded task might better explain the objectives. As a result of this, the second version of the environment has a practice mode involving making a cup of tea in a kitchen environment. This was received well by the participants at the next meeting, however some issues were still raised regarding the controls which will be addressed in the next iteration (Fig. 2).

Fig. 2. The first version (left) and the kitchen environment implemented as part of the second version (right)

Following the final co-design session, data collection will take place.

3   EEG Analysis to Validate Spatial Navigation in VR as an Assessment Tool

It has previously been shown that EEG data from the retrosplenal cortex can indicate when egocentric and allocentric navigation occur (Lin, Chiu, and Gramann 2015). Lin et al. also found that homing performance on a path integration task correlate with EEG power in the parietal, motor and retrosplenal cortex. We will therefore analyse the theta and alpha modulations occurring during the task to validate that the task is assessing spatial navigation.

A portable 32-channel wireless EEG device will be used for EEG data collection. Participants will wear the VR headset over the top of the EEG cap (it has previously been found that it is possible to collect good quality data using this method Haigh 2022). Saline solution is required to get good contact quality with this EEG cap (which can mean small amounts of solution running down the participant's scalp). Data will be recorded for the duration the participant is completing the spatial navigation task, and transmitted live over Bluetooth to a nearby laptop. Following this, the data will be analysed to identify the theta and alpha wave modulations in the aforementioned areas of the brain.

3.1   Potential Limitations

This study aims to use EEG data to validate the sensitivity of a virtual environment assessing spatial navigation which in turn could indicate MND. As previously stated, MND is characterised by deficits in one or more cognitive domain.

This assessment tool may be limited in its ability to assess cognitive functions not relating to spatial navigation. Therefore, even if it can be shown to effectively assess spatial navigation, a participant performing well in this task could be experiencing deficits in other cognitive functions. Episodic memory especially is a cognitive function commonly associated with MND and dementia. Therefore, if this task were to be used in a clinical setting, it would need to used alongside other tools assessing other cognitive domains.

4   Within Subjects Design over the Longer Term

Given that those with ID form a highly heterogeneous population, comparing results from a spatial navigational task between participants with ID is unlikely to yield reliable results. Therefore, using a "within subjects" design will be the most effective way of evaluating the effectiveness of this system (e.g. see Standen et al. 2020). This design also has the advantage of requiring fewer participants than a between subjects design.

If the co-designed application is accepted by the NICER group, this design could be used to assess the effectiveness of the tool over a longer period of time. This evaluation would be done through using a pre-existing cognitive measure to assess a baseline of cognitive performance such as MoCa LD (Edge et al. 2016), DSQIID (Deb et al. 2007), CAMDEX (Beresford-Webb et al. 2021) or DLD (Evenhuis et al. 2009). We aim to identify the most appropriate measure of these four to use with the NICER group.

5   Conclusion

So far, this methodology has already yielded useful feedback on the development of the virtual environment. Co-researchers are engaged in the design sessions. It is anticipated this method of using and collecting EEG data from the retrosplenal and parietal cortex will validate that the spatial navigation task recruits these areas of the brain. The task could form part of a larger battery of cognitive decline measures to use with those with intellectual disabilities to help identify cognitive decline sooner.

References

Barrash, J.: Age-related decline in route learning ability. Dev. Neuropsychol. 10(3), 189–201 (1994). issn: 8756-5641. https://doi.org/10.1080/87565649409540578+

Beresford-Webb, J., et al.: CAMDEX-DS-II: A Comprehensive Assessment for Dementia in People with Down Syndrome and Others with Intellectual Disabilities, 2 edn, Manual. Pavilion Publishing and Media Ltd. (2021). isbn: 978-1-914010-78-1.   https://www.pavpub.com/mental-health/camdex-ds-ii-the-cambridge-examination-for-mental-disorders-of-older-people-with-down-syndrome-and-others-with-intellectual-disabilities-version-ii-manual

Deb, S., et al.: Dementia screening questionnaire for individuals with intellectual disabilities. Brit. J. Psychiat. J. Mental Sci. **190**, 440–444 (2007). issn: 0007–1250. https://doi.org/10.1192/bjp.bp.106.024984. pmid: 17470960

Edge, D., et al.: The utility of the montreal cognitive assessment as a mental capacity assessment tool for patients with a learning disability. Brit. J. Learn. Disabil. **44**(3), 240–246 (2016). issn: 1354–4187. https://doi.org/10.1111/bld.12157

Evenhuis, H.M., Kengen, M.M.F., Eurlings, H.A.L.: The dementia questionnaire for people with intellectual disabilities. Neuropsychol. Assess. Dementia Down Syndr. Intell. Disabil., 39–51 (2009). isbn: 978-1-84800-248-7. https://doi.org/10.1007/978-1-84800-249-4_3

Fortea, J., et al.: Alzheimer's disease associated with down syndrome: a genetic form of dementia. The Lancet Neurology 20(11), 930–942 (2021). issn: 1474-4422, 1474-4465. https://doi.org/10.1016/S1474-4422(21)00245-3. pmid: 34687637. https://www.thelancet.com/journals/laneur/article/PIIS1474-4422(21)00245-3/fulltext. Accessed 15 Mar 2023

Gazova, I., et al.: Spatial navigation—a unique window into physiological and pathological aging. Front. Aging Neurosci. **4** (2012). issn: 1663–4365. https://www.frontiersin.org/articles/10.3389/fnagi.2012.00016. Accessed 14 Mar 2023

Haigh, M.: An investigation into to the use of a BCI in combination with a VR headset. Nottingham Trent University (2022)

Harris, M.C., Brown, D.J., et al.: A methodology for the co- design of shared VR environments with people with intellectual disabilities: insights from the preparation phase., p. 14 (2022)

Harris, M.C., Lewis, J., et al.: Assessing the usability of current generation virtual reality in adults with intellectual disabilities. In: Proceedings/the 13th International Conference on Disability, Virtual Reality and Associated Technologies, p. 9 (2020)

Heller, T., Scott, H.M., Janicki, M.P.: Care- giving, intellectual disability, and dementia: report of the summit work- group on caregiving and intellectual and developmental disabilities. Alzheimer's & Dementia: Transl. Res. Clin. Intervent. **4**, 272–282 (2018). issn: 2352–8737. https://doi.org/10.1016/j.trci.2018.06.002. pmid: 30090847. https://www.ncbi.nlm.nih.gov/pmc/articles/PMC6078103/. Accessed 10 Feb 2023

Hilton, C., et al.: Are age-related deficits in route learning related to control of visual attention? Psychol. Res. **84**(6), 1473–1484 (2020). ISSN: 1430-2772. https://doi.org/10.1007/s00426-019-01159-5. https://doi.org/10.1007/s00426-019-01159-5. Accessed 14 Mar 2023

Krinsky-McHale, S.J., Silverman, W.: Dementia and mild cognitive impairment in adults with intellectual disability: issues of diagnosis. Dev. Disabil. Res. Rev. **18**(1), 31–42 (2013). issn: 1940-5529. https://doi.org/10.1002/ddrr.1126. https://onlinelibrary.wiley.com/doi/abs/10.1002/ddrr.1126. Accessed 13 Mar 2023

Lin, C.-T., Chiu, T.-C., Gramann, K.: EEG correlates of spatial orientation in the human retrosplenial complex. NeuroImage **120**, 123–132 (2015). issn: 1053-8119. https://doi.org/10.1016/j.neuroimage.2015.07.009. https://www.sciencedirect.com/science/article/pii/1053811915006187. Accessed 25 Oct 2022

Musaeus, C.S., et al.: Electroencephalographic functional connectivity is altered in persons with down syndrome and Alzheimer's disease. J. Intellect. Disabil. Res. JIDR **65**(3), 236–245 (2021). issn: 1365-2788. https://doi.org/10.1111/jir.12803. pmid: 33336867

Neto, E., et al.: EEG spectral features discriminate between Alzheimer's and vascular dementia. Front. Neurol. **6** (2015). issn: 1664–2295. https://www.frontiersin.org/articles/10.3389/fneur.2015.00025. Accessed 14 Mar 2023

Paiva, A.F., et al.: Screening of cognitive changes in adults with intellectual disabilities: a systematic review. Brain Sci. **10**(11), 848 (2020). issn: 2076-3425. https://
doi.org/10.3390/brainsci10110848. pmid: 33198271. https://www.ncbi.nlm.nih.gov/
pmc/articles/PMC7698112/. Accessed 12 Sept 2022

Serrano-Pozo, A., Growdon, J.H.: Is Alzheimer's Disease Risk Modi able?. J.
Alzheimer's Dis. JAD **67**(3), 795–819 (2019). issn: 1387-2877. https://doi.org/
10.3233/JAD181028. pmid: 30776012. https://www.ncbi.nlm.nih.gov/pmc/articles/
PMC6708279/. Accessed 09 Feb 2023

Standen, P.J., et al.: An evaluation of an adaptive learning system based on multimodal
affect recognition for learners with intellectual disabilities. Brit. J. Educ. Technol.
51(5), 1748–1765 (2020). issn: 1467–8535. https://onlinelibrary.wiley.com/doi/abs/
10.1111/bjet.13010. https://doi.org/10.1111/bjet.13010. Accessed 04 Nov 2022

Strydom, A., Hassiotis, A., Walker, Z.: Clinical use of structural magnetic resonance
imaging in the diagnosis of dementia in adults with down's syndrome. Irish
J. Psychol. Med. **19**(2), 60–63 (2002). issn: 0790-9667, 2051-6967. https://doi.
org/10.1017/S0790966700006984. https://www.cambridge.org/core/journals/irish-
journal-of-psychological-medicine/article/abs/clinical-use-of-structural-magnetic-
resonance-imaging-in-the-diagnosis-of-dementia-in-adults-with-downs-syndrome/
E0475F240C5B1A09ACB7BFF7D141E58B. Accessed 14 Mar 2023

Strydom, A., Livingston, G., et al.: Prevalence of dementia in intellectual disability using dierent diagnostic criteria. Brit. J. Psychiat. **191**(2), 150–157
(2007). issn: 0007-1250, 1472-1465. https://doi.org/10.1192/bjp.bp.106.028845.
https://www.cambridge.org/core/journals/the-british-journal-of-psychiatry/
article/prevalence-of-dementia-in-intellectual-disability-using-different-diagnostic-
criteria/6A5C7A6665B8FD3B58D039C13506B195. Accessed 10 Feb 2023

Tan, R.H., et al.: Retrosplenial cortex (BA 29) volumes in behavioral variant fron-
totemporal dementia and alzheimer's disease. Dementia Geriatric Cogn. Disord.
35(3-4), 177–182 (2013). issn: 1421–9824. pmid: 23406695. https://doi.org/10.1159/
000346392

Wilkinson, H., Janicki, M.P.: The dinburgh principles with accompanying guidelines
and recommendations. J. Intell. Disabil. Res. **46**(3), 279–284 (2002). issn: 1365-
2788. https://doi.org/10.1046/j.1365-2788.2002.00393.x. https://onlinelibrary.wiley.
com/doi/abs/10.1046/j.1365-2788.2002.00393.x. Accessed 10 Feb 2023

Zakzanis, K.K., et al.: Age and dementia related differences in spatial navigation within
an immersive virtual environment. Med. Sci. Monit. **15**(4), CR140–CR150 (2009).
issn: 1234–1010, 1643–3750. pmid: 19333197. https://medscimonit.com/download/
index/idArt/869613. Accessed 29 Nov 2022

Zeilinger, E.L., et al.: Informant-based assessment instruments for dementia and their
measurement properties in persons with intellectual disability: systematic review
protocol. BMJ Open **10**(12), e040920 (2020). issn: 2044-6055, 2044-6055. https://
doi.org/10.1136/bmjopen-2020-040920. pmid: 33293393. https://bmjopen.bmj.com/
content/10/12/e040920. Accessed 13 Mar 2023

Mobility Link XR: Interspace Interaction System in Electric Wheelchair

Nozomi Hayashida[1]([✉])[iD], Hironori Shimosato[1][iD], Kenta Urano[1][iD], Takuro Yonezawa[1][iD], and Nobuo Kawaguchi[1,2][iD]

[1] Graduate School of Engineering, Nagoya University, Nagoya, Japan
{linda,shimo}@ucl.nuee.nagoya-u.ac.jp,
{urano,takuro,kawaguti}@nagoya-u.jp
[2] Institutes of Innovation for Future Society, Nagoya University, Nagoya, Japan

Abstract. This research proposes a communication system called Mobility Link XR that connects physical space and cyberspace with mobility. Mobility Link XR is a system that enables remote users to view panoramic video from a 360-degree camera attached to a mobility vehicle in different space by wearing a VR device, and mobility users to view the remote user as an avatar by wearing an MR device. In this way, sharing space in three dimensions using XR enables a higher level of human communication. In this paper, we apply Mobility Link XR to an electric wheelchair and design two types of scenarios: an assistance mode that reproduces the positional relationship of communication in a conventional wheelchair, and a passenger mode that reproduces the positional relationship inside a vehicle, which is said to be a suitable distance for conversation. We also evaluated the reproducibility of communication in the wheelchair and the effectiveness of communication using the avatar. The results showed that the reproducibility of voice and emotion was highly evaluated and that the side-by-side positional relationship enabled higher quality communication as the avatar was more easily seen and felt present.

Keywords: Virtual Reality · Mixwd Reality · Interspace Communication · Wheelchair · Remote Control

1 Introduction

Information technology extends our living space into cyberspace, virtual reality, or the so-called metaverse. Also, as a digital counterpart of physical space, the concept of digital twins has attracted many researchers, both in academia and industry, in the context of smart cities. Thus, methods to connect and integrate various spaces are becoming increasingly important to improve communication and services between spaces. We present Mobility Link XR, a communication system that connects physical and cyber spaces. Mobility Link XR provides a unified user experience for remote users and mobility users through mobility. Remote users can view panoramic video from a 360-degree camera attached to the mobility vehicle with a VR device, and mobility users can see the remote user as an avatar by wearing an MR device. In this study, Mobility Link XR is applied to an electric wheelchair to provide a communication method for two scenarios: assistance mode and passenger mode. The contributions of this paper are as follows

1. Proposal of Mobility Link, a new communication system that connects different spaces
2. Introduction of a scenario in a wheelchair using Mobility Link XR
3. User survey and discussion to evaluate the effectiveness of Mobility Link XR

2   Related Research

2.1   Interspace Communication

Bai et al. [1] proposed an MR remote collaboration system that shares a panoramic image of the user's surroundings with the remote user and elucidate that both users can provide a sense of co-presence by communicating not only verbally but also visually and gesturally through MR.

Cai et al. [2] proposed a mixed reality-based mobile communication system to connect two users in separate environments. Evaluations were conducted to investigate the system's usability and user performance, showing that both users can effectively communicate instructions related to the physical world and enable smooth remote collaboration.

Yonezawa et al. [6] proposed Metapo, a mobile robot equipped with a spherical display, a 360° camera image, and a robot hand, etc. Metapo functions as a portal to physical space, cyberspace, etc., and allows multiple remote users to communicate with each other through Metapo.

2.2   Teleoperation System

Ostanin et al. [4] proposed a framework to interactively control multiple robots using mixed reality interface technology. They experimentally demonstrated that the proposed framework can connect to and interactively control heterogeneous robots using multiple robots such as robotic arms, small mobility, and UAVs.

Hashizume et al. [3] proposed "Telewheelchair," an electric wheelchair with HMD-based teleoperation and operation assistance functions to reduce the caregiver's burden in wheelchairs. They investigate the user study of wheelchairs and the work time for each four tasks, the results showed that the operation mode using the HMD was superior to the other operation modes

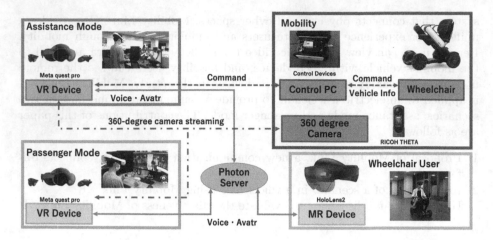

Fig. 1. System Design

3 Methodology

This section describes an overview of the Mobility Link XR system, which enables communication with remote persons through mobility, and two types of communication scenarios in an electric wheelchair using this system.

3.1 Mobility Link XR

Mobility Link XR is a system that enables users in different spaces to communicate with each other in mobility, a place where conversations are easily generated. In this system, a remote user can virtually ride in a mobility vehicle in a different space by wearing a VR device. The mobility vehicle is attached with a 360-degree camera, and the remote user can view the panoramic video to understand the surrounding conditions of the mobility vehicle. The mobility user can also see the remote user as an avatar by wearing an MR device. This enables the user to express not only language through speech, but also facial expressions, emotions, and three-dimensional physical expressions, making it possible for the user to communicate at a higher level.

3.2 System Design and Scenarios in Wheelchair

As described in the Stinzer effect [5], the positional relationship between people is one of the major factors in the quality and content of communication. In this paper, Mobility Link XR is applied to a wheelchair, which is a front/rear positional relationship and a special kind of communication, such as letting the person in the back drive, and two scenarios are designed as shown in Fig. 1.

Scenario 1: Assistance Mode. The first scenario is communication performed by the remote user as a caregiver. Wheelchairs are essentially an indispensable means of transportation for the elderly and physically disabled, and basically require the presence of a caregiver. On the other hand, the presence of a caregiver also creates opportunities for communication. To reproduce this communication, a remote caregiver can operate the wheelchair, and the wheelchair user can talk with the caregiver while leaving the wheelchair in the caregiver's hands. The positioning of the wheelchair user is not commonly seen in general communication, and we believe that this type of communication can be created.

Scenario 2: Passenger Mode. The second scenario is communication in which the remote user acts as a passenger. The interior of a car is said to be a suitable distance for conversation. Therefore, by reproducing the positional relationship between the wheelchair user in the driver's seat and the remote passenger in the passenger seat, we have created a place where communication can occur. In this scenario, the wheelchair user moves using a joystick attached to the wheelchair.

4   Evaluation

In this paper, two user surveys were conducted to evaluate the effectiveness of Mobility Link XR. This chapter describes the details of each survey and its results. Six students and staff members of the laboratory (four males and two females, average age of 25) participated in the user surveys. The survey was conducted in a 15-m straight corridor in the laboratory, as shown in the Fig. 2.

4.1   User Study1

The first user study compares a conversation while actually pushing a wheelchair with a conversation using the proposed system in order to investigate how well the Assistance mode described in Sect. 3.2.1 reproduces communication in an actual wheelchair.

Procedure. Subjects were first given a lecture on how to remotely operate the wheelchair and practiced for about 10 min to become familiar with the wheelchair. After that, the subjects were asked to talk with the facilitator while riding or pushing the wheelchair along the path shown in the Fig. 2. On the outward journey, the subject rode in the wheelchair and the facilitator pushed the wheelchair from behind as a caregiver. On the return trip, the subject pushed the wheelchair and the facilitator rode the wheelchair. On the outward journey, the subject rode in the wheelchair wearing the MR device. The facilitator remotely controlled the wheelchair with a VR device. On the return trip, the subject used the VR device to remotely control the subject's chair, and the facilitator talked with the subject while the subject was in the wheelchair. After the completion of all tasks, a 6-question questionnaire with a 5-point Likert scale and an open-ended questionnaire was administered.

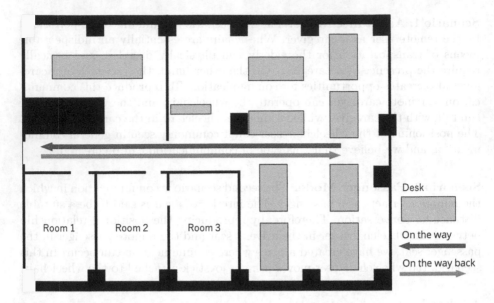

Fig. 2. Passage where the experiment was conducted

Result. The Fig. 4 shows the mean and standard deviation of the 5-point Likert scale for each evaluation index in User Survey 1. As shown in the Fig. 4, the five items except for operation were reproduced to some extent. The results were especially high for Talk and Emotions. The relatively low values for Gesture and Face despite the use of an avatar may be due to the fact that the wheelchair user rarely communicated non-verbally with the avatar since it was behind the user. In addition, the users in wheelchairs said that it was difficult to operate the device despite the practice. In this study, we used a joystick to remotely control the VR device, but we believe that a more intuitive method of remote control is needed.

4.2   User Study2

The second user study will investigate the effectiveness of using avatars by comparing video calls and this system (Scenarios 1 and 2) while both users are remote from each other.

Procedure. As in User Study 1, the subject was the wheelchair user and the facilitator was the remote user for the outward trip, and the subject was the remote user and the facilitator was the wheelchair user for the return trip. First, the subject held a tablet connected to the remote user via video call and engaged in conversation. Second, the conversation was conducted in the assistance mode, and finally, the conversation was conducted in the passenger mode. In all cases, the wheelchair was operated with a joystick attached to the wheelchair. After

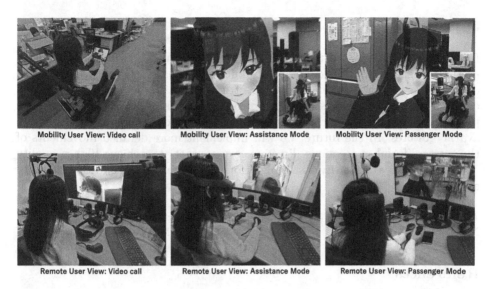

Fig. 3. Each user's view

all, tasks were completed, a four-question questionnaire and an open-ended questionnaire were administered to determine whether the communication was easier compared to the video call.

Result. The Fig. 5 shows the mean and standard deviation of the 5-point Likert scale for each of the evaluation indicators in User Survey 2. As the Fig. 5 shows, Talk and Gesture have higher values than the other items. This result indicates that the avatar improves the quality of communication not only through verbal expression but also through nonverbal expression. However, compared to video calls, the 360-degree panoramic image of this system has a low resolution, which makes it difficult to convey facial expressions. In addition, when comparing the Assistance mode and the Passenger mode, it was found that the Passenger mode is easier to see the avatar and feel the presence of the other party nearby, making communication easier.

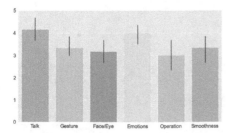

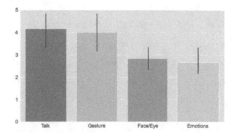

Fig. 4. Results of Likert scale in the User Study1.

Fig. 5. Results of Likert scale in the User Study2.

5   Conclusion

In this study, we proposed the concept of Mobility Link XR, which enables users in different spaces to connect and communicate with each other via mobility, and developed a prototype applied to an electric wheelchair. The evaluation results demonstrated that the system can reproduce communication through special positioning in a wheelchair and improve the quality of communication through avatar gestures. In the future, we will implement more detailed movements of the avatar (facial expressions, lip-sync, eye contact) to achieve higher quality communication and clarify its application and potential for various mobility applications.

Acknowledgements. This research is partially supported by NICT BG5 project, NICT DDT project and JST, CREST Grant Number JPMJCR22M4, Japan.

References

1. Bai, H., Sasikumar, P., Yang, J., Billinghurst, M.: A user study on mixed reality remote collaboration with eye gaze and hand gesture sharing. In: Proceedings of the 2020 CHI Conference On Human Factors In Computing Systems, pp. 1–13 (2020)
2. Cai, M., Tanaka, J.: Mixed-reality communication system providing shoulder-to-shoulder collaboration. Int. J. Adv. Softw. **12**(3 & 4), 2019 (2019)
3. Hashizume, S., Suzuki, I., Takazawa, K., Sasaki, R., Ochiai, Y.: Telewheelchair: The remote controllable electric wheelchair system combined human and machine intelligence. In: Proceedings of the 9th Augmented Human International Conference, pp. 1–9 (2018)
4. Ostanin, M., Yagfarov, R., Devitt, D., Akhmetzyanov, A., Klimchik, A.: Multi robots interactive control using mixed reality. Int. J. Prod. Res. **59**(23), 7126–7138 (2021). https://doi.org/10.1080/00207543.2020.1834640
5. Steinzor, B.: The spatial factor in face to face discussion groups. Psychol. Sci. Public Interest **45**, 552–555 (1950)
6. Yonezawa, T., Hayashida, N., Urano, K., Przybilla, J., Kyono, Y., Kawaguchi, N.: Metapo: A robotic meta portal for interspace communication. In: ACM SIGGRAPH 2022 Posters, pp. 1–2 (2022)

Alternatives for Designing Augmentative and Alternative Communication Systems for People with Disabilities and Older Adults

Janio Jadán-Guerrero[1]([✉]), Hugo Arias-Flores[1], Priscila Cedillo[2], and Marcos Chacón-Castro[3]

[1] Centro de Investigación en Mecatrónica y Sistemas Interactivos (MIST), Universidad Indoamérica, Av. Machala y Sabanilla, Quito 170103, Ecuador
`{janiojadan,hugoarias}@uti.edu.ec`
[2] Computer Science Department, Universidad de Cuenca, Cuenca, Ecuador
`priscila.cedillo@ucuenca.edu.ec`
[3] Grupo Investigación GIECO, Fundación Universitaria Internacional de La Rioja, Bogotá, Ecuador
`marcos.chacon@unir.net`

Abstract. Augmentative and Alternative Communication Systems (AACS) provide a variety of forms of expression used to improve the communication skills of people with disabilities and/or older adults. These systems consist of physical or digital communicator boards that use pictograms to represent an object, a person or an action. The objective of this article is to analyze some easy-to-implement alternatives of SAACs systems, including low-cost digital resources such as websites and Apps; as well as both high devices such as virtual assistants, AI chatbots like GPT, and tangible interfaces. The research analyzes the difficulties that older adults have in activities of daily living, and a proposal is presented that allows to adapt in a dynamic and scalable way. The prototypes generated allowed us to identify some strengths and weaknesses of the possible solutions. These results provide an opportunity for technology designers to take on board the recommendations and use them to design more robust systems adapted to their environment.

Keywords: SAAC · older adults · disabilities · Alexa · Makey-Makey · functional diversity · daily living activities · IA

1 Introduction

Augmentative and Alternative Communication Systems (AACS) refers to a range of tools and techniques used to support communication for people with disabilities and/or older adults who have difficulty speaking or writing. These systems provide alternative ways to express themselves, such as through visual aids, gestures, symbols, and electronic devices [1].

In the first case AACS can be used by individuals with a wide range of disabilities, including those with physical, cognitive, or sensory impairments. For example, someone who has a physical disability that affects their ability to use their hands or arms may benefit from a communication device that is operated with their eyes or mouth. Similarly, someone with a cognitive impairment may benefit from using picture symbols or a visual schedule to help them understand and communicate. The goal of AACS is to improve the communication skills of individuals with disabilities, enabling them to better express their wants, needs, and thoughts, and to participate more fully in their daily lives. AACS can also enhance social interactions, reduce frustration and anxiety, and improve overall quality of life.

Regarding the second case, it is important to highlight that numerous research studies are currently being carried out on the use of AACS in older adults, as it has traditionally focused on children. These tools include communication boards, speech-generating devices, manual signs, and other electronic and non-electronic supports [2, 3].

In this article, a comprehensive review of the latest advances and trends in the field of AACS is offered, exploring its use in various contexts such as healthcare, education, and social communication. In addition, innovative ideas are presented to create proposals with cutting-edge technological tools, such as virtual assistants, AI chatbots like GPT, and tangible interfaces. Finally, the challenges and opportunities posed by the use of AACS, as well as emerging technologies and future directions of research in this field, are discussed [4, 5].

2 Related Works

AACS (Augmentative and Alternative Communication System) is a tool that enables people with speech disabilities to communicate using images, videos, drawings, and writing. This system is designed to help people who face challenges in verbal communication due to cognitive impairments, physical disabilities, or other related issues. Prior to implementing AACS, it is important to assess the individual's communication needs, cognitive abilities, and interpretation skills to provide tailored support. Several studies have explored the effectiveness of AACS in improving communication outcomes for adults with communication problems (e.g., [2, 3, 6]). One of the latest studies by Johnson et al. [7] demonstrated that AACS can significantly enhance the communication skills of individuals with speech impairments, leading to better quality of life and social participation.

Similarly, the paper "Computational cognitive training for older adults: A systematic review" discusses previous research on computational cognitive training for older adults. The authors review several studies that have demonstrated the potential benefits of such interventions for improving cognitive functions, including attention, memory, and executive functions. They also highlight the importance of individualization and personalization in cognitive training, as well as the need for further research on the long-term effects of these interventions. The paper also addresses the potential use of assistive technologies, such as AACS, in cognitive training for older adults with communication difficulties. The authors suggest that AAC systems could enhance the effectiveness of cognitive training by providing tailored and interactive support for communication and cognitive skills. They emphasize the importance of developing AAC systems that are user-friendly and accessible to older adults, and call for further research to explore the potential of these systems in cognitive training. Overall, the paper provides valuable insights into the potential of computational cognitive training for older adults and the role of assistive technologies in enhancing the effectiveness of such interventions [8].

Based on the aforementioned documentary information, it can be identified that there is a critical need to create a method that integrates existing solutions with new intelligent assistive technologies based on Artificial Intelligence (AI) techniques to better adapt to the specific needs of older adults.

Artificial intelligence is an important complement for this type of application, as evidenced by several studies in the domain of AAC systems that employ AI and its techniques. Bautista et al. [9] presented a Spanish text-to-pictogram translator that used natural language processing (NLP) techniques, performing syntactic analysis followed by n-gram processing. The goal of this translator was to predict the pictogram(s) that best described the mentioned word or phrase with greater accuracy. Additionally, Pahisa-Solé and Herrera-Joancomartí [10] evaluated an AAC system that transformed pictograms into natural language. The system was tested with four participants with severe cerebral palsy over a total of 40 sessions. An interesting aspect of this article was that they were able to adapt the system to the linguistic characteristics of each person. Finally, they reported that quantitative results showed an average increase of 41.59% in communication rate compared to the same communication device without the compression system, as well as a general improvement in communication experience when the output was in natural language.

Therefore, this article aims to analyze and apply various forms of interaction in a pictogram-based AAC systems. The proposed solution should include multiple forms of HCI to promote a comfortable, transparent, and versatile use of technology, enabling effective communication for adult individuals.

3 Method

To identify different forms of interaction of AAC systems, we conducted a focus group discussion with an interdisciplinary group of 12 experts to obtain detailed information about their experiences, as well as to analyze existing solutions in depth, in order to establish their strengths and weaknesses in detail and, through the use of technology, enrich their usefulness.

3.1 Participants

The group of experts was composed of 12 researchers from four Ecuadorian universities. Among them were a neuroscientist, a specialist in technology development for people with disabilities, a visually impaired researcher, an expert in artificial intelligence, a data scientist, an expert in human-computer interaction, a communicator, an educator, a psychologist, and several software developers.

3.2 Instruments

For this study, a discussion guide was employed to gather qualitative data on the perceptions and experiences of a particular group of participants regarding the research topic.

The guide, which was specifically designed for this purpose, consisted of open-ended questions that aimed to explore the communication needs and preferences of older adults and people with disabilities. The guide was administered to a focus group composed of 12 experts, who participated in two online sessions that utilized a virtual chat board for brainstorming and defining the key characteristics that a new alternative augmentative communication system should possess, taking into account the various perspectives of the participants.

To analyze the data, the discussions from the focus group were transcribed, and emerging themes and patterns were identified. The insights gained from the discussion guide were then used to inform the development of a new augmentative alternative communication system for older adults and people with disabilities. In conclusion, the discussion guide proved to be a valuable tool in collecting in-depth qualitative data on the perceptions and experiences of a specific group of participants. Its use was crucial in understanding the communication needs and preferences of people with disabilities and in guiding the design of the new augmentative alternative communication system.

3.3 Procedure

This study was conducted using a six-phase approach to develop a new augmentative alternative communication system for older adults and people with disabilities. In Phase 1, the study team recruited and selected 12 experts who had experience working in the field of augmentative and alternative communication with this particular population. In Phase 2, the team developed a discussion guide specifically for this study to collect qualitative data on the communication needs and preferences of the participants. Phase 3 involved administering the discussion guide to the focus group in two online sessions, which were recorded and transcribed verbatim. In Phase 4, the data were analyzed using thematic analysis to identify emerging themes and patterns. The insights gained from the analysis were then used to inform the design of the new system in Phase 5. Finally, in Phase 6, the team conducted a validation and evaluation of the system with a separate group of participants to ensure that it met their communication needs and preferences. Overall, this multi-phase approach proved to be an effective method for developing a new augmentative alternative communication system that addresses the specific needs of older adults and people with disabilities.

4   Results

The results of this study provide valuable insights into the communication needs and preferences of older adults and people with disabilities, as well as the design and development of a new augmentative alternative communication system. In the upcoming section, we describe the study's findings and highlight some of the most innovative solutions that were discovered.

By utilizing emerging technologies, such as tangible user interfaces, RFID technology, augmented reality, voice assistants, and artificial intelligence, a range of alternative solutions were explored. One idea presented in the study involved the use of Makey

Fig. 1. Makey Makey as an AAC Strategy for older people

Makey to create a tangible augmentative board, which allows for the conversion of tangible pictograms into spoken words. Figure 1 shows an idea of the proposal.

The aim of using Makey Makey is to introduce the use of alternative augmentative boards to children with disabilities and older adults, in order to familiarize them with the system prior to utilizing a more complex system on a computer or tablet.

Other recommendations included implementing radio frequency cards to enhance scalability and enable customized pictograms for elderly users, as well as incorporating tangible components for children with disabilities. Figure 2 shows an idea of the proposal.

On the other hand, another proposal was put forth. For instance, by utilizing Alexa's skill configuration, individuals with speech impairments could benefit from the recognition of specific sounds, which would then be translated into pictograms and ultimately synthesized into complete sentences. Within this context, various applications can be utilized with Alexa, including "Speak2See," "AskSARA," and "SpeakIt!" These apps are highly customizable and programmable to meet the unique needs and preferences of individual users, empowering them to communicate effectively across diverse environments and situations.

Augmented reality is one of the emerging technologies that is gaining more and more ground in different fields. In the field of augmentative and alternative communication (AAC), augmented reality can be especially useful. Thanks to it, a board of pictograms can be created which, when scanned with the camera of a mobile phone or a tablet, is complemented with multimedia elements such as explanatory audios or videos. In this way, people with communication difficulties can access information in a more visual and intuitive way, which can be especially beneficial in situations where quick and effective communication is required. Additionally, being highly customizable, augmented reality can be adapted to the specific needs of each user, making it a very versatile and powerful tool.

We are currently witnessing a boom in artificial intelligence (AI), and this trend has opened up new opportunities for the implementation of Augmentative and Alternative Communication (AAC) systems. Several AI-powered applications, such as Chat GPT, Synthesia, Proloquo2Go, Eye-Gaze, and Speechify, have emerged as invaluable support tools for individuals with communication challenges.

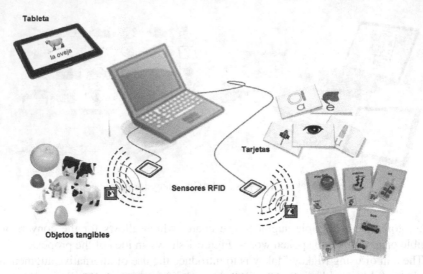

Fig. 2. RFID technology to build tangible pictograms

For example, Synthesia AI video creation allows the creation of avatars with text-to-speech capabilities, while Proloquo2Go features word prediction functionality that suggests phrases based on user input, streamlining communication and enhancing efficiency. Eye-Gaze employs cutting-edge AI algorithms to detect and track eye movement, converting it into commands for typing and communication. Furthermore, Speechify utilizes advanced speech recognition technology to adapt pronunciation and tone of voice to meet the unique needs and preferences of users.

These innovative applications represent significant advancements in augmentative and alternative communication, providing valuable resources for individuals with communication challenges. With the power of AI, we can now develop more personalized and effective communication strategies that can greatly improve the lives of those who rely on AAC systems.

5 Conclusions

In conclusion, the use of a discussion guide has proven to be a valuable tool for gathering in-depth qualitative data on the perceptions and experiences of a specific group of participants. Moreover, the integration of various technologies, such as tangible user interfaces, RFID technology, augmented reality, voice assistants, and artificial intelligence, has significantly impacted and improved the lives of older adults. Emergency technology, with its intuitive design and ability to stimulate long-term memory, is a prime example of how technology can enhance the quality of life for older adults. As technology continues to evolve, the potential for further innovations that empower and enrich the lives of older adults is truly exciting.

Overall, technology has opened up endless possibilities for older adults, allowing them to enjoy greater autonomy and improved quality of life. This transformative power of technology in the lives of seniors cannot be overstated. If we continue to embrace technological advancements, we can look forward to even more exciting breakthroughs that will enhance their well-being and enrich their lives. The integration of technology into the daily lives of older people has the potential to revolutionize their experiences, making everyday tasks more manageable and enjoyable. These exploratory results will provide a foundation for future work to design prototypes, evaluate their effectiveness in a given context, and identify the most suitable solutions for our environment.

Acknowledgments. The authors would like to thank the Coorporación Ecuatoriana para el Desarrollo de la Investigación y Academia- CEDIA for their contribution in innovation, through the "Fondo I+D+I" projects, especially the project I+D+I-XVII-2023-61, "Análisis y aplicación de formas de Interacción Humano – Computador (HCI) en una herramienta tecnológica de Comunicación Aumentativa y Alternativa (CAA) basada en pictogramas, que ayude a las personas adultas mayores a comunicarse con su entorno"; also the Universidad Tecnológica Indoamérica, Universidad de Cuenca, Universidad de las Fuerzas Armadas and Universidad del Azuay for the support for the development of this work.

References

1. Light, J. C.: Augmentative and alternative communication. Handbook of Autism and Pervasive Developmental Disorders, pp. 617–637. Springer (2014)
2. Andzik, N.R., Chung, Y.-C.: Augmentative and alternative communication for adults with complex communication needs: a review of single-case research. Commun. Disord. Q. **43**(3), 182–194 (2022). https://doi.org/10.1177/1525740121991478
3. Hillary, A., Dalton, E.: Augmentative and alternative communication for speaking autistic adults: overview and recommendations. Autism Adult **1**(2), 93–100 (2019). https://doi.org/10.1089/aut.2018.0007
4. Koul, R., Raj, S.: Augmentative and alternative communication systems: a scoping review of recent advancements and trends. Health Inf. Sci. Syst. **10**(1), 1–21 (2022)
5. Elsahar, Y., Hu, S., Bouazza-Marouf, K., Kerr, D., Mansor, A.: Augmentative and alternative communication (AAC) advances: a review of configurations for individuals with a speech disability. Sensors **19**, 1911 (2019). https://doi.org/10.3390/s19081911
6. Cedillo, P., Collaguazo-Malla, C., Sánchez, W., Cárdenas-Delgado, P., Prado-Cabrera, D.: VitaApp: augmentative and alternative communication system aimed at older adults. In: Salgado Guerrero, J.P., Chicaiza Espinosa, J., Cerrada Lozada, M., Berrezueta-Guzman, S. (eds.) TICEC 2021. CCIS, vol. 1456, pp. 75–86. Springer, Cham (2021). https://doi.org/10.1007/978-3-030-89941-7_6
7. Johnson, A., Smith, K., Williams, H., Brown, J.: Augmentative and alternative communication systems for individuals with speech disabilities: a systematic review. J. Commun. Disord. **101**, 108307 (2022). https://doi.org/10.1016/j.jcomdis.2022.108307
8. Cattani, A., Faria-Fortini, I., Wajman, J.R., Biazoli, C.E., Jr.: Computational cognitive training for older adults: a systematic review. Frontiers Aging Neurosci. **13**, 819285 (2022). https://doi.org/10.3389/fnagi.2021.819285
9. Bautista, S., Hervás, R., Hernández-Gil, A., Martínez-Díaz, C., Pascua, S., Gervás, P.: Ara-traductor: text to pictogram translation using natural language processing techniques. In:

Proceedings of the XVIII International Conference on Human Computer Interaction (Interacción 2017), pp. 1–8. Association for Computing Machinery, New York, NY, USA, Article 28 (2017). https://doi.org/10.1145/3123818.3123825

10. Pahisa-Solé, J., Herrera-Joancomartí, J.: Testing an AAC system that transforms pictograms into natural language with persons with cerebral palsy. Assist Technol. **31**(3), 117–125 (2019). https://doi.org/10.1080/10400435.2017.1393844

Visiting Supermarket Through Virtual Reality: An Opportunity for Rehabilitation of People with Disability

Manuel Lagos Rodríguez⊙, Javier Pereira Loureiro⊙,
María del Carmen Miranda Duro⊙, Patricia Concheiro Moscoso(✉)⊙,
and Thais Pousada García⊙

CITIC (Centre for Information and Communications Technology Research), TALIONIS
Research Group, University of A Coruña, Elviña Campus, 15071 A Coruña, Spain
{m.lagos,javier.pereira,carmen.miranda,patricia.concheiro,
thais.pousada.garcia}@udc.es

Abstract. The process of rehabilitation of physical or cognitive skills in people with disabilities can be long, monotonous and unmotivating. Exercises can often involve mechanical and repetitive movements, which can have a negative impact on adherence to the rehabilitation process. The aim of this work is the use of virtual reality (VR) environments for the improvement of physical and cognitive skills. The researcher's proposal is a work based on activities of daily living, which can facilitate the transfer of the improvements obtained to the person's daily life. The proposed environment represents a very realistic supermarket, which provides a high degree of immersion. Four activities are proposed to take place in different locations in the supermarket. These activities will involve the movement of different parts of the body to improve physical skills. Cognitive skills related to memory, coordination or mental agility will also be worked on. The application will track the person's movements and record various parameters related to the achievement of the activity. This data can be consulted by the health professional, which could contribute to a better evaluation of the user's progress.

Keywords: Virtual Reality · Disability · Virtual Supermarket

1 Introduction

Virtual reality (VR) is a type of technology that allows the generation of virtual environments with a certain degree of immersion. The more immersive the VR device, the greater the sense of realism for the person. Usually, VR equipment consists of a VR headset or glasses composed of a screen for displaying 3D environments and a set of sensors capable of capturing a person's movement and translating it into the virtual world. VR headsets also often provide 3D audio, which offers high-quality surround sound, and allows the person to identify the location of the sound source in the virtual environment. VR scenarios can be passive, in which the user is a mere spectator, or interactive, in which it is possible to interact with the elements of the environment. The most common

C. Stephanidis et al. (Eds.): HCII 2023, CCIS 1833, pp. 329–335, 2023.
https://doi.org/10.1007/978-3-031-35992-7_45

form of interaction is through two controllers, one for each hand. These controllers are equipped with various sensors to monitor the movement of the arms. Likewise, they have a set of buttons that enable multiple actions with the elements of the environment.

It is common to associate VR with entertainment, specifically with video games. However, this technology is showing promising results in many other fields such as education, tourism, industry and healthcare [1–4].

In concrete, VR has a place in various areas of health. It can be a powerful tool for the practical training of doctors and nurses [5, 6]. Its use as a medical test simulator is also of great interest, which could give patients greater peace of mind when faced with a real medical test [7]. Another possibility to highlight is its use as a tool for the rehabilitation of physical and cognitive abilities in people with disabilities [8, 9].

This paper proposes to continue this line of research but developing virtual environments that are based on the performance of activities of daily life. The use of VR scenarios can enhance the development of more enjoyable and motivating activities, moving away from mechanical or repetitive exercises. In addition, working through everyday tasks could be very beneficial as the exercise the person performs has a direct application in their life.

The activities proposed are not aimed at a single-person profile, but each activity can be customizable, allowing one to choose the skill to work on and regulate its complexity. This will allow the tool to be used by entities and organizations with people with different needs.

It is also important to be able to monitor the person's progress in carrying out an activity. In this respect, in addition to the therapist's supervision in real-time, the application records the movement of those parts of the body involved in the activity, as well as other values of interest such as the time taken to complete the task or the number of failures until the objective is achieved.

Thus, the objective of this work is the development of a virtual supermarket using VR technology. The application will have four usual activities in a supermarket, which will involve working on physical and cognitive skills. The researchers intend to evaluate the effectiveness of VR in the rehabilitation of people with disabilities based on environments that represent activities of daily living.

2 Materials and Methods

The application will consist of a highly realistic supermarket. It will have a large catalogue of products from the food, hygiene and household cleaning sections, among others. This will increase the possibilities when programming tasks, especially those related to cognitive skills. On the other hand, the environment will have the usual equipment of a real supermarket. Thus, it will have attended and self-service cash registers, shelves at different heights, fridges and freezers with different types of openings, and baskets and trolleys to store the shopping. The wide variety of furniture is very important as it facilitates the implementation of physical work tasks, as well as contributes to the realism of the exercise. An example can be found in reaching for products at different heights or opening refrigerators and freezers using different ways of grasping them with the hands.

In the initial stage of the project, several meetings have been scheduled with entities and organizations that work with people with disabilities. These meetings have been attended by both health professionals and people who need to work on some physical or cognitive ability, and who could be potential users of the proposed tool. The researchers presented the VR equipment available, as well as the different means of interaction and monitoring. After completing the scheduled meetings, the joint work between researchers, health professionals and users has allowed the virtual environment to be defined, as well as the tasks to be carried out in it.

To carry out this work, several hardware and software elements and an appropriate development process are needed. These are briefly described below:

2.1 Hardware

- HTC VIVE Pro 2 [10]: It is a virtual reality kit created by HTC. It consists of a kit made up of glasses, controllers and position sensors. The glasses have a screen that allows the visualization of virtual environments in 3D and a high-quality audio system that increases the immersion capacity. The controls allow interaction with the different elements of the scenarios. As for the sensors, they will be in charge of creating a game area, within which the person's movement will be tracked.
- Vive Tracker [11]: It is a tracking device that can be placed on different parts of the body or on real objects. The virtual reality system can detect your movement and translate it into the virtual environment.
- Leap Motion [12]: It is an optical hand and finger tracking system. It allows interaction with digital content with the hands, avoiding the use of a keyboard, mouse or controller. It is possible to integrate it into a virtual reality system, providing greater realism by being able to touch and grasp virtual objects.

2.2 Software

- Unity [13]: It is a real-time 3D content development platform. It allows the creation of interactive environments for a wide variety of devices such as computers, consoles or VR equipment.
- OpenXR [14]: It is a free and open API standard developed by Khronos. It facilitates the development of VR applications compatible with VR devices from different manufacturers.
- Unity Leap Motion Modules [15]: It is a set of libraries provided by the Leap Motion manufacturer to access the device API and to facilitate the development of functionalities in the VR application.

2.3 Development Process

The development process of the tool started with the search for a 3D model of a supermarket and its products and equipment. The selection process took into account the completeness of the product catalogue, the realism of the 3D objects and their configuration options.

Once the 3D models have been acquired, the distribution of the elements in the scene has begun. The placement of the objects in each scenario is carried out by taking into account the tasks to be programmed in the scenario. The aim is to obtain a realistic, intuitive and motivating scenario for the user. To enhance the motivational aspect and provide feedback to the user, animated elements will be used, as well as a screen on which instructions will be displayed to support the activity.

When the process of designing the environments has been completed, the necessary functionalities will begin to be programmed so that the scenario can be interacted with and each of the proposed activities can be carried out.

The next step will be to test the application. In addition to testing by the researchers themselves, it is proposed to organize test sessions with professionals and users from different organizations in the field of disability. The aim will be to detect possible errors and implement improvements that contribute to increasing the usability of the tool.

Once the final application is available, it is proposed to carry out a qualitative study through several work sessions with groups of users who require work on different physical or cognitive skills.

3   VR Scenarios

The design, programming and implementation of two VR environments representing a supermarket are proposed. Each environment will represent a location of the supermarket, and different tasks will be disposed. In the following, each of the scenarios will be described and the tasks linked:

3.1   Scenario 1

It will represent one of the aisles of the supermarket. The user will see a shelf of products on each side. Various types of products will be placed at different heights. In addition, a shopping trolley will be placed next to the user (see Fig. 1).

Two activities are proposed:

- **Activity 1:** It will consist of taking products at different heights and placing them on the trolley. The aim is for the person to work on mobility exercises that involve both the upper limbs when stretching to reach a product and the lower limbs when bending down and getting up.
- **Activity 2:** The user will be provided with a shopping list. He/she will have to take the correct products and place them in the shopping trolley. The aim is to train on cognitive skills such as memory and concentration.

3.2   Scenario 2

It will represent the checkout area of the supermarket. The user will stand in front of a checkout counter with a trolley with different products (see Fig. 2).

- **Activity 1:** The user must place the products in the checkout and then place them in a shopping bag. The objective is to work on the physical movement of both the lower

Fig. 1. Scenario 1

limbs when taking each product from the trolley and the upper limbs when placing them in the bag.

- **Activity 2:** This activity aims to train mental agility and to solve problems. The task consists of making the payment for the purchase made. To do this, the user will have bills and coins of different values in his left hand. The user will have to check the amount to be paid at the cash desk and select bills and coins to complete the amount to be paid.

Fig. 2. Scenario 2

4   Conclusions

The use of virtual environments in the process of physical or cognitive rehabilitation for people with disabilities could be a safe, motivating and enjoyable way to carry out different physical and cognitive activities.

The fact that the tasks are based on activities of daily life helps to transfer the results of the training sessions to the person's contexts. In addition, it may also mean greater adherence to the prescribed exercises.

The Leap Motion device can be a differentiating element compared to other virtual environments on the market. The fact of using the hands to interact with objects allows the activities to be used by a greater number of people, avoiding the exclusion of those who are not able to use the controls. In addition, the interaction with the hands allows for working on coordination and fine dexterity skills.

Health professionals can use the monitoring data from the app to assess the users and monitor them. Combining this data with live visualization of activity performance can be a powerful tool for tracking an individual's progress.

Acknowledgments. This work is supported in part by some grants from the European Social Fund 2014-2020: Centre for Information and Communications Technology Research (CITIC; Research Center of the Galician University System). Grant support for CITIC was provided by the Xunta de Galicia through a collaboration agreement between the Regional Ministry of Culture, Education, and Vocational Training and the Galician Universities for the work of the Research Centers of the Galician University System and the Handytronic chair. In addition, this work is supported in part by structural support for the consolidation and structuring of competitive research units and other promotion actions in the universities of the Galician University System, in the public research organizations of Galicia, and other entities of the Galician R&D&I System for 2022 (ED431B-2022/39); and the Ministerio de Ciencia e Innovación R&D&I projects in the framework of the national programs of knowledge generation and scientific and technological strengthening of the R&D&I system and challenges of the call R&D&I 2019 oriented to society (PID2019-104323RB-C33).

References

1. Pellas, N., Dengel, A., Christopoulos, A.: A scoping review of immersive virtual reality in STEM education. IEEE Trans. Learn. Technol. **13**, 748–761 (2020). https://doi.org/10.1109/TLT.2020.3019405
2. Oncioiu, I., Priescu, I.: The use of virtual reality in tourism destinations as a tool to develop tourist behavior perspective. Sustainability **14**, 4191 (2022). https://doi.org/10.3390/SU14074191
3. Naranjo, J.E., Sanchez, D.G., Robalino-Lopez, A., Robalino-Lopez, P., Alarcon-Ortiz, A., Garcia, M.V.: A scoping review on virtual reality-based industrial training. Appl. Sci. **10**, 8224 (2020). https://doi.org/10.3390/APP10228224
4. Pelargos, P.E., et al.: Utilizing virtual and augmented reality for educational and clinical enhancements in neurosurgery. J. Clin. Neurosci. **35**, 1–4 (2017). https://doi.org/10.1016/J.JOCN.2016.09.002
5. Barteit, S., Lanfermann, L., Bärnighausen, T., Neuhann, F., Beiersmann, C.: Augmented, mixed, and virtual reality-based head-mounted devices for medical education: systematic review. JMIR Serious Games **9**(3), e29080 (2021). https://games.jmir.org/2021/3/e29080. https://doi.org/10.2196/29080
6. Saab, M.M., Hegarty, J., Murphy, D., Landers, M.: Incorporating virtual reality in nurse education: a qualitative study of nursing students' perspectives. Nurse Educ. Today **105**, 105045 (2021). https://doi.org/10.1016/J.NEDT.2021.105045

7. Hudson, D.M., Heales, C., Vine, S.J.: Scoping review: how is virtual reality being used as a tool to support the experience of undergoing Magnetic resonance imaging? Radiography **28**, 199–207 (2022). https://doi.org/10.1016/J.RADI.2021.07.008
8. Domínguez-Téllez, P., Moral-Muñoz, J.A., Casado-Fernández, E., Salazar, A., Lucena-Antón, D.: Effects of virtual reality on balance and gait in stroke: a systematic review and meta-analysis. Rev. Neurol. **69**, 223–234 (2019). https://doi.org/10.33588/rn.6906.2019063
9. Lee, H.K., Jin, J.: The effect of a virtual reality exergame on motor skills and physical activity levels of children with a developmental disability. Res. Dev. Disabil. **132**, 104386 (2023). https://doi.org/10.1016/J.RIDD.2022.104386
10. HTC Corporation. HTC VIVE. https://www.vive.com/eu/product/vive-pro2-full-kit/overview/https://www.vive.com/eu/product/vive. Accessed 14 Mar 2023
11. HTC Corporation. HTC VIVE Tracker. https://www.vive.com/eu/accessory/tracker3. Accessed 15 Mar 2023
12. Ultraleap. Leap Motion. https://www.ultraleap.com/product/leap-motion-controller. Accessed 10 Mar 2023
13. Unity Technologies. Unity. https://unity.com. Accessed 15 Mar 2023
14. Khronos Group. OpenXR. https://www.khronos.org/openxr/. Accessed 15 Mar 2023
15. Ultraleap. Leap Motion Modules. https://developer.leapmotion.com/unity. Accessed 16 Mar 2023

Research Trend Analysis of Usability Evaluation in Exoskeleton Robots

Kyung-Sun Lee[1](✉), Jinwon Lee[2], and Jaejin Hwang[3]

[1] Department of Industrial Engineering, Kangwon National University, Chuncheon 24341, Republic of Korea
ksunlee@kangwon.ac.kr
[2] Department of Industrial and Management Engineering, Gangneung-Wonju National University, Wonju 26403, Republic of Korea
jwlee@gwnu.ac.kr
[3] Department of Industrial and Systems Engineering, Northern Illinois University, DeKalb, IL 60115, USA
jhwang3@niu.edu

Abstract. The development of exoskeleton robots by major ICT companies both domestically and internationally has been focused on augmenting or replacing human body capabilities. However, it is crucial to develop functions and technologies that can facilitate interaction with humans and to establish a proper evaluation system. To this end, this study aimed to derive detailed elements for user evaluation by synthesizing the functional characteristics, user evaluation method, and evaluation results of previously developed passive exoskeleton robots through literature review. The investigation focused on the functional characteristics, purpose, and user evaluation methods of passive exoskeleton robots. The study found that most of the test subjects were men in their 20s and the evaluation methods mainly involved joint angle, muscle activity, heart rate, and subjective questionnaires. However, there was a limitation that evaluation is performed only for specific body parts. As such, the study suggests that there is an urgent need for research to establish a methodology for the development and evaluation of exoskeleton robots that considers their characteristics, functions, use environment, and user class to advance in terms of safety, convenience, and usability. With the establishment of such methodology, exoskeleton robots can be optimized to cater to a wide range of users with different needs, ultimately enhancing their quality of life.

Keywords: Passive exoskeleton robot · Assessment methods · Research trend · Usability

1 Introduction

As individuals age, physical activity, which is linked to a better quality of life, tends to decrease as a result of various factors, including muscle loss, cardiac and respiratory disease, and other reasons [1]. Exoskeleton robots have emerged as a popular technology to enhance human movement and physical capabilities, with the potential to significantly improve the quality of life for a significant portion of the global population [2].

© The Author(s), under exclusive license to Springer Nature Switzerland AG 2023
C. Stephanidis et al. (Eds.): HCII 2023, CCIS 1833, pp. 336–340, 2023.
https://doi.org/10.1007/978-3-031-35992-7_46

Exoskeleton robots that assist, support, or supplement human functions and activities are becoming increasingly practical and widespread. One of the key benefits of exoskeleton robots is their ability to effectively combine human flexibility and robotic power without requiring extensive programming or training, making them useful in situations where traditional solutions are not effective or feasible. Despite their potential benefits, the number of exoskeleton robots in everyday use remains low due to limited availability on the market and challenges related to acceptance of the technology.

To expand the usage of exoskeleton robots in different areas, there is a need to enhance their usability during the development phase. At present, wearable robots do not have the perfect ergonomic properties. Prior to incorporating the device's control and actuation, it is important to ensure that the exoskeleton robot is user-friendly and comfortable to use. Although comfort is subjective, the smooth interaction between the device and the user is crucial for overall comfort; in essence, the device must not restrict the range of motion or add any burden to the user while using the device [3].

Several prior studies have aimed to assess the effectiveness and usability of exoskeleton robots. In one such study, Pinho and Forner-Cordero [4] investigated the level of shoulder muscle activity and perceived comfort among industry workers who used a commercial upper limb exoskeleton for simulated tasks. The researchers discovered that the exoskeleton robot increased the time required to complete the task but reduced the perceived effort, leading to greater overall comfort. Overhead work often leads to physical fatigue, which can contribute to musculoskeletal disorders. Exoskeletons offer support that reduces muscle activity in the arm-elevating muscles and partially alleviates the impact of fatigue [5].

Despite the multitude of studies mentioned earlier, there is still a lack of a uniform framework regarding the design and safety evaluation guidelines for wearable robots. Users' complaints about not having enough access to participate in the design phase of these robots still persist [6]. Therefore, the objective of this study was to extract specific elements for user evaluation by analyzing the functional features, user evaluation methods, and results of previously developed passive exoskeleton robots through a review of literature.

2 Methods

Procedures of literature reviews are classified in to six step such as 1) Choosing the target databases, 2) Selecting the keyword in the last 10 years, 3) Evaluation of titles, 4) Evaluation the abstract, 5) Available full-test articles, 6) evaluation methodology and related factors review and arrangement. Passive Exoskeleton, Upper/Lower Exoskeleton, etc. were used as search English keywords for evaluation methodology and key related variable investigation. For the data searched by keyword, the data judged to be highly relevant to this study were primarily selected through title review, and the abstract was reviewed for them. Afterwards, based on the review of the abstract, the data used for the evaluation methodology and the arrangement of key related variables were selected.

The titles of journal articles (recent 5 years, 2017–2022) were analyzed to select papers that fit the subject. After analyzing the abstracts of the selected papers, the final 79 papers (72 for industrial use and 7 for recycling) were reselected. The entire contents of the selected papers were analyzed, and the purpose and type of the exoskeleton robot was classified and organized according to items such as user evaluation method, subject information, and characteristic evaluation equipment measurement method.

3 Results

3.1 Exoskeleton Type and Aim of Development

The exoskeleton robots developed in the 79 selected papers were classified as follows according to the main supporting and supporting parts (Table 1).

Table 1. Exoskeleton type.

Type	Upper limb	Lower limb	Trunk
N(%)	23(29.1%)	29(36.7%)	27(34.2%)

Exoskeleton robots were mainly developed for lifting (39.1%), walking (25.6%), and overhead work (14.6%), and were also developed to assist carrying, squatting, and handling. The exoskeleton robots could be classified into 82.7% for muscle support and 17.3% for posture maintenance. A total of 22 tasks were used for usability evaluation in the research papers, and among them, Dynamic Lifting accounted for 23.3% and Walking accounted for the highest percentage at 20.3% (Table 2).

Table 2. Experimental task in usability task.

Dynamic lifting	Static lifting	Dynamic squatting	Static squatting	walking	Carrying
24(23.3%)	9(8.7%)	7(6.7%)	4(3.8%)	21(20.3%)	7(6.7%)
Overhead work	Running	Up & down stairs	Static trunk flexion	Stooping	Etc
8(7.7%)	1(0.9%)	1(0.9%)	4(3.8%)	4(3.8%)	13(12.6)

There were 7 types of measurement equipment used for usability evaluation in the research papers, among which EMG was used to evaluate usability in 47 papers. A total of 15 factors were measured, and among them, muscle activity was used in 47 studies and joint angle was used in 22 studies, making it the most frequently measured factor in usability evaluation. As a scale for subjective evaluation, the Borg scale was used in 11 studies and was the most frequently used evaluation scale.

3.2 Effectiveness and Usability Evaluation Results

The results of efficiency and usability evaluation were described only for muscle activity and subjective satisfaction in this paper. Summarizing the results of previous studies, when performing tasks while wearing an exoskeleton robot, muscle activity decreased by about 20.5% (9.8 ~ 31.2%) (Table 3).

Table 3. Muscle activities change rate in usability task.

Task	Body part	Muscle	Change rate(%)
Dynamic lifting	Upper limb	Biceps, Triceps	23.3%↓
		Deltoid, Trapezius	18.1%↓
	Back	Thoracic/Lumbar Erector spinae	9.8%↓
	Lower limb	Biceps femoris Quadriceps	25.0%↓
Overhead work	Upper limb	Deltoid, Trapezius	31.2%↓
Walking	Back	Thoracic/Lumbar Erector spinae	25.4%↓
Static Lifting	Lower limb	Biceps femoris Quadriceps	31.2%↓

Looking at the results of subjective satisfaction (Borg scale), about 64.5% evaluated the exoskeleton robot positively (Table 4).

Table 4. Subjective satisfaction rate in usability task.

Result	Positive	Neutral	Negative
Ratio (%)	64.5%	16.1%	19.4%

4 Discussion and Conclusion

The main objective of the research was to evaluate the effectiveness and feasibility of exoskeleton robots by conducting a thorough literature review. The study revealed that there are various types of exoskeleton robots being developed and their effectiveness is highly dependent on the intended use. In general, exoskeleton robots have the potential to reduce muscle activity. However, the studies that have been conducted in this regard only assess specific muscles, and their impact on other interacting muscles is not taken into account.

The currently available exoskeleton robots are designed for general use and not for specific tasks, which can result in decreased efficiency and usability problems in certain tasks. Therefore, it is recommended that customized exoskeleton robots be developed for specific tasks in the future. It is also important to comprehensively evaluate all muscles and factors that may be affected while using an exoskeleton during usability evaluation.

To address these limitations and improve the usability of exoskeleton robots, further research is necessary. The development of task-specific exoskeleton robots can enhance the efficiency and effectiveness of the device. Additionally, a comprehensive evaluation of all interacting muscles and factors that may affect the user's performance while wearing the exoskeleton should be conducted during usability evaluation. Such improvements will ensure that exoskeleton robots can be utilized safely and efficiently in various fields.

Moreover, it is essential to consider the comfort and ease of use of exoskeleton robots during their design and development. The ideal ergonomic characteristics of wearable robots have not been fully realized yet, and it is necessary to establish a proper evaluation system to ensure user comfort and ease of use even before implementing the device's control and actuation. The interaction between exoskeleton robots and humans is crucial, and the device must not limit the range of motion or burden the user while wearing it. Thus, it is recommended to develop an evaluation system and detailed elements that can be properly evaluated for the characteristics, functions, use environment, and user class of exoskeleton robots. Such a system can advance the safety, convenience, and usability of exoskeleton robots, and establish a methodology for their development and evaluation.

References

1. Kim, J., Chun, H., Lee, S.-H., Lee, H.-J., Kim, Y.-H.: Functional improvement and satisfaction with a wearable hip exoskeleton in community-living adults. Healthcare 11(5), 643 (2023)
2. Pons, J.L.: Wearable Robots: Biomechatronic Exoskeletons. John Wiley & Sons, Hoboken (2008)
3. Samuel, M.F.R., Tim, C.L., Lorenzo, T.D.: Individualized arm shells towards an ergonomic design of exoskeleton robots. In: IEEE International Conference on Systems, Man, and Cybernetics, pp. 5–8. IEEE, San Diego (2014)
4. Pinho, J.P., Forner-Cordero, A.: Shoulder muscle activity and perceived comfort of industry workers using a commercial upper limb exoskeleton for simulated tasks. Appl. Ergon. 101, 103718 (2022)
5. Bock, S.D., et al.: Passive shoulder exoskeleton support partially mitigates fatigue-induced effects in overhead work. Appl. Ergon. 106, 103903 (2023)
6. Ármannsdóttir, A.L., et al.: Assessing the involvement of users during development of lower limb wearable robotic exoskeletons: a survey study. Human Fact., 0018720819883500 (2020)

A Comparison of Digital Libraries for the Visually Impaired in the United States and Japan

Tomoya Matsumura[1]([✉]) and Yoichi Ochiai[2]

[1] Graduate School of Science and Technology, Division of Health Sciences, Course of Information systems, Tsukuba University of Technology, 4-11-7 Kasuga, Tsukuba 305-8521, Ibaraki, Japan
natarajgiri@icloud.com

[2] School of Informatics, University of Tsukuba, the College of Media Arts, Science and Technology, 1-2 Kasuga, Tsukuba 305-0885, Ibaraki, Japan

Abstract. Visually impaired individuals face significant challenges in mobility and acquiring information, resulting in difficulties with education, employment, and daily life. Human-computer interaction technology, such as screen readers and digital libraries, have the potential to improve accessibility and transform the lives of visually impaired people. In the US, Bookshare, National Library Service (NLS) and learning arai provides accessible content to people with print disabilities, while in Japan, the SAPIER Library and the Data Transmission Service for the Visually Impaired of the National Diet Library are major information services. The Americans with Disabilities Act defines a person with a disability more broadly than Japan's NLS, which issues certificates for fixed medical conditions. One significant difference between the US and Japan is music copyright, with the US allowing visually impaired individuals to use music materials, while Japan's accessibility to higher education and music lags behind. The author, a visually impaired person in Japan, is launching a digital library using HCI technology in collaboration with the National Diet Library to provide electronic books and music resources for higher education.

Keywords: Access to education and learning · Accessible documents and multimedia · Design for All education and training · Design for Children with and without disabilities · Design for Cognitive Disabilities · Design for Quality of Life Technologies · Design for well-being and eudaimonia · Evaluation of Accessibility Usability and User Experience · Inclusive affective technologies · Media Accessibility · Digital Libraries

1 Objective, Background and Methods

According to the Japan Rehabilitation Association, visually impaired people have substantial difficulties in mobility and information acquisition. Due to certain barriers, such as the inability to read bound books, the visually impaired face challenges in education, employment, and daily life. Improvements in accessibility through human–computer interaction technology have the potential to considerably change the lives of the visually impaired and are in the process of doing so. The author, who is also blind, uses a voice aid known as a screen reader to read and write papers. In human–computer interaction, digital libraries for the visually impaired that guarantee access to information are one of the most innovative technologies.

In recent years, systems for the visually impaired in many countries have become standardized with the enactment and ratification of the Convention on the Rights of Persons with Disabilities, commonly known as the Marrakesh Treaty [1, 2]. However, these systems vary depending on the circumstances and legal systems. In this study, we surveyed and compared digital libraries for the visually impaired in the United States (U.S.) and Japan through a literature review and suggested future models.

2 Definition of Persons with Disabilities

2.1 Definition of Persons with Disabilities in the U.S.

The Americans with Disabilities Act (ADA) defines a person with a disability in the U.S [3, 4]. According to it, a person with a disability is a person who has a record of having had a physical or mental impairment in the past that substantially limits one or more of their major life activities or is regarded as having such an impairment. It is believed that a larger percentage of the population is considered disabled in the U.S. because they view disability in the social sense of limiting activities of daily living, and they are considered disabled even if their activities of daily living are temporarily limited. In the past, the National Library Service (NLS) was only available to the physically challenged, but literacy and other disabilities were gradually added.

2.2 Definition of Person with Disabilities in Japan

In Japan, the definition of persons with disabilities by Ministry of Health, Labour and Welfare is narrower than in the U.S.[5] Japanese government issues a certificate for a fixed medical condition that allows the holder to receive welfare services and special measures for employment.

3 Digital Libraries for the Visually Impaired

3.1 Digital Libraries for the Visually Impaired in U.S.

Bookshare is an online library that provides accessible content to people with print disabilities [6, 7]. Launched in 2002 by Benetech, an American non-profit social enterprise, it is a online library for people with print disabilities, offering 1,139,341 titles. People in over 70 countries access Bookshare to pursue employment and education.

National Library Service (NLS) is a free braille and talking book library service for people with temporary or permanent low vision, blindness, or a physical, perceptual, or reading disability that prevents them from using regular print materials [8, 9]. Through a national network of cooperating libraries, NLS circulates books and magazines in braille or audio formats, that are instantly downloadable to a personal device or delivered by mail free of charge. Another organization, Learning Ally, is focused on educating people with visual impairment and dyslexia [9].

3.2 Digital Libraries for the Visually Impaired in Japan

The SAPIER Library and the Data Transmission Service for the Visually Impaired of the National Diet Library are two major information services for visually impaired persons in Japan [10–12]. University libraries, public libraries, and Braille libraries participate in these services, producing electronic books for the visually impaired. At the Sapier Library, more than 240,000 titles of Braille data and 100,000 titles of audio Daisy data can be downloaded from the website. The National Diet Library and Sapier Library share data with each other, and although they were not as diverse as the three types of services in the U.S., the National Diet Library's digital archives owned by the National Diet Library will be made accessible in the FY2022 budget; a full-text text conversion demonstration experiment will be conducted jointly with publishers and other organizations. The efforts are conspicuous.

4 Exception for Music Copyright

One of the major differences between the American and Japanese systems is music copyright. In the U.S., not only books but also music can be used by the visually impaired as an exception to copyright [13]. The NLS in America has a large collection of music materials for the visually impaired. It comprises around 25,000 titles and includes a wide variety of Braille and large print scores, Braille and large print textbooks and books, music, and private lessons on individual instruments. There is no equivalent system in Japan.

5 Next Model

In Japan, most visually impaired workers are acupuncture and massage therapists. While this is a positive aspect of social security, on the other hand, accessibility to higher education and to play music, in particular, lags far behind that of the United States. As a blind person in Japan, I launched a digital library by using HCI technology in cooperation with the National Diet Library. I will release electronic books and music resources at the level of higher education soon.

References

1. The Marrakesh Treaty to Facilitate Access to Published Works for Persons Who Are Blind, Visually Impaired or Otherwise Print Disabled, WIPO Doc. VIP/DC/8 (2013). Accessed 30 Sept 2016

2. Köklü, K.: The marrakesh treaty – time to end the book famine for visually impaired persons worldwide. IIC – Int. Rev. Intellect. Proper. Compet. Law **45**(7), 737–739 (2014). https://doi.org/10.1007/s40319-014-0266-z
3. ADA official website, ADA.govlast. Accessed 24 Mar 2023
4. Aldousari, A., Alghamdi, A., Alwadei, H.: The 1991 americans with disabilities act (ADA) standards for accessible design. Am. Res. J. Humanit. Soc. Sci. **4**, 59–62 (2021)
5. Ministry of Health, Labour and Welfare website. https://www.mhlw.go.jp/stf/seisakunitsuite/bunya/hukushi_kaigo/shougaishahukushi/shougaishatechou/index.html. (in Japanese). Accessed 24 Mar 2023
6. Bookshare website. https://www.bookshare.org/cms/. Accessed 24 Mar 2023
7. Cylke, F.K., Moodie, M.M., Fistick, R.E.: Serving the blind and physically handicapped in the United States of America. Libr. Trends **55**(4), 796–808 (2007)
8. NLS website. https://www.loc.gov/nls/. Accessed 24 Mar 2023
9. learning ally website, https://learningally.org/,last access 2023/3/24
10. Sapier library website. https://www.sapie.or.jp/. Accessed 24 Mar 2024
11. National diet library website. https://www.ndl.go.jp/. Accessed 24 Mar 2023
12. Takenori, N., Yashio, U., Ichiro, N., Susumu, M.: A empirical study on accessibility of erictorical books, Jinbunkagakunenpo (2014). (in Japanese)
13. Mary, A.: Resources for helping blind music students- A variety of resources is available to help educators teach blind students how to read music and become part of the music classroom. Music Educ. J. **8**(2), 23–45 (1998)

Improvement of User Interface of Blind Football Play-by-Play System for Visually Impaired Spectators-Tangible Sports

Hiroyuki Ohshima[1]([✉]) [iD], Makoto Kobayashi[2], and Shigenobu Shimada[1]

[1] Tokyo Metropolitan Industrial Technology Research Institute (TIRI), Tokyo, Japan
ohshima.hiroyuki@iri-tokyo.jp
[2] Tsukuba University of Technology, Tsukuba, Japan

Abstract. In the field of sports, visually impaired spectators are at a disadvantage in terms of understanding the precise developments in a game. This study proposes a blind football play-by-play system that combines a tactile graphic display and a position acquisition function to aid visually impaired spectators in understanding game developments. To evaluate the proposed system, we develop a prototype system, which detects the positions of players and balls using image processing technology and deep learning and shows these positions via a refreshable tactile display. Furthermore, the validity of the proposed system is established through subjective experiments. The results show that all participants are able to identify each team member and understand the formation of players using the proposed interface. The results provide significant suggestions for the major task of human interface research: the transmission of kinesthesia. Spectators report that they felt as if they were playing on the field and could determine details such as the position of the opposing player and the course from which the assisting player passed the ball to the scoring player. This system provides a rich user experience for spectators and is a powerful feedback tool for players.

Keywords: Tactile graphic display · Feedback tool · Support system

1 Introduction

Blind football (also known as blind soccer) has become increasingly popular in the field of para sports with worldwide championships being conducted regularly by the International Blind Sports Federation (IBSA) [1]. Additionally, it is broadcasted on the internet and even on TV in Japan. Consequently, the number of spectators attending these events has been increasing. These spectators can be categorized into three groups [2]: athletes participating in the game, individuals such as family members or friends of the athletes, and unrelated individuals with disabilities. In the case of blind football, many spectators are visually impaired. However, understanding the precise developments in these games is challenging for visually impaired spectators. Although employing a professional commentator for every game is infeasible, to provide them with such information, making play-by-play announcements during the live coverage of games is the best solution.

Therefore, Panasonic developed a support system to broadcast live announcements to smartphones or tablets of visually impaired spectators via available network [3]. However, this solution, albeit discreet and effective, requires a professional sports commentator and is challenging to realize in the case of local matches. Therefore, a blind football play-by-play system called "Tangible Sports" was proposed for visually impaired spectators [4, 5]. To verify the proposed system, a prototype system that detected the positions of players and ball on the field was developed using image-processing technology and deep learning. Afterward, it displayed these positions on a refreshable tactile display. The results established the possibility of displaying the positions of players and ball on a tactile display. The players of teams A and B and the ball were presented with tactile pins of different frequencies so that spectators could distinguish them. However, the participants reported that although the position of each player can be realized, players' formation is challenging to understand. Realizing players' formations is the best part of watching blind football. Therefore, this study proposes and verifies a method that assists visually impaired people in understanding players' formations.

2   System Configuration

As described in our previous study [5], this system consists of a position acquisition function and tactile graphic display. The position acquisition system tracks the position information of players and ball automatically using image-processing technology and deep learning. Most tactile graphic displays developed in the past were only capable of unidirectional communication [6–8]. In this study, four bimorph modules (SC–10, provided by KGS Inc.) were used to assemble the tactile display, which is widely employed in Japan, and the result that blinds can understand significant graphical information from the device is verified [9]. This section describes the playback function and quadrangle presentation method, which are additional specifications to improve UI.

2.1   Playback System

The position acquisition function and tactile graphic display control program were integrated as a playback system on the same PC. The position acquisition function outputs CSV files every 1/30 s, and the tactile graphic display control program reads the CSV files every second and sends the bumpy pattern to DV-II firmware via serial communication. The DV-II firmware controls the raising and lowering of the pins of the tactile graphic display. Figure 1 shows the user interface of the playback system. A position acquisition function is shown on the left side of the figure, which enables users to display images of a blind football game, display the acquired position results, open files, play/stop/frame-by-frame playback, and select scenes with seek bar. In the background, CSV writing of the position results, acquired by the position acquisition function, data conversion for the tactile graphic display, and serial communication management with the tactile graphic display, are performed as displayed in the upper right of Fig. 1. Finally, the position information is presented on the tactile graphic display at the lower right of the figure.

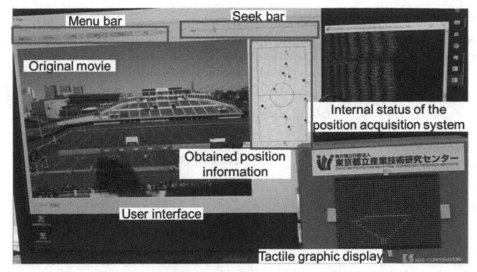

Fig. 1. User interface of the proposed system.

2.2 Quadrangle Presentation Method

On the tactile graphic display at the lower right of Fig. 1, the same position of the field players and ball shown in the actual blind football game is presented as a bumpy pin pattern. A 3×3 pin rectangle at the bottom of the quadrangle is the position of the ball. A white quadrangle is shown at the center of the tactile graphic display. The quadrangle is formed by connecting four field players of team A, that is, all players except for the goalkeeper. This newly proposed method is called the "quadrangle presentation method." Compared with our previous method, which uses different vibration frequencies for discrimination of the ball and players of both teams, this presentation method may facilitate spectators' understanding of player formations. We expect that the finger of a visually impaired spectators will touch somewhere on the quadrangle, even if they scan the presentation surface on the tactile graphic display casually with their finger. They can find the apexes as the positions of field players by following the lines of the quadrangle from where their finger hits. The formation represented by a quadrangle always has a certain size on the tactile graphic display. Therefore, they can track players' positions easily.

3 Experimental Setup and Results

An experimental setup was established to verify the quadrangle presentation method. The setup comprises a graphic tactile display and computer. The participants sat in front of the tactile graphic display while wearing a protective eye mask and earmuffs. The Ethics Committee of the authors' institution approves the experimental procedure. All participants provided informed prior consent based on institutional requirements.

3.1 Participants

Six males (aged 19 to 52 years, 28.8 ± 13.5) volunteered as participants in this study and were similar to subjects in a previous study [5]. Table 1 shows the characteristics of the participants. Three of them were blind, and three were visually impaired.

Table 1. Participants' characteristics.

Age	Visual acuity (yard-pound system)	Congenital/acquired	Type of characters used	Method to obtain information	Experience of habitually watching (hearing) sports	Remarks
19	under 20/2000	Acquired	Braille	Voice, braille	Yes	
19	under 20/2000	Congenital	Braille	Voice, braille	Yes	
20	20/1000–20/666	Congenital	Braille, printed	Voice, enlargement, braille	Yes	
20	20/1000–20/666	Congenital	Printed	Same as sighted person	Yes	Blind football player
52	under 20/2000	Congenital	Braille	Voice, braille	Yes	
43	under 20/2000	Acquired	Braille	Voice, braille	Yes	

3.2 Procedure

The participants verified if they could distinguish the players of the two teams and if they could understand the formation of team A, which changed over time dynamically. The players and ball positions extracted from real games were displayed on the tactile graphic display. For the game scene, a scene of 7 s until team A scored a goal was employed. As shown in Fig. 2, each player is displayed with one pin and ball is displayed with 3 × 3 pins. We used a quadrangular presentation for team A. The participants were not provided with instructions on how to scan the tactile graphic display with their fingers. The participants had a little prior experiences with tactile graphic displays for studies at school. However, they were using the proposed system for the first time to watch sports. They were allowed multiple chances with the 7 s game scene even though they were not given time to explore it prior to the experiments. After the experiments, the participants answered questions about if they could distinguish between the players of the two teams and if they could understand the formation of team A. Furthermore, they provided their impressions of the proposed system.

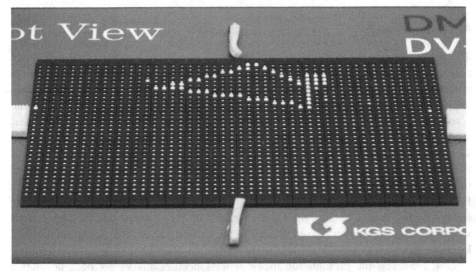

Fig. 2. Example of a display with ball (3 × 3 pins) and players (1 pin each).

3.3 Results

All seven participants could identify each team member and understood the formation of team A, which was represented by a quadrangle. Several participants commented that they could distinguish the detailed movements of players, which was not possible with live announcements. Other comments from the participants were as follows.

First, the following were positive opinions:

- The formation of players was easier to understand on the quadrangular presentation than in the vibration presentation.
- It was easier to understand the position of players in the entire field in the quadrangular presentation than in the vibration presentation.
- The quadrangular presentation was more fun than the vibration presentation because the line connecting the players always moved.
- It was easier to track the players in the quadrangular presentation than in the vibration presentation.
- I understood the flow of the game in the quadrangular presentation better than in the vibration presentation.
- The quadrangular presentation emphasized the player's position, which was easier to understand in this presentation than in the vibration presentation.

Additionally, the following specifications could be improved:

- When I was tracking the formation, it was difficult to track the ball.

- It was difficult to understand the players of team B.
- It would have been nice to have a function to show the players of team B.
- I lost the players of team B when they overlapped with the formation lines of team A.

4 Discussion

The para-sports lab developed a support device that shows the position of the ball in real time via tactile sensation such that spectators with visual impairments can follow the field situation by touch [10]. However, this solution does not provide information regarding the positions of the players from the supporting and opponent teams or the different team formations, which are some of the best parts of watching blind football. In a previous study [5], team members were presented with different vibrations, and most participants were able to identify them. However, the previous method could not convey the flow of the game, which is a crucial part of watching blind football. Understanding the flow of the game is not simply knowing the uniform numbers of players who scored or assisted. Feeling the flow of the game means that spectators feel as if they are playing on the field and can perceive details, such as the position of the opponent and the course from which the assisting player passed the ball to the scoring player. This sensation is called kinesthesia and is as significant for the quality of entertainment as visual and auditory senses. However, the presentation methods for kinesthesia have not been developed as much as those for visual and auditory senses. This is because the mechanisms of kinesthesia have not been clarified as much as those of the visual and auditory senses. The results show that all seven participants were able to identify each team member and understand the formation of Team A, which was presented in a quadrangle. This result provides important suggestions for the major task of human interface research, which is the transmission of kinesthesia. The experiment demonstrated the effectiveness of the quadrangle presentation method. In addition, the following requests were made by the participants in the experiment to further improve the user interface.

- Function to pause, slow-motion replay, zoom in/out
- Function to display the center line
- Function to switch quadrangular presentation from Team A to Team B
- Function to display the trajectory of the ball
- Function to move the viewpoint around the ball
- Function to show the height of the shoot

All suggestions were useful because they were the opinions of visually impaired parties that could not be conceived by sighted people. The opinions were adapted to their information acquisition characteristics, and very useful opinions were obtained for the improvement of the user interface of our proposed system. Moreover, this system is applicable not only to spectators but also to players as an effective method of sharing strategy. This system can be displayed simultaneously on four tactile graphic displays. This allows four field players to share the same scene at the same time, which helps to form a common understanding among the players.

However, issues with this system remain. The position of the camera must be set sufficiently high to capture the entire field at once, and positioning the camera on a tall pole might be dangerous and difficult to execute in a local game.

Therefore, it is necessary to identify workarounds to address this issue in future studies.

5 Conclusion

To develop a blind football play-by-play system for visually impaired spectators, we created a prototype system that detects the positions of the players and the ball on the field using image processing technology and deep learning. The system displays player positions on a refreshable tactile graphic display. A verification study was conducted, and the results suggest the possibility of transmitting kinesthesia to visually impaired spectators by displaying the positions of the players and the ball on the tactile display. In the future, we plan to add a synthesized voice to the output method.

References

1. Football - general information (IBSA web site). https://blindfootball.sport/. Accessed 2 Mar 2023
2. De Haan, D., Faull, A., Molnar, G.: Blind football: spectators' experience of the forgotten. In: Proceedings of 19th Conference of the European Association for Sport Management, pp. 185–186 (2011)
3. Panasonic Newsroom, 4 April 2017. Panasonic Demonstrated Spectator Solutions with VOGO Sport for Disabled Sports at Japan-Brazil Blind Football Match. http://news.panasonic.com/global/topics/2017/46362.html. Accessed 2 Mar 2023
4. Kobayashi, M., Fukunaga, Y., Shimada, S.: Basic study of blind football play-by-play system for visually impaired spectators using quasi-zenith satellites system. In: Miesenberger, K., Kouroupetroglou, G. (eds.) ICCHP 2018. LNCS, vol. 10897, pp. 23–27. Springer, Cham (2018). https://doi.org/10.1007/978-3-319-94274-2_4
5. Ohshima, H., Kobayashi, M., Shimada. S.: Development of blind football play-by-play system for visually impaired spectators: Tangible sports. In: Extended Abstracts of the 2021 CHI Conference on Human Factors in Computing Systems. Association for Computing Machinery, New York, Article 209, pp. 1–6 (2021). https://doi.org/10.1145/3411763.451737
6. Wellman, P.S., Peine, W.J., Favalora, G., Howe, R.D.: Mechanical design and control of a high–bandwidth shape memory alloy tactile display, In: ISER, pp. 56–66 (1997). https://doi.org/10.1007/BFb0112950
7. Shinohara, M., Shimizu, Y., Mochizuki, A.: Three-dimensional tactile display for the blind. IEEE Trans. Rehabil. Eng. **6**(3), 249–256 (1998). https://doi.org/10.1109/86.712218
8. Wagner, C.R., Lederman, S.J., Howe, R.D.: A tactile shape display using RC servomotors. In: Proceedings of 10th Symposium on Haptic Interfaces for Virtual Environment and Teleoperator Systems. HAPTICS 2002, pp. 345–355 (2002). https://doi.org/10.1109/HAPTIC.2002.998981
9. Kobayashi, M., Watanabe, T.: Multimedia communication system for the blind. In: Ichalkaranje, N., Ichalkaranje, A., Jain, L. (eds.) Intelligent Paradigms for Assistive and Preventive Healthcare. Studies in Computational Intelligence, vol. 19, pp. 165–181, Springer, Heidelberg (2006). https://doi.org/10.1007/11418337_6
10. Haptic Field. https://ponoor.com/projects/haptic-field/. Accessed 2 Mar 2023

User Experience in Virtual Reality from People With and Without Disability

Thais Pousada García, Javier Pereira Loureiro(✉), Betania Groba,
Laura Nieto-Riveiro, Jessica Martín, and Manuel Lagos Rodríguez

Center of Research in ITC, CITIC, TALIONIS Research Group, University of A Coruña, 15071
A Coruña, Spain
{tpousada,javier.pereira}@udc.es

Abstract. Virtual Reality (VR) is a resource for leisure and participation. Recently, VR applications have been introduced progressively into health interventions. The possibility of being immersed in virtual scenarios offers an opportunity to recreate real spaces in a rehabilitation room and to become more motivating. There exist interesting open-access games and applications in platforms such as STEAMVR, VIVEPort or META, that can be used during rehabilitation. Nevertheless, the main problem is the lack of usability and possibility to adapt these applications to demands of final users. The use of VR is conditioned, also, by the experience and perspective of the people. Purpose of research was to analyze and determine the possibilities of generic VR applications from the perspective of final users, based on their experience. A cross-sectional study was done, with sample divided into two groups: people with (N = 24) and without disability (N = 34). The Game Experience Questionnaire (GEQ) was applied. The applications analyzed were: IkeaVRPancake Kitchen, TheBlue, Adventure climb, Google EarthVR, Cube dancer, Blobby tennis and Richie's PlankExperience.

Results indicated that people without disabilities felt an experience more immersive in VR. No significant differences were obtained concerning the GEQ Post-game. The application with the higher score in terms of positive experience was Richie's PlankExperience (M = 2,32), and concerning competence was Google EarthVR (M = 2,6) In general, the game experience was positive, but there are still some difficulties detected to implement the games into rehabilitation: control manipulation, interface person-application and understanding instructions. So, is needed to implement adaptations into the games to facilitate their use by people with disabilities.

Keywords: Virtual reality · disability · user experience (UX) · accessibility · First Section

1 Introduction

Virtual Reality (VR) is a new resource for leisure and participation. Recently, VR applications have been introduced progressively into health interventions, especially in those focused on the rehabilitation of people with disabilities. The possibility of being immersed in a variety of virtual scenarios offers a great opportunity to recreate real spaces in a rehabilitation room and to become more motivating in the sessions for the patients. There exist interesting and open-access games and applications in commercial platforms such as STEAMVR, VIVEPort or META, that can be used during any rehabilitation process. Nevertheless, the main problem is the lack of usability and the possibility to adapt these applications to the demands of final users [1, 2]. The use of VR resources is conditioned, also, by the experience, perspective and interests of the people that can use this resource.

The goals of this research were: (1) to analyze and determine the possibilities of generic VR applications from the perspective of final users, based on their experience; (2) to check if there are differences between people with and without disability in their interaction with virtual scenarios.

2 Methodology

The study had a cross-sectional, transversal and prospective design. It was carried on during the academic course 2020/2021, and all tests and experiences with virtual reality were done in the same place: Research Center of Information and Communication Technologies (CITIC) at the University of A Coruña.

This center has facilities to use virtual environments, including HTC Vive Glasses, with Wi-Fi connection, and LeapMotion controller as an optical hand tracking module that captures the movements of the hands with unparalleled accuracy [3].

Sample. The sample (N = 58) was formed by people with (N = 24) and without disabilities (N = 34) who voluntarily decided to participate in the study.

People with disability came from a regional Non-Govermental Organization (NGO), whose mean of age was 34.5. The diagnosis of all of them was Spinal Cord Injury, being tetraplegic in 8 cases and paraplegic in 16 persons. In the case of participants without disability, the group was formed by students of the University of A Coruña. The mean age was 21.9 and all of them were familiar with the gaming experience, but only 6 people had tried VR in the past.

Measure Instrument. The Game Experience Questionnaire (GEQ) is an instrument that has been development to get information about user-experience using videogames and interactive applications [4]. This tool has widely been applied by games researchers and practitioners to a broad scope of game genres, user groups, gaming environments, and purposes [5]. The Game Experience Questionnaire has a modular structure and consists of a core questionnaire, Social Presence Module and Post-game module. In addition to these modules, a concise in-game version of the GEQ was developed [4]. In the present research, the in-game version and post-game module were applied.

The first one was developed for assessing game experience at multiple intervals during a game session, or play-back session and it allows to assess the game experience on seven components: Immersion, Flow, Competence, Positive and Negative Affect, Tension, and Challenge.

The post-game module assesses how players felt after they had stopped playing. This is a relevant module for assessing naturalistic gaming, but may also be relevant in experimental research. The components for this module are Positive experience, Negative experience, Tiredness and Returning to reality.

Each item of all modules is scored in a Likert scale from 0 (not at all) to 4 (extremely).

Procedure. In order to assess the user experience in virtual scenarios some commercial applications from the library of SteamVR and Vive Port were selected: IkeaVR Pancake Kitchen, TheBlue, Adventure climb, Google EarthVR, Cube dancer, Blobby tennis and Richie's Plank Experience. The criteria for choosing these ones and not another was due to they allow to reproduction of movements and actions related to activities of daily life and they can use to promote the process of rehabilitation of people with disability. Also these applications were easy to understand and to play by different groups of people. Its features are briefly described below:

- IkeaVR Pancake Kitchen [6]: In this application, the users can make some virtual pancakes, through the guide from IKEA to some of the key aspects of a well-planned kitchen.
- TheBlue [7]: Is a deeply immersive VR series that allows audiences to experience the wonder and majesty of the ocean through different habitats and come face to face with some of the most awe-inspiring species on the planet.
- Adventure climb [8]: It is a room-scale climbing experience suitable for anyone. The person achieves triumph through a combination of physically demanding climbing techniques and puzzle challenges that are designed by actual rock climbers.
- Google EarthVR [9]: This virtual reality app lets the user see the world's cities, landmarks, and natural wonders. The person can fly over a city, stand at the top of the highest peaks, and even soar into space. Also the app includes cinematic tours and hand-picked destinations.
- Cube dancer [10]: It is a short VR rhythm game, that puts the user in dance battles against mysterious opponents, each with its own unique dance style. The person has to hit all the cubes that are thrown at him/her.
- Blobby tennis [11]: The environment recreates a beach scene, controlling a tennis racket and ball, where the person can do tricks, play the ball back and forth over the net with Blobby or outplay him to score points.
- Richie's Plank Experience [12]: it is a psychological experience that the users will react to with exhilaration, fear or laughter. This game invokes a near-instant emotional reaction.

The procedure consisted of inviting participants to try one or more [respecting his/her preferences and interests) of the selected applications. The time for the game was the same for all participants, respecting the specified times in each game experience.

After the game, participants were invited to fill out the modules of Game Experience Questionnaire: in-game and post-game. These were digitalized and the research group used the Research Electronic Data CAPture [RedCAP] tool. This is a secure web application for building and managing online surveys and databases [13].

All participants gave their informed consent to involve in this study and all data were codified and anonymized.

3 Results

The main results analyzing the VR experience with all games derived from the application of GEQ are shown in Table 1 (in-game module) and Table 2 (post-game). They are broken down by categories of each questionnaire.

People with disability showed a feeling of a more immersive experience than those without disability, and in the experience post-game, it is relevant that people without disability returned to reality better than the other group.

The item with the higher score was "I was interested in the game's story" (3,2) for the in-game module, and "I felt satisfied" (2,64) for post-game module.

Table 1. Results obtained in GEQ (in-game module), according the group of participants

Components	People with disability (N = 24) Mean (SD)	People without disability (N = 28) Mean (SD)	p-value
Competence	2,4 (1)	2 (1,1)	0,169
Sensory and Imaginative Immersion	3,1 (1)	2,6 (1,1)	<0,05
Flow	2,9 (1,2)	2,5 (1)	0,113
Tension	0,7 (0,7)	0,4 (0,6)	0,87
Challenge	1,8 (1)	1,8 (1,2)	0,879
Negative affect	3 (0,6)	0,4 (0,5)	0,297
Positive affect	3,1 (1)	2,5 (1,4)	0,69

Table 2. Results obtained in GEQ (post-game module), according the group of participants

Components	People with disability (N = 24) Mean (SD)	People without disability (N = 28) Mean (SD)	p-value
Positive experience	1,98 (1,19)	1,53 (1,16)	0,151
Negative experience	0,5 (0,5)	0,3 (0,5)	0,129
Tiredness	0,7 (0,9)	0,3 (0,7)	0,69
Returning to reality	0,82 (0,64)	0,38 (0,39)	<0,05

Analyzing the results independently for each game, the games with the best immersive experience were Google EarthVR (M = 3,4) and Adventure Climb (M = 3,4), and the most positive affect was for IkeaVR Pancake Kitchen (M = 3,4). After the game, the one who reported the most positive experience was Richie's PlankExperience (M = 2,32), but it was also the one that reported more tiredness among the participants. The game that reported the biggest negative experience was Blobby tennis (M = 0,9), and the return to reality was easier for IkeaVR Pancake Kitchen (M = 0,11).

The reliability study of the Game Experience Questionnaire was high in both in-game module (α cronbach = 0,819) and post-game module (α cronbach = 0,730).

4 Conclusions

The main contribution of this work is the analysis of commercial applications of Virtual Reality, taking into account the user's experience and perspective, comparing its use by people with and without disability. The results that emerged can be used to guide the design and prototype of new virtual realities environment, mainly, for those which aim to be applied in rehabilitation intervention.

In general, the game experience was positive, but there are still some difficulties detected to implement the games into rehabilitation: control manipulation, interface person-application and understanding instructions. So, it is needed to implement adaptations into the games to facilitate their use by people with disabilities.

It is important to take into account opinions and relevant comments from users in order to develop and get more interesting, enjoyable and immersive experiences, using virtual scenarios. It is more relevant in the case of applying VR during rehabilitation treatment. So, the user experience, or UX, has to be implemented as a constant feature in order to get more success for clinical and health purposes. With this in mind, developers must consider not only the perspective of the final users (people with disabilities), but also the opinion of rehabilitation professionals.

Acknowledgments. This work is supported in part by some grants from the European Social Fund 2014-2020: Centre for Information and Communications Technology Research (CITIC; Research Center of the Galician University System). Grant support for CITIC was provided by the Xunta de Galicia through a collaboration agreement between the Regional Ministry of Culture, Education, and Vocational Training and the Galician Universities for the work of the Research Centers of the Galician University System and the Handytronic chair. In addition, this work is supported in part by structural support for the consolidation and structuring of competitive research units and other promotion actions in the universities of the Galician University System, in the public research organizations of Galicia, and other entities of the Galician R&D&I System for 2022 (ED431B-2022/39); and the Ministerio de Ciencia e Innovación R&D&I projects in the framework of the national programs of knowledge generation and scientific and technological strengthening of the R&D&I system and challenges of the call R&D&I 2019 oriented to society (PID2019-104323RB-C33).

References

1. Lagos, M., Martín, J., Gómez, Á., Pousada, T., González, M.A., Pereira, J., et al.: Virtual reality at the service of people with functional diversity: Personalized intervention spaces. Eng. Proc. **7**(1), 43 (2021). https://www.mdpi.com/2673-4591/7/1/43/htm
2. Miranda-Duro, C., et al.: Virtual reality game analysis for people with functional diversity: An inclusive perspective. Proc **54**(1), 20. https://www.mdpi.com/2504-3900/54/1/20

3. Ultraleap. Tracking | Leap Motion Controller | Ultraleap. Ultraleap. (2019)
4. Serda, M., Becker, F.G., Cleary, M., Team, R.M., Holtermann, H., The, D., et al.: The game experience questionnaire. Balint, G., Antala, B., Carty, C., Mabieme, J.-M.A., Amar, I.B., Kaplanova, A. (eds.) Uniw śląski **7**(1), 343–354 (2013). https://research.tue.nl/en/publicati ons/the-game-experience-questionnaire
5. Law, E.L.C., Brühlmann, F., Mekler, E.D.: Systematic review and validation of the game experience questionnaire (GEQ) – Implications for citation and reporting practice. In: CHI PLAY 2018 - Proceedings of the 2018 Annual Symposium on Computer-Human Interaction in Play (2018)
6. Ikea. IKEA Launches Pilot Virtual Reality (VR) Kitchen Experience for HTC Vive on Steam. Ikea's News (2016)
7. Steam Store. theBlu [Internet] (2022). https://store.steampowered.com/app/451520/theBlu/
8. Steam Store. Adventure Climb VR en Steam [Internet] (2020). https://store.steampowered. com/app/1040430/Adventure_Climb_VR/
9. Google. Google Earth Imagery. c 2016 Infoterra Ltd & Bluesky, Landsat, Google (2016)
10. VivePort. CUBE DANCER [Internet] (2019). https://www.viveport.com/apps/6852f553-5072-463b-bce3-2052d8e7700f
11. Steam Store. Blobby Tennis en Steam [Internet] (2017). https://store.steampowered.com/app/628530/Blobby_Tennis/
12. Steam Store. Richie's Plank Experience en Steam [Internet] (2017). https://store.steampowe red.com/app/517160/Richies_Plank_Experience/
13. Harris, P.A., Taylor, R., Minor, B.L., Elliott, V., Fernandez, M., O'Neal, L., et al.: The REDCap consortium: Building an international community of software platform partners. J. Biomed. Informat. **95**, 103208 (2019). Academic Press Inc.

Improving Web Accessibility Testing with Microsoft's Accessibility Insights for Web

Kewal Shah[(✉)], Ankur Garg, and Carrie Bruce

Georgia Institute of Technology, Atlanta, GA 30332, USA
{kshah365,carrie.bruce}@gatech.edu, ankur.garg26@gmail.com

Abstract. Browser extensions to evaluate web accessibility have been widely adopted by web developers for checking websites against various Web Content Accessibility Guidelines (WCAG) success criteria. However, most extensions rely on algorithms to quickly scan web pages and detect accessibility issues. These evaluations are often inaccurate and non-exhaustive. Accessibility Insights for Web, a relatively new open-source web extension developed by Microsoft, offers a unique solution by letting the user perform a combination of more than 50 automated and manual tests and easily document the detected issues. Although it contains some novel accessibility evaluation features, the tool itself faces some serious usability and accessibility issues. In this study, we conduct UX research and iteratively design the Accessibility Insights tool by receiving feedback from a diverse group of professionals with and without disabilities. Our goal is to generalize the findings so that they can serve as a reference for designers of future web accessibility evaluation tools.

Keywords: Web Accessibility Evaluation Tools · Microsoft · Accessibility Insights · WCAG

1 Introduction

The universality of the World Wide Web suggests a promise of access to everyone, irrespective of their disability. Web accessibility has the potential to aid individuals with disabilities in overcoming a multitude of obstacles and enable equitable experiences. For example, the use of larger fonts and high color contrast ratios can make content easily readable for people with vision impairments. This promotes social inclusion and brings economic benefits, as websites with higher usability are likely to rank higher in search engine results and reach a wider customer base [1].

The Web Accessibility Initiative (WAI) has defined several components that should function together for websites to be accessible - web content, browsers, assistive technology, user knowledge, developers, authoring tools, and evaluation tools [2]. Among these, developers play a critical role as they are ultimately responsible for creating websites that meet Web Content Accessibility Guidelines (WCAG). The WCAG documentation contains a total of 61 test success criteria for each guideline, but for developers having less accessibility expertise, testing these criteria can be overwhelming. Browser-based web accessibility testing tools can mitigate this issue by automatically detecting issues and providing an intuitive interface for developers to analyze and document the results.

In this paper, we evaluate and redesign a browser-based accessibility testing tool – Microsoft's Accessibility Insights for Web [3], using the Double Diamond design process [4]. We discover the tool's pain points, define the scope of our research, and redesign the tool's interface while receiving feedback from developers, designers, and accessibility experts at each stage.

2   Background

Browser extensions for accessibility testing have become increasingly popular among web developers. Web extensions like WAVE, Axe, and Lighthouse have more than 200,000 users each on the Chrome Web Store [5]. These tools focus on automated evaluation by scanning the target web page and identifying accessibility issues. However, the WAI states that one cannot solely depend on automated tools, and human judgment is essential [6]. Several studies have shown that automated checking tools can often fail to meet even 50% of the WCAG success criteria [7].

Microsoft's Accessibility Insights extension takes a unique approach by using three types of accessibility checks - automated, assisted, and manual. The automated checks consist of 57 predefined tests checking the target webpage for appropriate use of properties like aria attributes, links, etc., and automatically categorizing them as passed or failed. The assisted checks identify if instances of certain elements are present on a page, and it is the user's responsibility to categorize each instance. Finally, the manual tests provide instructions for users to find specific elements and add comments if they think a test failed. However, despite being comprehensive, the tool has some critical usability issues. We hypothesized that identifying these issues and redesigning Accessibility Insights could guide the design of future web extensions that also incorporate human judgment into the accessibility checking process.

3   Research Methods

The first step in our project was to explore Accessibility Insights and discover the pain points that the end users of the tool face while interacting with it. As our research was going to involve human subjects, we obtained approval from the Institutional Review Board (IRB) at the Georgia Institute of Technology. We explored how the existing tool functioned to establish a working model of the application. Concurrently, we framed our research questions and selected user interviews and heuristic evaluations as the appropriate research methods to help find answers to those research questions. We conducted ten user interviews and five heuristic evaluation sessions to identify user pain points with the tool.

3.1   Current System Analysis

As we had not used the tool before undertaking this study, we first needed to gain a thorough understanding of what it offered, how it functioned, and frame our perspective on its different aspects. Backed by our experience with web development and using other web accessibility evaluation tools [8], we began using the tool to find accessibility issues on various websites. While doing this, we keenly observed its current behavior and how it differed from our expectations. We then started documenting these findings on a digital board with Miro, a visual collaboration and whiteboarding tool. This activity helped us individually document our findings, group them, and merge them at the end. For each feature or function, we described the current behavior, how we expected it to behave, and high-level suggestions to improve it.

3.2 Semi-structured Interviews

Semi-structured interviews were the primary method for our user research. Guided by a predefined interview protocol, we aimed to understand our interview participants' use of and feedback about Accessibility Insights.

Participants. We interviewed 10 participants whom we recruited with the help of our professional network and by distributing a screener survey on LinkedIn. Two of the 10 study participants were graduate students at Georgia Tech, and the remaining eight were industry professionals. The reported profession of participants included web developer ($n = 7$), web accessibility expert ($n = 2$), and web accessibility tester ($n = 1$). Three of the 10 participants reported having a disability. Among them, one was blind; one had partial vision, partial hearing, and neurological impairments; and the third had a physical disability impacting fine motor and mobility skills.

Procedures. Each of our semi-structured interviews lasted approximately 60 min and was divided into two phases. The first phase focused on asking the participants about their experiences with web accessibility and evaluation tools, as well as their opinions about the utility of features in such tools. The second phase focused on participants using various features and functionalities of the Accessibility Insights for Web tool, followed by a question-and-answer session about their experience with the tool. As mentioned earlier, our interview protocol not only helped us to guide the overall flow of the interviews but also allowed us to dive deep into areas where the participants seemed frustrated while interacting with the existing interface.

3.3 Heuristic Evaluations

We conducted heuristic evaluation sessions to leverage the expertise of practitioners involved in web development, UX, and accessibility and validate several issues that surfaced during our interviews and uncover additional concerns. During these sessions, we asked our participants to complete a list of predefined tasks using Accessibility Insights and identify associated usability issues.

Participants. We conducted heuristic evaluations with five participants. Four of them were graduate students at Georgia Tech who previously worked in the industry as web developers. One of them was a web accessibility and UX expert working in the industry. As with the interviews, participation in the heuristic evaluations was voluntary, and no compensation was provided.

Procedures. Each of our heuristic evaluation sessions lasted for about 75 min. Our heuristic evaluation protocol consisted of five tasks, and each task consisted of two to five actions. For each action, the user was asked to provide a severity rating on a scale of 0 to 4 for various usability heuristics. We referred to the 10 usability heuristics by the Nielsen Norman Group [9] and used the following heuristics in our protocol: flexibility and efficiency of use; match between system and real-world; help and documentation; consistency and standards; aesthetic and minimalist design; and visibility of system status. We also requested our participants to think aloud while performing these actions. Think-aloud is a method in which the participants are asked to narrate everything that goes through their minds as they perform a task. This allowed us to capture additional feedback regarding their experience using the tool.

4 Results and Findings

After completing our research activities, we gathered the data collected from our research, grouped the data into chunks to make it easily understandable, and finally analyzed all the data. In this section, we will briefly explain the data analysis process and the resulting findings from our interviews and heuristic evaluations. The research activity for analyzing and exploring the existing system did not directly generate any findings. Instead, it helped us to gain a thorough understanding of the Accessibility Insights tool, which in turn helped us to effectively conduct other research activities.

4.1 Semi-structured Interviews

Analysis. We analyzed the data collected during our interviews with the help of a bottom-up affinity diagramming technique, as shown in Fig. 1. Roughly 400 participant quotes were documented on sticky notes, and similar notes were grouped to produce themes. This mapping was done on four levels. Going from bottom to top, the stickies with the user quotes are in level four. The stickies in level three represent the identified themes and the associated user pain points, motivations, characteristics, and opportunity areas relevant to the study. The stickies in levels two and one highlight the sub-features and the key features of the tool respectively. This affinity map helped us to identify features of the Accessibility Insights tool that presented the biggest opportunity for improvement. Furthermore, for each of the identified themes, we assigned a severity rating of high, medium, or low based on the number of users quotes under them and the total count of users associated with them.

Fig. 1. Affinity map for qualitative data gathered from the semi-structured interviews.

Findings. Some of the features of the Accessibility Insights tool that stood out in our affinity map were the overview page; sidebar navigation; triggering of automated checks; and text and interactive content elements in the various tests. Most users (n = 7) had trouble understanding the overall status and status of individual tests on the overview page. They also felt that the overview page lacked enough information to explain how to begin testing. Regarding the sidebar navigation, most users felt that the sidebar was not user-friendly, especially the representation of passed and failed tests within the sidebar. The triggering of automated checks is another problematic area where the users are not given sufficient control to execute various automated tests. Lastly, several interactive elements on the assisted and manual test pages were not intuitive, and the textual instructions on these test pages were difficult to follow.

4.2 Heuristic Evaluations

Analysis. From our heuristic evaluations, we generated quantitative data in the form of severity ratings and qualitative data in the form of participants' quotes. We plotted all the tasks, actions, and corresponding heuristics on a Miro board. Next, we decided to bring both the severity ratings as well as the user quotes on the board so that we could easily analyze the data. We defined different colors for our stickies with user quotes based on the associated severity ratings. We placed each participant's quote on a colored sticky and under its corresponding heuristic. This activity resulted in several groups of stickies with user quotes around the various actions and their heuristics. Depending on the size of these groups and how many high severity stickies were within the group, we classified the actions with a high, medium, or low priority.

Findings. Based on the analysis from our heuristic evaluations, the actions that felt the most painful to the users were making sense of the information on the overview page; triggering the automated tests; finding the passed and failed automated tests after executing them; understanding the information available on the various automated tests' pages; and understanding how to execute the various assisted tests. Almost all these findings were consistent with the findings from our interviews and reinforced the key issues present within the tool.

5   Design Methods

The next big step in our project was the design phase. Continuing from the prioritization of the research findings from the interviews and heuristic evaluations, we conducted four co-design sessions with users to generate design ideas. We then combined the ideas from these co-design sessions with the ideas from our own brainstorming sessions to design low-fidelity wireframes. After completing our wireframes, we conducted five user feedback sessions to get feedback on our wireframes.

5.1   Co-design Sessions

Having spent several months using Accessibility Insights, observing and listening to users while they interact with the tool, and then analyzing the good and bad points of the tool, we had several ideas for improving the various features of the tool. Nevertheless, we decided to conduct a few co-design sessions with developers and designers to bring in a fresh perspective for idea generation.

Participants. We conducted four co-design sessions with seven participants. Two of these sessions were conducted remotely and with one participant each. The other two sessions were conducted in person at the Georgia Tech campus. Among the two in-person sessions, one had two participants, and the other had three participants. All seven participants had web development experience. One of the participants, who had previously also participated in our interviews, had a physical disability impacting fine motor and mobility skills.

Procedures. Each of our co-design sessions lasted for approximately 60 minutes. We created separate protocols for the individual and group sessions. For both type of sessions, we selected four key features in the tool, and then explained the features individually as well as the research findings related to those features. We then asked our participants to generate design ideas on a Miro board. The slight difference for our group co-design sessions was that we distributed the different features amongst the participants and then asked them to individually generate design ideas on a Miro board. Later, we asked them to explain their ideas and give feedback on other participants' ideas. Overall, our co-design sessions were very helpful and led to the generation of several new design ideas which we had not thought of previously.

5.2 Low-Fidelity Prototypes

Guided by our medium and high-priority research findings and their corresponding design ideas, we began designing low-fidelity wireframes using Figma, a popular design and prototyping tool. We primarily focused on redesigning the overview page, the sidebar navigation, and the automated, assisted, and manual test pages. Figure 2 shows one of our wireframes with the redesigned overview page.

Fig. 2. One of our low-fidelity wireframes showing the redesigned overview page.

5.3 Feedback Sessions

We decided to get some quick feedback from a few users on our low-fidelity wireframes before we could start converting our wireframes into high-fidelity prototypes. For most of the features in the tool, our prior project work allowed us to generate multiple design ideas for various features. Thankfully, these feedback sessions allowed us to validate several possible design ideas with minimal effort.

Participants. We conducted a total of five sessions. Four of the five participants were HCI graduate students at Georgia Tech and had previously worked in the industry as UX designers. One of the participants was a software engineer at Microsoft, although not part of the Accessibility Insights team at the company.

Procedures. Each of our low-fidelity feedback sessions lasted for about 75 minutes. Because we had several design ideas to be validated for different features within the tool, we divided our five feedback sessions into two phases. In the first phase, which consisted of three sessions, we discussed our low-fidelity prototypes for the overview page and the sidebar navigation. During these sessions, we gave all our participants a brief overview of the tool and then went over each element of the overview page and the sidebar navigation that we had redesigned in our wireframes. We asked our participants to compare the existing tool with multiple wireframes showing the different designs. In the second phase, which consisted of the remaining two sessions, we discussed our low-fidelity designs for one of the assisted tests and one of the manual tests in the tool. Like phase 1, we gave a brief overview of the tool and reviewed each element of the assisted and manual test screens that we redesigned in our wireframes. Like earlier, we asked our participants to compare the existing tool with multiple wireframes showing our contrasting designs. These feedback sessions helped us gather additional data, which we are currently in the process of analyzing before we can effectively use the same in our high-fidelity prototypes.

6 Limitations

While we tried to follow a rigorous research process and make data-informed decisions at each stage, there were several limitations in our study. We did not have access to prior research conducted by Microsoft. Knowing the justifications for some of their design decisions early on could have helped us better define the scope of our research.

Our participant group did not have enough developers with disabilities. Although we included three such users, we believe we could have benefited by talking to more people with different types of disabilities to ensure the new design was accessible. Also, as there is a lack of accessibility testing tools that perform an in-depth accessibility evaluation by incorporating developer feedback, we could not get substantial data during our initial research stage when we tried to do a competitive analysis. Finally, since we did not have enough web development knowledge or formal training in web accessibility, we did not focus on changing the WCAG-related testing instructions across the tool. As pointed out earlier, during our research, many users felt that these instructions were complicated to understand.

7 Conclusion and Future Work

Web accessibility evaluation should be a meticulous process to ensure websites are highly accessible to support people with various disabilities. Comprehensive accessibility testing tools like Microsoft's Accessibility Insights for Web that use a combination of automated and manual testing methods have the potential to be adopted by many developers and organizations in the future. In our project's final stage, we plan to create high-fidelity designs and evaluate a prototype through usability testing and task-based heuristic evaluations with accessibility experts and developers working in the industry. We are planning to present our high-fidelity designs and findings to the Accessibility Insights team at Microsoft. However, we acknowledge that there is a possibility that they might not implement many of our proposed changes in the future. Therefore, we plan to concurrently publish the designs and research findings online so that our project is publicly available and can help inform the designers of similar accessibility testing tools in the future.

References

1. Jenny, C. Web Accessibility: Practical advice for the library and information professional. Facet Publishing (2008)
2. Essential Components of Web Accessibility, https://www.w3.org/WAI/fundamentals/compon ents/. Accessed 11 Mar 2023
3. Accessibility Insights for Web, https://accessibilityinsights.io/docs/web/overview. Accessed 12 Mar 2023
4. The Double Diamond: A universally accepted depiction of the design process, https://www. designcouncil.org.uk/our-work/news-opinion/double-diamond-universally-accepted-depict ion-design-process/. Accessed 13 Mar 2023
5. Chrome Web Store - Accessibility, https://chrome.google.com/webstore/search/Accessibility. Accessed 12 Mar 2023
6. Selecting Web Accessibility Evaluation Tools, https://www.w3.org/WAI/test-evaluate/tools/ selecting/. Accessed 12 Mar 2023
7. Abascal, J., Arrue, M. Valencia, X.: Tools for web accessibility evaluation. In: Yesilada, Y., Harper, S. (eds) Web Accessibility. Human–Computer Interaction Series, pp. 479–503. Springer, London (2019)
8. Web Accessibility Evaluation Tools List, https://www.w3.org/WAI/ER/tools/. Accessed 14 Mar 2023
9. Usability Heuristics for User Interface Design, https://www.nngroup.com/articles/ten-usabil ity-heuristics/. Accessed 16 Mar 2023

An Artificial Intelligence-Based Interactive Learning Platform to Assist Visually Impaired Children in Learning Mathematics

Muhammad Shoaib[1]($\boxtimes$) (iD), Shiyu Jiang[2], Luo Jin[3], Donal Fitzpatrick[4], and Ian Pitt[1]

[1] School of Computer Science and Information Technology, University College Cork, Cork, Ireland
muhammad.shoaib@cs.ucc.ie

[2] Whiting School of Engineering, Johns Hopkins University, Baltimore, USA

[3] Department of Computer Science, Wenzhou-Kean University, Wenzhou, China

[4] Centre for Excellence in Universal Design, National Disability Authority, Dublin, Ireland

Abstract. Visually impaired children mainly depend upon hearing and touch in the absence of vision. Smartphones are now relatively cheap and are in widespread use in almost all parts of the world, including by many people who do not have access to laptops or desktop machines. Smartphone-based applications provide a learning environment in which visually impaired children can enhance their educational skills in a similar way to other students. This paper introduces an artificial intelligence-based interactive learning platform that can enhance the mathematical skills of visually impaired children. This platform can assist teachers in the classroom to provide accessible and interactive materials to their visually impaired students. The proposed platform uses text-to-speech along with vibrotactile and auditory feedback to help visually impaired students arrive at a better understanding of mathematical material. Four participants were recruited to evaluate the prototype of this interactive learning platform. The results showed that understanding of mathematical content in visually impaired children was significantly improved. Furthermore, problem-solving skills and action awareness were enhanced with the help of a multimodal feedback approach. Participants also reported high levels of satisfaction with the proposed design. The paper concludes with a discussion of possible directions for future research aimed at overcoming barriers to learning faced by visually impaired children.

Keywords: Learning · Interactive · Mathematics · Visually Impaired · Smartphone

1 Introduction

Visually impaired students have difficulties in perceiving graphical information. They normally use the senses of hearing and touch to obtain information from their surrounding environment. With the help of technological advancement, many techniques and solutions have been introduced that could assist them to improve their learning skills.

C. Stephanidis et al. (Eds.): HCII 2023, CCIS 1833, pp. 366–373, 2023.
https://doi.org/10.1007/978-3-031-35992-7_51

Smartphone-based and computer-based solutions are prominent areas of solutions for visually impaired people and provide effective assistance to them in accessing information. In these solutions, artificial intelligence-based techniques are quite useful for visually impaired students. Shubham et al. [1] proposed a smart personal assistance by using the artificial intelligence technique that provided better access to the surrounding environment of visually impaired people. They used image recognization, text recognization and machine learning techniques together in form of a mobile application. This application helped visually impaired people in certain tasks i.e., accessing books electronically, currency and image recognization. Some tutoring applications are also available for visually impaired people that provide better ways to access and manipulate information during their learning process. The i-Math is an automatic math reader application which was designed for Thai Blind people and is quite useful for them to access mathematics material. It can read the mathematics content from documents in audio form with the help of a screen reader. Teachers also have the facility to prepare their assessments for students in the audio form [2]. Computer Haptics provided a new way to access information by touch, auditory and visual means. In this approach computer and haptic feedback controller were used by students to virtually explore the 3D shapes [3].

Interactive learning platforms are also becoming popular in education, especially for visually impaired students. Visually impaired students can easily use them in learning mathematics. These platforms used various technologies such as screen readers, braille displays, and audio instructions to present mathematical concepts in a way that was accessible to visually impaired students. One such platform is MathTrax [4], which was designed to offer accessible math materials to students with visual impairments. MathTrax used screen reader technology to read mathematical expressions aloud and allows students to navigate through equations using their keyboards. Another platform, MathSpeak [5], was a browser-based tool that can be used by both sighted and visually impaired students to learn math concepts through a combination of text, audio, and video instruction.

This paper introduced an Artificial Intelligence-Based Interactive Learning Platform for math tutoring of visually impaired children. This platform helped visually impaired children in learning mathematics by using text-to-speech and vibrotactile feedback. Visually impaired children can learn and practice linear and quadratic equations of mathematics by using this platform. The remainder of this article is organized as follows: Sect. 2 which defines previous work associated with visually impaired children learning mathematics. Section 3 describes the proposed methodology of the interactive learning platform. Section 4 presents the participants and results information. Lastly, Sect. 5 has a discussion and conclusion based on the results of this study.

2 Related Work

Ávila-Soto et al. designed a tangible user interface by using a multimodal method. This method used auditory feedback and tangible numbers to enhance the basic arithmetic skills of visually impaired students [6]. Bouck et al. proposed a computer-based Voice Input and Speech Output (VISO) calculator to help visually impaired students to solve basic mathematic calculations. Results showed that the VISO calculator reduced the time to perform the calculations. It also has some accuracy issues in the recognition of speech [7]. Bier et al. designed and implemented a multi-purpose math-to-speech translation system based on Lua script, which allows users to manually adjust translation rules, i.e., language change and focusing on the relevant requirements. Results illustrated that the overall success rate of the correct answers was about 83%. This system can be used for several purposes i.e., e-learning platforms for auditory representation and as an educational tool for non-native visually impaired users [8].

Buzzi et al. developed an accessible vibro-tactile-based android application to solve geometry problems. The design of this application is more accessible for visually impaired children because they can make freehand drawings and recognize geometry shapes based on vibration and touch senses [9]. Gulley et al. introduced an auditory approach to guide and evaluate mathematics learning named Process-Driven Math. It facilitates the visually impaired students who do not have enough experience in Braille to learn mathematics. Audio rendering of the algebraic expression was used to significantly reduce the complexity of mathematical expression. It also helped the visually impaired students to improve their understanding of mathematical expressions [10].

Murphy et al. designed auditory cues by using synthetic speech, non-speech and spearons. These newly designed cues were used to eliminate the ambiguity of mathematical formulas. They designed an online survey to evaluate the effectiveness of these auditory cues on 56 participants. Results demonstrated that visually impaired users better understand mathematical equations with the help of synthetic speech Their listing time is reduced with the help of modified speech (spearcons) [11]. MathPlayer is also an important platform for learning mathematics. It can read aloud mathematical formulas and has support for Internet Explorer, Mozilla Firefox and screen readers [12]. Furthermore, researchers have also proposed some theoretical methods for visually impaired students to learn specific kinds of mathematical problems i.e., algebra and calculus. Islam Elkabani and Rached Zantout proposed a framework that helped visually impaired people in learning linear algebra [13]. There is another framework that has been proposed to solve some simple calculus problems and achieve successful outcomes by Sebastian et al. [14].

3 Proposed Methodology

In this study, a prototype was introduced that can enhance the learning skills of visually impaired students more effectively. This prototype used a multimodal feedback approach that facilitates visually impaired students. This prototype has two main modules "interactive learning module" and "Practice module". In the interactive learning module, students can practice linear and quadratic equations. They can choose one type of mathematical question, and the proposed system automatically searches the related questions from the question bank. They can interact with the system through their voice. During the interaction, the user can explore all relevant information about the selected questions. Shown below is a step-by-step example for solving a linear equation with one variable in this module:

Solve for y, $y^2 + 4(y + 1) = 1$.

$y^2 + 4y + 4 = 1$ Multiply small parenthesis by 4

$y^2 + 4y + 4 - 1 = 0$ Move the right constant to the left side
$y^2 + 4y + 3 = 0$ Subtract both constant values
$y^2 + 3y + y + 3 = 0$ Factor the equation
$y(y + 3) + y + 3 = 0$ Take y value common from equation
$(y + 3)(y + 1)$ Splitting the equation for the solution
$y = -3, y = -1$ Final solution

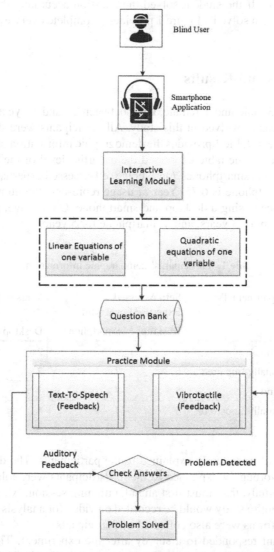

Fig. 1. Provides a basic overview of the proposed framework.

Once students have a proper understanding of the selected topic then they can proceed with the practice module to check their learning skills. Students can attempt to solve the questions in this module. They can acquire the information by using multimodal feedback which is the composition of text-to-speech and vibrotactile feedback. They have to select a question from the question bank. After selection, the text-to-speech function reads the selected question aloud which indicates the user is ready to solve the question. Users can give the step-by-step solution by speaking and the system can validate the solution. If there is something wrong then it generates vibrotactile feedback. Vibrotactile feedback indicates that something went wrong and the user can request a hint in this situation. If the student solved the question accurately then it generates a message that "problem solved". Figure 1 provides a complete overview of the proposed framework.

4 Participants and Results

Four participants 3 male and 1 female, aged between 12 and 14 years old (M = 12.5 and SD = 0.84), were involved in this study. All participants were desktop computer and smartphone users. Table 1 provides the demographic information of the participants. Self-assessed scores in the table expressed the expertise level of the participants with desktop computers and smartphones. On average self-assessed expertise level with desktop is 5.25 and smartphone is 6.75. Year of usage represents the number of years that a participant has been using a desktop and smartphone. On average, participants have been using a desktop for 3 years, and a smartphone for 5 years.

Table 1. Participants' demographic information.

PID	Age	Impairment Type	Self-Assessed Expertise Level with		Years of Usage	
			Desktop	Smartphone	Desktop	Smartphone
P1	12	Blind	5	6	2	4
P2	13	Visually Impaired	6	7	3	5
P3	12	Blind	5	7	3	5
P4	14	Visually Impaired	5	7	4	6

The study's goal was clearly explained to the participants. The details of application usage were thoroughly explained to them. Participants were told that in order to participate in this study, they must first attend a training session. All participants were informed that the entire study would be recorded on video for analysis purposes. Signed informed consent forms were also collected by participants.

Each participant responded to a survey after the experiment. The scores for this survey were reported as feeling pleasant (3)-unpleasant (1), like (4)-Dislike (0), enjoyable (4)-hurting (0), happy (4)-painful (0), and pleased (3)-irritating (1).

Figure 2 displayed word clouds made from a total of 24 words that our participants believed best captured their experience with our proposed application. Mostly **the** words

Fig. 2. Extracted word clouds from the comments of our participants (Designed from: https://www.wordclouds.com)

were positive i.e., "helpful", "pleasant," "enjoyable" "useful," and "interesting". As well as there were some words with negative responses i.e., "disturbing," "painful" "useless" and "irritation" (Fig. 2).

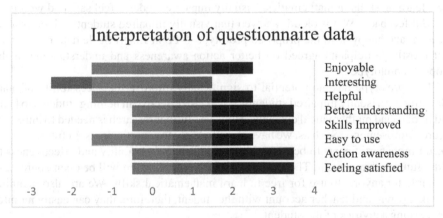

Fig. 3. Interpretation of participants behaviour after the experiments

After the experiments, we conducted a study with participants in which they had to fill out a questionnaire. We designed this questionnaire using the 5-Point Likert Scale (values as Strongly Agree, Agree, Neutral, Disagree, Strongly disagree). Questions were designed to measure several aspects of the participants i.e., satisfaction, action awareness, ease, skills improvement, understanding, helpful,interesting and enjoyable. Figure 3 provided an overview of the participants' behaviour after the experiments. Blue indicates that participants strongly agree, maroon indicates that they agree, cyan color indicates that they were neutral, light purple indicates that they disagree and dark purple indicates that they strongly disagree with this study. It was clearly illustrated that participants mostly agreed or strongly agreed with the proposed prototype.

5   Discussion and Conclusion

Teaching mathematics to visually impaired students is a very difficult task due to the rich visual information i.e., graphs, formulas and notations. With the help of advanced technology, visually impaired students can now access a more inclusive and personalized learning experience that caters to their requirements and adjusts to their learning styles. Previous studies showed that auditory and vibrotactile feedbacks were very useful for visually impaired students in learning mathematics. In this study, we have combined both feedbacks to provide better interaction and action awareness to visually impaired students. Our main focus was to solve linear and quadratic equations of one variable. The proposed prototype was mainly designed for visually impaired students who want to gain better mathematics skills.

Our proposed prototype plays an important role in making mathematics material accessible to visually impaired students. With the help of auditory and vibrotactile feedback, visually impaired students can receive audio descriptions of math problems, interact with the platform using voice commands, and access visual representations of math concepts through an audio form. This prototype can track the student's progress and provides personalized feedback, enabling them to learn at their own pace and adapt to their individual learning styles. Results from the questionnaire data and face-to-face interviews showed that the proposed prototype helped visually impaired students to improve their learning skills in mathematics. Visually impaired students feel satisfied with multimodal feedback. Words clouds showed that visually impaired students felt enjoyable, pleasant and happy with the proposed prototype. 5 Point Likert Scale data represented that mostly participants agreed on better action awareness and understanding of the proposed prototype.

This prototype has the potential to significantly improve the accessibility of math education for visually impaired students. It was also effective in helping students to learn and understand mathematical concepts. However, further research is needed to introduce future improvements. Such as, we have recruited only four participants. In future, we can recruit more participants to better assess the application's usability and effectiveness to add a future enhancement. The final release of this application will be open-source and available for anyone to use for free to learn mathematical skills. We are also planning to link a parent and teacher account with the student, therefore, they can easily monitor the learning activities of the student.

Acknowledgement. This publication has emanated from research conducted with the financial support of Science Foundation Ireland under Grant number 18/CRT/6222.

References

1. Felix, S., Kuamar, S.: 2nd international, and undefined 2018. A smart personal AI assistant for visually impaired people, ieeexplore.ieee.org (2018). https://ieeexplore.ieee.org/abstract/document/8553750/. Accessed 6 Mar 2023
2. Wongkia, W., Naruedomkul, K., Cercone, N.: i-Math: Automatic math reader for Thai blind and visually impaired students. Elsevier (2012) https://www.sciencedirect.com/science/article/pii/S0898122112003495. Accessed 6 Mar 2023

3. Darrah, M.: Computer haptics: a new way of increasing access and understanding of math and science for students who are blind and visually impaired, nfb.org (2013). https://nfb.org/images/nfb/publications/jbir/jbir13/jbir030202.html. Accessed 6 Mar 2023
4. Nguyen, D.M.: The Use of MathTrax in Algebra Teaching. search.ebscohost.com
5. Sauer, L.: Mathematics for Visually Impaired Students: Increasing Accessibility of Mathematics Resources with LaTeX and Nemeth MathSpeak, Senior Honors Theses (2020). https://digitalcommons.liberty.edu/honors/954. Accessed 6 Mar 2023
6. Ávila-Soto, A., del Carmen Valderrama Bahamóndez, E., Schmidt, A.: TanMath: a tangible math application to support children with visual impairment to learn basic arithmetic, dl.acm.org, vol. Part F128530, pp. 244–245 (2017). https://doi.org/10.1145/3056540.3064964
7. Bouck, E.C., Flanagan, S., Joshi, G.S., Sheikh, W., Schleppenbach, D.: Speaking math—a voice input, speech output calculator for students with visual impairments. J. Spec. Educ. Technol. **26**(4), 1–14 (2011). https://doi.org/10.1177/016264341102600401
8. Bier, A., Sroczyński, Z.: Rule based intelligent system verbalizing mathematical notation. Multimedia Tools Appl. **78**(19), 28089–28110 (2019). https://doi.org/10.1007/s11042-019-07889-3
9. Buzzi, M., Buzzi, M., Leporini, B., Senette, C.: Playing with geometry: a multimodal android app for blind children, dl.acm.org, vol. 28, pp. 134–137 (2015). https://doi.org/10.1145/2808435.2808458
10. Gulley, A.P., Smith, L.A., Price, J.A., Prickett, L.C., Ragland, M.F.: Process-driven math: an auditory method of mathematics instruction and assessment for students who are blind or have low vision. J. Vis. Impair Blind **111**(5), 465–471 (2017). https://doi.org/10.1177/0145482X1711100507
11. Murphy, E., Bates, E., Fitzpatrick, D.: Designing auditory cues to enhance spoken mathematics for visually impaired users. In: ASSETS 2010 - Proceedings of the 12th International ACM SIGACCESS Conference on Computers and Accessibility, pp. 75–82 (2010). https://doi.org/10.1145/1878803.1878819
12. Sorge, V., Chen, C., Raman, T., Tseng, D.: Towards making mathematics a first class citizen in general screen readers, dl.acm.org (2014). https://doi.org/10.1145/2596695.2596700
13. Elkabani, I., Zantout, R.: A framework for helping the visually impaired learn and practice math, ieeexplore.ieee.org (2015). https://ieeexplore.ieee.org/abstract/document/7426909/. Accessed 6 Mar 2023
14. Maćkowski, M., Brzoza, P., Spinczyk, D.: Tutoring math platform accessible for visually impaired people. Elsevier (2023).https://www.sciencedirect.com/science/article/pii/S0010482517301671. Accessed 6 Mar 2023

Sign Language Communication Through an Interactive Mobile Application

Andreas Stergioulas[1(✉)], Christos Chatzikonstantinou[1], Theocharis Chatzis[1],
Ilias Papastratis[1], Dimitrios Konstantinidis[1], Kosmas Dimitropoulos[1],
Klimnis Atzakas[2], George J. Xydopoulos[2], Vassia Zacharopoulou[2],
Dimitris Papazachariou[2], Vasilis Aggelidis[3], Kostas Grigoriadis[4],
and Petros Daras[1]

[1] Visual Computing Lab, Information Technologies Institute,
Centre for Research and Technology Hellas, Thessaloniki, Greece
[2] University of Patras, Patra, Greece
[3] Centre of Greek Sign Language – KENG, Thessaloniki, Greece
[4] MLS Innovation Inc., Thessaloniki, Greece

Abstract. Sign languages (SLs) are an essential form of communication for hearing-impaired people. However, a communication barrier still exists between the deaf community and the hearing population due to the lack of accurate automated SL communication systems. In this work, a novel SL communication system running as a mobile application has been developed to facilitate the bi-directional communication between hearing-impaired and hearing people. The proposed system utilizes Natural Language Processing (NLP) techniques, along with linguistic rules to convert between spoken language and signs, taking into account the grammatical structure of a sign language. Additionally, the system employs sign language recognition (SLR) algorithms to transform video sequences to signs, as well as hand and pose estimation algorithms to model the 3D motion of signs. Moreover, a 3D human avatar representation is employed to animate the motion of each sign in a seamless manner. Finally, a new partition of the Greek SL (GSL) dataset is formed with 1825 videos from 12 signers captured in the wild to evaluate SLR performance under realistic conditions. The proposed SL communication system and its components are validated quantitatively in GSLW as well as qualitatively by means of questionnaires, demonstrating the user satisfaction with the system.

Keywords: Sign language · Deep learning · Mobile application

1 Introduction

The primary form of communication among hearing-impaired people, as well as between hearing-impaired and hearing people is sign language (SL). However a

---

A. Stergioulas, C. Chatzikonstantinou, T. Chatzis, I. Papastratis—Equal contribution.

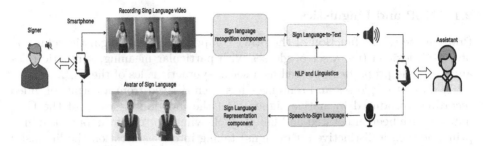

Fig. 1. Proposed SL communication system integrated in a mobile application.

few people among the hearing population can communicate with the SL community. As a consequence, communication barriers still exist that inhibit the social inclusion of hearing-impaired people. To promote inclusivity, automated methods [1] that convert SLs to spoken languages and vice versa have been developed with the help of recent advances in AI and machine learning [2,3].

In this work, we present a holistic approach to sign language communication, integrated in a mobile application. Sign language representation is performed through novel human and hand pose estimation algorithms that can robustly model human body, hand and finger movements. Furthermore, a 3D human avatar is employed to animate the extracted sign movements and perform the sign sequence corresponding to the initial spoken sentence. Novel continuous SLR methods were also developed, to efficiently recognise glosses in continuous sign language sentences. NLP models and GSL linguistics are finally employed to translate between GSL and spoken Greek language by utilizing the grammatical structure of GSL.

2   Overall System

The main goal of the proposed sign language communication system, shown in Fig. 1, is to facilitate the interaction between hearing-impaired and hearing people. To achieve its goals, the system consists of several components, each performing a specific task, necessary for the problem at hand.

The proposed system can accurately translate sign sentences to spoken languages and vice versa. In the Sign Language-to-Text scenario, the signs are recorded using the smartphone camera and the sign language recognition component is concerned with transforming the video sequence to glosses, employing a state-of-the-art SLR method. The glosses are then converted to structured sentences with the aid of the NLP and linguistics component. On the other hand, in the speech-to-sign language scenario, the NLP and linguistics component is utilized to transform speech to structured sentences and then to sign language glosses. The sign language representation component then transforms the glosses to body, hand and finger movements. Finally, the movement sequences are sent to a user's smart device for playback.

2.1   NLP and Linguistics

Prerequisite to the function of the other components is the linguistic definition of a GSL lexicon (i.e. a set of glosses with particular meaning, syntactic roles and semantic properties), as well as a set of syntactic rules of the GSL.

A dataset of glosses and sentences has been derived from a corpus of video recordings produced by native signers. All the individual glosses of the GSL dataset have been annotated and labelled following the "one form one meaning" principle (i.e., a distinctive set of signs) taking into consideration the linguistic structure of GSL. Solutions were provided for: a) compound words, b) synonyms, c) regional or stylistic variants of the same meaning, and d) agreement verbs [4]. The lexicon was further enriched with the syntactic role/es that each gloss has performed in the dataset (e.g. the role of verb/agent/patient, the possible number of complements, the possible types of complements), as well as their semantic properties (e.g. human/non-human, animate/inanimate, transitive/intransitive).

Furthermore, syntactic rules were established that describe and explain the structure of all sentences of the GSL dataset (Table 1). The above lexicon was used for training the SLR component. It also provided necessary semantic and syntactic information to the NLP component, that, in combination with the syntactic rules of the GSL, allows the correct interpretation of the meaning of GSL sentences, as well as the correct translation from the spoken Greek language to GSL.

2.2   Sign Language Recognition Component

This component is responsible for transforming video sequences to glosses. It utilizes a novel method, called Sign Language Recognition Generative Adversarial Network (SLRGAN) [5]. SLRGAN performs context-aware continuous sign language recognition utilizing a generative adversarial network architecture. The method has been further tuned for sign language conversations for both Deaf-to-Deaf and Deaf-to-hearing communication. This network architecture includes a generator that extracts spatiotemporal features from frame sequences and recognizes the corresponding glosses and a discriminator that measures the quality of the predicted glosses of the generator.

More specifically, the generator employs the Inflated 3D ConvNet (I3D) [4, 6] since 3D CNNs can learn spatiotemporal properties from frame sequences directly and it has shown excellent results on isolated SLR. Then, a BLSTM is used to encode short and long-term information of the video sequence. The discriminator is employed to differentiate between the predicted glosses and the actual glosses. This is achieved by modeling textual information at sentence and gloss levels and discerning between the ground truth glosses and the output of the generator.

A second configuration has also been employed by using a 2D-CNN (GoogLeNet [7]) to model the spatial information of each frame, followed by a TCL module to model motion characteristics of finger and hand movements.

Table 1. Statistics of Greek Sign Language datasets

Datasets	Characteristics				
	Signers	Classes	Video instances	Resolution	fps
GSL isolated	7	310	40,785	848×480	**30**
GSL SD	7	310	10,295	848×480	**30**
GSL SI	7	310	10,295	848×480	**30**
GSLW	5	310	1,736	640×480 – 1920×1080	**15–30**

2.3 Sign Language Representation Component

This component is concerned with transforming glosses (i.e., text input) to body, hand and finger movements. To this end, we utilized the vocabulary of the Greek Sign Language (GSL) dataset [4], consisting of 310 unique glosses. Body movement was extracted by applying the VIBE [8] model on the video instances of each individual gloss. For the extraction of the more challenging hand and finger movements, a novel 3D hand pose estimation method [9] was created that employs a GAN network to separate the input images into the 3D hand pose and RGB image information sub-spaces, as well as VAE mappers to bring the extracted 3D pose closer to the actual one. Additionally, two innovative loss terms were applied during training to avoid non-plausible poses, the KCS loss and GEO loss. In addition, a new VAE decoder architecture was proposed, that contributes to the creation of more robust sub-spaces by injecting latent space information into the intermediate decoder linear layers. The algorithm yielded the best results in two publicly available datasets, namely, Stereo Hand Pose Tracking (STB) [10] and Rendered Hand Pose (RHD) [11] datasets, with 13.88 mean End-Point-Error (mEPE) on RHD and 6.71 mEPE on STB. It is worth noting that the proposed method manages to alleviate finger overlap, which is one of the most important problems in this area [12].

After extracting the motion of signs, we transferred it to a fully rigged human avatar and created the required animations. The predicted 3D hand poses from the proposed method were aligned to the body's coordinate system and two temporal filters were applied, the moving average and median filters, to smooth motion between consecutive frames. The final SL representation system was achieved by creating an Android application on the Unreal Engine 4 platform [13].

2.4 Mobile Application

A smartphone application with a friendly user interface was developed for the sign language communication system. The application is responsible for the seamless connection of the several components comprising the overall system.

A video of a signer is recorded and uploaded to a server, which uses the SL recognition component to recognize the gloss sequence and respond back with the predicted output. The recognised sequence is then processed by the NLP and linguistics component and is transformed to the spoken Greek language. A hearing person can respond using the voice recorder button and the NLP and linguistics component converts the speech to a gloss sequence. Finally, the gloss sequence is uploaded to the signer's smart device where the SL representation component displays the signs with the use of the 3D Avatar. Figure 2 presents screenshots from a) the mobile app interface and b) the 3D Avatar performing a sign sequence.

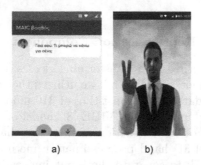

a)   b)

Fig. 2. Screenshots from a) the mobile app interface and b) the 3D SL avatar.

3   Experimental Results

3.1   Sign Language Recognition

In this section, two backbone configurations for SLRGAN are evaluated quantitatively. Both variants are initially trained on GSL dataset and then evaluated on the new GSL in the wild (GSLW) dataset. GSLW contains videos captured using mobile cameras by a group of 12 native GSL signers. The dataset has been recorded under various background and lighting variations and with different smartphones. In addition, the camera position and orientation are gently varied among subsequent recordings to increase video diversity. Similarly to the GSL dataset [4], 15 cases of hearing-impaired people dealing with public services have been recorded. The resulting test dataset has 1,736 videos that were annotated both at individual gloss and sentence level. Cropped frames from the collected videos are shown in Fig. 3.

Performance comparisons of the two backbone configurations for SLRGAN, i.e. GoogleNet and I3D, for videos of 5 s (150 frames) on GSLW indicate that the 2D-CNN setup requires less GPU memory (2109 MB compared to 6601 MB of GPU memory) while running faster than the 3D-CNN setup (152.59 ± 0.27 ms compared to 205.57 ± 1.09 ms). However, a significant drop in performance is noticed when the 2D-CNN setup is employed. To this end, the model that was chosen relies on I3D as a backbone network and achieves a WER of 36.91% in continuous SL recognition and a Top-1 accuracy of 81.72% in identifying the correct signed sentences.

3.2 Sign Language Representation

To evaluate the quality of the animated sign sentences and the appearance of the avatar, a questionnaire was created based on the evaluation standard introduced by the H2020 EasyTV European-funded program [14]. Participants were asked to evaluate the representation quality on five randomly selected sign sentences, the avatar's signing capabilities and give feedback. All questions were rated on a scale of 1 to 5, with 5 representing the best given score. Figure 4 presents a graph of the average score that each participant gave to randomly selected sign sentences. On average, the participants gave a score of 3.8 out of 5, meaning that they are satisfied with the proposed application and its components. More specifically, the content understanding and avatar realism were rated by users with a score of 3.9, while the hand movement accuracy was rated with a score of 3.3. These results indicate the robustness of the SL representation component and its potential for real-life applications.

3.3 SL Communication System

The evaluation of the entire SL communication system was driven by the goal for measuring its usability and potential for growth. As such, the System Usability Scale (SUS) [15] and the Net Promoter Score (NPS) [16] were adopted in the form of a questionnaire, that was handed to early testers of the application. Following the SUS model, the questionnaire contained 10 questions, half of which are positive statements while the rest are negative, alternated and presented in a fixed standardized order. Participants were asked to express whether they agree with the statements in the questionnaire by selecting one of five available options, ranging from 'strongly disagree' to 'strongly agree'.

The overall score ranges from 0 to 100 with higher scores indicating better usability. Figure 5 presents a graph of the overall scores given by the participants in the SUS scoring scale. It is observed that all users rated the system highly, with an overall score of 81.46, which on the SUS scale is considered Excellent.

The user satisfaction scale NPS is calculated based on responses to the question, "How likely is it for you to recommend this service to a friend or colleague on a scale of 0 (not at all likely) to 10 (would definitely recommend it)?". In the NPS score scale, individuals responding from 0 to 6 are considered "detractors", those responding from 7 to 8 are considered "neutrals" and individuals responding with 9 or 10 are labeled "promoters". The total NPS score is calculated

Fig. 3. Sample images from the recorded dataset GSLW.

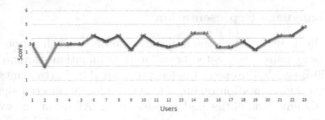

Fig. 4. User evaluation of SL representation component.

by subtracting the percentage of detractors from the percentage of promoters, with neutrals being ignored. The NPS scale ranges from -100 to 100, with values above 0 being considered "Good". The NPS score for the proposed system is 14.3, revealing that 3 participants became promoters and none detractors of the system. Thus, the proposed SL communication system is viewed positively from the SL community, which realizes the value and potential of such a system.

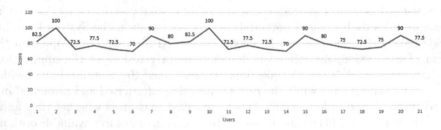

Fig. 5. User evaluation of the proposed SL communication system in the SUS scale.

4   Conclusions

In this work, a novel SL communication system, integrated in a mobile application, to promote Deaf-to-hearing communication is introduced. The system consists of an NLP and linguistics component to transform speech to signs and vice versa, a SL recognition component for accurately recognizing glosses from videos and a SL representation system to robustly transform glosses to body and hand movements. Leveraging on the findings of this work, the future goals are to improve upon them and create a even more powerful application that will facilitate the day-to-day communication of hearing-impaired people on more broad conversational scenarios, towards improving their social inclusion.

Author contributions. Andreas Stergioulas, Christos Chatzikonstantinou, Theocharis Chatzis and Ilias Papastratis: equal contribbution

References

1. Papastratis, I., Dimitropoulos, K., Konstantinidis, D., Daras, P.: Continuous sign language recognition through cross-modal alignment of video and text embeddings in a joint-latent space. IEEE Access **8**, 91 170–91 180 (2020)
2. Papastratis, I., Chatzikonstantinou, C., Konstantinidis, D., Dimitropoulos, K., Daras, P.: Artificial intelligence technologies for sign language. Sensors **21**(17), 5843 (2021)
3. Stefanidis, K., Konstantinidis, D., Kalvourtzis, A., Dimitropoulos, K., Daras, P.: 3d technologies and applications in sign language. Recent Advances in 3D Imaging, Modeling, and Reconstruction, pp. 50–78 (2020)
4. Adaloglou, N.M., et al.: A comprehensive study on deep learning-based methods for sign language recognition. IEEE Trans. Multimedia (2021)
5. Papastratis, I., Dimitropoulos, K., Daras, P.: Continuous sign language recognition through a context-aware generative adversarial network. Sensors **21**(7), 2437 (2021)
6. Carreira, J., Zisserman, A.: Quo vadis, action recognition, a new model and the kinetics dataset. CoRR, abs/1705.07750, vol. 2, p. 3 (2017)
7. Szegedy, C., et al.: Going deeper with convolutions. In: Proceedings of the IEEE Conference on Computer Vision and Pattern Recognition, pp. 1–9 (2015)
8. Kocabas, M., Athanasiou, N., Black, M.J.: Vibe: video inference for human body pose and shape estimation. In: Proceedings of the IEEE/CVF Conference on Computer Vision and Pattern Recognition, pp. 5253–5263 (2020)
9. Stergioulas, A., Chatzis, T., Konstantinidis, D., Dimitropoulos, K., Daras, P.: 3d hand pose estimation via aligned latent space injection and kinematic losses. In: Proceedings of the IEEE/CVF Conference on Computer Vision and Pattern Recognition, pp. 1730–1739 (2021)
10. Zhang, J., Jiao, J., Chen, M., Qu, L., Xu, X., Yang, Q.: A hand pose tracking benchmark from stereo matching. In: 2017 IEEE International Conference on Image Processing (ICIP), pp. 982–986. IEEE (2017)
11. Zimmermann, C., Brox, T.: Learning to estimate 3d hand pose from single RGB images. In: Proceedings of the IEEE International Conference on Computer Vision, pp. 4903–4911 (2017)
12. Chatzis, T., Stergioulas, A., Konstantinidis, D., Dimitropoulos, K., Daras, P.: A comprehensive study on deep learning-based 3d hand pose estimation methods. Appl. Sci. **10**(19), 6850 (2020)
13. Unreal engine: The most powerful real-time 3d creation tool. https://www.unrealengine.com. Accessed 24 Feb 2022
14. Easytv: Easing the access of europeans with disabilities to converging media and content, deliverable 6.5 (2020). https://easytvproject.eu/files/D6.5.pdf. Accessed 24 Feb 2022
15. Brooke, J.: Sus: a retrospective. J. Usabil. Stud. **8**(2), 29–40 (2013)
16. Yüksel, A., Rimmington, M.: Customer-satisfaction measurement: performance counts. Cornell Hotel Restaurant Administ. Quar. **39**(6), 60–70 (1998)

Applying APCA and Huetone for Color Accessibility of User Interfaces

Kirill Ulitin(✉) (iD)

MyOffice, Nevsky pr. 104, 191025 Sankt-Petersburg, Russia
`kirill.ulitin@myoffice.team`, `kirill@ulitin.ru`

Abstract. Over the 15 years since the adoption of WCAG 2.0, user interface design and interface devices have changed substantiallys. However, many interface guidelines still employ the old color contrast formula. In the last few years, the range of color accessibility tools has expanded with a variety of newcomers: LCH and HSLuv, enhanced color models adapted to human perception, have been developed; Advanced Perceptual Contrast Algorithm (APCA) has been implemented as part of WCAG 3.0; Tools for creating color palettes have been developed based on its implementation, such as Accessible Palette and Huetone. These new tools were used during a redesign of an office suite to change the color scheme. The purpose of this paper is to demonstrate practical results of using these tools. Despite the fact that WCAG 3.0 has not yet been adopted, APCA shows more accurate results for measuring color contrast. Huetone Color Tool provides capabilities of palette analysis using the LCH color space model with easy color contrast and color distance calculation.

Keywords: User interface · Color contrast · APCA · LCH · Huetone

1 Introduction

1.1 Color Models

Well known color models are based on red, green and blue, the colors used for pixels on computer screen matrices. The transformation of RGB to polar coordinates produces HSL (Hue, Saturation, Lightness), HSB (Hue, Saturation, Brightness) color models – a more natural way of understanding and selecting colors [1]. Unfortunately, these color models commonly used in design tools are not adapted to human perception. As shown in Fig. 1, in the process of creating a uniform palette with numerous colors via the HSL color model, designers must adapt the lightness of each color, because HSL does not have a uniform lightness.

To solve this issue, color models adapted to human perception have been developed, such as LCH, HSLuv, HPLuv. [2] LCH is already supported in CSS 4.0 [3] and has been recently added to the Chrome browser [4]. The future of using LCH on the web looks promising.

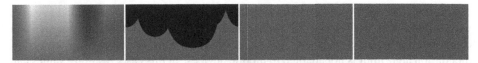

Fig. 1. Comparison of HSL, LCH, HSLuv, HPLuv color models

1.2 Color Contrast

Contrast between the color of an element and the background is a key metric for readability; studies confirm the effect of contrast on reading speed [5]. Interestingly, depending on the display device, the preferred color combinations also change. While on CRT monitors the best result is a pair of yellow on black, on LEDs it is black on white [6].

The WCAG 2.1 accessibility standard describes a formula for calculating contrast and offers a calculator for it; the same formula and methodology is used in many other contrast estimation solutions [7]. However, in some cases the imperfect algorithm produces incorrect results. Ericka O'Connor even tested controversial points on people with color perception disorders and found WCAG 2.1 imperfection for white and black text on orange background [8].

In 2019, Andrew Somers published an issue on the W3C's GitHub page with the problems he found [9]. Later, he also developed a new adaptive algorithm and a calculator to estimate the APCA (Advanced Perception Contrast Algorithm) contrast. APCA replaced the previous contrast calculation algorithm and was included in the development version of the WCAG 3.0 [10].

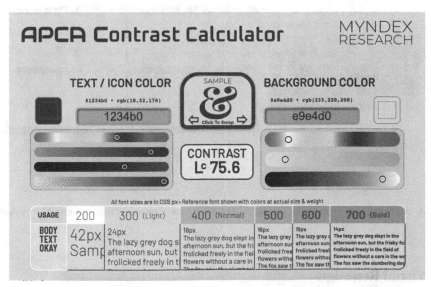

Fig. 2. Screenshot of APCA Contrast Calculator, URL: https://www.myndex.com/APCA/, author: Andrew Somers

APCA contrast (Fig. 2) depends on color polarity and shows positive and negative values depending on whether the background is light or dark. It also recommends a minimum font size, depending on the thickness of the font. However, the font recommendation algorithm is not adapted to mobile devices. In this case, resulting values can be divided by 2, since when working on a mobile device, the distance from the eyes to the screen is about 2 times less than when working at a monitor [11, 12]. The values can also be interpreted according to Table 1.

Table 1. Mapping of WCAG and APCA contrast values

WCAG 2.1	3:1	4.5:1	7:1
APCA	60	75	90

1.3 Huetone Color Tool

The Huetone web app was created by Alexey Ardov [13] (Fig. 3). It allows to create a color palette, measure contrast via WCAG 2.1 and APCA between a selected color and the whole palette at once, to visualize the palette with different LCH channels, as well as to import and export the palette.

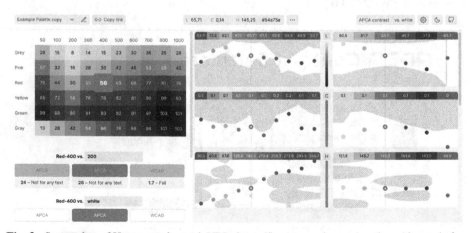

Fig. 3. Screenshot of Huetone color tool, URL: https://huetone.ardov.me/, author: Alexey Ardov

2 Visual Redesign

The redesign of MyOffice web applications has started in the beginning of 2020. One of the goals was to increase the color accessibility and reduce the influence of accent colors. At first, the design team relied on the WCAG 2.1 contrast formula. However, during the redesign of the color scheme the team faced the issue of conflicting accent and status colors [14]. After an investigation, a new color contrast formula was discovered. APCA and later Huetone were added to internal design guidelines.

3 Results

After examination author has found the lack of previous contrast values. WCAG 2.1 formula shows extreme contrast values that are almost twice as big as APCA figures. Colors were tuned in order to increase contrast. In Table 2 difference between formulas can be found. Final design is shown in Fig. 4.

Table 2. Comparison of contrast calculation #121212 to color in table cells

Palette created with WCAG 2.1	WCAG 2.1 contrast	11	11.5	11	10.9	10.6	9.8	9.4	9.3
	APCA contrast in WCAG 2.1 range	5.1	5.4	5.1	5.0	4.9	4.4	4.2	4.2
Palette created with APCA	WCAG 2.1 contrast	12.1	12	12	12.2	11.9	12	12.3	12.2
	APCA contrast in WCAG 2.1 range	5.8	5.7	5.7	5.9	5.7	5.7	5.9	5.8

The comparison algorithm for the check mark color in Table 3 shows even more serious problems with the old contrast formula.

The Huetone color tool provides the ability to analyze palettes in order to understand color patterns. Figure 5 shows a chroma channel graph of colors used to indicate users collaborating in a popular online document editor. It is clearly seen that adjacent colors have shifts in the chroma value. These shifts also help increase color distance between adjacent colors and in theory improve color recognition.

Fig. 4. Applications' color coding with error state, author: Alexander Gusar

Table 3. Comparison of color choosing dialogs

black check mark if WCAG 2.1 contrast color to black more 4.5	black check mark if APCA contrast color to black more 60 (4.5 WCAG 2.1 equivalent)
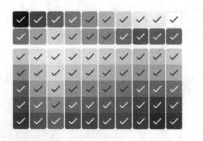	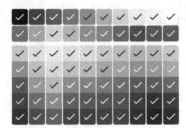

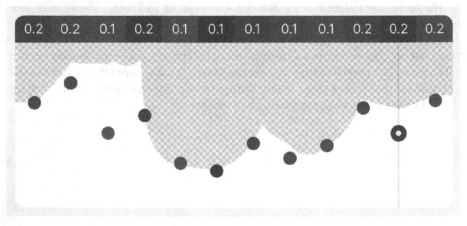

Fig. 5. Chroma channel graph

4   Discussion

This paper provides information about practical application of the APCA and Hue-tone color tools. During the redesign of the MyOffice applications, the design team ran into issues with the old contrast formula. After analysis, a new approach to calculating contrast was adopted. The calculations and examples provided in this paper show the disadvantage of the WCAG 2.1 contrast formula in comparison with APCA. Currently APCA is included in the development version of the WCAG 3.0. But the main problem is that WCAG 3.0 has not yet been widely adopted. Many color accessibility tools and regulations are still based on WCAG 2.1 and therefore an old contrast formula. It can lead to misinterpretation, especially with auto testing software.

The Huetone color tool, which incorporates the LCH color model, APCA contrast and color distance calculation, allows to streamline the color palette creation and testing processes.

Acknowledgement. Author would like to thank Olga Resetnaka, Artem Verkhogliadov for their help with text editing and Arthur Savchenko for idea of initial analysis.

References

1. Boronine, A.: Color spaces for human beings. https://www.boronine.com/2012/03/26/Color-Spaces-for-Human-Beings/. Accessed 10 Mar 2023
2. Zeileis, A., Hornik, K., Murrell, P.: Escaping RGBland: selecting colors for statistical graphics. Comput. Stat. Data Anal. **53**, 3259–3270 (2009). https://doi.org/10.1016/j.csda.2008.11.033
3. Verou, L.: LCH colors in CSS: What, why, and how?. https://lea.verou.me/2020/04/lch-colors-in-css-what-why-and-how/. Accessed 10 Mar 2023
4. LCH(): Can I use... support tables for HTML5, CSS3, etc, https://caniuse.com/?search=lch%28%29. Accessed 10 Mar 2023
5. Ohnishi, M., et al.: Effects of luminance contrast and character size on reading speed. Vision. Res. **166**, 52–59 (2020). https://doi.org/10.1016/j.visres.2019.09.010
6. Humar, I., Gradisar, M., Turk, T., Erjavec, J.: The impact of color combinations on the legibility of text presented on lcds. Appl. Ergon. **45**, 1510–1517 (2014). https://doi.org/10.1016/j.apergo.2014.04.013
7. Contrast (minimum): understanding SC 1.4.3. https://www.w3.org/WAI/GL/UNDERSTANDING-WCAG20/visual-audio-contrast-contrast.html. Accessed 10 Mar 2023
8. O'Connor, E.: Orange you accessible? A mini case study on color ratio. https://www.bounteous.com/insights/2019/03/22/orange-you-accessible-mini-case-study-color-ratio. Accessed 10 Mar 2023
9. W3C: Contrast ratio math and related visual issues · issue #695 · W3C/WCAG. https://github.com/w3c/wcag/issues/695. Accessed 10 Mar 2023
10. W3C Accessibility Guidelines (WCAG) 3.0. https://www.w3.org/TR/wcag-3.0/. Accessed 10 Mar 2023
11. Charness, N., Dijkstra, K., Jastrzembski, T., Weaver, S., Champion, M.: Monitor viewing distance for younger and older workers. Proc. Hum. Fact. Ergon. Soc. Ann. Meet. **52**, 1614–1617 (2008). https://doi.org/10.1177/154193120805201965
12. Bababekova, Y., Rosenfield, M., Hue, J.E., Huang, R.R.: Font size and viewing distance of handheld smart phones. Optom. Vis. Sci. **88**, 795–797 (2011). https://doi.org/10.1097/opx.0b013e3182198792

13. Ardov, A.: Huetone: A tool to create accessible color systems. https://github.com/ardov/hue
    tone. Accessed 10 Mar 2023
14. Ulitin, K.: Color in Interface. Int. Culture Technol. Stud. **6**, 225–234 (2022). https://doi.org/
    10.17586/2587-800x-2021-6-4-225-234

TACTILE DESIGN: Touching The Light of Art in a Dark World

Dingwei Zhang(✉) ⓘ, Xiaotong Zhang ⓘ, and Hongtao Zhou(✉) ⓘ

College of Design and Innovation, Tongji University, Shanghai, China
zhangdingwei@tongji.edu.cn

Abstract. Based on the sensory design of emotional interaction, the blind art product design is studied with the help of modern technology to enhance the tactile emotional cognition of the blind and to explore and construct an immersive interactive cognitive system oriented to tactile design. To introduce design and art into the development of tactile cognitive product design for the blind, to transform two-dimensional flat information into different three-dimensional recognizable cognitive learning interfaces through 3D printing technology, and to improve tactile cognition and art appreciation for the blind with a unique blind reading and exhibition approach. On the premise of the a priori nature of blind people's tactile and auditory qualities and their bodies, we use materials, shapes, emotions and spatial mapping methods to compensate for the congenital lack of art experiences of blind people. At the same time, through the emotional translation between the blind and the art space, we explore the way to recreate the "blind art space". Modern technology (mainly 3D printing) is used to develop new tactile cognitive art interfaces for the blind, which are innovative and sustainable in improving the emotional perception of blind people and broadening the design style of artworks. Tactile design-oriented immersive interactive art space design for the blind provides new design ideas and empirical references for exploring art for the blind.

Keywords: Tactile Design · Immersive Interactive Experience · Haptic Cognition · Humanistic Care for Blind Art · Emotional Interaction · 3D Printed Products

1 Introduction

Generally speaking, the treatment of the disadvantaged reveals the height of civilization in that society. In recent years, the topic of visual arts for the blind has attracted increasingly widespread attention. Blind people have a unique way of cognition and appreciation, and due to their own defects are hardly able to appreciate art activities as ordinary people do. How to make blind people like ordinary people, also appreciate and share modern art in some form, as well as the study of the mechanism of perception of art space and the way of perceiving art by blind people, is one of the important tasks of our workers engaged in design and art.

China is one of the countries with the largest number of blind people in the world. According to national authorities, as of May 2020, there are approximately 5 million

C. Stephanidis et al. (Eds.): HCII 2023, CCIS 1833, pp. 389–399, 2023.
https://doi.org/10.1007/978-3-031-35992-7_54

blind people in China, accounting for 18% of the world's blind [1], and growing at a rate of 450,000 blind people per year [2]. The disabilities of blind and low-vision people lead to their inability to receive appropriate public resource services, and the severe shortage of cognitive design products for blind people in daily life leads to a single life situation for blind people, while blind people need to enrich their inner world. However, culture and art have become an unattainable luxury and a regret in their lives. They need a form of communication that is easy to understand, expresses emotions and conveys spiritual joy, and provides feedback through feelings (visual, auditory and tactile). Tactile Cognition provides cultural and artistic products that enrich the learning lives of blind people, creating art products and art space experiences that are more suitable for the cognitive learning and emotional communication of blind and low vision groups.

2   Tactile Cognition and Emotional Interaction

Cognition is a human perception of information that is perceived, learned, and thought about. Blind people perceive the world around them mainly by connecting Braille interfaces and books in their daily lives. The only way to obtain information is by touching Braille or by having someone else relay it to them through language, forming a corresponding cognitive image in their minds. Each person perceives and identifies in a different way, just as a hundred people reading Shakespeare's Hamlet will have a hundred different perceptions. To improve the practice of tactile cognition for the blind and to improve the existing cognitive aids for the blind, the product is designed with art and design interventions in tactile cognition art products through design reconstruction, the introduction of artistic design and parametric design innovations to quickly achieve grounded use, reconstructing the tactile cognition product model for the blind, and exploring the possibility of art and design interventions in tactile cognition.

Expression of emotion is the natural flow of inner feelings of each of us in life, a spontaneous neurological response through expressions, gestural reactions and body language. Professor Arlie Russell Hochschild of the United States argues that it is within situational norms and broad cultural concepts that an individual's emotions can be perceived and expressed and that emotional interactions all have specific limiting effects that reflect the emotional culture and emotional concepts required for the interaction [3]. Blind people are afraid to interact with normal people due to their physical defects. It is necessary to explore the value and role of tactile cognition in human-centered design based on the theory of emotional interaction combined with the concept of design empathy to develop design for the advantages of blind people's sense of touch, to design tactile products and artworks for blind people from theoretical and practical perspectives, and to conduct redesign research on tactile spaces for blind people. Reconstruct the model of tactile cognitive products for the blind, and explore the possibility of art design intervention in tactile cognition. Through 3D printing technology, we will transform two-dimensional flat information into different three-dimensional recognizable cognitive learning interface styles to improve the tactile cognition and artwork appreciation ability of blind people.

3 Touching the Art World in the Dark

3.1 Tactile Interface to Perceive Things

Blind people perceive the world in their daily lives mainly by touching two-dimensional flat objects and books with Braille. The text is perceived by touch and transformed into mental images in mind by individual imagination. The current stage of tactile mental products for the blind is based on their sensory advantages and application habits for tactile cognitive redesign to improve the quality of spiritual and cultural life of the blind as a cultural and artistic cognitive tool to solve the problem of art education for the blind. Tactile text cognition, symbol cognition, interface cognitive tools, and cognitive artwork are studied from the aspects of tactile text cognition, symbol cognition, and interface cognitive tools. Using 3D printing technology to convert flat pictures in Braille books into semi-dimensional touchable books to enhance cognitive education for the blind [4]. The author's team developed cognitive learning products for the blind based on their cognitive habits, improved the design of existing cognitive learning aids for the blind, and cooperated with schools for blind children and institutions with Braille art education aspirations. We use various materials such as resin, silicone, nylon, and acrylic to realize 3D printing product design (Fig. 1), conduct printing material exploration and practice, design efficient, low-cost, and sustainable learning cognitive tools, and promote the development and dissemination of cognitive products for the blind.

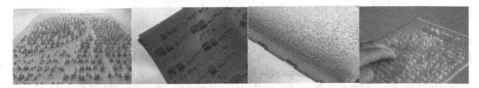

Fig. 1. 3D printed nylon and PLA materials (photo by the author)

The "Touch Text" project is a tactile cognitive tool for blind children based on their habits, learning styles, and cognitive characteristics (Fig. 2). The team developed a series of touch characters based on the traditional Chinese family name culture. It is difficult for blind people to recognize their own family names through Chinese characters. The team used touch symbol design and 3D printing technology to quickly translate Chinese characters into touchable 3D forms, combined with the aid of teacher dictation to stimulate blind children's curiosity and exploration of the unknown. The application scenario of this product is schools for blind children and special education schools, which is very friendly to the cognitive learning of the first blind or low vision group. Firstly, it allows for design sharing, special customization and 3D printing for rapid prototyping. Secondly, the product is made of biodegradable material, which is safe, durable, sustainable, not easily damaged, small in size and easy to carry.

Fig. 2. Touching the text - "Hundred family names" (photo by the author)

3.2 Touch the Product, Feel the Life

Based on the theory of emotional interaction and the concept of design empathy, the designer explores the value of tactile cognition in design and its role in design, targeting the sensory advantages of blind people, such as touch, hearing, and smell. From theoretical and practical perspectives, the designer designs tactile cognition for blind people in various aspects, such as tactile symbols, words, and graphics, and seeks to develop and improve existing learning tools and art products and to improve the tactile cognitive ability of blind people by transforming two-dimensional flat information into different three-dimensional recognizable cognitive learning interfaces through 3D printing technology innovation design.

Touchable three-dimensional objects are indispensable tools for blind people to form object concepts and spatial forms, etc., in the creation of their minds. They are designing products that are suitable for them to help them perceive the world so that they can forget about their physical barriers and psychological inferiority complex and live their lives as normal people. Through haptic-emotional interactive cognitive design research, we learn in-depth cognitive styles and build design principles and design methods based on haptic cognition for blind people. Their own physiological defects have deprived them of a colourful life, and design can make them feel the beauty of the world again, as shown in Fig. 3. Creative products for the blind that make their daily life easier.

Fig. 3. Braille products (images from the web)

In order to solve the limitation of vision for the blind, Wang Xiaogu and others designed a sticky note for the blind with additional information, which can be printed for the visually impaired through the simple operation of the ROTATA Braille note printer. The "Universal gravitation" Magnetic Tableware - Designed for The Blind" is a solution to the problem of blind people's lack of vision, which makes it difficult for them to find their way around the table. The magnetic tableware was designed to solve the problem of the blind not being able to find the silverware or the side dishes in the bowl (Fig. 4). In order to reduce the burden of eating for the blind, Zhao Rong from Wuhan Light Industry University analyzed the psychological and emotional aspects of blindness and the service experience of eating and designed the "Gravity" magnetic tableware, which solves the problem of blind people being unable to distinguish the function and position of tableware and easily knocking over dishes when eating (Fig. 5). This design also allows the able-bodied to experience the inconvenience of living with a visual disability so that they can give more care and help to these blind people in their future lives.

Fig. 4. ROTATA Braille memo printer (image from the web)

Fig. 5. "Gravity" magnetic tableware design (image from the web)

Our team solved the cognitive and art interface derivative product design for the blind by developing additive manufacturing technology, proposing a cognitive art interface research system for the blind, and building a shared art and design platform. The team designed a high-end Shanghai book box themed on the middle section of the Huangpu

River and the Oriental Pearl and other landmark architectural complexes in Shanghai (Fig. 6). The design of Ping Pong Shanghai ornaments show the spirit of Shanghai's national sports (Fig. 7). The team's attempt to integrate commercial space, creative education and technological innovation across the border with Starbucks China to present futuristic tactile art - Tea Cloud series (Fig. 8).

Fig. 6. Shanghai Design Capital Book Box (Photo by the author)

Fig. 7. Ping Pong Shanghai Photosensitive Resin (Photo by the author)

Fig. 8. Tactile Art Derivative Design - Tea Cloud Series (photo by the author)

3.3 Touching Art, Understanding the World

The team attaches importance to the emotional world of the blind and strives to explore artworks that can be read by the blind and enhance the aesthetic level of art that enriches them. Based on the Hundred Family Names series of products, the team artistically designed the Chinese character names to incorporate the features of their hometown terrain patterns and worked with blind people to create exclusive 3D artworks with local sentiments [5], such as Fig. 9, which shows Li Zhihao, a student at the Shanghai School for the Blind, whose hometown is a city of tall buildings on the southern plains. Blind people can share with their peers by touching the 3D-printed artistic cognitive interface to mentally decipher their names and depict what their hometown looks like. To let blind people understand different cities, the author's team developed "Braille City" and "City Skyline" tactile cognitive art interfaces (see Fig. 10), which use other countries' written languages and landmarks of different cities as artistic expressions. The artwork uses the language of different countries and the landmarks of different cities as the carrier of creative expression, using artistic processing techniques to describe the local urban landscape and human history, such as the Eiffel Tower in Paris, France, Berlin, Germany, and the Oriental Pearl in Shanghai, China......, typical city architectural landmarks, allowing blind people to touch and understand different world cities.

Fig. 9. Blind Student - Name Artwork by Li Zhihao (Photo by the author)

Fig. 10. Braille urban artwork & City skyline - Beijing (photo by the author)

Marc Dillon, the founder of Unseen Art, is committed to making art more accessible to the blind and visually impaired by launching a number of art projects, including "Unseen Art Unseen Art" is an art project that will change the art experience for the blind by printing two-dimensional classical artworks such as the Mona Lisa as 3D models [6]. The project allows blind and visually impaired people to experience artworks through touch, making them more accessible and understandable (Fig. 11).

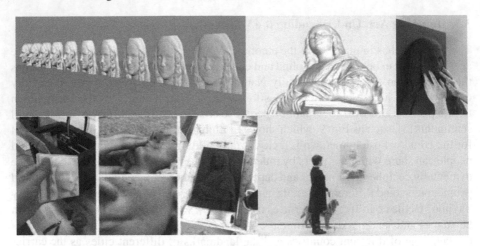

Fig. 11. 3D model of "Mona Lisa" (Photo credit: Phoenix Art)

3DPhotoworks uses micro-sculpting technology to make the museum's classic two-dimensional flat art collection into a three-dimensional installation that can be touched directly by visitors. By connecting the artworks, blind people visiting the museum can "appreciate" the art themselves without the need for docents to help them interpret it. In addition, the surface of these devices is covered with sensors that automatically trigger an audio explanation when you touch a part, enhancing the emotional interaction between the blind and the artwork (Fig. 12).

Fig. 12. Raised Surface; Virginia Museum of Fine Arts diorama installation; Blind Touch Art (image source web)

3.4 Touching Culture, Expressing Emotions

With the unique tactile cognitive art expression form, the team tries to explore its deeper connotation of traditional Chinese cultural expression. Using the new tactile art form as the carrier of traditional culture, the Touch Culture series: the Chinese character "Five Grains of Plenty" with auspicious symbolic meaning is used in the idyllic landscape of mountains and hills to express people's beautiful symbolic meaning of good wind and rain and good harvest (Fig. 13). The classical poems from the ancient Chinese classic literature "Tang Poetry" and "Song Lyrics" are selected and transformed into readable and appreciable 3D traditional cultural artworks (Fig. 14). The creative transformation of design ideas through 3D printing and molding technology has become an important way for blind people to inherit and develop traditional Chinese culture. 3D printing and moulding technology have practical significance for blind people's cognitive style, 3D conversion of 2D graphics, improvement of art cognitive level, expansion of art space for blind people, design sharing platform and new era development of blind people's cultural career.

Fig. 13. Folk culture - "Five Grains of Plenty" (Photo by the author)

Fig. 14. Classical poetry works of the ancient Chinese "Tang Poems" and "Song Lyrics" (Photo by the author)

3.5 Touch Space and Perceptual Art Experience

Based on empathy-based experience design, the blind touch art perception, many countries are increasingly focusing on the attention of the blind, while many blind touch experience museum projects have become attempts to focus on special people [7]. Figure 15 shows a blind child touching the wall sculpture and caressing the bronze statue in the Chinese Writing Museum to experience the charm of Chinese writing art and the demeanour of ancient Chinese literati.

Figure 16 shows Croatians visiting the "Touch, Smell, Hear Art Exhibition for the Blind" on May 18, Museum Day, in Zagreb, Croatia, to experience the perception of art by the blind. The format of the exhibition is that the viewer is blindfolded and has to touch the work, smell it and listen to the sound in order to experience an immersive, tactile aesthetic experience due to different materials, forms and textures. Through the combination of touch, hearing and smell, a new interactive experience of art appreciation is formed, realizing the possibility of allowing blind people to appreciate artworks. Ordinary viewers can also imagine and experience the infinite charm of art through their own touching sensations. Curator Werner Biocchi hopes that more people can understand the blind's perception of art through this form of art exhibition and thus give them more support and assistance. Similarly, the exhibition "Dialogue in the Dark" at the Experience

Fig. 15. Chinese Writing Museum, photo source: Anyang civilization network

Fig. 16. "Touch, Smell, Hear the Art of the Blind Exhibition" at the Museum of Kravice Vidvorj

Center for the Blind in Frankfurt, Germany, allows people with no disabilities to try to perceive and experience only by hearing, touch, smell, and taste, based on an empathetic design that makes people respect and care for the blind (Fig. 17).

Fig. 17. Frankfurt Experience for the Blind

4 Conclusion

For blind people, using tactile cognition to understand the world is not only from words but also from 3D tactile art, so that they can "see" the world in their own way. The team will develop new cognitive interfaces, tactile cognitive art products and exhibition spaces for the blind to promote the enjoyment of art and a better spiritual and cultural life for the blind, allowing them to touch art in the dark and experience the charm of art in an immersive way. The team, together with the China Disabled Persons' Federation Apparatus Aids Center and the Shanghai School for Blind Children, has developed a preliminary theory of tactile cognitive design guidelines for art aids for the blind and a complete set of social practice methodology and can think about and solve the art mental problems of the blind from multiple perspectives and dimensions, and at the same time propose practical ways of implementation and corresponding think-tank solutions for the country to enhance services for the disabled.

References

1. China Disabled Development Research Center. Annual overview of the development and social progress of the disabled in China. Qiuzhen publishing house, Beijing (2020)

2. Chai, L.X., Wang, X.G, Du, B.: Research on the design of blind simulation navigation system based on AR technology. J. Bus. Inform. **37**, 164 (2019)
3. Chen, T.: Literature review and theoretical reflection on the research of emotional mobilization in network action. Southeast Commun. **02**, 144–147 (2016)
4. David Lee Kuo, C, Deng, R.: How 3D Printing Will Change the Future of Borrowing Lending and Spending. Academic Press (2017)
5. Tang, X.: Research on social innovation from the perspective of participatory design. Hunan University (2017)
6. Wu, S.Y.: Research on interaction design of thematic exhibition hall in the era of Internet of Things. Donghua University (2015)
7. Zhang, X.T., Tian, J., Yan, N.: Research on the design of movable art space for the blind based on cognitive psychology. J. Furniture Interior Decor. **05**, 5–9 (2022). https://doi.org/10.16771/j.cn43-1247/ts.2022.05.002

A Positive Design Based Intervention Product for Mild Cognitive Impairment

Shiqian Zou and Zhang Zhang[✉]

College of Art Design and Media, East China University of Science and Technology, Shanghai, China

15618746761@qq.com

Abstract. With the rapid development of China's economy and the extension of the average life expectancy of the people, China has entered an aging society. And the elderly, as a high incidence of mild cognitive impairment (MCI), their health problems have become the focus of attention. MCI is a transitional phase between normal aging and dementia, and early diagnosis and intervention in this transitional phase is currently the most effective treatment due to the irreversible development of dementia and the absence of effective treatment. Therefore, this paper studies the design of MCI intervention products by combining positive design methods and frameworks. Finally, with the goal of enhancing subjective well-being, "MCI Intelligent Intervention Training Musical Instrument", an intervention product, that can meet the three design elements of pleasure, personal significance and virtue, delay the decline of patient cognitive function and reduce the pressure of caregivers is designed. The design helps to improve society's attention to MCI, and has a positive guiding effect on the improvement of the positive design theory system and the field of cognitive impairment intervention.

Keywords: Positive Design · Positive Experience · Subjective Well-being · MCI · Intervention Training

1 Introduction

MCI is a transitional stage between normal aging and Alzheimer's disease [1]. The elderly at this stage have different degrees of impairment of memory and/or other cognitive functions, and their daily living ability has not been affected too much, but they have not met the diagnostic criteria for dementia. The prevalence rate of MCI among the elderly aged 60 and above in China is 15.54%, and the number of patients is about 38.77 million, which is 2.5 times the number of dementia patients. It can be seen that the number of patients with MCI in China is extremely large [2].

So far, dementia is an irreversible process, and drug treatment has not made breakthrough achievements. Therefore, it is particularly important to analyze and study the risk factors of MCI, which helps to distinguish high-risk groups at the early stage, complete the early diagnosis of elderly MCI patients, effectively intervene and delay dementia, so as to effectively prevent the disease and development of MCI, and further reduce the

C. Stephanidis et al. (Eds.): HCII 2023, CCIS 1833, pp. 400–407, 2023.
https://doi.org/10.1007/978-3-031-35992-7_55

incidence rate of dementia. At a time when the prevalence of MCI remains high, we should pay more attention to the popularization of relevant medical knowledge, improve the design of corresponding cognitive impairment intervention products, and create a better and more complete treatment and intervention environment.

2 Overview of Positive Design

Pieter Desmet, a professor at Delft University of Technology in the Netherlands and founder of the Institute of Positive Design, first proposed the concept of "positive design" in 2013 [3]. Positive Design is a design concept based on positive psychology and combining positive psychology with a series of design theoretical knowledge. It focuses on people's positive aspects, takes improving people's subjective well-being as the design goal, stimulates the positive aspects and overcomes the impact of negative aspects, improves positive emotions, brings people happy and meaningful experience and life, and it not only promotes human progress but also social prosperity.

After Desmet put forward the concept of positive design, he took the pleasure, personal significance and virtue of subjective well-being as the three elements of positive design, and constructed the framework of positive design. The framework of positive design can be divided into three levels, namely, design for pleasure, design for personal significance and design for virtue. When the three elements are achieved at the same time, the fundamental goal of the positive design will be achieved, that is to promote the progress and prosperity of human beings and society; When only one or two factors are realized without negative impact on other factors, it can also be called positive design, which helps to improve subjective well-being [4].

3 User Research of MCI Intervention Products

3.1 Analysis of Characteristics of Patients with MCI

Physiological Characteristics of Patients with MCI. The most significant physiological characteristics of the group with MCI are memory decline, and the initial performance is forgetfulness, often forgetting time, and getting lost in familiar places; In the medium term, they forget the recent events seriously, appear in a trance, and get lost at home; In the late stage, it is accompanied by severe memory impairment, unable to recognize relatives and friends, completely dependent on others' care, and even aggressive. In the early and middle stages, patients can maintain basic self-care ability. However, a series of cognitive abilities such as attention, executive ability, logical thinking ability, visuospatial ability and orientation ability of patients will decline with the development of the disease, and physiological abilities such as walking ability, language ability and eating ability will also decline [5].

Psychological Characteristics of Patients with MCI. With the decline of physiological and cognitive functions caused by MCI, patients may have psychological problems indirectly. On the one hand, the difficulty of accepting new things and the decline of learning ability make it difficult for them to adapt to the changes in life and the fast-paced lifestyle and electronic technology, resulting in negative emotions, such as lone-liness and weariness. On the other hand, the physiological barrier and memory decline caused by cognitive impairment will also lead to a serious decline in the quality of life of patients, making it difficult to communicate with their families, and bringing care pressure to their children, while generating a sense of guilt. These various physiological and psychological reasons are likely to lead to the outbreak of psychological diseases such as depression, autism and bipolar disorder.

3.2 Interventional Treatment of MCI

In recent years, due to the advantages of low cost, low threshold and significant effect of non-drug treatment, it has become more and more popular with patients' families and medical and nursing staff, and has become the research focus of intervention therapy for MCI, mainly including nostalgic therapy, art therapy, music therapy, multi-sensory stimulation therapy, etc. In this study, the intervention therapy of music therapy can not only soothe the emotion, but also improve the cognitive disease of patients. At present, Boone music therapy, which is mainly used by training institutions, proposes a new musical instrument, simplifies fingering and music theory, drives patients to exercise coordination ability, concentration, promote communication and self-identity, and improve multiple cognitive abilities through changes in music. Boone musical instrument can enable cognitive patients without any playing experience to learn at once, which is an excellent care therapy [6].

4   User Demand Extraction Based on Positive Design

4.1   Analysis on the Needs of Patients with MCI

First of all, a semi-structured interview was used to deeply understand the needs of MCI elderly and their caregivers for the function and intelligence of intervention products. Secondly, the situational observation method was selected to record the frequency, process and habits of the elderly using products, and compare the behavior of the elderly at different MCI stages. Finally, based on the user journey map tool (see Fig. 1), the pain points and design opportunities are obtained, the typical user portrait of MCI patients is refined, and the service motivation, contact points and pain points in the intervention product system are clarified.

4.2   Analysis on the Needs of MCI Caregivers

Considering the use scenarios and user objects of the intervention products for MCI, the caregivers were subdivided into family caregivers and intervention training volunteer caregivers, and two types of typical users were selected for in-depth interviews. The interview found that many caregivers said that it was necessary to carry out intervention training activities at home. The training intensity once a week could not meet the treatment effect. The cognitive impairment intervention training products that could be portable and brought to home were a good direction. In addition, caregivers attach great

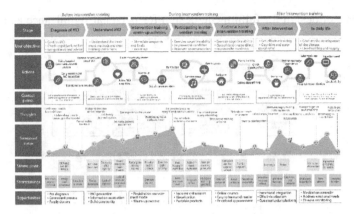

Fig. 1. Patient User Journey Map

importance to the visualization of disease monitoring and pre-diagnosis function, and propose that the APP should be able to configure relevant training courses online to facilitate the exchange of course learning and disease between volunteers and patients and their families. According to the interview results, the user journey map of the caregiver side (see Fig. 2) can be constructed.

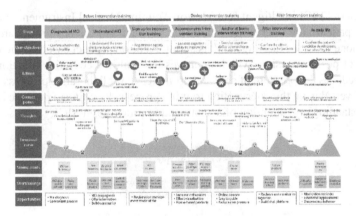

Fig. 2. Caregiver User Journey Map

4.3 Demand Analysis Based on Positive Design

Based on the previous research on MCI, use scenario research, and the needs of caregiver users and patient users, taking "MCI intelligent intervention training musical instrument" as the design direction, five needs can be summarized, which are intervention training needs, interesting needs, communication needs, emotional needs, and medical needs, and further subdivided into 12 categories (see Fig. 3). Then use the design method of positive design to sort out the above requirements and check whether they meet the requirements of design for fulfillment, design for personal significance and design for virtual.

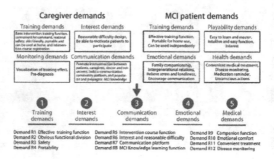

Fig. 3. User demand analysis

5   Design Practice of Intervention Products for MCI Based on Positive Design

5.1   Design Scheme

The design of "MCI Intelligent Intervention Training Musical Instrument" includes the design of patient-side intervention hardware product and the design of caregiver-side mobile phone software (see Fig. 4). It is an intervention product based on the theoretical guidance of positive design, which improves the multiple cognitive functions of MCI patients, reduces the pressure of care and promotes the collaborative progress of patients and caregivers during the intervention training process. Its ultimate purpose is to arouse the understanding and attention of society and families about MCI.

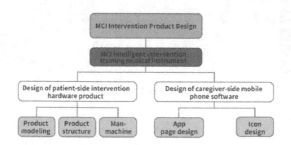

Fig. 4. Framework for MCI intervention Product design

5.2   Design of Patient-Side Intervention Hardware Products

The hardware product of "MCI Intelligent Intervention Training Musical Instrument" has four major functions: intervention training (see Fig. 5 and Fig. 6), emotional comfort, building communication platform and disease monitoring. The product size data of "MCI Intelligent Intervention Training Instrument" is as follows: the total length is 60cm, the total height is 10cm, and the total width is 29cm.

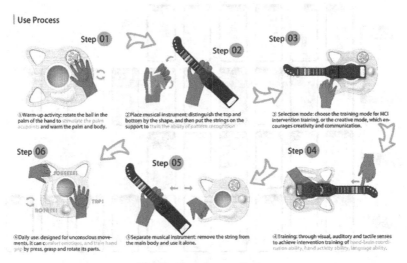

Fig. 5. Use process display

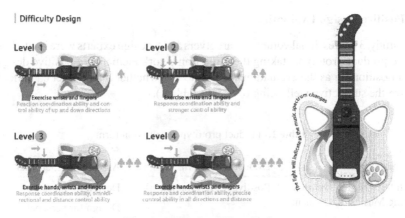

Fig. 6. Difficulty design display

5.3   Design of Caregiver-Side Mobile Phone Software

According to user needs and product functions, "MCI Musical Instrument Assisted APP" is designed for caregivers with MCI. It integrates four modules: intervention training, communication platform, intervention course, and disease monitoring (see Fig. 7). It aims to reduce the care pressure of caregivers, and cooperate with MCI musical instrument to better conduct intervention training for patients with MCI.

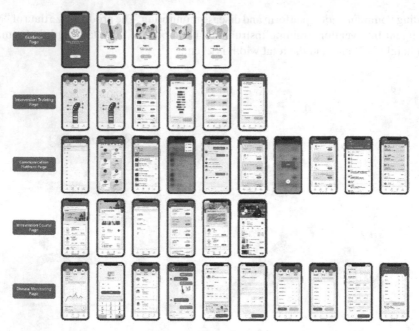

Fig. 7. APP page display

5.4 Positive Design Evaluation

In this study, 3 professional volunteer caregivers and 5 design experts were invited to evaluate the product prototype, taking the three framework elements of positive design and design positioning as the evaluation criteria, to test whether the product can effectively improve the subjective well-being of users (Table 1).

Table 1. Product prototype evaluation form

Evaluation Object	Evaluation Criteria	Assessment Elements
MCI Intelligent Intervention Training Musical Instrument	Positive design framework	Design for pleasure
		Design for personal significance
		Design for virtue
	Design position	Improve MCI patients' cognitive function
		Reduce the care pressure of MCI caregivers

From the perspective of positive design framework, the product appearance design and the process of intervention training can attract the patients' use interest and make them obtain immediate positive experience under reasonable difficulty design, which is in line with the design for pleasure. It integrates a series of functions, such as intervention courses, communication platforms and disease monitoring, to help realize personal meaning and achieve a sense of achievement and subjective well-being. The ultimate goal is to call for attention to the MCI group, promote understanding, communication and companionship, which meets the design standards of cultivating virtue [7].

When it comes to design positioning, the intervention training function can effectively exercise patients' multiple cognitive functions, and appease patients' negative emotions such as loneliness, worldliness, anxiety, etc. With the help of product hardware and software, caregivers can scientifically guide and accompany patients to carry out intervention training, and obtain positive experience through learning the latest MCI care knowledge, information sharing, community assistance, disease monitoring and other functions, so as to better care for patients and improve subjective well-being.

6 Conclusion

Against the background of increasingly serious aging problem, MCI deserves continuous attention from the family and society. Applying the theory of positive design to the field of intervention product design with cognitive impairment has high research value and practical significance, which can make up for the problems such as the relatively blank application field of positive design in China and the immature market of intervention products. Based on the positive design theory, under the guidance of the three elements of the positive design framework of design for pleasure, design for personal significance and design for virtue, this paper explores a new model to improve the user's positive experience and subjective well-being, and provides new design directions and ideas for the innovation of intervention products with MCI [8].

References

1. Huang, M., Liu, X., Zhang, M., Meng, J., Mu, W.: Research progress on risk factors of MCI in the elderly. Chin. Massage Rehab. Med. 9(21), 87–90 (2018)
2. Jia, L., et al.: Prevalence, risk factors, and management of dementia and mild cognitive impairment in adults aged 60 years or older in China: a cross-sectional study. The Lancet. Public health 5(12), e661–e671 (2020)
3. Zhang, X.: Positive Design Participate in the Research of Rural Mutual Pension Products. Donghua University (2021)
4. Desmet, P., Pohlmeyer, A.: Positive design an introduction to design for subjective well-being (2013)
5. Ma, H., et al.: Research on design of educational products for elders with mild cognitive impairment. Chin. Indust. Des. 11, 62–63 (2021)
6. Xing, W., et al.: Research progress of music therapy in the treatment of post - stroke cognitive impairment. Chin. Henan Med. Res. 30(29), 5565–5568 (2021)
7. Dai, Y.: Research on the design of children's financial quotient educational products based on positive design theory. East China University of Science and Technology (2021)
8. Zhang, P., et al.: Product design based on the prevention of mild cognitive impairment for older adults. Chin. Design 35(05), 132–134 (2022)

Interactive Technologies for the Aging Population

Communication Support for Older Adults Through Pictograms

Hugo Arias-Flores[1](✉) ⓘ, Mireya Zapata[1] ⓘ, Sandra Sanchez-Gordon[2] ⓘ, and Priscila Cedillo[3] ⓘ

[1] Centro de Investigación en Mecatrónica y Sistemas Interactivos - MIST, Universidad Indoamérica, 170103 Quito, Ecuador
hugoarias@uti.edu.ec
[2] Department of Informatics and Computer Science, Escuela Politécnica Nacional, 170525 Quito, Ecuador
[3] Departamento de Ciencias de la Computación, Universidad de Cuenca, 01.01.168 Cuenca, Ecuador

Abstract. Changes generated by the pandemic have stimulated new forms of communication through technological devices. Thanks to these, augmentative and alternative communication through the use of pictograms has allowed the development of communicative capacity for people who face health problems, such as speech, limited motor skills, hearing, among others. In particular, for segments of the elderly population with limited communication and technology management skills, it is important to consider usability and accessibility criteria in technological support interfaces design, in order to provide a satisfying and non-intrusive user experience. Support activities must be pleasant and transparent for the effective users' communication with their environment. In this context, the article presents a methodology for the design of an augmentative communication solution based on pictograms, with the purpose of transmitting the message from the user to the receiver. This article proposes a systematic review of the literature on augmentative and alternative communication, as well as the use of existing pictograms and technologies. The systematic review protocol considered the choice of four digital libraries for the search. The method of search and selection of technological solutions was based on the search for Apps and websites for the use of pictograms through technology to automate and support the communication of elderly.

Keywords: older adults · pictograms · augmentative and alternative communication · technology

1 Introduction

Communication is a basic need for everyone. It is an exchange of feelings and needs and develops from childhood to adulthood through natural language [1]. In this sense, language has the function of representing ideas about the world, adding values and concepts to communicative symbols, allowing face-to-face interpersonal interactions. When conveying a message, people use a language that, whether spoken, written, or signed, encompasses a system that expresses meaning [2].

C. Stephanidis et al. (Eds.): HCII 2023, CCIS 1833, pp. 411–417, 2023.
https://doi.org/10.1007/978-3-031-35992-7_56

With aging, certain cognitive abilities tend to decline. Some people may experience mild cognitive impairment, which makes it difficult to correctly execute some cognitive processes. However, there are many people who have a disability that prevents communication through natural language [3]. The most common problems faced by an older adult are related to communication and particularly to speech, among these are: dysarthria, apraxia, stuttering, voice disorders [4].

This phenomenon became even more visible during the COVID-19 pandemic, since family contact was lost as a precaution against contagion, creating greater vulnerability, since their abilities to take advantage of the opportunities offered by digital transformation are relatively lower than those of the youngest groups [5].

In this sense, communication through new technologies becomes a challenge for the elderly, given certain motor or visual restrictions; Hence, every time an older adult needs to communicate through text messages through the different existing services, it is complicated due to the imprecision of their movements or the lack of vision typical of their age, compared to interfaces with buttons or small texts not suitable for their reality. In general, the performance deficit of the elderly using technology is not due to a lack of experience or usability problems, but rather to their cognitive conditions [6].

Augmentative and Alternative Communication (AAC) technologies for people with communication needs within society have substantially increased expectations for participation and engagement in a wide range of settings [7, 8]. Computer solutions have been developed that include the use of iconographic symbols that support the communication of whoever requires it. Particularly, these systems have been used for social skills development in people with autism spectrum disorder or intellectual disabilities [9], such as the proposal of the Sc@ut communicators that include three types of language: pictograms, spoken language and animations that show gestures, and are especially intended for communicative learning. They are an attractive medium for training, increase motivation and facilitate communication for people with intellectual disabilities [10].

Despite advances in high-tech research, existing methods and technologies are still insufficient to meet the functional communication needs of older adults who need support. Hence, this research sought to consolidate the findings of current research on the intervention of specific AAC for these people. A systematic review was conducted to identify and assess relevant research.

2 Method

This research used literature systematic review methodology on augmentative and alternative communication, such as the use of pictograms and existing technologies, with the aim of understanding the topic analyzed, in order to synthesize the evaluated studies, contributing to automate and support the communication of older adults. The steps followed for the construction of the review were: definition of the research question, establishment of the inclusion and exclusion criteria through a bibliographic search, definition of the information to be extracted from the studies, evaluation of the included studies, results interpretation and review presentation [11].

To guide the research survey and discussion, the following research question was raised: What technologies, methods, strategies and tools are used for the implementation of AAC for older adults communication?

2.1 Research Strategy

For the articles survey, a period from 2013 was considered, in the following databases: Public Medicine Library (PubMed), Scientific Electronic Library Online (SciELO), Scopus (Elsevier) and Web of Science. A search was made for the descriptors in English: 'alternative and augmentative communication', 'elderly adults' and 'pictograms'. The terms used were combined with the Boolean AND operator in each database.

2.2 Inclusion Criteria

Full access articles available in the databases published in English, studies from the last 10 years (2013 to 2022) that addressed the topic of augmentative and/or alternative communication, older adults, and pictograms.

2.3 Exclusion Criteria

Duplicate articles, articles carried out with children, reviews, and those that were not available in open access in the databases were discarded.

2.4 Data Collection and Analysis

The articles were searched and identified, the titles and abstracts were evaluated, followed by the complete reading and the final selection of the articles by the authors, considering the inclusion and exclusion criteria proposed for the review.

3 Literature Revision

The systematic review protocol considered the choice of four digital libraries for the search. The authors searched for articles published from 2013, considering the studies that used augmentative and/or alternative communication for older adults and their impact on communication. With these selection and exclusion parameters, eight articles were included in the analysis.

From the search in the selected databases, 79 articles were found. Of these, 36 were excluded because the full text was not available and also because it was not in English. After reading the titles, 25 were discarded for not addressing the topic "augmentative and/or alternative communication" and 6 after reading the abstracts, for the same reason.

After the complete reading of the articles, one was excluded for not using the strategies of interest and one was a review work.

Regarding the country of publication, two were developed in the United Kingdom [12, 13] (25.0%) and two in South Africa [14, 15] (25.0%) and only one study was identified for each of the following countries: Japan [16], Australia [17], South Korea [18] and Italy [19]. Regarding the family environment, three [12, 14, 15] (37.5%) addressed issues of friendship, conversation as a couple and quality of life and two [17, 18] (25.0%), considered care in hospital environments.

Regarding the research participants, six studies (75.0%) were carried out with people with some communication disability, two studies (25.0%) with people without disabilities and two studies (25.0%) included support staff and family members.

Table 1. Characterization of the studies selected for this review (n = 8)

Ref	Document title	Author	Year	Country	Participants	Strategies	Results
[13]	A voice-input voice-output communication aid for people with severe speech impairment	Hawley et al.	2013	United Kingdom	People with dysarthria	Voice input and voice output communication support (VIVOCA)	The test highlighted some issues that limit the performance and usability of the device when applied in real use situations, with an average recognition accuracy of 67%
[16]	Comparison of Four Control Methods for a Five-Choice Assistive Technology	Halder et al.	2018	Japan	Healthy people	Comparison of two visual systems (a visual P300 brain-computer interface (BCI) and an eye tracker) and two non-visual systems (an auditory and a tactile P300)	The performance between the eye tracker and the visual BCI was strongly correlated, the correlation between the tactile and auditory BCI performance was less
[12]	Voice banking for people living with motor neurone disease: Views and expectations	Cave et al.	2021	United Kingdom	People living with motor neuron disease	Voice banking, voice that creates an approximation of the person's own voice	Preserving identity is the main motivation in decision-making for voice banking, which limited the decision to use it in the participants
[17]	An exploration of communication within active support for adults with high and low support needs	Iacono et al.	2019	Australia	People living in group homes	Communication for people in group homes with high and low support needs	Receiving good communication was associated with higher levels of engagement

(*continued*)

Table 1. (*continued*)

Ref	Document title	Author	Year	Country	Participants	Strategies	Results
[14]	The self-determined and partner-predicted topic preferences of adults with aphasia	Beringer et al.	2013	South Africa	People with aphasia	The Talking Mats™ framework was used to score 37 topics	Adults with moderate to severe aphasia in this study were able to communicate their topic preferences when provided with the Talking Mats™ framework
[15]	Friendship Experiences of Young Adults Who Use Augmentative and Alternative Communication	Dada et al.	2022	South Africa	People with physical disabilities	Semi-structured interviews	Four themes were identified, namely companionship, friendship quality, the desire for independence, and the role of technology in mediating friendships
[18]	The Effect of AAC Display Types on Message Production and Its Relationship with Reading Ability in Patients with Cognitive-Communication Disorders	Kim et al.	2022	South Korea	Patients with cerebrovascular accidents	Message production capabilities were examined by measuring accuracy scores and response times in three AAC viewing conditions	The graphic symbol-based GRID showed significantly high accuracy scores and short response time compared to the text-based VSD
[19]	Writing with the Eyes: The Effect of Age on Eye-Tracking Performance in Non-Disabled Adults and a Comparison with Bimanual Typing	Caligari et al.	2021	Italy	Healthy people	Eye tracking communication devices and a standard keyboard were used	Age had a negative impact on performance: as age increased, typing speed decreased and error rate increased

Three studies used low-tech strategies (37.5%) and referred to pencil, paper, gestures, and pictograms. Six studies (75.0%) used high-tech strategies, with voice-generating devices, eye tracking, and software. The synthesis of the articles covers the following data: author, year, country of publication, title, participants, strategies used and results, which are presented in Table 1.

4 Discussion and Conclusions

From the articles analyzed, it was possible to identify that the impossibility of verbal communication compromises the family and social relationship, which generates frustration. The use of augmentative and alternative communication technologies is an effective communication option in the environment of people with communication problems, generating an improvement in their quality of life, this goes in harmony with the intervention that should consider strategies functional and non-linguistic clues for communication [20].

The use of high-tech tools employs symbolic means in association with resources, such as voice-generating devices, specific software, and some resources that have automatic scanning [1, 7]. Evidence suggests that these tools increase communication, improve quality of life and psycho-emotional issues, in addition to allowing communication exchanges between the patient and their environment [3, 10].

Acknowledgment. The authors would like to thank the Corporación Ecuatoriana para el Desarrollo de la Investigación y Academia-CEDIA for their contribution in innovation, through the "FONDO I+D+i" projects, especially the project I+D+I-XVII-2023-61, "Análisis y aplicación de formas de interacción humano – computador (HCI) en una herramienta tecnológica de comunicación aumentativa y alternativa basada en pictogramas, que ayude a las personas adultas mayores a comunicarse con su entorno"; also the Universidad Tecnológica Indoamérica, Universidad de Cuenca, Universidad de las Fuerzas Armadas and Universidad del Azuay for the support for the development of this work.

References

1. Carvalho, D., Queiroz, Í., Araújo, D., Barbosa, S., Carvalho, V., Carvalho, S.: Augmentative and alternative communication with adults and elderly in the hospital environment: an integrative literature review. Rev. CEFAC **22**(5), e16019 (2020)
2. Moreschi, C.L., Almeida, M.A.: A comunicação alternativa como procedimento de desenvolvimento de habilidades comunicativas. Rev. Bras. Educ. Espec. **18**(4), 661–676 (2012). https://doi.org/10.1590/S1413-65382012000400009
3. Hervás, R., Bautista, S., Méndez, G., Galván, P., Gervás, P.: Predictive composition of pictogram messages for users with autism. J. Ambient Intell. Hum. Comput. **11**(11), 5649–5664 (2020). https://doi.org/10.1007/s12652-020-01925-z
4. MedlinePlus. Deterioro del lenguaje en adultos (2023). https://medlineplus.gov/spanish/ency/article/003204.htm
5. BBVA. La brecha digital que desconecta a nuestros mayores en la crisis del coronavirus (2020). https://www.bbva.com/es/es/la-brecha-digital-que-desconecta-a-nuestros-mayores-en-la-crisis-del-coronavirus/. [Último acceso: 15 12 2022]
6. Callari, T.C., Ciairano, S., Re, A.: Elderly-technology interaction: accessibility and acceptability of technological devices promoting motor and cognitive training. Work **41**, 362–369 (2012). https://doi.org/10.3233/WOR-2012-0183-362
7. Light, J., et al: Challenges and opportunities in augmentative and alternative communication: Research and technology development to enhance communication and participation for individuals with complex communication needs. Augmen. Altern. Commun. **35**(1), 1–12 (2019)

8. Fager, S.K., Fried-Oken, M., Jakobs, T., Beukelman, D.R.: New and emerging access technologies for adults with complex communication needs and severe motor impairments: State of the science. Augmen. Altern. Commun. 35(1), 13–25 (2019). https://doi.org/10.1080/07434618.2018.1556730

9. Morin, K.L., et al.: A systematic quality review of high-tech AAC interventions as an evidence-based practice. Augmen. Altern. Commun. (Baltimore, Md.: 1985) 34(2), 104–117 (2018)

10. Rodríguez-Fórtiz, M.: Sc@ut: developing adapted communicators for special education. Procedia – Soc. Behav. Sci. 1(1), 1348–1352 (2009)

11. Mendes, K. Silveira, R., Galvão, C.: Revisão integrativa: método de pesquisa para a incorporação de evidências na saúde e na enfermagem. Texto contexto enferm 17(4), 758–764 (2008)

12. Cave, R., Bloch, S.: Voice banking for people living with motor neurone disease: views and expectations. Int. J. Lang. Commun. Disorders 56(1), 116–129 (2021)

13. Hawley, M.S., et al.: A voice-input voice-output communication aid for people with severe speech impairment. IEEE Trans. Neural Syst. Rehabil. Eng. 21(1), 23–31 (2013). https://doi.org/10.1109/TNSRE.2012.2209678

14. Beringer, A., Tönsing, K., Bornman, J.: The self-determined and partner-predicted topic preferences of adults with aphasia. Aphasiology 27(2), 227–251 (2013). https://doi.org/10.1080/02687038.2012.744809

15. Dada, S., Tonsing, K., Goldbart, J.: Friendship experiences of young adults who use augmentative and alternative communication. Int. J. Disabil. Develop. Educ. 69(3), 951–975 (2022). https://doi.org/10.1080/1034912X.2020.1746246

16. Halder, S., Takano, K., Kansaku, K.: Comparison of four control methods for a five-choice assistive technology. Front. Hum. Neurosci. 12,(2018). https://doi.org/10.3389/fnhum.2018.00228

17. Iacono, T., Bould, E., Beadle-Brown, J., Bigby, C.: An exploration of communication within active support for adults with high and low support needs. J. Appl. Res. Intellect. Disabil. 32(1), 61-70 (2019)

18. Kim, M., Shin, S.: The effect of AAC display types on message production and its relationship with reading ability in patients with cognitive-communication disorders. Commun. Sci. Disorders 27(1), 107–118 (2022)

19. Caligari, M., Giardini, M., Arcolin, I., Godi, M., Corna, S., Colombo, R.: Writing with the eyes: The effect of age on eye-tracking performance in non-disabled adults and a comparison with bimanual typing. Comput. Intell. Neurosc. 2021, 1–9 (2021). https://doi.org/10.1155/2021/9365199

20. von Tetzchner, S., Øvreeide, K., Jørgensen, K., Ormhaug, B., Oxholm, B., Warme, R.: Acquisition of graphic communication by a young girl without comprehension of spoken language. Disabil. Rehabil. 26(21), 1335–1346 (2004)

Technology to Reduce Social Isolation Among Older Adults: A Move from Digital to Tangible

Pallabi Bhowmick⬥ and Erik Stolterman Bergqvist(✉)⬥

Indiana University, Bloomington, IN 47405, USA
{pbhowmic,estolter}@iu.edu

Abstract. The population of older adults (aged 65+) is rapidly increasing worldwide and about one in four older adults are considered to be socially isolated in USA alone. It is associated with increased risk of depression, dementia, heart disease, and premature mortality. The COVID-19 pandemic and social distancing has only increased the risk of isolation. Digital technologies have made communication easier, but traditional screen-based interfaces are not suitable for older adults because they do not offer intuitive, accessible mediums of communication. This results in a steeper learning curve, which eventually leads to non-adoption. Researchers have explored tangible user interface design in the past, but only a few have explored its potential for older adults. This paper presents a comprehensive review of previous research efforts that concentrate on enhancing social connections among older adults. Additionally, it delves into the exploration of tangible user interfaces as a promising alternative solution. We conclude the paper with a framework that suggests design considerations for HCI researchers designing tangible user interfaces for older adults to improve social connection.

Keywords: older adult · social isolation · tangible user interface

1 Introduction

Older adults are the fastest-growing population in the United States [1]. According to a recent report from National Academies of Engineering, Sciences, and Medicine (NASEM), about one in four older adults report of social isolation in the US [2]. Social isolation is associated with poor physical and mental health leading to depression, heart diseases, and an increased risk of premature mortality [3]. The Harvard Longitudinal Study of Adult Development [4], which is almost 80 years old and one of the world's longest studies, has showed that the key to quality of life is embracing community and maintaining meaningful social contacts. HCI researchers have historically investigated the use of social technologies, which are digital technologies used by people to interact socially, for improving communication and reducing isolation. While social technologies are associated with better subjective health and well-being [5], they are not developed keeping the needs of older adults in mind. Digital screen-based user

C. Stephanidis et al. (Eds.): HCII 2023, CCIS 1833, pp. 418–425, 2023.
https://doi.org/10.1007/978-3-031-35992-7_57

interfaces do not offer intuitive, accessible mediums of communication, making it difficult for older adults to learn and use them [6].

Additionally, older adults prefer to age independently in their own homes. According to the latest American Association of Retired Persons (AARP) survey, older adults express aging in place as a primary goal [7]. Independence, in case of older adults, is often guided by agency. Aging-in-place technologies include sensor-equipped smart homes [8], digital location tracking apps in smartphones [9] to track movements, physical in-home systems that share well-being information [15], or wearables to monitor various health parameters [10]. However, such passive monitoring takes away agency and control from older adults, which is dehumanizing [11]. Furthermore, institutionalization incurs a significant increase in cost of care, and older adults living in care facilities experience more psychological decline, reduced autonomy, and quality of life [12].

There is a need to address bias and ageism in technology design for older adults by giving back agency to older adults and making them active users of technology, instead of mere passive recipients of care. In this paper that builds on a preliminary review [13], we will investigate how tangible technologies can provide a familiar, intuitive interface for older adults, help older adults become active users of technology to stay connected with loved ones, reduce social isolation, and increase technology adoption.

2 Methodology

We conduct a scoping review motivated by the following research question - a) What are the challenges with existing technologies for older adults to address isolation? b) How can tangible technologies potentially emerge as an alternate solution? The ACM Digital Library was searched with the keywords, *("older adult" OR "elder" OR "senior" OR "aged") AND ("isolation" OR "loneliness")* since the year 2000, which returned 3502 results. Post title, abstract, and full text screening, we further excluded all those papers that did not describe any technology use, design, or development. Papers were then filtered based on whether the technologies were tangible or not. Screen-based technologies that did not include a physical component that older adults could interact with, were excluded. We found 115 papers, out of which only 23 papers [Table 1] focused on using tangible user interfaces primarily for increasing social interaction among older adults.

3 Existing Research on Tangible Technologies

In this section, we will discuss our results from the scoping review on existing tangible technologies to improve social connection among older adults.

The influential paper on "Tangible Bits" by Ishii et al. [14] opened new opportunities of interaction with tangible, physical objects. Their paper first proposed a move beyond the dominant Graphical User Interface (GUI) to Tangible User Interface (TUI) by augmenting real physical objects with digital information. Digital Family Portrait [15] and CareNet [16] were one-way communication systems, and early works that sparked interest in tangible technologies for improving social communication of older adults with their families. ABRA system [17]

Table 1. List of Existing Work on Tangible Technologies to Improve Social Connection among Older Adults.

Paper Title	Author(s)
Digital Family Portraits: Supporting Peace of Mind for Extended Family Members	Mynatt et al. [15]
Casablanca: Designing Social Communication Devices for the Home	Hindus et al. [31]
The CareNet Display: Lessons Learned from an In Home Evaluation of an Ambient Display	Consolvo et al. [16]
Shared Family Calendars: Promoting Symmetry and Accessibility	Plaisant et al. [19]
MoviPill: Improving Medication Compliance for Elders Using a Mobile Persuasive Social Game	Oliveira et al. [25]
Affect- and Behaviour-related Assistance for Families in the Home Environment	Peter et al. [17]
Tangible Interfaces As a Chance for Higher Technology Acceptance by the Elderly	Spreicer et al. [32]
Social Yoga Mats: Designing for Exercising/Socializing Synergy	Nagargoje et al. [24]
Stitchtures: Interactive Art Installations for Social Interventions in Retirement Communities	Rebola et al. [33]
Audio-enhanced Paper Photos: Encouraging Social Interaction at Age 105	Piper et al. [34]
Bridge: Senior Citizen Care Through Facilitating Reciprocal Awareness	Choudhury et al. [35]
Sympathetic Devices: Designing Technologies for Older Adults	Rebola et al. [36]
From Checking on to Checking in: Designing for Low Socio-economic Status Older Adults	Arreola et al. [22]
SonicAIR: Supporting Independent Living with Reciprocal Ambient Audio Awareness	Baharin et al. [21]
BUMP: Bridging Unmet Modes of Participation	Chu et al. [18]
Promoting Active Aging with a Paper-based SNS Application	Cornejo et al. [37]
Sensor-based and Tangible Interaction with a TV Community Platform for Seniors	Herrmanny et al. [23]
Augmenting Everyday Artefacts to Support Social Interaction Among Senior Peers	Nazzi et al. [38]
Towards an Analysis Framework of Technology Habituation by Older Users	Soro et al. [27]
Nettle: An Exploration of Communication Interface Design for Older Adults	Fox et al. [28]
The multisensory interactive window: immersive experiences for the elderly	Angelini et al. [30]
Supporting intergenerational memento storytelling for older adults through a tangible display: a case study	Li et al. [26]
InSight: Kick-Starting Communications for Elderlies Ageing in Place	Zhide et al. [20]

and BUMP [18] were also one-way systems that allowed family to received data on older family members through passive sensing. But, one-way communication takes away agency from older adults because older adults are not allowed to actively use the technology to receive well-being information of their family.

Shared paper calendars [19] allowed older adults to write with a digital pen and transfer data into a digital format in a two-way exchange. InSight [20] and SonicAIR [21] offered two-way information sharing of older adults with family members and caregivers. The Check-in Tree [22] offered a peer-to-peer morning check-in functionality to connect older adults with their loved ones. Other research-based systems such as, Smart TV [23], Social Yoga Mats [24], and MoviPill [25] facilitated the creation of a social circle for older adults. Memento [26] facilitated inter-generational communication, while Messaging Kettle [27], a smart communicating device and Nettle [28] improved social connection of older adults over a mundane, routine task of making tea.

4   Findings

This work is a scoping review to explore the potential of tangible user interfaces for the older adult population. In this section, we will discuss the benefits tangible user interfaces offer over digital user interfaces and what makes tangible user interfaces particularly suited for older adults. However, it may be observed that we found only 23 papers that used tangible technologies to improve social connection for older adults. Considering the idea of tangible user interfaces were introduced 20 years earlier, the results indicate lack of evidence in this particular area of research. We present a framework (Fig. 1) suggesting design considerations for HCI researchers developing tangible technologies for facilitating social connection for older adults. We argue that there is a need for more integrated work on reducing social isolation for older adults with the use of tangible technologies. Such tangible systems improve social connectedness, address ageism by restoring agency, meet accessibility and aesthetic needs, thereby encouraging technology adoption. They also empower older adults to maintain their independence, instill in them a strong sense of community, and improve quality of life.

Functional Qualities. The functional qualities of a system can be defined as the attributes that determine the system's ability to carry out its intended tasks or functions effectively. These qualities relate to the system's performance and intended capabilities, and serve as indicators of whether the system functions as intended. In essence, they measure the system's affordances or its ability to perform in the manner it was designed to.

Social Exchange Theory [29] states that isolation occurs from an unequal exchange of "investments and returns". It is important to ensure that the system offers a two-way exchange of information in an asynchronous manner between older adults and their families and friends. As much as family members want to know about the older member of the family's well-being, the emotion is entirely reciprocal. Furthermore, asynchronous exchange ensures practicality and facilitates knowledge sharing despite schedule and time zone differences. Tangible

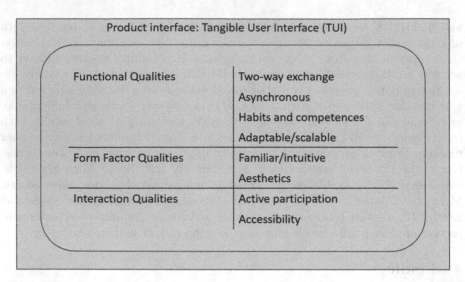

Fig. 1. Framework for designing tangible technologies for older adults to improve social connection.

systems must also leverage existing habits and competences of older adults. Technologies that leveraging existing habits such as making tea or picking up newspaper, are easier to integrate in daily routine. Finally, tangible technologies should be customizable and scalable to adapt to older adults' changing needs or preferences. USe of Maker technologies could be beneficial in this regard.

Form Factor Qualities. Form factor refers to the physical features, size, shape, and design of the system. It is a critical aspect that can affect the ergonomics and usability of a system, and can also influence the system performance.

One of the affordances of tangible systems is its ability to use off-the-shelf materials or everyday objects as user interfaces. This aspect of tangible interfaces is highly beneficial for older adults in particular because this can help achieve familiarity in user interface design. A familiar interface is easy to learn and adopt. Intuitiveness stems from familiarity and results in a shorter learning curve, thereby facilitating quicker integration and adoption. Additionally, this can also address aesthetic needs of older adults. Age-related declines do not affect an older adult's sense of aesthetics. Tangible technologies can be designed keeping the aesthetic needs of older adults in mind because they can leverage the use of any physical artifacts or common objects as interfaces.

Interaction Qualities. Interaction qualities refer to the desirable attributes of the system that support and enhance the user experience. These qualities are characteristics that are required to ensure the user's needs and goals are met when it comes to interacting with the user interface of the system. Incorporating these qualities into the design process can lead to more successful and satisfying interactions between users and systems.

Technology design should include older adults as active participants as end users of technology. One-way passive monitoring is demeaning and takes away agency. It reduces self-esteem and independence. By allowing older adults to be end users of the system facilitates a non-stigmatizing technology design, which in turn, can improve technology adoption. Finally, researchers have previously used childlike buttons and fonts to make digital technologies more accessible. But, such designs again cater to bias and ageism, and should be avoided. Switching to tangible everyday interfaces that leverage natural gestures, is therefore, a more dignified solution.

References

1. United States Census Bureau. 2018. Older People Projected to Outnumber Children for First Time in U.S. History. Accessed 18 May 2022. https://www.census.gov/newsroom/press-releases/2018/cb18-41-population-projections.html
2. Engineering National Academies of Sciences and Medicine. Social isolation and loneliness in older adults: Opportunities for the health care system. National Academies Press (2020)
3. Steptoe, A., Shankar, A., Demakakos, P., Wardle, J.: Social isolation, loneliness, and all-cause mortality in older men and women. Proc. Natl. Acad. Sci. **110**(15), 5797–5801 (2013)
4. Mitchell, J.F.: Aging well: surprising guideposts to a happier life from the landmark harvard study of adult development. Am. J. Psychiat. **161**(1), 178–179 (2004)
5. Chopik, W.J.: The benefits of social technology use among older adults are mediated by reduced loneliness. Cyberpsychol. Behav. Social Netw. **19**(9), 551–556 (2016)
6. Neves, B.B., Franz, R.L., Munteanu, C., Baecker, R.: Adoption and feasibility of a communication app to enhance social connectedness amongst frail institutionalized oldest old: an embedded case study. Inf. Commun. Soc. **21**(11), 1681–1699 (2018)
7. Vasold, K., Binette, J.: 2018 home and community preferences: a national survey of adults ages 18-Plus. AARP Research (2019). Accessed 7 Feb 2020. https://www.aarp.org/research/topics/community/info-2018/2018home-community-preference.html
8. Morris, M.E., et al.: Smart-home technologies to assist older people to live well at home. J. Aging Sci. **1**(1), 1–9 (2013)
9. Saare, M.A., Hussain, A., Jasim, O.M., Mahdi, A.A.: Usability evaluation of mobile tracking applications: a systematic review. Int. J. Interact. Mob. Technol. **14**(5), 119–128 (2020)
10. Nath, R.K., Thapliyal, H.: Wearable health monitoring system for older adults in a smart home environment. In: 2021 IEEE Computer Society Annual Symposium on VLSI (ISVLSI), pp. 390–395. IEEE (2021)
11. Lorenzen-Huber, L., Boutain, M., Camp, L.J., Shankar, K., Connelly, K.H.: Privacy, technology, and aging: a proposed framework. Ageing Int. **36**(2), 232–252 (2011)
12. González-Colaço Harmand, M., et al.: Cognitive decline after entering a nursing home: a 22-year follow-up study of institutionalized and noninstitutionalized elderly people. J. Am. Med. Direct. Assoc. **15**(7), 504–508 (2014)

13. Bhowmick, P., Stolterman, E.: Exploring tangible user interface design for social connection among older adults: a preliminary review. In: Extended Abstracts of the 2023 CHI Conference on Human Factors in Computing Systems, pp. 1–9 (2023)

14. Ishii, H., Ullmer, B.: Tangible bits: towards seamless interfaces between people, bits and atoms. In: Proceedings of the ACM SIGCHI Conference on Human Factors in Computing Systems, pp. 234–241 (1997)

15. Mynatt, E.D., Rowan, J., Craighill, S., Jacobs, A.: Digital family portraits: supporting peace of mind for extended family members. In Proceedings of the SIGCHI Conference on Human Factors in Computing Systems, pp. 333–340 (2001)

16. Consolvo, S., Roessler, P., Shelton, B.E.: The CareNet display: lessons learned from an in home evaluation of an ambient display. In: Davies, N., Mynatt, E.D., Siio, I. (eds.) UbiComp 2004. LNCS, vol. 3205, pp. 1–17. Springer, Heidelberg (2004). https://doi.org/10.1007/978-3-540-30119-6_1

17. Peter, C., Bieber, G., Urban, B.: Afect-and behaviourrelated assistance for families in the home environment. In: Proceedings of the 3rd International Conference on PErvasive Technologies Related to Assistive Environments, pp. 1–5 (2010)

18. Chu, C., Rebola, C.B., Kao, J.: BUMP: bridging unmet modes of participation. In: Proceedings of the 2015 British HCI Conference, pp. 261–262 (2015)

19. Plaisant, C., Clamage, A., Hutchinson, H.B., Bederson, B.B., Druin, A.: Shared family calendars: promoting symmetry and accessibility. ACM Trans. Comput.-Hum. Interact. (TOCHI) 13(3), 313–346 (2006)

20. Loh, Z., Zhang, E., Lim, Z.Y.: InSight: kick-starting communications for elderlies ageing in place. In: Proceedings of the 33rd Annual ACM Conference Extended Abstracts on Human Factors in Computing Systems, pp. 25–30 (2015)

21. Baharin, H., Viller, S., Rintel, S.: SonicAIR: supporting independent living with reciprocal ambient audio awareness. ACM Trans. Comput.-Hum. Interact. (TOCHI) 22(4), 1–23 (2015)

22. Arreola, I., Morris, Z., Francisco, M., Connelly, K., Caine, K., White, G.: From checking on to checking: designing for low socio-economic status older adults. In: Proceedings of the SIGCHI Conference on Human Factors in Computing Systems, pp. 1933–1936 (2014)

23. Herrmanny, K., Gözüyasli, L., Deja, D., Ziegler, J.: Sensor-based and tangible interaction with a TV community platform for seniors. In: Proceedings of the 7th ACM SIGCHI Symposium on Engineering Interactive Computing Systems, pp. 180–189 (2015)

24. Nagargoje, A., Maybach, K., Sokoler, T.: Social yoga mats: designing for exercising/socializing synergy. In: Proceedings of the Sixth International Conference on Tangible, Embedded and Embodied Interaction, pp. 87–90 (2012)

25. De Oliveira, R., Cherubini, M., Oliver, N.: MoviPill: improving medication compliance for elders using a mobile persuasive social game. In: Proceedings of the 12th ACM International Conference on Ubiquitous Computing, pp. 251–260 (2010)

26. Li, C., Hu, J., Hengeveld, B., Hummels, C.: Supporting intergenerational memento storytelling for older adults through a tangible display: a case study. Pers. Ubiq. Comput. 26, 1–25 (2020)

27. Soro, A., Brereton, M., Roe, P.: Towards an analysis framework of technology habituation by older users. In: Proceedings of the 2016 ACM Conference on Designing Interactive Systems, pp. 1021–1033 (2016)

28. Fox, A.M.: Nettle: an exploration of communication interface design for older adults. In: Proceedings of the Twelfth International Conference on Tangible, Embedded, and Embodied Interaction, pp. 506–510 (2018)

29. Hooyman, N.R., Kiyak, H.A.: Social Gerontology: A Multidisciplinary Perspective. Pearson Education, Boston (2008)
30. Angelini, L., Caon, M., Couture, N., Khaled, O.A., Mugellini, E.: The multisensory interactive window: immersive experiences for the elderly. In: Adjunct Proceedings of the 2015 ACM International Joint Conference on Pervasive and Ubiquitous Computing and Proceedings of the 2015 ACM International Symposium on Wearable Computers, pp. 963–968 (2015)
31. Hindus, D., Mainwaring, S.D., Leduc, N., Hagström, A.E., Bayley, O.: Casablanca: designing social communication devices for the home. In: Proceedings of the SIGCHI Conference on Human Factors in Computing Systems, pp. 325–332 (2001)
32. Spreicer, W.: Tangible interfaces as a chance for higher technology acceptance by the elderly. In: Proceedings of the 12th International Conference on Computer Systems and Technologies, pp. 311–316 (2011)
33. Rebola, C.B., Vela, P.A., Palacio, J., Ogunmakin, G., Saurus, C.: Stitchtures: interactive art installations for social interventions in retirement communities. In: Proceedings of the 30th ACM International Conference on Design of Communication, pp. 71–78 (2012)
34. Piper, A.M., Weibel, N., Hollan, J.: Audio-enhanced paper photos: encouraging social interaction at age 105. In: Proceedings of the 2013 Conference on Computer Supported Cooperative Work, pp. 215–224 (2013)
35. Choudhury, P.R., Patel, K., Chakravarty, A., Saraf, A., Bagalkot, N.: Bridge: senior citizen care through facilitating reciprocal awareness. In: Proceedings of the 11th Asia Pacific Conference on Computer Human Interaction, pp. 195–198 (2013)
36. Rebola, C.B., Jones, B.: Sympathetic devices: designing technologies for older adults. In: Proceedings of the 31st ACM International Conference on Design of Communication, pp. 151–156 (2013)
37. Cornejo, R., Weibel, N., Tentori, M., Favela, J.: Promoting active aging with a paper-based SNS application. In: 2015 9th International Conference on Pervasive Computing Technologies for Healthcare (PervasiveHealth), pp. 209–212. IEEE (2015)
38. Nazzi, E., Sokoler, T.: Augmenting everyday artefacts to support social interaction among senior peers. In: Proceedings of the 8th ACM International Conference on PErvasive Technologies Related to Assistive Environments, pp. 1–8 (2015)

Towards Augmented Reality-Based and Social Robot-Based Social Integration of Older Adults: A User Requirements Analysis

Melisa Conde⬚, Veronika Mikhailova⬚, and Nicola Döring⁽⊠⁾ ⬚

Technische Universität Ilmenau, Ehrenbergstr. 29, 98693 Ilmenau, Germany
`nicola.doering@tu-ilmenau.de`

Abstract. Background: Older adults are at risk of social isolation and loneliness. As part of the CO-HUMANICS (Co-Presence of Humans and Interactive Companions for Seniors) project, augmented reality (AR)-based and telepresence robot-based systems are to be developed to support social integration of older adults.

Aim: Following a human-centered approach, this study aims to identify requirements of older adults towards AR-based (RQ1) and telepresence robot-based (RQ2) communication that fosters social integration.

Methods: Semi-structured individual interviews were conducted between May and October 2022 with N = 30 older adults (60–74 years old, 37% women) from Germany. Participants were presented with storyboard illustrations of hypothetical interpersonal communication scenarios involving an AR system and a telepresence robot and gave their detailed evaluations (mean interview duration 43 min).

Results: Older adults had ambivalent and nuanced requirements for an AR system and a telepresence robot. Technology-specific and general requirements emerged from the data and were grouped into four dimensions: 1) technological requirements (ease of use, effortless contact initiation, realistic avatar design, intuitive movement control, anthropomorphism, and robot size), 2) emotional requirements (warmth, intimacy, companionship, and empowerment), 3) social requirements (potential for joint activities, multiparty interaction, and multitasking), and 4) administrative requirements (privacy, data protection, and affordability).

Conclusions: Older adults recognized the potential of AR systems and telepresence robots to support their social integration; however, ease of use, privacy and data protection issues, and affordability remain an obstacle for technology acceptance.

Keywords: Innovative technologies · Ageing · Human-centered design · Telepresence robot · AR

1 Introduction

It is estimated that by 2030, one in six people in the world will be aged 60 years or over [1]. The ageing process can be accompanied by life changes that bring on social isolation or feelings of loneliness among older adults: widowhood, death of friends and relatives,

C. Stephanidis et al. (Eds.): HCII 2023, CCIS 1833, pp. 426–432, 2023.
https://doi.org/10.1007/978-3-031-35992-7_58

retirement, reduced mobility, and health issues, among others [2, 3]. Therefore, several potential solutions aimed at fostering the *social integration* of older adults are being developed and researched. Technology-based interventions carried out by researchers and self-directed behaviors carried out by older adults have shown potential for loneliness and social isolation reduction in old age [4]. In consequence, studies focusing on communication mediated by innovative technologies –such as *augmented reality (AR)* and *telepresence robots*– are increasingly becoming part of the research landscape [5, 6]. However, data show technologies developed for older adults are often discarded due to factors such as stigmatization or lack of adaptiveness to physical and cognitive changes that come with age [7]. To overcome this technology adoption barrier, user-centered design is paramount when creating technologies for the ageing population. Considering individual characteristics of older adults (both physical and psychological) and adapting technologies to their values, has proven effective for technology acceptance [8, 9]. It is against this backdrop that the current study aims at identifying the requirements older adults have towards AR-based and telepresence robot-based interpersonal communication that fosters social integration.

1.1 Augmented Reality for Older Adults

Augmented reality (AR) is a technological system that incorporates virtual objects into the real world in real time as the user experiences them [10]. These objects can range from a simple shape to the real-time rendering of another person ("avatar"), with whom the user can interact socially via an AR headset [11]. Hence, AR systems can enable vivid interpersonal communication over distance.

Recent studies already highlighted potential benefits that AR can provide for the wellbeing of older adults [12], and a number of AR applications have been developed to foster their independence. These applications mostly address the physical [13] and cognitive [14] health of older adults, or they provide assistance in everyday activities such as cooking or cleaning [15]. Social features of AR, however, remain under-researched for this target group, even though experimental studies with younger adults showed AR's overall potential to improve social connectedness among individuals [16]. To address this research gap, the specific requirements of older adults towards AR-based interpersonal communication need to be explored. Therefore, the present study aims at answering the following research question (RQ1):

What requirements do older adults have for innovative interpersonal communication via an augmented reality (AR) system to be developed?

1.2 Social Robotics for Older Adults

Social robots are robots that interact with ordinary users and have capabilities to assist them in everyday life [17]. Telepresence robots are a subset of social robots that are designed to enable interpersonal communication over distance. Telepresence robots consist of a remotely controllable mobile platform with video conferencing equipment that allows remote users to move around a local environment and interact socially with others [18].

Telepresence robots are being increasingly used to provide support, promote healthy ageing, and foster the social wellbeing of older adults [19, 20]. Robot technology can connect older adults to social networks, such as their relatives, friends, and healthcare workers [17]. Previous studies have tested telepresence robots as tools to help social inclusion of older people with positive results [21–23].

Nevertheless, technology acceptance among the older population is still a challenge [7]. To increase the acceptance of robots, researchers are now employing human-centered approaches that invite older adults into the design and evaluation process [24]. In line with this human-centered approach, the present study aims at answering the following research question (RQ2):

What requirements do older adults have for innovative interpersonal communication via a telepresence robot to be developed?

2 Methods

An interview study with $N = 30$ older adults (60–74 years old, $M_{age} = 67.1$, $SD_{age} = 4.3$, 37% women) living in Germany was conducted between May and October 2022. Participants were active senior citizens without cognitive impairments and all of them signed an informed consent form. The study was granted approval by the ethics committee of Technische Universität Ilmenau, Germany, on July 19, 2021, and was pre-registered through the Center of Open Science (https://osf.io/fxp6r/). The individual, semi-structured interviews had an average duration of 43 min.

Participants were asked about their current use of communication technologies and their potential use of innovative communication technologies, namely AR systems and telepresence robots. To familiarize older adults with the innovative technologies, the use of an AR system and a telepresence robot were presented through storyboard illustrations that visually depicted a hypothetical interpersonal communication scenario between a grandparent and an adult grandchild. Each participant viewed 2 storyboards, one from the grandparent's and one from the grandchild's perspective. Women were shown an older female and men an older male character (see Fig. 1).

Fig. 1. Excerpts from storyboard illustrations depicting AR-based and telepresence robot-based grandparent-grandchild communication scenarios.

Interviews were audio-recorded, transcribed, and anonymized. Subsequently, several rounds of thematic coding of the transcripts were done with the software MAXQDA.

3 Results

Participants had technology-specific and general requirements for the AR system and the telepresence robot. Four requirement dimensions emerged from the coded interviews: 1) technological, 2) emotional, 3) social, and 4) administrative. A summary of all main requirements included in each dimension can be seen in Table 1.

Table 1. Requirements of older adults for an AR system and a telepresence robot.

Dimension	AR requirements	Telepresence robot requirements
Technological	Ease of use Effortless contact initiation Realistic avatar design	Ease of use Intuitive movement control Anthropomorphic medium-sized
Emotional	Warmth Intimacy	Companionship Empowerment
Social	Joint activities Multiparty interaction	Joint activities Multitasking
Administrative	Privacy/data protection Affordability	Privacy/data protection Affordability

3.1 Technology-Specific Requirements for an AR System

To answer RQ 1, technology-specific requirements related to the AR-system were collected. The very term "augmented reality" was not familiar to older adults, therefore the requirements for the AR-system centered around the emotional response to the presented scenarios. Apart from general concerns regarding wearability of AR headsets and their compatibility with health-related aids (e.g., hearing device or glasses), participants expressed doubts that AR-based communication will fulfill their requirements for intimacy and warmth during mediated communication: *"If I want to have contact, then I want to have contact the way I see you now. The way I can look into your eyes. That would be important to me"* (male participant, 72 years old).

In connection to this, participants expressed the requirement of realistic avatar design. Having an avatar that would look as similar to the real person as possible would help them feel more comfortable during AR-based communication, as would the possibility to move around the room freely without any wires attached to the headset and the option to initiate contact in an effortless manner. The potential for interacting with several avatars at once also added value to the AR-based communication in the eyes of older adults: *"It's like a virtual family reunion. That's really cool, I like it"* (male participant, 68 years old).

3.2   Technology-Specific Requirements for a Telepresence Robot

To answer RQ 2, technology-specific requirements related to telepresence robots were collected. All participants had previous knowledge of robots mostly acquired from different fictional and non-fictional media. Furthermore, all of them were acquainted with videoconferencing applications and most of them had first-hand experience with them. Given this familiarity with robots and their functions, older people had very specific requirements related to size and form: anthropomorphic, medium sized robots were preferred: *"It must be a robot that doesn't take up too much space. Not too big, not too small"* (female participant, 61 years old). Additionally, the movement control of the robot was expected to be intuitive as participants associated a sense of empowerment with their ability to control the robot independently.

Related to anthropomorphism was the perception that a telepresence robot that resembles a human could serve as a companion and help against loneliness: *"When a machine like that scurries around in your house [...] then you have the feeling that there is someone else. I don't necessarily have to hug it, but you have the feeling [...] 'I am not alone here'"* (male participant, 68 years old). The ability to communicate with others while performing daily activities was also perceived by older adults as an attractive function.

3.3   General Technology Requirements

Older adults expressed concerns regarding ease of use and wished for both technologies to be as effortless to operate as possible: *"I know it works when I turn it on and I don't have to do much. There's always a lot of talk about 'it's very simple, you plug it in, and it works', but it's not"* (male participant, 62 years old). Participants also expressed doubts about the safety of innovative technologies in areas such as privacy and data protection: *"Can someone hack into it [the robot]? [Then they] can basically explore my apartment with it"* (female participant, 61 years old). The topic of affordability was also raised, since AR systems and telepresence robots were perceived by older people as very expensive devices beyond the budget of the general population.

Finally, the possibility of engaging in joint activities with loved ones (conversations, meals, virtual celebrations, etc.) was highly valued in both the AR system and the telepresence robot. Older adults saw potential in both technologies to foster social contact and, therefore, social integration in older age: *"[I would use the robot] with my grandchild [...] while cooking food, talking about school [...]. We do math homework together, maybe it would also be possible to do that"* (female participant, 63 years old).

4   Discussion

Older people have technological, emotional, social, and administrative requirements for AR systems and telepresence robots.

Specific requirements for an AR system were related to the technology fulfilling the need for warmth and intimacy during communication while conveying others through realistic avatars. This is in line with studies by Lee et al. [12] and Puri et al. [25] showing AR can provide older people with an emotionally rich communication experience and stressing older adults' preference of realistic avatars to represent themselves.

Since older adults were already familiar with the type of mediated communication provided by a telepresence robot (videoconferencing) their requirements were connected to the robot's appearance (size and anthropomorphism), the ease to control it, and the feeling of empowerment associated to its use. Accordingly, previous research has determined that the use of technology for communication purposes gives older adults a feeling of empowerment and control over their lives [26].

The most common general requirements were ease of use and social functions: Older people prefer technologies that are intuitive and allow for virtual social activities they can share with loved ones. On the other hand, two obstacles for technology acceptance still remain: privacy and data protection issues as well as affordability.

The scope of the requirements presented in this study confirms the importance of adapting technologies to their users and avoiding "one-size-fits-all" solutions as suggested in previous research [8, 9]. Older people recognize the potential of innovative technologies for social integration, but developers need to include this target group in the early stages of design in order to discover and address issues that can deter technology acceptance in the older generation.

Funding. This study is a part of the CO-HUMANICS (Co-Presence of Humans and Interactive Companions for Seniors) project. The CO-HUMANICS project is supported by the Carl-Zeiss-Stiftung within the framework of the "Durchbrüche 2020" program (https://www.carl-zeiss-sti ftung.de/programm/czs-durchbrueche).

References

1. World Health Organization. https://www.who.int/news-room/fact-sheets/detail/ageing-and-health. Accessed 15 Mar 2023
2. Chipps, J., Jarvis, M.A., Ramlall, S.: The effectiveness of e-interventions on reducing social isolation in older persons: a systematic review of systematic reviews. J. Telemed. Telecare **23**, 817–827 (2017). https://doi.org/10.1177/1357633X17733773
3. Dahlberg, L., Agahi, N., Lennartsson, C.: Lonelier than ever? Loneliness of older people over two decades. Arch. Gerontol. Geriatr. **75**, 96–103 (2018). https://doi.org/10.1016/j.archger.2017.11.004
4. Döring, N., et al.: Can communication technologies reduce loneliness and social isolation in older people? A scoping review of reviews. Int. J. Environ. Res. Public Health **19**, 11310 (2022). https://doi.org/10.3390/ijerph191811310
5. Döring, N., et al.: Digital media in intergenerational communication: status quo and future scenarios for the grandparent–grandchild relationship. Univers. Access Inf. Soc. (2022). https://doi.org/10.1007/s10209-022-00957-w
6. Tsai, T.-C., Hsu, Y.-L., Ma, A.-I., King, T., Wu, C.-H.: Developing a telepresence robot for interpersonal communication with the elderly in a home environment. Telemed. e-Health **13**, 407–424 (2007). https://doi.org/10.1089/tmj.2006.0068
7. Heerink, M., Kröse, B., Evers, V., Wielinga, B.: Assessing acceptance of assistive social agent technology by older adults: the Almere model. Int. J. Soc. Robot. **2**, 361–375 (2010). https://doi.org/10.1007/s12369-010-0068-5
8. Baisch, S., et al.: Acceptance of social robots by elder people: does psychosocial functioning matter? Int. J. Soc. Robot. **9**, 293–307 (2017). https://doi.org/10.1007/s12369-016-0392-5
9. Frennert, S., Östlund, B.: Review: seven matters of concern of social robots and older people. Int. J. Soc. Robot. **6**, 299–310 (2014). https://doi.org/10.1007/s12369-013-0225-8

10. Cipresso, P., Giglioli, I.A., Raya, M.A., Riva, G.: The past, present, and future of virtual and augmented reality research: a network and cluster analysis of the literature. Front. Psychol. **9**, 2086 (2018). https://doi.org/10.3389/fpsyg.2018.02086
11. Li, Y., Ch'ng, E., Cobb, S., See, S.: Presence and communication in hybrid virtual and augmented reality environments. PRESENCE: Virtual Augmented Reality **28**, 29–52 (2021). https://doi.org/10.1162/pres_a_00340
12. Lee, L.N., Kim, M.J., Hwang, W.J.: Potential of augmented reality and virtual reality technologies to promote wellbeing in older adults. Appl. Sci. **9**, 3556 (2019). https://doi.org/10.3390/app9173556
13. Mostajeran, F., Steinicke, F., Ariza Nunez, O.J., Gatsios, D., Fotiadis, D.: Augmented reality for older adults: exploring acceptability of virtual coaches for home-based balance training in an aging population. In: Proceedings of the 2020 CHI Conference on Human Factors in Computing Systems (2020). https://doi.org/10.1145/3313831.3376565
14. Lee, I.-J., Chen, C.-H., Chang, K.-P.: Augmented reality technology combined with three-dimensional holography to train the mental rotation ability of older adults. Comput. Hum. Behav. **65**, 488–500 (2016). https://doi.org/10.1016/j.chb.2016.09.014
15. Rohrbach, N., et al.: An augmented reality approach for ADL support in Alzheimer's disease: a crossover trial. J. Neuro Eng. Rehabil. **16**, 1–11 (2019). https://doi.org/10.1186/s12984-019-0530-z
16. Miller, M.R., Jun, H., Herrera, F., Yu Villa, J., Welch, G., Bailenson, J.N.: Social interaction in augmented reality. PLoS ONE **14**, e0216290 (2019). https://doi.org/10.1371/journal.pone.0216290
17. Søraa, R.A., Tøndel, G., Kharas, M.W., Serrano, J.A.: What do older adults want from social robots? A qualitative research approach to human-robot interaction (HRI) studies. Int. J. Soc. Robot. **15**, 411–424 (2022). https://doi.org/10.1007/s12369-022-00914-w
18. Almeida, L., Menezes, P., Dias, J.: Telepresence social robotics towards co-presence: a review. Appl. Sci. **12**, 5557 (2022). https://doi.org/10.3390/app12115557
19. Chen, S.C., Jones, C., Moyle, W.: Social robots for depression in older adults: a systematic review. J. Nurs. Scholarsh. **50**, 612–622 (2018). https://doi.org/10.1111/jnu.12423
20. Orlandini, A., et al.: Excite project: a review of forty-two months of robotic telepresence technology evolution. Presence: Teleoper. Virtual Environ. **25**, 204–221 (2016). https://doi.org/10.1162/PRES_a_00262
21. Coşar, S., et al.: ENRICHME: perception and interaction of an assistive robot for the elderly at home. Int. J. Soc. Robot. **12**, 779–805 (2020). https://doi.org/10.1007/s12369-019-00614-y
22. Niemelä, M., van Aerschot, L., Tammela, A., Aaltonen, I., Lammi, H.: Towards ethical guidelines of using telepresence robots in residential care. Int. J. Soc. Robot. **13**, 431–439 (2019). https://doi.org/10.1007/s12369-019-00529-8
23. Wu, Y.-H., Wrobel, J., Cornuet, M., Kerhervé, H., Damnée, S., Rigaud, A.-S.: Acceptance of an assistive robot in older adults: a mixed-method study of human–robot interaction over a 1-month period in the living lab setting. Clin. Interventions Aging **9**, 801 (2014). https://doi.org/10.2147/CIA.S56435
24. Lee, H.R., Riek, L.D.: Reframing assistive robots to promote successful aging. ACM Trans. Hum.-Robot Interact. **7**, 1–23 (2018). https://doi.org/10.1145/3203303
25. Puri, A., Baker, S., Hoang, T.N., Zuffi, R.C.: To be (ME) or not to be?. In: Proceedings of the 29th Australian Conference on Computer-Human Interaction (2017). https://doi.org/10.1145/3152771.3156166
26. Blok, M., van Ingen, E., de Boer, A.H., Slootman, M.: The use of information and communication technologies by older people with cognitive impairments: from barriers to benefits. Comput. Hum. Behav. **104**, 106173 (2020). https://doi.org/10.1016/j.chb.2019.106173

Design of Elderly Assisted Wheelchair Based on KJ-Technique and Analytic Hierarchy Process (AHP)

Wei Ding and Yu Ming Zhou[✉]

East China University of Science and Technology, Shanghai, China
1291467680@qq.com

Abstract. With the aging problem becoming more and more serious today, the design and research of age-appropriate products has gradually become a hot topic. With the advent of the aging society, the elderly have more and more say in the whole social market. Aging life, aging interaction, community for the elderly and other social hotspots have emerged. The aging travel problem is a very important part of it. In the past, most wheelchairs commonly used by the elderly were driven by manpower, and the circulation time of power-assisted wheelchairs in the market is relatively short. Therefore, most of the power-assisted wheelchairs in the market now have problems such as unreasonable structure, not suitable for most elderly people, and rigid appearance. In addition to the problems in the shape and structure, the elderly also have some obstacles in the interactive learning of wheelchairs, so it is necessary to pay more attention to the interface and operation mode of wheelchairs. In order to help the elderly design an ergonomic model and effectively solve the difficult problems in their travel process, this paper, from the perspective of the elderly and designers, understands their real views and needs on the power wheelchair, and then summarizes and classifies these needs through scientific methods and transforms them into design entities.

Keywords: Age-appropriate design · KJ-technique · Analytic Hierarchy Process (AHP)

1 Introduction

With the development of society and the improvement of human civilization, people, especially the elderly, need to use modern high technology to improve their quality of life and freedom of life. Because of the vigorous development of social production and the rapid arrival of an aging society, it is urgent to solve the travel problem of some elderly people with insufficient physical strength. Therefore, the research on robotic wheelchairs used to help the elderly walk has gradually become a hot spot.

According to data from China's Knowledge Infrastructure Project, the number of literature on ageing has shown a rapid upward trend in the past decade, with only 20 articles in 2012 and 1,210 articles on ageing topics in 2022. Among them, age-appropriate transformation and age-appropriate design are popular words. Such a growth rate reflects the fact that the issue of suitable aging has become a hot spot in society.

C. Stephanidis et al. (Eds.): HCII 2023, CCIS 1833, pp. 433–441, 2023.
https://doi.org/10.1007/978-3-031-35992-7_59

2 Research Status of Ageing

The concept of age-appropriate design began from the field of environmental design and architectural design, and the designer considered that there will be continuous communication and interaction between people in the social environment, so how to ensure the rights and basic needs of the elderly as a vulnerable group in society under such circumstances has slowly aroused everyone's thinking, and the field of age-appropriate design gradually covers many aspects such as community buildings, medical products, household products and life aids, such as aging blood glucose meters and blood pressure monitors in the medical field [1, 2]. Elderly aisles, handrails, and more in public spaces. Although China's aging design started late, with the acceleration of the aging society, more and more elderly groups have spawned a huge market and application scenarios, and the surge in demand has further promoted the development of related industries and aging design [3].

Cui Dunrui proposed to build a barrier-free kitchen for the elderly suitable for the elderly through the construction of the mental model of the elderly [4]. Bi Yifei added research on perceptual engineering on the basis of traditional robot design to design the appearance of escort robots suitable for the elderly [5]. Kong Lin proposed that behavior is the external manifestation of the physical function of the elderly, so taking the behavior of the elderly as the starting point, considering the age-appropriate design from the behavior of the elderly, closer to the needs of the elderly, closer to the human-oriented design concept (age-appropriate design - Kong Lin) [6], Li Yongfeng based on the rough set theory analyzed the needs and difficulties of the elderly when using the web page, and sorted out and modified the relevant design elements [7].

3 Research Status of KJ-Technique and Analytic Hierarchy Process (AHP)

The Kj method was developed by the Japanese anthropologist Kawakita Jiro as a tool used to quickly solve problems related to the field in which one is beginning to work. kj method starts from the internal connection of things, excavates the commonalities and advantages hidden in these connections and summarizes them to find out the optimal path to achieve the purpose [8–10].

This method is one of the seven management and planning tools of total quality management. KJ can integrate people's opinions and attitudes about a class of things and turn them into distinct, coherent modules. If kj is the collection and sorting of information from scratch, then ahp is the artificial demand classification of the collected information, which is a combination of quantitative and qualitative importance classification of demand. Analytic hierarchy process (AHP) is a data analysis method combining quantitative and qualitative methods. By establishing a goal, factors related to the goal are grouped according to their relevance, and different factors are compared to determine the degree of influence of different factors on the goal. By combining the kj method and the kano model, Mu Yun used the kano model for secondary analysis on the basis of the demand list collected by kj method, and successfully explored the external and potential product demands of consumers [11]. Zhou Feng combined the interaction elements of the excavator interface collected by kj method with the usability evaluation scores of the human-machine interaction interface of mechanical products by ahp method, and corresponding to the specific operation interface elements, so as to put forward the shortcomings and corresponding suggestions for improvement. In the early stage of the design of cultural and creative souvenirs [12], Wen Yuxin used kj method to collect users' wishes so as to excavate the perceptual image of red cultural and creative products with a goal [13].

4 Research Paths

To establish a clear understanding of the needs of wheelchairs and grasp the real needs of users and the designer's basic cognition of products and the half-segment demand model, it is first necessary to go deep into the consumer group, starting from the personal attributes of the consumer as the subject, and firmly grasp what consumers need and what consumers want. In this principle, in order to build a certain product concept for consumers and explore product functions and details that are difficult for them to notice, it is necessary to not only explain and popularize the wheelchair function of the interviewed consumers when collecting data in the early stage, but also investigate and study the relevant designer groups.

The main purpose of establishing a list of product functional requirements is to obtain the functional characteristics of a product object. Using the KJ method to obtain the user needs of the wheelchair function, the specific operation steps are as follows.

(1) Identify 30 respondents for interviews. The respondents were 20 consumers and 10 designers with wheelchair support needs and experiences.

(2) Collect the basic personal information of the respondents, and inform the respondents that the main body of this seminar is the functional design of assistive wheelchair products, and carry out a simple science popularization of unified wheelchair functions and structures for the respondents, so as to ensure that the respondents' choice is not affected, and try to let the respondents have a certain understanding of the assistive wheelchair. At the same time, considering that the respondents have certain thinking limitations on assisting wheelchairs, the respondents were asked to collect language and text materials related to the topic of the discussion through various channels.

(3) Collecting information, considering that there are conflicting schedules of respondents, the KJ method adopts the practice of collecting information at different locations and at different times in the process of specific implementation, and then each respondent screens and classifies needs. When collecting information, respondents are now asked to write down the information that can be associated with wheelchairs in the form of terms or short sentences, which the organizers will summarize. After that, the organizer will ask the interviewee to explain the unclear part to ensure the accuracy of the entry.

(4) Hierarchical information classification, the first step, the organizer will summarize the collected terms, and send the summarized questionnaire to each respondent, requiring them to classify the terms according to their own cognition of different terms according to certain internal connections. In the second part, the organizers

put together the list of categories, examined whether there were overlapping parts in the modules classified by different respondents, retained the overlapping parts, and screened out the non-overlapping parts of the entries into a new questionnaire. The third step asks respondents to fill in the terms that do not overlap in the new questionnaire into the terms that have already formed modules. Repeat steps two and three until the terms for each module overlap completely. Excluding terms with the same or similar content, and discussing the similarities of each module, named the module, the "three-level demand indicator" is collected. Categorize upwards by grouping related groups into a module, each with the name of the "Level 2 Requirements Indicator". In the same way, the middle group is classified again to form a large group, that is, the "first-level demand indicator".

5   Obtain the List of Requirements Based on the KJ-Technique

The KJ method can explore the intrinsic connections in people's subjective views and vague impressions of an unknown field, classify the vague similarities in the chaotic information, and summarize the relatively reasonable set of associations in the articles full of personal assumptions and subjective feelings. This approach can help non-professionals in the field to quickly participate in experiments.

The first round first informed these 30 users that the theme of this KJ method is the improved design of the assistive wheelchair, and after giving each participant two days to understand the product, each participant is asked to list 15 items for the characteristics they think the assistive wheelchair should have, each entry exists in the form of words or short sentences, and the ambiguous items are required to be re-summarized by the proposer, and a total of 450 items were collected in the first round.

The second round is to classify the similarity of the collected entries and find certain correlations between the entries. The 450 entries collected in the first round were redistributed to the 30 participants in the experiment, and they were asked to group according to the 450 items of relevance, and then we collected the entries in the group, because different people have different understandings of the correlation between the wheelchair articles, so there are differences between the classification of the collected items, so we then screened the groups with high similarity, retaining the 18 groups with high similarity, and excluding 12 groups with excessive differences. The remaining 18 groups of entries can be roughly divided into four categories, and then the remaining 18 groups are corrected, and the overlapping items are retained, and the redundant entries are eliminated and reselected.

In the third round of screening, we first analyzed the intrinsic relationship of the four groups that have been formed, and concluded that the classification of the four groups is classified according to "functional characteristics", "appearance", "interoperability" and "security", that is, the secondary demand indicators, we inform 30 participants of these four groups, and ask them to fill the unfilled items into the existing groups according to these four classification methods. Among them, "Features" contains 168 entries, "Appearance" contains 120 entries, "Interoperability" contains 82 entries, "Security" contains 63 entries, and 17 items cannot be filled into these four groups, so they are discarded. Subsequently, items with the same or similar content are eliminated to form detailed corresponding requirements under four groups, that is, "three-level demand indicators" (Fig. 1).

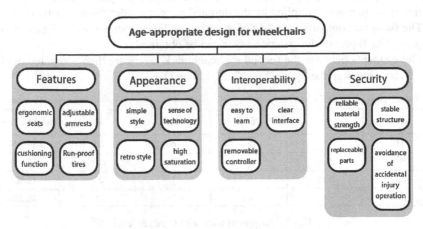

Fig. 1. Progressive structural hierarchical model

6 AHP Method for User Needs Analysis

6.1 (1) Build a Demand Hierarchy Model

The progressive hierarchy model of the design requirements of the assist-assisted wheelchair constructed by the KJ method is constructed, and the structural hierarchy model is divided into three layers according to the AHP method, the target layer, the criterion layer and the second criterion layer. The target layer is to build this model to hope to achieve the purpose, that is, to assist the wheelchair aging design, the wheelchair itself is for all the products of the same travel population caused by physical disability, this study shifts the design focus to the elderly group, is to consider that the elderly population in the overall physical function decline and psychological ability decline is different from other travel disabled people, but has certain similarities, so the study of the elderly population can also form targeted results in the development of wheelchair products. The criterion layer is summarized by the second quasi-test layer, which represents the attention of the participants in the design of assistive wheelchairs to the four levels of "functional characteristics", "appearance modeling", "interactive operation" and "safety". The 11 items of the second criterion layer were summarized by surveying users and summarizing in the experiments of the KJ method.

The hierarchical hierarchy model was constructed, and the age-appropriate design of the target layer assist wheelchair was represented by C. The criterion layer is represented by Bi (i = 1, 2, 3); The secondary criterion layer is represented by Ai (i = 1, 2, 3), and the 1–9 scale method is used to assign the factors in the hierarchical model. In order to make the decision-making results more objective, the assignment work was jointly completed by 8 designers, 2 elderly users who assisted wheelchairs, and 3 family members of users who assisted wheelchairs. The two-pair comparison matrix of the criterion layer is completed first, and then the two-pair comparison matrix of the secondary criterion layer is completed. After the consistency test, the demand weights of the features under the criterion layer are multiplied by the demand weights under the sub-criterion layer.

The two-pair comparison matrix of the criterion layer is shown in the figure, and the weights of each part of the criterion layer can be obtained.

The elements between the secondary benchmark layers are then compared, and the weights are shown in the figure (Figs. 2, 3, 4, 5 and 6).

C1	B1	B2	B3	B4	Weight value (%)
B1	1	2	4	0.5	30.602
B2	0.5	1	0.5	0.25	10.819
B3	0.25	2	1	0.5	15.301
B4	2	4	2	1	43.278

Fig. 2. Judgment matrix of C target level

Features(B1)	A11	A12	A13	A14	Weight value (%)
A11	1	0.5	0.25	0.25	9.121
A12	2	1	2	0.5	25.798
A13	4	0.5	1	0.5	21.694
A14	4	2	2	1	43.387

Fig. 3. Judgment matrix of B1 target level

Appearance(B2)	A21	A22	A23	A24	Weight value (%)
A21	1	0.167	0.333	2	10.548
A22	6	1	3.03	5	56.414
A23	3	0.33	1	4	25.773
A24	0.5	0.2	0.25	1	7.265

Fig. 4. Judgment matrix of B2 target level

6.2 Consistency Test

After constructing the two-by-two comparison matrices of the criterion layer and the secondary criterion layer, the content of each matrix is checked for consistency. Calculate the consistency indicator CI as well as the maximum eigenvalue root λmax in the matrix.

$$CI = \lambda \max -n/n - 1 \qquad (1)$$

Interoperability(B3	A31	A32	A33	Weight value (%)
A31	1	0.25	0.333	12.196
A32	4	1	2	55.842
A33	3	0.5	1	31.962

Fig. 5. Judgment matrix of B3 target level

Security(B4)	A41	A42	A43	A44	Weight value (%)
A41	1	3.03	5	6.993	56.735
A42	0.33	1	5	3.003	26.384
A43	0.2	0.2	1	0.333	6.009
A44	0.143	0.333	3	1	10.872

Fig. 6. Judgment matrix of B4 target level

The calculation is performed by the following formula. Then, the consistency index CI was compared with the random consistency index RI to obtain the consistency ratio CR. Generally, when the consistency ratio CR < 0.1, pass the consistency test. If it does not pass, the judgment matrix needs to be reconstructed.

$$CR = CI/RI \tag{2}$$

The results of the consistency test of each judgment matrix are shown in the figure, and each judgment matrix has passed the consistency test, indicating that the experimental results are effective and feasible. Then, according to the weight of each design element displayed by the model, the design trend of helping wheelchair design in the future can be obtained (Fig. 7).

	CI	RI	CR	RESULT
C	0.083	0.882	0.094	pass
B1	0.062	0.882	0.07	pass
B2	0.04	0.882	0.045	pass
B3	0.009	0.525	0.017	pass
B4	0.08	0.882	0.09	pass

Fig. 7. Consistency test judgment table

7 Design Example Conversion

According to the above KJ method and analytic hierarchy method on the demand level and priority of assistive wheelchairs, combined with the general characteristics and advantages of existing wheelchair products, a assistive wheelchair for the elderly group is designed. According to the primary needs of safety, the load-bearing structure of the assistive wheelchair is strengthened, and high-strength alloy materials are used to ensure the stability of the wheelchair, and the components that are prone to loss, such as hubs, backrests, and handles, adopt modular design methods to ensure that users can replace them immediately. In terms of functional characteristics, we have adopted a seat design that meets the sedentary habits of the elderly, and uses adjustable seats for different body shapes of the elderly, and the adjustment parts correspond to the three key parts of the human neck, spine and tail vertebrae. At the same time, considering that users often encounter terrain with undulating and drop differences during wheelchair use, the wheels and seats of the wheelchair are connected through a special spring structure to achieve the effect of cushioning. In terms of styling, it adopts a nostalgic style that conforms to the aesthetics of the elderly, and matches bright color combinations, so that the elderly have a more satisfactory psychological experience in the process of traveling. In terms of the use operation and interactive experience of the elderly, taking into account the learning cost and learning ability of the elderly, the operation interface of most wheelchairs on the market is specially referred to in the wheelchair design of this time, and the simple and clear operation button form is summarized and extracted. These design details can also help the elderly to better use assistive wheelchair products.

References

1. Peng, H.: Visualization analysis of Chinese aging design research based on CNKI in recent 20 years. Packag. Eng. **43**(4), 7 (2022)
2. Yang J.: General discussion on demographic dividend – and the realization of demographic dividend in aging China. Econ. Theory Manag. **V**(008), 12–16 (2009)
3. Wu, C., Wang, L., Miao, R.: The process, prospect and countermeasures of population aging with Chinese characteristics. Popul. Res. **28**(1), 8 (2004)
4. Cui, D., Li, W.: Research on kitchen furniture design based on mental model of elderly users. For. Prod. Ind. **57**(11), 5 (2020)
5. Bi, Y., Whang, N., Zhu, Y.I.: Modeling design of elderly care robot based on Kansei Engineering. Packag. Eng. **39**(2), 6 (2018)
6. Kong, L.: Age-appropriate Design. Central Academy of Fine Arts (2014)
7. Li, Y., Zhu, L.: Application of Rough Set Theory in product image modeling design. Packag. Eng. **31**(18), 4 (2010)
8. Hou, S., Zhou, Y., Xiao, S.: Development and practice of community health education curriculum for Senile dementia based on KJ method. Nurs. Res. (2009)
9. Qiu, B., Li, X., Min, S.: Innovative design of Storage cabinets in office area based on TRIZ Theory and KJ Method. Packag. Eng. **43**(24), 7 (2022)
10. Jiang, Y., Song, L., Liu, L.: Application of KJ method in improved design. Art Des.: Acad. Edn. **000**(009), 95–97 (2015)
11. Mu, Y., Zhang, J., Wang, A.: Research on trench coat product design based on KJ method and Kano model. Wool Sci. Technol. **48**(5), 7 (2020)

12. Zhou, F., Zhou, J., He, Y.: Research on usability of human-computer interaction interface based on KJ method and ANP method. Sci. Technol. Eng. **6**, 5 (2015)
13. Wen, Y., Song, S.S., Wan, W.: Research on purchase perception image of Red Cultural Creative Users based on KJ. Design **34**(22), 3 (2021)

AI to Design Care-Taking Home Appliances for Older Adult's Perceived Value and Happiness

Yifang Gao[✉]

Tongji University, Shanghai 200092, China
1911185@tongji.edu.cn

Abstract. With the rapid development of technology, the application of smartphones and computing networks has been continually innovated, occupying every moment of life and reflecting the excellent comfort of the Internet. Through the design of home products, we will integrate the life of older adults, not only solve a few small things in life, but expand the goal and make a design that can improve the current situation with integrated thinking. As service design combines space and time, tangible entities and intangible services may be included. Therefore, many products that can improve the quality of life of older adults and reduce the burden of life are gradually developing, so that older adults can still live healthily and have a happy life in the process of aging. Over the last few years, the search for happiness has progressively become a subject of our modern people. Design itself is an area created to improve people's lives, and how happy design practices will also be an important indicator of future design. Consequently, this study explores the impact of the design of home appliances on the perceived value and happiness of older adults, and hopes to help older adults design and development of products. In addition to meeting the needs of tomorrow's society, it has the potential to reduce the impact of an aging society.

Keywords: Product Design · Home Appliance · Perceptual Value · Happiness · Artificial Intelligence

1 Introduction

Population aging is an important trend of social development. According to the statistics of the World Bank, as early as 2014, there were more than 35 countries in the world, and the proportion of older adults over 65 years old accounted for more than 15% of the total population. According to the United Nations standards, an aging society is defined as a city where older adults aged 65 account for 7% of the total population or older adults aged over 60 account for 10% of the total population. According to the seventh population census of China, the population aged 60 and above is 264.02 million, accounting for 18.70% (of which, the population aged 65 and above is 190.64 million, accounting for 13.50%) [1]. This is both a challenge and an opportunity. On the one hand, population aging reduces the supply of labor force, increases the burden of family pension and the

C. Stephanidis et al. (Eds.): HCII 2023, CCIS 1833, pp. 442–454, 2023.
https://doi.org/10.1007/978-3-031-35992-7_60

pressure of basic public service supply, on the other hand, it promotes the development of "silver economy" and expands the consumption market of elderly intelligent products based on artificial intelligence, mobile internet and other technologies. Intelligent nursing household appliances play an important role in the daily life of older adults, health care, information acquisition and communication. However, the old home product design can no longer meet the needs of older adults in the new era [2]. For example, the function of the product is not consistent with the expectation, the operation is cumbersome, and the answer is wrong, which not only affects the user experience of older adults, but also is not conducive to the development of older adults product market. Therefore, through design thinking and artificial intelligence technology, product services can be closer to the psychological and physiological needs of older adults. Relevant research shows that comfortable care experience can improve the perceived value and happiness of older adults [3]. Therefore, this study aims to provide older adults with a good product user experience by exploring the impact of smart home appliance design on the perceived value and well-being of older adults, and proposes design strategies for older adults.

2   Discussion of Literature

Product design and scientific and technological innovation are important ways to empower the current contradiction of elderly care. By using artificial intelligence, mobile internet, internet of things and other technologies, we can realize the integrated development of elderly care, health, medical care and life services at home [9]. Product design for older adults should pay more attention to user experience. Designer Donald Norman pointed out that the perception and response generated by users in the whole process of contacting with products, systems or services is the user experience [4]. Compared with the past, the emphasis on the usability of elderly products is more on the subjective feelings of elderly users. For older adults, positive user experience can not only meet the needs of product functions, but also meet psychological needs and self-perceived value. Perceived value refers to the overall evaluation of the effectiveness of products or services after the balance between the perceived benefits of users and the costs they pay when acquiring products or services. For older adults, the purpose of using AI nursing appliances is to delay and maintain the decline of physical and mental functions, which reflects the expectation of older adults for healthy aging [5]. The self-perception of older adults is the subjective perception and emotional response generated by the threat of psychological, physical and social aging [7].

From the perspective of the perceived needs of older adults and the development of science and technology, the design and application of intelligent products for older adults are mainly in kitchen appliances, household appliances, bathroom appliances, cleaning appliances, sports and health, leisure and entertainment, communications, etc.; From the perspective of application fields, smart products for older adults are mainly concentrated in communication, container, control and data processing, medical targeting and auxiliary appliances; From the perspective of technology, intelligent products for older adults are usually represented as wearable technology, remote monitoring technology and intelligent robots [9]. The design of these intelligent products involves all aspects of the physical needs and psychological care of older adults. They are all designed to enhance the ability of older adults to live independently and enable them to live safely, independently and comfortably in their own homes or communities. Therefore, this study proposes the following hypothesis:

Hypothesis H1: Product design has a significant positive impact on perceived value.

The penetration of intelligent nursing products into the daily life scene of older adults can monitor older adults's blood pressure, heart rate, exercise and physical activity, blood sugar, fall risk, sleep duration and quality, weight, diet, posture, mood, etc. at any time in the aspect of health care. And easy to wear will not affect normal life. Therefore, older adults can monitor vital signs and provide remote diagnosis and treatment assistance through daily necessities. In terms of functional health care, intelligent products can manage movement posture, collect movement data, assess movement risk, analyze training data and other intelligent products. Through intelligent analysis of relevant data, appropriate suggestions can be given to make functional health care more scientific [10]. Through the "partners" of these smart products, a smart home environment for care and health care is formed to improve the perceived value of older adults. Self-perception can be used as an internal psychological factor of older adults to reflect the mental state of older adults. Mental well-being refers to the joyful spiritual experience of value, strength and other feelings from the depths of the heart when individuals deal with the relationship between themselves and others, society and the environment [6]. The sense of spiritual well-being can evaluate the sense of spiritual experience of older adults when they coordinate the relationship between themselves and the outside world. The positive attitude of older adults towards their own aging can effectively promote their communication with the external environment, which is beneficial to obtain positive support [8]. Therefore, this study proposes the following hypothesis:

Hypothesis H2: Perceived value has a significant positive impact on happiness.

Happiness comes from people's psychological experiences. The psychological theory of positive experience originated from optimism put forward by psychologist Jung. In recent years, studies in the fields of psychology, philosophy, economics and politics have shown that people are increasingly interested in happiness. This concern for human happiness has entered the field of design. Desmet applies the positive experience theory of psychology to product design, endows users with positive experience through correct design intervention, thus improving users' subjective well-being [11]. Kai Eckoldt and other scholars use daily life cases to show how to use positive experience in daily products to improve people's subjective well-being, and use an illustrative case to outline the design process of positive experience [12]. Hassenzahl M applied positive experience to the interaction design of the computer interface, proving that positive experience can guide users to complete meaningful target activities, such as relieving loneliness and stress in emotional needs [13]. From this, we can feel that product design, from emphasizing the appearance design in the past to focusing on the invisible part of the internal users of the product [14], is also a process for designers to select the level for each significant attribute contained in the product [15]. Among them, the efficacy of the product is the basis to achieve the user's happiness perception, and also the first step to bring basic material happiness to older adults [16]. Secondly, in terms of the sensory attributes of older adults, whether the "aesthetic" products are pleasant or not, when the sense of pleasure exceeds the user's expectations, it will trigger the user's emotional enjoyment experience, that is, the comfort of the sensory attributes drives the happiness of the emotional attributes, which is a psychological enjoyment satisfaction [17]. Therefore, this study proposes the following hypothesis:

Hypothesis H3: Product design has a significant positive impact on happiness.

3 Method

3.1 Research Object and Basic Data

In this study, from May to July 2022, older adults from Shanghai Community Health Service Center were selected as the subjects of the questionnaire. The researcher promised to keep the interview data confidential and alleviate the concerns of the interviewees. This study was reviewed and approved by the Ethics Committee of our hospital. In this study, 360 questionnaires were distributed and 223 valid questionnaires were collected. The recovery rate is 62%. Inclusion criteria: (1) Community residence ≥ 1 year; (2) Age ≥ 60 years old; (3) Have a certain understanding of intelligent nursing appliances; (4) Informed consent and voluntary participation in this study. Exclude those who cannot express the meaning correctly. Finally, 360 elderly people were included in this study. Among the surveyed groups, the proportion of male and female elderly groups is 46.6% and 53.4%, and the proportion of married elderly groups is relatively higher, accounting for 96.4%. The proportion of older adults with junior high school education and lower junior high school education is relatively high, but there are also a considerable proportion of older adults with higher education level. According to the analysis of the use of intelligent nursing appliances by older adults, the response rates of household appliances, kitchen appliances and sports health appliances are 24.3%, 17.1% and 15.5%, respectively, indicating that the three types of intelligent nursing appliances with high popularity among older adults are household appliances, kitchen appliances and sports health care appliances, and the range of other types of nursing appliances is low. See Tables 1, 2 and 3 for the basic data of the respondents.

Table 1. Correlations.

	Correlations	Frequency	percentage	Cumulative percentage
Effect	M	104	46.6	46.6
	F	119	53.4	100
	Total	223	100	

Table 2. Education Level.

	Education level	Frequency	percentage	Cumulative percentage
Effect	Below junior high school	56	25.1	25.1
	Junior high school	83	37.2	62.3
	High school	28	12.6	74.9
	University and above	56	25.1	100
	Total	223	100	

Table 3. Usage Information of Intelligent Nursing Appliances.

		Responses		Percent of Cases
		N	Percent	
$Aa	Cleaning appliances	64	10.00%	29.50%
	Household appliances	155	24.30%	71.40%
	Kitchen appliances	109	17.10%	50.20%
	Sanitary appliances	55	8.60%	25.30%
	Recreation & Entertainment	56	8.80%	25.80%
	Transportation	75	11.80%	34.60%
	Sports health	99	15.50%	45.60%
	Other	24	3.80%	11.10%
Total		637	100.00%	293.50%

a. Dichotomy group tabulated at value 1.

3.2 Reliability and Validity Test of the Scale

Reliability Test of the Scale. According to the reliability test of the questionnaire, the reliability analysis of the full sample data of customers' actual perception in terms of ease of use, understandability, security, perception and satisfaction of intelligent nursing appliances showed that the Cronbach's alpha values in terms of ease of use, understandability, security, perception and satisfaction were 0.915, 0.768, 0.848, 0.958 and 0.929, respectively The dimensions of the five research variables of safety, perception and satisfaction are greater than 0.8. If the value of the Cronbach reliability coefficient is greater than 0.8, it means that the consistency of the internal measurement items that reflect the meaning of the latent variables in each research variable is high, the reliability of the test or scale is very good, and the quality of the data collection of the perception questionnaire meets the requirements of the questionnaire test, and subsequent analysis can be carried out, as shown in Table 4.

Table 4. Item-Total Statistics.

	Scale Mean if Item Deleted	Scale Variance if Item Deleted	Corrected Item-Total Correlation	Cronbach's Alpha if Item Deleted	
A1	6.14	6.232	0.812	0.894	0.915
A2	6.07	6.571	0.83	0.878	
A3	5.98	6.477	0.848	0.863	
B1	2.75	1.547	0.625		0.768
B2	2.98	1.342	0.625		
C1	3.29	1.052	0.736		0.848
C2	3.2	1.069	0.736		
D1	14.9058	26.987	0.794	0.958	0.958
D2	15.1211	26.692	0.849	0.952	
D3	15.2556	26.272	0.895	0.947	
D4	15.1435	25.844	0.916	0.944	
D5	15.0179	26.045	0.863	0.95	
D6	15.0717	26.445	0.885	0.948	
E1	9.61	9.366	0.806	0.917	0.929
E2	9.96	9.588	0.862	0.9	
E3	9.88	9.026	0.818	0.914	
E4	9.62	9.128	0.858	0.9	

Validity Test of the Scale. The validity of the scale is usually analyzed by factor analysis, which is divided into exploratory factor analysis (EFA) and confirmatory factor analysis (CFA). The prerequisite for factor analysis to test the validity of the questionnaire is that KMO > 0.6, p < 0.001, after the questionnaire data is extracted by factor analysis. This shows that the existing questionnaire data can be tested by factor analysis. According to the KMO and Bartlett test results of the Perception Questionnaire, KMO = 0.888, KMO > 0.7, P < 0.001, and the factor analysis method is suitable for the validity test, and the research data is more suitable for extracting information, with good data validity, as shown in Table 5. This study uses SPSS 25.0 software to rotate through the maximum variance method. The extraction requirement is that the extraction factor can explain more than 80% of the variable information. Based on this principle, four common factors are extracted, namely, ease of use, ease of understanding, security, and perception. After rotation, the cumulative variance interpretation rate is 84.304%, and more than 50% indicates that the scale used has good interpretation ability, and the information loss is small in the process of dimensionality reduction of high-dimensional data, The exploratory factor load matrix is obtained by the orthogonal rotation of variance maximization. When the factor load coefficient of each measurement item is greater than

0.5, the convergence validity is acceptable, and when it is greater than 0.7, the convergence validity is very good. The results are shown in the following table, and the load of measurement factors in the dimensions of ease of use, ease of understanding, security and perception ability all exceed 0.7, and there is no cross-load phenomenon. The scale of perception questionnaire in this study has good validity, as shown in Tables 6 and 7.

Table 5. KMO and Bartlett's Test.

Kaiser-Meyer-Olkin Measure of Sampling. Adequacy		0.888
Bartlett's Test of Sphericity	Approx. ChiSquare	2912.273
	Df	78
	Sig	0

Table 6. Total Variance Explained.

Component	Initial Eigenvalues			Extraction Sums of Squared Loadings			Rotation Sums of Squared Loadings		
	Total	% of Variance	Cumulative %	Total	% of Variance	Cumulative %	Total	% of Variance	Cumulative %
1	7.419	57.068	57.068	7.419	57.068	57.068	4.82	37.076	37.076
2	1.96	15.078	72.146	1.96	15.078	72.146	2.692	20.708	57.784
3	0.947	7.288	79.434	0.947	7.288	79.434	1.897	14.589	72.373
4	0.633	4.869	84.304	0.633	4.869	84.304	1.551	11.93	84.304
5	0.45	3.458	87.762						
6	0.358	2.751	90.513						
7	0.302	2.324	92.837						
8	0.276	2.126	94.964						
9	0.212	1.633	96.596						
10	0.164	1.258	97.855						
11	0.14	1.078	98.932						
12	0.117	0.898	99.83						
13	0.022	0.17	100						

Extraction Method: Principal Component Analysis.

3.3 Correlation Analysis of the Scale and Questionnaire

Through the correlation analysis of the questionnaire, it can be seen that the correlation coefficients between older adults's satisfaction perception and perception of intelligent nursing home appliances, the ease of use, understanding and safety of intelligent nursing

Table 7. Rotated Component Matrix a.

	Component			
	1	2	3	4
D4	0.883			
D6	0.869			
D3	0.866			
D2	0.806			
D5	0.8			
D1	0.755			
A3		0.924		
A1		0.889		
A2		0.885		
C1			0.872	
C2			0.821	
B2				0.792
B1	0.498			0.681

Extraction method: principal component analysis.
Rotation method: Caesar normalization maximum variance method.
a. Converged after 5 iterations of rotation.

home appliances are 0.692 * *, 0.420 * *, 0.645 * * and 0.594 * *, respectively, indicating that older adults's satisfaction perception and perception of intelligent nursing home appliances, the ease of use of intelligent nursing home appliances There is a positive correlation between comprehensibility and security. There is a positive correlation between the perception ability of older adults to intelligent nursing appliances and the ease of use, understanding and safety of intelligent nursing appliances, as shown in Table 8.

3.4 Regression Analysis

It can be seen from Table 9 that this hierarchical regression analysis involves three models. In model 1, the ease of use, understandability and safety of smart home appliance product design are used as the core independent variables, and satisfaction is used as the dependent variable for linear regression. As can be seen from the following table, the R-square value of model 1 is 0.515, which means that only putting control variables and only putting exclusion in the model can explain the change of 51.5% of the dependent variable. The model passed the F test (F = 79.448, p < 0.05), which means that the ease of use, understandability and safety of smart home appliance product design will have a positive impact on user satisfaction. The regression coefficients of ease of use, understandability and safety on satisfaction with use are 0.142, 0.364 and 0.341, respectively. Among them, the understandability of intelligent nursing home appliances has the highest satisfaction level for older adults group using intelligent nursing home appliances.

Table 8. Correlation.

		Satisfaction	Perception	Ease of use	Comprehensibility
Perception	Pearson Correlation	.692**			
	Sig. (2-tailed)	0			
	N	223			
Ease of use	Pearson Correlation	.420**	.403**		
	Sig. (2-tailed)	0	0		
	N	223	223		
Comprehensibility	Pearson Correlation	.645**	.734**	.393**	
	Sig. (2-tailed)	0	0	0	
	N	223	223	223	
Security	Pearson Correlation	.594**	.615**	.275**	.560**
	Sig. (2-tailed)	0	0	0	0
	N	223	223	223	223

**.Correlation is significant at the 0.01 level (2-tailed).

In model 2, the ease of use, understandability and safety of smart home appliance product design are taken as the core independent variables, and the perception ability is taken as the dependent variable for linear regression. It can be seen from the following table that the ease of use, understandability and safety of smart home appliance product design will have a positive impact on the perception ability. The regression coefficients of ease of use, understandability and safety on perception ability are 0.096, 0.4984 and 0.307, respectively. Among them, the understandability and safety of intelligent nursing appliances have the highest impact on the perception ability of elderly people using intelligent nursing appliances.

In model 3, on the basis of the ease of use, understandability and safety of the independent variable smart home appliance product design, the perception ability of the intermediary variable is added. The R-square value of model 3 is 0.558, and compared with model 1, the explanatory variable's explanatory power to the dependent variable is enhanced. Further combining the regression coefficient, we can see that the ease of use, understandability and safety of the design of smart home appliances will have a positive impact on the use satisfaction, and the perception ability will have a level of 0.333 for older adults to obtain satisfaction when using nursing home appliances, which means that the stronger older adults's perception ability in the process of using nursing home appliances, the easier it is to obtain satisfaction.

Table 9. Coefficients.

Model	Satisfaction				
	Unstandardized Coefficients		Standardized Coefficients	t	sig.
	B	Std. Error	Beta		
(Constant)	0.674	0.182		3.698	0
Ease of use	0.142	0.041	0.176	3.453	0.001
Comprehensibility	0.364	0.055	0.393	6.644	0
Security	0.341	0.059	0.326	5.762	0
Perception					
R Square	0.521				
Adjusted R Square	0.515				
F	79.448				
Sig.	0				
Model	Perception				
	Unstandardized Coefficients		Standardized Coefficients	t	sig.
	B	Std. Error	Beta		
(Constant)	0.303	0.168		1.807	0.072
Ease of use	0.096	0.038	0.116	2.532	0.012
Comprehensibility	0.498	0.05	0.527	9.881	0
Security	0.307	0.054	0.288	5.654	0
Perception					
R Square	0.611				
Adjusted R Square	0.606				
F	114.647				
Sig.	0				

(continued)

Table 9. (*continued*)

Model	Satisfaction (Happiness)				
	Unstandardized Coefficients		Standardized Coefficients	t	sig.
	B	Std. Error	Beta		
(Constant)	0.573	0.175		3.271	0.001
Ease of use	0.11	0.04	0.137	2.766	0.006
Comprehensibility	0.198	0.063	0.214	3.154	0.002
Security Perception	0.238	0.06	0.228	3.946	0
R Square	0.566				
Adjusted R Square	0.558				
F	71.094				
Sig.	0				

4 Conclusion

It can be seen from this study that with the accelerated development of science and technology and the improvement of educational level, older adults have raised their requirements for quality of life in the era of adequate supplies. They pay attention to physical and mental health. Therefore, the prevalence of intelligent nursing appliances among older adults is relatively high. The ease of use, understandability and safety of the design are the key factors for older adults to use artificial intelligence nursing appliances, which is conducive to enhancing the perception ability of older adults; The enhancement of older adults's perception ability will improve the satisfaction of product use, thus improving the quality of life and happiness; Intelligent nursing home appliances with older adults experience as the design orientation have significantly enhanced the life and spiritual well-being of older adults.

5 Suggestions

While solving the basic needs of older adults, designers should explore the needs of users at a higher level with empathy. Take the explicit needs of older adults as the "face" to explore the "point" of the deeper hidden needs. Connect the small functions in the product design experience map to complete the deep user interaction intelligent experience. Improve the perceived value and happiness of older adults. In this regard, this study has the following suggestions:

1. The design of intelligent nursing products for older adults needs the principle of humanization. In human-computer interaction, people are given emotional interaction and experience, and the visual information conveyed by the product shape design should be closer to the user's portrait and life scene.
2. The application of emerging technologies needs to follow the design principle of safety. Technologies that have not been scientifically tested for a long time may cause potential harm to users. In view of the particularity of older adults, the product design needs to highlight reliable safety at the physical and psychological levels.
3. The principle of fault-tolerance should be strengthened in the use of elderly product design. Improve the confidence and enthusiasm of older adults in the process of use, and strengthen the fluency and validity of product use. So as to interpret the "spiritual communication" between products and users.

References

1. Bulletin of the Seventh National Population Census (No. 8). http://www.stats.gov.cn/ztjc/zdt jgz/zgrkpc/dqcrkpc/ggl/202105/t20210519_1817701.html. Accessed 11 May 2021
2. Zhou, Y., Zhang, J., Luo, T., et al.: Research on the design of smart home products for aging bedrooms. West. Leather **43**(18), 87–88 (2021)
3. Picard, R.W.: Affective Computing. MIT Press, Cambridge (1997)
4. Norman, D., Miller, J., Henderson, A.: What you see, some of what's in the future, and how we go about doing it: HI at Apple Computer. In: Conference Companion on Human Factors in Computing Systems, p. 155. Association for Computing Machinery, New York, NY, USA (1995)
5. Sarkisian, C.A., Hays, R.D., Berry, S.H., et al.: Expectations regarding aging among older adults and physicians who care for older adults. Med. Care **39**(9), 1025–1036 (2001)
6. Xu, X., Sun, C., Wang, F.: Mental well-being: concept, measurement, related variables and intervention. Prog. Psychol. Sci. **25**(2), 275–289 (2017)
7. Bunt, S., Steverink, N., Olthof, J., et al.: Social frailty in older adults: a scoping review. Eur. J. Ageing **14**(3), 323–334 (2017)
8. Chen, K., Chen, L., He, J., et al.: The intermediary role of spiritual well-being in the self-perceived aging and aging expectations of older adults in the community. Joint Serv. Mil. Med. **37**(01), 60–66 (2023). https://doi.org/10.13730/j.issn.2097-2148.2023.01.013
9. Chen, F., Jiang, Z.: Application prospect and ethical risk of smart products for older adults. J. Shandong Univ. Sci. Technol. (Soc. Sci. Edn.) **23**(01), 21–28 (2021). https://doi.org/10. 16452/j.cnki.sdkjsk.2021.01.003
10. Yan, Y., Zou, H., Zhou, L., et al.: Development of wearable technology. Chin. J. Biomed. Eng. **2015**(6), 644–653 (2015)
11. Desmet, P.M.A., Pohlmeyer, A.E.: Positive design: an introduction to design for subjective well-being. Int. J. Des. **7**(3), 5–19 (2013)
12. Hassenzahl, M., Eckoldt, K., Diefenbach, S., et al.: Designing moments of meaning and pleasure. Experience design and happiness. Int. J. Des. **7**(3), 21–31 (2013)
13. Hassenzahl, M.: Experience design: technology for all the right reasons. Synth. Lect. Hum. Centered Inform. **3**(1), 1–95 (2010)

14. Creusen, M.E.H., Schoormans, J.P.L.: The different roles of product appearance in consumer choice. J. Prod. Innov. Manag. **22**(1), 63–81 (2004)
15. Camm, J.D., Cochran, J.J., Kannan, S., et al.: Conjoint optimization: an exact branch and bound algorithm for the share-of-choice problem. Manag. Sci. **52**(3), 435–447 (2006)
16. Jordan, P.W.: Human factors for pleasure in product use. Appl. Ergon. **29**(1), 25–33 (1998)
17. Wu, X., Xu, G.: Research on the concept, connotation and level of product happiness design. Packag. Eng. **40**(12), 1–7+11 (2019). https://doi.org/10.19554/j.cnki.1001-3563.2019.12.001

A Hospital MR Navigation Design for Elderly People's Medical Needs

Bailu Guo(✉) and Xiaolei Mi

Beijing City University, Beijing, China
13521505946@163.com

Abstract. As China has a large population with a large elderly group, in first-tier cities with a concentrated population, medical resources do not match the population. In particular, the average daily outpatient reception is large in tertiary hospitals. Taking a hospital in Beijing as an example, the average daily outpatient reception is about 10,400 person-times. The complex medical environment and various procedures also lead to patients need to constantly look for the next target department for a long time. Even if there are a few volunteers in the lobby to guide, the medical treatment process is still a challenge for elderly patients. The guidance of hospital departments is generally based on conventional text signs and some hospitals also try to use the indoor positioning and navigation system of smart phones to give instructions, but the difficulties of unaccompanied elderly people in smart phone applications are not taken into account. Mixed Reality (MR) holds the promise of presenting navigational instructions directly into the patient's field of vision, creating a humanoid sign of a virtual guide in the patient's vision, thus achieving the same effect as a human guide. From the beginning of entering the hospital, the virtual guide sign will automatically plan the medical route for the patient, which can save the time for the elderly to ask the medical staff for directions and understand the guide sign and the medical treatment process; moreover, the sense of companionship generated by the virtual humanoid sign based on Mixed Reality (MR) can alleviate the anxiety of the elderly patients when they seek medical treatment to some extent. Although there are still many problems to be discussed in the specific application and practical operation of the technology, the virtual humanoid guide sign with the nature of companion can still become an important design direction of the future hospital navigation system.

Keywords: Mixed Reality · Virtual Sign · Outpatient Guidance

1 Background

China is a country with a large population. According to "the Main Data of the Seventh National Census" released by the National Bureau of Statistics of China, China had a population of 1.412 billion in 2021, among which the elderly population over 60 years old was 267 million, accounting for 18.9% of the national population [1]. In 2050, the elderly population of China will reach 30% of the total population. China's first-tier cities have a relatively concentrated population, which does not match existing medical resources; especially, the outpatient departments of first-class hospitals need to receive a large number of patients. Taking a hospital in Beijing as an example, the average daily outpatient reception is about 10,400 person-times, among which the elderly over 60 years old account for 57%. The huge population also poses challenges to China's entire medical system and many problems exist in the medical treatment process improvement for the elderly. One of them is that how department navigation signs of the outpatient department can help the elderly find the target departments more effectively (Figs. 1 and 2).

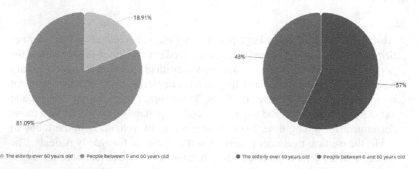

Fig. 1. Proportion of the elderly population in China and the figure of proportion of average daily receptions in outpatient department of a hospital in China

2   Current Navigation Design of Hospital Outpatient Service

2.1   Basic Navigation Board Design

It is the most basic and currently the most widely used in outpatient navigation design with the combined use of icons, arrows and texts to produce physical navigation board to guide patients in the department. It's very practical, convenient and easy to understand, but because of the varied design level, some navigation board design is confusing. For example, in the design of navigation boards, if the font is too small and too fine, it is not eye-catching enough. This problem may cause little confusion for young people, but for the elderly patients, with the growth of age, the function of various organs of the body declines and the vast majority of them have varying degrees of visual decline.

2.2   3D Panoramic Navigation

To click to enter the panoramic navigation can display panoramic information for patients to guide patients to the destination through directional arrows, department prompts and other information. In the hospital, users can compare the panoramic view with the real hospital scene they see, find the way according to the direction guided by the panoramic navigation and finally reach the destination. Such panoramic navigation is available not only in the hospital but also in the home for patients to get familiar with the internal environment of the hospital in advance. It's an innovative endeavor in the

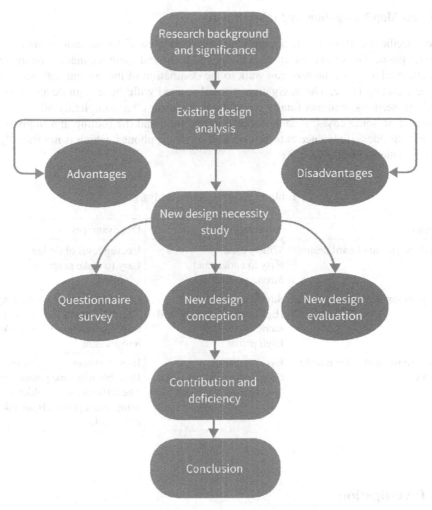

Fig. 2. Research frame diagram

medical environment that takes advantage of popular technology at the moment. In most surveys, it is highly rated. However, the weakness is that when entering the panoramic navigation, sometimes the system cannot locate in real time in the hospital. Therefore, patients visiting the hospital cannot locate their own position in real time, which may cause the inconsistency between the panoramic map and the user's position, leading to the user being confused and lost. As a result, the user will waste time in the walking process of looking for the position in the panoramic navigation, thus reducing efficiency [2]. The design also fails to take into account how difficult it is for elderly patients to operate electronic devices alone to some extent.

2.3 2D Map Navigation by Mobile Phone

The specific locations of all departments are "transported" to the indoor map of the mobile phone. Generally, the starting point, end point and route are marked on the two-dimensional map, so the user can walk to the destination of the current path according to the traveling route. The navigation is synchronized with the text guide and through guide in sections, patients finally reach the destination after completing all the paths. However, in some cases, it cannot locate in real time and the routing algorithm is not perfect. Besides, it also needs to be operated by smart phones, which is not friendly to elderly patients (Table 1).

Table 1. Existing design analysis.

Design	Advantages	Disadvantages
Basic navigation board design	Widely used Easy to understand Strong practicality	Uneven level of design Easy to make people get confused
3D panoramic navigation	Strong intuitiveness High contrast with the real scene High praise	Unstable real-time positioning The difficulty of the elderly in using smart phones is not taken into account
2D map navigation by mobile phone	Easy to operate Commonly used map mode	Imperfect routing algorithm Unstable real-time positioning The difficulty of the elderly in using smart phones is not taken into account

3 Investigation

In order to understand the guiding effect of navigation signs in existing outpatient departments of hospitals on the elderly group, 500 questionnaires were conducted for the elderly group over 60 years old in first-tier cities. The sample data showed that 75.45% of this group came to the outpatient clinic two to three times a year on average, of which 61.07% were accompanied by family members. The reasons for needing family companionship mostly come from that the complicated medical treatment process bothers elderly patients, the accompanying people can relieve the anxiety of medical treatment and the hospital signs cannot give clear directions to elderly patients, so patients need family members to constantly consult medical staff.

The guiding signs of various departments in the hospital are generally based on conventional text signs. However, there are many problems in the design of text navigation signs, such as the small and thin font and not bold colors in navigation signs. In 500 questionnaires, as many as 61.46% of the elderly could not find the target department quickly and accurately through text signs. Some hospitals try to use smartphone apps for indoor positioning and navigation systems, but it does not take into account the difficulties of unaccompanied elderly people who are unfamiliar with smartphone apps. Similarly, they not only have some difficulties in smart phone applications; in the 500 questionnaire survey, 58.7% of elderly patients also had trouble with the application of self-service registration and payment machines in hospitals. In the 500 questionnaire reports, only 4.15% of patients never asked the medical staff for directions even when the hospital had clear navigation bar for floors, departments and medical procedures (Fig. 3).

4.15%

95.85%

● Person never asking a medic for directions
● Person needing to ask a medic for directions

Fig. 3. Chart of the percentage of people who have never approached a health care provider for directions

The hospital outpatient environment is complex and crowded, so the medical process remains a challenge for elderly patients even with volunteers serving as guides in the halls. The process of medical treatment generally includes taking the number, waiting at the triage table for diagnosis, seeing the doctor, paying the examination fee, arriving at the target examination department, seeing the doctor again for diagnosis and examination results, paying for medicine, leaving the hospital, etc. Among them, patients need constantly switch between the correct target department, examination room and

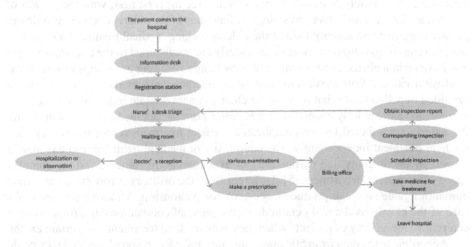

Fig. 4. Outpatient's medical treatment process

treatment room to complete the treatment process. The constant questioning of medical staff in this process is also a waste of medical resources to some extent (Fig. 4).

4 Design Concept of New Hospital Outpatient Navigation

It is an important issue to be solved that how to provide more intuitive and effective guidance for patients in the process of seeing a doctor and improving their medical experience. As can be seen from the above, the two main reasons why the elderly need to be accompanied in outpatient treatment are the need to constantly ask medical staff caused by the complicated medical treatment process and confused signs as well as the need for companionship to relieve the anxiety of seeking medical treatment.

For the above two reasons, Mixed Reality (MR) provides us with a new way of designing hospital outpatient navigation. Mixed Reality (MR) technology builds an interactive feedback information loop between the real world, virtual world and users by presenting virtual scene information in the real scene, thus enhancing the sense of reality of user experience [3]. With the development of Mixed Reality (MR) technology, blending virtual elements with the physical world can provide a navigational instruction directly integrated into the user's field of vision, especially when always-online devices are used such as head-mounted displays (HMD) and head up displays (HUD) [4].

In the navigation design of hospital outpatient department, a humanoid navigation sign can be designed based on Mixed Reality (MR) technology. The patient can use the head-mounted display (HMD) to display the sign directly in the field of vision and then simply walk with the navigation sign during the whole process of medical treatment. From the moment a patient enters the hospital, virtual navigational signs automatically plan the medical route without patients having to ask medical staff for directions or trying to understand the complex signs, different medical processes and the environment of each hospital (Fig. 5).

The elderly are more prone to anxiety than others in the process of seeking medical treatment. This anxiety is mostly derived from three aspects: first, with the growth of age, the audiovisual and other physiological functions of the elderly decline, resulting in greater cognitive and activity load of the elderly seeking medical treatment alone. Second, in terms of psychology, most of the elderly are accustomed to the existing lifestyle and have certain obstacles to contact with new things, resulting in feelings of insecurity, confusion and fear. With the development of the Internet, many medical service items are provided in online forms, but most of the elderly cannot operate independently, leading to more and more elderly people's reduced enthusiasm to seek medical treatment. Third, the elderly are affected by the complicated medical treatment routes when they seek medical treatment independently. The complexity of medical treatment route is mainly caused by the diversity and particularity of examination instruments and the complex space of outpatient department [5]. Different from the ordinary arrow sign, the virtual humanoid guide sign can produce a sense of companionship. Although it cannot take care of the elderly as the real person does, the sense of companionship produced by it can relieve the anxiety of patients when they seek medical treatment to a certain extent.

According to the data from 500 questionnaires, 68.3% of respondents said they could accept the virtual humanoid navigation if technology conditions allow.

Fig. 5. Models

5 Contribution and Limitations

First, it can be confirmed in this survey that most elderly patients are accompanied by someone in the process of outpatient treatment. The reasons for accompanying elderly patients are largely from the complicated medical treatment process and confused guidance signs causing trouble to them, which determines the necessity of designing a new outpatient guide. Second, it confirms the acceptability of Mixed Reality (MR) identification by the elderly, so that later work can be carried out.

The sample in the survey is aimed at the elderly over 60 years old seeking outpatient treatment in first-class hospitals in first-tier cities, so the acceptance degree of the design among the elderly living in small cities or small hospitals cannot be determined. That whether the use of head-mounted displays (HMD) in specific implementation will cause new problems for the elderly is unknown. In the future design process, more attention should be paid to the emotional design and it is also worth studying that how to make the design provide more real companionship to relieve patients' anxiety in medical treatment.

6 Conclusions

It is very necessary to provide new hospital navigation design to provide more intuitive and effective guidance for patients in the process of medical treatment and improve patients' medical experience, especially for elderly patients without family companion. Humanoid navigation signs based on Mixed Reality (MR) are suitable for complex

462   B. Guo and X. Mi

hospital outpatient environment, with a promise to effectively save time and effort for patients and medical staff. Although there are still many problems to be solved in the practical application of the technology, virtual humanoid navigation sign is still likely to become an important design direction of hospital navigation system in the future.

References

1. Ning, J.: Main data of the 7th national census (2021)
2. Jin, Y.: Study on goal-oriented interaction design – interior navigation design of large hospitals. Beijing Institute of Fashion Technology
3. Cheng, S., Pei, L., Zhang, W., Guo, L., Wang, B.: Study on application advantages of mixed reality technology in architectural heritage practice teaching. Surv. Educ. **12**(01), 87–89+105 (2023). https://doi.org/10.16070/j.carolcarrollnkicn45-1388/g4s2023.01.021
4. Lee, J., Jin, F., Kim, Y., et al.: User preference for navigation instructions in mixed reality. In: 2022 IEEE Conference on Virtual Reality and 3D User Interfaces (VR), pp. 802–811. IEEE (2022)
5. Li, Z., Xu, J., Nie, Q.: Research on the interface design of medical companion app for the elderly. Chin. Art **2023**(01), 72–78 (2023)

Automatic Identification of Daily Life Activities and Prediction of Falling Accidents Caused by Behavior

Seiji Hayashi[1](✉) and Akira Nakajima[2]

[1] Department of Electronics and Computer Systems, Faculty of Engineering,
Takushoku University, Tokyo, Japan
shayashi@es.takushoku-u.ac.jp
[2] Mechanical and Electronic Systems Course, Graduate School of Engineering,
Takushoku University, Tokyo, Japan

Abstract. In the present research, we developed an application that measures acceleration by a smartphone located at the waist, along with a deep learning system that automatically detects six behavioral activities (walking, running, standing, walking downstairs, walking upstairs, and falling). Specifically, we use a human activity database provided by the University of California–Irvine (UCI) to create a deep learning model with the UCI data. Next, transfer learning was applied to the learning model for the measurement data obtained by the acceleration acquisition application developed in this research. Using Sony's Neural Network Console development environment as a deep learning tool, in recognition experiments, our proposed method for automatic identification of activities and prediction of falling accidents caused by behavior achieved a high accuracy rate of almost 95%.

Keywords: human activity detection · falling accidents prediction · transfer learning · Neural Network Console

1 Introduction

Knowing behavior types and how often they are performed in daily life activities helps to evaluate one's own health condition, and can be a factor in increasing health consciousness. In addition, if this is used in nursing care facilities, it will be possible to measure the amount of residents' exercise. Concurrently, due to the aging of developed societies, the number of sudden fainting and other accidents among the elderly has tended to increase year by year. Previous research on fall detection used smartphones, wearable inertial sensors, and radar as input devices, and several papers have been published on effective methods using long short-term memory (LSTM) neural networks [1, 2]. Other methods, such as fall detection based on the OpenPose skeleton [3] and systems based on multiple ultra-wideband radar to detect falls [4], have also been proposed.

C. Stephanidis et al. (Eds.): HCII 2023, CCIS 1833, pp. 463–470, 2023.
https://doi.org/10.1007/978-3-031-35992-7_62

In this study, we constructed a network using the Sony Neural Network Console (NNC) tool for discriminative classification by transfer learning with the LSTM architecture. As one countermeasure to detect these incidents at an early stage, it should be possible to immediately judge human activities by machine learning from measurement data obtained through smartphones equipped with acceleration sensors. Additionally, it may be possible to issue a warning in response to sudden falling accidents. In the present study, we developed an application that measures acceleration by a smartphone located at the waist, along with a deep learning system that automatically detects six behavioral activities (walking, running, standing, walking downstairs, walking upstairs, and falling). Specifically, using a human activity database provided by the University of California–Irvine (UCI) [5], we created a deep learning model using the UCI data. Next, transfer learning was applied to the learning model for the measurement data obtained by the acceleration acquisition application developed in this research. We applied our method in recognition experiments using Sony's NNC development environment [6] as a deep learning tool.

2 Equipment, Programs, and Data Used in This Research

2.1 Measurement Equipment

In this research, we acquired acceleration data using a common smartphone and a sensor developed for measurement.

- ASUS ROGphone2: Smartphone with built-in TDK InvenSense ICM4x6xx accelerometer. Measurements were conducted using an application that was modified to function in AndroidStudio.
- IMS-SD data logger type inertial sensor [7]: Developed by TEC Giken, the IMS-SD can measure three-axis acceleration, angular velocity, and geomagnetism. Data can be saved to a PC or SD card using control software.

2.2 Acceleration Measurement Application

The application developed in this research was created with a horizontal screen, as shown in Fig. 1. The sampling frequency of the smartphone's acceleration sensor can be adjusted using the application, and acquired data can be saved in CSV format in the main storage. Example CSV data are shown in Fig. 2. Column A records the date and time of measurement down to the unit of 1 ms. The B-th to D-th columns are the X-, Y-, and Z-axis acceleration data, respectively, and are recorded to the sixth decimal place.

The save function is mainly used to collect training data for machine learning. In this study, to detect falling accident behavior in addition to the five behaviors performed in everyday life in real time, by inputting the IP address and PORT number, the acquired data are directly communicated by the User Datagram Protocol to the PC.

	A	B	C	D
1	22.02.06_16:26:55:462	-1.60808	9.449661	1.848282
2	22.02.06_16:26:55:481	-1.5183	9.466415	1.747726
3	22.02.06_16:26:55:501	-1.59131	9.650772	1.860245
4	22.02.06_16:26:55:462	-1.75652	9.705841	2.159531
5	22.02.06_16:26:55:481	-1.81757	9.750137	2.134384
6	22.02.06_16:26:55:501	-1.64758	9.68309	1.823135
7	22.02.06_16:26:55:462	-1.61166	9.667526	1.64238
8	22.02.06_16:26:55:481	-1.58533	9.552612	1.292831
9	22.02.06_16:26:55:501	-1.74814	9.606476	1.193466
10	22.02.06_16:26:55:462	-1.61285	9.675919	1.078537
11	22.02.06_16:26:55:481	-1.3902	9.675919	0.8918
12	22.02.06_16:26:55:501	-1.51709	9.902161	0.833145
13	22.02.06_16:26:55:462	-1.28845	9.92012	0.588928

Fig. 1. Interface screen of application developed in this research

Fig. 2. Example of saved data

3 Obtaining Acceleration Data

3.1 Acceleration Measurement

Acquisition of acceleration data is the same as that in the UCI method [5]. Figure 3 shows the wearing position of the smartphone. To attach a smartphone, we used a rubber band and a smartphone pouch, and attached the sensor so that the movable range of the sensor was within 3 cm and the inclination of the sensor was within 15° [8]. The orientation of the three axes of the sensor is shown in Fig. 4.

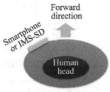

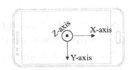

Fig. 3. Wearing position of the smartphone

Fig. 4. Three-axis sensor orientation

The data measurement cycle was set to 50 Hz, and 5 sets of 20 s were measured for each action. In addition, various measurement locations, such as asphalt pavement outdoors, inside a house, and inside a school building, were used.

3.2 CSV Data of Measured Acceleration

Preprocessing is performed on training data and test data measured by smartphones. The CSV files used in NNC datasets need to match the number of rows and columns appropriately. Because the data used in this research are only the numerical values of acceleration, it is necessary to remove the time record in the first column from the CSV file shown in Fig. 2. Also, the numerical value of the XYZ acceleration data is changed to double type, and then changed to the unit of gravitational acceleration (1 G = 9.80665 m/s^2)[8], and multiple frames were generated by performing 50% overlap every 2.56 s.

4   Creating Learning Models and Transfer Learning

First, a machine learning model is created using the acceleration data in the UCI Machine Learning Repository [5]. After that, transfer learning is applied to the data actually measured in this research.

4.1   Machine Learning Using UCI Acceleration Data

UCI Acceleration Dataset. The first model was created using the acceleration data shown in Table 1, which are available from the UCI Machine Learning Repository.

Table 1. UCI acceleration dataset details

Subject, Age	30 Volunteers, 19–48
Type of behavior	Walking, running, standing, walking downstairs, walking upstairs, lying down
Labeling method	Manually generated from video
Total frames	Learning: 7352 frames, verification: 2947 frames

Network Structure. Among the recurrent neural networks that can extract time-related features, we used networks including LSTMs, which can handle long time series data. Figure 5 shows the network with a LSTM. In addition, to create a network structure with higher accuracy and less computational complexity, we used NNC's automatic structure optimization function, which can change the network structure in various ways, for learning. As a result, the network structure shown in Fig. 6 was obtained, and a UCI learning model with a high accuracy rate was constructed.

Transfer Learning. When data from the five behaviors (walking, running, standing, walking downstairs, and walking upstairs) measured in this study were applied with transfer learning to the optimal network structure of the six behaviors obtained in Fig. 6, the numerical values of the network parameters were partially changed from 6 to 5. Figure 7 shows the parameters changed for transfer learning from the model in Fig. 6. The affine weight W was changed from (64,6) to (64,5) and bias b was changed from (6,) to (5,). Also, the parameters of b, gamma, mean, and var of BatchNormalization below affine were changed from 6 to 5.

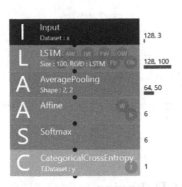

Fig. 5. Network structure including LSTM

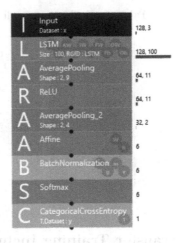

Fig. 6. Learning model with high accuracy rate

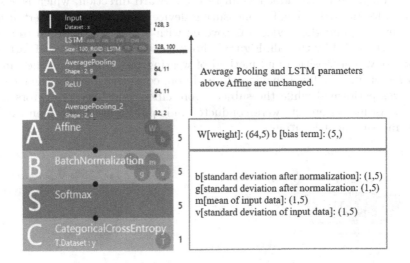

Average Pooling and LSTM parameters above Affine are unchanged.

W[weight]: (64,5) b [bias term]: (5,)

b[standard deviation after normalization]: (1,5)
g[standard deviation after normalization: (1,5)
m[mean of input data]: (1,5)
v[standard deviation of input data]: (1,5)

Fig. 7. Modified parameters for transfer learning

4.2 Results of Transfer Learning

From the results of the mixture matrix in Table 2, we obtained a high accuracy rate of 95.71% for five actions, a precision rate of 95.96%, and a recall rate of 95.71%.

Table 2. Evaluation results for transfer-trained learning model

	y'__0	y'__1	y'__2	y'__3	y'__4	Recall	
y:label=0	14	0	0	0	0	1	walk
y:label=1	0	13	0	1	0	0.9285	run
y:label=2	0	0	14	0	0	1	up
y:label=3	2	0	0	12	0	0.8571	down
y:label=4	0	0	0	0	14	1	stand
Precision	0.875	1	1	0.923	1		
F-Measures	0.9333	0.9629	1	0.8888	1		
Accuracy	0.9571						
Avg.Precision	0.9596						
Avg.Recall	0.9571						
Avg.F-Measures	0.957						

5 Transfer Training Including Fall Behavior

5.1 Measurement of Acceleration Data Including Fall Behavior

In this study, we newly added a fall in the forward direction, which is easy to measure, for fall detection. The measuring device was an IMS-SD inertial measurement unit, and the device was covered with cushioning material to absorb the impact caused by the fall. Figure 8 shows a diagram of the IMS-SD attached to the body. The position and method of wearing the IMS-SD are the same as when measuring the five behaviors. In addition, considering safety, the measurement was performed while the subject wore elbow and knee protectors and a helmet. All measurements were conducted indoors. Figure 9 shows an example of the measurement location.

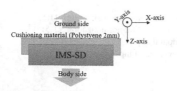

Fig. 8. Wearing setup of IMS-SD

Fig. 9. Example of measurement location

The data were acquired at 50 Hz, and each action was performed in 3 s to capture the moment of falling. The capture the state before falling, the three behaviors of running, walking, and stopping were performed a certain number of times. In addition, the last 0.44 s of the 3-s measurement data were omitted to make each 2.56-s frame the same as that in the five-action data acquisition. Figure 10 shows an example visualization of fall behavior data.

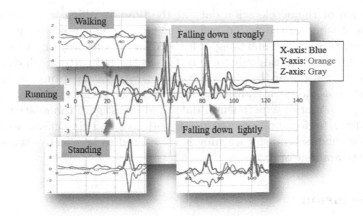

Fig. 10. Example visualization of fall behavior data

5.2   Machine Learning of Six Behaviors Including Fall Behavior

The learning model before transfer learning uses the network and parameters of the learning model in Fig. 6. The training data of six actions (walking, running, standing, walking downstairs, walking upstairs, and falling) were used to perform transfer learning by only deleting the parameters below the affine of the learning model in Fig. 6.

Table 3. Evaluation results of six behaviors including fall behavior (label 5 indicates fall behavior)

	y'__0	y'__1	y'__2	y'__3	y'__4	y'__5	Recall	
y:label=0	28	0	0	0	0	0	1	walk
y:label=1	1	27	0	0	0	0	0.9642	run
y:label=2	0	0	26	2	0	0	0.9285	up
y:label=3	3	0	3	22	0	0	0.7857	down
y:label=4	0	0	0	0	28	0	1	stand
y:label=5	0	0	0	0	1	43	0.9772	tentou
Precision	0.875	1	0.8965	0.9166	0.9655	1		
F-Measure	0.9333	0.9817	0.9122	0.8461	0.9824	0.9884		
Accuracy	0.9456							
Avg.Precis	0.9422							
Avg.Recall	0.9426							
Avg.F-Mea	0.9407							

The results of the mixture matrix in Table 3 show that we were able to obtain a high accuracy rate of 94.56% for the six behaviors including the fall behavior, a precision rate of 94.22%, and a recall rate of 94.26%. The transfer learning model, which was used to classify the five actions, obtained a high accuracy rate even when falling was included. The first reason for this high accuracy is that the variation of the acceleration data at the time of falling was characteristic, regardless of whether the action before the fall behavior was walking, running, or standing. Second, the matching of learning in transfer learning was excellent. However, this method uses only forward falls as the fall pattern, which is considered to be the reason for the higher recognition rate. In the future, we would like to conduct trial-and-error transfer learning based on various behavioral patterns and a large amount of experimental data, and investigate the relationship with detailed data. As for the learning speed, both five and six actions were significantly shortened, so transfer learning is considered to be effective when dealing with a large amount of data.

6   Conclusion

In this research, a model using UCI data was used for transfer learning of five behaviors obtained from actual measurements, and behavior detection was performed by combining the fall behavior data obtained from an IMS-SD sensor with five common behaviors. As a result, high accuracy rate and fast learning speed were obtained for both five and six actions. Future tasks include increasing the number of measurement subjects and increasing both the learning data and verification data. In addition, when measuring fall behavior, the impact on the body is somewhat large, so measures should be taken to include not only falling on a mat but also falling on the ground or in a forward direction.

References

1. García, E., Villar, M., Fáñez, M., Villar, J.R., de la Cal, E., Cho, S.-B.: Towards effective detection of elderly falls with CNN-LSTM neural networks. Neurocomputing **500**, 231–240 (2022)
2. Li, H., et al.: Bi-LSTM network for multimodal continuous human activity recognition and fall detection. IEEE Sens. J. **20**(3), 1191–1201 (2019)
3. LIN, C.-B., et al.: A framework for fall detection based on OpenPose skeleton and LSTM/GRU models. Appl. Sci. **11**(1), 329 (2020)
4. Maitre, J., Bouchard, K., Gaboury, S.: Fall detection with UWB radars and CNN-LSTM architecture. IEEE J. Biomed. Health Inform. **25**(4), 1273–1283 (2021)
5. Dataset of Human Activity Recognition Using Smartphones, UC Irvine Machine Learning Repository. https://archive-beta.ics.uci.edu/dataset/240/human+activity+recognition+using+smartphones. Accessed 12 Jan 2023
6. Neural Network Console. https://dl.sony.com/. Accessed 12 Jan 2023
7. IMS-SD: Data logger type inertial sensor (IMU: Inertial measurement Unit). https://www.tecgihan.co.jp/products/ims-sd-imu. Accessed 11 Feb 2023
8. Kawaguchi, N., et al.: HASC challenge 2010: construction of wearable accelerometer sensor corpus for activity recognition. In: Proceedings of Multimedia, Distributed Cooperation and Mobile Symposium, vol. 2011, pp. 69–75 (2011)

Biographical Patterns for Technology Use in Older Adults - A Case Study

Ines Himmelsbach(✉), Christina Klank, Tjard de Vries, and Michael Doh

Catholic University Freiburg, Karlstr. 63, 79104 Freiburg, Germany
ines.himmelsbach@kh-freiburg.de

Abstract. This qualitative study aims to display a case of 80-year-old Mrs. Blade and her attitude towards technology and education. A biographic-narrative interview with PZI questions was conducted. The approach of reconstructing narrative identity was used for step-by-step analysis. After a brief explanation of Mrs. Blade's biography, the case itself will be portrayed. Biographical aspects regarding education and technology will be shown. Results yielded that fear of mis-takes prevent Mrs. Blade to further using or engaging with technology. However, high educational interest may serve as an amplifier of technology use. Additionally, contextual conditions may force individuals to interact with technological devices.

Keywords: Qualitative biographical research · ICT use of older adults

1 ICT Use and Older Adults

Learning on how to use ICT for older adults on the one hand leads to various advantages, e.g. as it holds great potential for improving access by adults to a variety of learning opportunities and promoting equity and inclusion [1]. On the other hand, challenges arise, such as being overwhelmed with devices or underestimating one's own abilities [2]. Regarding the technology acceptance model, perceived usefulness, ease of use to engage with ICT [3], and internet self-efficacy are furthermore identified as key factors [4]. Lastly, following van Deursen, van Dijk and Peters [5], it results that there is a gap between exploring ICT at the first place and continuously using ICT to reach certain outcomes.

The context of education and learning of older adults is predominantly informal [6]. Biography inhabits a pivotal role in education for older adults. Older adults' learning in present day is largely influenced by past learning experiences [7]. Focusing on the individual perspective, biographical research provides necessary tools to map these educational and learning experiences across the life span [8]. Taking a closer look in terms of education and ICT use, it results that analyzing biographical patterns help to better understand ICT non-use in older age. To our understanding, this perspective especially if we want to address non-use is often neglected [9]. In this study we thus aim to analyze whether biographical learning behavior explains (non-)use of ICT. We further address contextual factors that appear relevant to (non)-use. Also, we elaborate factors which – beyond age – shape ICT rejection.

C. Stephanidis et al. (Eds.): HCII 2023, CCIS 1833, pp. 471–477, 2023.
https://doi.org/10.1007/978-3-031-35992-7_63

2 Method

This case study provides first insights on patterns connecting biography, education as well as learning and ICT (non-)use. The case of Mrs. Blade shows that learning experiences develop over the life course and that these have an impact on learning how to use ICT.

Mrs. Blade was interviewed using a combination of narrative interview according to Schütze [10] as well as the problem-centered interview method (PCI) [11]. The narrative interview starts with an open narrative question and does not interrupt the biographical narrative. Afterwards an inquiry phase with immanent questions on past and present life continues the interview. Lastly, PCI questions regarding the research questions were asked. Material was fully transcribed in German. The material was analyzed following Lucius-Hoene and Deppermann's [12] approach of reconstructing narrative identity. The method can be defined as identity work of a person in concrete interactions, narrative representation and production of aspects of his or her identity that are relevant to the respective situation [12]. Analyzing starts off with a structural analysis, focusing on the overall structure of the narrative. Based on these results, decisive text excerpts are then selected for a detailed line-by-line analysis. The present case was derived from the data set of the project DiBiWohn ("Digital educational processes for older residents in assisted living arrangements and care facilities" funded by the "Federal Ministry of Education and Research" in Germany; 2020–2025).

3 Results

3.1 The Narrative of Mrs. Blade

Mrs. Blade was born as the third child of her family. Four years later, the father returns from being a prisoner of war from Russia, but soon dies. Having four children, the family has to cope with life without a head of the family. Despite limited financial resources, all children graduate and complete an apprenticeship. Mrs. Blade starts working in administration until she gets married ten years later. The couple has two sons and a daughter. The family enjoys doing outdoor activities and takes regular vacation trips to France, also because of Mrs. Blade's French language skills. Two of the children spend an exchange year abroad, which leads Mrs. Blade's to enhance her English skills. Encouraged by her husband, she starts language classes which she maintains for ten years. Finally, after about 20 years of being a housewife, she starts a job and works for another eight years. The sudden death of her younger sister and her husband's retirement status ultimately cause her to retire early. Due to the husband's health conditions, the couple decides to sell the house and moves into an assisted living apartment. There, the husband dies after a short illness. As a widow, Mrs. Blade finds her way back to life. She receives regular support in daily hassles from her sons, e.g. in online cash transfer. She spends her daily life going to the cemetery to visit her husband, reading or doing crossword puzzles. She also devotes time to her hobby of learning French. Mrs. Blade is grandmother to nine grandchildren.

The narrative itself follows a mostly chronological storyline, beginning at birth and ending on the day of the interview.

3.2 A Case of Biographical Continuity Preventing ICT Learning

Family of Origin and Affinity for Education Lead to Status Despite All Circumstances. The biographical narration begins with two different story lines, which are strongly intertwined and appear simultaneously within the narration. the two topoi cover narrations of Mrs. Blade's father and the four siblings' background. The father seems to have struggled from the consequences of his imprisonment during the second world war which thus had an impact on the family. The interpretation is that he has not complied with paternal attributions and therefore had a possibly negative impact on his children growing up. The father remains distant in the narrative of Mrs. Blade, no emotional bond is shown rather an icon of a world war II father is depicted. This dynamic explains the separate story lines. In contrast to the distant father stands the unity of the siblings, expressed by the interviewee in constantly using the pronoun "We" when addressing topics that include her siblings. There seems to be a strong bond between the siblings, most likely due to the circumstances. Only very few notions characterize the mother whose country of birth is France. Nevertheless, her role is of great importance to Mrs. Blade which can be detected later on. for example, Mrs. Blade describes a strong interest in learning French. Her own family takes regular vacations in France and surprisingly her own daughter nowadays lives in France. due to the difficult (economic) background, Mrs. Blade's mother strongly focuses on her Children's education. As a result, all children pass school and complete an apprenticeship. Mrs. Blade herself passes this attitude for Education on to Her Children and, Alike Her Mother, She was successful in doing so. proudly, she reports on school and academic development of all of her three children.

Overall Biographical Patterns. Being mother and wife is an essential factor for Mrs. Blade's biography. Her narrative is aligned with her Children's and Husband's careers. Even her interests (the Violin, English class) or experiences refer to at least either one. She seems to comply with the middle-class image of women at that time (in central Europe) with a corresponding gender image. After getting married, she quits her job with her husband continuing his career as breadwinner. There are only few notions in the interview, where Mrs. Blade seems to contradict her Husband's opinion – at least in the way she positions him and herself.

Mrs. Blade's descriptions can be characterized as status driven (husband in public service, house, backyard, big car, children going abroad), although over the course of the interview, this tendency seems to fade. Still, it is noticeable that her actions as a parent, her statements and views are constantly justified with former societal norms. She wants to act within what is expected from her role, and thus positions herself, her husband and her children's actions adapted towards her attitude. Referring to her children, she taught them how important it is to continue even though things might not work out as planned.

Her perspective on aging is positioned within the same view on societal norms. For her, it is unthinkable to show weakness, complain or be a burden to her children. She seems to have an overall optimistic and positive (albeit socially desirable) attitude.

Education Matters. In this study, we define education as the holistic acquisition of self and world and thus both in terms of self-positioning towards appropriation as well as in terms of the contexts within which education (world) takes place, following Humboldt

[13]. Accordingly, we define education with the corresponding German term *Bildung*. The term depicts a process that results in the individuals' transformation.

Self-positioning: Education and Learning. Mrs. Blade defines education and learning as „very important" (02_79w) which is what she internalized from her mother and passed on to her children. From her perspective, education includes: knowledge acquisition, decent behavior and a variety of programs.

Knowledge acquisition. Can mainly be identified regarding formal education and learning situations. As the only child in her grade, she transfers to an upper secondary level school (Gymnasium) although she graduates early to start an apprenticeship. After that she begins her job and does not obtain other degrees.

Acting according to societal norms makes *decent behavior* (both in society and at home) mandatory for Mrs. Blade. Her importance of one's role in society is again evident. She aims to act according to her role and to not cause attention or go against, as she taught her children. Therefore, an informal perspective on education can be added as education takes place in her daily life or at least has an impact on it.

Finally, she mentions different *educational interests:* The variety of possibilities seems only to be limited by one's interests, following Mrs. Blade. She herself prefers learning languages and listening to presentations on travels to France. When looking at her learning methods, she confirms that she has established her personal learning procedure for languages over years.

A Focus on Technology. Mrs. Blade was selected because she described herself as having no prior experience or interest in engaging with ICT. However, the interview shows that her self-perspective and our perspective differ. From a technology perspective, Mrs. Blade reports that she owns a telephone, a basic mobile phone and a CD player including a radio. Her daily routine includes listening to the radio. The mobile phone is used solely in the occurrence of a crisis when she is away. Only when asked on how she communicates with her daughter does it emerge that she uses ICT regarding video calls on her tablet. In general, she seems to have a basic knowledge of tablet use, as she is familiar with terms related such as facetime or apps.

Self-positioning: ICT Use Over the Life Course and Age. Mrs. Blade acknowledges that there is no possibility nowadays to live without ICT. Nonetheless, she assigns this task to the younger generation E.G. like her grandchildren. However, she seems to be skeptical: "it is a = different world" (02_79w). as a result, she neither identifies the need to further interact with her tablet or a smartphone nor change her position in the future as it is not vital for her. she adds metaphorically: "I BELIEVE this ship has sailed." (02_79w).

Learning, ICT, Biography – Missing Biographical References for Mrs. Blade. She enjoys learning languages. She acknowledges that learning how to use ICT can be a hobby when someone enjoys doing so. However, this is not the case for her. following Mrs. Blade's narrations, she describes how new topics should be learned in three steps: getting to know a topic, getting further informed about it and finally attending classes. She became familiar with this path at school, received information and content and later on attended a language class. Most importantly in her case is that this path is accompanied by a biographical reference or connection. As we know, Mrs. BLade's mother and daughter biographically connect her to France. She got to know the language, received information and continued learning due to her interest. Knowing about French culture and the country itself allows her to behave decently (similar her interest in the English language). in regard to ICT use, her background is different. She has no previous experience in this field and no support from her husband. Rather, He turned her proposal to use ICT down. Later on, she got partially familiar with it on behalf of her kids. However, the Husband's nonexistent legitimacy seems to outweigh this. Thus, she did not get beyond becoming familiar and does not want to receive further information.

Additionally, she does not want to participate in ICT classes. Her position seems to be defensive, above all as she is afraid to embarrass herself. It is interesting, though, that she is not interested in language classes either. Nevertheless, her prior knowledge allows her to compensate. That enables her to implement her developed learning method and continue to practice on her own – as opposed to ICT learning where she will not be able to catch up. In sum, Mrs. Blade portrays herself as a person with a strong affinity for education, but ICT use came too late in life and has no connection in her biography.

Externalizing Reasons for (Non-)use of ICT. Mrs. Blade's previous experience with technical devices can be summarized briefly: "not much (3.0)" (02_79w). Instead, she reports a variety of reasons why this is so and why she does not want any change:

- *No previous experiences in ICT use.* Contradiction to her previous learning patterns
- *Lack of necessity for use (rationale).* Mrs. Blade needs ICT for cash transfer, however her son takes care of that. Besides, she does not mention a specific need for ICT use.
- *Arthritis.* Her fine motor skills in her fingers limit her in controlling the tablet: "i push a different button and i get all anxious and and (…) there's no point" (02_79w)
- *Emotional factors.* She generally mentions her insecurity as well as the hurdle that ICT presents. Another concern is to cause damage due to a wrong action, e.g. for cash transactions. Referring to her view on societal norms, she is afraid of embarrassing herself in front of others.

4   Conclusion

Fang and colleagues [14] show that education has the greatest impact on ICT use. However, this case illustrates that education is not a matter of achieving a missed goal, but rather to shape life according to one's own interests and preferences and focusing on topics that are important for everyday life.

Therefore, informal learning activities are preferred and are interpreted as connecting to biographical interests and expanding one's own preferences. In addition, they can protect against the danger of 'embarrassment' – unlike possibly in non-formal learning contexts. The case highlights that one's own pace, own demands and self-control are important. Additionally, it can be shown that educational activities in old age break away from a status-driven ideal and a change towards personal interests and relevance to everyday life occurs. It will now be interesting to see to what extent this relationship between educational understanding, learning patterns, and technology use will be corroborated or expanded in further analyses with other biographical cases.

Accordingly, one's biography provides valuable key factors for education with older people [7]. As a result, we propose to consider biographical aspects when planning and designing educational programs. One method are peer learning methods, which are applied in the project DiBiWohn [15].

Perceived usefulness, ease of use [3], perceived value [16] and internet self-efficacy [4] cannot be detected in this case. Han and Nam [3] point out that it is necessary to address those factors among older adults. The overall questions now are, how biographical aspects can influence the understanding of ICT and its use. And second, to what extent biography can be used to better understand ICT learning.

In future studies, what needs to be addressed first and foremost is "the process moving from exploring new technologies to a more robust use of new technologies" [17, p. 729]. Thus, on the one hand, simply testing out is a much lower hurdle than continuously retaining and using ICT. On the other hand, this is precisely the transition that needs to be positively designed or guided for long-term use.

References

1. UNESCO Institute for Lifelong Learning: 4th Global Report on Adult Learning and Education (2019)
2. Rathgeb, T., Doh, M., Tremmel, F., Jokisch, M., Groß, A.-K.: Ergebnisse der SIM-Studie 2021 Medienumgang von Menschen ab 60 Jahren. [Results of the SIM study 2021 media use by people aged 60 and older]. Media Perspektiven, pp. 389–402 (2022)
3. Han, S., Nam, S.: Creating supportive environments and enhancing personal perception to bridge the digital divide among older adults. Educ. Gerontol. (2021). https://doi.org/10.1080/03601277.2021.1988448
4. Jokisch, M.R., Schmidt, L.I., Doh, M., Marquard, M., Wahl, H.-W.: The role of internet self-efficacy, innovativeness and technology avoidance in breadth of internet use: comparing older technology experts and non-experts. Comput. Hum. Behav. (2020). https://doi.org/10.1016/j.chb.2020.106408
5. van Deursen, A.J., van Dijk, J.A., Peters, O.: Rethinking Internet skills: the contribution of gender, age, education, Internet experience, and hours online to medium- and content-related Internet skills. Poetics (2011). https://doi.org/10.1016/j.poetic.2011.02.001
6. Tippelt, R., Schmidt-Hertha, B., Friebe, J.: Kompetenzen und Kompetenzentwicklung im höheren Lebensalter. [Competenices and developmpent among older adults. Study results]. In: Friebe, J., Schmidt-Hertha, B., Tippelt, R. (eds.) Kompetenzen im höheren Lebensalter. Ergebnisse der Studie "Competencies in Later Life" (CiLL). DIE spezial, pp. 11–22. W. Bertelsmann Verlag, Bielefeld (2014)
7. Schmidt-Hertha, B.: Kompetenzerwerb und Lernen im Alter. [Competence acquisition and education of older adults], 1st edn. Studientexte für Erwachsenenbildung. Bertelsmann, Bielefeld (2014)
8. von Felden, H.: Zur Erforschung von Lern- und Bildungsprozessen über die Lebenszeit aus biographieanalytischer Perspektive. In: Hof, C., Rosenberg, H. (eds.) Lernen im Lebenslauf. Springer Fachmedien, Wiesbaden (2018)
9. Rohner, R.: Digitale Bildung und digitale Kompetenzen im Alter. [Digital education and digital competencies in aging]. In: Kolland, F. (ed.) Bildung in der nachberuflichen Lebensphase. Ein Handbuch, 1st edn., pp. 189–200. Kohlhammer Verlag, Stuttgart (2023)
10. Schütze, F.: Biographieforschung und narratives Interview. [Biographical research and narrative interviews]. Neue Praxis. Kritische Zeitschrift für Sozialarbeit und Sozialpädagogik (1983). https://doi.org/10.2307/j.ctvdf09cn.6

11. Witzel, A.: Das problemzentrierte Interview. Forum Qualitative Sozialforschung / Forum: Qualitative Social Research **1**, Art. 22 (2000)
12. Lucius-Hoene, G., Deppermann, A.: Rekonstruktion narrativer Identität. Ein Arbeitsbuch zur Analyse narrativer Interviews. [Reconstruction of narrative identity: A workbook on analyzing narrative interviews]. VS Verlag für Sozialwissenschaften, Wiesbaden (2002)
13. von Humboldt, W.: Theorie der Bildung. [Theory of education]. In: Humboldt, W. von (ed.) Werke in fünf Bänden, Band 1. Wiss. Buchgesellschaft (1969)
14. Fang, M.L., Canham, S.L., Battersby, L., Sixsmith, J., Wada, M., Sixsmith, A.: Exploring privilege in the digital divide: implications for theory, policy, and practice. Special issue: technology and aging: review article. Gerontol. **59**, e1–e15 (2019)
15. Doh, M.: Auswertung von empirischen Studien zur Nutzung von Internet, digitalen Medien und Informations- und Kommunikations-Technologien bei älteren Menschen. Expertise zum Achten Altersbericht der Bundesregierung. [Evaluation of empirical studies on the use of the Internet, digital media, and ICT among older people. The Expert Commission of the Eighth Government Report on Older People]. In: Hagen, C., Endter, C., Berner, F. (eds.). Deutsches Zentrum für Altersfragen, Berlin (2020)
16. Jung, Y., et al.: Low-income minority seniors' enrollment in a cybercafé: psychological barriers to crossing the digital divide. Educ. Gerontol. (2010). https://doi.org/10.1080/036012 70903183313
17. Tsai, H.-Y.S., Rikard, R.V., Cotten, S.R., Shillair, R.: Senior technology exploration, learning, and acceptance (STELA) model: from exploration to use – a longitudinal randomized controlled trial. Educ. Gerontol. (2019). https://doi.org/10.1080/03601277.2019.1690802

Effects of Conversational AI Assistance and Decision Stages on the Flow Experience of Older Users' of an e-Healthcare Decision Tool

Xiao Huang[1]([⊠]) [iD], Wi-Suk Kwon[2] [iD], Ebenezer Nana Banyin Harrison[3] [iD], Nick McCormick[2] [iD], and Salisa Westrick[2] [iD]

[1] Zhejiang Fashion Institute of Technology, Zhejiang 315000, China
huangxiao_cici@outlook.com
[2] Auburn University, Auburn, AL 36849, USA
[3] University of North Carolina Asheville, Asheville, NC 28804, USA

Abstract. Many older users find it challenging to use Medicare Plan Finder (MPF), an interactive online decision support tool for Medicare plan selections without assistance due to the diversity of plan options and their low internet competency. This study implements an artificially intelligent decision assistant (AIDA) to support older users' Medicare Part D plan selections on MPF and applies the flow theory to examine (1) the effects of AIDA on older users' perceptions of online flow (control, concentration, and enjoyment) during a Medicare Part D plan selection on MPF and (2) the moderating role of the decision stage for these effects. Data were collected through an online experiment with a 2 (AIDA: present vs. absence) x2 (Decision Stage: need recognition vs. alternative evaluation) between-subjects design with a U.S. national sample of 420 older (ages of 65 +) Medicare beneficiaries. Structural equation modeling results revealed that AIDA improved the perception of flow in control, which in turn further enhanced the perceptions of flow in concentration and enjoyment. Further, the AIDA effect on flow was significantly stronger in the alternative evaluation stage (vs. the need recognition stage). The findings suggest positive effects of the AIDA intervention in driving older users' superior online flow experience, especially at the stage closer to the final plan selection and provide significant theoretical and practical implications.

Keywords: Flow · Intelligent Decision Assistant · Decision Stage

1 Introduction

The Medicare Outpatient Prescription Drug Coverage Program (Part D) served over 48 million beneficiaries in 2022, the majority of whom are older adults (65 + years old) [1]. However, choosing an optimal Medicare Part D plan can be challenging and frustrating for older adults due to a large number of plan choices, diverse plan attributes (e.g., monthly premiums, out-of-pockets, deductibles, and star ratings), complicated and changing health conditions, and limited health literacy [2]. Medicare Plan Finder

(MPF), an interactive decision support tool available on the Medicare website (www. medicare.gov), is the only place where comprehensive plan comparisons is possible [3]. However, older users' MPF use can be challenged by their low internet competency coupled with the high level of complexity required for the decision due to the large number of alternatives and attributes to be considered for an optimal decision.

Researchers have argued that well-designed interactive interfaces can enhance users' online flow experiences by providing feelings of control, enjoyment, and concentration of interacting with the interface [4]. Although online flow has been widely investigated in the online shopping context [4], research on online flow experiences in online healthcare decisions is rare. Recent literature shows that human counselors' real-time assistance during older Medicare beneficiaries' use of MPF for Medicare plan selection processes enhances positive user experience outcomes, such as increased use of MPF functions and diverse decision strategies [5, 6]. In this study, we propose that using an artificially intelligent decision assistant (AIDA) embedded in the MPF website which provides real-time assistance conversationally may produce similar positive user experiences. The role of conversational AI in helping older adults has received much attention in various contexts, such as shopping [7], exercise [8], and healthcare [9]. However, no research has attempted to implement conversational AI in Medicare decision-making contexts, and little research has examined conversation AI effects on users' online flow experiences. Older adults adopt a five-stage decision-making process in Medicare plan selections, including (1) need recognition, (2) information search, (3) alternative plan evaluation, (4) plan selection decision, and (5) post-decision evaluation [2]. This study focuses on two of these decision stages, namely need recognition (the initial stage in which beneficiaries identify what plan attributes and criteria are important to consider to meet their financial and medication needs) and alternative evaluation (the later stage in which beneficiaries compare actual plan alternatives in terms of their relative advantages and disadvantages). Therefore, the purpose of this study was to examine (1) the effects of AIDA on older Medicare beneficiaries' perceptions of online flow (control, concentration, and enjoyment) during a Medicare Part D plan selection on MPF and (2) how these AIDA effects may vary between the aforementioned two decision stages.

2   Literature Review and Hypotheses

2.1   Online Flow: Control, Concentration, and Enjoyment

According to the flow theory [10], flow refers to "the holistic sensation that people feel when they act with total involvement (p. 36)." Individuals experience a flow when they are highly concentrated on the activity, control their own performance in it, enjoy it, be less self-conscious, and have nothing else that is important anymore [10]. Flow happens when an individual acquires prompt responses/feedback and has skills/capabilities to reach an achievable yet challenging goal [10]. Flow can be experienced during an activity in computer-mediated environments, which is known as online flow [11]. Online flow experiences have been known to enhance positive outcomes, such as favorable website or brand attitudes, revisit and purchase intentions, and purchase behaviors [4, 10, 12]. Similarly, users of MPF may reach an online flow state if they experience that the Medicare plan selection task on MPF is challenging yet doable [11], and this flow experienced on a MPF task may motivate them to continue to reuse MPF for future Medicare plan selections, which will help them make optimal Medicare plan selections.

As the concept of flow is relatively complicated and abstract, many researchers treated flow as a multi-dimensional concept using a set of sub-concepts, among which control, concentration, and enjoyment have been found to represent dimensions of flow experiences in human-computer interaction contexts [e.g., 10, 13]. Therefore, this study focuses on examining these three dimensions of online flow during Medicare plan selection tasks on MPF. First, *control* refers to the extent to which users' perceptions of their ability to use an online tool or performing an action online to achieve a goal [11]. Previous research demonstrated that communication, interaction, or instant feedback through chats or comments in the virtual environment enhanced users' feeling of control [14]. As such, a Medicare plan selection task assisted by AIDA (vs. without AIDA) may make users feel more in control of using MPF as AIDA can provide information, instant feedback, or task instructions to help users complete tasks.

Next, *concentration*, also known as attention focus or immersion, refers to the extent to which users focus their attention on the online activity while ignoring other irrelevant situations [10]. Researchers found that imbalance between task challenge and the user's skill may affect their concentration [15]. According to cognitive aging theories, older adults with low computer literacy are more likely to be influenced by interruptions than younger people in the computer-mediated environment [16]. However, goal/task-related information or signals help users focus on the task [17]. For example, researchers found that virtual agents could effectively help users in interface navigation, avoid being lost, and make them focus on their tasks [17]. Therefore, we predict that AIDA (vs. without AIDA), which provides necessary and instant information/feedback to guide older users, will help them stay concentrated on the Medicare plan selection task on MPF.

Finally, *enjoyment* refers to the level of pleasure received from involving in an online activity, regardless of the outcome of the activity [13]. Enjoyment has been frequently examined as a key flow dimension in the computer-mediated context [12]. For example, conversational AI agents were found to increase older users' perceived enjoyment of online shopping tasks [18], and user-to-automated chatbot interactions heightened users' enjoyment in the online service context [19]. Similarly, AIDA's assistance during a Medicare plan selection task on MPF is likely to help older users enter a flow state, making it a more enjoyable task. Based on the aforementioned literature, we propose the first hypothesis:

H1: Medicare beneficiaries perceive a higher flow on MPF in terms of (a) control, (b) concentration, and (c) enjoyment with (vs. without) AIDA's assistance.

2.2 The Mediating Role of Control

Previous research shows that concentration and enjoyment may come as the consequence of the feeling of being in control [20, 21]. For example, perceived control was found to mediate the relationships between consumers' level of skill and concentration and enjoyment for both computer-mediated and face-to-face tasks [20, 21]. Similarly, consumers' feeling of control over a system (e.g., website, online store) was found to be a precondition for their excitement and concentration on using the system [22]. Based on these empirical findings, we propose the following hypothesis:

H2: The AIDA effects on flow in (a) concentration and (b) enjoyment are mediated by control.

2.3   The Moderating Role of Decision-Making Stage

The traditional consumer decision model includes five decision-making stages—need recognition, information search, alternative evaluation, purchase decision, and post-purchase evaluation [23], whereas recent literature demonstrates that information search occurs throughout the other four stages of the decision-making process [24]. Information sought in the initial stage (i.e., need recognition) tends to be abstract, holistic, and exploratory, while it becomes more concrete, analytic, structured, and goal-directed as it becomes closer to the final decision stage (e.g., alternative evaluation) [25]. An optimal online flow state requires three antecedent conditions, including a clear but challenging goal, a certain level of user skills to achieve the goal, and immediate responses from the online medium [10, 11]. As compared to MPF tasks in the exploratory need recognition stage, MPF tasks in the alternative evaluation stage are likely to be more goal-directed, more complex, more analytical, and thus more cognitively challenging to older users, suggesting a more ideal environment for the immediate responses provided by AIDA to contribute to their flow experience. Therefore, we hypothesize the following moderating role of the decision stage for the AIDA effects on users' online flow:

H3: The AIDA effects on online flow, including (a) control, (b) concentration, and (c) enjoyment, are stronger during the alternative evaluation (vs. need recognition) stage.

3   Method

To test the hypotheses, an online experiment with a 2 (*AIDA:* present vs. absent) × 2 (*Decision Stage:* need recognition vs. alternative evaluation) between-subjects design was conducted. For manipulating the four experimental conditions, simulation videos were created which captured the screen and audio of a male older user's MPF task in either the need recognition or alternative evaluation stage of Medicare plan decision-making, which was performed either with or without the conversational assistance of AIDA. The four simulation videos were pretested with a convenience sample of 98 students from a Southeastern university. Pretest results showed that the manipulation was successful. Pretest participants were more likely to perceive that the user in the need recognition condition video was exploring Medicare plan features and criteria, whereas the user in their video was narrowing down and comparing Medicare plan alternative for a final decision, as expected. In addition, pretest participants recognized AIDA's presence in the AIDA-present condition whereas they did not in the AIDA-absent condition.

Given the successful pretest results of the stimulus videos, the main experiment was conducted with a national sample of 420 Medicare beneficiaries (65 + years old; M_{age} = 72.45, SD = .40; 210 men and 210 women) recruited among the Qualtrics consumer panel. The majority of the participants were non-Hispanic White (93.3%) with an average monthly gross income below $5,000 (55.0%). Participants first watched a randomly assigned video among the four simulation videos representing the four experimental conditions, and then completed manipulation check measures, followed by measures for flow experiences of control (3 items; e.g., "I would clearly know the right things to do on MPF"), concentration (3 items; e.g., "I would have total concentration while using MPF"), and enjoyment (3 items; e.g., "I would have fun using MPF"), adapted from existing scales [26, 27] and rated on a five-point Likert scale (1 = Strongly Disagree, 5 = Strongly Agree).

4 Results

4.1 Manipulation Check and Measurement Properties

All participants identified correctly whether AIDA was present or absent in their assigned video stimulus. Further, participants in the need recognition condition were more likely to rate the user in their video was figuring out Medicare plan features ($M_{NR} = 4.55$; $M_{AE} = 4.05$) and less likely to rate that the user in their video was trying to narrow down Medicare plan choices ($M_{NR} = 4.31$; $M_{AE} = 4.72$) or compared Medicare plans ($M_{NR} = 3.55$; $M_{AE} = 4.75$) than participants in the alternative evaluation condition. Therefore, the manipulations were successful.

Confirmatory factor analysis (CFA) of the dependent measures, conducted using AMOS 23.0, showed a good model fit ($\chi^2/df = 2.45, p < .001$; CFI = .988, TLI = .982, NFI = .980, GFI = .969; RMSEA = .059). All factor loadings were above .80, the average extracted variance (AVE) values for all three flow factors was above .50, and composite reliability for each factor was above .80, all of which established the convergent validity. The unconstrained CFA model showed a significantly ($ps < .001$) superior fit to the constrained models with unity factor correlations, and the 95% confidence intervals for all three factor correlations did not include one, which established the discriminant validity [28]. Finally, the internal consistency of the measures was also assured through Cronbach's αs larger than .80.

4.2 Hypotheses Testing

The hypotheses were tested using structural equation modeling (SEM) based on the maximum likelihood estimation method and 5,000 bootstrap samples ($\chi^2/df = 1.79$, $p < .001$; CFI = .990, TLI = .985, NFI = .978, GFI = .970; RMSEA = .043). SEM results revealed that the presence of AIDA significantly improved perceived online flow in control ($\gamma = .33, p < .01$), supporting H1a; however, the effects of AIDA on perceived flow in concentration ($\gamma = -.11, p = .177$) and enjoyment ($\gamma = -.01, p = .899$) were non-significant, rejecting H1b and H1c, respectively. Further, the AIDA × Decision Stage interaction effect was significant and positive for control ($\gamma = .64, p < .001$), meaning that the AIDA effect was stronger in the alternative evaluation stage compared to the need recognition stage, supporting H3a. However, non-significant interaction effects were found for concentration ($\gamma = .01, p = .907$) and enjoyment ($\gamma = .14, p = .242$), rejecting H3b and H3c, respectively. Finally, AIDA had positive and significant indirect effects on concentration (IE = .21, 95% CI [.08, .37]) and enjoyment (IE = .34, 95% CI [.13, .57]), fully mediated by control, supporting H2a and H2b, respectively. Additionally, although not hypothesized, results also showed significant and positive indirect effects of the AIDA × Decision Stage interaction on concentration (IE = .42, 95% CI [.22, .64]) and enjoyment (IE = .67, 95% CI [.35, 1.00]) fully mediated by control.

5   Discussion and Implications

The effects of conversational AI on older users' navigation task completion have been widely examined in previous studies. However, its effectiveness as a decision assistant for older decision-makers has been rarely studied, and no literature exists on its role in Medicare plan selection decision tasks. The findings of this study demonstrate that AIDA's assistance enhances Medicare beneficiaries' perceived online flow in control, which in turn positively impacts the concentration and enjoyment dimensions of online flow perceptions. The findings echo previous research findings that dimensions of flow could happen in order [20, 21], particularly highlighting the critical role of control as the precondition for concentration and enjoyment in online flow [20, 21].

Further, this study offers a novel finding that AIDA's contribution to users' flow experience may depend on the decision stage. Specifically, AIDA's role is significantly stronger as it becomes closer to the final decision-making. In the initial stage where decision-makers are in the mode for exploration, AIDA's assistance may be more intrusive, inhibiting them from reaching a flow; whereas as decision-makers become more goal-directed and analytical in the final stages of decision-making, AIDA's immediate responses when assistance is needed for concrete information directly relevant to the alternatives considered help the decision-makers feel in control and thus help them stay concentrated on the decision-making task and even enjoy the decision-making process. These findings are novel in human-computer interaction research as no previous empirical studies have ever examined the effects of conversational AI's role in user experiences based on the decision-making stage.

Our findings provide valuable implications for the development of the Medicare decision-support system. Though MPF offers a wealth of information and functions to ease beneficiaries' Medicare plan selection process, given the effect of cognitive aging on the older user's declining abilities to learn a new web interface and make complex decisions, it is of critical importance to this major intended user group of MPF to have access to ongoing real-time decision assistance. Conversational AI, such as AIDA designed for this study, can provide a feasible solution to address this need by helping older users experience online flow during their Medicare plan decision-making using MPF, which can enhance the possibility for finding an optimal plan that best meets their financial and medical needs. Further, our findings on the moderating role of decision stages for AIDA effects have farther-reaching implications for conversational AI designs for diverse consumer decision-making contexts by providing a key recommendation for prioritizing the implementation of an intelligent decision assistant in a more concrete, analytic, goal-directed, and structured decision stage close to the final decision to maximize the utility of the decision assistance.

Acknowledgments. This study was supported by the Auburn University Intramural Grant Program, the Alabama Agricultural Experiment Station, and the Hatch program of the National Institute of Food and Agriculture, U.S. Department of Agriculture.

References

1. Cubanski, J., Damico, A.: Key facts about Medicare Part D enrollment and costs in 2022 (2022). https://www.kff.org/medicare/issue-brief/key-facts-about-medicare-part-d-enrollment-and-costs-in-2022
2. Zhao, Y.: Qualitative exploration of factors influencing the plan selection process by Medicare beneficiaries. J. Manag. Care Spec. Pharm, **27**(3), 339–353 (2021). https://doi.org/10.18553/jmcp.2021.27.3.339
3. Stults, C.D., Baskin, A.S., Bundorf, M.K., Tai-Seale, M.: Patient experiences in selecting a Medicare Part D prescription drug plan. J. Pat. Exp. **5**(2), 147–152 (2018)
4. Kazancoglu, I., Demir, B.: Analysing flow experience on repurchase intention in e-retailing during COVID-19. Int. J. Retail Distri. Manag. **49**(11), 1571–1593 (2021). https://doi.org/10.1108/IJRDM-10-2020-0429
5. Kader, M.S., Kwon, W.S., Westrick, S., Ross, K., Zhao, Y., Huang, X.: What functions on the Medicare plan finder do older Medicare beneficiaries use? In: Stephanidis, C., Antona, M., Ntoa, S. (eds.) HCI International 2021 - Posters. HCII 2021. Communications in Computer and Information Science, vol. 1419. Springer, Cham (2021). https://doi.org/10.1007/978-3-030-78635-9_36
6. Ross, K., Kwon, W.S., Westrick, S., Kader, M.S., Zhao, Y., Huang, X.: Medicare plan decisions: what strategy do older adults use for e-healthcare decision-making and what intelligent assistance do they need? In: Stephanidis, C., Antona, M., Ntoa, S. (eds.) HCI International 2021 - Posters. HCII 2021. Communications in Computer and Information Science, vol. 1419. Springer, Cham (2021). https://doi.org/10.1007/978-3-030-78635-9_41
7. Chattaraman, V., Kwon, W.-S., Gilbert, J.E., Ross, K.: Should AI-based, conversational digital assistants employ social - or task-oriented interaction style? A task-competency and reciprocity perspective for older adults. Comput. Hum. Beh. **90**, 315–330 (2019). https://doi.org/10.1016/j.chb.2018.08.048
8. Bickmore, T., Caruso, L., Clough-Gorr, K., Heeren, T.: It's just like you talk to a friend' relational agents for older adults. HCI Older Pop. **17**(6), 711–735 (2005)
9. Morrow, D.G., Lane, H.C., Rogers, W.A.: A framework for design of conversational agents to support health self-care for older adults. Hum. Factors: J. Hum. Fact. Erg. Soc. **63**(3), 369–378 (2021). https://doi.org/10.1177/0018720820964085
10. Csikszentmihalyi, M., Larson, R., Prescott, S.: The ecology of adolescent activity and experience. J. Youth Adole. **6**(3), 281–294 (1977)
11. Hoffman, D.L., Novak, T.P.: Locus of control, web use, and consumer attitudes toward internet regulation. J. Pub. Policy **22**(1), 41–57 (1986)
12. Kaur, P., Dhir, A., Chen, S., Rajala, R.: Flow in context: development and validation of the flow experience instrument for social networking. Comput. Hum. Beh. **59**, 358–367 (2016)
13. Domina, T., Lee, S.-E., MacGillivray, M.: Understanding factors affecting consumer intention to shop in a virtual world. J. Retail. Con. Ser. **19**(6), 613–620 (2012). https://doi.org/10.1016/j.jretconser.2012.08.001
14. Wang, L.C., Baker, J., Wagner, J.A., Wakefield, K.: Can a retail web site be social? J. Market. **71**, 143–157 (2007)
15. Moneta, G.B., Csikszentmihalyi, M.: The effect of perceived challenges and skills on the quality of subjective experience. J. Pers. **64**(2), 275–310 (1996)
16. Tams, S., Thatcher, J.B., Grover, V.: Concentration, competence, confidence, and capture: an experimental study of age, interruption-based technostress, and task performance. J. Asso. Info. Sys. **19**(9), 2 (2018)
17. Frémont, V., Phan, M.T., Thouvenin, I.: Adaptive visual assistance system for enhancing the driver awareness of pedestrians. Int. J. Hum.-Comput. Interact. **36**, 856–869 (2020). https://doi.org/10.1080/10447318.2019.1698220

18. Kwon, W.-S., Chattaraman, V., Shim, S.I., Alnizami, H., Gilbert, J.: Older user-computer interaction on the internet: how conversational agents can help. In: Jacko, J.A. (ed.) HCI 2011. LNCS, vol. 6762, pp. 533–536. Springer, Heidelberg (2011). https://doi.org/10.1007/978-3-642-21605-3_58

19. Balakrishnan, J., Dwivedi, Y.K.: Role of cognitive absorption in building user trust and experience. Psy, Market. **38**(4), 643–668 (2021). https://doi.org/10.1002/mar.21462

20. Chen, H.: Exploring web users' on-line optimal flow experiences. Unpublished Ph.D. Dissertation, Syracuse University, New York (2000)

21. Ghani, J.: Flow in human computer interactions: Test of a model. In: Carey, J. (ed.) Human Factors in Information Systems: Emerging Theoretical Bases, pp. 291–311. Ablex Publishing Corp, New Jersey (1995)

22. Ward, J.C., Barnes, J.W.: Control and affect: the influence of feeling in control of the retail environment on affect, involvement, attitude, and behavior. J. Bus. Res **54**, 139–144 (2001)

23. Bettman, J.R., Luce, M.F., Payne, J.W.: Consumer decision making: a choice goals approach. In: Haugtvedt, C.P., Herr, P., Kardes, F.R. (eds.) Handbook of Consumer Psychology. Lawrence Erlbaum Associates, New York (2008)

24. Chang, J.Y., Kwon, W.-K.: Social media information search behavior in consumption decisions: consumer segmentation and discriminant factors. In International Textile and Apparel Association Annual Conference Proceedings, vol. 77, (1) (2021)

25. Steenkamp, J.B.E., Baumgartner, H.: The role of optimum stimulation level in exploratory consumer behavior. J. Con. Res. **19**(3), 434–448 (1992)

26. Shim, S.I.: Enhancing brand loyalty through brand experience: application of online flow theory. Unpublished Ph.D. Dissertation. Auburn University, Auburn, AL (2012)

27. Heshan, S., Ping, Z.: Causal relationships between perceived enjoyment and perceived ease of use: an alternative approach. J. Asso. Info. Sys. **7**(9), 618–644 (2006)

28. Garbarino, E., Johnson, M.S.: The different roles of satisfaction, trust, and commitment in customer relationships. J. Market. **63**(2), 70–87 (1999)

Accessibility of Health Data Representations for Older Adults: Challenges and Opportunities for Design

Peterson Jean[1](✉) ⒾⒹ, Emma Murphy[1] ⒾⒹ, and Enda Bates[2] ⒾⒹ

[1] Technological University Dublin, Dublin, Ireland
D22126863@mytudublin.ie
[2] Trinity College Dublin, Dublin, Ireland

Abstract. Health data of consumer off-the-shelf wearable devices is often conveyed to users through visual data representations and analyses. However, this is not always accessible to people with disabilities or older people due to low vision, cognitive impairments or literacy issues. Due to trade-offs between aesthetics predominance or information overload, real-time user feedback may not be conveyed easily from sensor devices through visual cues like graphs and texts. These difficulties may hinder critical data understanding. Additional auditory and tactile feedback can also provide immediate and accessible cues from these wearable devices, but it is necessary to understand existing data representation limitations initially. To avoid higher cognitive and visual overload, auditory and haptic cues can be designed to complement, replace or reinforce visual cues. In this paper, we outline the challenges in existing data representation and the necessary evidence to enhance the accessibility of health information from personal sensing devices used to monitor health parameters such as blood pressure, sleep, activity, heart rate and more. By creating innovative and inclusive user feedback, users will likely want to engage and interact with new devices and their own data.

Keywords: Health data representation · Accessibility · Older adults

1 Introduction

Wearable devices offer new potential benefits to help older adults directly improve their health behaviours by monitoring and measuring their physiological parameters. Wearable health and well-being devices can be defined as off-the-shelf consumer products [8, 14] that track physiological parameters like activity, sleep, heart rate, blood pressure and other vital signs over time. They can also present the collected data in graphs or text through applications on smartphones or computers. Unlike medical devices mainly used by health care providers [9], wearable devices offer direct access to health information to end consumers.

Health information is often complex and diverse and can come from various sources and domains in the health system. Health data representations convey health information to different users, such as clinicians, patients, policymakers or other experts. Health data representations can include visual or textual formats that show trends, patterns or insights from the data. Health information can come from clinical, public and personal health data. Clinical when health care providers collect it during diagnosis or treatment, public when collected by government agencies or organisations for monitoring or improving population health, or personal when collected by users using devices like wearables.

In 2010, the introduction of a large-scale National Health Information Infrastructures exploration plan predicted many research opportunities for healthcare information [1]. In this plan, experts suggested that the health infrastructure consisted of three main components: clinical, public, and personal health data. They also identified research opportunities for personal health data, such as promoting better health conditions and supporting patients with acute or chronic diseases. These research opportunities implicitly target older adults who may face more challenges in managing their own health [1]. However, more effort has been put into public and clinical health information than personal health information [2]. Therefore, there is a gap in how to represent and interact with personal health data effectively and efficiently for different users and purposes.

Personal health data is mainly sourced from Patient-Generated Health Data (PGHD). PGHD is data users collect using input devices like wearables or smartwatches. PGHD can help users self-manage their health and communicate with their healthcare providers [9]. However, there is a challenge in effectively representing and interacting with PGHD for different users and purposes, which is especially pronounced for older adults who may face challenges such as low digital literacy, impairments or cognitive decline [8, 9]. These challenges create a digital divide gap between users and technology. Older adults' use of health applications and devices is increasing due to their potential benefits for self-managing chronic conditions or preventing diseases.

In this paper, we propose a need for a more inclusive consideration of how health data is conveyed to the end user, particularly older users. According to current estimates, the 65 + age group represents 10% of the world's 8 billion people and is expected to equal the 12 + age group by 2050 [4]. According to UN recommendations, healthcare and long-term care systems must be anticipated. These significant demographic changes motivate the empowerment, independence, and involvement of older adults by enabling them to understand and self-manage their own health. We aim to identify accessibility issues with current feedback data representation and harness opportunities for innovation and improvement. We first explore the narrative on health data and the possible digital gap to understand digital competencies. Then we describe data representation in the context of health app systems. We analyse and outweigh challenges and opportunities and finally anticipate limitations for future work.

2 Health Data and the Digital Divide

The digital divide refers to the gap between those with access to and use of technology and those without [12]. This gap is particularly pronounced among older adults due to digital literacy, impairments, or cognitive decline, which often affect their confidence in using technology. To better understand the divide between older adults and health applications, a top-bottom approach can help conceptualise the importance of data representation within the development of these applications [12]. Health data representation is crucial at the intersection of clinical, public, and personal health within national health infrastructure [1]. This infrastructure is crucial for individual and global health goals, and its societal impact is critical in achieving a human-centred focus.

Based on cycles of injustice [3], all stakeholders may influence digital applications or solutions, potentially reinforcing the power dynamics of experts and creating discrimination or unfairness towards end-users in general. This discrimination can further extend the accessibility gap for older adults. These cycles of injustice patterns are particularly relevant to technology based on Data and rely on within the healthcare domain [3]. These technologies can have ethical and societal implications that affect different stakeholders of society, such as individuals, groups, communities, organisations, or governments. However, these technologies can also create or exacerbate existing inequalities, biases, or harms that affect people's rights, dignity, or well-being.

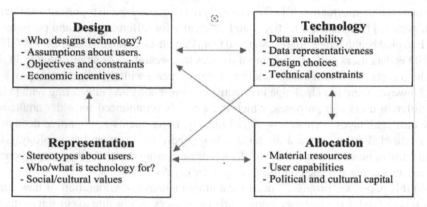

Fig. 1. Representation of cycle of injustice pattern to highlight unfairness and discriminations in the context of development, application and understanding of Data based systems. It emphasises ethical and societal implications for the different stakeholders in the process [3].

We can better consider a potential health application to understand the cycles of injustice in healthcare technology. Depending on its scale, it may be developed by actors like researchers and developers, applied by others like policymakers or practitioners, and understood by other actors like users or beneficiaries. This standard-design approach for health applications, as seen in Fig. 1, means that each stage introduces different values, interests, and perspectives that may conflict or align with each other. For instance, policymakers may have different criteria or standards than practitioners when implementing data-based technologies, and users may have different expectations or experiences than beneficiaries when using these technologies.

The cycles of injustice can be influenced by various factors such as power dynamics, accountability mechanisms, transparency measures, participation opportunities, and feedback loops. Power dynamics determine who controls the technology and who influences its development. Accountability mechanisms set who is responsible for outcomes and impact, while transparency measures determine who has access to its information. Participation opportunities define who is involved in decision-making about the technology, and feedback loops determine how the technology is evaluated and improved over time. These factors can affect how data-based technologies are perceived and accepted by different stakeholders of society.

One concept that can help explain the acceptance of technological innovation is self-efficacy [14]. Self-efficacy refers to belief in one's ability to perform a task or achieve a goal using a specific tool or resource. It can affect one's motivation, effort, and persistence in using a new technology and trust, satisfaction, and loyalty towards a new technology. Various sources, such as personal experience, social influence, verbal persuasion, and emotional arousal, can influence self-efficacy. Exploration of challenges and perceptions within the health data representation may empower different stakeholders of society, like our older adult groups, to use data-based technologies effectively and responsibly. Consequently, self-efficacy can play a role in breaking injustice cycles, hence reducing the digital divide.

3 Data Representations and Ageing in Health Application Systems

As health application systems continue to gain popularity, there is an increasing digital gap for older adults regarding using wearable devices and accessing health data output, which may prevent them from benefiting from personalisation. Rather than creating technologies that widen this gap, we must reduce it. While most research has attempted to address this gap by evaluating self-efficacy [14] with digital literacy and cognitive decline, it may only mitigate rather than eradicate the gap in health systems, considering the circle of justice. Shifting power dynamics to older adults, such as involving them in building solutions tailored to and by them, could be a more practical approach. Ultimately, empowering older adults to guide the process by capturing how they interpret health data representation is crucial to reduce the digital divide in health applications.

Personalisation within health applications heavily relies on Patient-Generated-Health-Data (PGHD) [9]. While it could benefit the quality of care and reduce its associated cost, it also reveals an increase in the misinterpretation of symptoms or collected data, often by older adults [9]. Theodore et al. focus on a subset of the cause of this misinterpretation: the collection of data by older adults [11]. They argue that as sensing devices become ubiquitous and extend traditional health data collection, the digital divide for older people should be addressed and reinforced with new innovative data input and analysis that adapts to the challenges of age-related impairments [11]. Although this study covers the first challenges in health data interaction with older adults, the authors don't address closing the data feedback loop by focusing on how to convey these analyses to our older adults. Therefore, we propose an extended model of their process in Fig 2 with Output and Usage criteria, which can identify the challenges and opportunities towards "health data by and for older adults".

3.1 Output

Data output is a critical aspect of digital health systems, and the enormous volume of multi-source input sources makes the possible representation even more complex. The information is often presented to users through visual [5], auditory, and haptic feedback. The feedback cues are meant to inform users about their health status. Commercial

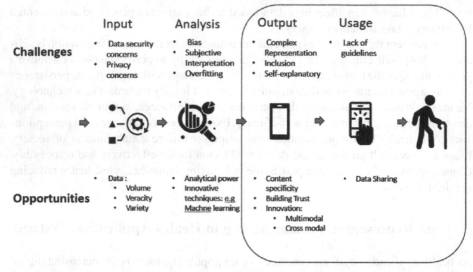

Fig. 2. Extension of mheatlh data collection loop [11] to include Output and Usage as key components to find challenges and opportunities potentially closing the data feedback loop. It integrates older adults as key stakeholders in health data representation design.

sensing devices and applications, such as Fitbit[1], Withings[2], iHealth[3] devices, present the monitored physiological parameters like activity, sleep, and heart rate through these data representation cues. However, the design of data feedback in digital health systems poses significant challenges.

One major issue is *the complex representation* of data, which can visually be overwhelming for non-expert users like older adults. This also motivates the adoption of simple visual graphs which limits proper representation of metadata or multi-faceted data [5]. In the Withings (Fig. 3), a physiological sensing device suite for critical data like Blood Pressure (BP), the health app in Fig. 3, relies on visual cues like graphs and text to present the BP data over time to users. In this case, a minimalistic style and emphasis on aesthetics hinder the multi-facet layer of the BP data. Considering the importance of threshold and time here, no time is properly indicated, the colour variation has no reference for a reminder, the gridlines are not clearly visible and can add confusion for the threshold. This cognitive load may add extra difficulty for older adults to share this information with their general practitioners. Hence increasing the telemedicine trust gap between patients and GP. Such pattern within the data representation exposes *inclusion* challenges which affect older adults facing chronic and cognitive conditions. The need for inclusive data feedback should therefore consider the diversity of users. The data representation should be self-explanatory and accessible without a focus on digital competencies but rather understanding.

---

[1] https://www.fitbit.com/global/ie/home.

[2] https://www.withings.com/ie/en/.

[3] https://ihealthlabs.eu/en/.

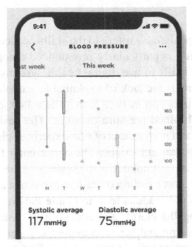

Fig. 3. A screen of Withing Blood pressure app showing a graph of different threshold measures for a user.

These challenges open opportunities for improving data feedback in digital health systems. The *self-explanatory* issues may be explored through *content specificity* in visual feedback ensuring the applications tailor user understandings. Another opportunity is building trust in health digital systems through explainable and non-confusing feedback. Users should be able to understand the feedback and have confidence in the system. Furthermore, there is room for innovation in the design of new data feedback. Doyle et al. explored an extended representation of sensing data over a clock-style plot 24h, as seen in Fig. 4, which tracks emotional behaviour based on in-home activity of older adults [7]. The *content specificity* is that each spiral represents a sensor measure and the green colour measures in a clockwise style. But further limitation could be an increased number of sensors, affecting readability. Existing data cues could be extended and used to create new and more effective feedback cues [6].

Fig. 4. Clock plot representation of activity sensing data within older adults' homes. Each spiral represents sensor data measurements over 24 h [7].

3.2 Usage

The *second level of the digital divide* refers to the skills needed to use digital technology effectively [11]. This divide is particularly pronounced among older adults who may lack the necessary digital skills to use digital health systems. One major challenge in using digital health systems is the lack of explainable guidelines [10] for non-experts. For example, in the Withings app in Fig. 3, there is a lack of a clear explanation for the time metadata for each blood pressure measure. The design of health applications should consider the needs and preferences of non-experts, such as older adults, who may require more detailed and clear guidelines. The opportunity from this is to explore the relationship between trust and confidence in the system. In the systematic review of clear guidelines, Liu et al. [10] report a feeling of guilt as proof of a lack of confidence in using the health applications, as older adults tend to blame the difficulties for understanding on themselves. Addressing the clarity and accessibility issue may increase accuracy for better condition monitoring and hence increase the potential of intersecting PGHD into national health information infrastructure. Overall, it may reduce the e-health gap between GP and older adults.

4 Conclusion

As the world's population ages, the need to empower older adults to self-manage their own health becomes increasingly important. Wearable devices offer new potential benefits to help older adults directly improve their health behaviours by monitoring and measuring their physiological parameters. However, health information can be complex and diverse. There is a gap in how to represent and interact with personal health data effectively and efficiently for different users and purposes. This paper explored the need for a more inclusive consideration of how health data is conveyed to end-users, particularly older adults. Our analysis highlights the challenges and opportunities in data representation within the context of health app systems. We have also identified the need to differentiate competencies from the understanding within the health app and explored how more accessibility studies could help outline and guide participatory opportunities with an older adult exploration of possible new data representation, reducing the digital divide. Future work will focus on harnessing these opportunities for innovation and improvement to promote better health conditions and support older adults in managing their own health.

Acknowledgements. This work was supported by Science Foundation Ireland Centre for Research Training in Digitally Enhanced Reality (d-real).

References

1. Hesse, B.W., Hansen, D., Finholt, T., Munson, S., Kellogg, W., Thomas, J.C.: Social participation in health 2.0. Computer **43**(11), 45–52, November 2010. https://doi.org/10.1109/MC.2010.326

2. Shneiderman, B., Plaisant, C., Hesse, B.W.: Improving healthcare with interactive visualization. Computer **46**(5), 58–66, May 2013. https://doi.org/10.1109/MC.2013.38
3. Whittlestone, J., Nyrup, R., Alexandrova, A., Dihal, K., Cave, S.: Ethical and societal implications of algorithms, data, and artificial intelligence: a roadmap for research. Nuffield Foundation, London
4. United Nations Department of Economic and Social Affairs, Population Division (2022). World Population Prospects 2022: Summary of Results. UN DESA/POP/2022/TR/NO. 3
5. Ola, O., Sedig, K.: Beyond simple charts: design of visualisations for big health data. Online J. Publ. Health Inform. **8**(3), e195, December 2016. https://doi.org/10.5210/ojphi.v8i3.7100
6. Merminkides, M.: Sound Asleep. Miltonline (2021). Accessed 16 November 2022. https://www.miltonline.com/hm-compositions/sound-asleep/
7. Doyle, J., O'Mullane, B., Knapp, B.: Emotional Wellbeing of Older Adults within Aware Homes – Detection and Intervention. 3
8. Piwek, L., Ellis, D.A., Andrews, S., Joinson, A.: The rise of consumer health wearables: promises and barriers. PLOS Med. **13**(2), e1001953, February 2016. https://doi.org/10.1371/journal.pmed.1001953
9. Kim, B., Ghasemi, P., Stolee, P., Lee, J.: Clinicians and older adults' perceptions of the utility of patient-generated health data in caring for older adults: exploratory mixed methods study. JMIR Aging **4**(4), e29788 (2021). https://doi.org/10.2196/2978
10. Liu, N., Yin, J., Tan, S.S., Ngiam, K.Y., Teo, H.H.: Mobile health applications for older adults: a systematic review of interface and persuasive feature design. J Am Med Inform Assoc. **28**(11), 2483–2501 (2021). https://doi.org/10.1093/jamia/ocab151.PMID:34472601; PMCID:PMC8510293
11. Cosco, T.D., Firth, J., Vahia, I., Sixsmith, A., Torous, J.: Mobilising mHealth data collection in older adults: challenges and opportunities. JMIR Aging **2**(1), e10019 March 2019. https://doi.org/10.2196/10019
12. Chang, B.L., et al.: Bridging the digital divide: reaching vulnerable populations. J. Am. Med. Inform. Assoc. **11**(6), 448–457, November 2004. https://doi.org/10.1197/jamia.M1535
13. Pan, X.: Technology Acceptance, Technological Self-efficacy, and attitude toward technology-based self-directed learning: learning motivation as a mediator. Front. Psychol. **11** (2020). Accessed 16 March 2023. https://www.frontiersin.org/articles/https://doi.org/10.3389/fpsyg.2020.564294
14. Khan, S.R., Mugisha, A.J., Tsiamis, A., Mitra, S.: Commercial off-the-shelf components (COTS) in realising miniature implantable wireless medical devices: a review. Sensors **22**(10), 3635, January 2022.https://doi.org/10.3390/s22103635

Experiences of Community-Dwelling Older Adults Participating in an Occupation-Focused Distance Exchange Program: A Qualitative Study

Akihiko Koga[1,2]([✉]) [iD], Kunihiko Yasuda[2] [iD], Shinpei Saruwatari[3], Hiroki Murakami[3], Kazuki Takeshita[3], and Shinya Hisano[4] [iD]

[1] Second Stage of Doctoral Program, Graduate School of Comprehensive Scientific Research, Prefectural University of Hiroshima, Hiroshima, Japan
koga.aki@fmt.teikyo-u.ac.jp
[2] Department of Occupational Therapy, Faculty of Fukuoka Medical Technology, Teikyo University, Tokyo, Japan
[3] Shirakawa Hospital, Shirakawa, Japan
[4] Department of Occupational Therapy, Faculty of Health and Welfare, Prefectural University of Hiroshima, Japan

Abstract. This study aimed to explore the experiences of community-dwelling older adults by piloting a smartphone-based, occupation-focused distance exchange program.

The program was conducted over 8 weeks, via the use of smartphones and consisted of remote and three face-to-face sessions, in which older adults and university students interacted in pairs. The first half of the program focused on the use of smartphones, while the second half of the interaction focused on occupation. Semi-structured interviews were conducted with 12 community-dwelling older adults after the program, and data were analyzed using the KJ method. Our study found that the total number of labels was 102, through which six categories were extracted: "participation with positive motivation," "change in daily living performance triggered by COPM," "acquisition of knowledge of smartphone use," "expansion of smartphone use," "things to do with smartphones," and "benefits and challenges of this program." Extant literature had identified multiple issues which served as impediments to older adults acquiring smartphone proficiency. Through our program, we delivered lectures on practical ways to use smartphones that met the needs of individual older adults. We were able to demonstrate an increase in smartphone usage among older adults through our program. In addition, the benefits of this program were formulated by incorporating the impact of intergenerational interactions involving university students and older adults.

Keywords: Community-dwelling older adults · Qualitative study · Information and Communication Technology

© The Author(s), under exclusive license to Springer Nature Switzerland AG 2023
C. Stephanidis et al. (Eds.): HCII 2023, CCIS 1833, pp. 494–499, 2023.
https://doi.org/10.1007/978-3-031-35992-7_66

1 Introduction

1.1 Research Background

In recent years, the Internet has enabled easier information gathering, and the use of smartphones has increased [1]. However, evaluating the percentage of mobile device ownership by age group reveals a low degree of usage among older adults, indicating a generational disparity and the problem of an information gap (digital divide) among older adults [2]. Based on this, we believed that there was a need to develop and conduct research on a distance exchange program for community-dwelling older adults, aimed at assisting them in exploring new occupational opportunities and social interaction. Therefore, a preliminary study was conducted to explore the experiences of community-dwelling older adults who participated in a trial occupation-focused distance exchange program.

In occupational therapy, occupations refer to the everyday activities that people do as individuals and as part of both, families, and communities to occupy time and bring meaning and purpose to life. Occupations include things people need to, want to, and are expected to do [3]. By "occupation-focused," we mean to use COPM to ascertain the client's occupation [4].

1.2 Purpose of the Study

The purpose of the study was to explore the experiences of community-dwelling older adults by using a smartphone, occupation-focused distance exchange program. The research question for this study is "What was the experience of the community-dwelling older adults who participated in this program?"

The research methodology was conceptualized by referring to the Standards for Reporting Qualitative Research (SRQR) [5], which serves as a benchmark for qualitative research.

2 Methods

2.1 Ethical Considerations

This study was conducted with the approval of the Research Ethics Committee of the Faculty of Fukuoka Medical Technology, Teikyo University (Approval No. 21-14).

By the Declaration of Helsinki [6], the participants were fully informed about the study beforehand consent was obtained.

2.2 Research Design

This study employs the use of qualitative research methods. In particular, the KJ method was deployed to structure the data [7].

2.3   Recruitment of Participants

The participants of this study were community-dwelling older adults, who were aged 65- years- or- older, excluding those who are certified as requiring long-term care and residing in long-term care insurance facilities. We included those older adults whom 1) owned a smartphone and 2) wished to take a smartphone course; we excluded those whom 1) could not understand the content of the study, and 2) those who could not voluntarily express their willingness to cooperate with the study. Participants who joined the study midway through the course were eligible to participate, but were excluded from the analysis. Recruitment for the study began two months prior to implementation and was conducted between October 1, 2021 and July 30, 2022.

2.4   Intervention

The program consisted of a two-month long remote session and three face-to-face sessions using a smartphone, setting up a situation in which older adults and university students could interact in pairs (see Fig. 1).

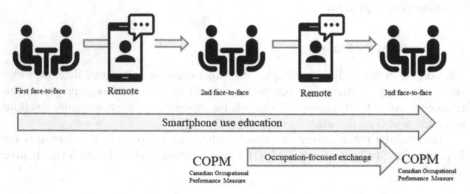

Fig. 1. Program structure (8 weeks)

Both parties used their smartphones remotely, and the free application LINE was used to platform this interaction. The face-to-face sessions were structured into three sessions: initial, intermediate, and final. The first half of the program consisted of an exchange on how to use the smartphone, and towards the end of the first half and the entire second half of the program, in addition to the aforementioned sessions, university students administered the Canadian Occupational Performance Measure (COPM) [8] to community-dwelling older adults, encouraging an occupation-focused interaction (see Fig. 2).

2.5   Data Collection

We conducted semi-structured interviews using an interview guide at a location convenient to the participants. The interviews were recorded through an IC recorder.

remote session   face-to-face sessions

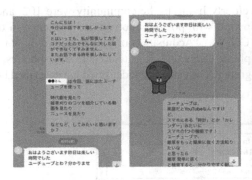 

Fig. 2. Program Scenery

2.6 Data Analysis

The analysis was conducted using the KJ method, which involved the following steps: (1) carding, (2) grouping, and (3) arranging and illustrating.

3 Results

3.1 Target Attribute

The number of participants was 12 (see Table 1).

Table 1. Demographic characteristics of participants

community-dwelling older adults	
Number of participants	12 (5 males 7 women)
Age (Mean ± SD)	77.4 ± 5.6
HDS-R (Mean ± SD)	27.8 ± 2.0

HDS-R: Hasegawa's Dementia Scale-Revised

3.2 Interview Duration

The interviews lasted an average of 18 min and 23 s (12 to 28 min) per participant, and amounted to a total of 3 h, 40 min, and 37 s.

3.3 Analysis Results

The total number of labels for the elderly living in the community were 102, and six categories were identified: "Participation with positive motivation," "Change in occupational performance triggered by COPM," "Acquisition of knowledge on how to use smartphones," "Expansion of smartphone usage," "Things to do with smartphones," and "Benefits and challenges of this program." The categories identified are described below (see Fig. 3).

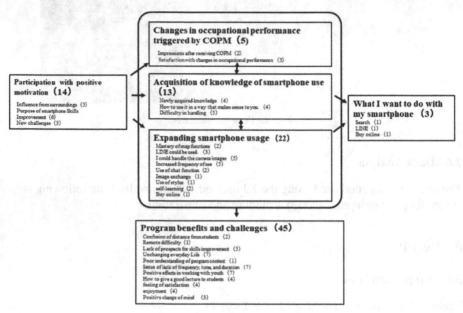

Fig. 3. Framework for the experience of community-dwelling older adults who participated in this program

4 Discussion

4.1 Findings

The results of this study showed that older adults who participated in this program "expanded their smartphone usage methods." A previous study [9] reported that following two issues for smartphone classes for the elderly: "there was no practice of direct communication between the participant and instructor via the smartphone" and "there was no process of operation with tasks thought up by the user." As this program dealt with practical communication and individual tasks for the elderly, we believe that it led to an expansion of usage among older adults. In addition, positive effects were cited in the "benefits and challenges of this program" about young people. Our findings were similar to a previous study that conducted an intergenerational exchange program [10], corroborating the suggested benefits of this program.

4.2 Clinical Applications

Healthy community-dwelling older adults were found to be willing to try new occupations, therefore, we believe programs like ours and similar to it can be utilized to broaden the horizons of older adults to help them lead a more productive life.

5 Conclusion

We explored the experiences of older adults who participated in an occupation-focused distance exchange program. As a result, six categories were extracted, including "expansion of smartphone usage" and "advantages and challenges of this program," suggesting positive experiences with this program and the advantages and challenges of this program.

Acknowledgments. We would like to thank Editage (www.editage.com) for English language editing.

References

1. Ministry of Internal Affairs and Communications: Communications usage trend survey (2021). https://www.soumu.go.jp/johotsusintokei/statistics/data/220527_1.pdf. Accessed 21 May 2022
2. Aung, M.N., et al.: Digitally inclusive, healthy aging communities (DIHAC): a cross-cultural study in Japan, Republic of Korea, Singapore, and Thailand. Int. J. Environ. Res. Public Health **19**(12), 6976 (2022)
3. American Occupational Therapy Association: Occupational therapy practice framework: domain & process-fourth edition. Am. J. Occup. Ther. **74**(2), 1–87 (2020)
4. Fisher, A.G.: Occupation-centred, occupation-based, occupation-focused: same, same or different? Scand. J. Occup. Ther. **20**(3), 162–732 (2013)
5. O'Brien, B.C., Harris, I.B., Beckman, T.J., Reed, D.A., Cook, D.A.: Standards for reporting qualitative research: a synthesis of recommendations. Acad. Med. **89**(9), 1245–1251 (2014)
6. World Medical Association: Declaration of Helsinki: ethical principles for medical research involving human subjects (2008). https://www.wma.net/policiespost/wma-declaration-of-helsinki-ethical-principles-formedical-research-involving-human-subjects/. Accessed 6 Nov 2020
7. Scupin, R.: The KJ method: a technique for analyzing data derived from Japanese ethnology. Hum. Organ. **56**(2), 233–237 (1997)
8. Law, M., Baptiste, S., McColl, M., Opzoomer, A., Polatajko, H., Pollock, N.: The Canadian occupational performance measure: an outcome measure for occupational therapy. Can. J. Occup. Ther. **57**(2), 82–87 (1990)
9. Koga, A., Hisano, S.: Scoping review on rehabilitation support for community-dwelling older adults using information and communication technology (ICT) in Japan: issues in the field of occupational therapy. Occup. Ther. Fukuoka (in press)
10. Hayashi, H., Takeda, M.: An intergenerational program for local elderly individuals and nursing students. J. Hum. Care Sci. **7**, 59–65 (2018)

Elderly Houniao for Challenges and Service Design of Social Integration Within the Context of Relocated Retirement

XiaoYang Luo[(✉)] and Wen Ye

Hunan University, Changsha 410082, Hunan, People's Republic of China
2219965818@qq.com

Abstract. Increasingly more retired elderly people with financial means have chosen the retirement option of migrating from the north to the south in winter and returning to their hometown in summer, just like the so-called migratory birds. However, the social integration challenges such as socialisation and identity that come with migration can directly affect their well-being in the place they move to. Consequently, this study aims to improve the social integration of older houniao by incorporating an interdisciplinary approach-service design. Firstly, we constructed a social integration indicator system applicable to elderly houniao based on literature research and used this sociological model to conduct semi-structured interviews with them during the study, in order to sort out their key needs. In addition, user portraits and user journey maps were drawn to summarise user characteristics and reproduce life scenarios, exploring the importance of enhancing the interconnection between elderly houniao and their neighbours. In the end, a community support service system for elderly houniao was developed with the theme of 'neighbourhood mutual assistance' and three design strategies were proposed: neighbourhood information mutual aid platform, talent mutual exhibition and hometown 'dining table'. The service system has changed the isolation of elderly houniao in the integration process, and more importantly, explored the new vibrancy of the mutual assistance service mode in cross-cultural retirement communities, thus creating an inclusive and friendly community environment.

Keywords: Relocated Retirement · Social Integration · Elderly Houniao · Service Design · Mutual Assistance

1 Introduction

As China's ageing process intensifies and modern attitudes to old age change, the need for new modes of retirement is becoming more and more prominent. One of the more typical modes is the relocated retirement mode, which refers to the elderly people who, like migratory birds, change their place of residence as the seasons change [1]. This mode attracts a large number of elderly people with a certain financial base due to factors such as the pleasant climate and slow pace of life in the retirement location [2].

A successful social integration requires strong interaction between the migrating population and the society in which they move. However, migrant elderly people, as a special group that is both 'migratiability' and 'ageing', have very limited ability to adapt to society on their own initiative [3]. Moreover, there are conflicts between them and the local population in terms of rhythm of life and folk culture [4], making it difficult for them to reconstruct their identity in their place of migration. The social integration affects the continuation of migratory retirement living and the well-being index, as well as the social harmony and stability of the societies to which they move.

Therefore, based on literature research, this study firstly reconstructed a social integration indicator system applicable to migrant elderly people in four dimensions: economic, living, cultural and psychological, and conducted semi-structured interviews with ten groups of elderly houniao to understand the current integration situation. Three key requirements were identified: 'access to local information', 'things to do in daily life' and 'relief of homesickness'. Secondly, the concept of 'neighbourhood mutual assistance' was explored through the use of persona mapping and user journey maps. Finally, based on the research, a community service system and three strategies for it were developed with the theme of 'neighbourhood mutual assistance'. The results can help strengthen the connection between the elderly houniao and the local community, so as to ensure a sense of belonging and sustainability of the elderly houniao's retirement life.

2 Literature

2.1 Social Inclusion Indicator System

Yang Juhua's social inclusion indicator system for the migrant population has a strong universal applicability. The system provides a more comprehensive overview of the integration factors of the migrant population in four dimensions, including economic integration, behavioural adaptation, cultural acceptance and identity [4]. However, the system is not fully applicable to older migrant populations such as the elderly houniao, who find it difficult to participate in socio-economic construction and are influenced by past habits and preconceptions, which make them attempt to recreate familiar socio-cultural networks in the local area in order to seek some degree of resettlement [5].

2.2 Community-Based Mutual Assistance for the Elderly from a Service Design Perspective

The social integration of elderly involves a variety of factors, including their own, the residents of the place they are moving to, the economy, the system and the culture. Service design is good at taking into account the needs of other stakeholders while being user-centred [6]. Therefore, The use of a service design approach to social integration of elderly houniao allows for a more systematic consideration of how interactions between elderly houniao and their place of migration impact. Thus, they will have a better experience and the service process will become more coordinated, efficient, and holistic.

Mutual assistance for the elderly is a unique model of ageing service that focuses more on the mutual help and comfort of elderly groups, allowing them to act as both recipients and providers of services. Older people can feel respected as they exercise their agency as contributors, thus gaining a new experiential value [7]. Studies have found that elderly who participate in the mutual help model of ageing have lower levels of depression, higher self-esteem and greater satisfaction [8]. Thus, from a service design perspective, the mutual aid model of ageing, in improving the social integration of migratory elderly, not only fully enhances the self-efficacy of older people, but also provides a rich environment for building social networks and creating a sense of community belonging.

3   Method

3.1   Building a Social Integration Indicator System of Elderly Houniao

Based on Yang Juhua's model for the migrant population, this study takes into account the dual characteristics of migrant elderly people's 'migratiability' and 'ageing', and constructs a social integration indicator system for elderly houniao in four dimensions: economic, living, cultural and psychological. (see Fig. 1).

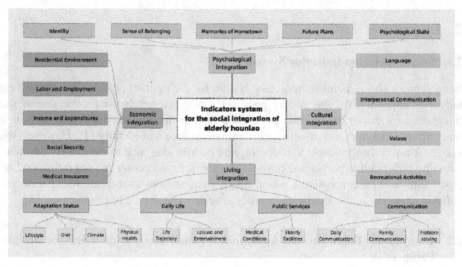

Fig. 1. Social integration indicator system.

3.2 User Interviews and Requirements Analysis

Based on the social integration index system developed above, semi-structured interviews were conducted with ten groups of migrant elderly in a mixed community (mixing of local and problems of social integration of elderly houniao. At the end of the interviews, the main problems in each dimension were summarised and sorted out.

Economic Integration. (1) Difficulty in screening and matching to suitable medical services; (2) Lack of opportunities to participate in productive activities; (3) Cumbersome social welfare processing process.

Living Integration. (1) No one to contact in case of emergency; (2) Significant differences in eating habits.

Cultural Integration. (1) Lack of interpersonal interaction; (2) Lack of cultural and recreational activities in daily life.

Psychological Integration. (1) Loneliness caused by homesickness; (2) Lack of sense of belonging due to being a foreigner.

Based on the above analysis, three key requirements in the social integration process of migratory elderly are summarised:

Access to Local Information. Migrant elderly can feel disappointed and frustrated by the lack of local resources and services, especially in terms of medical conditions. However, after gaining an understanding of the local situation, local resources, including medical resources, are abundant in Sanya. Most of the problems are caused by the migrant elderly due to lack of local information.

Something to do in Their Daily Lives. The unfamiliar environment and estranged interpersonal relationships make migrant birds bored and lonely in their daily lives. The daily lives of migrant elderly are more fixed and revolve around family and going for walks, with nothing to do most of the time being the norm for them.

Alleviates Homesickness. Because of the impact of widely differing cultural customs, migratory birds can perceive a loss of emotional ties to their homeland, which, combined with the influence of inherent memories of their place of origin, leads migratory elderly to fall into depression from time to time as they miss their loved ones back home. (see Fig. 2).

3.3 Persona

After summarizing the results of the interviews, this study deduces a typical persona. Both pessimistic and optimistic elderly houniao suffer from depression and would like to make new friends and receive assistance in a newly relocated location. Persona 1 also shows that they have some expertise and are keen on recreational activities. (see Fig. 3).

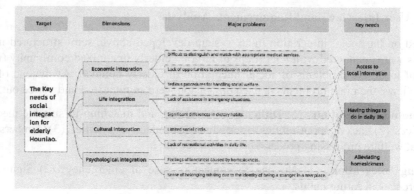

Fig. 2. Requirements analysis diagram.

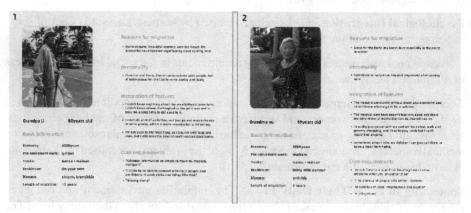

Fig. 3. Persona.

3.4 User Journey Map

After understanding elderly houniao's key needs and characteristics, we dismantled the daily life trajectory of them and summarised the journey map. Through scene reproduction, we identified the significance of strengthening the interconnection between houniao and between houniao and local residents. We have therefore developed a community support service system for migrant elderly people, with 'neighbourhood mutual assistance' at its core, to help elderly houniao integrate better into the local community by enhancing interaction between community residents. (see Fig. 4).

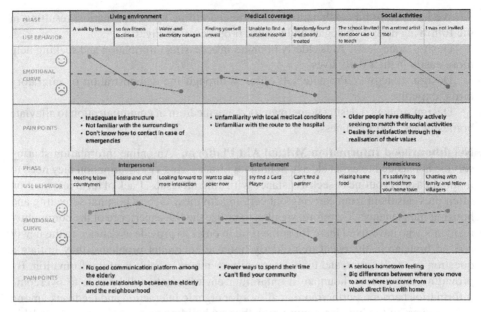

PHASE	Living environment			Medical coverage			Social activities		
USE BEHAVIOR	A walk by the sea	So few fitness facilities	Water and electricity outages	Finding yourself unwell	Unable to find a suitable hospital	Randomly found and poorly treated	The school invited next door Lao Li to teach	I'm a retired artist too!	I was not invited
EMOTIONAL CURVE									
PAIN POINTS	• Inadequate infrastructure • Not familiar with the surroundings • Don't know how to contact in case of emergencies			• Unfamiliarity with local medical conditions • Unfamiliar with the route to the hospital			• Older people have difficulty actively seeking to match their social activities • Desire for satisfaction through the realisation of their values		
PHASE	Interpersonal			Entertainment			Homesickness		
USE BEHAVIOR	Meeting fellow countrymen	Gossip and chat	Looking forward to more interaction	Want to play poker now	Try find a Card Player	Can't find a partner	Missing home food	It's satisfying to eat food from your home town	Chatting with family and fellow villagers
EMOTIONAL CURVE									
PAIN POINTS	• No good communication platform among the elderly • No close relationship between the elderly and the neighbourhood			• Fewer ways to spend their time • Can't find your community			• A serious hometown feeling • Big differences between where you move to and where you come from • Weak direct links with home		

Fig. 4. User journey map.

4 Result

4.1 Building a Design Strategy

Based on the concept of 'neighbourhood mutual assistance', and taking into account the three key requirements: access to local information, things to do in their daily lives and relief of homesickness. A service design framework has been developed with the aim of improving the social integration of elderly houniao. (see Fig. 5).

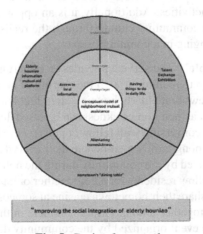

Fig. 5. Design framework.

We have chosen a combination of online and offline service scenarios, resulting in the following design strategies and service proposals (see Fig. 6):

Design strategies 1. Aids elderly houniao in accessing information and seeking help more easily in their daily lives.

Design strategy 2. Promote self-efficacy through the demonstration of migratory birds' expertise.

Design strategy 3. Using hometown food as a medium of communication to alleviate homesickness and loneliness.

Neighbourhood Information Mutual Aid Platform. An online information sharing service is intended to assist elderly houniao with accessing key information they need to maintain a daily routine or seek assistance with difficult issues. Lack of local information often prevents them from carrying out certain activities, such as hospital screening and housing maintenance. Therefore, we plan to utilize the life experience of the community residents who have lived there for some time in order to provide assistance to the newly arrived houniao.In the event that elderly houniao encounter problems, they initiate a question on the Internet, and then community members provide useful information. By providing this service, houniao in unfamiliar environments will be able to overcome information barriers. Furthermore, it allows for organic interaction and feedback among the members of the houniao community, thereby building an atmosphere of friendship and cooperation.

Talent Exchange Exhibition. Through the creation of an offline environment where recreational and social interaction can be initiated, facilitated, and carried out among the residents of the houniao community. In their daily lives, elderly houniao experience boredom and sleepiness due to a lack of cultural activities, interpersonal interaction, and other spiritual worlds. It was found in the study that most migratory elderly possess a high level of artistic literacy and are eager to display and communicate. Community managers arrange for the houniao with special skills to demonstrate or teach their skills in this environment, and others have the opportunity to learn and communicate with them. Attracting elderly houniao out for face-to-face socialising and enriching their spiritual world through cultural activities; Additionally, it is an opportunity for elderly houniao to actively participate in community culture through the realisation of their self-worth, creating a sense of belonging in a community space.

Hometown 'Dining Table'. The service provides an opportunity for groups of elderly from the same hometown to reunite through the sharing of hometown food. It has been revealed through interviews that elderly houniao often feel lonely due to the loss of ties to their hometowns, but that their homesickness can be eased through the consumption of hometown foods and the conversing with fellow countrymen. Most of the time, the event is a small get-together among family members in their everyday lives, but it can also be a large-scale event organized by the community during the holiday season. The Houniao send out invitations to fellow residents for a get-together online, and when a response is received, they cook and share their hometown cuisine at someone's home. In most cases, the event is a small get-together among family members in their everyday lives, but it can also be a large-scale event organized by the community during the holiday season. When Houniao residents receive an invitation to a get-together online, they cook and share their hometown cuisine at the home of another resident. Through comfort food and shared memories, they recreate the emotional attachment to their hometown.

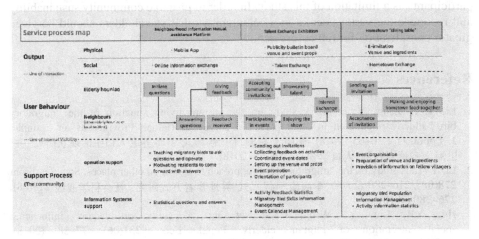

Fig. 6. Service process map.

Those three services complement each other, ranging from the satisfaction of individual needs to the building of community culture. These processes allow migrant birds to feel the warmth of others and their self-worth in a mutually supportive community, and to rediscover the joys of daily life.

The community serves primarily as a manager, assisting the elderly houniao with registering and managing their information. (1) In Neighbourhood Information mutual aid Platform. Staff are responsible for teaching elderly houniao how to ask questions, motivating them to answer questions and tallying questions and answers to figure out key information gaps. (2) In Talent Exchange Exhibition. The community seeks out and invites capable houniao to act as hosts and they provide the venue and props for the cultural activities. It is also necessary to advertise the event and coordinate the schedule among residents before the event and collect feedback on the event afterwards. (3) In Hometown 'Dining Table'. As an information provider, helping fellow villagers find each other; or as an organiser, providing participants with ingredients for the venue.

5 Conclusion

Using sociological model and service design tools, this study explores the living patterns of elderly houniao in their place of migration, culminating in the creation of a community service system based on neighbourhood mutual assistance.

As a result of the service, elderly houniao have been able to transition from a difficult adjustment to being alone to a positive integration process with mutual support, which has enabled them to feel at home again in relocating surroundings. Furthermore, the mutual assistance model creates a unique and inclusive community, due to multicultural integration that stimulates a new vitality in the community cultural atmosphere. This not only reduces tension in resource allocation, but also creates a unique and inclusive community. Nevertheless, the lack of consideration of local residents, who were also participants, is a limitation of this study. In order to promote community sustainability and reconcile the various actors in a community, other stakeholders should be given greater consideration for future research.

References

1. Li, Y.-T., Zeng, Y., et al: A study on the current living situation of the "migratory bird" elderly population in other places: a survey in Hainan Province as an example. J. Popul. (1), 56–65 (2018). 李雨潼,曾毅,等: "候鸟式"异地养老人口生活现状研究——以海南省调查为例. 人口学刊 (1), 56–65 (2018)
2. Li, Y.-T.: A study on the "migratory bird" approach to ageing in other places. Soc. Sci. Front **278**(08), 276–280 (2018). 李雨潼: "候鸟式"异地养老方式研究. 社会科学战线 **278**(08), 276–280 (2018)
3. Hu, Y.P., Liu, Y., Wang, C,-K., et al.: A study on factors influencing social integration of migrant elderly. Popul. Econ. **231**(06), 77–88 (2018). 胡雅萍,刘越,王承宽,等流动老人社会融合影响因素研究.人口与经济 231(06), 77–88 (2018)
4. Yang, J,-H.: An indicator system for the social integration of migrant population in the inflow area - a further study based on social integration theory. Popul. Econ. **179**(2), 64–70 (2010). 杨菊华: 流动人口在流入地社会融入的指标体系——基于社会融入理论的进一步研究. 人口与经济 **179**(2), 64–70 (2010)
5. Chen, J.-f.: Displacement, emplacement and the lifestyles of Chinese 'snowbirds' and local residents in tropical Sanya. Soc. Cult. Geogr. **21**(5), 629–650 (2020)
6. Suoheimo, M., Vasques, R., Rytilahti, P.: Deep diving into service design problems: visualizing the iceberg model of design problems through a literature review on the relation and role of service design with wicked problems. Des. J. **24**(2), 231–251 (2020)
7. Pahk, Y., Baek, J.-S.: Design opportunities in mutual support service for the elderly. In: DS 87–3 Proceedings of the 21st International Conference on Engineering Design (ICED 17), Product, Services and Systems Design, Vancouver, Canada, vol. 3, pp. 359–368 (2017)
8. Bowers, H., Mordey, M., Runnicles, D., et al.: Not a one way street: research into older people's experiences of support based on mutuality and reciprocity. Joseph Rowntree Foundation, York (2011)

Universal Design of ICTs and Equal Right for Elderly People

Qian Meng[1], Eva Hadler Vihovde[2], and Huilin Yin[3(✉)]

[1] University of South-Eastern Norway, 3184 Borre, Norway
[2] Oslo Metropolitan University, 0130 Oslo, Norway
[3] Tongji University, Shanghai 200092, China
yinhuilin@tongji.edu.cn

Abstract. There is a big gap between the digitalization level of the whole world and the ICT systems the elderly use in the whole Europe. Faced with this challenge, Universal Design (UD) as sustainable design has become the guiding concept to achieve the sustainability goals by helping the elderly to improve their life quality. ICT systems general characteristics of robustness, stability, resilience, flexibility and performance comply with the seven principles of UD. This paper aims for a conceptual study to explore the concept of UD of ICTs as a significant aspect of social sustainability, especially the Norway Norwegian ICT policy for securing an information society for all, emphasizing the importance of technology for all, including the elderly and disabled people. This study also illustrates the design process of UD of ICTs and some practice in Norway which shows UD has evolved as a significant component for the elderly to achieve a better life.

Keywords: Universal Design · ICTs · Equal Right · Elderly People

1 Introduction of the Equal Right for Using ICTs

Nowadays people use more digital tools in their daily life. One of the common activities on the internet was participation in social networks, for example, using Facebook, Instagram, TikTok or Twitter. While according to Eurostat research for the elderly people in 2021, close to three-fifths (57%) of the EU's population participated in social networks during the three months. The participation rate for youths aged 16–29 years (83%) was almost four times as high as the corresponding rate for older people aged 65–74 years (23%) [1]. There is a big gap between the digitalization level and the ICT systems the elderly use.

Faced with this challenge, Universal Design (UD) for the ICT systems can play a significant role to make a friendly interface for the expansion of ICT among aged people, thus to achieve the sustainable goal. In 1997 the North Carolina State University (NCSU) Center for Universal Design(UD) [2] defined UD as "the design of products and environments to be usable by all people, to the greatest extent possible, without the need for adaptations or specialized design", following by seven principles of UD that were developed by NCSU.

C. Stephanidis et al. (Eds.): HCII 2023, CCIS 1833, pp. 509–514, 2023.
https://doi.org/10.1007/978-3-031-35992-7_68

Software systems and the connected hardware, together with other ICT technologies, such as Internet of Things, Big Data, Artificial Intelligence, Cloud Computing, should take equal status, equal treatment and equal merit as the central notion to achieve sustainable goals during the ICT system design, development, implementation and maintenance life cycle. The study [3, 4] also put the individual equal right at the first place in the five interrelated dimensions for a technical system's objective of sustainability, in which the individual dimension refers to individual freedom and agency (the ability to act in an environment), human dignity, and fulfillment. It includes individuals' ability to thrive, exercise their rights, and develop freely, which means the elderly people aged over 65 years should be taken into account for the design and use of ICTs.

2   ICT Systems General Characteristics

All ICT systems are in line with the seven principles [2] of UD. ICT systems, their characteristics of robustness, stability, resilience, flexibility and performance have the correspondent relationship with the seven principles of UD as displayed in Table 1.

Table 1. The seven principles of Universal design and ICT systems characteristics

Principle	Definition	ICT system
Equitable use	The design is useful and marketable to people with diverse abilities	Stability
Flexibility in use	The design accommodates a wide range of individual preferences and abilities	Flexibility
Simple and intuitive use	Use of the design is easy to understand, regardless of the user's experience, knowledge, language skills, or current concentration level	Performance
Perceptible information	The design communicates necessary information effectively to the user, regardless of ambient conditions or the user's sensory abilities	Robustness
Tolerance for error	The design minimizes hazards and the adverse consequences of accidental or unintended actions	Resilience
Low physical effort	The design can be used efficiently and comfortably and with a minimum of fatigue	Performance
Size and space for approach and use	Appropriate size and space are provided for approach, reach, manipulation, and use regardless of the user's body size, posture, or mobility	Performance

ICT systems are considered as useful tools to promote the equality for the elderly. ICT systems can empower the elderly to gain a stronger voice for their economic, social and political rights in their communities, their government and at the global level. ICT technologies have made more space for the elderly to communicate, network and collaborate on a more global scale than before. E.g., the internet provides both for anonymity and solidarity, for self-expression and for building connections. They can amplify the voices from the elderly and help publicize their experiences and perspectives.

For example, automatic driving vehicles meets all the 7 principles. They provide equal access for individuals with diverse abilities and needs (Principles 1 and 2) and show stability and flexibility. They are very simple and intuitive to use (Principle 3). The built-in software in the car relays robust information visually through pictures and audibly through speakers (Principle 4). The sensors in the car also ensure that the car will get immediate accurate information, minimizing the risk of crashing with other cars and ensuring a safe and resilient driving line (Principle 5). Automatic driving cars show good performance since they require no physical effort to operate (Principle 6). Finally, automatic driving cars have enough place for the people to sit in and easy to manipulate the control panels (Principle 7). For the elderly who no longer have good sights for driving and those who even don't manage to move freely, automatic driving cars enable them significantly to travel a long distance and enlarge their activity domains.

3 ICT Systems for the Elderly and Disabled in Norway

From a universal design perspective for sustainable goals, ICTs can be seen as architectural building blocks for new social systems and as system integrators. As building blocks, they allow institutions to reinvent themselves and reconfigure the existing system logic, ie., allowing development processes and structures to coordinate intuitively, creating possibilities for decentralized design and decisions, and expanding institutional capabilities for accountability. From a citizenship perspective, these attributes enhance the democratic potential through new modes for participation and citizenship [5]. ICTs can facilitate the building of a more inclusive public sphere: enabling all people, the aged, the disabled, and the discriminated to communicate, to network, and to reach policy makers.

The considerations for the elderly and disabled people should be central to the ambition of ICT system design. In Norway, the elderly population is expected to increase in the coming decades, at the same time, there will be an increase in the prevalence of age-related diseases, such as dementia and cerebral stroke. It is estimated that 60–80% of elderly people with dementia and stroke live at home in Norway [6]. The study [7] shows that the ICT-based ACTION emphasizes the importance of providing appropriate support in the caring process while recognizing experienced family carers as experts with regards to their own caring situation. The Norwegian State Council on Disability also illustrated in the report [8] in 1997 that new ideas and practical solutions must be sought to bring society closer to the ideal of full participation and equality of status for all the people. There is a clearly defined ambition in the ideology and practical work with universal design that: all products, buildings and surroundings shall be made to be used on equal terms by as many as possible.

Norwegian ICT policy aims at securing an information society for all, emphasizing the technology for all, including the elderly and disabled people. ICT has become a central facilitator in Norwegian inclusion policy as the digital inclusion policy. This policy has three main pillars: digital access for everyone, universal design of all ICT, and digital skills e. g. by enhanced use of digital learning resources in education [9]. Two different strategies are used to promote access to ICT for all. The first strategy, which emphasizes the universal design of ICT, has focused on public Web sites, open standards, and open sources [10]. The second strategy is a rights-based national assistive technology diffusion system. Each Norwegian county houses an Assistive Technology Center that provides assistive technologies, free of charge, to people whose ability to function in everyday life is considerably and persistently reduced. These centers provide assistive technology solutions for use at home, school, work, or leisure, and for people of all ages [11].

4   Design Process and Practice in Norway

Universal design of ICT aims to create solutions in information and communication technology such that it can be used by as many as possible. Norwegian regulation for universal design of ICTs which entered into force July 1st 2013 is with the purpose of ensuring universal design of ICTs without causing an undue burden on businesses, mainly for net based solutions and automatic devices [12]. The regulation applies in cases where the ICT solution supports the ordinary functions and constitutes part of the enterprise's main solution.

4.1 Design Process

Zimmermann and Vanderheiden [13] proposed a 4-step methodology for the development of ICT application development that is closely aligned with best practices of ICT engineering:

1. Using user cases and personas to capture accessibility requirements and make them real and comprehensible.
2. Making user requirements real concrete through the use of scenarios and guidelines.
3. Using manual and automated testing techniques based on test cases and checkpoints.
4. User testing and expert review.

As digital solutions become more widespread, it is argued [14] that a design approach is needed to provide early user feedback since there was a change from mainly doing late large-scale usability testing in plan-based development, to agile and iterative process models. Meanwhile, the concept of user (human) centered design (UCD) has been widely accepted. During the design process, the developer and designer initially worked away from the user with a focus on user needs. The developer and designer observe, designs, improves and tests the product. User needs specification are expressed through the step of description of requirements which is the key to sustainability; systems designed using UML models.

UCD is founded on user needs and focused on understanding the user in contexts of use, especially for the elderly. UCD understands users and their requirements, conducting iterative prototyping and evaluation, and are typically quite task focused.

4.2 Practice in Norway

Under the government's framework, ICT and Internet-of-Things (IoT) have been widely used for independent living and social engagement for older adults in Norway.

With a set of physical devices, vehicles, home appliances with electronics, software, sensors, actuators, and connectivity which connect and exchange data between the devices, the elderly people can control those devices via the internet, therefore they can live more comfortably and independently. For example, Norwegian Institute of Public Health has argued [15] that universal designed remote patient monitoring devices may result in little to no difference in the resource use in the specialized health services compared with standard of care for the elderly with cardiovascular disease, chronic obstructive pulmonary disease, or asthma. A risk assessment [16] of the IoT devices for the elderly living alone at home was performed using a risk assessment model.

In addition, the award Innovation Award for Universal Design [17] has been presented since 2011 on behalf of the Norwegian Ministry of Children and Equality (BLD), which coordinates government universal design efforts. The award aims to put the spotlight on innovative, low-threshold and user-friendly solutions. This encompasses all types of solutions, such as buildings, outdoor spaces, landscapes, transport, interior design, products, visual communication, service design, ICT and digital platforms. The award has a total of eight categories.

5 Conclusion

In this paper we have outlined the principles of universal design and how the ICTs comply with the seven UD principles. As to the United Nations' sustainability goals of human equal rights, ICTs are useful tools to achieve the equality by building the elderly capacity, dissemination of equal right information through ICTs channels and amplifying their voice and perspectives. Then the universal design process of ICT is studied and the practice in Norway is presented.

More work will be done for the case study of how UD helps the elderly and reducing inequality by implementing ICTs in different areas. User (human) centered design (UCD) also needs further study.

References

1. EU regions: how did people use the internet in 2021? https://ec.europa.eu/eurostat/web/products-eurostat-news/-/edn-20210517-1. Accessed 12 Mar 2023
2. The Center for Universal Design North Carolina State University: The Principles of Universal Design Poster (1997)
3. Penzenstadler, B., et al.: Safety, security, now sustainability: the nonfunctional requirement for the 21st century. IEEE Softw. 31(3), 40–47 (2014)
4. Becker, C., et al.: Requirements: the key to sustainability. IEEE Softw. 33(1), 56–65 (2016)
5. Gurumurthy, A.: Gender equality through ICT access and appropriation: taking a rights-based approach. IT for Change (2008)
6. Engedahl, K., Haugen, P.K.: Lærebok Demens: Fakta og Utfordringer. The Norwegian Center for Dementia Research, Sem, Norway (2004)

7. Nolan, M., Grant, G., Keady, J.: Understanding Family Care. Open University Press, Buckingham (1996)
8. Askalen, F., Bergh, S., Bringa, O.R., Heggem, E.K.: Universal design: planning and design for all. GLADNET Collection, 12 January 1997. The Norwegian State Council on Disability (1997)
9. The Norwegian Ministry of Modernization: e-Norge 2009-det digitale spranget (e-Norway 2009-the digital leap), Oslo, Norway (2005)
10. Fossestøl, K.: Stairway to Heaven? ICT-Policy, Disability and Employment in Denmark, The Netherlands, United Kingdom and Norway. FAFO/Work Research Institute (2007)
11. Söderström, S.: Disabled pupils' use of assistive ICT in Norwegian schools. In: Assistive Technologies, Croatia (2012)
12. Norwegian Ministry of Government Administration, Reform and Church Affairs: Regulation for universal design of information and communication technology (ICT) solutions, 21st June 2013 pursuant to Act 20 June 2008 No. 42. https://www.regjeringen.no/globalassets/upload/fad/vedlegg/ikt-politikk/regulation_universal_design_ict_solutions.pdf. Accessed 12 Mar 2023
13. Zimmermann, G., Vanderheiden, G.: Accessible design and testing in the application development process: considerations for an integrated approach. Univ. Access Inf. Soc. 7(1–2), 117–128 (2008)
14. Begnum, M.E.N.: Universal design of ICT: a historical journey from specialized adaptations towards designing for diversity. In: Antona, M., Stephanidis, C. (eds.) HCII 2020. LNCS, vol. 12188, pp. 3–18. Springer, Cham (2020). https://doi.org/10.1007/978-3-030-49282-3_1
15. Meneses-Echavez, J.F., Johansen, T.B., Holte, H.H., Harboe, I., Underland, V., Zinöcker, S.: Remote patient monitoring and resource use in the specialized health service: an overview of systematic reviews (revised edition). Norwegian Institute of Public Health (2022)
16. Paupini, C., Giannoumis, G.A., Gjøsæter, T.: A user-centered approach to digital household risk management. In: Stephanidis, C., Antona, M. (eds.) HCII 2020. CCIS, vol. 1226, pp. 82–88. Springer, Cham (2020). https://doi.org/10.1007/978-3-030-50732-9_12
17. DOGA homepage. https://doga.no/en/activities/priser/innovation-award/this-is-the-innovation-award-for-universal-design/. Accessed 12 Mar 2023

Research and Development of a Bingo Game Using Dice to Prevent Dementia

Sakura Mizobuchi📵 and Hiroshi Suzuki(✉) 📵

Kanagawa Institute of Technology, Atsugi, Kanagawa, Japan
S2023095@cco.kanagawa-it.ac.jp, hsuzuki@ic.kanagawa-it.ac.jp

Abstract. Recent years, the number of patients with dementia is on the rise. Dementia is a disease where the brain cells can't function normally for various reasons. The onset of it causes damage to memory and judgment, which makes it difficult for people to live their daily lives. But dementia can be prevented by taking measures. It is considered to be effective to do brain training, exercise and communication, to prevent dementia.

The proposed system is an interactive bingo game that requires the use of dices. The main target of this system is the elderly population which contains the most cases of dementia patients. The aim of this game is to get a bingo faster than your opponent while matching the numbers displayed on the screen with help of simple mathematical combinations using blocks with numbers. This is an effective measure against dementia, exercising the brain and body using calculation, coordination moving big dices and communication through a competition.

Before full scale implementation, we created the protype using blocks of 10^3 cm^3. And displayed this protype at two facilities to check the concept of this system. Everybody could easily experience because it is easy to understand how to exchange numbers by moving blocks with numbers and making simple equations. When the participants blocked their opponent's bingo or conversely or when their own bingo was blocked, they communicated actively with smiles.

As a conclusion, we have assumed that this system played a good role in brain training and communication.

Keywords: dementia · interactive · brain training

1 Introduction

As the life expectancy in our society increases, the incidence of dementia is on the rise. Dementia is a neurodegenerative disorder caused by various factors that impair the normal functioning of brain cells. The onset of dementia results in memory and judgment impairments, which make daily living difficult for patients. Although medication is available for treatment, it only slows the progression of symptoms. In severe cases, it may be challenging for patients to live independently. In Japan, as of 2020, there were about 6 million patients with dementia over 65 years old, and the number is expected to rise to about 7 million by 2025. This means that approximately one in five elderly individuals will have dementia [1]. It is well established that the risk of developing

C. Stephanidis et al. (Eds.): HCII 2023, CCIS 1833, pp. 515–522, 2023.
https://doi.org/10.1007/978-3-031-35992-7_69

dementia increases with age, particularly in an aging society like Japan, which urgently needs to address this issue. Fortunately, preventive measures such as brain training, exercise, and communication are effective in preventing dementia. Therefore, we propose a system that incorporates these three measures in this study.

2   Related Case Studies

2.1   Brain Training and Dementia

Kawashima [2] discovered a learning therapy to prevent the decline in brain function of elderly individuals with dementia. The training to increase cognitive speed was customized to each patient's symptoms by adjusting the level of difficulty. The training included tasks such as reading sentences quickly, solving simple math problems, and counting numbers rapidly. In an experiment conducted at a care facility in Fukuoka, patients with dementia showed improvement in symptoms such as no longer wandering at night and being able to wear diapers.

2.2   Exercise and Dementia

Sato [3] stated that exercise can prevent the deposition of abnormal proteins in the brain. This is because exercise causes the heart to work harder, which increases cerebral blood flow and affects the nerves.

Asada [4] noted that dual task (DT) is gaining attention as a dementia prevention measure. DT involves performing two tasks at the same time, particularly exercise and intellectual work. Examples of such tasks include solving simple math problems while walking, or performing different actions with the right and left hands and switching between them instantly when signaled. Many exercises activate the prefrontal cortex, but DT also activates the lower part of the frontal lobe, which is involved in the ability to sense direction. This brain region has also been linked to the wandering seen in Alzheimer's patients.

2.3   Communication and Dementia

Abe [5] said that conversations are effective in preventing dementia because they stimulate multiple brain regions. Different areas of the brain are used to express what you want to say and to understand what the other person is saying. Furthermore, while these language functions are located in the left brain, the right brain is responsible for reading the emotion and intention of words. Therefore, just talking with people can stimulate the entire brain.

Life review, proposed by Robert Neil Butler, a psychiatrist in America in the 1960s, is known as psychotherapy for dementia. In this therapy, patients discuss old memories.

3 Description of This System Features

The proposed system is an interactive bingo game that uses dice, as shown in Fig. 1. The main objective of this system is to target the elderly, the demographic most affected by dementia. The object of the game is to match the numbers on the screen using simple mathematical combinations and numbered blocks to achieve bingo faster than your opponent. We call our proposed system "SancoroBingo," and we believe it is effective in combating dementia by promoting brain and body exercise through calculation, coordination, and the movement of large dice, as well as communication through competition. The name "SancoroBingo" is derived from the fact that the three dice used in the game can be turned into bingos through calculation.

Fig. 1. The schematic diagram of this system

4 Prototype Implementation

Before full scale implementation of SancoroBingo, we created the protype using blocks of 10^3 cm^3. Figure 2 shows the system configuration. To realize the prototype, the following five conditions were necessary.

1. Selection of dice rolls
2. Determination of formulas
3. Recognizing the results of calculations and the numbers on the bingo card
4. Bingo determination
5. Output of content such as video and audio

To meet the above requirements, Uniry Technology's Unity game engine was used to output the content. In 1, RFID cards are placed inside the dice so that when the dice are placed on the RFID reader, it reads the roll of the dice. A physical button is prepared in 2. After the dice have been lined up, the player presses the button to determine the mathematical formula and performs the process described in 3. When the result of the calculation matches the number on the bingo card, a marker of player's color is placed in the square on the bingo card. In 4, a bingo is considered to be a bingo only when a marker of the player's color fills a square in the bingo card horizontally, vertically, and diagonally. The player receives 10 points for each bingo square filled, and 100 points for a bingo. The game ends when one of the players gets a bingo or when the time limit of 3 min is exceeded.

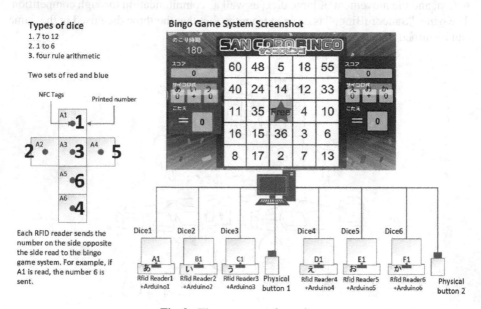

Fig. 2. The system configuration

5   Prototype Experiment 1

We displayed this protype at the Kawasaki Senior Citizens Welfare and Community Center on November 25, 2022 to check the concept of this system. Figure 3 shows the experimental situation. In this experiment, we set two points to be confirmed: 1. Whether this system is acceptable to the elderly, and 2. Whether it is an enjoyable experience as a game. These two points were confirmed by observing the participants.

For checkpoint 1, the elderly people who are good at math or interested in digital contents participated actively. In terms of age, the early elderly understood the rules better than the late elderly, and seemed to enjoy the game without any resistance to calculation.

For the Checkpoint 2, we had the impression that the game became more exciting when the players had opponents. For the Checkpoint 2, I had the impression that the game became more exciting when the players had opponents. The game became more exciting when the players searched hard for the necessary numbers from the dice in order to get a bingo faster than their opponents, or when their bingo plan was interrupted by opponents. Spectators who were watching the game also said to the players, "You are using the wrong operator".

Fig. 3. The experimental situation.

6 Survey by Questionnaire

In experiment 1, the authors obtained only subjective data based on observations of the people who experienced the system. In order to obtain a more objective data, we decided to make a questionnaire to those who experienced this system. Table 1 shows the questionnaire items. The questions were determined with the aim of researching the factors that make the experience of this system interesting to the participants and the relationship between their usual exercise habits and their feelings of the intensity of the system's exercises.

Q1 to 3 were asked to investigate the factors that make this system interesting. The response method for question 1 was a two-choice "yes" or "no" response. Q2 and 3 were asked using a 5-point scale: "5. enjoyed, 4. rather enjoyed, 3. neither, 2. rather not enjoyed, 1. not enjoyed" and "5. liked, 4. rather liked, 3. neither, 2. rather disliked, 1. disliked," respectively.

Q4 and 5 were asked to investigate the feeling of the exercise intensity of this system. Q4 was answered by using a five-point answer system, with "5. agree, 4. somewhat agree, 3. neither 2. somewhat disagree, 1. disagree" as the response method. Q5-1 was conducted using a four-option answer system "Almost every day, 2 or 3 times a week,

Table 1. The questionnaire items

question
1. Did you have a bingo?
2. Did you enjoy Sancoro Bingo?
3. Do you like puzzles?
4. Do you think that playing Sancoro Bingo helped you to move your body?
5-1. Do you have a habit of physical exercise?
5-2. What kind of exercise do you do?

once a week, and almost never", and Q5-2 was conducted by circling all the exercise items such as walking, calisthenics, and golf.

7   Prototype Experiment 2

In order to obtain an objective evaluation of the concept, an experiment was conducted on March 1, 2022 at the Aso Senior Citizen Welfare Center using the same prototype used in experiment 1, and a questionnaire was sent to those who experienced the system. 18 questionnaires were collected from participants in their 60s to 80s. The number of valid responses was 17 for Q1, 16 for Q4, and 18 for the other questions.

The process of constructing equations and bingo in this system includes elements of puzzle game combinations. We hypothesized that people who like puzzle games would enjoy playing the game more, and created Q3. Figure 4 shows the results of the questionnaire. The results show that there is an almost positive relationship between the liking of puzzles and the enjoyment of the experience of this system. Many of the participants this time liked puzzles, and some of them usually play puzzle games such as Kanji Cross. If this system is to be used for dementia prevention in the future, people who do not like puzzles must be able to enjoy participating in the game. It is necessary to adjust the difficulty level according to the ability of each player.

Next, we hypothesized that the intensity of the system's exercise might change depending on one's usual exercise habits, and created Q5. Figure 5 shows the results of the questionnaire. In this prototype, the dice were only moved with the hand, so those who exercised almost every day felt that it was not enough at all. On the other hand, some people who rarely exercise felt that just standing up was a good exercise. This survey will be used as comparative data when the exercise component is added to the system in the future.

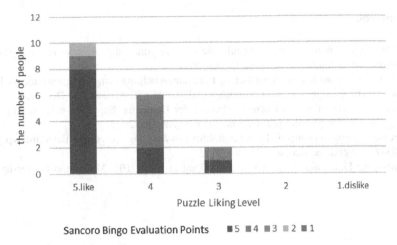

Fig. 4. Relationship between the enjoyment of the system and puzzle liking level

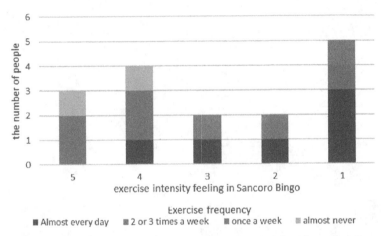

Fig. 5. Relationship between usual exercise habits and perceived intensity of exercise

8   Conclusion

This paper describes a system for dementia prevention. We proposed a calculation bingo system using dices, "Sancoro Bingo" and implemented prototype of this system. Using the implemented system, we showed the results of an experiment using subjective evaluation and an experiment using questionnaire evaluation as a research experiment to confirm whether this system is acceptable to the elderly.

Based on the findings from this prototype experiment, we plan to implement a system that includes an exercise component. In addition, we would like to evaluate the effects of including the three elements that are effective in preventing dementia at the same time.

References

1. MHLW. Comprehensive mental health site for everyone. https://www.mhlw.go.jp/kokoro/know/disease_recog.html. Accessed 18 Dec 2022
2. Brain training, a method for strengthening the brain, is helping many dementia patients. https://www.kyotobank.co.jp/houjin/report/pdf/special201905.pdf. Accessed 18 Dec 2022
3. Effects and Mechanisms of Exercise Therapy for Dementia. https://www.jstage.jst.go.jp/article/jjrmc/55/8/55_55.658/_pdf/-char/ja. Accessed 26 Dec 2022
4. Exercise Therapy in Dementia Prevention. https://www.jstage.jst.go.jp/article/faruawpsj/55/9/55_838/_pdf/-char/ja. Accessed 18 Dec 2022
5. Kazuho, A.: Dementia: What You Really Want to Know 101. Musashino University Press (2017)

Evaluating Privacy Policies and User Agreements of Smart Home Devices from the Perspective of the Aging Population

Manasi Vaidya(✉) , Chaiwoo Lee , Lisa D'Ambrosio , and Joseph F. Coughlin

AgeLab, Massachusetts Institute of Technology, Cambridge, MA 02139, USA
manasiv@mit.edu

Abstract. Smart home technology has the potential to support several tasks in the home, especially for older adults who are likely to increasingly experience difficulties with everyday activities. Trade-offs between privacy and autonomy, security, and comfort have been an ongoing discussion for over a decade. Although there have been significant advances in the technology available today compared to a few years ago, privacy communications to users accompanying these technologies have changed little. Much existing research in the smart home technology space focuses on the design of the technology itself; less has been done to ensure that older adults know where their data is going so that adoption of the technology is better informed, and so they feel more secure about using it. In this work a total of 30 documentations including 24 privacy policies of individual smart devices and 6 privacy terms and policies from platform providers were reviewed to understand their commonalities and shared limitations. Our evaluation revealed that the length of each ranged between 9 to 49 pages, and that such policies are rarely displayed to maximize user access and legibility, contributing to user confusion and concern. The results suggest a need for user agreements and privacy policies to be more easily accessible. Companies publishing privacy documents should be more mindful of how these are presented to the user, whether online or printed. This study recommends that companies should adhere to usability and readability guidelines and follow accessibility standards published by the Web Content Accessibility Guidelines. For older adults to successfully utilize smart home technology, adoption should happen in an informed manner. Sustained usage may also be encouraged with practices that make users feel confident and in control of their data. It is important that companies build their trust ethically, and ensure that older adults are not required to trade off their privacy for autonomy and security.

1 Introduction and Background

While populations are not aging at the same rate in every nation, people across nearly all nations are experiencing longer lifespans. By 2050, it is projected that a significant proportion of the population in many countries across Africa, Asia, and South America will be aged 60 and over, with one in five people in these regions falling within this age group (United Nations 2019, p. 2). The United Nations also predicts that the global population of older persons is projected to surpass the number of children and young people aged 0–14 by 2050.

C. Stephanidis et al. (Eds.): HCII 2023, CCIS 1833, pp. 523–530, 2023.
https://doi.org/10.1007/978-3-031-35992-7_70

Previous research has shown that privacy is one of the major barriers when it comes to older adults adopting smart home technology. Along with the usual privacy concerns, older adults are also interested in being informed and having control over not just what kind of data is collected, but also who the recipients of that data are. Older adults want to know who has access to and accesses their data, what exactly they are looking for in the data, and how frequently they access this data (Cahill et al. 2017). Setting up a new electronic or smart device might often require creating or already having an account with the company, which could mean that older adults might be needed to share their existing login credentials with the person setting up the device for them or that the person setting up the device creates the login credentials for them.

This paper extracts insights regarding the privacy and ethics taken into consideration from a review conducted of a total of 30 documentations including 24 privacy policies of individual smart devices and 6 privacy terms and policies from platform providers.

2   Method

A secondary data analysis/archival study and literature review were conducted. This study undertook a purposive selection of 24 distinct privacy policies of smart home devices and 6 user agreements belonging to various companies. The sample was deliberately chosen to be representative of the most prevalent devices available on the market today. The study also considered the policies of companies utilizing third-party voice assistants, as well as those with proprietary voice assistant technology.

The dataset considers various aspects of user agreements and privacy policies including but not limited to: type of installation; hub requirement; supported voice assistants; type of device; product description; product name; name of company; the updates policy; the number of products the companies have; user friendliness of their agreements and policy pages; number of voices the voice assistant recognizes; who has access to the data collected by the smart device; ability of the user to make changes and set preferences around the kind of data collected; the kind of data collected and its storage location; false wake frequencies; type of customer support; and what happens to the data after the user terminates or deletes the service.

3   Results

3.1   Current Use of AI in Home Tasks

While there are some devices used in the home space, like the August Smart Lock, that do not leverage artificial intelligence (AI; e.g., machine learning, deep learning, and natural language processing), the smart home category in Mozilla Foundation's *Privacy Not Included* series concludes that AI is currently being used by most of the companies in this space[1]. Most of the data that a device collects acts as the database for the AI to function and respond to requests made by the user. AI supports many tasks

---

[1] Mozilla Foundation. Privacy Not Included: https://foundation.mozilla.org/en/privacynotinclu ded/.

at home, such as managing energy usage, controlling the home climate, and various entertainment purposes. AI is used to respond to requests and questions that users have when they use voice assistants like Amazon Alexa, Apple Siri, Google Assistant, and Microsoft Cortana. Voice assistants use natural language processing to listen to the users and understand requests to provide responses. When it comes to performing tasks in the smart home, AI is used in thermostats, for example, to learn what temperature the user likes at different times of day, which is then leveraged to auto-schedule the temperature in the home. In some smart thermostats, AI is also leveraged to switch to clean energy whenever available to generate cost savings. A second example is camera-based motion-detection, in which motion is used as a cue to start recording in doorbells that have video enabled in them.

One of the most common uses of AI is in technologies with voice assistants. The way older adults would use a voice assistant differs from the way younger adults would use it; a voice assistant only gets activated when the wake word is used, followed by a pause and then the command. In her paper, Sunyoung Kim (2021) concludes that older adults find it difficult to stick to the pause after saying the wake word and struggle with the correct pronunciation of the wake word. The participants in Kim's study also expressed frustration because they would often speak lengthy sentences with a command somewhere in between, then after completing the sentences realize that the voice assistant was not even activated because they did not follow the activation pattern. The feedback that many voice assistants give when they are activated is often subtle (for example, Amazon Alexa's blue ring around the speaker lights up when it starts listening or is activated). Giving more direct feedback on when the device starts listening and when it stops is important not just in terms of the interactions with older adults, but also to ensure that users know when their voice is being recorded and stored in the cloud (or not, depending on the voice assistant) to address privacy and false wake concerns.

Amazon Alexa has more than 5 wake words, and a number of additional wake words can be added. On the other hand, Google Assistant and Apple HomeKit have only one wake word each. The number of wake words is directly proportional to the number of false wakes a smart device might experience.

Voice assistants are typically continuously listening to the conversations they hear if they are plugged in, and with the help of AI they decide whether to switch on or not based on the presence of the wake word within the conversation. Because of the numerous wake words the three major voice assistants have today, false wakes are very common, which means the AI thinks the user is asking it something and starts listening, saving this audio and transcript to the cloud eventually. Companies often use this saved data to train the AI the voice assistant uses and the database it refers to; depending on the company, it is either used in an audio recording format or converted to transcripts. Which company's voice assistant is used also affects whether the data will be deidentified with the user's profile or not. While most companies do de-identify this data, they also use it to deliver to users personalized advertisements that they are paid to place.

3.2 Smart Home Technology Adoption Amongst Older Adults

Previous research in the field of older adults adopting technology, particularly smart home technology, has been limited. Anderson and Perrin (2019) discuss the various adoption barriers concerning technology. Pireh et al. (2022) highlighted the low adoption rates of smart technology among older adults despite various enhancements and the introduction of new assistive services particularly designed for older adults.

Francois Portet et al. (2014) reported that because smart home devices are often used by older adults for health-related monitoring, like falls or movement detection, for which video sensors that are often considered highly intrusive are used, the devices contain data that is of vital importance and extremely private. It is important that these smart devices provide reassurance to older users about to whom all the collected data will be accessible, if and when the data will be discarded, whether it will be stored anonymously or not, and if changes can be made to the default storage and collection settings. According to Pireh et al. (2022), technology designed for older adults is more likely to be adopted if researchers prioritize user-friendliness and seamless integration with daily routines. To achieve this, the design of a monitoring system for smart homes should include interfaces via smart devices that enable easy control and configuration and offer user feedback. Additionally, the system should incorporate various sensors and devices to provide a comprehensive smart home solution that seamlessly integrates into daily life. Finally, it is essential to establish clear policies and guidelines regarding data ownership to ensure the privacy and security of user data.

3.3 User Agreements and Privacy Policies

According to a study by the Pew Research Center (2019), only 9% of adults say they always read privacy policies, and 13% say they occasionally read them before agreeing to their terms and conditions; only 22% of these say they read such policies completely and *all the way* through to the end before signing. More than 36% of U.S. adults responded to the survey mentioning they have never read a privacy policy before signing it. It has been reported that a substantial number of Americans may be unknowingly sharing their personal information due to frequent privacy policy agreements. Specifically, around 25% of the U.S. population acknowledges being asked to agree to these policies nearly every day, potentially indicating a lack of understanding of the terms and consequences of individual agreements. In addition, there are concerns over the government's use of the data it collects, with a significant proportion of U.S. adults, around 78%, indicating they have limited or no understanding of these practices. These findings highlight the importance of increased transparency, education, and regulation to address the challenges associated with data privacy and security in today's digital landscape.

Older adults fear regarding companies selling their information to third parties is not unfounded. A majority of the 24 user agreements in this study included the phrase *'We do not sell your information to third parties'*, but if these agreements are read in detail, in the next few paragraphs the policies itemize the various details the companies collect in order to help decide which advertisements will suit the users better. These details include the frequency of use, time and duration of access, location of access, use of one/many devices for accessing, links clicked while accessing, and links clicked while going through any other emails/ advertisements sent by the company to the user.

Every user agreement examined as part of the review of the 24 smart home devices includes another phrase: *'We have the right to collect information regarding the device(s) you use to access the service they provide.'* This essentially means the companies have the right to access information about computers, tablets, smartphones or any other electronic devices the user uses to connect to the service, details about the type of device used, model of the device and manufacturer, unique device identifier number (e.g., Google ad ID, unique ID for advertisers, Windows advertising ID), mobile carrier used, operating system (e.g., OS) of the mobile brand used, phone number of the user, any browsers and applications connected to the service, internet service provider used, IP address, and the device's telephone number (if it exists).

Consider this statement from Google: 'We do not sell your information to third parties' – but Google has the right to place Google ads based on the user's personal information and all information collected, which in turn may entice users to make purchases. Google is paid by these third parties for placing their advertisements. Further, every device that is connected to use Google Assistant as the voice user interface (VUI) collects all the same information that the Google device itself would collect.

3.4 Voice Assistants and Their Connection to Third Party Smart Devices

All companies that manufacture smart devices that do not have their own voice assistant in order to operate the device require users to onboard a voice assistant of their choice, if they want to have the ability to operate these devices through voice commands. When a user decides to use a voice assistant that is not created by the company whose device they are using, they automatically implicitly agree to all the user and privacy agreements that the voice assistant creator company has. For example, a user of Philips Hue's smart home lights is automatically and implicitly signing the user and privacy agreements of Amazon if they decide to use Amazon Alexa as the device's way of communication.

3.5 Updating Privacy Settings of Smart Home Devices

Many manufacturers of smart home devices using AI state that the settings can be changed based on the user's preferences. Some of these settings define how the AI behaves, collects, and stores information in the cloud (or not). The default settings of most of these devices are set to collect the data and store it in the cloud, but these settings can be changed in the smart home device's application. This makes it problematic for many older adults, as many may depend on their children or grandchildren or even a third party for the set up required for the smart home devices. All the individuals who lack the technical expertise required to modify settings through a smartphone application, which has been established by the company or a third-party, were not given due consideration during the service design process.

User agreements are often now not included in written form in the device's packaging, and companies that do include the agreements in the packaging usually print them in extremely small text (8 pt or 9 pt), which is difficult for older adults to access as a majority of this population experiences at least one form of vision impairment. The question of what format is best suited for this audience needs further investigation. In the case of a printed booklet, older adults' preferences for whether they want larger text with potentially more pages in the booklet, or keeping the smaller text with fewer pages, is unknown. The current most common format of user agreements, however, is digital. In many of these, the agreement contains various hyperlinks to additional pages that include 'Privacy Policies,' 'Exceptions,' and 'Additional Data,' which a user may not always end up reading - should they even choose to read the agreement in the first place. Default settings that a device comes with are almost universally biased toward allowing the manufacturing company to gather user data without reference to user preferences, hence these settings need to be changed if users (including older adults) want to change what data these devices capture and what companies do with the data. If there is an easier way to make changes to these settings for this population, that will support older users making more informed adoption decisions that are sustainable and comfortable for them in the long run.

4   Conclusions

Smart home technologies today have the potential to support several tasks in the home on a regular basis. If older adults opt to use these technologies, they can potentially prolong their ability to live independently in their homes and delay the need to move into a care facility or assisted living. Older adults' technology adoption and their comfort with using the technology involve creating and designing devices they are comfortable using. The Pew Research Center reported that the rates of older adults who own smart technology and technology in general have increased sharply, but the report also notes that just 26% of older adults report being comfortable using the technology they own. As a result, long-term use of such technologies could be affected by various factors including comfort with the technology, and privacy could be one of the reasons why 74% of the older adults say they are not comfortable with using technology they own. There is a need for user agreements and privacy policies to be more easily accessible; companies publishing user agreements and privacy documents should be more mindful of how these are presented to the user, whether online or hardcopies. Companies should try at minimum, for example, to adhere to accessibility standards published by the Web Content Accessibility Guidelines (WCAG)[2]. For older adults to fully utilize smart home technology, we need to make sure they are adopting it in an informed manner. They may also be able to use it in a sustained manner once they see its value and feel confident about being in control what data is collected about them and how the data are used. It is important that companies build their trust ethically, and ensure that older adults are not required to trade off their privacy for autonomy and security.

5   Future Work

Further studies that try to uncover how people understand user agreements and privacy policies best, and the format best suited for these, is needed. In addition, it will be helpful to think of new ways to offer and obtain consent, so that users may better comprehend the information and make informed choices of what data they share and what they do not share.

---

[2] World Wide Web Consortium. (2018). Web Content Accessibility Guidelines (WCAG) 2.1. https://www.w3.org/TR/WCAG21/.

Acknowledgements. This study was supported in part by the MIT AgeLab's C3 Connected Home Logistics Consortium.

References

Anderson, M., Perrin, A.: Tech Adoption Climbs among Older Adults. Pew Research Center: Internet, Science & Tech. Pew Research Center (2020). https://www.pewresearch.org/internet/2017/05/17/tech-adoption-climbs-among-older-adults/

Anderson, M., Perrin, A.: 2. barriers to adoption and attitudes towards technology. Pew Research Center: Internet, Science & Tech. (2019). https://www.pewresearch.org/internet/2017/05/17/barriers-to-adoption-and-attitudes-towards-technology/. Retrieved 18 Sept 2022

Beaudin, J., Intille, S., Morris, M.: To track or not to track: user reactions to concepts in longitudinal health monitoring. J. Med. Internet Res. **8**, e29 (2006)

Cahill, J., McLoughlin, S., O'Connor M., Stolberg, M., Wetherall, S.: Addressing issues of need, adaptability, user acceptability and ethics in the participatory design of new technology enabling wellness, independence and dignity for seniors living in residential homes. In: Zhou, J., Salvendy, G. (eds.) International Conference on Human Aspects of IT for the Aged Population, pp. 90–109. Springer, Cham (2017). https://doi.org/10.1007/978-3-319-58530-7_7

Coughlin, J., D'Ambrosio, L., Reimer, B., Pratt, M.: Older adult perceptions of smart home technologies: implications for research, policy & market innovations in healthcare. In: Proceedings of 29th Annual International Conference on IEEEEMBS, pp. 1810–1815 (2007)

Courtney, K.: Privacy and senior willingness to adopt smart home information technology in residential care facilities. Methods Inf. Med. **47**, 76–81 (2008)

Courtney, K., Demiris, G., Rantz, M., Skubic, M.: Needing smart home technologies: the perspectives of older adults in continuing care retirement communities. Inform. Primary Care **16**, 195–201 (2008). https://doi.org/10.14236/jhi.v16i3.694

Demiris, G., Hensel, B.K., Skubic, M., Rantz, M.: Senior residents' perceived need of and preferences for "smart home" sensor technologies. Int. J. Technol. Assess. Health Care **24**, 120–124 (2008)

Demiris, G., et al.: Older adults' attitudes towards and perceptions of "smart home" technologies: a pilot study. Med. Inform. Internet Med. **29**, 87–94 (2004)

Mihailidis, A., Cockburn, A., Longley, C., Boger, J.: The acceptability of home monitoring technology among community-dwelling older adults and baby boomers. Assist. Technol. **20**, 1–12 (2008). Spring

Mozilla Foundation. Privacy Not Included (n.d.). https://foundation.mozilla.org/en/privacynotincluded/. Retrieved 10 Sept 2021

Pal, D., Funilkul, S., Vanijja, V., Borworn, P.B.: Analyzing the elderly users' adoption of smart-home services. IEEE Access **6**, 51238–51252 (2018). https://doi.org/10.1109/ACCESS.2018.2869599

Pew Research Center. Americans and Privacy: Concerned, Confused and Feeling Lack of Control Over Their Personal Information (2019). https://www.pewresearch.org/internet/2019/11/15/americans-attitudes-and-experiences-with-privacy-policies-and-laws/. Accessed 23 Sept 2022

Pirzada, P., Wilde, A., Doherty, G., Harris-Birtill, D.: Ethics and acceptance of smart homes for older adults. Inform. Health Soc. Care **47**(1), 10–37 (2022). https://doi.org/10.1080/17538157.2021.1923500

Portet, F., Vacher, M., Golanski, C., Roux, C., Meillon, B.: Design and evaluation of a smart home voice interface for the elderly – acceptability and objection aspects. Pers. Ubiquit. Comput. **17**(1), 127–144 (2014). https://doi.org/10.1007/s00779-011-0470-5

Steele, R., Secombe, C., Brookes, W.: Using wireless sensor networks for aged care: the patient's perspective. In: Proceedings of Pervasive Health Conference and Workshops, pp. 1–10 (2006)

Sunyoung, K.: Exploring How Older Adults Use a Smart Speaker-Based Voice Assistant in Their First Interactions: Qualitative Study. JMIR mHealth and uHealth. JMIR Publications (2021). https://www.ncbi.nlm.nih.gov/pmc/articles/PMC7840274/

Townsend, D., Knoefel, F., Goubran, R.: Privacy versus autonomy: a tradeoff model for smart home monitoring technologies. In: 2011 Annual International Conference of the IEEE Engineering in Medicine and Biology Society, pp. 4749–4752 (2011). https://doi.org/10.1109/IEMBS.2011.6091176

Tyrer, H., et al.: Technology for successful aging. In: Proceedings of 28th Annual International Conference on IEEE-EMBS, pp. 3290–3293 (2006)

United Nations. World population prospects 2019: Highlights (ST/ESA/SER.A/423). Department of Economic and Social Affairs, Population Division (2019). https://population.un.org/wpp/Publications/Files/WPP2019_Highlights.pdf

Wild, K., Boise, L., Lundell, J., Foucek, A.: Unobtrusive in-home monitoring of cognitive and physical health: reactions and perceptions of older adults. J. Appl. Gerontol. **27**, 181–200 (2008)

World Wide Web Consortium. Web Content Accessibility Guidelines (WCAG) 2.1 (2018). https://www.w3.org/TR/WCAG21/. Retrieved 10 Sept 2021

Research on Digital Products and Service Design for Health Elderly Under the Concept of Smart Health and Wellness

Fei Wang(✉) and Cong Gu

China Academy of Art, 218 Nanshan Road, Hangzhou, Zhejiang, China
16792174@qq.com

Abstract. Based on the concept of smart health care, in the technology-led solutions for the elderly's smart health care, this paper finds that there is a lack of attention to and research on the health elderly group, and many factors such as society, family and self make the health elderly suffer from various troubles. The article breaks the contents of economic support, life care and spiritual comfort under the traditional endowment concept and way, discusses the health care of the health elderly from a new perspective, emphasizes that the health elderly are no longer treated in a special way, focuses on the various needs of the health elderly in daily life, and combines the case of the wisdom health care creation camp cooperated by China Academy of Art and Panasonic Group. From five dimensions, such as spirit sharing, habit continuation, value sharing, health care and creation of happiness, the design concept of "suitable for the old and the young" is proposed, and the value proposition of multi-dimensional comprehensive construction of "integration of the old and the young" life scene is constructed, reflecting the care for the health elderly and proposing new solutions for the aging society.

Keywords: Smart Health and Wellness · health elderly · Humanistic Care · Integration of All Ages

1 Smart Health and Wellness

According to the National Bureau of Statistics of China, the number of people aged 60 or above will reach 264 million in 2021, accounting for 18.7 percent of the total population, and the number is expected to reach 380 million in 2050. Population aging is the basic national condition of our country for a long period of time, which is both a challenge and an opportunity. In addition, the elderly aged between 60 and 69 account for 55.83% of the elderly group. Most of these elderly people have the advantages of knowledge, experience and skills. They are in good physical condition and have great potential to play the role of waste heat [1].

1.1 Smart Technology Enables Old Age

With the development of information technology, products and services for the elderly have moved into the smart sector. Smart technology-enabled solutions are emerging in the elderly market segment. For example, digital products designed specifically for the elderly, with intelligent voice features and touch interaction designs, bring good usage experience and humanistic care to the elderly, while also meeting their social needs. Healthcare Enterprise offers a full range of smart healthcare platforms for the elderly. Through the elderly care intelligent system and command and dispatch center, they provide emergency rescue, online services and home services, as well as professional, safe and convenient medical care services. There is also an APP that provides aging services specifically for the elderly by integrating audio-visual to address reading disorders such as vision loss and fatigue in the elderly.

Digital products suitable for aging are becoming more abundant, bringing more convenience to the lives of the elderly. How to give older people more equal access to information, services and emotional companionship to fill their lives, acquire new knowledge, enjoy convenient services and achieve happiness and security in the development of information technology has also become a goal of the current design.

1.2 Smart Elderly Care Has Become a New Concept

With the development of information technology and the rising economic level of society as a whole, people's perceptions of pensions are changing. The first is economic development and scientific and technological progress. As income levels increase, more solutions to the living and physical problems of older people will be provided. A life of affluence will provide more older people with social and family care and security. Second, government policy guidance and the establishment of social security mechanisms have made pension levels an important part of social progress amid the aging trend. The third is a change in the concept of child support and old age care, which gradually shifts the financial support, life care and spiritual comfort of the elderly from a single aspect to a diversified pursuit of creating a happy home and spiritual pleasure. The fourth is the change of the old people's self-concept, from the traditional social concept of "raising children for old age", gradually formed a new idea of self-independence, self-value realization, independent pension.

The concept of intelligent elderly care, shaped by the development of advanced and new technologies, has gradually gained attention. Meiyun Zuo believes that Smart care for the aged refers to the use of information technologies such as the Internet, social networking, Internet of Things, mobile computing, etc., to support the elderly's life and management in various aspects such as life, security, medical care, health care and rehabilitation, entertainment, leisure, learning and sharing. Automatic monitoring, early warning and even proactive disposal of information related to the elderly can enable friendly, autonomous and personalized intelligent interactions between these technologies and the elderly. On the one hand, it can improve the quality of life for older people, and on the other hand, it can make good use of the experience and wisdom of older people, so that their wisdom and technology complement each other. The aim is to make older people live happier, more dignified and more valuable lives [2].

1.3 The Relationship Between Intelligent Technology and People

The rapid development of information technologies such as the Internet, big data, artificial intelligence and the Internet of Things have changed the way people live and improved efficiency. At the same time, people's lives are constantly affected by technology, which has become a prominent contradiction between technology and human relations. With the development of technology, the concept of intelligent health care increasingly emphasizes the role of the elderly as the main part and the play of value. The concept of intelligent health care is to deal with various relations of the life of the elderly under the progress of technology, but also to meet the spiritual world and value needs of the elderly under the domination of technology, and to present the ethical balance between human and technology.

In the digital age, older people crave psychological and spiritual satisfaction, personal fulfillment and social recognition, as well as a healthy lifestyle. The essence of the gap created by technology is the lack of research into the user as a complete person and a comprehensive consideration of human needs in terms of natural, social and spiritual attributes. We should think about how digitalization and intelligence can be used to realize the emotional connection of family members, so that health elderly will no longer be lonely in a digitalized intelligence society. With the concept of humanistic care, the integration of smart technology and the approach of digital intelligence design, healthy living at home can reflect the emotions and temperatures of computing.

2   Design of Digital Products and Services for the Health Elderly

2.1   The Needs and Troubles of the Health Elderly's Smart Health and Wellness

The modern age group is much broader, not just for those in need of care at the back end, but also for those in their 60s entering retirement in good health. Health elderly is a term of geriatric medicine published in 2017. It refers to elderly people who are physically healthy, functioning normally, free of disease, mentally healthy and fit to meet the five criteria of society. With the development of urbanization and changes in family structure, living space and lifestyle, health elderly are left out in the middle between the prime of life and illness or need to care for the elderly. Social factors, family factors, and ego factors cause the spiritual needs, value realization, emotional communication, and health care of health elderly to be inadequately met.

In terms of social factors, health elderly groups are uniformly classified as "elderly groups", belonging to a group of people who need special care. However, regular rehabilitative and therapeutic products for the elderly may not be suitable for them, and there is a lack of products and services for them in life and emotional aspects. In terms of the family factor, under the China's policy of encouraging two and three children, the modern health elderly still bear the onerous responsibility of helping their children in some way to raise the next generation. Multi-generational living under the same roof and home-based endowment patterns make the values and lifestyles of elderly and their children inconsistent, and there is a lack of effective communication between families. In terms of self-factors, the social circle of health elderly shrinks rapidly after retirement. They are physically fit and have normal mobility, but they cannot continue to participate in social production and service, and there is a wide gap between their actual situation and their ideal state. Moreover, with the advent of the digital age and technological advances, health elderly are faced with the re-learning of digital products and application scenarios, and they are uncomfortable with smart home products and networked management [3]. Digital products and abundant online content have reduced emotional communication and communication among family members.

2.2 The Value of Digital Product and Service Design for Health Elderly

First of all, with the rapid development of social economy, the living standards of the elderly are constantly improving, which puts forward higher requirements for the quality of life. On the whole, the new generation of older people are more eager to enrich their spiritual world. Through the development and service of digital products, improve the ease of use of digital products and services, think from the perspective of ethics, help the elderly to cross the digital divide, and meet the psychological demands of the new generation of health elderly people to pursue new things and keep pace with The Times. Second, digital products and services have entered the lives of the elderly under the concepts of intelligence and healthcare. Digital technologies can help elderly prevent or minimize many of the risks posed by physical and cognitive changes, assist in the self-management of chronic diseases, and give them greater access to health monitoring and health assessments to meet the needs of daily life and health. Establishing trust and trustworthiness of digital products through the design of digital products and services, and taking full care of the digital marginalization of special groups are at the core of the design. Third, the use of advanced information technology, supported by digital products and services, means developing Internet of Things systems platforms for home-based elderly people, communities and institutions to provide real-time, fast, efficient and intelligent services for the elderly. With intelligent scene construction and design, it can meet the diverse needs of health elderly in terms of recreation, learning and sharing, communication and mutual assistance, and social value [4].

3   Design Strategy Under the Concept of Smart Health and Wellness

The difference between the smart health and wellness and the traditional pension concept is health care for the health elderly. First, social well-being and policy guidance are only the external factors in building a good and healthy life, while the internal factors are the relationships and emotional maintenance of the health elderly in the family. Second, intelligent health care under smart technology, with more emphasis on humanistic care, highlighting the wisdom of people and the wisdom and value of the elderly, rather than relying solely on scientific and technological means to solve the problems of the elderly. Third, wisdom and health care can enhance interaction and engagement among older subjects, rather than blind giving.

In 2021, China Academy of Art cooperates with Panasonic Group. As one of CAA's professional tutors, the author and industry experts of Panasonic Group jointly participate in and guide the creation camp plan entitled "Wisdom and Health". In response to the changes of the digital age, focusing on the needs of the health elderly as the "middle zone" group, with the goal of building a new scene of "integration of the old and the young", breaking the digital divide in the elderly's health care life as the starting point, with the concept of digital technology integration of humanistic care, from the aspects of products, services, scenes, space, etc. The study focuses on the relationship between the young and the old, active learning, health management, fun of life, value of life and other aspects to provide new scenarios for the elderly health care, and explore the new concept of Chinese home health care. Finally, the creative camp produced a series of health elderly life topics under the concept of wisdom and health, which was highly praised by Panasonic Group.

3.1 Spiritual Joy and Emotional Joy

In modern society, with the gradual change in the concept of pension, the main body of pensioners is diversified, and children still play a dominant role in the pension of the elderly [5]. Some studies have shown that when it comes to pension content, younger and older people are more focused on financial support, followed by life care and mental comfort. Young people are more concerned with the environment in which they live and their physical health, but in reality older people are more concerned with spiritual pleasure, the companionship of family and friends, and the usefulness of old age in the hope of making their own value and social contribution.

In the author's opinion, spiritual comfort is still the traditional concept of treating the elderly as a special group, and it is a kind of psychological and emotional comfort given by the "other" group of society. Spiritual comfort is a low-level care, which can no longer adapt to the psychological needs of contemporary elderly people, especially health elderly people, on the basis of pursuing "intergenerational equality". More importantly, it is necessary to advocate the spiritual and emotional enjoyment between the young and the old, change the understanding and values of the health elderly, enhance the sense of independence, and continue to release the energy of contribution to society, so as to encourage them to pursue the spiritual and emotional enjoyment in life, and further improve the life happiness index.

The beating of the back is the oldest Chinese way of keeping fit and healthy. The beating of the elders' backs is also a reflection of honoring the elderly and carrying forward the traditional virtues of the Chinese nation. *The Beating Back Game Between the Old and the Young* (Fig. 1) is a fun interactive backbeat product that can be "shared by all ages". By beating, the elderly and the children can have fun with each other, expressing the care and love for the elderly in ways the children like. "Generational parenting" has been a common phenomenon in the current society, and grandparents have become an important force to take care of children. How to create the joy between grandparents and grandchildren becomes the thinking point of creation, so that grandparents and grandchildren can live together, establish a chaperone relationship and become each other's "playmates". *P-Dancerl* (Fig. 2) connects the bridge of equal interaction between the elderly and children. It provides simple and cheerful music, dance and game experience in the indoor and home environment, as well as soothing and healthy light health massage service, making the elderly and children become "partners" of common entertainment, common exercise and common life between generations, so that the elderly people who love life can change their heavy and tired "nursing" role in children's life and meet their needs of mutual integration and entertainment.

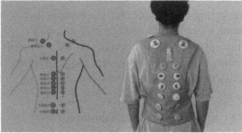

Fig. 1. The *Beating Back Game Between the Old and the Young* Designed by: Yuwei Yuan, Ruoyun Yan, Kai Fang, and Yiqing Lian.

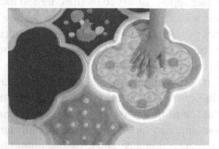

Fig. 2. P-Dancerl Designed by: Shipei Yu, Yinan Yang, Qingyun Wang.

3.2   Habit Continuation and Value Sharing

Technological development changes the mode of social production and reorganizes the structure of social production. People's accumulated life experiences of the past will be replaced and eliminated by new technologies, new methods and new ways of life. How to give full play to the advantages and skills of the old people's life experience, create a scene of "integration of the old and the young", enhance the old people's sense of value and satisfaction, but also be respected and valued, has become the focus of this topic.

In the initial discussions at the creation camp, the research team focused on the family diet and conducted the study by exploring the relationship between diet and family individuals. In China, food maintains the relationship of every family, and our taste always carries the memory of "home". The goal of *Home Cooking* (Fig. 3) provides a new way of communication between the young and the old. Through cooking, it connects the younger generation to their parents, broadens the topics of life exchange and increases the exchange of emotions. The product can be connected to other smart household appliances in the home. If the family suffers from high blood sugar, the cloud will give advice on reducing oil and controlling sugar intake based on the user's health status, thus ensuring the health of the family. The kitchen is an important part of food breeding, the food processing plant, and the maintenance of family relationships.

Growing flowers, grass and vegetables is a way of life for the elderly. *Happy to Grow* (Fig. 4) is a product for the health elderly to plant vegetables at home. Each watering process is a scene of interaction and recreation with grandchildren, sharing the joy of the harvest with the family, making growing flowers and vegetables easy and fun. The upper and lower parts of the disc are extended by a ring of dial handles, which can be easily grasped and rotated at different heights. When the bottom of the dish is rotated, multiple spouts shoot out of the holes around the dish to water the plant. The rotational motion of the disc also allows the plant to receive full sunlight, which is conducive to growth. The farmers' market is a daily necessity for the elderly and a place for them to socialise.

Fig. 3. *Home Cooking* Designed by: Jiayi He, Shuangying Chen, Tongyao Liu, Yuxin Ding, Xinda Chen, and Yuao Wang.

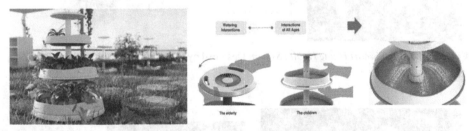

Fig. 4. Happy *to Grow* Designed by: Shijie Wang, Bing Kong, Minhua Guan, Ruiyun Feng, Qingshan zhou.

3.3 Health Care and Create with Happiness

Elderly, the creation camp attempts to humanize the collection and monitoring of home health data of health elderly through an obscure and more natural approach.

The Yilian Smart Home Health System (Fig. 5) aims to enable the health elderly to realize more natural, considerate and gentle health monitoring anytime and anywhere in the smart home environment, reduce the frequency of going to the hospital, and visually reflect the health status of family members and convey emotions in the way of a health farm themed game. For high blood pressure, diabetes, cardiovascular disease, night sickness and other common problems among the elderly, it can enable data collection through casual movements in daily life and complete health detection. It is easy to maintain health, maintain family ties, and let the elderly no longer be treated as a "special group" by using obscure and implicit emotional expression of Chinese style to convey mutual care.

When researching the needs of health elderly, the creative camp found that singing and dancing were popular among health elderly and wanted to create a different exercise experience product for health elderly through smart technology. *The Instrument between the Hands* (Fig. 6) is a new micro-exercise wearable device specially designed for the health elderly. It combines entertainment with exercise items, based on music "performance", supplemented by the realistic sense capture and rhythm prompt of "magic mirror", and gives feedback when the elderly wear gloves and make corresponding movements. Through simple interactive forms and feedback mechanisms, the elderly can get rid of the obstacles of "digital divide" and intelligent technology, exercise their nervous response ability, and achieve the health exercise effect of micro-exercise.

Fig. 5. *The Yilian Smart Home Health System* Designed by: Yutong Jiang, Shiyu Zhou, Jiani Zhu, Qingyi Sun.

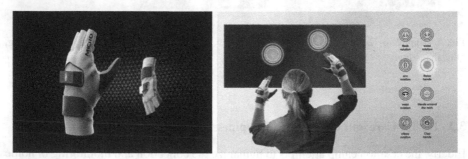

Fig. 6. *The Instrument between the Hands* Designed by: Chenhui Zheng, Zhongjian Su, Zhizhi Wang.

4   Epilogue

In the next decade, the post-70s generation, the mainstay of today's society, will also enter retirement and join the ranks of the health elderly. They are well educated, have rich economic conditions, pursue a high quality of life, put forward a higher demand for a healthy life, and expect to release energy to the society again. How to think about the scene and form of future wisdom and health care through the iteration of design concepts and methods, so as to promote the design and research in the field of wisdom and health care in the future, and provide more comfortable and better health and wellness experience for the elderly has become an important proposition of smart health and wellness.

First, the design concept of smart health and wellness should change thinking away from treating the elderly as a special group, which is the foundation of smart health care design. Starting from the philosophical nature of human beings, this paper examines the living needs of the elderly and moves further from the basic standpoint of caring and friendliness to the thinking of empowering and creating value for the elderly.

Second, smart health and wellness will present updated content based on the development of smart technologies. In the wide-area society filled with technology, both the government, enterprises and designers should be more clearly aware of the "double-sided" of technology, and emphasize the necessity and importance of humanistic care in the field of elderly health care. Based on the needs of humanity, humanistic care in technology is highlighted to create a better experience and service for the health care of the elderly.

Finally, with the rapid development of machine intelligence in the future, human-machine cooperation and human-machine integration are the most important future development trends. As digital technology moves into the age of the meta universe, escorts of smart people and digital people will be the choice of many more older people in the future. In the face of intelligent and virtual character companionship, design should always stand on the human-oriented AI as the core, and respond to the needs of the elderly in a more intelligent way.

References

1. People's Daily Online. National Bureau of Statistics. https://baijiahao.baidu.com/s?id=169943 3233776674836&wfr=spider&for=pc. Accessed 10 Mar 2023
2. Zuo, M.: Connotation, mode and opportunity of intelligent pension. China Public Security (10), 48–50 (2014)
3. Gu, C., Wang, F.: Smart Design - a new form of design in the digital age. Zhuangshi (12), 52–65 (2021)
4. Huang, C.: The present situation. Challenge and countermeasure of digital divide in the aged. People's Tribune (29), 126–128 (2020)
5. Cao, X.: The Consensus, difference and integration of young people and old people's pension concept. J. Sichuan Univ. Sci. Eng. (Soc. Sci. Edn.) 33(03), 21–41 (2018)

What Affects the Continued Use of Smart Wearable Devices in Older Adults?

Mengke Xie, Chengxiang Chu, and Cong Cao(✉) [iD]

School of Management, Zhejiang University of Technology, Hangzhou, China
congcao@zjut.edu.cn

Abstract. From the perspective of elderly users, this paper discusses the specific factors that influence the continuous use behavior of intelligent wearing devices and constructs a model. Based on the integration of the perceptual-emotion-behavioral willingness (CMC) model framework, the model increases behavioral activation variables. This model comprehensively analyzes the influence factors of persistent behavior from two aspects: affective intention and behavioral activation, and has wide applicability. Multi-faceted thinking provides support to the government in solving population aging problems and enterprises to develop intelligent pension products.

Keywords: Elderly group · Smart wearable device · Perceived emotional response · Behavioral activation

1 Introduction

With the rapid development of big data, the Internet of things, and other technologies, smart wearable devices and related services have been widely concerned. The increasingly serious problem of aging has increased the outbreak of age-related diseases and is a huge medical challenge to society [1]. The smart wearable device has the function of sports data statistics and health data monitoring, which can provide all kinds of valuable information about the body and is a strong predictor of morbidity and mortality [2]. The aging population has an increasing demand for smart wearable devices. A variety of smart products have entered the elderly market, and smart health care opened a new situation of social elderly care.

However, with the increasing use of the elderly, there are more and more problems, such as inadequate page design aging, and privacy issues. These problems will have a negative impact on users' use of the device, resulting in the further development of smart wearable devices hindered. Therefore, it is important to understand the factors influencing the continued use of smart wearable devices by the elderly. This will not only help alleviate the medical problems of the aging society but also help enterprises and individuals develop better.

In this paper, a comprehensive sustainable use model is established by integrating the perceptual-emotion-behavioral willingness (CMC) model framework. By establishing this model, the emotional state and behavior activation effect of the elderly group

C. Stephanidis et al. (Eds.): HCII 2023, CCIS 1833, pp. 540–546, 2023.
https://doi.org/10.1007/978-3-031-35992-7_72

are expressed abstractly, and the nature of users' continuous use behavior is revealed. Through the continuous use model, enterprises can grasp the specific factors that affect consumer behavior. And then to improve the product, and make the product meet the market development. To sum up, the continuous use model helps enterprises better understand the needs of elderly consumer groups, enhance the application of smart wearable devices, and bring better medical monitoring and prevention services.

2 Literature Review

As a device with computer intelligence technology, smart wearable devices can be used to collect and monitor information data to help users complete various daily tasks. The functions of smart wearable devices are different for different users. For example, Li, Xiao Qing et al. have designed smart health bracelets for pregnant women to monitor fetal heart rate, blood sugar, blood pressure, and other indicators [3]. Chang, Wan Jung, et al. have designed an intelligent assistant system for visually impaired people based on wearable glasses and smart walking sticks [4].

With the application of smart wearable devices, scholars begin to focus on the value of their diffusion and success at the user level. Wu, Liang Hong et al. based on three user-oriented theories (innovation diffusion theory, TAM, and the unified theory of acceptance and use of technology (UTAUT)) explore users' behavioral intentions when using smart wearable devices [5]. Li, Jun De et al. pointed out the factors for the acceptance of smart wearable systems and constructed a device acceptance model [6]. Abouzahra, M. et al. adopted a qualitative method to summarize the factors affecting the adoption of wearable devices by the elderly [7]. At the same time, some scholars have studied technological innovation and extended applications [8, 9].

In summary, there are some kinds of literature on the user level of smart wearable devices, but there are a few kinds of literature on the elderly. In addition, existing literature pays more attention to the influence factors before user adoption but lacks research on user experience and behavior after adoption.

3 Theory Development

It is generally accepted in academia that people usually have a series of thoughts and plans before they do something [10]. For this reason, scholars have carried out a lot of research on the influencing factors of behavior. During this period, the Cognition-Affect-Conation Pattern (CAC) emerged. This model mainly discusses the interaction among perception, emotion, and behavioral intention, and reveals the essential influencing factors of people's behavioral intention. Previous studies have demonstrated the effectiveness of the CAC model for behavior prediction [11]. Since its emergence, this model has been applied to many fields. Some scholars use it to predict user stickiness and loyalty, and some also use it to predict users' continuous usage behavior. Qin, Hong et al. extended the CAC model to provide a comprehensive perspective of continuous use and purchase intention [12].

With the development of technology, scholars have looked at different models and perspectives to find out what causes users' continuous use. Based on the theory of diffusion of innovation and U&G, Yen, W.C. et al. proposed the factors of users' intention to continue using social network service applications [13]. Park, EUNIL explored the motivation factors for the continuous use of smart devices by using ECM and TAM [14]. Tam, C. et al. revealed the factors influencing the willingness to continue using mobile applications through ECM and UTAUT2 [15].

In fact, there have been many achievements in the research on the intention of continuous use of smart devices. However, more achievements are concentrated in the middle-aged and young groups, there is still a gap in the study of the elderly groups. At the same time, most of the previous studies focused on the use of ECM theory, relatively single and fixed. Therefore, this paper extends the CAC model to explore the impact of elderly consumer groups on the sustainable use of smart wearable devices.

4 The Proposed Model

In this paper, by integrating the CMC model framework, a comprehensive sustainable use model of smart wearable devices for the elderly group is constructed. From four dimensions of perceived value, perceived fitness, privacy concern, and health consciousness, the interactive impact of personal perception on continuous use intention is explored. At the same time, the process from intention to behavior is further explored, as shown in Fig. 1. Integrated continuous-use model. Through this model, this paper comprehensively expounds on the influencing factors of the continuous use behavior of the elderly population.

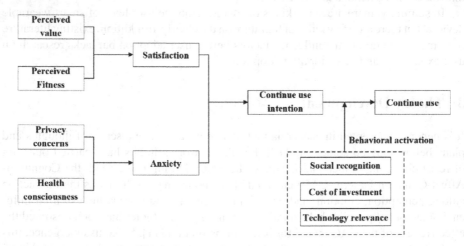

Fig. 1. Integrated continuous-use model

4.1 Perceived Value

Perceived value is the overall evaluation of a product or service by consumers. In the model, perceived value refers to the elderly users' trade-off evaluation after using the smart wearable device. Satisfaction is a psychological concept of users after purchasing and using. The study found that satisfaction is an important factor in the willingness to continue to use [16]. The improvement in satisfaction will lead to the enhancement of the will to use continuously.

Perceived value positively affects satisfaction, while perceived value is influenced by online and offline purchasing channels and product quality [17]. For Enterprises, mining how users use the purchase channels to achieve a balance of quality and price is very important. Enterprises should try their best to eliminate the price difference caused by different purchasing channels, and also should actively maintain the high-quality development of products, so that users feel that their cost is worth paying.

4.2 Perceived Fitness

Perceived fitness refers to the user's overall assessment of the user experience after using the device. Simply put, is whether the device is easy to use, or whether the use of products is in line with the target user's habits and group characteristics. When the product is not suitable for users to use, users will have a negative psychology, resulting in lower product satisfaction.

Smart wearable devices for the elderly must cater to their unique living habits and physical characteristics. At present, some products have this problem: the page settings are not suitable for the elderly to use. Enterprises should fully understand the use of the target population characteristics, and focus on the shortcomings of products to improve the applicability of the elderly.

4.3 Privacy Concerns

Privacy concerns reflect an individual's sense of boundaries and security. In recent years, more and more smart devices need users to provide personal information, and privacy problems have increased significantly. Research shows that consumers' privacy concerns can have a negative impact on the use of smart wearables [18].

Anxiety is a kind of irritability caused by excessive worry, which can weaken the intention of continuous use [19]. Therefore, this study takes anxiety as an emotional mediator and adds the dimension of privacy concern. Users' privacy concerns can lead to anxiety and negative emotional reactions to the use of the device.

4.4 Health Consciousness

Health consciousness refers to people's beliefs and concepts about health. Health-conscious people tend to pay more attention to health information and are more likely to learn and use relevant technology and equipment [20]. Such users are more likely to use smart wearable devices to help themselves manage health problems and control health actions.

Due to the influence of health awareness, users buy and use smart wearable devices. But if the device doesn't do a good job of managing its health, users may become anxious and balk at continuing to use smart wearables. Therefore, this study believes that the health awareness of the users will promote anxiety and reduce the intention of continuous use of the smart wearable device under the premise of health management problems.

4.5 Behavioral Activation

The transition from intention to behavior is a thought process. The change from intention to behavior requires some factors. This paper analyzes activation from three dimensions: social recognition, cost of investment, and technology relevance.

In this model, social recognition refers to the acceptance of the device by the user's surrounding group, cost of investment refers to the cost of the user's use of the device, and technology relevance refers to the follow-up service of the device, for example, the degree to which the medical device is connected to the hospital system. When the intention of continuous use occurs, better social recognition, greater investment, or better technology relevance will promote the continuous use of the device.

5 Conclusion

Based on the research of previous literature and theory, this paper proposes a continuous-use behavior model based on the CMC model framework. Based on the CMC framework, the model explores how the four dimensions of perceived value, perceived fitness, privacy concern, and health consciousness interact with the two emotional mediators (satisfaction and anxiety) of users, then it explains the nature of users' continuous use intention. At the same time, behavioral activation variables are added to the model, which is analyzed from three aspects: social recognition, cost of investment, and technology relevance.

At a time of increasing aging, we need to pay more attention to the health of elderly users. Smart wearable devices are a powerful tool for dealing with aging medical problems. There are few studies on the continuous use of smart wearable devices by the elderly in the academic circle Therefore, with the help of the sustainable use model proposed in this paper, enterprises can better analyze the needs of the elderly users, comply with national policies, and actively promote the development of intelligent endowment industry.

The existing continuous-use model is insufficient to study the elderly population. Based on the existing theory and the development of intelligent devices, this paper proposes a continuous usage model. The model further enriches the understanding of promoting smart wearable devices in a health service-related interactive marketing. Enterprises can balance the relationship between price and quality and improve the suitability of products to enhance users' continuous use intention, at the same time, it can also promote the continuous use behavior of users by strengthening the technical innovation and information feedback of products.

Based on the existing literature and data, this paper proposes a continuous usage model based on the CMC model. In future research, this paper will focus on the collection and analysis of relevant data, to adjust and verify the model more appropriately, and provide better support for the decision-making of the relevant enterprises of intelligent wearable devices.

Acknowledgments. The work described in this paper was supported by grants from the Zhejiang Province University Students Science and Technology Innovation Activity Program (Xinmiao Talent Program); the Zhejiang Provincial Federation of Social Sciences, grant number 2023N009; the Humanities and Social Sciences Research Project of Zhejiang Provincial Department of Education, grant number Y202248811; and the Zhejiang Province Undergraduate Innovation and Entrepreneurship Training Program, S202210337022.

References

1. Fang, E.F., Scheibye-Knudsen, M., Jahn, H.J., et al.: A research agenda for aging in China in the 21st century. Ageing Res. Rev. **24**, 197–205 (2015)
2. Alevizos, A., Lentzas, J., Kokkoris, S., et al.: Physical activity and stroke risk. Int. J. Clin. Pract. **59**(8), 922–930 (2005)
3. Li, X., Lu, Y., Fu, X., et al.: Building the Internet of Things platform for smart maternal healthcare services with wearable devices and cloud computing. Future Gener. Comput. Syst. Int. J. Esci. **118**, 282–296 (2021)
4. Chang, W.-J., Chen, L.-B., Chen, M.-C., et al.: Design and implementation of an intelligent assistive system for visually impaired people for aerial obstacle avoidance and fall detection. IEEE Sens. J. **20**(17), 10199–10210 (2020)
5. Wu, L.-H., Wu, L.-C., Chang, S.-C.: Exploring consumers' intention to accept smartwatch. Comput. Human Behav. **64**, 383–392 (2016)
6. Li, J., Ma, Q., Chan, A.H.S., et al.: Health monitoring through wearable technologies for older adults: smart wearables acceptance model. Appl. Ergon. **75**, 162–169 (2019)
7. Abouzahra, M., Ghasemaghaei, M.: The antecedents and results of seniors' use of activity tracking wearable devices. Health Policy Technol. **9**(2), 213–217 (2020)
8. Kyriakopoulos, G., Ntanos, S., Anagnostopoulos, T., et al.: Internet of Things (IoT)-enabled elderly fall verification, exploiting temporal inference models in smart homes. Int. J. Environ. Res. Public Health **17**(2) (2020)
9. Choi, E.P.H.: A pilot study to evaluate the acceptability of using a smart pillbox to enhance medication adherence among primary care patients. Int. J. Environ. Res. Public Health **16**(20) (2019)
10. Hutton, C., Heider, F., Blanco-Gomez, A., et al.: Single-cell analysis defines a pancreatic fibroblast lineage that supports anti-tumor immunity. Cancer Cell **39**(9), 1227 (2021)
11. Tsiotsou, R.H.: Sport team loyalty: integrating relationship marketing and a hierarchy of effects. J. Serv. Mark. **27**(6), 458–471 (2013)
12. Qin, H., Osatuyi, B., Xu, L.: How mobile augmented reality applications affect continuous use and purchase intentions: a cognition-affect-conation perspective. J. Retail. Consum. Serv. **63** (2021)
13. Yen, W.C., Lin, H.H., Wang, Y.S., et al.: Factors affecting users' continuance intention of mobile social network service. Serv. Ind. J. **39**(13–14), 983–1003 (2019)
14. Park, E.: User acceptance of smart wearable devices: an expectation-confirmation model approach. Telemat. Inf. **47** (2020)
15. Tam, C., Santos, D., Oliveira, T.: Exploring the influential factors of continuance intention to use mobile apps: extending the expectation confirmation model. Inf. Syst. Front. **22**(1), 243–257 (2018). https://doi.org/10.1007/s10796-018-9864-5

16. Liu, H.H., Shao, M.M., Liu, X.H., et al.: Exploring the influential factors on readers' continuance intentions of e-book APPs: personalization, usefulness, playfulness, and satisfaction. Front. Psychol. **12** (2021)
17. Hult, G.T.M., Sharma, P.N., Morgeson, F.V., III., et al.: Antecedents and consequences of customer satisfaction: do they differ across online and offline purchases? J. Retail. **95**(1), 10–23 (2019)
18. Zhu, Y., Lu, Y., Gupta, S., et al.: Promoting smart wearable devices in the health-AI market: the role of health consciousness and privacy protection. J. Res. Interact. Mark. (2022)
19. Wu, Y.F., Chen, M.Y., Ye, J.H., et al.: The relationship of breathing and COVID-19 anxiety when using smart watches for guided respiration practice: a cross-sectional study. Front. Psychol. **13** (2022)
20. Cho, J.: The impact of post-adoption beliefs on the continued use of health apps. Int. J. Med. Inf. **87**, 75–83 (2016)

The Effect of Face-to-Face Interaction on Older Adults' Attitudes Toward Robots in Human-Computer Interaction

Chien-Chun Yang[1,2]([envelope]), Su-Ling Yeh[1,3,4,5], Sung-En Chien[1], Tsung-Ren Huang[1,3,4], Yu-Ling Chang[1,3,4,6], Joshua O. S. Goh[1,3,4,5], Yi-Chuan Chen[2], and Li-Chen Fu[7,8,9]

[1] Department of Psychology, College of Science, National Taiwan University, Taipei, Taiwan
{r06227142,suling,trhuang,ychang,joshuagoh}@ntu.edu.tw
[2] Department of Medicine, Mackay Medical College, New Taipei City, Taiwan
ycchen@mmc.edu.tw
[3] Center for Artificial Intelligence and Advanced Robotics, National Taiwan University, Taipei, Taiwan
[4] Neurobiology and Cognitive Science Center, National Taiwan University, Taipei, Taiwan
[5] Graduate Institute of Brain and Mind Sciences, College of Medicine, National Taiwan University, Taipei, Taiwan
[6] Department of Neurology, College of Medicine, National Taiwan University Hospital, National Taiwan University, Taipei, Taiwan
[7] Department of Computer Science and Information Engineering, National Taiwan University, Taipei, Taiwan
lichen@ntu.edu.tw
[8] Department of Electrical Engineering, National Taiwan University, Taipei, Taiwan
[9] MOST Joint Research Center for AI Technology and All Vista Healthcare, Taipei, Taiwan

Abstract. Interpersonal interactions are often expected to be polite and follow communicative norms to avoid potential social conflicts by employing strategies such as face work. Although face work has been well-documented in human-human interactions, it is unclear whether people would be polite to the robots and give them higher ratings in face-to-face interactions than in paper questionnaires. In addition, according to the Socioemotional Selectivity Theory, older adults are more likely to be polite to reduce potential interpersonal tensions and maintain emotional harmony, which causes them to respond kindly to others. The current study investigated how face-to-face human-robot interactions influence people's subjective evaluations of the robot and, more critically, whether older and younger adults perform differently. We recruited older and younger adults and assessed their attitudes toward the robot through face-to-face interaction and a paper questionnaire. The results revealed that the older adults rated the robot more positively than the younger adults. Critically, the older adults rated the robot's personal association and perceived ease of use higher when responding to the robot directly than when answering the paper questionnaire; however, the younger adults did not show this difference. The findings emphasize the importance of face-to-face interaction and social norms in human-robot interactions, especially for older adults. Our findings have implications for human-computer interaction researchers and practitioners who are interested in developing social robots that are sensitive to social norms for different age groups.

C. Stephanidis et al. (Eds.): HCII 2023, CCIS 1833, pp. 547–554, 2023.
https://doi.org/10.1007/978-3-031-35992-7_73

Keywords: Human-Robot Interaction · Face work · Social Norm

1 Introduction

Interpersonal communication is rarely straightforward; when interacting with others, people are expected to act politely and follow communicative norms to avoid potential social conflicts by employing strategies such as face work [1–3].

Face work refers to the ways in which people mitigate and deal with the negative effect of their actions on others' sense of self-esteem, autonomy, and belongingness in conversation [1–3]. For instance, people may praise others' abilities before asking for a big help, or they may express their intimate emotions before starting to criticize in order to minimize the hurt and disrespected feelings caused by their words [2]. Among these strategies, directly giving approval or avoiding criticism of others' performance is one of the most common and powerful ways to avoid social conflicts in human-human interactions. However, very few studies have tested whether people apply for similar face work when interacting with social robots face-to-face; furthermore, it is unclear any age difference in such human-robot interactions.

Rosalia et al. (2005) showed that young adults tend to disregard robots' feelings [4]. Older adults, however, according to the Socioemotional Selectivity Theory, are more likely to be considerate of and use face work with others to maintain emotional harmony and avoid potential interpersonal tensions than young adults [5–7]. The goal of the current study was, therefore, two folds: First, we examined whether people generalize the face work to the face-to-face human-robot interactions; second, whether older adults use face work greater than young adults.

2 Methods

2.1 Participants

49 participants were recruited. One older female was excluded from the analysis because of the missing data in her basic demographic information, giving rise to 20 younger adults (9 males, age range: 18–26 years old) and 28 older adults (12 males, age range: 58–86 years old) remained in the data analysis. All participants gave informed consent before participating and were naïve to the purpose of the experiment.

2.2 Apparatus and Procedure

The experiment was conducted in a well-lit classroom. The participants were instructed to orally reply to the questions asked by the robot as in daily conversation (i.e., the robot condition) and then answer the same questions presented in the paper questionnaires (i.e., the paper condition). A service robot, Zenbo Jr. (ASUS), was used to interact with the participants automatically.

In the beginning of the experiment, a robot named "Little Cutie" introduced himself and explained the experimental procedure to the participant. Then, the participant interacted with the robot, followed answering a set of questions that were queried by the robot. Afterward, the participants were asked to complete a set of paper questionnaires at the end of the experiment.

A total of eight attitude measurements were both asked by the robot and presented in paper questionnaires, including Perceived Usefulness (4 questions) [8, 9], Perceived Ease of Use (3 questions) [8, 9], Intention to Use (1 question) [8, 9], Social Presence (4 questions) [10], State Curiosity (2 questions) [11, 12], Personal Association (1 question) [11], Human Likeness (1 question), and Social Contagion (1 question). These questionnaires were measured by a three-point Likert-like scale (0 = disagree; 0.5 = neutral; 1 = agree), except for the two questions regarding State Curiosity and Human Likeness. The two questions, one was a question in State Curiosity measurement (SC1), "Are you curious about this robot?," which was measured by a five-point Likert-like scale (1 = very incurious; 5 = very curious), and the other was the only question in Human Likeness measurement that "How humanlike do you think Little Cutie is?" which was rated by a 100-point scale (1 ~ 100 points).

3 Results

We first estimated the internal reliabilities of the questionnaires used in the current study to decide whether to analyze them as unidimensional scales or as individual questions. Then, we performed a two-way mixed Analysis of Variance (ANOVA) on each attitude measurement with the between-subject factor of Group (younger adults, older adults) and within-subject factor of Form (asked by the robot, presented in paper questionnaires).

3.1 The Internal Reliabilities of Questionnaires

We calculated Cronbach's alpha for the multi-item questionnaires to test their internal reliabilities. The results showed that the measurements of Perceived Usefulness, Perceived Ease of Use, and Social Presence had acceptable internal consistencies regardless of the forms of the questionnaires (all Cronbach's alpha $\geq$ .79). However, the internal reliabilities of the State Curiosity questionnaire in the robot and paper conditions were both poor (Cronbach's alpha: -.03 in the robot condition; .25 in the paper condition) indicating that the two questions in the measurement surveyed two different constructs in our investigation. Thus, we would treat Perceived Usefulness, Perceived Ease of Use, and Social Presence as unidimensional scales while analyzing the two questions in State Curiosity (SC1: "Are you curious about this robot?"; SC2: "How likely would you be to spend time watching a video that introduces this robot?") individually to prevent misinterpretation of the results.

3.2 Attitude Toward the Robot

We performed a two-way mixed ANOVA on each attitude measure with the between-subject factor of Group (younger adults, older adults) and within-subject factor of Form (asked by the robot, presented in paper questionnaires). The results were summarized in Table 1.

The results revealed that all attitude measures had a significant main effect of Group (all $ps < .05$), except for the SC2. This indicated that the older adults were more friendly and had a more positive attitude toward the robot than the younger adults. Critically, unlike other measurements, the main effect on Group did not reach be significant on SC2, $F(1,46) = 1.55$, $p = .219$, $\eta_p^2 = .03$. This result suggests that the older adults were willing to get information from the introductory videos of products, and so was their younger counterparts even when they hold more negative attitudes toward the robot.

Table 1. The results of ANOVA for the attitude measurements. Significant results ($p < .05$) are marked in bold.

Questionnaire	Main effect of Group	Main effect of Form	Interaction effect
Perceived Usefulness	**$F(1,46) = 43.89$, $p < .001$, $\eta_p^2 = .49$**	$F(1,46) = 1.20$, $p = .279$, $\eta_p^2 = .03$	$F(1,46) = 3.75$, $p = .059$, $\eta_p^2 = .08$
Perceived Ease of Use	**$F(1,46) = 33.56$, $p < .001$, $\eta_p^2 = .42$**	**$F(1,46) = 11.75$, $p = .001$, $\eta_p^2 = .20$**	**$F(1,46) = 4.42$, $p = .041$, $\eta_p^2 = .09$**
Intention to Use	**$F(1,46) = 9.11$, $p = .004$, $\eta_p^2 = .17$**	$F(1,46) = 1.52$, $p = .224$, $\eta_p^2 = .03$	$F(1,46) = 2.13$, $p = .151$, $\eta_p^2 = .04$
Social Presence	**$F(1,46) = 60.75$, $p < .001$, $\eta_p^2 = .57$**	$F(1,46) = 3.27$, $p = .077$, $\eta_p^2 = .07$	$F(1,46) = 3.00$, $p = .090$, $\eta_p^2 = .06$
SC1	**$F(1,46) = 5.47$, $p = .024$, $\eta_p^2 = .11$**	$F(1,46) = 0.47$, $p = .499$, $\eta_p^2 = .01$	$F(1,46) = 2.68$, $p = .108$, $\eta_p^2 = .06$
SC2	$F(1,46) = 1.55$, $p = .219$, $\eta_p^2 = .03$	$F(1,46) = 0.80$, $p = .375$, $\eta_p^2 = .02$	$F(1,46) = 0.21$, $p = .652$, $\eta_p^2 < .01$
Personal Association	**$F(1,46) = 45.09$, $p < .001$, $\eta_p^2 = .50$**	**$F(1,46) = 30.45$, $p < .001$, $\eta_p^2 = .40$**	**$F(1,46) = 6.41$, $p = .015$, $\eta_p^2 = .12$**
Human Likeness	**$F(1,46) = 22.35$, $p < .001$, $\eta_p^2 = .33$**	$F(1,46) = 0.71$, $p = .403$, $\eta_p^2 = .02$	$F(1,46) = 0.05$, $p = .821$, $\eta_p^2 < .01$
Social Contagion	**$F(1,46) = 12.56$, $p < .001$, $\eta_p^2 = .21$**	$F(1,46) = 0.89$, $p = .350$, $\eta_p^2 = .02$	$F(1,46) = 1.25$, $p = .270$, $\eta_p^2 = .03$

Note: SC: state curiosity

For Perceived Ease of Use, the main effect of Form was significant, $F(1,46) = 11.75$, $p = .001$, $\eta_p^2 = .20$. Critically, the interaction effect between Group and Form was also significant, $F(1,46) = 4.42$, $p = .041$, $\eta_p^2 = .09$. The follow-up post-hoc tests showed that the older adults significantly evaluated the robot higher on Perceived Ease of Use when asked face-to-face than when presented in the paper form, paired $t(27) = 3.52$, Holm adjusted $p = .003$, whereas the younger adults' scores on Perceived Ease of Use were unaffected by the form of questionnaires, paired $t(19) = 0.78$, Holm adjusted $p = .894$ (Fig. 1A). For Personal Association, similarly, both the main effect of Form, $F(1,46)$

$= 30.45, p < .001, \eta_p^2 = .40$, and the interaction effect between Group and Form were significant, $F(1,46) = 6.41, p = .015, \eta_p^2 = .12$. The follow-up post-hoc tests showed that the older adults' scores on Personal Association were significantly higher in the robot condition than in the paper condition, paired $t(27) = 5.67$, Holm adjusted $p < .001$, whereas the scores of the younger adults were unaffected by the form of questionnaires, paired $t(19) = 1.71$, Holm adjusted $p = .207$ (Fig. 1B). The main effect of Form and the interaction between Group and Form were not significant in other attitude measures, all ps $> .05$.

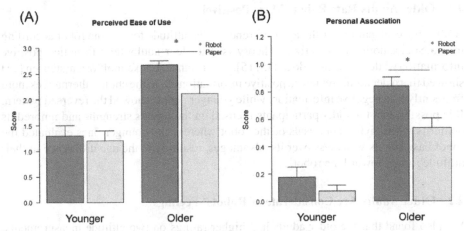

Fig. 1. The scores of (A) Perceived Ease of Use and (B) Personal Association measurements for the younger and older adults in the robot and paper conditions. The symbol* indicates that the scores between the robot and paper conditions differ significantly (Holm adjusted $p < .05$).

The results demonstrated a face-to-face benefit in the older adults' ratings on the Perceived Ease of Use and Personal Association measurements in terms of that they rated the robot higher on these two aspects when the robot face-to-face asked them for their evaluation than when being queried by the paper questionnaires; however, the youngsters did not show this tendency. Such results indicate that the older adults, unlike the younger ones, could be considerate of the robot's face, preventing negative feedback, and are polite when answering their appraisal toward the robot face-to-face. This tendency could be rooted in the older adults' characteristics that they tend to avoid potential interpersonal conflicts and maintain their emotional harmony [6, 7, 13, 14].

4 General Discussion

The present study compared how face-to-face human-robot interaction influenced older and younger adults' subjective evaluations of the robot with which they interact. According to the Socioemotional Selectivity Theory, we expected that older adults are more likely to be polite in the context of social interactions in order to avoid potential interpersonal tensions and maintain emotional harmony, which causes them to respond kindly to people and may extend to robots. We instructed the older and younger adults to interact with a robot and assessed their attitudes toward the robot through face-to-face interaction and a paper questionnaire. The results revealed that the older adults generally rated the robot more positively than the younger ones; critically, the older adults rated the Personal Association and Perceived Ease of Use to be higher when the questions were asked face-to-face by the robot rather than in the paper questionnaire, whereas younger adults did not show such a difference. The findings emphasize the importance of face-to-face interaction and social norms in human-robot interactions, particularly for older adults.

4.1 Older Adults Rate Robots More Positively

A possible explanation for the age difference in the attitude toward the robot according to the Socioemotional Selectivity Theory is that older adults tend to notice positive information while youngsters do not [5, 15]. For instance, Löckenhoff & Carstensen [15] showed that older adults reviewed positive information about the choice alternatives more frequently than negative information, while younger people showed the reversed pattern. It is possible that the older participants focused on the robot's strengths and ignored its demerits when giving appraisals of the robot whereas the younger ones evaluated the robot based on its weakness over its advantages, resulting in the age difference in their attitude ratings toward the robot.

4.2 Older Adults Are Considerate of Robots' Feelings

We also found that the older adults had higher ratings on two attitude measurements, Personal Association and Perceived Ease of Use when the questions were asked face-to-face by the robot rather than in the paper questionnaire, while the younger adults did not show this tendency. These face-to-face benefits could be the results of face work, reflecting the fact that the older adults were more considerate of the robot's feelings than the young adults [1–3].

Face work, by definition, would be applied in conversation when people feel their actions or opinions would be aggressive or impolite to others. To save face for the receiver, the speaker would take action such as giving approval or diminishing criticism to soften their language [2]. Similar behaviors were observed in the present study that the older adults raised their ratings in the Perceived Ease of Use and Personal Association measures when directly replying to the robot to prevent hurting its self-esteem rather than when replying in the paper questionnaire (Fig. 2). The ratings on the Human Likeness measurement were an exception to this face-work framework, probably because discussing "how humanlike a robot is" is not in our social norm. The very few experiences with this situation could make the participants difficult to prettify their answers. Another explanation is that the older participants did not feel sorry to tell a robot they are not humanlike (given that it is true) and felt it unnecessary to prettify their replies. In sum, the social norms in human-human interaction could bias older people's responses when directly replying to robots.

The fact that the older participants applied face work to the robots while their younger counterparts did not use the same strategy could be rooted in the older adults' characteristics that they tend to avoid potential interpersonal conflicts and maintain emotional

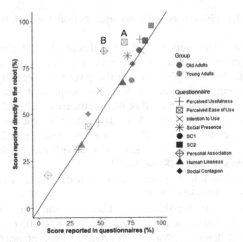

Fig. 2. The percentages of scores the participants rated on each attitude measurement toward the robot are plotted as a function of the percentages of rated scores of the paper condition (x-axis) in that of the robot condition (y-axis). The face-to-face benefits were represented by the older adults' ratings on the (A) Perceived Ease of Use and (B) Personal Association measurements.

harmony [6, 7, 13, 14]. According to Socioemotional Selection Theory, aging people compared to their younger counterparts optimize positive social experiences and minimize social conflicts to maintain their emotional well-being [5–7]. As a result, older adults prioritize emotional-related goals and reduce social tensions in social interactions. In contrast, youngsters prioritize knowledge acquisition and pursue them even at the cost of emotional well-being [6]. These age discrepancies may have contributed to the observed age difference in face-work usage. The present study provides empirical evidence showing that older adults, unlike their younger counterparts, were considerate of the social robots and considered the robots as social agents with self-esteem rather than just treating the robots as mechanical tools.

5 Conclusion

The present study found that older adults rated the robot more positively than younger adults. Critically, the older adults had higher ratings when directly responding to the robot rather than reporting in the paper questionnaire on two measures, whereas the younger adults did not show this tendency. The findings highlight the importance of face-to-face interaction and social norms in human-robot interactions, especially for older adults. Our findings have implications for human-computer interaction researchers and practitioners who are interested in developing social robots that are sensitive to social norms.

References

1. Brown, P., Levinson, S.C.: Politeness: Some Universals in Language Usage, vol. 4. Cambridge University Press, Cambridge (1987)

2. Lim, T.S., Bowers, J.W.: Facework solidarity, approbation, and tact. Hum. Commun. Res. **17**, 415–450 (1991)
3. Spiers, J.A.: The use of face work and politeness theory. Qual. Health Res. **8**, 25–47 (1998)
4. Rosalia, C., Menges, R., Deckers, I., Bartneck, C.: Cruelty towards robots. In: Robot Workshop-Designing Robot Applications for Everyday Use, Göteborg (2005)
5. Carstensen, L.L., Fung, H.H., Charles, S.T.: Socioemotional selectivity theory and the regulation of emotion in the second half of life. Motiv. Emot. **27**, 103–123 (2003)
6. Charles, S.T., Piazza, J.R., Luong, G., Almeida, D.M.: Now you see it, now you don't: age differences in affective reactivity to social tensions. Psychol. Aging **24**, 645–653 (2009)
7. Luong, G., Charles, S.T., Fingerman, K.L.: Better with age: social relationships across adulthood. J. Soc. Pers. Relatsh. **28**, 9–23 (2011)
8. Davis, F.D.: Perceived usefulness, perceived ease of use, and user acceptance of information technology. MIS Q **13**, 318–340 (1989)
9. Davis, F.D., Bagozzi, R.P., Warshaw, P.R.: User acceptance of computer technology: a comparison of two theoretical models. Manag. Sci. **35**, 982–1003 (1989)
10. Heerink, M., Kröse, B., Evers, V., Wielinga, B.: Assessing acceptance of assistive social agent technology by older adults: the almere model. Int. J. Soc. Robot. **2**, 361–375 (2010)
11. Chien, S.E., et al.: Age difference in perceived ease of use, curiosity, and implicit negative attitude toward robots. ACM Trans. Hum.-Robot Interact. **8**, 1–19 (2019)
12. Park, S.H., Mahony, D.F., Kim, Y., Kim, Y.: Curiosity generating advertisements and their impact on sport consumer behavior. Sport Manag. Rev. **18**, 359–369 (2015)
13. Birditt, K.S., Fingerman, K.L.: Age and gender differences in adults' descriptions of emotional reactions to interpersonal problems. J. Gerontol. - B Psychol. Sci. Soc. Sci. **58**, P237–P245 (2003)
14. Birditt, K.S., Fingerman, K.L., Almeida, D.M.: Age differences in exposure and reactions to interpersonal tensions: a daily diary study. Psychol. Aging **20**, 330–340 (2005)
15. Löckenhoff, C.E., Carstensen, L.L.: Socioemotional selectivity theory, aging, and health: the increasingly delicate balance between regulating emotions and making tough choices. J. Pers. **72**, 1395–1424 (2004)

Correction to: Interactions Afforded by Mobile Telepresence Robots in Health Care Settings

Alejandra Rojas🆔 and Sladjana Nørskov🆔

Correction to:
Chapter "Interactions Afforded by Mobile Telepresence
Robots in Health Care Settings" in: C. Stephanidis et al.
(Eds.): *HCI International 2023 Posters*, **CCIS 1833,**
https://doi.org/10.1007/978-3-031-35992-7_20

Chapter 20 "Interactions Afforded by Mobile Telepresence Robots in Health Care Settings" was previously published non-open access. It has now been changed to open access under a CC BY 4.0 license and the copyright holder updated to 'The Author(s)'.

The updated original version of this chapter can be found at
https://doi.org/10.1007/978-3-031-35992-7_20

Author Index

558

Printed in the United States
by Baker & Taylor Publisher Services